PANAMA ODYSSEY

PANAMA ODYSSEY

by William J. Jorden

To my old friend Bill Jossup —
This is about one of the few battles
we didn't have to fight together.
But you will understand it all.
With highest regard.

Bill Jorden

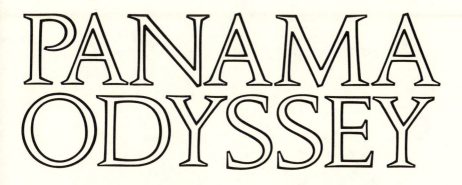

UNIVERSITY OF TEXAS PRESS, AUSTIN

Publication of this book was made possible by a grant from the
Sid W. Richardson Foundation.

First Edition, 1984

LIBRARY OF CONGRESS CATALOGING
IN PUBLICATION DATA

Jorden, William J. (William John), 1923–
   Panama odyssey.

   Bibliography: p.
   Includes index.
   1. Panama Canal Treaties, 1977—History.   2. United
States—Foreign relations—Panama.   3. Panama—Foreign
relations—United States.   4. Canal Zone—History.
5. Panama Canal (Panama)—History.   I. Title.
JX1398.73.J67   1984   972.87′5052   83-22291
ISBN 0-292-76469-3

This book is dedicated to the Americans and Panamanians

—*whose wisdom and imagination produced the Panama Canal Treaties;*
—*whose courage transformed them into law;*
—*and whose dedication and skill are making them work.*

Contents

Preface

ODYSSEUS' arduous and adventure-filled journey to the peace of home after the rigors of the Trojan War required some ten years. The journey from the bloody riots of 1964 in Panama to the completion of the Panama Canal Treaties took somewhat longer. But it was, most certainly, an odyssey—for the two nations concerned and their governments, especially for the individuals involved most directly. For those who lived it, it was a long and harrowing transport through countless risks and frequent danger, and marked regularly by a large measure of excitement. It was an adventure that none who took part will ever forget.

The central subject in what follows is the protracted search for a new arrangement between the United States and Panama to replace that under which the two countries had been working for more than seventy years—since the 1903 treaty was approved. I will not rake over the coals of that notorious convention, written and signed (for Panama) by a Frenchman, Philippe Bunau-Varilla, in collaboration with our then Secretary of State John Hay.* Nor will I go into the many ways in which we interpreted the treaty over the intervening years to our great advantage—and to the total frustration of our Panamanian friends. These and other more remote matters emerge herein in the words of Panamanians and Americans who raised them in talking about more pressing current business. But one hears the tone of bitterness in those words. As in all history, the shadow of earlier times and events hangs always over what men later do and say.

The cast of characters who played important roles in this drama of treaty making was extensive. But it was an interesting assemblage, one I hope you will enjoy getting to know. There are presidents on this stage, some more active than others but each playing some key part in the Panama drama: Lyndon Johnson, who really started it all in 1964, backed by

---

*The remarkable story of that earlier U.S.-Panama Treaty, its origins, and its meaning has been beautifully detailed in David McCullough's fascinating book, *The Path between the Seas*.

Truman and Eisenhower; Richard Nixon, who revived the Panama treaty effort when it seemed moribund; Gerald Ford, who worked to advance the treaty cause—then became gun-shy when the "Panama issue" began to look like a major liability in the 1976 presidential campaign; finally, Jimmy Carter, who met the problem head on, made its resolution the subject of his first foreign policy decision, and fought hard for its approval—with some stumbles and near disasters along the way.

At the other end, Panama's President Roberto Chiari figured in the events of 1964 that began the treaty-making process—but he overplayed his hand. For Panama, the key player (and producer and stage manager) was General Omar Torrijos Herrera, the military ruler of his country from 1968 to 1981. He was the mastermind of Panama's negotiating plan throughout the crucial years that ended with a signing ceremony in Washington in September 1977. Torrijos was without a doubt one of the most interesting, yet enigmatic, rulers in recent Latin American history. Tough, shrewd, egotistical, ill-educated, charismatic, incredibly patient, yet often volatile, he orchestrated the Panamanian game plan with great finesse—and, on occasion, endangered the whole process with snap judgments and emotional outbursts.

The real heroes in this adventure, those who carried the heaviest burdens, who manned the trenches day in and day out, month after trying month, who suffered the slings and arrows of their opposite numbers—and often of colleagues in their own governments—were the negotiators themselves. For the United States that meant Ellsworth Bunker, a patrician, New England sugar merchant in earlier years, and a veteran of the diplomatic wars—from Buenos Aires to Rome, from New Delhi to New Guinea to Saigon. Bunker was tapped by President Nixon and Secretary of State Henry Kissinger to direct the treaty effort in September 1973, soon after his return from Vietnam. Former Secretary of the Treasury Robert D. Anderson, Lyndon Johnson's choice to work out a new arrangement in 1964, had submitted his resignation in July 1973.

In the first months after moving into his seventh-floor office in the Department of State, Bunker led the way in formulating a set of eight principles—agreed to by the Panamanians—that would henceforth guide the labors of the two nations' diplomats in making the treaties. After that, the real work began. A major slowdown developed, however, in 1975 when the U.S. government bureaucrats, concerned with the new treaties, spent more time fighting among themselves than they did negotiating with the Panamanians.

Once the internal haggling was largely resolved, Bunker and his colleagues moved forward. But they did so at a measured pace. The ambassador was operating under presidential guidelines that called for him to "proceed with all deliberate speed." Bunker, a canny observer of politics and a veteran of the Washington scene, knew without being told directly that, in the atmosphere of the primary campaigns of 1976, the emphasis was on "deliberate" rather than on "speed." He conducted his diplomatic campaign accordingly.

With the election of Jimmy Carter, the Panama treaty exercise received a higher priority. To reflect that new status—and to put his own imprint on the proceedings—President Carter asked Sol Linowitz, an experienced international lawyer and a campaign adviser, to join Bunker as co-negotiator of the Panama treaties. Linowitz, former president of Xerox Corporation, had headed the so-called Linowitz commission, which prepared a detailed report on Latin America in 1976. The need for a new deal for Panama was emphasized in the commission's statement.

Linowitz was a brilliant activist, a man who suffered fools with profound impatience, a lawyer with the gift of all first-class lawyers—the ability to see quickly to the heart of the matter at hand. He injected new life into the treaty talks, pushing "deliberate" aside and putting his emphasis on "speed." He and Bunker made a superb team—one, the seasoned diplomat, the veteran of countless fracases with chancelleries around the world, a master of the bureaucratic maze, an astute observer of the ways and foibles of the Congress, the elder statesman; the other, younger, more active, brilliant in debate, yet with a sensitivity to the feelings of his adversaries, an indefatigable worker who insisted on no less from those who served him as advisers and staff members.

Facing Bunker and Linowitz across the negotiating table were two similarly talented though very different men. Rómulo Escobar Bethancourt was one of Panama's better lawyers and among its best orators. A champion of the poor and oppressed, he went into the books of some members of the business community and residents of the Canal Zone as a "Communist." But the allegation came from people who didn't know Rómulo very well. Certainly he had a profound sympathy for leftist causes, and he was an admirer of Fidel Castro. But he was a pragmatist, and above all a dedicated follower of Omar Torrijos. Let's just say that he preferred Johnny Walker Black to Stolichnaya.

His partner in the treaty talks was Aristides Royo, later president of Panama at age 38. Like Escobar, Royo was a well-known lawyer. Royo had been a member of the Panamanian Assembly in the early 1970s; then Torrijos made him minister of education, a post he held throughout the treaty talks. Royo was one of the most organized people I had ever known. He worked long hours, but always had his tasks well defined, and he covered ground prodigiously. He was tense, high-strung, proud, but steady and disciplined, a perfect partner for the volatile, emotional Rómulo.

Enough, for the moment, of people. Those already mentioned—and many more on both sides who made crucial contributions—will be onstage in many scenes as the history unfolds. Beyond the characters were the scenes on which they played their roles. Much of the early work was done on the island of Contadora, today Panama's best-known tourist playground. But in 1973 and 1974, when Bunker and his colleagues first went there, it was a relatively quiet, exceedingly beautiful tropic island. Not many modern treaties are negotiated on palm-studded islands anymore. But there were long sessions in other settings—in the study of the ambassador's residence (my home for four and a half years) in Panama; in the sitting room of the home of my counterpart, Ambassador Gabriel Lewis Galindo, in Washington; in the Panamanian foreign minister's office (his "bunker" as we called it); and most often—especially in the critical months of May through July of 1977—across the polished table in the conference room of the deputy secretary of state. Other critical encounters took place around the luncheon tables at Le Provençal and Sans Souci, in the offices of senators, and in the White House itself.

And so the stage is set for what follows, not the product of imagination but real events as they transpired in the real world.

We have two leaders—Jimmy Carter, president of the United States, and Omar Torrijos, a military man and political leader of Panama, one of the smallest countries on earth. Two men so very different in outlook and life style. Carter, a deeply religious man who was in church each and every Sunday; Torrijos, who rarely bowed his knee before the altar except on state occasions or at funerals of old friends. Carter, who alienated three-fourths of Washington by eliminating hard liquor from the White House bill of fare; Torrijos, whose thirst for the hard stuff was legendary. Carter, graduate of a prestigious military school (Annapolis) and familiar with the applications of nuclear power to modern warfare; Torrijos, graduate of the tiny military school in El Salvador and thoroughly familiar with the .45 Colt. Carter, who made a notable effort to learn some useful Spanish; Torrijos, who thought that admitting he knew some words of English marked him as less than a patriot.

So very unlike, those men; and yet . . .

Both were born in rural backwaters and rose to the top of their societies. Both had a profound respect for men who tilled the soil—and felt much closer to them than to the captains of industry or the intellectual elite. Both were born of parents who placed a high priority on education and personal advancement. Both assigned more value to what they personally perceived in another man than to all the briefing papers they received about him. Both had an unshakable faith in their own judgment of men and events. Both believed that God would somehow smile on their endeavors—because their motives were just and their hearts were pure. And both, strangely, were seen by their fellow citizens in a similar light—as men who wanted the best for their countries and for their compatriots, yet who often seemed not quite to know how to achieve that end.

Those two men guided the destiny of countries vastly different in size and strength, in history, in outlook and psychological makeup. One of them was a world power with a vast and complex economy, with awesome military strength, and with heavy investments and involvements in every continent, almost every country; the other, a Lilliputian country, smaller than South Carolina in size, than Houston in population. Panamanians hate the thought, but must grudgingly admit that the independence they achieved in 1903 from Colombia was significantly the product of encouragement by the United States, and the timely intervention of U.S. military power that frustrated Colombian reconquest. Through the years of the digging of the canal and since the opening of that great waterway in 1914, Panama has lived in a symbiotic relationship with its huge hemispheric neighbor to the north. It sells most of its products there, starting with the principal one, Chiquita bananas. And it buys most of its imports from U.S. suppliers. Panama's unit of currency is the balboa, but that means dollars, literally (there is no paper balboa). And U.S. colleges and universities remain the academic Mecca for the vast majority of Panamanian students studying abroad—especially in the technical fields of medicine, dentistry, engineering, and architecture, as well as in law and business administration.

These many ties, this intricate web of interdependence, have made it possible for Panamanians and Americans to understand each other better than any two nations in the hemisphere, except for our Canadian neighbors. At the same time, this multitude of connections and linkages made it all the more imperative that the two countries get together and solve the one overwhelming irritant in their relations—the elimination of the foreign enclave, the "colony" if you will, in the very heart of a small and friendly country. The last eight former presidents of the United States, starting with Franklin D. Roosevelt, recognized the need for change— some belatedly, to be sure, but eventually they came around to the obvious requirement. This book recounts how that requirement was eventually met, after seventy-five years of tension and thirteen years of negotiation.

We deal here not simply with two countries of disparate power and history and temperament. We must also be concerned with two quite different political systems. On the U.S. side, as we shall see, the Congress played a decisive role, indeed, an indispensable role. If, for example, Sen. Robert Byrd of West Virginia had acted differently, there would now be no treaties between the two countries. If there had been no Sen. Howard Baker of Tennessee, or if he had shown less courage, there would be no treaties. In any case, the Senate, acting on its constitutional mandate to give or withhold its advice and consent, held the power of life or death over the Panama treaties. And the way it performed this vital function is an essential part of the treaty tapestry.

The picture was very different in Panama. In pre-1968 years (i.e., before the Torrijos coup), the National Assembly was a traditional legislative body—initiating laws, helping or hindering the executive, and planning for the next elections. That ended when the National Guard took power and suspended the old constitution. In place of the small Assembly with specific powers, the new regime installed an Assembly of Community Representatives with 505 members—and virtually no power. The Constitution of 1972 specified that any treaty dealing with the Panama Canal had to be approved by a plebiscite of the entire electorate. Thus, in Washington, President Carter had to win the support of two-thirds of the Senate for any new treaty; Omar Torrijos had to secure the backing of a majority of his entire voting population. And, as we shall see, that plebiscite requirement caused endless anguish and deep concern for both negotiating teams.

Other individuals enter the scene at times, some for only a cameo appearance but others in a more sustained way. Costa Rica's President Daniel Oduber, for example, was a trusted adviser to General Torrijos through most of this period. And Venezuela's volatile, emotional, brilliant President Carlos Andrés Pérez involved himself from Caracas as well as during a visit to Washington. Colombia's scholarly, conservative Alfonso López Michelsen was sought out frequently for advice by Torrijos and played host to a gathering of Latin American presidents, a meeting that intervened decisively in treaty affairs at one crucial junction in August 1977.

When the slowness of negotiations became too much to bear for Panama's high-strung leader, he frequently turned to international organizations as an outlet for his dammed-up emotions. His representatives in the United Nations in New York and the Organization of American States in Washington grew accustomed to receiving orders from the boss to "let the gringos have it." That meant attacking the United States for recalcitrance or injustice, or extolling the virtues of Panama's patience and "reasonable" stand, usually both. Those resorts to international bodies were, I always felt, designed to do several things—to get rid of built-up steam generated by frustration among Torrijos and his closest aides, to "prove" to the Panamanian people that its government was doing something to advance its cause, and to create added pressure on the United States to mend its ways and move ahead on the treaty path. One such intervention, a U.N. Security Council meeting in Panama in March 1973, came close to blowing the whole treaty-making effort out of the water. Henry Kissinger's sense of history and Ellsworth Bunker's quiet, unflappable diplomatic style later that year helped heal the deep wound the U.N. meeting had inflicted. Some of my Panamanian friends are still inclined to regard the U.N. Security Council meeting as a great triumph for their cause. They don't know how near to the brink they walked, nor how close that exercise in chauvinism came to producing an unmitigated disaster for all who wanted a rational settlement. We shall see just how near a thing it was.

No description of any major event in recent history can ignore the role that the press plays in shaping opinions and affecting attitudes. Certainly it would be unthinkable for this long-time journalist to pass over that aspect of Panama events. But in the case of the Panama problem, we had a situation quite unlike that of some other recent crises in our national life. It was no Vietnam, where the loudest and most influential voices of the media were arrayed against the administration. Nor was it a Watergate, where the president himself became the central target. For the most part, the American press took an enlightened view of Panama and the proposed treaties. I should quickly say that I refer to that portion of the media that worked hard to find out what the Panama problem was all about. The major newspapers and the television networks and a few less-than-major newspapers took the trouble, and expense, to send their representatives to Panama to look at the situation first-hand, to listen to every available point of view, and to report on them. They did a good job.

I have little patience for those editorial writers around the country who did not know a thing about Panama, or the issue, or the history of the problem, who sat back in their chairs on a slow afternoon and took it upon themselves to tell their people what was *really* going on and how they should think. I read hundreds of those outpourings, trivial in thought, unsupported by fact or reason, designed, I suppose, to appeal to what the writers thought was the emotional bias of their readers—or to implant such a bias.

This is a social and philosophical problem that should be of concern to all who share strongly the sentiments expressed by Thomas Jefferson two hundred years ago about the importance of a free press. The central point is that a press cannot pretend to inform its readers—and that, after all, is its central function—if it is not itself well informed. And that means digging for information, knowing the facts, not writing off the west wall.

Enough by way of preamble. It is time to get into the real story.

This is an account of a portion of history, of the way in which a great world power tried and succeeded in working out new arrangements for dealing with a small, nearby nation in an effort to maximize the benefits for both. It is a story about overcoming the prejudices and injustices of a past that its people hardly knew. It is a description of the way treaties are negotiated and approved. It is a chronicle of the interactions between a large country and a small country in facing their differences and working them out to mutual satisfaction.

Beyond that, the reader will find herein a detailed account of the way modern diplomacy works—or *can* work if the conditions are right and the spirit is willing. He or she will also find considerable detail about the Congress and the way it copes with a major foreign policy problem, and how the executive and legislative branches work together—and oppose each other—to meet a national need. There is also in these pages considerable evidence relating to the role of individuals who feel deeply about a problem and are convinced that its fair settlement is good for them and for their countries, for their children and for the future. I speak not only of the politicians and diplomats, the generals and admirals, the businessmen, lawyers, and technicians. I refer as well to the Bill Buckleys and John Waynes, the Angier Biddle Dukes and Cleveland Amorys, and the hundreds and hundreds of lesser known who came to Panama to see for themselves, to ask and listen, to learn and feel, and then to fight for what they believed was right.

What this is all about is the story of men and women of imagination and political courage who knew the right, as God gave them to see the right, and who fought to see it through.

In relating these events, I have been guided by an earlier and wiser historian who, in introducing his account of another major event, wrote:

> With reference to the narrative of events, far from permitting myself to derive it from the first source that came to hand, I did not even trust my own impressions, but it rests partly on what others saw for me, the accuracy of the report being always tried by the most severe and detailed tests possible. My conclusions have cost me some labor from the want of coincidence between accounts of the same occurrences by different eyewitnesses, arising sometimes from imperfect memory, sometimes from undue partiality for one side or the other . . . I shall be content if it is judged useful by those inquirers who desire an exact knowledge of the past as an aid to the interpretation of the future, which in the course of human things it must resemble if it does not reflect it.
>
> Thucydides, *The History of the Peloponnesian War*

Austin, Texas   William J. Jorden
September 1983

Acknowledgments

WHEN I retired from government and settled in Austin, Texas, to write this book, I had expected the task would require about two years. That was five years ago. The delay, though totally necessary and useful, was a trial for friends and family and all concerned. I am most grateful for their forbearance, which was Job-like.

In 1978, the board of the Lyndon Baines Johnson Foundation approved a generous grant, which made me the first scholar-in-residence at the LBJ Library and an adjunct professor at the LBJ School of Public Affairs. The award provided me with an office and secretarial assistance. Even more important, it sustained me during two years of intensive research and the writing of early drafts. I hope the members of the board will consider this work the fruit of their investment and will realize that it reaches them with the author's profound gratitude.

The foundation stones of this history are the numerous and lengthy interviews given by all the principal players who were involved in these events. Their names are listed in the interviews section in Sources and I take this occasion to thank them once again for their willingness to search their memories and give freely of their time. I am particularly thankful to those who not only relived their particular experiences but also supplied documentation that filled in several interstices.

Three old friends read almost every word of the manuscript in one draft or another and made invaluable suggestions. Walt W. Rostow brought to the reading an exceptional sense of history and of economic realities and much more. My Panamanian brother, Gabriel Lewis Galindo, read from the vantage point of one who knew intimately what was happening on the Panamanian side at every important juncture. His strong patriotism never beclouded his fair-mindedness. The most detailed and meticulous critiques came from Mike Kozak, who was associated with the Panama treaty talks both before and after most other Americans. His prodigious memory, lawyerlike precision, and command of detail, combined with a rare sensitivity to moods and meanings, produced comments and advice that render any characterization as trivial. Without Mike, this would have been a different and poorer account.

My thanks go, too, to those friends and colleagues who read portions of the manuscript, in most cases reviewing events in which they played a central role. They helped me avoid some errors of fact and improved many descriptions of events. I recall particularly Nicolás Ardito Barletta, Ellsworth Bunker, Gerri Chester, Sol Linowitz, Fernando Manfredo, and Ambler Moss. Other friends not associated with the Panama treaty story read parts of the narrative and made useful suggestions on style and historiography. These included Robert Hardesty, James Michener, Harry Middleton, and John Roche.

I want the staff at the LBJ Library in Austin to know how much I appreciate their extensive help in delving into the pertinent papers of the Johnson presidency, to say nothing of other materials—newspaper files, *Congressional Records*, microfilms, books, and other sources. I am grateful to Bob Pastor and the staff of the National Security Council, who made some requested papers available and cleared my notes on same. I also wish to thank my old friend Dick Wyrough, who made arrangements for me to review many of the files on treaty negotiations during the 1970s. He also made sure I received unclassified reports on canal operations and congressional developments after 1978.

In addition to the librarians and archivists at the LBJ Library, I want to extend my special thanks to Lou Anne Missildine. During the two years she worked for me, she converted random papers and assorted documents into orderly files. She also typed most of the first drafts of these chapters. All this she did with great efficiency and amazing cheerfulness. Another LBJ Library stalwart, Ted Gittinger, was responsible for the grueling but invaluable task of compiling the index, which he accomplished with great professionalism.

My old friend Howard Handleman had just retired from *U.S. News* when I began this work. He generously gave up his leisure to go to the Library of Congress for many weeks to carry out valuable research into materials that were not available to me in Austin. I want him to know what a difference it made.

My three children—Tabby, Telly, and Tem, all wise beyond their years—read chunks of the book. They made some useful suggestions and, in any case, made me feel that what I was doing mattered. Tabby took part of a holiday to proofread a dozen chapters—which was a great help.

A word about Omar Torrijos. He is gone and so he will not be reading these words. I think he knows, nonetheless, how I feel. He talked with me several times at length and answered my questions candidly. He had the courage not to shy away from matters that he knew would not make him look good. Most important, he passed the word through government channels that he would be pleased if all hands would cooperate in helping make this book as accurate as possible. That stimulated help from some quarters that might not otherwise have been so forthcoming.

I have left until last the expression of my largest debt and my most profound gratitude. My wife, Melpo (or Mili), lived through the researching and writing of this book with amazing fortitude and unfailing good cheer. Her good spirits survived not only the burning of midnight oil but also the tapping of the midnight typewriter. She assumed without a grumble all the burdens of household engineering while I was in Washington or Panama or elsewhere interviewing participants in the Panama adventure. She deferred many hoped-for trips and activities in the interest of this history. And on top of everything else, she patiently, skillfully typed all the final drafts of every chapter. In short, an irreplaceable partner.

PANAMA ODYSSEY

CHAPTER I

When Presidents Negotiate

"Can't we wrap this thing up?"
—Gen. Omar Torrijos in Bogotá, August 5, 1977

AUGUST 5, 1977, was a sizzler in Washington. It was Friday, crab-cake day at my favorite watering hole, the Black Steer Restaurant, a block north of the White House. I had enjoyed an excellent meal and good talk with two old friends, Howard Handleman of *U.S. News & World Report* and Serban Vallimarescu of the U.S. Information Agency. I had known Howard for almost thirty years, since our days as foreign correspondents in Japan and Korea. Val was the son of a prewar Rumanian foreign minister, Harvard graduate, fluent in four languages. We met in Paris when I was a member of the U.S. delegation trying to reach a peace settlement with the Vietnamese and he was a senior officer in the U.S. Embassy.

Back at State, I was sitting in the tiny office the Panama Desk had provided, enjoying the afterglow of good food, excellent companionship, and a couple of splendid martinis. I leaned back in my chair watching the heat waves bounce off the roof just below my window. "Compared to this," I thought, "Panama is in the temperate zone." That was heartening, because I would be back in Panama the next day.

I thought about the preceding months. The Carter administration wanted new Panama Canal treaties, and we had been struggling intensively for six months to get them. Instead of working in my large, comfortable office in the embassy on Avenida Balboa, looking out over the Bay of Panama, I had been operating from this cubbyhole on the fourth floor of the Department of State.

I had come to Washington in early May, mainly to prepare the way for the new Panamanian ambassador to the United States, my good friend Gabriel Lewis Galindo. The post had been vacant since February, when Gabriel's predecessor, Nicolás González-Revilla, had been called back to his homeland to become (at 31) the youngest foreign minister in his country's history. General Torrijos had picked Gabriel, a longtime friend and adviser, as the successor. The selection proved not merely good, but a stroke of genius on Torrijos' part. Lewis became the most effective ambassador that Panama had had in Washington during its seventy-five years as an independent nation. I have never seen any foreign envoy move so adroitly through the Washington jungle, avoiding the social and political traps that usually ensnare the unwary new envoy. Among other things, he never got bogged down in the endless requirements of protocol—to the chagrin of many colleagues in the diplomatic corps who waited confidently for him to stub his toe on the rocks of tradition. They waited in vain. He quickly became one of the best known diplomats in the U.S. capital.

I came to Washington not only to help Gabriel but also to consult with my American colleagues and treaty negotiators: the tall, white-haired Vermont patrician and diplomatic veteran, Ellsworth Bunker, then 83 years and showing no more than 65 of them, and his co-negotiator, Sol Linowitz, a dynamic international lawyer and former board chairman of the Xerox Corporation, who became the trail boss of the treaty-making drive. They wanted a detailed report on the internal situation and the mood in Panama as they prepared an intensive diplomatic campaign to create a new treaty arrangement with Panama.

I had expected to be in Washington five days, which turned into eleven weeks. What happened was one of those juxtapositions of time and place and people that changes the normal course. We discovered—not surprising to Gabriel and me, but perhaps to others—that there was a level of trust, communication, and mutual confidence between the new ambassador and me that made it possible to overcome in hours problems and disputes that might have taken weeks or months. During the day, the negotiators met. Every evening, Gabriel and I got together to chew over what our colleagues had been discussing. We were able to convey the heart of our countries' positions on certain issues in ways that did not always translate across the negotiating table.

"Look, Bill," Gabriel said to me one night, "for you, Ancon Hill is a piece of land, a dot on the map. And you've got antennas on the top of it, so it's important to you. But Ancon is something else for us. It's the highest piece of land in Panama City. It looks over everything. It's like Mt. Everest for us. And since 1903, it's been a visible symbol of the Canal Zone, of foreign power in the middle of our country. It's not just geography we're talking about, it's history and emotion. You can keep your damn antennas, but give us the hill." The next morning, I explained to Bunker and Linowitz why the argument about Ancon Hill was dragging on and on, and creating so much ill will. They soon settled it to both sides' satisfaction.

On another occasion, I told Ambassador Lewis: "Look, Gabriel. You claim Panama has been shortchanged for 65 years. You've let us use one of the most valuable pieces of real estate in the world, and we've made money from it, and given you peanuts. All true! But I tell you this, my friend: we may be able to convince the Congress and the American people to make a new arrangement and eventually give Panama the canal. But you have to understand we can never convince anybody that we should pay you for the privilege." The ambassador then went to his negotiators and laid out the reasons why a seemingly logical case simply could not be sold.

And so it went. Day after day, night after night. The U.S. and Panamanian negotiators came to realize they had a useful, constructive channel that made their labors considerably easier. So I stayed in Washington from early May until June's end. But I had to get back to Panama for the Fourth of July. That is the biggest day in U.S. embassies around the world, our national birthday. For the American community in a foreign country, it is a time for drawing together and remembering home, and flag, who we are as a people, what we are trying to do, and why. It's also a time when ambassadors invite Americans and the friends of their country to share with them a glass, and fellowship, and a renewed dedication to ideals and ideas —however hard that may be for some who do not live under governments that believe in "life, liberty, and the pursuit of happiness." So I had to be there. But I was on a Braniff jet returning to Washington a few days later.

Soon it was early August, and I was preparing to return again to home base. Jean Puhan, the efficient secretary on the Panama Desk, had made our reservations and secured our tickets. My wife, Mili, was with me on this trip and we had taken a small apartment in Foggy Bottom, just behind the State Department on Virginia Avenue. She was busy with last-minute shopping, calls, and final packing. We were leaving a day in advance to be on hand to welcome Ambassadors Bunker and Linowitz and their entourage when they arrived in Panama on Sunday for what we all thought would be the decisive round in the treaty talks. But we reckoned without Omar Torrijos. He had gone to Bogotá, Colombia—and the treaty talks were about to take a quite bizarre turn.

I heard the phone ring in the outer office and then the intercom buzzed. It was Jean telling me Ambassador Lewis wanted to talk with me. I switched over to the lighted connection.

"Hello, Gabriel. What's up?"

"Look, Bill," he said, "we've got a problem. I just talked with Omar in Bogotá. He wants us to get to work. I don't know if it's possible. But you and I better talk about it. Can you come over?"

"Sure," I said. "Give me twenty minutes. Anything I need to bring along?"

"No," he said, "just bring yourself—and your imagination."

"I'll be there *muy pronto*."

I hung up and looked at my watch. It was 4:10 P.M. I stuffed papers and plane tickets in my briefcase and walked out. I told Jean I was off to the Panamanian Embassy and thanked her for all her help over the weeks of wild confusion. I walked down the hospitallike corridor to the bank of elevators and punched the "Down" button. "What in the name of God can Torrijos be thinking of now," I wondered. I had thought that the Bogotá meeting would be a "love feast," a gathering of Latin American leaders who would show their solidarity and stand firmly behind Panama's "just demands." Then, when Bunker and Linowitz got to Panama on Sunday, the real business of hammering out a final agreement would begin. What had happened. Why had Torrijos called from Bogotá?

I walked out the diplomatic entrance on C Street and hit it lucky. A cab pulled up just as I got to the curb, and discharged its passenger. I climbed aboard, gave the driver the address, and we took off. In fifteen minutes we were at the Panamanian ambassador's residence.

A white-clad maid let me in. I walked up the carpeted stairs and into the living room, then back to the comfortable sitting room in the rear, Gabriel's "headquarters" and the warmest, friendliest room in the house. It was surrounded on three sides by windows looking over the backyard and the swimming pool. The fourth wall was taken up by two sets of French doors separated by tiered stones from floor to ceiling, the rear side of the huge fireplace in the living room. My friend Ambassador Lewis was obviously tense. He is built like a linebacker with a neck as broad as his head, strong shoulders, and powerful arms. But there is nothing stolid or slow about him. He paces constantly, a kind of perpetual-motion machine. His face is mobile and his eyes crinkle often in humor. We shook hands and he put his scotch aside while he poured me a vodka.

"Christ," he said. "What are we going to do?"

"Look, my friend, you better tell me what's happening, then maybe I'll have an idea."

He handed me a vodka-and-water, grabbed his own glass, and sat down in an easy chair next to the phone. I took off my coat and sat next to him at the end of a long couch.

"Omar just called me before I called you," he said. "He's in Bogotá, as you know, with López Michelsen [Alfonso López Michelsen, president of Colombia] and Andrés Pérez [Carlos Andrés Pérez, president of Venezuela] and the others [the "others" being José López Portillo, president of Mexico; Daniel Oduber Quiros, president of Costa Rica; and Michael Manley, prime minister of Jamaica]. And Torrijos is asking me: 'Can't we wrap this thing up?' What he would like to do, Bill, is to finish the main problems and announce in Bogotá that the treaty is completed."

I took a sip, looked at my friend, and thought fast. "Gabriel," I said, "there is no way to do that unless we get the negotiators here and talk about it. And even then . . ." and I let it hang. "Well, let's get them here," he said impatiently.

I located Ambassador Bunker by phone. He was understanding when I explained that Torrijos had called from Bogotá and that I thought a meeting at the Panamanian Embassy was necessary. He said he would come in an hour. Meanwhile, Gabriel had tracked down Sol Linowitz at the White House and convinced him to come over, too. We told both of them we thought about an hour would take care of the problem.

Bunker and Linowitz arrived at the Panamanian Embassy at the same moment, 6:00 P.M. I met them at the door, and as we walked up the stairs and through the house, I told them all I knew: "Torrijos is in Bogotá. He's meeting with the other Latin American presidents. And he wants to wrap up some key issues. I don't have any specifics. But Gabriel thinks it's important—and he's usually right on these things."

Gabriel welcomed them warmly as we walked in. He had been joined by two colleagues—Díogenes de la Rosa, a wise and gentle man, a septuagenarian whose memory of treaty talks and problems went back farther than that of any of his fellow Panamanians; and Arnaldo Cano, a young, intelligent Panamanian, graduate of West Point, an engineer who understood the technical and geographic problems that were so crucial.

By the time Bunker and Linowitz arrived, there had been several exchanges between the Panamanians in Washington and the top-level team with Torrijos in Bogotá. The main spokesman for the Bogotá group at that moment was Aristides Royo, a sharp lawyer, then minister of education and later president of Panama. Royo told Ambassador Lewis that several key issues needed to be straightened out, and he asked Gabriel to work for a solution right away. First, the Panamanians wanted to be absolutely certain that the new treaties would replace all previous treaties and agreements regarding the canal. Some economic issues were still pending and Panama wanted to nail them down. There were other technical issues on the Panamanian agenda, matters mainly of interest to specialists or scholars.

The real centerpiece of the Bogotá meeting and the talks between Washington and Bogotá that evening was the issue of the sea-level canal. It was a problem that figured importantly in the negotiations of the treaties of 1967, and in the calculations of the U.S. administration then. But by the middle 1970s, it counted very little in the thinking of the treaty negotiators of either country. In the 1960s, American planners focused heavily on the idea of a new canal to be dug by nuclear explosion. By the mid-1970s that seemed out of the question. On the Panamanians' side, the existing canal was what counted. They calculated that if a new canal were ever built, it would have to be in Panama, and they could drive their bargain when it became a real possibility.

What moved it to the front burner was a meeting in the White House in early July. Alaska Sen. Mike Gravel had looked deeply into the pluses and minuses of a sea-level canal. His central concern, naturally, was how to get the newly found oil of his home state most efficiently and cheaply to the refineries of the Gulf and East coasts. His conclusion was that we needed a sea-level canal in Panama—one the Panamanians would own and operate, but whose use would benefit us greatly. On July 7, Gravel had an appointment with President Carter. He took with him the accumulated data of months of study and research. He laid it out for the president in painstaking detail. "Here's what a sea-level canal would do for us," he explained. "Here's what it would cost and this is the benefit we would get." Gravel is an effective salesman, with an intelligent mastery of complicated details and an eloquent flow of language. In his Oval Office encounter with a naval-minded, engineer president, the senator from Alaska obviously was in rare form. He left behind a Jimmy Carter who was beginning to think like Theodore Roosevelt, possibly dreaming of the great achievement a new canal would surely represent.

Two weeks after meeting Gravel, the president was in Yazoo City, Mississippi, for the second "town meeting" of his presidency. Some 1,500 Yazoo City residents jammed into the high school auditorium to ask the new president questions and listen to his answers. It was a warm night, especially inside the meeting place, which had no air conditioning. Ten minutes into the give-and-take session, the president doffed his coat and rolled up his sleeves. A thoughtful, and ad-conscious, local undertaker had provided the audience with hand fans (Carter called them "southern, hand-propelled air conditioners") and they were being waved energetically to provide a little relief. Inevitably, in the question period, the Panama treaty issue was raised by one listener. How, he asked, could U.S. military needs be met if the existing canal were turned over to Panama?

"My guess," the president replied, "is that before many more years go by, we might well need a new canal at sea level." He added: "I would say we will need a new Panama Canal." He explained that such a canal could provide the solution to our problems of quickly transporting crude oil from Alaska to Gulf Coast and East Coast refineries. It would also allow the navy's largest aircraft carriers—which cannot transit the lock canal—to pass readily between the Atlantic and the Pacific. Two days later, after visiting an off-shore oil rig off the Louisiana coast, the president made the same points to an audience in New Orleans.

Scholarly works on the presidency rarely treat the presidential speech as an instrument in policy formulation. But anyone who has worked in the White House knows that getting an idea into a talk by the president is one of the better ways to ensure that the proposal gets broad exposure and immediate attention. The very fact that the president talked publicly about a sea-level canal drove it into the public domain and pushed it forward on the treaty makers' agenda. When they were writing the draft treaty for the Panama Canal in July 1977, the U.S. negotiating team put in a rigidly worded article that would have given the United States an exclusive option to build a sea-level canal. That option became the big bone of contention during the Bogotá gathering of Latin American presidents.

Several things helped make the sea-level canal issue central to the proceedings in Bogotá. One was the reaction of a key legal adviser to the Panamanian team, Carlos López-Guevara. Carlos, or "Fello" to good friends, was an astute lawyer (a doctorate from Harvard Law) and a veteran of the treaty-making campaigns. He had flown back to Panama from Washington two days before with a copy of the U.S. treaty draft in his briefcase. On the long flight across the Caribbean he studied the draft with care. When he read the sea-level canal article, he blew up—at least as much as a restrained intellectual like Carlos can "blow." Once he arrived in Panama, he contacted General Torrijos' party and expressed his strong opposition to the one-sided option in the U.S. draft. He was equally irritated by his own country's effort to require that the United States talk only to Panama about a sea-level canal, and build it there. "On the one hand," he later explained, "we were saying the U.S. should leave our country. On the other, we were saying, 'Don't leave. Build another canal in our country.'" It was, he insisted, politically and psychologically inconsistent.

A principal reason the dispute about a sea-level canal rose to such prominence at that particular moment was that the Panamanians, when they went to Bogotá, knew that some of their neighbors—especially Carlos Andrés Pérez, the fiery Venezuelan president, and López Michelsen, Colombia's scholarly leader—were convinced the biggest reason for the treaty delay was Panama's demand for exorbitant payments. Torrijos and his colleagues wanted desperately to convince the summit participants that the United States, too, was making extravagant proposals. So the sea-level proposition became both a real issue and a pawn on the diplomatic board as the wild evening continued.

When Aristides Royo had called Ambassador Lewis in Washington that afternoon, the sea-level canal option figured importantly in their talk. Royo told the ambassador that Panama had, in fact, decided to give the new canal option to the United States. "But," he said, "it has to be made more palatable. It is much too one-sided in its present form." He mentioned raising Panama's revenues in return for the new canal option. He also insisted Lewis make clear to Bunker and Linowitz that any new canal would have to be subject to the same conditions governing the old canal under the treaty. In other words, there would not be U.S. control *after* the year 2000. The education minister also told Lewis that the Americans should be told that if Panama made this concession, we should not consider building a new canal any place but Panama. Gabriel was sitting in his study, holding the phone and frantically writing the instructions he was getting from Bogotá.

I had arrived at the embassy a few minutes after the Royo call. Gabriel had already huddled with de la Rosa and Cano, the only members of the Panamanian negotiating team left in Washington, passing along the orders he had just received. Gabriel knew he had a tiger by the tail. So, very adroitly, he pointed out that he was not a negotiator but that his role was "behind the scenes." He asked veteran lawyer de la Rosa to lay out for Bunker and Linowitz what was happening.

The two U.S. diplomats were both wearing dark suits, appropriate for the dinners they had planned to attend later that evening. Outside it was steaming, but Gabriel had turned down the thermostat and the air conditioner was pouring cold air into the room. Ambassador Bunker moved to the center of the couch to avoid the icy blast behind him. Linowitz was sitting to his left, his eyes darting from de la Rosa to Gabriel to me. His foot kept tapping the carpet in impatience. De la Rosa droned on in his soft, gentle voice, going through the list from Bogotá. I was having trouble following Díogenes' exposition, which was muted and in less-than-fluent English. Ellsworth Bunker, whose hearing was not perfect, was having even more trouble. Sol Linowitz was having about the same difficulty I was—and he had a considerably shorter fuse.

Gabriel was in and out of the room, answering the red phone that connected him on a direct line from Washington to Panama to Bogotá. He sensed the two American negotiators were getting impatient, and he called de la Rosa out of the room so I could placate them. Sol turned to me and asked: "What the hell are we doing here?" I told him he knew as much as I did, but my understanding of Torrijos told me it was important and that we would get into real business soon. "We have to be patient," I said, "until we get a better sense of the game." Gabriel came back and Ellsworth turned his cold blue eyes on his host. "What is the agenda, Gabriel?" he asked. Lewis stressed that six heads of government were at the other end of the line and they wanted to iron out some of the problems we had been discussing. "I guess," he said with emphasis, "the real agenda is: *are we going to have a treaty or aren't we?*" He felt it was terribly important to go through the items that had been relayed to him, and he told us more details would be coming through any minute.

Bunker and Linowitz were somewhat taken aback. "I didn't think we came here to negotiate," Linowitz said. But he and the rest of us were quickly realizing that that was precisely why we were there and that the pressures from Bogotá had to be met. It was also clear by that time that we needed more precise and accurate interpretation. I called the State Department and had them locate Tony Hervas, the superb official interpreter who had worked most of the negotiating sessions over the past months. He soon joined us and that smoothed the communications flow significantly.

Meantime, some 2,500 miles due south, the scene in Bogotá was only slightly less chaotic. The visitors from the five countries had been welcomed individually at the airport by President López Michelsen—with honor guard, national anthems, speeches, and flag-waving school children. The national leaders then climbed into their Mercedes limousines and headed off to the center of Bogotá behind their police escort and its wailing sirens. They passed through the Plaza de Bolívar and roared to a stop at their destination, the Palacio San Carlos. Colombian presidential guards in colorful dress uniforms snapped to attention as the visitors entered the palace.

The meeting place was a large and opulent room, filled with priceless art. Crystal chandeliers bathed it in a warm glow that one witness said made the antique wood panels look like tooled leather. In one of the phone calls to Washington, General Torrijos told Ambassador Lewis they were working in the room where Simón Bolívar, the fabled Liberator of Latin America, had housed and enjoyed the favors of his favorite mistress, Manuelita. True or not, it added a touch of glamor. I thought: leave it to Omar Torrijos to introduce a little mystery and sex into the affairs of state. The man was many things, but never dull.

In the center of the room was a large, heavy conference table. López Michelsen, the soft-spoken, scholarly host for the Latin American summit, sat at the head of the long table. To his right was Carlos Andrés Pérez, the emotional, suave, socially conscious leader of oil-rich Venezuela. Pérez had followed the treaty negotiations with close attention and, only a few weeks earlier, he had been in Washington where he had several very candid meetings with President Carter. Sitting at the host's left was the recently installed president of Mexico, José López Portillo, balding and intense, a fiercely nationalistic man, as are all Mexican politicians. He was new to the treaty business but felt strongly about some key issues. Across the table and to the right of Venezuela's Pérez was Daniel Oduber, a staunch democrat, a thoughtful man, and a close friend of General Torrijos. He headed the government of Costa Rica, the most truly democratic of all Latin American countries. Torrijos sat opposite Oduber and next to the Mexican president. To Oduber's right was the sixth participant in the summit, Michael Manley, leftist prime minister of Jamaica. Manley led one of the most populous and troubled nations in the Caribbean.

That was the cast of characters for the Bogotá summit, the leaders of the only civilian-led, democratically elected governments south of the Rio Grande—plus Torrijos, who was not a civilian and had not been elected.

Aware of the contrast, the Torrijos delegates aboard the plane bound for the Colombian capital decided to award their leader an honorary doctorate. For the next two days, in the company of his well-educated, civilian fellow leaders, Torrijos would be called by his colleagues not General but "Doctor" Torrijos. There is no indication what effect this had on the others around the table in Bogotá, if any. But the Panamanians enjoyed it.

The seat at the other end of the table, opposite host López Michelsen, became a kind of witness chair. Members of the Panamanian treaty team sat there in turn as they explained to the Latin American chiefs the status of the negotiations. Each presentation was brief, about ten or fifteen minutes. The foreign minister, who despite his youth occupied the position of *canciller* (chancellor) in the Panamanian cabinet, led off with a general description of the background of the treaty discussions. Aristides Royo followed with a more specific description of the issues, especially the more contentious ones. Architect Edwin Fábrega Velarde, a soft-spoken Cal Tech graduate who had been working with us on the technical problems of land areas and facilities—*which* were absolutely necessary for canal operations; *which* would be turned over to Panama—described what we had long called "Lands and Waters" issues. Adolfo Ahumada, the left-leaning minister of labor and another of the impressive array of lawyers who dominated the Panamanian team, laid out the defense issues, the meaning of the "neutrality" treaty, the bases that would be retained by the United States, and the long-range plans for joint defense of the canal. The continued presence of U.S. military bases and military personnel in the heart of Latin America made this one of the most sensitive issues confronting the heads of governments at the Bogotá conference. It was a measure of General Torrijos' political acuity that he picked a political radical like Ahumada to be his spokesman on this delicate matter before his nationalistic confreres in Colombia. Then, Nicolás Ardito Barletta, a graduate of North Carolina State with a doctorate from Chicago, and one of the top economists in the Western Hemisphere, described the numerous economic issues—the payments Panama would receive under the treaty and the vastly greater economic benefit Panamanians felt was justified by history and equity.

The summation of the Panamanian case was made by the principal treaty negotiator, Rómulo Escobar Bethancourt—a brilliant choice, and certainly not accidental, for Escobar was perhaps Panama's most eloquent advocate. He was a lawyer by training and a poet by inclination. His exposition showed the discipline of the former and the passion of the latter, beautifully blended into compelling argument. He was also a supremely gifted political tactician. At Bogotá he used all his skill and wiles to impressive effect. One purpose of the Bogotá summit—as a Torrijos intimate later explained to me—was to find out if the Latin American leaders really were convinced that a treaty with the United States was possible and whether, from their viewpoint, it was a good idea. But Rómulo decided that, to get an honest answer, the Panamanians should not appear as too-eager salesmen. Rather, it would be better to let their neighbors sell *them* on the advantages of a new relationship with the United States. He had explained all this to Torrijos on the plane en route to Colombia. The general quickly saw the point, and bought it.

When Rómulo took the "witness chair" at the end of the long conference table in the *palacio* that night, he was not his usual lively and optimistic self. Up to that point, what the Latin American leaders had heard was an explanation, in some detail, of what a new treaty would provide and why it was advantageous, at least on balance, to Panama. Rómulo looked down the table and said quietly: "Gentlemen, Mr. Presidents, I am afraid that I do not feel that we can have a successful negotiation with the North Americans." It was like a bolt of lightning passing through the quiet conference room. The Venezuelan president looked at his Colombian neighbor with a puzzled frown. Costa Rica's Oduber raised eyebrows and glanced across the table at an impassive Torrijos. The Panamanian negotiators—not in on the Torrijos-Escobar stratagem—looked at each other, puzzled. What was Rómulo talking about? Had something happened that they didn't know about?

Escobar then proceeded to lay out a gloomy catalog of negatives—U.S. refusal to provide the kind of payments Panama really deserved; American insistence on keeping troops and bases in the heart of the hemisphere; the implied U.S. right to intervene in Panama; the demand for an option to build a sea-level canal in Panama whether that country liked it or not. "No," he concluded, "we won't arrive at any successful result with them."

It was totally unexpected, catching the conferees by surprise. The first to recover was President Pérez. The Venezuelan leader had been with President Carter in July. He half-stood, then settled back in his chair, but his tension was evident. He glanced around the table at his colleagues and said: "Look, I have been in Washington and I talked with President Carter just a few weeks ago. I know the man wants a treaty, a fair treaty. You [looking at Torrijos] have to keep on negotiating. We just have to insist that the United States reach a reasonable agreement with Panama."

There were nods and mumbles of agreement. But Rómulo continued to take a negative stand. As one participant told me later, "He seemed in a very bad mood. A very disappointed man—not angry, but disappointed." The reaction was what Escobar and Torrijos wanted: sympathy for the Panamanian cause, irritation with the United States, and encouragement to push hard for a reasonable accommodation.

To Pérez, it seemed that the sea-level canal problem was central to the difficulty. An astute politician, he judged that if that contretemps could be overcome other matters raised around the table could be settled reasonably. He reached for a scratch pad and began to play with words. He asked for suggestions. Mexico's López Portillo was the most adamantly opposed to anything that would give the United States unilateral rights, and the Venezuelan leader tried to bring him into the effort to find a compromise solution.

Meantime, another bit of behind-the-scenes playacting was going on. Rómulo decided that "Doctor" Torrijos had to speak very strongly to his fellow leaders. To make the case Rómulo felt had to be made, his general needed to be angry. Rómulo spoke quietly to López Michelsen. "Look," he said, "we are going to write a counterproposal. But we need to have my general speak strongly to the other presidents, because they are going to be in touch with President Carter. So we need to have General Torrijos angry so he will make the case powerfully." López Michelsen understood.

In the exchanges that followed, the Colombian president took a sweetly reasonable position—"this is not all bad," he said, and "the United States has a certain amount of justice on its side," and "let us not be unreasonable." The more he spoke in that vein, the madder Torrijos got. And the angrier he was, the more eloquent he became. He looked in amazement at his friend, who had always been so sympathetic to Panama's cause. To counteract the appeals for caution and restraint from his neighbor, he spoke with passion and great persuasiveness—so those present say. His words had tremendous appeal to the others. Mexico's president strongly backed the view Torrijos was advocating. Manley thought it was justified. He said: "This is crazy. How can the United States think that we came here to approve this kind of thing?" And Torrijos was saying to the presidents: "I came here to announce the conclusion of the treaty—and to have a rest. But this is an *entierro* [a funeral]."

Having listened to the full exchange, Rómulo suggested that he and Royo retire and try to work something out. They moved aside and started to put words on paper, working from the suggestions that Andrés Pérez and the others had been discussing.

Meantime, in Washington, two frustrated ambassadors, Bunker and Linowitz, were trying to stay calm. And they were getting hungry and thirsty. Ambassador Lewis' lovely wife, Nita, pulled her husband aside and said: "We should give our guests some food; I have some chicken in the kitchen."

"No," he said. "If I give them a drink, they will relax. And if we feed them, they'll get comfortable. I want them to concentrate on working. It's the only way we'll finish this thing. Besides, I'm sure they would have indigestion if they ate now."

And so the Americans, having by now canceled their Friday evening dinner dates, stayed hungry. Thanks to Ruffino, the ambassador's efficient man-of-all-work, we, at least, did not die of thirst. But the air conditioner stayed on high, and we all got up now and then to restore our circulation. The phone calls with Colombia continued.

In one conversation with Bogotá, Ambassador Lewis was told by Foreign Minister González-Revilla that if the Americans wanted the sea-level canal option so badly they should pay for it. He suggested that the Panamanians in Washington tell Bunker and Linowitz that, if they raised the tonnage payments to Panama by five cents a ton (to 35¢), Panama might consider easing its opposition to the U.S. proposal. Gabriel swallowed hard, and passed that idea on to poor Dr. de la Rosa. "Handle it diplomatically," he said, "because that's a tough thing to bring up." In fact, it was outrageous, as I'm sure the Panamanians knew. And of course it was doing precisely what Torrijos and his advisers had been saying all along they did not want to do—trade a political concession for cold hard cash. When he heard it, I thought Sol Linowitz was going to have an attack. He jumped up and said: "You're mad! You're all mad. I would never raise such a point with the president." And it died right there.

Again the phone rang. Gabriel came in from his study, and said that Nicky Barletta was on the line and wanted to talk to Linowitz. Sol went to the phone, still shaking with irritation. This and the other calls from Bogotá were coming from an alcove just outside the men's room in the palace. It was the nearest available phone outside the chamber where the presidents were conferring. The Panamanian delegation used it to avoid interfering with the discussions going on among the heads of governments. Later, they would joke about the "Men's Room Connection."

Barletta, Panama's leading economist, had three items in mind. He began by explaining again why Panama thought larger economic benefits were justified. In a sense it was unnecessary. Linowitz had heard and been impressed by the detailed economic and historical arguments presented by Barletta and his lieutenants over the past month. He and the other members of the U.S. team knew the Panamanians had an excellent point, that their country had been grossly underpaid for seventy-four years. But we also knew—as did Barletta, I am sure—that we were under severe political constraints. Anything paid to Panama under a new treaty would *have* to come from income provided by the users, and that was not, of course, an infinitely expandable resource. Asking Congress for money to be paid directly to Panama was simply out of the question. Barletta was trying to operate within that limitation, but also trying to get a better deal for his country.

He raised the first item on his agenda: how would the United States feel, he asked Linowitz, about raising by one cent the per ton revenue that Panama would receive a year? He didn't realize it, but his timing was atrocious. Linowitz had just heard—and reacted violently against—the five-cent-a-ton increase proposed by the foreign minister. Barletta's one-cent boost stimulated the same reaction. "That's out," he told Barletta. "It would be an insult to President Carter and I wouldn't even raise it." He explained that he had pushed the president hard to get the previous increase—from 27 cents to 30 cents a ton—and that was as far as he was willing to carry this issue. Barletta sensed immediately the strong feelings he was encountering, and dropped the subject.

He went to his second point. We all know, he explained, what inflation does to fixed payments. When the original treaty was signed in 1903, the annual payment of $250,000 a year sounded substantial. Thirty years later, it was paltry. Panama thought it would only be fair if the per ton payments it received were related to some kind of cost-of-living or other inflation index. That way, he said, if inflation continues and canal revenues increase, and world prices rise, Panama's payments from the operation will keep pace. Otherwise, he said, what we receive will decline every year in terms of real dollars. Ambassador Linowitz considered that a reasonable argument, and he agreed to take it up with the president.

Barletta's final point was the most difficult. In the July discussions, the United States had agreed to pay Panama $10 million a year from canal revenues. Barletta said he believed strongly that $20 million would be a fairer figure. Linowitz told him that he did not think that could be sold. And, he added, the experts on canal traffic doubted that income from ship transits would sustain that kind of payment. The discussion went back and forth, each man supporting his case with all the arguments he could muster. Linowitz told Barletta he would back either a guaranteed $10 million a year or a conditional $20 million a year—if it were available from canal company profits. Barletta then raised what proved to be the final settlement. Can we say that Panama will get $10 million guaranteed, he asked, and an additional $10 million if it is available from the revenues? In fact, Linowitz had, at that moment, White House approval for just such an arrangement. We had suspected this might well be the Panamanian bottom line, and so Sol had raised it with Vice President Mondale the previous day. He had also talked about it with Zbigniew Brzezinski, the president's National Security adviser. As a result, Sol had prepared a memo recommending this variation in the economic package, and it had come back to him the afternoon of August 5 with the president's black-inked OK. Sol did not, however, want to give away this card without something in return. So he told Barletta that *if* the other issues then being debated could be settled, he would recommend the economic package they were discussing. That generated pressure on the Panamanians to try to work out the other matters quickly.

Linowitz had consulted Ambassador Bunker periodically during the talk with Barletta. He hung up the phone at that point and rubbed his arm, which was nearly numb from holding the phone for forty minutes.

We went into the next room for a break, but the red phone suddenly jangled again. It was Edwin Fábrega wanting to discuss some land issues and the transfer of facilities. There was a housing area in Curundu, within a stone's throw of the Zone border with Panama. Fábrega argued it would create problems if that remained an exclusive U.S. military housing area. Couldn't we put our people in some less conspicuous place? Then there was the U.S. Navy pier at Rodman, which the navy rarely needed. Couldn't this seldom-used facility go to Panama? Another problem, on the Atlantic side, involved housing and the high school at Coco Solo. Couldn't we be a bit more generous on that?

Throughout the treaty talks, the U.S. negotiators were impatient with the tendency of the Canal Zone authorities and the military to try to hold on to as much as possible of what they had regardless of real need. When matters like that arose, Linowitz especially was inclined to seek quick solutions. Bunker's experience, on the other hand, convinced him that Defense Department cooperation was essential and that we should not alienate the men in uniform if it could be avoided. As the talk with Fábrega progressed, Bunker excused himself and put in a call to Gen. Tom Dolvin, the deputy negotiator who represented the Defense Department on the U.S. team. Bunker wanted Dolvin to know, at least in a general way, what was going on. He also wanted to assure him that no final decisions would be made on these Lands and Waters issues—Dolvin's specialty—without his knowledge and concurrence. Dolvin appreciated the ambassador's call and offered to join the group. But Bunker told him it was late (10:00 P.M. by then). He promised to consult Dolvin in the morning. The final response to Fábrega in Bogotá was that the United States was favorably disposed to the points he had made. But, of course, they would have to be checked out with the Defense members of the U.S. team. General Dolvin to this day refers to the meeting at the Panamanian Embassy that night as the "Friday Night Massacre" because of the implied promises that were made. He spent the next four days pulling back from some of the things the Panamanians thought, with excessive optimism, they had been promised.

By that time, negotiators in both Bogotá and Washington were optimistic. Some issues had been settled; others seemed well on the way to solution. There was a growing feeling at both ends of the line that a few more days of that kind of serious negotiating could make the difference between a treaty and no treaty. But the hardest issue—the keystone of the Bogotá chapter—had not yet surfaced fully at the Washington terminus of the long-distance connection. That was the option for the United States to build a sea-level canal. After all the talk about economics and payments, and housing areas and other matters, it came to the fore.

The phone rang and Gabriel grabbed it. Royo was on the other end. He explained that the Latin American presidents were unhappy with the U.S.

proposal. They thought it was completely one-sided. They had a counter-proposal—on which they were unanimously agreed—and they hoped President Carter would accept it in the spirit in which it was offered. The ambassador turned the phone over to Tony Hervas, who dictated to us, as Royo read the Bogotá text: "The Republic of Panama and the United States of America recognize that a sea-level canal can be important for international navigation in the future. Consequently, after ratification of the actual treaties and during the term of same, both countries agree to study jointly the feasibility of a sea-level canal. In the event they determine favorably the need for a sea-level canal, they will negotiate for its construction on terms agreeable to both countries." Linowitz got on the phone with the scribbled text in his hand. In other words, he said, having quickly caught the central meaning, you're not giving us an exclusive option. Panama would have as much say as we about building a new and more modern canal. "Is that right?" Linowitz asked. "Correct," said Royo. The presidents assembled in Bogotá, he explained, believed no country should have the right to do anything as major as building a new canal in another country without the full approval of that country.

Royo said the Latin American presidents thought the proposal they were making was fair to both sides. Would it be possible to get President Carter's approval that night, he asked? Then the U.S. president could cable his acceptance to the Bogotá summit, and everyone would be happy. Linowitz told him it was impossible. President Carter was in Plains and asleep. He and Bunker did not want to wake him in the middle of the night with anything as sensitive as this. Obviously, it would take careful consideration. He promised Royo to contact the president first thing the next morning and to reply to Bogotá as quickly as possible. Royo said he understood and would pass that message to General Torrijos and the others—who by that time were enjoying a sumptuous banquet.

Linowitz hung up the phone. We looked at each other in silence. The Panamanians were trying to read our expressions. There was little to read. Linowitz and Bunker and I went into the next room. We reread the Bogotá wording. Sol said he saw no real problems with it, except it would be hard to give up the exclusivity of our earlier proposal. Bunker agreed. I recalled the strong case that had been made in the 1960s for an open U.S. option to build a new canal—as well as the emotional feelings of some members of Congress—and suggested we might have political problems with the new proposal. But I thought that could be overcome—if the White House took a strong lead.

With that, one of the wilder nights in U.S.-Panamanian diplomacy drew to a close. It was nearing midnight and we had been at it for six hours. Ambassador Lewis was feeling particularly optimistic at that point. He offered Bunker and Linowitz the chicken dinner that Nita had been holding ready. But they were both exhausted and had lost all appetite. They politely declined. It was time to call it a night. Everyone shook hands, and I walked them to the door and down the steps to the sidewalk. "That was one unusual night," I said. "You're right, Bill," Bunker said. "But worth it in the end." Linowitz thought it had been "a good night's work." And they climbed into their cars.

"Are we going to be arrested for kidnapping?" Gabriel asked with a grin when I returned. "I don't think so," I said. "Actually, my colleagues are quite happy with the results."

"So are we," Gabriel said.

We had a nightcap and reviewed the bidding. It truly had been a good night's work, one none of us was going to forget. No one was likely to be party again to a negotiation with five presidents at the other end of a phone line.

Engineer Cano offered me a ride back to my Virginia Avenue apartment. It was 1:00 A.M. by then and there was little traffic along Rock Creek Parkway. The downtown streets were almost deserted—only a few cruising cabs, some late partygoers. As we neared my temporary address, due north of the State Department, I pointed to the east. "The White House is over there a few blocks," I said, "and that's where it all began thirteen years ago." Cano asked what I meant. I told him that in 1964 an American president named Lyndon B. Johnson had said that the time had come for a new arrangement between the United States and Panama. And that's what we had been trying to work out over the past thirteen years.

But there were still a few loose ends. Saturday morning was a time for follow-up on the previous night's events. Bunker and Linowitz had sent to the White House the wording we had received from the presidents in Bogotá. It was forwarded quickly to Plains for the president to study. We also had several questions pending on the economic package. Sol Linowitz had explained the state of play to his assistant, Ambler Moss (a lawyer Sol had brought with him into the treaty business from Coudert Brothers, the prestigious law firm). Moss drafted a memo for the White House on the two key items—the $10 million guarantee with the additional $10 million on an "if available" basis,* and the matter of the inflation index. Moss had studied the matter and found that the Industrial Wholesale Price Index was probably the most reliable and stable of all those available. He put it into the memo as the negotiators' recommendation. It was, he admitted later, very much an end run around the bureaucracy. But it was the only way to get things done in the time available. The memo came back from the White House in a few hours with presidential approval. Linowitz

---

*This was raised again because it ran into some Defense Department resistance that Saturday morning. Defense officials did not know that the president had already approved it.

passed the word to Ambassador Lewis, who relayed it to General Torrijos and his advisers in Bogotá.

The sea-level canal option was more difficult for the president and the White House staff. As he studied the Bogotá wording at his home in Plains, the president saw no real problem with its basic thrust—that the two countries would have to agree on any plans for a new canal. That was only fair, since it was Panamanian territory we were talking about. But he had one nagging worry. What if Panama decided to work out a deal with someone else? What if a consortium of foreign powers made a deal to build a new canal in Panama, leaving the United States out in the cold? Even more worrisome—what if Panama made an arrangement with the Soviet Union, or Cuba? Clearly the Congress would want to know that couldn't happen. So he wrote some words and discussed the problem with his advisers.

The message went back to Bogotá via Ambassador Lewis: "President Carter accepts the text of the six leaders in Bogotá. But he asked that additional language be added to allow him to sell the treaty to the Senate of the United States." The additional text was: "A new interoceanic canal will not be built in the territory of the Republic of Panama during the term of this treaty if it is not in accordance with the provisions of same or any other agreement entered into between the parties." The Bogotá formula said that no U.S. canal would be built unless Panama and the United States agreed on the terms. With the added words, the United States would have a veto over a canal proposed by other builders. In relaying the message, Ambassador Linowitz told Lewis that President Carter was asking his presidential colleagues in the Colombian capital to "take his problems into account." And he explained the congressional difficulty.

The Latin American leaders in Bogotá were at that moment assembled in a country house (technically, a state farm) some twenty miles from Bogotá. It was a beautiful, rambling ranch house built in traditional Spanish style—lovely tile floors, open terraces, high ceilings, a fantastic view of the surrounding countryside. President López Michelsen had invited his four guests* there for a relaxed lunch. They were sitting on the terrace, enjoying preluncheon drinks and talking about the night before. All eyes turned, however, when the phone rang. Ambassador Lewis in Washington was relaying the message from President Carter. Royo took it down, then passed it to Torrijos and the others. The reaction was less than favorable. They understood the U.S. president's problem, but this was Latin America and they could never approve anything that looked, or was, one-sided for

*The fifth leader, Jamaican Prime Minister Manley, had left after the previous evening's meeting and late dinner in order to be in Kingston in time for a previously scheduled session with Andrew Young, the U.S. ambassador to the United Nations, who was touring the Caribbean.

their neighbor Panama. The heart of the matter, as they saw it, was that Panama could not make any arrangement with another country to build a canal on its own territory, but the United States was free to make a deal with some other country in Central America for a new canal if it wished.

Once again the tension mounted. Mexico's López Portillo called the one-sided proposal unacceptable. Panama's foreign minister grabbed the phone and told Ambassador Lewis to tell the Americans that if this was their position, "Don't come to Panama." (They were due to arrive the following day, August 7.) Lewis was wise enough not to report this remark to the U.S. team.

Torrijos looked around, sensed the temper of the group, and said, in effect: "You, my friends, draft something. Whatever it is, I will accept it—and I hope that Carter will accept it, too." Led by Venezuela's Andrés Pérez, new additional wording was drafted. It came to be known as "Paragraph B," and it was dictated to Lewis: "That during the term of the Canal Treaty, the United States will not negotiate with third countries regarding the construction of an interoceanic canal over any other route within the territory of the Americans, nor will it undertake construction of a canal within the territory of the Americas."

Lewis called Linowitz at State and gave him this wording. Sol immediately passed it on to Hamilton Jordan at the White House. Within minutes the Situation Room teletype was clattering urgently, and the counterpart machine in Plains kept pace with the words from Bogotá. It was in the president's hands in minutes. President Carter thought it over and discussed it with some of his closest advisers—Jordan, Zbig Brzezinski, a few others. Then he placed a conference call to Bunker and Linowitz, standing by in their seventh-floor suite at the southeast corner of the State Department Building. They talked back and forth, and the president gave the ambassadors his decision. He asked them to relay it to Torrijos and his colleagues in Bogotá. Conveyed by Ambassador Lewis, the Carter message was: "Tell General Torrijos that I accept, without taking out a single comma, the text of the proposal made by Torrijos and his friends, the presidents. What was added in Washington [the U.S. paragraph] will not go, nor will Paragraph B [the Bogotá addition]."

Carter said to congratulate Torrijos on "the courage he has shown." The president also expressed his gratitude to Colombia's President López Michelsen, the Bogotá host, and told him he was "glad we have reached an agreement." The presidents in Bogotá were delighted. They issued a joint communiqué that said the end of U.S. control over the Canal Zone meant the end of a colonial vestige in the Western Hemisphere. As could have been easily forecast, the Latin American leaders expressed strong support for Panama's claims in the bilateral negotiations. But the presidents surprised many readers of their communiqué—and pleased the U.S. president and his key associates—by adding significant praise for Carter. They said that "the spirit which has guided President Carter in the negotiations . . . will serve to strengthen friendship and cooperation in the hemisphere." They had heard, and were reacting to, Carter's request to them to take his problems into consideration. They were passing the word to the American people and to the U.S. Congress that a new arrangement with Panama would make friends for the United States in Latin America, and that rejection of Panama's aspirations would only make enemies south of the border.

Everything seemed to be coming up roses. Ambassador Lewis asked Foreign Minister González-Revilla if he could tell Ambassadors Bunker and Linowitz that "we have a treaty." Nico replied: "Not yet. There are no problems in sight. But we have to be very careful to have good people draw up the final text." It was but a small cloud in an otherwise clear and shining sky. Major difficulties had been overcome. The presidents in Bogotá had proved to be able negotiators. And the president in Plains had risked much to buy their compromise. Bunker and Linowitz and their team would be on a plane the next day bound for Panama and the wrap-up sessions.

Mili and I were at Washington National Airport when I got the word that the Bogotá-Washington talks had produced a last-minute solution. I was leaving for home base to be on hand to welcome the U.S. team for what looked like surely the final round. I felt exceedingly good. But somewhere inside was a nagging question: what else can happen to break this thing up? I had no way of knowing then how very close we would come to that break in the next few days. Nor did I foresee how many chasms we would approach, and nearly topple into, during the following eight months, particularly as we crossed the cratered Senate landscape.

As we rose over the Potomac, I glanced down at the familiar monuments of our capital city. The sun was shining brightly and all seemed fair and promising. I leaned back and closed my eyes. "Quite a day," I thought. And then I began to relax. There would be some tough ones ahead, I knew. But Scarlett O'Hara had the right idea. I would worry about it tomorrow.

CHAPTER 2

Prelude to Crisis

"The present contains nothing more than the past, and
what is found in the effect was already in the cause."

—Henri Bergson, *Creative Evolution*

IT began in an unlikely way. But most of history is the result of the
unexpected, small sparks thrown into tinder made dry and flammable over
long years. Who in Boston realized that a group of painted men were
changing the world by throwing bales of tea into the icy harbor? How
many foresaw that the assassination of an obscure archduke would produce the most massive bloodletting in human history? Who imagined that
a hunger strike by one man, even one so holy, would mean the end of empire in the Indian subcontinent? In Panama in 1964, no one thought a
small group of unthinking American students could, by raising their country's flag in front of their high school, assure the beginning of the end of a
way of life they and their parents wanted eagerly to preserve. It was not
what they expected, even less what they wanted. Nonetheless, an ill-
conceived prank and a display of false bravado turned into a nightmare for
them and for all around them.

The Christmas holidays were over. On January 2, 1964, the students of
the Canal Zone school system trudged back to their classes. As with students in most places, the postvacation blues were upon them. But a special
grievance was eating away at some of the students at Balboa High School.
A few days earlier, on December 30, the governor of the Canal Zone, Robert J. Fleming, Jr., had announced that henceforth U.S. and Panamanian
flags would fly together at seventeen selected sites in the Canal Zone. And,
he added, the American flag would *not* fly at some other places—the
American schools, the district court, and a few others. The governor was
carrying out a policy begun by President Dwight Eisenhower and expanded by President John Kennedy. In so doing, he became a target for
many of his subordinates in the Zone.

Fleming was a rarity among those who had occupied the governor's office—a man who believed it was both right and wise to establish good working relations with Panama. Unlike the insecure and nervous folk who were his charges, he did not believe a powerful nation like the United States had to prove how strong it was by using an iron hand with a small and basically friendly country. It may be, too, that Fleming was aware that the first in his line of governors, Maj. Gen. George Davis, had told a committee of the Senate in 1906 that the U.S. flag was not flown in the Canal Zone and that, in his opinion, it never would be "in view of Panama's basic sovereignty over the territory." Unfortunately, by the time Fleming became governor, most Zonians had forgotten that they were living within another country.

In the corridors of Balboa High School that January day, the flag issue was a lively subject. Obviously it had produced heated comments in many living rooms and across backyard fences over the Christmas holidays, and the students were filled with their parents' emotions and prejudices. "Why," they were asking, "can't our flag fly as it always has? Why is the governor giving in to 'those people'?" Before nightfall, some students prepared a petition addressed to President Lyndon Johnson protesting the flag decision. The petition was circulated the next day, and by sundown had more than four hundred signatures.

That same day, January 3, a Canal Zone policeman named Bell took it on himself to raise an American flag over the small war memorial in Gamboa at the center of the Zone. Gamboa was one of the seventeen sites where the flags of the two countries were to be flown together. Bell's was the first act of defiance of the governor's order. That it was done by a policeman diminished respect for authority in the Zone. Bell became a one-day hero, especially when the Canal Zone government backed down and said the Gamboa flag could continue to fly "because it is the responsibility of a veteran's organization." The example of successful defiance was not lost on the students.

The following day was Saturday. With schools closed, authorities hoped that emotions would recede and the crisis disappear. But in Panama City, countervailing pressures were building. Newspapers lambasted Zone authorities for not allowing Panamanian flags to fly at more places. More important than editorial attacks was the decision of Panama's most magnetic politician to use January 4 to announce his candidacy for president. Arnulfo Arias had served twice before as his country's chief executive, and twice he had been ousted (in 1941 and 1951). The son of a middle-class family from Panama's interior, he was an excellent student, and with scholarships managed to attend college in the United States and to graduate from the Harvard Medical School. But politics was more to his liking than medicine. Distrusted by many in the oligarchy, and feared by old-line politicians, he had appeal for the common people, the underprivileged, and the downtrodden. When he appeared in Santa Ana Plaza that Saturday, forty thousand people—mostly from the nearby urban slums—showed up to hail him.

Arias won cheers with his violent attacks on the government, the traditional parties, economic moguls, and intellectuals. He promised he would erase injustices in relations with the United States. Roars of approval swept the plaza. It was a brand of rabble-rousing politics Panamanians had not experienced for years. Many in Santa Ana Plaza that afternoon would be, in a few short days, out in the streets again—shouting their hatred, destroying property, fighting, looting, and, some of them, shooting.

The issue that so riled sentiment in 1964 was not something that had erupted overnight. Display of the flag was linked directly to the question of sovereignty, and that had been a source of controversy since the 1903 treaty was negotiated. More than any other single factor, what shaped Panamanian attitudes in the twentieth century was the central feature of the Hay–Bunau-Varilla agreement: turning over to control of the United States that which Panamanians always regarded as their principal natural asset, their unique geographic position. That outlook had persisted from the earliest days of Panama's links to the Spanish Empire.

Panama never had the gold that Peru could offer, or the silver of Mexico, or Colombia's emeralds—none of the natural wealth that Spanish monarchs drained from their far-flung colonies. What Panama did provide was the shortest overland route between the Pacific and the Caribbean, the easiest way for the treasures of the west coast of South America and the spices and silk of the Orient to reach Spain.*

From the days of Columbus and Cortez and Balboa, for more than four hundred years, Panamanians considered their unique location to be their most precious national resource. They always assumed that if Charles V's dream of a canal from the Atlantic to the Pacific was realized, it would be through their homeland and would become part of their heritage. No wonder, then, that the most galling aspect of the 1903 treaty was the fact that it turned over more than five hundred square miles in the very heart of their country to a foreign power. The specific purpose was "construction, maintenance, operation, sanitation and protection" of a transisthmian canal. But with that concession, Panama also gave the United States "all the rights, power and authority" in the new zone that it would have "if it were

---

*Incidentally, the dream of a canal across the isthmus goes back to those early sixteenth-century days when Spanish galleons were returning to Spain with their treasures. Charles V commissioned a search for a strait that might connect the eastern and western shores of the New World. Reporting the results of his search, Hernando Cortez wrote to the king and queen: "We have not found as yet a passage from Iberia to Cathay, but we must cut it. At no matter what cost, we must build a canal at Panama." That was in 1529.

the sovereign of the territory." That sweeping authorization, and the fact that it was *forever*, was a bone in the throat of the Panamanians ever after.*

Panamanians never forgave the United States for letting a shrewd and dapper Frenchman, Philippe Bunau-Varilla, negotiate and sign the 1903 accord. He had credentials as their official agent, to be sure. But he also had a massive interest in the bankrupt French canal company which benefited greatly by the final settlement. Panamanians were outraged that a matter so vital to their national life should have been dealt with in such haste and with so little consideration for their sensibilities. (The treaty was signed by Secretary of State John Hay and Bunau-Varilla in Hay's Washington home just two hours before a delegation of leading Panamanians arrived in the U.S. capital to negotiate a treaty.) But however indignant they were, the Panamanians were boxed in and knew it. Refusal to accept the new treaty—though its provisions were onerous—would have meant loss of U.S. support for their independence. Surrender of nationhood was the one price they would not, could not, pay. So they acquiesced, but they never forgot.

Not that Panamanians did not welcome the idea of a major shipping route being built across their country. They did. Obviously, little Panama could not itself build a canal. They had seen a strong, technologically advanced France come to grief in the previous decades as it struggled in the jungle to duplicate its feat at Suez. So if the United States would build such a waterway, all to the good. It would bring world commerce to their country. All those ships would need supplies and fuel. Building the canal would provide thousands of jobs. Workers would need food, clothing, and recreation. It would be a bonanza. Panamanians and Americans would join hands in the great adventure, and both would share in the rewards.

Sadly, it did not work that way. The Americans who arrived to launch the massive undertaking had strong ideas about how to do it, and treating Panamanians as partners was not part of their plan. The new rulers of the Canal Zone charged ahead, setting up their own small empire. They took over and improved ports at both ends of the canal route, established customs houses, and launched a postal system—using U.S. stamps. The surprised Panamanians watched with growing amazement. What, they asked, did all this have to do with digging and running a canal? Finally, in exasperation, they sent Secretary of State Hay a long and detailed bill of complaint. That was in August 1904.† Ten weeks later, Secretary Hay re-

---

*Ironically, a similar grant of sovereign authority extracted by Imperial Germany from an enfeebled China only a few years earlier had been vigorously condemned by the United States.

†Any reader who assumes that differences between the United States and Panama are of recent origin should note the date. The Panamanian complaint against illegal procedures was written less than six months after the Isthmian Canal Convention went into force.

sponded with an even longer, more legalistic note. In effect, it said: "We intend to interpret the treaty to our maximum advantage."

The Panamanian plaint received short shrift at the Department of State but attracted attention in another part of town. President Theodore Roosevelt read the grievances and became convinced a political crisis was building in Panama. To set things right, he turned to his secretary of war, William Howard Taft, who was responsible for overseeing the Panama enterprise. In a letter to Taft on October 18, 1904, Roosevelt noted that the people of Panama were fearful the United States might set up a "competing and independent community" in the Canal Zone that would injuriously affect their business, reduce their revenues, and diminish their prestige as a nation. He asked Taft to go to Panama and reassure its people that "we have not the slightest intention of establishing an independent colony in the middle of the state of Panama, or of exercising any greater governmental functions than are necessary to enable us conveniently and safely to construct, maintain, and operate the canal under the rights given us by the treaty." Roosevelt then added words that should have been required reading for every Canal Zone employee and every member of Congress from that day to this: "The exercise of such powers as are given us by the treaty within the geographical boundaries of the Republic of Panama may easily, if a real sympathy for both the present and future welfare of the people of Panama is not shown, create distrust of the American Government. This would seriously interfere with the success of our great project in that country." *

Taft sailed off to Panama to carry out the president's instructions. The three-hundred-pound future president established excellent rapport with Panama's leaders. More important, he worked out fair solutions to many of the problems the Panamanians had raised. Taft assured them that the Canal Zone would import only the machinery and other supplies vital to the work of building the canal. Everything else brought into the country should properly go through Panamanian customs, he agreed. Panamanian goods would enter the Zone duty free. He even ruled that Panamanian stamps should be used on letters from the Zone. The Panamanians were delighted with Taft's fairness and understanding. When they waved goodbye to their genial visitor from the Cristóbal dock in December 1904, the Panamanians were convinced the U.S. government would henceforth deal with them with justice, and that future relations would be based on trust and cooperation.

---

*Text of the Roosevelt letter is in *Background Documents Relating to the Panama Canal*, prepared by the Congressional Research Service of the Library of Congress.

That hope gradually disintegrated as a result of the slow erosion of individual actions and interpretations. Despite the friendly words of Roosevelt and Taft, it became clear the fundamental U.S. goal was not to meet Panamanians halfway, but rather to assure that nothing happened that might disrupt the fabulous engineering project. Within a few years, the Taft agreements were abandoned. Under Presidents Wilson, Harding, Coolidge, and Hoover,* what Teddy Roosevelt said would never happen did happen: we created a colony.

The United States intervened in Panama numerous times to maintain public order and to oversee elections. North American businesses flourished by supplying the huge canal enterprise. Panamanian suppliers could not compete with the U.S.-subsidized commissaries that catered to the work force. And the Zone postal system began using its own stamps. The Canal Zone became a "company town" not unlike those established by the coal companies in West Virginia and Ohio or the copper producers in Montana before the turn of the century. Panamanians could work on the canal with a pick or shovel alongside the thousands of blacks brought in from Caribbean islands to dig "the Ditch." Later, they could handle hawsers and unload ships stopping in the Zone. But technical or administrative positions were closed; they were the exclusive territory of white North Americans.

Racial attitudes prevailing in the United States were reflected, even exaggerated, in the Canal Zone. The black work force—three-fourths of the laborers who built the canal—suffered not only the disadvantages of skin pigmentation. They were also mostly non-U.S. citizens. So they were not a constituency any representative or senator or president had to be much concerned with. U.S. citizens were paid in gold; all others, in silver. The "gold and silver" distinction may have seemed less obvious than "black and white," but that is what it meant. And it carried over into most aspects of life—housing, transportation, recreation, restrooms, virtually everything. Perhaps it was unreasonable to expect Canal Zone authorities and the U.S. Congress to be more farsighted and humane than were politicians in the towns and states of the continental United States in those days. Still, the pattern of prejudice and segregation was solidly established over the years; and there was considerably less pressure to change in Balboa and Colón than there was in Birmingham or Chattanooga. In any case, the fact that no Panamanian was ever permitted to work into the upper levels of

---

* President Franklin Roosevelt and President Eisenhower both tried to correct major flaws in the 1903 arrangement and to meet some of Panama's aspirations. There were major treaty revisions in 1936 and 1955. But no U.S. president before Lyndon Johnson faced up to the central problems: sovereignty over the Canal Zone and an arrangement drawn up to last forever.

canal management and administration was just one more source of friction between the Zone and the Republic.

Despite all the frustration and points of irritation—perhaps because of them—the fact was that relations with the United States dominated Panamanian political and economic life from the birth of the Republic on. I occasionally asked Panamanian friends how they explained this national preoccupation with one other country. They pointed out the obvious things—the canal and the large North American community, U.S. military bases, the common currency, an influential U.S. business colony, all the elements that created a special relationship. But one perceptive friend stressed another factor: "You have to remember," he said, "even though it is painful to us, that our independence was not something we fought and died for. It was a result of U.S. political and military intervention at a crucial moment in 1903. That made it possible for us to break with Colombia."

He was not arguing that independence was handed to Panama on a silver platter. Throughout the nineteenth century, when they chafed under Bogotá's heavy-handed domination, Panamanians repeatedly revolted against Colombian rule. There were at least forty attempts to restore Panamanian independence, and many Panamanians fought in those battles.

Nonetheless, the hard historic truth was that the U.S. gunboat *Nashville* in the harbor at Colón on November 3, 1903, and its armed sailors in the city were vital to the Panamanian independence move just launched. Colombian troops in the Caribbean port city could not get to the Pacific side to rescue their commanding officers—who had been ceremoniously welcomed to Panama City, then unceremoniously put in jail. In a speech to his miniature army, the leader of the independence movement, Dr. Manuel Amador Guerrero, proclaimed: "President Roosevelt has made good . . . Long live President Roosevelt." Within ten days, four U.S. Navy warships were at anchor in Panama City, and five others had joined the *Nashville* at Colón. That show of force provided the final assurance that the infant republic would survive.

From that day, a complicated love-hate ambience characterized U.S.-Panama relations. Panamanian appreciation for the U.S. role in their independence was profound. During three-quarters of a century after that momentous event, Panamanians knew that the Colossus of the North was the most reliable guarantor of their continued freedom. But, while one may take comfort from the protection nearby friendly power affords, no one likes to be beholden, even to a parent, to say nothing of a mighty neighbor. As Balzac said: "Gratitude is a charge upon the inheritance which the second generation is apt to repudiate."

By the mid-1950s, Panamanians were two generations removed from their day of independence. In the intervening years, pride and irritation gradually overwhelmed any thankfulness. Panamanians still realized that what the United States had done in 1903 had helped them to nationhood, but they became convinced that it had helped the United States vastly more.

In 1958, Dr. Milton Eisenhower, the president's brother and a man well versed in Latin American affairs, made a long visit to Panama. He returned to Washington with, as he said, "a feeling of impending disaster." He made the rounds of the capital talking to all who would listen—in the State Department, the Pentagon, and the Congress—arguing for urgent steps to better Panama's sad economic condition. To improve the political atmosphere, he suggested that the Panamanian flag fly in the Zone on a regular basis, or at least on ceremonial occasions. His proposals generated violent protests from some members of Congress as well as from the secretary of the army and the Canal Zone governor.*

A year later, Washington received reports that Panamanian students and some political leaders planned to march into the Canal Zone with their national flag on November 3, Panama's day of independence. A worried Army Secretary Wilber M. Brucker called in Eisenhower, described the problem, then laid out a course of action he thought the United States could and should take. Eisenhower reported that "I tried to appear placid as he repeated a plan nearly identical to the one I had urgently proposed thirteen months earlier." Eisenhower described the plan and urged his brother Ike to adopt it that weekend. A meeting was hastily called at the White House on Monday morning and the plan was launched. But there was no time to put it into effect. It was overtaken by events in Panama.†

Aquilino Edgardo Boyd was 38 years old in 1959. A member of a distinguished Panamanian family, he graduated from Holy Cross College in New Orleans, and studied law at the University of Havana. In the Cuban capital, he also worked in the Panamanian Embassy; then he went to the embassy in Washington as first secretary. At some point, the talented Boyd succumbed to a virus that attacked most intelligent sons of Panama's oligarchy—the conviction that he should and could be president of his country.

He won elections to Panama's National Assembly four successive times, beginning in 1948. He resigned his Assembly seat in 1956 to accept appointment as foreign minister. He led Panama's delegation to the United

---

* Eisenhower's account of his visit to Panama and of the events that followed is in his perceptive book, *The Wine Is Bitter*.
† Why there was such procrastination in Washington is unclear. There was nothing secret about Panamanian intentions. The plan to march into the Zone with the Panamanian flag had been announced in August, but Brucker did not summon Milton Eisenhower to discuss the crisis until early October.

Nations General Assembly in 1956 and 1957. (He later served with great skill as Panama's full-time representative to the U.N. for more than 13 years.) He resigned in 1958 as the result of student disorders, went off to Mexico as ambassador, and then left that post in five months. The call of politics was too strong. From the Assembly seat which he reassumed, the fiery, nationalistic Boyd became a champion of causes that attracted popular support—and U.S. opposition, which was the name of the game. In January 1958, for example, he called for a 50-50 split of canal revenues between the United States and Panama.

With a presidential election coming up in 1960, Boyd decided to promote his candidacy with dramatic action. He announced in August that on November 3, the anniversary of Panama's founding (his grandfather Federico Boyd had been one of the founders), he and his followers would parade the Panamanian flag through the Canal Zone. Zone authorities, using arguments they had relied on for years, decided to prohibit Boyd's incursion. They showed no sensitivity to Panamanian sentiment. On the contrary, they hastily erected an eight-foot-high cyclone fence along the border separating the Canal Zone from the downtown area of Panama City. (In a few years, Panamanians were calling it "the little Berlin wall.")

What would have happened if, instead of fencing themselves in and Panamanians out, the Zone authorities had announced that November 3 was U.S.-Panama Friendship Day, or Good Neighbor Day, and if on that day Panamanians had been free to march behind their flag wherever they pleased? I suspect it would have pulled the ultranationalist fangs rather painlessly. But nothing of the sort was tried, or even considered.

Instead, early on November 3, a large crowd, led by Boyd and Ernesto Castillero Reyes, Panama's best-known historian, assembled on Fourth of July Avenue. They asked to enter the Zone with their flag. The Zone police said no. A small group, carrying their national banner, crossed the avenue and tried to force their way into the Zone anyway. The police pushed them back. The flag fell to the ground and was torn. That sight made tempers flare. Rocks were thrown. The leaders disappeared but the mob, armed with clubs, bottles, and rocks, surged forward, pelting the police.

Boyd left the battle at the Zone perimeter. Then, he gathered a second crowd and led them to the defenseless U.S. Embassy, a stately old building on Avenida Balboa. The mob broke many of the embassy windows with rocks. The U.S. flag was hauled down and witnesses said Boyd and others tore it into pieces.

Two miles away, on the Zone border, the confrontation continued. Two policemen were severely beaten. The Panamanian National Guard was called out; then the U.S. Army. Many rioters were injured. Tear gas discouraged the outburst until the troops arrived. With bayonets fixed, the soldiers formed a wedge and moved the shouting crowd back to the street.

There, the young soldiers stood their ground though they were the targets of rocks and bottles. Not one shot was fired and no one died. The most serious encounters were between Panamanian police and rioters.

There is an axiom in Latin American politics: "If you want to get Uncle Sam's attention, you have to scream and raise hell, and even threaten to go to the Russians for help." There is another that many governments have acted on repeatedly: "If internal problems become intractable, divert the people's attention by getting into a fight with outsiders—the 'imperialists,' the multinational companies, the Colossus of the North." In Washington, there is a countervailing axiom: "We cannot appear to be giving in to pressure."

Nowhere have those clichés been more evident than in U.S.-Panama affairs. Leaders of the 1959 riots believed the outbreak would catch Washington's eye and perhaps produce some changes. At least, leading the fray against the *yanqui* devils would enhance their domestic political standing. At the other end of the line, an administration that was about to launch a nine-point program to help Panama economically, moved it to the back burner. "We can't cave in to pressure."

But the atmosphere soon quieted in Panama. President Eisenhower was asked about the flag issue at a press conference in December. Reflecting the advice of his brother Milton, the president said he believed "we should have visual evidence that Panama does have titular sovereignty" over the Canal Zone. That set off a minor explosion among the superpatriots on Capitol Hill. Led by the irrepressible Daniel Flood of Wilkes Barre, Pennsylvania—surely the most colorful of all congressmen with his waxed moustache and flowing black cape—the House in February 1960 voted 380 to 12 against permitting Panama's flag in the Canal Zone. It was only a "sense of the House" resolution and had no binding effect on the president. Nevertheless, it was a gauge of the prevailing mood in the lower house, where whim and passion often prevail over detached judgment. By April, the Eisenhower administration was moving forward with its new Panama program. Wages were raised for unskilled and semiskilled workers. The Zone government was told to stop buying beef and lamb from faraway Australia and New Zealand and to purchase its meat in the United States or Panama, even if it cost slightly more. Luxury items—hardly necessary to operate the canal—disappeared from commissary shelves. Sales of jewelry and perfume rose in Panama. And a start was made on a low-cost housing program.

Four months before he left the White House, President Eisenhower carried out the most controversial item of his nine-point Panama program—flying the Panamanian flag in the Canal Zone. The site selected for that historic act was a small, wedge-shaped piece of the Zone known as

Shaler Triangle,* located on Fourth of July Avenue just next to Panama's legislative palace. There, on September 21, 1960, Canal Zone police raised the flag of Panama alongside the Stars and Stripes. It was the first time since 1906 that Panama's national banner had flown over Canal Zone territory. The action produced a highly favorable response among Panamanians, but it was a different story for the rabid, pro-Zonian group in Congress. Dan Flood likened it to Britain's weakness at Munich and called for Eisenhower's impeachment.

In 1960, a mild-mannered, extremely wealthy, and not too robust Roberto Chiari was elected president of Panama. His father had been president earlier in the century and was one of the nation's abler chief executives. Roberto himself had served as acting president for a few days in 1949. Clearly, his dearest wish was to follow in his father's footsteps with a full term of his own. He was a proud man when he donned the colorful presidential sash and walked up the long stairway in the Herón Palace for the first time in October 1960. One month later, the people of the United States elected a new president, John F. Kennedy. Thus, by the third week in January 1961, new men were in charge of both countries—the huge, wealthy, powerful United States and the least populous country in the Western Hemisphere, yet the "crossroads of the world," Panama.

Relations between the two countries were tranquil for the moment. The Eisenhower program, which met some of Panama's more obvious complaints, was moving forward. Meantime, President Kennedy was facing several important tests, the Berlin Wall, for example. Panama did not figure at all in Kennedy's calculations. But for the Panamanians, including President Chiari, the United States continued to be Problem No. 1. In a long letter to Kennedy in September 1961, Chiari set forth the many ways in which unilateral U.S. interpretation of the treaty between the two countries had been less than fair to Panama, in his view, and why adjustments were needed. Chiari's brother Rudolfo, who went to Washington on an economic mission, delivered the letter on September 15. Kennedy finally answered on November 2. The U.S. president told Panama's leader that, when one treaty partner was unhappy about parts of their pact, "arrangements should be made to permit qualified representatives of both nations to discuss these points of dissatisfaction with a view to their resolution." He also told Chiari that he had instructed departments and agencies concerned with Panama and the canal to make "a complete re-examination of

---

*Named for Col. James Shaler, head of the Panama Railroad in 1903 and a key figure in the events that gave Panama its independence. Shaler, by all accounts, loved Panama. He probably would have been pleased that land named for him was used for this purpose.

our current and future needs with respect to Isthmian canal facilities." He
promised to contact Chiari when the study was finished.

But another "study group" was not what the Panamanians wanted.
They saw it as a way to further postpone real action, which it probably
was. So the Panamanians kept pressing wherever they could—with U.S.
diplomats in Panama City, through their embassy in Washington whenever
a U.S. official could be buttonholed, at cocktail parties and across dinner
tables, at the United Nations, on the golf course. The upshot was an invitation to President Chiari to visit Washington in June 1962.

When Chiari flew to Washington to meet the young U.S. president, his
briefcase was filled with papers on all the issues dividing Panama and the
United States. The two men and key assistants met in the Oval Office on
June 12, and again on the thirteenth. On the second day, they issued a joint
communiqué. Its central point was the principle that Kennedy had mentioned seven months earlier—when one treaty partner is unhappy with the
way the contract is being handled, "arrangements should be made to permit both nations to discuss these points of dissatisfaction." Chiari and
Kennedy agreed to appoint "high-level representatives" to carry out the
discussions. And they agreed the representatives should "start their work
promptly." *

A communiqué is like a biographic sketch in *Who's Who*—it gives essentials but leaves out much that is interesting. The Kennedy-Chiari report
was no exception. It did say that the presidents had instructed their representatives to find ways for Panamanian business to supply more to the
Zone market. It promised to improve employment opportunities and to
boost wages for non-U.S. workers. And it said the two countries would
arrange to fly the Panamanian flag "in an appropriate way" in the Zone.

The joint statement did *not* mention some things Chiari had pressed on
Kennedy that were of profound significance for Panama. One was the
question of Canal Zone land. The Zone comprised some 550 square
miles—only a fraction directly occupied by the canal itself and the services
essential to its operation. Even when housing areas, town sites and recreation grounds, airbases and training fields were deleted, a good deal was
left. Why, the Panamanians asked, can't some unused land be returned to
us, or at least turned over to our use? They were especially interested in
areas adjoining urban centers in Panama City and Colón where existence
of the Zone prevented or distorted normal city development.

Another issue was the desirability of a mixed court system, with both
U.S. and Panamanian judges. Many defendants appearing before Zone

---

*The men picked were, for the United States, Ambassador Joseph Farland and Canal Zone
Gov. Robert Fleming; for Panama, Foreign Minister Galileo Solís and Dr. Octavio Fábrega.

courts were Panamanians, yet they were tried by North American judges under U.S. law. Would it not serve the interests of justice to have at least some Panamanian representation in the legal machine? When this issue was raised, the dominant reaction of the Zonians was outrage. They considered the Zone part of the United States; U.S. law and justice were part of the natural order. They did not know, or care, that the first Canal Zone court, the "supreme court" as it was designated, had a distinguished Panamanian jurist as one of its three members. Secretary of War Taft, appearing before a congressional committee in 1906, vehemently defended both the jurist and the concept. Judge F. Mutis Durán, Taft noted, was one of Panama's leading lawyers and "an authority on civil law." He further argued that "in a jurisdiction of such anomalous character as that which the United States exercises in the midst of another people, in the belly of another country, so to speak, . . . it seems just and fair that upon a court of three, one Panamanian should be appointed."

Chiari raised with Kennedy the vexed question of postage stamps on mail from the Zone. It had been a bone of contention since 1904. Chiari's question was: If Panama has basic sovereignty, shouldn't Panama's stamps be used on all mail from its territory? What do stamps have to do with running the canal? Kennedy added it to the list of areas of discontent the two countries' representatives would consider.

By far the most sensitive issue on Chiari's agenda was the matter of "sovereignty in perpetuity." That, for Panama, had always been the gut issue whenever treaty matters were discussed. That most central of the issues brought up in the Oval Office, unmentioned in public, was obviously the hottest of several hot potatoes Chiari introduced.

The issue was not bypassed, however, in talks between Kennedy and Chiari aides who picked up where the two presidents left off. The aides met on June 14 and 15. On the latter date, they signed a "secret" memorandum. It noted that the presidents had agreed bilateral talks would go forward, and while talks were underway, it said, "the question of perpetuity becomes less important." That was so, the memo claimed, because studies were then going forward that would "enable the United States to come to a definite decision to build a sea-level canal or continue with the present one." The memo then added the intriguing conclusion that that decision "will make the question of perpetuity obsolete because a new treaty will have to be negotiated *in either case* [emphasis added]." In other words, if the United States decided to build a sea-level canal, it obviously would have to work out a new treaty. But even if a sea-level route were ruled out, the two countries would have to write a new treaty to govern the old canal.

The memorandum remained secret until the crisis of January 1964. In the midst of that diplomatic contretemps, Panama's ambassador to the OAS produced it as evidence that the United States had, under President Kennedy, committed itself to negotiate a new treaty on the canal. When the memorandum leaked, the *Washington Post* found one U.S. official who said President Kennedy "never led Chiari to believe . . . that the United States was prepared to agree to a new treaty." Another official told the *Post* that it was "clear" no time limit had been set, but that a new treaty "was deemed desirable as a long-range goal."* It was the usual waffling that occurs when any administration makes a decent but impolitic promise in confidence which then is revealed.

The presidential commission initiated by Kennedy and Chiari went to work immediately, and the first subject taken up was the matter of flags. Governor Fleming compiled a list of fifteen sites where the two countries' ensigns should be flown together, and U.S. Ambassador Farland concurred. The list included Shaler Triangle, where the national banners had been flying side by side for almost two years. The list was given to the Panamanian commissioners on July 20, 1962. They welcomed it and suggested no additions or changes. The first real action under the agreement came with the inauguration of the Thatcher Ferry Bridge, a huge span over the canal linking Panama City with western Panama. It replaced the outmoded ferry, for which it was named, that once provided the only connection for people and freight traveling from the provinces to the capital city. It was dedicated on October 12, 1962, with Under Secretary of State George Ball representing the U.S. government. At each end of the long, graceful bridge, the flags of the United States and Panama flew together. They have flown there ever since.

The goodwill generated by the bridge opening was dissipated greatly in two weeks. On October 26, a Zone resident named Gerald Doyle filed suit in the federal district court seeking an injunction to prevent flying the Panamanian flag in the Zone. Doyle, a branch chief of the Canal Company's Engineering Division, named the secretary of the army and the Canal Zone governor as defendants in his suit. Doyle became an overnight hero to many Zonians and his action produced a flood of congratulatory mail. Conservative members of Congress commented favorably in the *Congressional Record*. The reaction in Panama was expectably negative. The National Assembly passed a resolution declaring that flying the Panamanian flag in the Canal Zone was "an inalienable right of the Republic of Panama." Despite the curdled atmosphere, bilateral talks went forward, but no additional Panamanian flags were raised while the suit was pending.

After nearly nine months of argument and judicial study, Doyle's case was dismissed. Federal Judge Guthrie Crowe ruled that the flying of flags

---

*The text of the "secret" memorandum and the comments thereon were printed in the *Washington Post* on February 9, 1964.

was a matter for decision by the executive branch of government. Nothing was done, however, for ten additional weeks, the time allowed for filing an appeal. Doyle apparently decided an appeal was useless. He resigned from his job on the canal and returned to the United States.

Once the legal hurdle was passed, Governor Fleming went forward with the scheduled flag raisings. New flagpoles had to be erected at the remaining sites, and that took time and money. But on October 24, 1963, the national banners of the United States and Panama were raised over the locks at Miraflores. On November 9, they went up at Gatun. Then successively, at intervals of a few days to two weeks, the national banners flew together at the Coco Solo Hospital, the Corozal Hospital, the Palo Seco Leprosarium, and the town of Margarita. The whole process covering all seventeen sites (raised from the original fifteen) was to have been completed by February 7, 1964. Each time the flags went up in tandem, the Panamanians cheered and the Zonians became more disheartened. The mood of frustration and indignation was palpable in many Zone households over the Christmas holidays. Students at Balboa High School listened to the vitriolic comments around them and absorbed their parents' anger. They were in an ugly mood when they went back to school on January 6. They were mad at the governor, disenchanted with the Pentagon, furious at the whole Washington establishment.

The first Monday of the year passed without incident, but storm warnings were evident. Students gathered in clusters between classes and muttered their discontent. An unusual number of flags were displayed in classrooms. The usual joking and good humor were absent. By evening, school officials learned that some students planned to raise the U.S. flag the next morning. They alerted higher authorities and two Zone policemen went to the high school at 6:00 A.M. Their orders were to maintain order and prevent damage to government property. They were not told, apparently, to see to it that the governor's instructions were carried out, that the flag should not fly outside the school.

By 6:40 A.M., some 25 students had gathered at the flagpole and the number increased by the minute. They found the halyard locked, and some young men tried unsuccessfully to climb the pole. Soon there were more than 200 students and a dozen adults. But the police reported that most were simply watching the affair, taking no direct part. The active element, about 80 students, finally got the halyard loose and raised the flag. It was 7:25 A.M. and the students then drifted off to their classes.

Two Canal Zone officials, B. I. Everson and Frank Castles, arrived at the scene. They met with the school principal, David Speir, and the three men lowered the flag. Twenty minutes later, the first class period ended. Students poured out of the school. One took out another, smaller flag and raised it to the top of the flagpole. By then, about 150 students were on the school steps and the lawn. They recited the pledge of allegiance, then went back to classes.

At noontime, someone produced a larger flag and it was substituted on the pole. After school, about 100 students and adults remained in the area. At sunset, 6:05 P.M. according to the police, the flag was lowered by six students. But two dozen youngsters remained on watch all night. They wanted to make sure the authorities did not remove the flagpole. Parents and friends supplied them with blankets and food.

The whole situation put Governor Fleming in a box. In carrying out the dual-flag policy, he was following the directions of his government. But his own people were defying him. As a soldier, he believed in obeying orders, and having them obeyed. But it was a nightmare to imagine the headlines he would generate if he imposed his will: "U.S. General uses force to lower U.S. flag!" So he temporized, hoping some solution could be found, perhaps by flying both flags.

Across Fourth of July Avenue, in the Republic, news of the flag raising at the school spread rapidly, and emotions rose. Wednesday morning, January 8, Radio Miramar forecast that tension between students in Panama and the Zone would surely worsen. At 7:45 A.M., the Balboa students returned to the flagpole and raised the U.S. flag once more. The flag craze spread. One went up at Coco Solo High School on the Caribbean side. Flags were also hoisted at several elementary schools—mainly by high school students and adults. When classes were over at Balboa, students marched around the flagpole and school yard with placards demanding that the U.S. flag continue to fly at their school. They circulated a petition addressed to senators they thought would favor their cause.

The harassed governor grew more worried. The problem was spreading, not easing. He issued a statement reminding Zone citizens of their responsibility to carry out "the official commitments of their government." He said there was a special responsibility in the Canal Zone "where our actions are subject to direct view by citizens of other countries." He then went on to explain that the list of sites where two flags would be flown was not final. He left the door ajar for readjustment, obviously meaning flying the two flags at schools. But, by then, the students were feeling very potent, and confident they would suffer no serious repercussions. The governor's appeal fell on deaf ears. A band of emotional students seemed determined to make the governor back down. They were urged on by their elders and their parents.

January 9, 1964, was one of those clear, bright days typical of the dry season. A cooling breeze was blowing from the south. In downtown Panama City, store clerks and government employees were on their way to work in Panama's colorful, always crowded buses known as *chivas*. The more affluent helped fill the streets with their Buicks and Fords. At the Panama Golf Club, a few of the privileged had gathered for an early morning round of golf. Shops were opening. Telephones were starting their daily clang. Students were walking to school. In the Canal Zone, the first ships of the day were approaching Miraflores Lock on the Pacific side and Gatun on the Atlantic. Shops were opening there, too. And students were going to school.

No one in Panama and no one in the Canal Zone imagined on that beautiful morning that the day would be remembered henceforth as the Day of the Martyrs. No one foresaw that before that day was out, the emergency room at Santo Tomás Hospital would be filled with injured and dying.

A worried Canal Zone governor was not troubled enough to prevent him from packing his bags for a trip to Washington that day.

The successor to a murdered president sat in the Oval Office at that hour reading the morning papers and thinking of the day's heavy load of business. He had no idea he was about to face his first major foreign policy crisis.

And students at Balboa High School and at Panama's Instituto Nacional would never have guessed that they were about to change history at the crossroads of the world.

By sunset some of them, by midnight all of them, knew differently.

CHAPTER 3

Blood in the Streets

"Where passion rules, how weak does reason prove!"
—Dryden, *The Rival Ladies*, Act II

I T was 7:30 in the morning, January 9, 1964. A handful of students at Balboa High School raised the U.S. flag in front of their school, as they had the previous two days. Scattered applause came from fellow students and adults who had gathered to watch approvingly. Then the teenagers walked into the school to their classes. The majority of students were not taking part in the display of inflated patriotism, but peer pressure induced silence. Any student would have found it difficult to dissent openly on flying one's national emblem. Those who disapproved of the clear violation of their government's avowed position remained silent and went about their normal routine, insofar as anything was "normal" that day. There was no excuse for the grownups involved—teachers, school authorities, and parents who either applauded the students' actions or looked the other way. They owed the younger generation a better example.

Gov. Robert Fleming was at that moment wondering what he could do to ease matters. He felt confident the affair would pass without incident. Fleming was considering adding the high school to the list of sites where flags of both countries should fly. But his mind was also on his long-planned trip to Washington that day. He had lunch with Foreign Minister Galileo Solís before leaving, but neither was aware they were sitting on a powder keg.

Fleming went over a statement his staff had prepared for him, made some changes, then taped it for broadcast by the U.S. Armed Forces Radio later in the day. That done, he went to the airport and took off for Miami and Washington. It was execrable timing, something like the captain of the Titanic going to bed after the first iceberg warning. Before Fleming's plane landed at Miami International Airport, his domain was besieged—and he was 1,200 miles away. He caught the next available plane and arrived back in the Zone in the middle of the night.

If the talk at Balboa High that morning was mostly about flag raising, the same subject dominated conversation at another high school, Panama's Instituto Nacional, located just across Fourth of July Avenue. For several days, Panamanian newspapers and radios had been filled with reports of the flag mania in the Zone. Editorials castigated Zone authorities for their decision not to fly the two countries' flags at the schools and at official buildings, such as the district court and the police station. When the students raised the Stars and Stripes at Balboa High, the Panamanian press attacked the move as a violation of the agreement reached by the presidential commissioners. In part, the press campaign was a natural outpouring of Panamanian pride and national zeal. But with most of the press controlled by political parties and ambitious individual politicians, there was a question as to what part of the effort was genuine patriotism and what part was political opportunism.

A national election was coming up in May. During the electoral season in Panama, parties and candidates vied with each other to raise the national banner highest, to outdo one another in proving how patriotic they were. A government that was in its final year of office and scared to death by the threat of Arnulfo Arias' candidacy was not above turning domestic frustration away from itself and toward the traditional scapegoat, the "Yankee imperialists." Whatever the reasons—and there were many—the mood in Panama that first week of January was increasingly emotional and explosive.

It was natural, probably inevitable, that the decision to "do something about it" was made by students of the Instituto Nacional. That academic institution had long been a hothouse for political activism. It was a training ground for many who later became leaders in the Federation of Revolutionary Students and other groups at the huge National University. Moreover, the institute was next door to the Zone and therefore especially sensitive to the overwhelming U.S. presence.

That January morning, institute students in their black trousers and white shirts could talk of little except the flag flying at Balboa High. One could almost hear young student leaders haranguing fellow students: "The gringos have forgotten that their precious Zone is part of our country. They fly their flag but not ours. They need to be taught a lesson." And so it went through the day. Books and lessons were forgotten.

By midafternoon, their plans were made. Student leaders went to see the director and explained their position. They won his support and permission to carry the precious institute flag in a march through the Zone. He did not ask whether they had approval from Canal Zone authorities to stage such a march. Like many educational administrators of his time, he found it easier to go along than to question. The flag he turned over had special meaning for institute students as well as for many Panamanians, for it was the flag of their country with the seal of the institute affixed at the center. It had been carried in the massive student outbursts of 1947 when young Panamanians overwhelmingly opposed a pact to continue U.S. military bases in their country outside the Canal Zone. A meek government had backed down; the huge student demonstrations made the agreement politically impossible. That flag was, for students at the institute, something like the flag raised over Mount Suribachi for U.S. Marines. It was precious; it was history; it stirred their blood.

At 4:45 P.M., when classes were over, between 150 and 200 institute students walked out of their school, crossed Fourth of July Avenue and entered the Canal Zone, marching up Gorgas Road. At their head, four students carried the treasured flag. Others carried a large banner that read *Panamá es soberana en la Zona del Canal* ("Panama is sovereign in the Canal Zone"). They were singing, cheering, laughing. But they were surely nervous, too. Most realized there was an ordinance prohibiting any parade of more than sixty persons. Would it be enforced? If so, how? Would they be rounded up and jailed? They didn't know.

In fact, no effort was made to interfere with their march. Zone authorities had decided the Panamanian students should be allowed to express their feelings, as long as they remained peaceful. So the police merely watched from a distance and reported their progress. They walked up Gorgas Road, past the well-known Gorgas Hospital, and on to the governor's residence, waving placards that urged the governor to "go home" and insisted "Panama is not a protectorate, it is free and sovereign." At the governor's house, the students paused long enough to sing the Panamanian national anthem. Then they continued on, chanting "Gringos go home" and waving their signs. They came to the imposing administration building where the governor and principal officers of the Zone government had their offices. They walked around the building, then down a long flight of more than one hundred steps, which carried them to the street level where Balboa High School was located. On the way down, they passed between two flagpoles where their national banner and the Stars and Stripes were flying together.

Across from the U.S. school, the institute marchers were met by Capt. Gaddis Wall, chief of the Balboa police, backed by a dozen of his troopers. Wall halted the young Panamanians and asked what their plans were. A spokesman, 15-year-old Guillermo Guevara Paz, told the big policeman they wanted to display their flag in front of the Balboa school and sing their national anthem. Balboa school principal David Speir and another Zone official joined the group. Speir got the impression that the

Panamanians wanted to have a discussion with the Balboa students, so he walked back across the street and convinced some of the Balboa teenagers to go to the school library for that purpose. That meeting, which might have cleared the air, unfortunately never took place. The Panamanian students were by then in the middle of heated discussion among themselves and with Captain Wall. Meantime, the crowd around the flagpole had grown larger and angrier.

Captain Wall proposed that five institute students accompany him and some of his men to the flagpole area. There, he assured them, they could display their flag and sing their anthem. This produced a long debate and heated words among the Panamanians. They argued that more, or all, of them should be allowed to go to the flagpole. But after forty-five minutes of dispute, the institute students accepted Wall's proposal.

By that time, the crowd in front of Balboa High had increased to about five hundred, both students and adults. They were irritated and vocal, shouting insults at the Panamanians. Those were returned in kind. U.S. accounts stressed the nasty mood of the young Panamanians and the insults they were casting at the Americans in front of the school. Panamanian descriptions underlined the threatening mood of the American crowd and their derogatory comments about Panama and its citizens. Both were accurate. The police and Zone authorities were caught in the middle—sympathetic to the American crowd but trying to be fair and to avoid serious trouble.

The five institute students—four carrying the flag, and another the student federation banner—walked across the street toward the flagpole escorted by Wall and his men. A sixth Panamanian, carrying a "sovereignty" placard, joined them. The flag bearers held their national emblem by the top edge; the bottom edge was at ankle level. Some witnesses insisted the Panamanian flag had a vertical split of about six or eight inches at its top center, and that one of the bearers held the split portions together in one hand. Panamanians argued the flag was torn by the Americans. An impartial study later concluded that neither claim was proved. With wonderful judicial balance, three foreign legal scholars who investigated the affair concluded: "It is quite likely that the flag, made of silk, was not able to resist the stress and strain of the occasion."

The school principal begged the students and adults to restrain themselves and to show courtesy toward the young Panamanians. But they ignored him. Some thirty U.S. students formed a double ring around the flagpole and sat down on the concrete pedestal. As the institute delegation and its police escort approached, the American men and women set up a chant: "No. No. No!" Soon the Balboa students joined in. Then they started singing "The Star Spangled Banner."

The frustrated Panamanians said they wanted to raise their flag on the flagpole. Captain Wall explained there was only one pole and the U.S. flag was already flying there. The students suggested the U.S. flag be lowered so they could raise theirs. Wall knew that would produce an outburst, so he told the Panamanians it was impossible. The noise level rose; so did bitter feelings on both sides. The American crowd closed in around the institute students and their flag. A shouting match developed, then pushing and shoving. The young Panamanians were pushed, or tripped on the hedge surrounding the flagpole pedestal, and one fell to the ground. The small rip in the flag grew larger. The rest of the institute crowd began to move across the street toward the school yard. Sensing real trouble was moments away, Captain Wall ordered his men to form a line between the Americans and the Panamanians. Then, with riot sticks held ahead of them, the police began to press against the institute group, urging them to leave and pushing to make sure they did. Some young Panamanians fell to the ground to express their protest. They were picked up by the police. Shouts and jeers from both sides filled the air. Suddenly, as if on a signal, the Panamanian students broke contact and began to run away. Up the long one hundred steps to the administration building they ran in disorder. Some went to the flagpole where the American flag was flying and started to undo the halyard. Panamanian reports said fellow students dissuaded them. U.S. accounts claimed Canal Company employees prevented the flag being lowered. Both were probably true.

In frustration, the students picked up rocks and started pelting the building. Several windows were broken. Some students were shouting: "You will live to regret this." The Panamanian students continued down Gorgas Road, spilling garbage cans, breaking street lights. At Gorgas Hospital, they swarmed over an unfinished addition where piles of lumber and steel reinforcing bars provided new weapons. In the parking lot, students slashed the top of a convertible. It belonged to a Panamanian doctor.

The Canal Zone police did nothing to prevent the vandalism, for they were under orders not to interfere—as long as the students kept moving out of the Zone. Finally, what was by then a mob spilled out of the Zone on Fourth of July Avenue, smashing street lights and traffic signals at that busy intersection. It was about 6:45 P.M. The entire affair had lasted two hours; but it was only the first act.

As the institute students were making their destructive way down Gorgas Road, the U.S. Armed Forces Radio was carrying the statement Governor Fleming had taped that morning. The governor explained that the flag agreement was "a valid commitment of our government." He told the primarily U.S. audience: "We Americans in the Zone have an obligation as citizens to support that commitment regardless of our personal beliefs." He concluded: "I hope that we Americans will conduct ourselves with reason, and, in an emotional situation, successfully avoid emotionalism." It was a perfectly good statement, reasonable, calm. But by the time it reached the airwaves, no one was listening. The emotions he was trying to calm had already exploded.

The Panamanian students arrived back at the National Institute eager to tell their welcomers about their "ordeal." Those welcomers included not only fellow students at the institute but also many from other schools in the city, including some from the university. There was a large representation from the Panamanian Federation of Students and from the leftist Federation of Revolutionary Students. How did the march into the Zone by a small group of high school students become so widely known so quickly? Obviously, word had spread as soon as they began walking up Gorgas Road two hours earlier. The purpose of the institute students was patriotic but also peaceful, by all indications. Clearly, extremists in the Panamanian student movement decided that it might not turn out that way, and they wanted to be on hand to take advantage if it didn't. The rudeness and immaturity of the Americans at Balboa High School—adults and students— provided the catalyst that helped turn a peaceful march into a revolutionary event.

Accounts by the returning students, undoubtedly wildly exaggerated, inflamed those gathered along Fourth of July Avenue. But word of the confrontation at Balboa and the news that the Panamanian flag had been torn had already spread. There were a few incidents of violence even before the students rushed down Gorgas Road back into the Republic. Several cars bearing Canal Zone license plates were overturned and burned on Fourth of July Avenue. Clearly, some Panamanians expected trouble, wanted trouble, went out of their way to make it happen.

People kept pouring into the street along the Zone border. Student ranks were augmented by hundreds of young people—and some not so young—from nearby Chorrillo, where tin-roofed shacks were jammed up against each other and narrow streets were the only access. A housing project under construction in the area provided a supply of bricks and clubs. The mob was screaming obscenities and throwing bottles and rocks at the Zone police. Captain Wall moved his men back from the fence to give them some protection.

Americans and Panamanians noticed that not a single Panamanian policeman was in sight. Everyone wondered why. The police captain went to the nearest phone and called Maj. Bolívar Urrutia, third in command of the National Guard. He described what was happening and urged that troops be sent to Fourth of July Avenue to bring the mob under control. The major promised help, but it never appeared. Urrutia dutifully called his superior after Wall's appeal. Col. Bolívar Vallarino, first commandant, listened to the report, then called President Chiari, who agreed the National Guard should remain aloof. It was an appalling abdication of responsibility. In effect, it said: let the mobs take over the streets; let passion make policy.

The explanation for that incredible display of indecision was fear, unadulterated, numbing fear. President Chiari and the National Guard were desperately afraid that, if they intervened, the hatred of the mob would be turned against them. The president was already in a weak position because of the widespread, and generally believed, stories of corruption in his government. The widely popular Arnulfo Arias had just announced his candidacy for president on a platform condemning the Chiari regime and the entire ruling class in Panama. The nightmare of screaming, outraged Panamanians being pushed from Fourth of July Avenue only to converge on the *presidencia* (only five minutes away) was enough to make Chiari's blood curdle—and for his advisers to prescribe inaction.

The National Guard itself was not eager for action. Vallarino and his colleagues recognized that many lower- and middle-rank officers harbored deep feelings of guilt because of their actions in suppressing popular demonstrations in 1947, in 1958, and again in 1959. In a force that was becoming increasingly politicized, they did not want the Guard to be—or seem to be—acting against popular wishes.

Both concerns were real, but there was a cynically political foundation beneath the decision to do nothing. Panama was in the midst of an electoral campaign. The voting would take place in May. The quadrennial exercise of "anti-Yankeeism" was well underway, and President Chiari had given tacit blessing to the familiar strategy. How would it look if, in the midst of an anti-American outburst, he used force to quell it? It would be a debacle, whispered the voices of political opportunism. Chiari agreed. And events moved inexorably toward disaster.

While President Chiari paced the floor of his office wondering what to do, while his and every other official voice was silent, another voice was being heard by half the population of Panama. It was that of a radio commentator named Homero Velásquez. That voice, conveying distorted reports to the people of the capital and the rest of the country, did more than almost anything else—except for the violence itself—to push matters to the fringe of chaos. Even before all the institute students had left the Canal Zone, Velásquez was on the air reporting the "brutality" the Canal Zone police had inflicted on the hapless students. In his account, the Panamanian flag had been "torn to shreds." The Zone police had savagely clubbed the Panamanian youths. Accounts of bloody encounters and Zonian inhumanity poured out over the airwaves from Radio Tribuna. At the time, the worst violence had been some broken windows, a couple of cars burned, and streetlights knocked out by rocks. But Velásquez put so much color and emotion into his reports that listeners assumed he was an eyewitness to all that was happening.

In fact, he was comfortably ensconced in a bar called the Cantina la Palma, well away from the center of things. He sat at a corner table with his microphone before him passing on tales of tragedy that soon helped bring that tragedy to pass. People ran into the bar to relay the latest rumors flying through central Panama. Velásquez elaborated on and magnified those reports for his increasingly inflamed audience. What made a radio journalist set up shop in a bar conveniently located to the scene of coming violence? What foreknowledge encouraged him to make the arrangements necessary for live broadcasts from downtown Panama on that fateful day? So far as I could learn, no one in authority ever asked why he was where he was, when he was.

The scene of the action in Panama City that night was a two-mile stretch of road (Fourth of July Avenue) dividing the Canal Zone from Panama. On the north side was Balboa Road and the entrance to Quarry Heights, headquarters for the U.S. Southern Command (SOUTHCOM). On a hillside, about one hundred feet from the border fence, was the residence of U.S. District Judge Guthrie Crowe. Then came Gorgas Road, the route Panamanian students had taken into the Zone that afternoon. The Tivoli Guest House, a stately old hotel built in turn-of-the-century French style, stood on high ground looking out over the avenue. Beyond the Tivoli, to the northwest, were the railroad station, the Ancon Laundry, and the Little Theater. Each would be attacked before the night was out.

The Panamanian side of that same arc was very different. Across from Judge Crowe's house was the writhing, noisy slum of Chorrillo. Close by, its bland back wall facing the street, was the National Institute. Then came the shops—gift shops, stores selling cameras and hi-fi equipment, souvenirs, clothing, all manner of things. They catered mainly to American tourists. Farther along was the recently built Pan American Airways building and the modernistic, uninspiring Legislative Palace. Beyond were shabby apartment houses with small stores and cantinas at street level. Avenida Nacional intersected with Fourth of July Avenue at that point of the arc. Along its length, and bordering Albrook Field, was another depressed slum, the area known as Calidonia. It provided many volunteers for the rampage that was coming.

That entire stretch of avenue, from the National Institute to the railroad station, had gradually filled with people—mostly students but many others as well: residents of nearby areas and the plainly curious attracted by the scent and sounds of violence. The fever among those hundreds of people built steadily, stimulated by the constant shouting, the sound of breaking glass as street lights were shattered, the odor of burning rubber and upholstery in the cars that had been set ablaze.

At 6:50 P.M., Acting Gov. Dave Parker called Southern Command to suggest some troops be alerted—just in case. Half an hour later, he called again to say he thought the situation was under control and that there was no need to position the troops just yet. He went out along the Panama-Zone border to see for himself.

By then, three thousand people were crowded along the border. Only a few minutes before, five hundred of them had rushed across the street from the National Institute and with wire cutters had breached the steel wire fence. The first structure in their path was Judge Crowe's home. They pelted it with rocks and threw Molotov cocktails against the wooden house. Several fires were started, but Judge Crowe and a few policemen managed to put them out. As they beat out the flames, they heard several shots from the Panamanian side. Later, the judge retrieved a .32-caliber bullet from the woodwork of his porch. It was probably the first shot fired in anger that shattering night.

What Colonel Parker saw on his reconnaissance convinced him matters were going from bad to worse. In addition to the attack on Judge Crowe's home, the bus terminal near Shaler Triangle was afire. Parker called Gen. Andrew P. O'Meara, commander-in-chief of the Southern Command at one minute before 8:00 P.M. He told the general that three thousand or more rioters were attacking the Zone and there was no way he could hold them back with the eighty policemen at his command. One of the most difficult things for any soldier is to admit he cannot handle the situation he faces. But Colonel Parker had both the guts and the wisdom to recognize reality. He asked General O'Meara to take command of the Canal Zone and assume responsibility for its safety. O'Meara agreed.

The situation the SOUTHCOM commander faced was serious. Firemen called to put out several fires were being pelted with rocks and could not get close enough to do their job. The police had used tear gas to discourage the mob, but their supply of gas grenades was limited.

In the center of the line, along Fourth of July Avenue, a thousand shouting, rampaging rioters tried to force their way into the Zone and attack the Tivoli Guest House. The police threw tear gas. Then they used both shotguns and pistols, firing into the ground and over the heads of the mob. Panamanians claimed they fired into the crowd as well; that some policemen did was unmistakable. In that area, the first Panamanian was killed and thereby became a martyr in the national cause.

Ascanio Arosemena was 20 years old. Before the end of the month, he would have graduated from the Escuela Profesional and he planned to continue his studies at the National University. Those who knew him described him as a serious young man and superior student. He was also an athlete, captain of his school's soccer team. He had no record of political activism. On the night of January 9, he had left home to see a movie. But as he walked toward the theater, he heard the noise of the rioting crowd on Fourth of July Avenue and joined the onlookers. He was wearing his red soccer jersey. Some who saw him in the crowd that night said he kept busy helping the injured escape from the scene. Sometime between 7:30 and 8:00 P.M., a .38-caliber bullet struck him in the back near his right shoulder. It passed through a lung, severed the aorta, and lodged in his chest. In a minute or two, he was dead. His body was taken to Santo Tomás Hospital, but it was too late.

The radio reporter Velásquez announced Arosemena's death, calling the Canal Zone police "assassins," but he devoted little time to it. He was too busy with other things. About the time the young soccer player was killed, a shouting gang of people was pushing its way down Avenida Nacional. At their head, carrying a Panamanian flag, was a friend of Velásquez. The broadcaster praised them as great heroes marching to "the front" to do battle with the Yankee "murderers." It was in that area—where Avenida Nacional intersected Fourth of July Avenue—that the largest, most costly confrontation of the evening took place. The mob, numbering some two thousand persons by that time, pushed into the Zone. The police formed a line to prevent them from moving on the Ancon housing area just behind. As the rioters approached, the police lobbed tear gas grenades in front of them. Coughing and crying, the Panamanians staggered back. They immediately fell on the nearby railroad station and the laundry, trying to set fire to both. Fire trucks from Balboa Fire Station roared up and the firemen, though pelted by rocks, managed to put out the worst fires.

But the angered crowd, egged on by rabble-rousers in their midst, refused to give up their orgy of violence. They advanced again on the railroad station, throwing rocks and Molotov cocktails into railroad coaches parked at the station and setting fire to the freight office. Soon the police had exhausted their supply of tear gas. They began using shotguns whenever the mob got too close, firing over the heads of the crowd and then into the ground and street in front of them. Some used their pistols. Thousands of people were gathered in the area, either demonstrating or watching. Moreover, that part of Panama City in a direct line from the embattled police and over the heads of the demonstrators was a heavily populated sector. The shots, though not aimed at those in front, did injure people standing farther off. It was almost certainly one such wild shot from a police .38 that killed Ascanio Arosemena. Dozens of other Panamanians were hit by shotgun pellets and bullets. A 36-year-old workman named Alberto Oriol was struck by birdshot in the face and upper body, one pellet severing his jugular vein. A 14-year-old student named Crance was killed by a

.38-caliber bullet that pierced his abdomen. Through much of that night, private cars and ambulances raced through the streets on their way to Santo Tomás Hospital with the wounded.

When General O'Meara took control of the Zone, he made a quick survey, then issued his first order. Anyone who did not live or work in the Zone was instructed to leave immediately. Those who did were told to go home and stay there. The general sent a plane over the troubled area, its loudspeaker carrying his message in English and Spanish. Everyone was urged to stop the violence and go home. The Panamanian government later complained that the tiny aircraft had intruded into its airspace. It probably did, but one can hardly imagine a more justified technical violation than trying to end bloodshed.

O'Meara ordered his troops to try to restore order in the threatened areas. At 8:35 P.M. a company of soldiers arrived at the Tivoli Guest House in 2½-ton trucks. They moved into position along the fence line on Fourth of July Avenue in front of the Tivoli. The crowd backed away before them. But the soldiers were hit with rocks, and Molotov cocktails fell among them. The troops retaliated with tear gas and quickly established their position along the avenue, from Gorgas Road beyond the Tivoli.

Meantime, O'Meara sent a trusted officer to the most troubled area, the intersection near the railroad station. He was Brig. Gen. George Mabry, a short, feisty, courageous South Carolinian who had won the Congressional Medal of Honor, and almost every other award for bravery, during World War II. At the intersection, Mabry found a violent, shouting mob. From behind barricades, the police were trying to fend them off. Mabry immediately ordered the police to stop shooting. Then, with fifteen soldiers behind him, Mabry advanced on the crowd. The sight of the determined officer and his men in battle dress, rifles held high and topped with bayonets, had the desired effect. The mob fell back, crowding into nearby streets in the Republic. U.S. Army troops replaced the police throughout the area.

The rioters quickly spotted the only place along the two-mile stretch of the avenue where army troops had not yet supplanted the police. It was Balboa Road, southwest of Judge Crowe's house. The mob surged up the road, penetrating the Zone for about one-fifth of a mile. Faced with a thousand yelling, rock-throwing Panamanians, the police fell back in some panic. There was a great deal of gunfire. The international jurists who later investigated found that in that area the shooting was not all directed into the ground or over the rioters' heads; some went into the mob. An 18-year-old student named Estanislao Orobio was hit in the throat by a revolver shot. He died thirty-six hours later. When U.S. troops finally arrived, they fired tear gas grenades and pushed the mob back to the avenue. They did not fire a shot. The soldiers spread coils of barbed wire across the road and, with that, violence in the sector largely ended.

With American troops controlling all main entrances to the Zone, frustration settled over the rioters, and rage, as well. They looked for other targets. The largest, most obvious, and most accessible was the relatively new office building of Pan American Airways, the most modern building in Panama City. To Panamanians bent on destruction, it was the next best thing to something in the Zone, a symbol of American power and foreign influence. No one apparently realized it was owned by Panamanians. In their heated state, it was enough that the big blue-and-white sign in front was that of a major U.S. company. So they attacked with the most destructive weapons they had: Molotov cocktails.

Two men at a corner of Cinco de Mayo Plaza had established a supply point for gasoline. They had a large drum of it and were passing it out to all who came by with empty coke bottles or wine jugs, glass containers of any kind. All it took then was an old rag, a piece of undershirt, anything that would serve as a wick. Add a match and you had a lethal weapon. Sometime between 8:30 and 9:00 P.M., a dozen or more of those missiles were tossed into the first floor of the Pan American building. Its builders had described the structure as fireproof. And it was, except . . . In all such buildings, there are upholstered sofas and chairs, carpeting, desks, woodwork, and paper, lots of paper. The gasoline thrown into the first floor started fires. For a time, they were confined to the lower floor and, before long, died out, leaving only a smoldering residue. With that, a swarm of people poured into the building. Soon they emerged carrying typewriters, adding machines, chairs, tables, lamps, whatever came to hand. Witnesses saw one man run through the smoking lobby with a small safe or strongbox in his hands. Another rioter killed him with either a knife or a gun, grabbed the metal container, and disappeared into the night.

Outside, several hundred people milled about, shouting, angry, looking for some way to destroy the building. They located a car with Canal Zone plates, set it afire, and pushed it into the building. Others continued to toss Molotov cocktails into second-floor windows. The fire blazed up again, and that time it did not stop. Firemen tried to approach but were hemmed in by the crowd and prevented from doing their jobs. Soon, the Pan American building was a flaming torch in Panama's night sky. Six bodies were later found in the wreckage, burned almost beyond recognition. They were either looters or arsonists, but they were entered in the list of "martyrs" compiled over the next days by those who wanted to make the riot the beginning of a new revolution.

The attack on the Pan American building whetted the appetite of the rioters. They fanned out to vent their outrage on other targets, which were not hard to come by. Offices of Braniff International and KLM, the Dutch airline, were looted and burned out. Panamanian shops on Fourth of July Avenue and nearby side streets became fair game for the looters. Store fronts and display windows were smashed. People rushed into darkened stores to grab what they could. Out they came—with radios and TV sets in their arms, and cameras, clothing, anything they could carry. One looted sporting goods store had a supply of guns and ammunition that added considerably to the firepower of those shooting into the Canal Zone over the next three days. Another target was a large pharmacy, where looters discovered the main drug vault and carried off the contents. One of the better jewelry shops lost its entire stock of gems, watches, and other jewelry. The looting fever spread, and the mob moved along Avenida Central and smashed its way through many side streets.

The National Guard was carefully avoiding the area of the worst rioting. But as looting became epidemic, the police did their best to protect property in other parts of town. They guarded such installations as the National Bank, the main hotels, the telephone office, and the city's electrical plant. When the mob attacked the power and light company, the Guard drove them back. The Guard also protected a sizable number of Americans—mostly young servicemen who had gone to backstreet cantinas for a night on the town. When rioting erupted, those Americans were effectively cut off from the Canal Zone. The police found many wandering through side streets and alleys trying to find a way out. The Guard took them to their headquarters building, then slipped them into the Zone in the middle of the night.

Hundreds of cases of Panamanians helping Americans occurred that night. Panamanian families took American neighbors under their own roofs to protect them. Cars with Canal Zone license plates were a special target for the rioters. Helpful Panamanians removed Zone plates from their friends' cars and replaced them with Panama plates. There were countless incidents of friendly cooperation in the city. Panamanian employees of Sears Roebuck joined the American manager to defend it against attack by the mob. Faced with that show of force, the mob looked for more vulnerable victims. Some Americans unlucky enough to get caught in the center of the storm were dragged from their cars and beaten while their vehicles were set to the torch. Many had to be treated at the hospital. One young man, taking his girl home from an early dinner, was set upon by the mob and was hit in the eye with a rock. He gunned the motor of his car and forced his way through his attackers, finally reaching the safety of the Zone. But he lost his eye, and spent a long time in the hospital.

The entire episode was a very mixed bag. Panamanians were attacking Americans here; and there, protecting them. Often the two were not widely separated in either time or space. In that kind of incident, where violence rules, there is always a tendency to think and write about it in black-and-white terms. But the truth is generally gray. It is not true that "there are two sides to every question"—an old Anglo-Saxon *idée fixe*— but probably five or six legitimate sides, and sometimes more.

Among those who thought that there were only two sides to the question—and that their's was right—were the Communists in Panama that night. They were not in the vanguard that went against the police and, later, the soldiers. But they were busily urging others on to brave deeds. They were the cheerleaders, the activists. As they roamed around the dark and frightened city that night, they found a suitable target. It was the U.S. Information Service library. Standing unguarded on Vía España far from the main riot scene, its library was regularly frequented by Panamanians doing research. Its books, films, and magazines were a treasure trove for students who needed information beyond that available in their crowded school libraries.

A Panamanian communist named Floyd Britton decided the USIS library was an appropriate place to display how *macho* he was. He led his portion of the mob to the USIS building and urged his followers to a frenzy of destruction. Rocks whistled through the air and smashed glass windows. What more satisfying sound to the rioter than that of breaking glass! Then Britton's troops stormed into the building to wreak total destruction. Things of obvious value—typewriters, recording machines, cameras, and the like—disappeared into the night. But the most precious asset of any library, its books, were torn from the shelves and tossed into piles in the street. There, the king of mob destruction, fire, took over. In front of the USIS library that night, some twelve thousand volumes went up in smoke.

On the other side of the isthmus, in the city of Colón, the wild exaggerations spread over the airwaves and by local inciters had stirred emotions to fever pitch. Colón offered even more fertile soil for violence than did Panama City. It had a higher percentage of unemployed; its slums were shabbier; the level of hope lower than elsewhere. It was ideal ground for a revolutionary outburst.

At 8:00 P.M., a dozen yelling, singing Panamanians marched down Bolívar Street waving a Panamanian flag. It was only an overture. In an hour, a crowd of fifteen hundred people had assembled and crossed over into the Canal Zone at the corner of Eleventh and Front streets. Nine or ten police were at the intersection, but did nothing. The crowd moved down Roosevelt Avenue to the administration building of the Canal Company. A small group carrying their national flag went into the building, climbed the stairs, and appeared at a second-story window. They raised the Panamanian flag on one of the twin flagpoles to loud shouts of approval from the crowd. Ironically, the flags of Panama and the United States had been flying together on those same poles for a week during daylight hours. They had been lowered together and folded for the night only a few hours earlier. Once the flag was raised, the crowd loudly sang the national anthem.

The Canal Zone police displayed remarkable patience, although they were subjected to a steady stream of insults and jeers. The Cristóbal* police chief, Captain Howerth, and Colón's mayor, Daniel Delgado Duarte, spoke to the crowd, begging them to remain orderly. But agitators kept moving through the gathering urging the opposite. One was a communist organizer trained in Cuba and the Soviet Union. Nonetheless, the large crowd began to disperse, albeit in disorderly fashion. They headed north, back along Roosevelt Avenue to Colón.†

The lull was short-lived. Several hundred who had left the Zone quickly reformed on Eleventh Street. They were halted briefly by the National Guard, but a segment of the mob broke off and surged down Balboa Avenue. While police tried to calm those in the front rank, windows could be heard shattering in the Canal Company offices nearby. That stirred the crowd further. They forced their way into the offices and the company's storage building. Furniture was dragged into the street. Typewriters and other office equipment were smashed on the pavement or carried off. While police attention was focused on Balboa Avenue, another crowd ran to the YMCA a block away. They forced their way in, looted the gift shop, ransacked offices, threw files and records on the floor, carried off anything of value. Through it all, the Zone police used no ammunition, fired no shots. They did arrest four of the looters. The police held the mob at bay around the railroad station, using tear gas when the rioters pressed in too close. At about 10:30 P.M., U.S. soldiers of the Fourth Battalion, Tenth Infantry, replaced the police along the riot-torn border.

The battalion commander spaced his troops along the border. On the opposite side of the narrow streets were stores and buildings, no open areas. It was like putting a border along lower Broadway or Washington, D.C.'s K Street. The young soldiers along that line were bombarded by bricks and bottles and Molotov cocktails. Soon, sniper fire from nearby

---

*Cristóbal was the municipal area of the Canal Zone on the Caribbean side. Colón is the Panamanian city.
†It was noteworthy that in Colón, unlike Panama City, there was regular contact and considerable cooperation between the Colón government and its police department and the police authorities in the Zone. That included frequent communication with José Bazán, second vice-president of the Republic and chief of the Colón Fire Department. During the days and nights of rioting, Colón firemen evacuated several hundred Americans from the inflamed city to the Canal Zone. Many others were assisted by the National Guard. Relations with the Canal Zone were always better in Colón than in Panama City.

buildings added to their danger. Pfc. Peter Juino was hit in the foot by a .22-caliber bullet as his outfit was forcing rioters out of the YMCA. Spec. Paul Boyd took a bullet in his right leg. A short time later, Sgt. Edward Rodriguez, standing in front of the YMCA, felt a sniper's bullet smash into his shoulder. Soon after, Pvt. James Willis was shot in the leg. Finally, at 1:00 A.M., Pvt. David Haupt was killed by a shot fired from across Bolívar Avenue. Through it all, the American forces did not fire a single shot in retaliation. It was an awesome display of courage and restraint.

The streetlights made it easy for snipers to spot the troops. The sector commander contacted Southern Command and received permission to take out the lights. Ten shots were fired; ten streetlights shattered. It gave the soldiers some protection. After that, the only light was the wavering flames from cars that had been set afire and the Molotov cocktails that sporadically arced across the darkened streets toward buildings on the Zone side and the troops that guarded them.

The absence of streetlights helped the defenders, but not enough. At 2 o'clock in the morning, S. Sgt. Luis Jimenez Cruz of Company B was shot in the head and killed instantly while leading his men to positions at Thirteenth Street and Bolívar. Two hours later, Sgt. Gerald Aubin of the same company was shot and killed by a sniper. His company commander, 1st Lt. Alexander Evans, was wounded at Aubin's side.

By late afternoon on the ninth, most of official Washington knew there was serious trouble in Panama. When the National Institute students began their march into the Zone, Lieutenant Governor Parker called the Pentagon and talked with Harry McPherson, then deputy under secretary for international affairs. "There's trouble down here," the lieutenant governor began. Parker told him of the students' march, and of the sour mood of the Americans. He assured McPherson that he planned to respond in a measured way; but he wanted Washington to know what was happening. McPherson passed the word to Under Secretary Stephen Ailes.

Back at the office later, McPherson phoned Parker. The lieutenant governor told him of the incident at Balboa High School and the destructive retreat of the Panamanian students down Gorgas Road. He also described the violence that had begun on Fourth of July Avenue. Parker said he thought things could be kept under control, but he was not sure. McPherson went home to look after his ill wife, but his nursing chores were brief. A call from the Pentagon told him that, as he recalled, "things were going to hell in a handbasket in Panama." He went back to the Pentagon, to the War Room, which is always center stage in a crisis.

Ailes arrived. Then Army Secretary Cyrus Vance wearing a tuxedo (he had been at a dinner party). The army's general counsel, Joe Califano, was on the phones along with McPherson, trying to piece together what had happened. The Situation Room at the White House was alerted. The State

Department's Operations Center was standing by, ready to pass along information from the embassy. McPherson and Califano stayed all night in the War Room, reading all the reports from Southern Command and other sources. Together, they drafted a detailed account. As new information arrived, the report was revised. By 7 o'clock in the morning, their summary—McPherson recalls it was fifteen to twenty pages in length—was finished. Secretary Vance took it to the White House for a 9:30 A.M. meeting with President Johnson.

There were many tired eyes around the table. The president and many of the others had been up late getting phone reports of developments on the isthmus. The president asked his CIA director for an intelligence assessment. John McCone reminded the group that the CIA had been forecasting trouble in that part of the world for six months—not just in Panama, but in Peru, Ecuador, and parts of Central America. The agency knew that Fidel Castro had been sending both money and agents into the area with the goal of stirring up as much trouble as possible. CIA had the names of certain activists who had been assigned to exacerbate any violence that erupted, however innocent or whatever the cause. Those agents had gone to work as soon as the flag incident occurred. So McCone, and others around the cabinet table, tended to view the events in Panama as a possibly planned outburst. Lyndon Johnson shared that suspicion. When the president asked for a rundown on exactly what had happened, Army Secretary Vance distributed copies of the Califano-McPherson report and summarized the main events.

Secretary of State Dean Rusk and Assistant Secretary Tom Mann both urged Johnson to contact Panamanian President Chiari directly. The president asked Pierre Salinger, who was still running the White House press office, to see if Chiari was available. While Salinger was gone, the president made several decisions. He told Tom Mann, the senior man on Latin American affairs, and Cy Vance to get ready to travel to Panama. Then he asked Secretary Rusk to urge the Organization of American States (OAS) to have its Inter-American Peace Committee investigate the affair immediately. He instructed Under Secretary of State George Ball to go quickly to the Hill and inform congressional leaders what was going on and what the president was doing about it.*

Salinger returned to say that Chiari was waiting for the president's call. Johnson went to the Oval Office and picked up the phone. After an exchange of greetings, Johnson stressed the two things uppermost in his mind—the need for both sides to do all they could to restore order, and a

---

*For President Johnson's account of the Panama crisis, see his memoirs, *The Vantage Point*, pp. 180–184.

reminder to Chiari that "elements unfriendly to both our governments" would probably try to exploit the violence. Chiari blithely ignored both Johnsonian points and raised the matter most on *his* mind—the need for a total revision of the 1903 treaty that governed U.S.-Panama relations. His countrymen's dissatisfaction with that outmoded arrangement, he claimed, was the direct source of the explosion that had just occurred. He recalled his meeting with President Kennedy in 1962 and complained that nothing had been done since to correct the inequalities and injustices he had described.

Lyndon Johnson knew political pressure when he felt it. And in that instant, he knew he was being pushed, and tested. He parried the Chiari thrust. That moment, he told the Panamanian, was no time to look into the past; violence was no way for friendly nations to try to solve their problems. Once order was restored, he said, we could go over all the differences and find ways to bridge them. That basic position—restore law and order first, then sit down and negotiate without preconditions on either side—was what Johnson would insist upon unwaveringly for the next months. To meet Chiari's demand for early action, President Johnson told him he was sending a personal representative and a top-level team to Panama "in thirty minutes" and that they would be on the isthmus that afternoon. Chiari said he was happy to know he was dealing with a man of deeds, not just words.

After their night-long vigil, Califano and McPherson went home to shower and take a nap. They had time for the former, not the latter. At 10:00 A.M., the phone rang in McPherson's bedroom and he was asked to get back to the Pentagon. A group of officials was going to Panama, he was told, and he would have to brief them. Califano got the same message. They were in their offices in half an hour. Soon after, they were told: get on the helicopter! What for? You're going to Panama! They both were wearing winter-weight suits, suitable for Washington in January, not designed for Panama's 90-degree clime. McPherson, like a foresighted Scotsman, stuck a toothbrush in his pocket. All the other essentials for an overseas mission would have to be picked up at the other end.

The air force jet carrying the U.S. mission took off from Andrews before noon, landed in San Juan, Puerto Rico, for fuel, then flew on to Howard Air Force Base in the Canal Zone. The members of the special presidential mission, in addition to Mann and Vance, were former Assistant Secretary of State Edwin Martin; Special Assistant to the President Ralph Dungan, a holdover from the Kennedy years; Assistant Secretary of State for Public Affairs Robert Manning; McPherson and Califano from the Pentagon; and assorted staff people. Immediately after landing, Mann contacted Panamanian authorities and asked to meet with President Chiari. He was told there was no safe way to go directly to the *presidencia*. The direct route would have been down Fourth of July Avenue through the riot-torn heart of the city. Mann was told he should fly to Panama's main airport (some twenty miles east of town) and that the National Guard would get him safely from there to the Presidential Palace. Mann and Cy Vance boarded a small U.S. plane and flew to Tocumen International.

What followed, Mann later described in his report to President Johnson as "pure theater." The Mann-Vance plane rolled up to a hangar at Tocumen and they alighted to find themselves surrounded by a large contingent of Panamanian soldiers. They were guided to a nearby office. An officer explained that the heavily armed escort was for their protection, that they were "in great danger." The officer got on the phone to make sure it would be safe to move the visitors to "the first checkpoint." It was. Mann and Vance were assigned a sedan and driver, and the convoy wheeled out of the airport area—two jeeps filled with *guardia* in front, and a similar armed party to the rear. Five miles down the road to Panama City, the convoy screeched to a halt at the checkpoint. The Panamanian officer went to a phone to get a report on the route to the second checkpoint. Mann and Vance remained in the sedan, surrounded by glowering armed men. Mann thought the whole procedure was deliberately calculated to intimidate the American visitors. Of course, those armed men had, for twenty hours, been listening to radio reports about the Zone police and U.S. troops "slaughtering" their fellow citizens. I doubt their demeanor was the result of careful coaching. More likely they were tired, nervous, and angry. They also faced the possibility of having to defend two gringo officials from their own people. A few scowls were understandable.

The convoy proceeded in that fashion, stopping periodically to check ahead to see if the path was clear. Finally, after what seemed to Mann and Vance several hours, they arrived at the *presidencia*. The small plaza in front was empty. Inside, around the graceful fountain and its surrounding pool, armed men of the National Guard were milling. The two Americans were escorted through and walked up the long stairway to the second floor. There they were greeted by President Chiari. He showed them to a sitting room in the front of the palace where large plate-glass windows faced the street. Next to the windows, two divans faced each other with a coffee table between. The conversation was barely underway when a crowd of several hundred shouting demonstrators appeared (possibly by prearrangement) in the plaza in front of the *presidencia*. Almost immediately, small stones began to strike the windows. There were no bricks or bottles, which would have shattered the windows; just pebbles, the right size to create noise, to harass the president and his visitors, not large enough to do real damage. It was like negotiating a contract in a hailstorm.

Chiari made one central point: the disturbances were the result of long frustration on the part of the Panamanian people over the presence of a foreign enclave in their midst; that, and the prospect that the foreign presence might continue forever. There had to be "structural revision" of the onerous treaty of 1903, he said, or there could never be real peace between the two countries. Unless positive steps were taken, he might have to break off relations with the United States. The threat was interesting because, at that moment, many Panamanians thought relations had *already* been broken. That is what they had been told by the radio.

Obviously, it was not the canal treaty that caused Panamanian rioters to take to the streets. It was the presumed insult to their flag, plus the wildly exaggerated reports of U.S. attacks on their fellow citizens. But Chiari was a shrewd politician. The treaty problem had rankled in Panamanian breasts for decades. He saw a chance to use the immediate crisis to achieve a long-standing national goal. Mann and Vance listened politely to Chiari's exposition, promised to report in detail to Washington, and urged that steps be taken to restore order to the streets. They underlined what President Johnson had emphasized that morning: no solutions could be found in the midst of chaos.

Both Mann and Vance were irritated by the needless time and complications of reaching the Presidential Palace. Mann closed the meeting by saying that if Chiari could not safely leave the *presidencia*, and if they could not safely get to it, it might be better for the president to send his foreign minister or anyone else in whom he had confidence to confer at a site in Panama that both sides could easily reach. Chiari agreed and picked the International Hotel in downtown Panama. Mann and Vance returned to the Canal Zone to send their report.

They described their long conversation with Chiari, and the bizarre atmosphere—the shouting mob outside and the steady pelting of the windows. They relayed Chiari's demand for "structural revision" of the Canal treaty and made their own recommendations. On treaty revision, they suggested telling Chiari they could not agree in advance that there would be a new treaty, but they would not close the door on future negotiations that might produce that result. On the vexed flag question, they suggested expanding the existing agreement to include flying U.S. and Panamanian flags at *all* Zone schools. After sending their cable, Mann and Vance went to get some needed sleep.

While the two chiefs of the special mission were dealing with the Panamanian president, the other Washington visitors conducted their own reconnaissance. After a briefing on the day's events at U.S. Army headquarters, they decided to see for themselves what was happening. They went in sedans to a point about one hundred yards behind and above the Tivoli Guest House. The cars parked behind a low building on Frangipani Street. As they huddled behind the building, the visitors could hear shots. They decided to make their way to the darkened Tivoli where the army had its advance command post. One by one, they walked across the grassy hillside, holding their breath and trying to make themselves as inconspicuous as possible. McPherson recalls turning up his coat collar to conceal his white shirt. At one point, he looked back at Ralph Dungan, who was following him. Dungan was walking along casually, swinging a cigar in one hand. Its lighted end was making visible red arcs in the night. McPherson shouted at his companion: "Put that goddamned thing out. I don't know if you care about getting shot; but I do!" Dungan dropped the cigar.

Inside the Tivoli, there was controlled confusion. Radios and walkie-talkies were squalling. Headquarters was asking questions; those on the scene were answering with what they knew. The sound of bullets hitting the outside walls was an occasional reminder of the lethal exercise being played out. Now and then a window shattered. The Washingtonians soon realized they were not helping, only adding to the confusion. They retreated back up the hill to the sedans, but they went knowing that the events they came to witness were deadly.

In the early morning hours, the U.S. representatives had President Johnson's answer to their cable. On the flag matter, he said, by all means agree that *both* flags should be flying at all schools. But on the first question, that there should be a basic revision of the relationship, the president told Mann and Vance the United States could not negotiate under pressure of violence. Therefore, they could not accept the idea of "structural revision." Johnson told his representatives to tell the Panamanian government that, as soon as peace was restored, the United States would "consider sympathetically" discussion of *all* problems between the two countries.

It took time to contact the Panamanian authorities. But finally a meeting was arranged that afternoon (January 11) at the International Hotel with President Chiari's selected spokesmen, headed by Foreign Minister Galileo Solís. When Mann passed on President Johnson's views, Solís called the *presidencia* and talked with Chiari. The Panamanian leader was adamant. Johnson and the U.S. government had to understand, he said, that, unless the basic rules of the game were changed, there could be no peace between the two countries. Mann responded that, unless there were peace, there could be no serious effort to solve the problems. It was a stalemate.

Meantime, the political fire started at the Balboa High School flagpole was fanning out in all directions. Panama and the United States had both appealed to the Organization of American States for its intervention in the dispute. Delegates of the Inter-American Peace Committee flew to Panama the day after the Mann mission. They were talking with both Panamanians and Americans—to get the truth and to make recommendations that might ease the problem.

Soon after the rioting exploded, President Chiari sent Aquilino Boyd, his country's U.N. representative, hurrying back to New York. In a stopover at Miami, Boyd told newsmen that "Panama has been the victim of unjustified oppression for fifty years." By the time he reached New York, the rhetoric had escalated. "We are the victims of a terrible aggression," he told reporters at La Guardia Airport. Boyd had a four-point solution—all things the United States should do, nothing Panama should do. The United States, he insisted, must: (1) take all measures to stop the violence (how the United States could stop the rioting without intervening in Panama's affairs was unclear); (2) "apologize" to Panama (why the United States should "apologize" for having the Canal Zone attacked was left to the imagination); (3) make "proper indemnification" (a better case could have been made that damage wrought by Panamanian mobs should be paid for by Panama); and, finally, (4) work out "a basically fair agreement" with Panama. The last was Panama's fundamental objective, as Boyd well knew; the rest was a smoke screen.

Boyd contacted the U.N. leadership and insisted on an emergency meeting of the Security Council. The session was convened late Friday evening. Ambassador Boyd laid out the Panamanian case, charging the United States with flagrant aggression against his little country. He urged the council to take all actions necessary to halt the bloodshed. He suggested that might include dispatch of a U.N. police force to Panama. At least some kind of U.N. representation might help, he said. Then, after the appeal to emotion, he got down to Panama's basic contention. "The Panama Canal Zone must not continue in its present status," he told the council. "This is cause for permanent discord. Panama cannot continue subject to iniquitous treaties." He proposed the canal be either nationalized (i.e., given to Panama) or internationalized (some form of multinational control under which Panama would have "special privileges").

Adlai Stevenson, the U.S. representative at the U.N., argued that the United States was "doing everything humanly possible to help restore the situation." He said that neither he nor Ambassador Boyd knew all the facts. But, he added: "I know neither the police nor the U.S. Army ever went outside the Zone. They stayed inside the Zone to protect U.S. citizens against snipers and an onrushing crowd." Then, in a pointed reference to the inaction of the Panamanian National Guard, Stevenson said: "I devoutly hope that the Panamanian authorities are being equally vigorous in their efforts to restrain lawlessness and to maintain order and prevent further incidents."

Brazilian Ambassador Carlos Alfredo Bernardes urged the president of the council to call for an immediate halt to the fighting and for both sides in Panama to restrain themselves. The council president, Bolivia's Renán

Castillo Justiniano, took the advice. The council approved his action and both Boyd and Stevenson welcomed his appeal. The council also agreed with Stevenson that no further action should be taken at the world body until the results of efforts then underway between the two countries and by the OAS were known.

Communist propaganda outlets around the world leapt on the story from Panama. Radio Moscow's news bulletin the day after the rioting began stated: "United States troops shoot Panamanian patriots." It labeled defense of the Canal Zone against rioters and snipers a "bloody act of repression" and claimed all of Panama was "in the grip of a wave of violent protest demonstrations." Newspapers in Havana that same morning used such headlines as "American Troops Machine-gun Panamanian People" (in *Hoy*); "Yankee Massacre in Panama" (in *El Mundo*); "Yankee Forces Kill in Panama" (in *Revolución*). A few days later, the Soviet Union's aggressive premier, Nikita Khrushchev, lashed out at U.S. actions in Panama. Speaking to workers at a textile factory, with Cuba's Fidel Castro at his side, Khrushchev ridiculed reports that Castro had helped organize the Panamanian demonstrations. "These events," the Soviet leader said, "are a result of the predatory policy of United States imperialists in Panama." He then advised the Americans: "Display some reason, gentlemen. Get out before you are tossed out." The speed with which communist propagandists jumped on the Panama story, and the prominence they gave it, strengthened the belief in the United States that the Communists, especially the Castroites, were more than innocent observers of Panamanian events.

In Panama, the level of violence was ebbing. Simple exhaustion took its toll among many who had taken to the streets. But hardcore demonstrators, egged on by agitators, refused to abandon their rampage. Panamanians with rifles and handguns continued sniping, confident, for the moment, that their police would not interfere. From midnight until dawn, the sniper fire was countered by a special U.S. Army marksmanship team operating from windows in the Tivoli Guest House. Using night-scopes and accurate rifles, the marksmen set out to eliminate the snipers or to at least harass them enough to diminish their effectiveness. Witnesses believed several snipers were either killed or wounded by the marksmen. By 4:00 A.M., firing into the Zone dropped off sharply. By then, the majority of rioters had left the streets and gone home to bed.

As the sun came up, soldiers looking out across the avenue saw store fronts without windows, the glass spread across the sidewalk; smoke still drifting from shops that had been fire-bombed; dozens of burned cars, many lying on their tops, some still smoking; the blackened hulk of the Pan American building; rocks and broken bottles and pieces of lumber and other riot debris strewn over the street. It was as though a tornado had touched down, moved through ten or twelve blocks, then passed on.

By 6:00 A.M. on the tenth, authorities in the Zone thought the storm had passed. Entrances to the Canal Zone were opened to traffic. Troops pulled back from the border. The only enforcement authority consisted of two military policemen stationed at each entry point. People entering the Zone were detained only long enough to ensure they were not carrying weapons. But within two hours, it became clear the trouble had not ended. Crowds once again gathered along the riot-torn avenue. The more audacious shouted insults and hurled rocks at the troops who had pulled back but had not disappeared. By 9 o'clock, snipers began again to shoot into the Zone. With that, those who had gone to the area merely to gawk ran for cover. In the back streets, looting was resumed. In one of those back streets, a plainclothes policeman who had been chasing a looter accidentally shot a 50-year-old man named Murgas. The killing was subsequently blamed on the Americans and Murgas became another one of the "martyrs" of the short-lived rebellion.

A few blocks away, on M Street, just across from the Tivoli, one of the most tragic events of the whole affair occurred. A couple of snipers had been firing from an apartment house. U.S. marksmen watched them rise up from a window, fire a round, then disappear, only to show up at another nearby window. Just at that moment, 11-year-old Rosa Elena Landecho poked her head out a window to see what was happening. A bullet felled her and she died. When other tenants learned what had happened, they ordered the armed Panamanians who had been using the building as a snipers' nest to leave. But it was too late to help the little girl. She, too, became a "martyr."

As the shooting became more intense, President Chiari called U.S. authorities and asked that countersniper fire be halted so the National Guard could move against the snipers. At a few minutes before noon, General O'Meara issued the order, and from that moment on U.S. troops fired no more rifle rounds into Panama. But the National Guard never showed up to halt the sniping as Chiari had promised. If anything, shooting from the Panamanian side became more intense. Judicial authorities who studied all the evidence after the riots estimated that between 400 and 500 rounds had been fired by Zone police and U.S. riflemen from beginning to end. That number of shots or more were fired from Panama into the Zone on each of the four nights of violence. When it was over, 465 bullets were found in the siding and woodwork of the Tivoli Guest House alone.

On Saturday, the eleventh of January, the size of the crowds and the level of violence diminished. Small groups of Panamanians rushed into the Zone along Fourth of July Avenue to plant miniature Panamanian flags. The troops made no effort to hinder them. About noon, at the eastern end of the Thatcher Ferry Bridge, a crowd of five hundred people assembled and began pelting a nearby Canal Zone housing area with rocks and bottles and damaged some parked cars. Three times they were repelled by Zone police using tear gas. They finally fled when U.S. Army troops arrived. Starting at 8:00 P.M. and continuing through the night, snipers using rifles and a few automatic weapons poured bullets into the Zone from atop the Legislative Palace and the burned-out Pan American building. The firing was not returned by the U.S. troops.

On Sunday, the area was even quieter than the day before. One reason was that, on that day, the "martyrs" of the rioting were carried to the cemetery in a huge funeral procession. Thousands of Panamanians turned out to take part or to watch, while thousands more watched on television. In the front row of the procession were six Panamanians who had been most active in fomenting the violence and in promoting the anti-American theme. Their names, and those of four others, had been given to the Panamanian police the day before. But the authorities did not pick them up. That afternoon, a lone group of seventy-five demonstrators penetrated the Zone, but they were discouraged by tear gas and fled. That night, shooting from Panama continued. Between 8 o'clock at night and 4 in the morning, an estimated 800 rounds were fired into the Zone.

In Colón, on the other side of the isthmus, the same general pattern was repeated. However, because of the crowded conditions and the proximity of targets to the area of rioting, fire became more a weapon for the mob, and more of a problem for the defending soldiers. Just before noon on Saturday, a crowd of two hundred Panamanians set fire to railroad ties in the pier area. Two fires burst out in the Canal Company office and storage building on Front Street. They roared out of control because snipers made it impossible for firemen to approach the blaze. The building was destroyed. At mid-afternoon, a mob of three hundred tried to force their way into the dock area to set fire to the piers and warehouses. Troops using tear gas forced them back. Sniper fire in Colón was, if anything, heavier than in Panama City. In part it may have been because U.S. soldiers on the Caribbean side never used rifle fire in retaliation. Saturday afternoon, the U.S. military commander in Colón asked for and received permission to use shotguns to help discourage the snipers. But heavy sniper fire continued through the night.

Early Sunday morning, a National Guard jeep drove west on Eleventh Street headed for the harbor area. At Balboa Avenue, opposite the Masonic Temple, the jeep stopped when its wheels became entangled in barbed wire. At that moment, a *guardia* sergeant named Celestino Villareta, sitting in the jeep next to the driver, was hit by a rifle bullet and killed. The shot came from his front, from the harbor area. The U.S. troops were not using rifles. The National Guard commander contacted the U.S. colonel in charge and asked for a cease-fire so an ambulance could pick up the body of the dead Panamanian soldier and rescue another member of the Guard who had been wounded. All shooting immediately stopped on the U.S. side. But when the ambulance stopped at the intersection, it was fired on—again from the harbor area. The only other Panamanian fatality in Colón was a six-month-old infant who reportedly died from the effects of tear gas. The evidence surrounding that unfortunate death was never made available to outside investigators. The child joined the list of "martyrs."

On Sunday, there was heavy sniper fire and hundreds of Molotov cocktails were thrown in the Masonic Temple area. A Red Cross driver was shot as he tried to evacuate wounded from the Masonic building. The sniping and fire-bombing continued until midnight.

At dawn on Monday, January 13, troops of the National Guard finally moved into the riot-torn areas of Panama City and Colón. They moved quickly through all buildings on or near the Zone border, flushed out the snipers, and picked up any guns they found. Within two hours, the situation was declared "under control." There was no more shooting; no more fires; no more looting. It was over. On January 16, the U.S. Army returned control of the Zone to Governor Fleming.

The casualties had been extensive. Three U.S. soldiers had been killed by sniper fire in Colón. Another was killed in a jeep accident while on patrol. One American civilian was hit and killed by a car whose driver was escaping the rioters. Thirty Americans were wounded by gunfire from snipers: 15 soldiers and 3 civilians in Colón; 9 army men and 3 civilians on the Pacific side. In addition, 126 U.S. soldiers and civilians received injuries from rocks, bottles and clubs, and burns from Molotov cocktails serious enough to require hospital treatment. On the Panamanian side, it was claimed that 24 persons died but a detailed accounting was never published. The Investigating Committee of the International Commission of Jurists studied all the information it could uncover with the help of the Panamanian Government and the authorities in the Zone.* The committee found that 95 injured Panamanians had been treated at Santo Tomás Hospital in Panama City during the riot period[†] and that 18 of those had been fatalities. Of those, 6 apparently died of asphyxiation when trapped in the burning Pan American building. They were undoubtedly looters. Six of the dead were probably victims of shooting by the Canal Zone police or U.S. troops. The committee did not receive reports on the other 6 in enough detail to reach any conclusions. They noted, however, that some Panamanians had fired on other Panamanians during the violence "for dif-

---

*The ICJ committee was in Panama from March 1 to March 14, 1964. It went at the request of the National Bar Association of Panama. Its report, titled *Report on the Events in Panama, January 9–12, 1964*, was published by the ICJ in Geneva.

[†]Many were treated at other hospitals or by their families or friends. The total of injured was between 200 and 300.

ferent reasons." And shopkeepers and others used weapons to protect their property and stop the looting. Nonetheless, all the dead entered the ranks of the "martyrs" and are honored to this day as heroes of the nation.

The dead were buried. The injuries to the other casualties gradually healed. But neither side fully recovered from the psychological wounds inflicted during those three and a half days of violence and bloodshed. They created a trauma that remained just beneath the surface of American-Panamanian relations for the next decade and a half. They left the kind of scar that General Pershing and his troops inflicted on Mexican-American relations when they invaded our southern neighbor in 1916 in unsuccessful pursuit of Pancho Villa. Or that Pearl Harbor left on the American psyche. Anyone working in the world of diplomacy, or commenting on it from afar, should become an expert in scars. Yesterday's wounds tell a great deal about present-day illnesses.

Throughout the rioting and the shooting, and after the National Guard finally restored order, the search for a peaceful formula went on. It was the main objective of the Mann-Vance mission. But that effort had two strikes against it from the beginning. First, emotions were high because Panamanians and Americans were shooting at each other, and many had died or been wounded. Second, both sides were being pushed by internal political considerations that made any compromise difficult. The best hope lay in third parties. And the third party then in Panama was the Inter-American Peace Committee of the OAS. The committee was composed of ambassadors from Venezuela, Argentina, Chile, Colombia, and the Dominican Republic. They went to Panama on January 10 and returned to Washington on January 15.

As part of its investigation, the OAS committee heard testimony from witnesses representing both the United States and Panama. Spokesmen from the United States—Tom Mann, Ed Martin, and Ralph Dungan—provided the facts of the riots as they knew them, described the steps the United States had taken to defend the Canal Zone, and emphasized the need to restore law and order. Assistant Secretary Mann also shared with the committee the U.S. suspicion that the rioting then going on was a result of communist plotting and agitation. By then, the OAS ambassadors had talked to many Panamanians and to their colleagues in the diplomatic corps in Panama. The committee chairman, Ambassador Enrique Tejera París of Venezuela, bluntly told the Americans: "We are satisfied that it was *not* communist prompted. Instead, it is a typical example of nineteenth-century nationalism . . ." The U.S. allegations were no doubt exaggerated and oversimplified. But to describe what was then happening in Panama as old-fashioned nineteenth-century nationalism was equally simplistic. There was no available evidence that the Communists planned the whole deadly affair; there was considerable evidence that they encouraged the violence and tried to keep it going. One Panamanian described it aptly: "The Communists," he said, "weren't there when the fire started. But once it had started, they dashed in and threw gasoline on the flames." Perhaps the truth is most evident in one simple fact: two weeks after the rioting, the Catholic hierarchy celebrated a "Mass for the Fallen" and forty thousand Panamanians took part; on the same day, a communist-led student federation held a rally for the martyrs, and three hundred people attended.

The major contribution of the Inter-American Peace Committee was a formula for getting Panama and the United States to the negotiating table to work out their differences. Tom Mann and his group returned to Washington on January 13, but Ed Martin remained in Panama to deal with the problem. The OAS consulted with him at great length, and with Panama Foreign Minister Solís and his colleagues. After long discussion, and interminable wrangling over each word, a formula was finally agreed to. It invited the two countries to reestablish diplomatic relations as soon as possible, and said both "have agreed to accept this invitation." Once relations were restored, Panama and the United States had agreed to talks within thirty days by special representatives "to discuss without limitations all existing matters of any nature which may affect the relations between the United States and Panama." The OAS committee issued its communiqué containing the agreement on January 15.

There was one hook in the formula. The English version said "to discuss." The Spanish version said *negociar* (which can mean either "discuss" or "negotiate"). President Chiari and the Panamanian government chose to interpret it to mean that the United States had promised to "negotiate a new treaty." When the Panamanian interpretation reached Washington, U.S. officials were upset. The person most furious was Lyndon Johnson. He had carefully avoided any such blanket commitment in advance. The spokesman for the State Department called in the press to clarify the U.S. position. He pointed out that the U.S. was prepared to "discuss" anything, but that did not mean a commitment to "negotiate." When his statement hit Panama, it created consternation. Chiari had taken a chance by saying that the U.S. had agreed to work out a new treaty. The long limb he had walked out on had been sawed off. And with that, the carefully engineered deal fell through.

The "suspension" of relations became a real break. Panama pulled all its diplomatic personnel out of Washington and insisted, on January 17, that the United States do the same in Panama. U.S. diplomats and their families moved into the Canal Zone, and some returned to the United States. The only exceptions were a handful of officers who continued to handle U.S. consular business, Peace Corps volunteers, and members of the U.S. Aid

Mission. Panama said they could continue their activities. The Panamanian government apparently thought the gesture of breaking relations would somehow "punish" the United States for its lack of consideration toward Panama. In fact, it created more problems for Panama than it did for Washington. Within days, the Panamanian government awoke to that reality. The shooting had ended, but the political struggle had just begun.

CHAPTER 4

Breaking the Deadlock

"Each goodly thing is hardest to begin."
—Spenser, *Faerie Queen*

JANUARY is the worst month for any U.S. president. He is obligated to report to the Congress on the state of the Union. He must submit his budget for the next fiscal year. He has to deal with members of the legislative body who have just returned from home districts and states certain they know better than any president what the people *really* want. He needs to shake up and revive a huge bureaucratic machine that is filled with Christmas turkey and New Year spirits. He looks out on a city generally dominated by snow and torpor and new-found arrogance. He has to pull it all together again and get it back to work. It is a time when leadership meets its severest test.

January of 1964 was no exception. In some ways, it was more demanding than usual. President Lyndon B. Johnson had been in the White House for only six weeks. He had picked up the reins of government from a murdered predecessor, a leader whose memory was still vivid for most of those who surrounded the new chief. The tall and vigorous Texan was, for most Americans, an unknown quantity. Because of that and the circumstances in which he took office, he had less room for maneuvering than most chief executives. Presidents normally move into the White House to the accompaniment of cheers and lively music and exaggerated hopes. This president had moved in with muffled drums and a dirge in the background. When he looked around him, he saw shattered dreams, pain, frustration in the eyes of many who were there to serve him.

He wanted desperately to dispel all that, to push the clouds aside. He settled on the prescription that had served him so well for so long: work; work hard; work harder than anyone else. And so, in those early days, the Johnson White House became a frenzy. The president led the way and he once said, speaking of those first months of his administration: "If I had a single moment when I could go off alone, relax, and forget the pressures of business, I don't recall it." With the president setting the course, the staff followed his direction. As did the cabinet. So, too, did the senior levels of the bureaucracy. Before long, half the government was working a twelve-hour day, or longer.

The Panama crisis exploded in the midst of that frenetic effort. The new president had delivered his State of the Union address the day before the rioting in Panama began. As Panamanian students were preparing to march into the Canal Zone, President Johnson was busy contacting old friends in the Senate to urge them to cut the withholding rate on a major tax bill. He met with two committees, one from business and the other a citizens group, both favoring tax reduction. He gave instructions to a U.S. delegation about to go to Geneva to revive the eighteen-nation disarmament conference. And he was reading his briefing book in preparation for the coming visit of Italian President Antonio Segni. All that and more was going on when, in the early evening of January 9, an aide handed the president a short note that said rioting had erupted on the border of the Canal Zone.

The news of trouble in Panama set off an alarm bell in the president's mind, he once told me. He had been getting reports from his intelligence briefers about Castroite agents preparing outbursts in Latin America, and Panama had been mentioned; so had Peru, Ecuador, and Venezuela. The president thought those warnings might be turning into reality. There was nothing in the early reports to substantiate his concerns, but Lyndon Johnson was by nature a suspicious man, likely to imagine the worst until he had every reason to know otherwise. Over the next few days, as accounts came in from the Canal Zone noting the presence of communist and leftist agitators among the rioting mobs, Johnson's misgivings were not allayed. His doubts were shared and expressed publicly by top administration officials during those first days of the crisis, by Secretary of State Rusk, Army Secretary Vance, and others. That preoccupation with communist involvement hindered the president from seeing that the Panama situation was immeasurably more complex and deep-seated than the simplistic estimates he was getting. That tilt in perception was corrected early on, but it delayed a solution. In the end, President Johnson came to realize that the roots of the Panama problem were nourished more by the heritage of Roosevelt and Taft, and Amador and Boyd than by Fidel Castro. The Cuban dictator was more a reaper than a sower. But Johnson never doubted that if he had mishandled the situation, or given it only passing attention, Castro might well have been a beneficiary. He was quite right.

In Washington, the Panama crisis was one of the many burdens the new president had to carry. It was, as he said, the first overseas test of his administration. But it contested with budgetary problems, taxes, civil rights, medicare, Vietnam, disarmament, and countless others for his attention. In Panama City, a possible breach with the United States was *the* problem. The Panama Canal—and all the political and economic effects that flowed therefrom—was central to Panamanian political life. The $1.9 million annual fee paid to Panama for use of its valuable territory was the least of it. More important were the ten thousand Panamanians who worked on the Canal and spent their money in local grocery stores and shops. Panamanian businessmen and farmers were selling products through the Canal Zone commissaries. Most important, the United States was Panama's principal trading partner and its main source of needed capital. Chase Manhattan, National City, and Bank of America dominated Panama's growing financial complex. As a Panamanian friend once told me: "When the U.S. catches a cold, Panama doesn't just sneeze, it gets pneumonia."

For Lyndon Johnson, the outburst in Panama was a worrisome, nagging problem. It already had raised some congressional hackles, and it would have caused political trouble if it got out of hand. But for LBJ's counterpart in Panama, President Roberto Chiari, the conflict with the United States was a potential disaster. The mild-mannered, indecisive Chiari was caught in a cruel vise. In his office and at the Union Club, old friends and advisers from the oligarchy and the business community were urging him to settle quickly with the North Americans, to restore normal relations. But in the streets, it was a different story. Chiari was being harassed daily by crowds of leftist students who gathered outside the *presidencia* demanding to meet with him, and threatening more violence if he refused. At those sessions, he was bombarded with demands to break relations totally with the gringos (at first they had been merely "suspended"). The students, and the agitators amongst them, insisted Chiari take a rigid stand, that relations with Washington be severed until the Americans committed themselves to negotiate a new treaty. Finally, on January 15, the beleaguered Chiari said just that. The corner into which he was painting himself shrank further.

That same day, the Inter-American Peace Committee's mediation effort fell apart. Even as Chiari was insisting the United States *must* negotiate, a spokesman for the U.S. government was saying in Washington that the Johnson administration would "discuss" anything, but not "negotiate." When news accounts from Washington reached Chiari, he was disconsolate. He believed the Americans were being truculent and had no sympathy whatsoever for his plight or Panama's. Meantime, from his office he could hear the shouting of the violence-prone mob. What shall I do, the embattled president wondered; what can I do? A Latin American diplomat who saw Chiari that day described him as "a man on the verge of being driven from office."

The U.S. Embassy staff had been gathering information and comments, and that afternoon they filed a report to the State Department. Pressure on Chiari to restore relations, it said, was increasing from the Panamanian and foreign business community. It emphasized that Panama's vulnerable economy could not stand any extended cut-off from its major partner without severe repercussions. In Washington, analysts were writing memos arguing that Panama would have to be reasonable, and soon.

No one realized that better than Panama's own politicians and business leaders. Those men were patriots and dedicated Panamanians as much as, perhaps more than, the mindless mob that was content to survive on slogans and flag-waving. Unlike the Communists, they did not want to break with the United States. As one of them explained: "Our problem was how to manage our marriage with the United States on a better footing in order not to generate the basis for a divorce that none of us wanted."

After relations were severed, a small group of those leading Panamanians met secretly with President Chiari and laid out for him the cruel truth: if all links to the United States were cut, Panama's economy would remain viable for only a short time. The government did not have the necessary reserves to pay its civil servants, its National Guard, the heavy service on its overseas debts. Among those in that painful session were men like Fernando Eleta, a radio and television entrepreneur, whose family had opposed Chiari's election, and Ricardo Arias, a former president and also a major political foe. Nonetheless, Chiari begged them to help him find some financing that would allow Panama to survive long enough to work things out with the Americans.

Those at the meeting went home and packed their bags. They fanned out to major world capitals in pursuit of financial backing. Former President Arias went to Japan. Others went to London, Paris, and Rome. Eleta, son of a distinguished Spanish family, went to Madrid. He met immediately with his brother-in-law, the Marquis de Castillo, and others. An interview was arranged with Generalissimo Franco's closest friend and second-in-command, Capt. Gen. Agustín Muñoz Grande. Eleta explained his country's plight to the austere old Spaniard. He emphasized that Panama did not want funds to launch any kind of campaign against the United States. Rather, he said in elegant Spanish, Panama wished only to be able to have an opportunity to reach an agreement with the Americans *en una forma digna* (in a dignified way) without "the pressure of economic survival."

The grandee listened closely with no change of expression. His heart obviously was with Panama, a daughter of the old Empire, that tiny territory where Christopher Columbus had landed on his third voyage to the New World. He felt the obligation that Mother Spain subconsciously responds to when one of her children is in difficulty. But he had to consider other matters, in all fairness to the modern Spain. He reminded Eleta that the Franco government was about to commence talks with the United States on the renewal of air base rights outside Madrid and at Rota, near Cadiz. Spain did not wish Washington to think a loan to Panama was in any sense an act of unfriendliness to them. Perhaps it would be best if this were kept a matter of confidentiality, he suggested with Old World subtlety. He would, of course, have to take it up with Generalissimo Franco, and he would let Eleta know.

The Panamanian envoy left his meeting with Don Agustín in a dispirited mood. Obviously, the Spanish government had to think of its own interests first. The military bases agreement with the United States was a major piece of business. But at least Don Agustín had promised to talk the matter over with Generalissimo Franco the next day. Eleta spent an uneasy Saturday. On Sunday, his prayers were for Spanish understanding. Early Monday morning, at 7:30 A.M., an unheard-of hour in Madrid for any serious business, Eleta was summoned to Don Agustín's headquarters. The distinguished old man welcomed the Panamanian representative, offered him coffee, then told him of Franco's decision. Spain would provide Panama with $5 million from its Central Bank. The loan was to be repaid whenever Panama could do so, up to fifteen years. No interest would be charged. But please, the grandee said, let us keep this as a matter among gentlemen. Eleta understood and, of course, agreed. The whole transaction was a superb example of Spanish *hidalguía* (a sense of dignity, of noblesse oblige, that has no good English translation). Spain had nothing to gain, much to lose, with its gesture. It made it, nonetheless. The U.S. Embassy and Washington authorities never learned of Spain's generosity. Panama's ability to hold out despite short-term economic adversity puzzled them greatly. In the world of 1964, $5 million was not really very much money. But in a small country like Panama, it was just enough to see them through the crisis.

At that moment, a man who would figure importantly in relations between the United States and Panama for the next fourteen years entered the scene. He was Ellsworth Bunker, a Vermonter of 69 years who had served his country as ambassador in major capitals (Buenos Aires, Rome, and New Delhi) through the 1950s. In 1962, he mediated the dispute between Indonesia and the Netherlands over West New Guinea. President Johnson once described Bunker as a man of "skill, judgment, and coolness under fire." For those reasons, and others, the president had picked him to be the U.S. representative to the Organization of American States. He was named a week before the riots broke out in Panama, but the Congress was not in session. By the time the Senate approved the nomination and Bunker could be sworn in, it was January 23. That same day, President Johnson, together with Bunker, Mann, and others, met with the Inter-American Peace Committee. The president wanted to introduce his new envoy to the OAS representatives. He also wanted to thank the Latin Americans for trying to find a way for Panama and the United States to get back together. That afternoon, the president spoke to a hastily summoned gathering of the White House press corps in the Fish Room.*

The president's statement was conciliatory. "There have been excesses and errors on the part of both Americans and Panamanians," he said. He suggested that actions by "imprudent students from both countries" had played into the hands of "agitators seeking to divide us." Johnson praised the restraint of U.S. military forces in defending the Canal Zone from attack. But he quickly added that "the security of the Panama Canal is not inconsistent with the interests of the Republic of Panama." The United States recognized, he said, that "there are things to be done" and said his administration was "prepared to talk about the ways and means of doing them." It was a gesture of friendliness to which he hoped Panama would respond. But he did not vary an inch from his basic stand, that diplomatic relations had to be restored and that the United States would accept no preconditions for any talks.

Johnson hoped his statement would get a favorable response from Chiari. He was disappointed. Perhaps the Panamanians were feeling new confidence because of the loan from Spain. Moreover, Chiari was still being bombarded by the student activists who assembled daily outside his residence. The press, largely controlled by opposition politicians, was striking the same theme in editorials and cartoons: "A new treaty—or nothing." At that moment, Chiari, his foreign minister, and others around him felt that accepting open-ended talks with no guarantees about a new treaty would be a major setback, and possible political suicide for them.

Panama did not react to Johnson's gesture. And Panama's representative to the United Nations, Aquilino Boyd, continued his energetic campaign for world recognition of the justice of Panama's cause. He told Adlai Stevenson at lunch during those strenuous days that Panama would settle for nothing less than recognition of its full sovereignty over the Canal Zone, an end to the perpetuity clause in the 1903 treaty, and a fairer share of economic benefits from canal traffic.

Ambassador Bunker used his maiden speech to the OAS to define the U.S. position. The tall, white-haired diplomat told his colleagues from Latin America: "We have made it abundantly clear that, in the discussions which we propose, each government would be free to raise any matters it wished, and that each government must be equally free to take any posi-

---

*A comfortable sitting room near the Oval Office, sometimes used for conferences. Its name came from its outstanding feature, a large mounted sailfish caught by President Franklin D. Roosevelt.

tion it deems necessary on any issue raised by the other." Then Bunker underlined what his government saw as the main problem: "The United States feels that the principal stumbling block at the moment is the insistence of one of the parties on a precondition of treaty revision."

Bunker's words were a precise reflection of the viewpoint of the man he served, the president of the United States. He was also voicing a position that, at that moment, had considerable support on Capitol Hill. Bunker had good reason to know what that attitude was because of a secret session that had taken place at the White House two days earlier.

No president before him, and none since, did as much as Lyndon Johnson to keep his links to the Congress strong. No president realized so well that no chief executive can turn his dreams into reality without the backing of the legislative branch. And no president before or since made anywhere near the number of phone calls that he did to his friends in the Senate and the House. When the Panama crisis exploded, he sought the advice of countless members of the Congress. His compulsion to stay close to the Hill led him, on January 29, 1964, to invite leaders of the Congress to meet with him in the Cabinet Room and "reason together," as he liked to say.

At a little before 5:00 P.M., the guests began to assemble. Their cars drove up to the south entrance (the so-called Diplomatic Entrance) of the White House. They walked through to the West Wing, circling the Rose Garden, and gathered in the Cabinet Room. Almost all the "big guns" in the Congress were there—leaders from both parties, chairmen of key committees and subcommittees concerned with foreign or military affairs or with Panama. Except for a few legislators who were out of Washington on business, it was a Who's Who of the 89th Congress. Executive branch officials concerned with Latin America were also present.

The president told the senators and representatives he had asked them to join him to discuss Panama. Tom Mann gave a brief account of what had happened and what was then happening. He noted Panama's insistence there be some kind of U.S. commitment in advance to negotiate a new treaty. When Mann concluded, the president looked around at the familiar faces of his one-time colleagues on Capitol Hill. Now, he said, I want you to tell me what you think. What do you think we should do?

Hubert Humphrey told the president he thought some way should be found to get to the negotiating table with the Panamanians, but without making any pledge that there would definitely be a new treaty. But he felt that the Panamanians should be free to raise any grievance or problem they wished, and the United States should give their views careful and sympathetic consideration. Humphrey was one who felt there had been great inequalities and unfairness in the U.S.-Panama relationship, and that corrections were long overdue. Senator William Fulbright, chairman of the powerful Foreign Relations Committee, supported the Humphrey position emphatically. So did Senator Wayne Morse, who had been following developments in Panama and Latin America closely. Most around the room seemed to agree.

The contrary view came from two senators who were assured of getting the president's close attention. One was Richard Russell of Georgia, head of the potent Armed Services Committee and the senator whom President Johnson respected above all others. Russell's attitude toward Panama was rigid and simplistic. We made a treaty in 1903, he said, and we should stick to it. Contracts should be lived up to. We should not mislead the Panamanians into thinking there was any hope of working out a new treaty. We could take care of Panama's frustrations by other means, that is, by paying her more money.

The second voice of dissent was an equally powerful one. Everett Dirksen of Illinois was the minority leader in the Senate. He had worked closely with Johnson when the Texan was Democratic leader in the Senate. Dirksen's view of things was more immediate than Russell's, less traditional, and considerably less legalistic. Dirksen's concern was the example that would be given if the United States caved in to Panamanian pressures. If that happened, he said, other small countries would get the idea that the way to influence Washington would be to break off relations, attack U.S. installations, and make demands. It was the same view Dirksen had expressed on the Senate floor immediately after the Panama riots occurred: "We are in the amazing position of having a country with one-third the population of Chicago kick us around. If we crumble in Panama, the reverberations of our actions will be felt around the world."

The attitude reflected by Russell and Dirksen told President Johnson he could expect trouble from the Congress if he made any abrupt moves. It reinforced his determination to resist pressure from Panama to accede to the idea of a new treaty in advance. Much more work would have to be done before any such major step was taken. But he realized, too, that if the time came for any major revisions in our working relations with Panama, there would be considerable backing from key lawmakers.

The main absentee from the secret White House conference was Senate Majority Leader Mike Mansfield. On his return to Washington, the Montanan received a briefing on the session, and a request to give the president his views. Mansfield wrote a long, thoughtful memo to Johnson on January 31. He urged the president to welcome mediation by the OAS. Obviously thinking of the hassle that had developed two weeks earlier, he said it should be made clear that the leader of the greatest nation on earth "does not quibble over words such as 'discussion' or 'negotiation.'" The president's position, Mansfield wrote, should be "that if changes are desirable, as well they may be, we are prepared to sit down and discuss, to negotiate, and to agree, on a mutually acceptable basis." Mansfield then drew a bead on the widely circulated theory of a "communist plot" in Panama. He told Johnson the administration should "avoid boxing ourselves in at home against change through the fanning of our own emotions by crediting Castro and Communism too heavily for a difficulty which existed long before either had any significance in this hemisphere, and which will undoubtedly continue to plague us after both cease to have much meaning." Aware of the heavy lobbying going on at that moment in Congress by entrenched civil servants in the Canal Zone, Mansfield leveled a broadside in their direction. The U.S. government should, he told the president, "stress with our own involved bureaucracy that our national interest is a trouble-free water passage, not the safeguarding of an outdated position of privilege."

There is no record of President Johnson's reaction to the Mansfield memo. We know that he read it. We also know that, as the president worked out his solution, the wisdom of the Montana senator was clearly reflected.

At that point, President Johnson had been in office only nine weeks. Panama was but one item on a very long agenda. At a jammed press conference on February 1, the president listed Panama among eight major areas of activity in the previous week. The others included a political crisis on the island of Cyprus, continuing aggression by the Vietnamese communists in South Vietnam, a dispute between Indonesia and Malaysia, and problems in East Africa. An unarmed American plane had been shot down over East Germany. France had just recognized Communist China. And a Saturn rocket had carried into space the largest payload in missile history. In the questioning, reporters showed more interest in domestic politics than in any of the foreign problems the president had mentioned. There was not one question about Panama. Nonetheless, President Johnson was giving events on the isthmus his close attention.

The Panamanians continued to haggle through February, still hoping Washington would bend to their demand for a new treaty. But they did so with decreasing energy, diminishing expectations. They began to see that Lyndon Johnson would not give ground under pressure. Moreover, while the money from Spain had been a godsend, it would not last very long. Finally, their hopes for international condemnation of the U.S. role in the riots were fading fast. The game, they felt, was turning against them.

Part of the Panamanian plan was to enlist the international legal community in their cause. If jurists from third countries would indict Washington for actions during the rioting, Panama's cause would be enhanced internationally. They reasoned that then Washington would *have* to pay attention. With that in mind, Jorge E. Illueca, president of Panama's National Bar Association, sent off a letter on January 21 to a friend on the International Commission of Jurists: Fernando Fournier, a distinguished lawyer from neighboring Costa Rica, and a former ambassador to the United States. The Illueca letter accused the United States of violating Articles 3, 5, and 20 of the U.N.'s Universal Declaration of Human Rights. Those articles provided:

Art. 3: "Everyone has the right to life, liberty and security of person."
Art. 5: "No one shall be subjected to torture or to cruel, inhuman or degrading treatment or punishment."
Art. 20: "Everyone has the right to freedom of peaceful assembly and association."

Specifically, the Panamanians charged the United States had violated those provisions:

—in the case of Art. 3, by "opening fire on the defenseless Panamanian civil population . . . resulting in 15 deaths."*
—regarding Art. 5, "by shooting at the Panamanian civil population."
—as to Art. 20, by firing small arms and tear gas "for the purpose of preventing the free use of such a right [to peaceful assembly]."

The International Commission of Jurists selected three distinguished legal figures to investigate the Panamanian charges: Professor A. D. Belinfante of Amsterdam University, Judge Gustaf Petren of Sweden, and Navroz Vakil, a lawyer from Bombay, India. The legal scholars met in Geneva on February 28 and left for Panama on March 1. During their investigation, which took two weeks, they questioned many Panamanian and American witnesses. They met President Chiari and Foreign Minister Galileo Solís, Canal Zone Gov. Robert Fleming, and the U.S. military commander, Gen. Andrew P. O'Meara.

Panamanian hopes that the three visiting jurists would provide them with a propaganda success died quickly. The Dutch, Swedish, and Indian legal scholars were interested only in proof of allegations, in evidence that would support charges. They were not impressed by emotional speeches or appeals to nationalist sentiments. The search for facts and insistence on strict and fair procedure were hallmarks of the ICJ investigation. All documents or other evidence submitted by one party were immediately given to the other for comments and reactions. Witnesses were subject to questioning by both Panamanian and U.S. lawyers. The hearings occupied about

---

*It is interesting that the Panamanian Bar Association cited 15 deaths attributable to U.S. actions, when the Panamanian government and press during and after the riots repeatedly used a death toll of 24—and still cite that as the number of "martyrs" in the 1964 riots. It is also significant that, in presenting their case to the international jurists, the Panamanian legal authorities provided evidence of only 6 specific cases. The foreign legal specialists found not all of those 6 "proved."

one hundred hours and twenty-six witnesses were examined by the committee. It was a superb example of intelligent and honorable men searching for honest answers to complicated questions.

The commission left Panama on March 14, and its final report was not published until June 9. Nonetheless, by the time the ICJ representatives left for Geneva, the Panamanians knew the findings would not be what they had hoped for. A Panamanian lawyer told me later: "We quickly knew we were getting nowhere. Our lawyers were eloquent and good patriots. But the jurists were interested only in facts. And our 'facts' could never sustain the sweeping charges we were making." When the ICJ report was issued that summer, it proved how correct the Panamanian assessment had been.

The international jurists criticized both the Panamanian and Canal Zone authorities. They found the Panamanian government derelict in not taking steps to control the rioters or to restore peace during the first three days of violence. They were persuaded that radio and television broadcasts and newspaper stories and editorials had served to "incite and misinform the Panamanian public" while the government did nothing to curtail or moderate those activities. They also noted that while 400–500 shots had been fired by the U.S. Army into Panama, Panamanians had fired more than 1,000 bullets into the Zone. On the other hand, the jurists criticized the handling of the Panamanian students who marched peacefully into the Zone on January 9. Zone authorities were not strict enough with their own people, they believed. And they should have used fire hoses and more tear gas rather than bullets to control the mobs. For these and many other things, the international lawyers criticized both sides in the dispute.

But on the specific allegations that the U.N. Declaration of Human Rights had been violated by the Americans, the ICJ panel concluded in each case that, based on the facts presented to them, "we are unable to come to this conclusion." The lawyers ruled there had been no such violations; Panama's complaint was denied.*

In the course of investigating the specific complaints, the Dutch, Swedish, and Indian jurists came to realize there were deep emotional and historical reasons for the violence that had erupted on the isthmus. They cited those factors in the concluding section of their report. They lamented the fact that two societies—one Panamanian, the other American—had been living next to each other for more than half a century yet had proved unable to promote good and friendly relations. Indeed, they said, "tension and resentment have increased in a vicious circle . . ."

The concluding paragraph of the jurists' report was the careful assess-

---

*For details of the allegations and the findings, see *Report on the Events in Panama, January 9–12, 1964.*

ment of eminently thoughtful men who could look at the Panama situation with neutral eyes and sympathy for both sides. The international jurists wrote:

> We cannot help feeling that the United States, having regard to the special situation it occupies in the world, and with its resources and ideals, should reflect upon these sad facts and take effective steps to make possible a reorientation and change in the outlook and thinking of the people living in the Canal Zone. Undoubtedly this is a difficult and uphill task, but it would yield rich dividends in healthier relations with the people of Panama. The Government of Panama and the life and economy of Panama is [*sic*] in many ways so closely tied to the Panama Canal that it would not be out of place to suggest that the Panamanian Government and Panamanian people should also reflect upon the facts as they appear to impartial observers, and should exercise tolerance, moderation and understanding in their relations with the United States and Canal Zone authorities.

Slowly but inexorably, pressures were building on Panama to reach some accommodation with Washington. Spain's small loan would not sustain even tiny Panama for too long. The campaign to win world support—at the United Nations and through the international jurists—was collapsing. The new U.S. president, who had just rebuffed Fidel Castro over Guantánamo, was surely not going to back down before Panamanian pressure. Meantime, bankers and businessmen were quietly urging President Chiari to seek some kind of reconciliation. The election of a new president was coming near and even Chiari's bitterest foe, the once rabidly anti-American Arnulfo Arias, was blaming the current mess on Chiari more than on the United States. Prospects for Chiari's chosen successor, Marco Robles, seemed to shrivel visibly with each passing day. Chiari edged toward a settlement.

With relations between the two countries severed, the best place for serious contacts was in Washington. The Organization of American States was headquartered in the U.S. capital and its members were still trying to find a formula for settlement. Panama and the United States both attended its meetings, and Ellsworth Bunker could take Panama's Miguel Moreno off for a quiet lunch at the sedate F Street Club without attracting too much attention. Washington became the venue for the intricate diplomacy of the time.

One of those most active in the search for reconciliation was Tom Mann, the veteran diplomat and lawyer whom President Johnson had picked to deal with Latin America. Mann had taken over his post in early January, after serving as ambassador to Mexico. With their Washington house still occupied by tenants, he and Mrs. Mann were living at the Fairfax Hotel on Massachusetts Avenue. Some intense negotiations took place in the Mann sitting room at the Fairfax, and in the dining room down-stairs. One of the principal participants in that secret diplomatic exercise was Vicente Sánchez Gavito, Mexico's veteran ambassador to the OAS. He and Mann were old friends.

Throughout February, while President Johnson was busy with innumerable other problems, efforts to resolve the Panama question were going on behind the scenes. Bunker was talking with Panama's Moreno and Mann was meeting with Sánchez Gavito. The diplomats were exploring various formulas. At his press conference on February 29, President Johnson was asked about Panama and whether he saw any hope for an agreement before national elections in Panama in May. His reply disclosed his thoughts and his minimal requirements.

"I would hope that we could reach an agreement as early as possible," he said. He added that he realized the basic treaty was written in 1903 and that "problems are involved that need to be dealt with and perhaps would require adjustment." He went on to say he was not ready to "make any precommitments, before we sit down, on what we are going to do in the way of rewriting new treaties with a nation that we do not have diplomatic relations with." Once those relations were restored, Johnson said, "we will be glad . . . to discuss anything, anytime, anywhere, and do what is just and what is fair and what is right." If ever a clear signal was sent by a president that he was ready to work things out, that was it. Sadly, no one in the Panamanian government at that crucial moment knew Lyndon Johnson, knew what kind of a man he was, or could interpret what his words really meant.

The fault for the U.S.-Panama crisis of 1964 and the failure to resolve it quickly can be laid on several doorsteps. The Panamanians misunderstood grossly what was happening in Washington and what kind of president they were dealing with. Lyndon Johnson did not understand how deeply Panamanian sensibilities were aroused by the rioting and offended by the U.S. response.

Tom Mann, a dedicated and experienced Foreign Service veteran, was caught in the middle. He was working on the assumption that the president had picked him to deal with Latin America, and that his many years of experience there should be used to find a rational solution. But he underestimated what Lyndon Johnson perceived as a highly sensitive, potentially explosive, domestic problem. Contacts with the Congress—exemplified by the meeting with Hill leaders on January 29—told the president he could not deal with the difficulty in a way that made it appear he was backing down on any central issue. For him, the unacceptable point was agreement, in advance, to work out a new treaty. And the alarm word was "negotiate"—as he had clearly showed on January 15.

Mann, a good diplomat and lawyer, realized that agreement to "negotiate" did not mean all that much. One can "negotiate" forever and not reach agreement if the terms are wrong, or the solution disadvantageous. He had been working quietly with Sánchez Gavito, and by the second week of March they thought they had an agreement. Under their formula, the United States and Panama would reestablish diplomatic relations. Then representatives "with sufficient powers to carry out discussions and negotiations" would get together to reach a "just and fair agreement" to eliminate the causes of conflict between their countries. Mann told his Mexican colleague that formula would work. But when Lyndon Johnson saw the wording, he exploded. The cap that set off his dynamite was the word "negotiations." He called Secretary of State Rusk and erupted. Rusk and Mann went to the White House. It was 1:26 P.M. on March 12 when they walked into the Oval Office. The president was irritated. Mann was livid. The president was pulling the rug from under his designated representative. Johnson was sitting on a couch next to the fireplace; Rusk sat opposite on a matching couch. Mann was standing. As the Texas lawyer paced, he said he thought he had been picked to resolve the problem. If the president who had asked him to do the job could not support what he had worked out, Mann said, he did not think he could any longer be useful. He thought he should leave.

Lyndon Johnson was not used to having people resign. He regarded it as a kind of disloyalty (and, deep down, as a sign of his own failure). When Mann said he thought he should leave his post, President Johnson responded: "You can't quit; you're fired." Mann said that was fine, that it didn't really matter, and he turned toward the door. The president moved quickly to change the atmosphere, to soften the tension that had risen. "Can't you take a joke?" he asked his fellow Texan. "Neither of us was joking, Mr. President," Mann said. The president laughed and motioned Mann to sit down. And so the moment passed. President Johnson's estimate of Mann probably rose as a result of the encounter. He respected men who couldn't be bulldozed. What he could not abide were people who heartily agreed with him in person, then walked out to support the reverse behind his back.

What bothered Mann most about the affair was that he then had to go to the Mexican ambassador and apologize, to admit he had been wrong. Mann later admitted candidly: "I don't like apologies." In any case, he did it. That threw the OAS behind-the-scenes efforts into confusion. The Latin American diplomatic scenario had been carefully written, and was about to be presented. The diplomats, even though warned, decided to go ahead with their project. They reasoned that the Panamanians would be happy with the formula they had worked out. They also decided—more emotionally than rationally—that President Johnson would relent once he saw that most of the hemisphere was back of the new formula. They were wrong on both counts.

The Latin American diplomats relied on an additional factor in calculating that the North Americans would do nothing to upset matters at that late moment. Monday, March 16, would be the third anniversary of President Kennedy's introduction of the Alliance for Progress, the joint effort—with heavy U.S. economic backing—to raise Latin American levels of health and education and living standards. President Johnson was scheduled to address a special session of the OAS on that day. Good feelings, fine words, and champagne toasts would be in order. Surely, they reasoned, the U.S. president would not, on the eve of such an occasion, repulse their efforts to find an accord on such a "minor" issue as Panama. That perfectly sound Latin reasoning appealed to all the key players on the OAS stage. And so they went ahead. At 6:45 P.M. that Sunday evening, the OAS released to the press its "diplomatic triumph," an agreement between Panama and the United States. It said:

> The Governments of the Republic of Panama and of the United States of America have agreed to reestablish diplomatic relations as soon as possible to seek the prompt elimination of the causes of conflict relative to the Panama Canal and to attempt to resolve other problems existing between them, without limitation or preconditions of any kind.
>
> Consequently, within 30 days following reestablishment of diplomatic relations, both Governments will designate Special Ambassadors with sufficient powers to carry out discussions and negotiations with the objective of reaching a just and fair agreement which will eliminate the above-mentioned causes of conflict and resolve the other problems referred to above. Any agreements that may result would be subject to the constitutional processes of each country.

The announcement clattered out on the international news service ticker machines. In seconds, it was in the hands of editors around the world. It was also in the hands of Fabian Velarde, President Chiari's press secretary in Panama. Before long, the duty officer of the White House Situation Room had sent it to Lyndon Johnson. The president already knew what was in the works. Tom Mann and his associates were closely following developments in the OAS. A few minutes before 5:00 P.M., Mann called the president to tell him what was happening. He called again twenty-five minutes later with the final text.

At that crucial moment, the Panamanians made still another tactical mistake. Stories began to come in from the isthmus saying the new agreement meant there would be a new treaty. It appeared Chiari and those around him were absolutely deaf to what had been said in Washington for two months. It proved anew that no one in the Panamanian capital who was advising the government had the vaguest notion what kind of man was sitting in the White House, what he could accept, what he would have to reject. The Panamanians had a good hand, but they trumped their own ace.

When McGeorge Bundy, the president's national security assistant, reported on the stories coming in from Panama, President Johnson told him to alert Press Secretary Salinger, and have him call in the White House press corps, at least the wire service representatives and some of the "regulars." The president wanted to make it clear that there was no real agreement. He had *not* agreed to work out a new treaty. Salinger carried out the instructions. At about 11:00 P.M., he told the handful of assembled reporters that there had not been any "meeting of the minds" between the United States and Panama, regardless of what the OAS statement said. He told the newsmen they could attribute his words to "U.S. sources," but not to the White House. The resulting stories, throwing cold water on the OAS claim and the consequent optimism, were another bombshell thrown into the political mix. The story only made the late editions of Monday morning's newspapers, but it was carried on the early morning news broadcasts. The word spread quickly in Panama and at OAS headquarters.

As the OAS ceremony marking the third anniversary of the Alliance for Progress approached, everyone in the organization realized what had happened overnight. It was apparent the peace initiative had collapsed. Most of the diplomats were holding their breath. But President Johnson arrived a few minutes after noon, smiling to one and all, and shaking hands with the dignitaries who welcomed him to the Pan American Union Building, the sedate old marble edifice on Constitution Avenue. The diplomats breathed a sigh of relief. So did Dean Rusk, Tom Mann, and Ellsworth Bunker, who were there to escort their chief to the council chamber. They all relaxed too quickly.

On the podium, President Johnson launched into his prepared remarks. He paid tribute to Franklin Roosevelt and the era of the "good neighbor." He hailed the Alliance for Progress. He told the assemblage they were all working to make the alliance a success. He promised "substantial external help" to the needy neighbors to the south in their struggle to improve their own lot. The applause rang out. Everyone was delighted. The crisis seemed just a worrisome memory.

Then it came. Just as the assembled diplomats were beginning to relax, thinking perhaps of the excellent lunch that was ahead, the president looked up from his text and his cold blue eyes swept across the assemblage.

"Let me now depart for a moment from my main theme," he said, "to speak of differences that have developed between Panama and the United

States." Suddenly all eyes were riveted on the lanky, powerful man who stood before them. What is happening? What has this to do with the Alliance for Progress? they were asking themselves.

"Our own position is clear, and it has been from the first hour that we learned of the disturbances," he said. "The United States will meet with Panama any time, anywhere, to discuss anything, to work together, to cooperate with each other, to reason with one another, to review and to consider all of our problems together, to tell each other all our opinions, all our desires, and all our concerns, and to aim at solutions and answers that are fair and just and equitable without regard to the size or the strength or the wealth of either nation."

The president was telling the assembled diplomats what they knew perfectly well. There was no great solicitude in that group for the game Panama was playing. The primal drive among them was to find a quick and mutually agreeable solution. But they questioned the propriety of raising such a sensitive issue in that forum. Didn't the president realize that they understood his problem, that they wanted to help? But didn't he know, too, that pushed into an open contest, they would have to back their small Latin American "brothers"?

The president went on. He used the same words Salinger had the night before: "As of this moment, I do not believe that there has been a genuine meeting of the minds between the two presidents of the two countries involved."

President Johnson was, by then, carrying a full head of steam. His irritation of the night before—and of the long weeks that preceded the latest moves—impelled him forward. At the same time, he must have realized he was alienating his listeners. He was much too sensitive to audience reactions not to know that he was not bringing them along. Irritation and conciliation were mixed in his next sentences: "Press reports indicate that the government of Panama feels that the language which has been under consideration for many days commits the United States to a rewriting and to a revision of the 1903 treaty. We have made no such commitment and we would not think of doing so before diplomatic relations are resumed and unless a fair and satisfactory adjustment is agreed upon." Then he went back to his prepared words, back to the Alliance for Progress and to hemispheric unity. The storm was over. The president concluded his remarks, shook hands with his hosts, and walked out, down the long marble staircase and through the front door to his car. He was back at the White House in plenty of time for a 1 o'clock lunch with Henry Luce of the Time-Life empire. He probably did not realize the chaos he had left behind in the Pan American Building. There was talk of little else over the hors d'oeuvres among Latin American diplomats than the impropriety of a

U.S. president bringing a bilateral problem into what should have been, they felt, a festive occasion. No one seemed to have noticed that, in his emotional statement, the president of the United States had, for the first time, said that he and his administration would at least consider rewriting the treaty of 1903. A few subtle minds may have perceived the landmark. If so, their views were lost in the flood of chatter about gaucherie in high places.

The next day was St. Patrick's Day, and the president went to New York City for some light politicking and a scheduled speech to the Loyal Sons of St. Patrick. But he had time to think more about the Panama issue. The "reviews" were coming in on his address to the OAS, private assessments from diplomats and from the press as well. They were generally negative. There were comments that the president had "shot from the hip."

Lyndon Johnson, never one to bow easily to criticism, had to admit that he might have been wrong. He recalled his disagreement with Tom Mann, the expert whose views on Latin America he respected greatly. The words from Mike Mansfield's memo went through his mind: "The President of the United States does not quibble over words such as 'discussion' or 'negotiation.'" And he was stung by the adverse reaction of so many Latin American diplomats. Johnson believed, with good reason, that he had more sympathy for and understanding of the southern half of the Western Hemisphere than any previous U.S. president. He was not going to have that impression besmirched by his own recalcitrance.

The next day the president met in the afternoon with five new Latin American ambassadors who were taking up their duties in the OAS. Witnesses said the president was in top form—laughing, joking, being sweetly reasonable, having what he would have called "a good visit." He was not, the diplomats felt, the same irritated man they had seen only two days before. They were quite right. The president was mellowing. By week's end, he had a statement he planned to send to the secretary general of the OAS. Johnson wondered how best to make it public, and chose the most direct course he could think of. He went to the White House press office and announced it himself.

The press office was under new management. Salinger had resigned two days before. He told the president he planned to run for the Senate in California. Then he packed his bags, emptied his desk, and flew to the Golden State—and political disaster. The new press secretary was George Reedy, a rumpled, intelligent, gray-haired former newspaperman who had served Lyndon Johnson since the early 1950s as a staff assistant on the Hill and press secretary during the vice-presidential years. Reedy was having one of his first sessions with his media clients that Saturday afternoon when the president walked in on them.

"Is it all right with you folks if I monitor your press conference?" the president asked as he ambled in. There was some confusion as Reedy welcomed his boss and the assembled reporters jumped up and said, "Hello, Mr. President." The president greeted a few old acquaintances. Then he went immediately to what was on his mind. He was sending a special message to the OAS that afternoon, he said, and he thought it might be of interest to the reporters. Then he began to read: "The present inability to resolve our differences with Panama is the source of deep regret." He went on to outline for the newsmen what those differences were—starting with the recent riots and moving up to date. He then rendered a quite remarkable paean to the glories of the inter-American system in general, and to U.S. friendship for Panama in particular. He recalled that when the Japanese attacked Pearl Harbor, Panama had declared war against the Empire of the Rising Sun even before the U.S. Congress took action. He emphasized the "special relationship" with Panama that flowed directly from sharing "the benefits, the burden, and trust of maintaining the Panama Canal." Then came the heart of the president's proposal:

> We are well aware that the claims of the Government of Panama, and of the majority of the Panamanian people, do not spring from malice or hatred of America. They are based on a deeply felt sense of the honest and fair needs of Panama. It is, therefore, our obligation as allies and partners to review these claims and to meet them, when meeting them is both just and possible.
> We are ready to do this.
> We are prepared to view every issue which now divides us, and every problem which the Panamanian Government wishes to raise.
> We are prepared to do this at any time and at any place . . .

He did not use the words *treaty* or *negotiate*, to be sure. But he did say, of the special representative he was ready to appoint, that "his instructions will not prohibit any solution which is fair, and subject to the appropriate constitutional processes of both our governments." That made it obvious the president was thinking of a possible treaty.

The reporters were surprised, especially those who had heard Johnson, a very different Johnson, at the Pan American Union Building five days before. The first question raised was whether he thought the American people outside the Washington area would support his new stand. "I am not going to make any evaluation of the American people outside the Washington area," the president replied, trying to push emotion and politics aside. One sharp reporter then asked the central question: "Mr. President, when you say his [the special representative's] instructions will not bar any solution which is fair, would that include, sir, a renegotiation of the 1903 treaty?"

"That would mean just what the statement says," the president answered. "We will discuss any problem that divides us in any way, and then we will come up with a solution that is fair." He could have said he did *not* mean treaty discussions, but he did not. He left that up to the reporters'— and the readers'—imaginations. When the news broke in newspapers the next day, everyone concerned with the Panama affair realized an important corner had been turned.

From then on, the pace accelerated. The following Thursday, the president flew to Texas for the long Easter weekend. Before he went, however, he approved giving the Panamanians a formula that embodied his statement to the press. That same day, Ellsworth Bunker took Mike Moreno to a quiet lunch at the F Street Club. After talking around the issue over the meal, the two diplomats retired to a private room for serious talk. Bunker gave Moreno the new U.S. proposal. The United States was ready to resume diplomatic relations "today." Ambassadors could be exchanged "forthwith." The two countries should pick special representatives and they would "review all issues between the two countries (including those related to the Panama Canal) and . . . seek a fair and just resolution of those issues."

Moreno hurried to his embassy and put in a call to President Chiari, to pass along the new U.S. proposition. Chiari said he would consult his advisers and be back in touch. Later in the afternoon, he called Moreno, and the ambassador then went to see Bunker. The Panamanian government found the new formula "too imprecise," he explained. He kept returning to the word "negotiate." Bunker patiently explained why that word was unacceptable. Moreno probably could have explained it equally well, but it was clear the Panamanians wanted to try to get the last concession they could extract. Chiari and his staff had read—and been heartened by— President Johnson's statement five days before. They thought perhaps the gringos were softening up, and that they might soften further. It was worth a try.

A disheartened Bunker reported the latest development to Secretary Rusk and Tom Mann. Rusk passed the news to the president. The president's orders were clear: don't budge another inch. He was sure other Latin Americans would soon be putting subtle pressure on the Panamanians to be reasonable. He was confident enough that the next afternoon he put in a call to New York to another fellow Texan, Robert B. Anderson, a business executive who had been secretary of the treasury under President Eisenhower. Johnson described the Panama situation in great detail. He said he might soon have to name a special representative to deal with the problem, to try to work things out with the Panamanians, and he needed someone from outside government. It had to be someone of distinction; someone who was tough-minded; someone whose selection would persuade the Panamanians beyond any doubt that the U.S. government and its president were serious about finding a solution; someone, in short, like Robert Anderson of Texas. Would Anderson please think it over and the president would get back to him later. Anderson promised to do so.

The following Tuesday, Johnson had a conference call with Tom Mann and Under Secretary of State George Ball. He wanted to settle the Panama issue once and for all, he told them. The United States would make one final offer, and that was it. He asked his advisers to work out the formula and have it ready for him when he got to Washington. He left Texas late in the day aboard *Air Force One*, and was back in the White House by 8:30 P.M.

Early the next morning, he read and approved the proposal State had worked out. It was very close to the offer Ambassador Bunker had made the previous week, but shorter. It avoided any reference to the Panama Canal and spoke only of the "causes of conflict" between the two countries. With the president's assent, Ambassador Bunker went in search of a breakthrough. He invited Ambassador Moreno to lunch again at the F Street Club.

Bunker gave the Panamanian diplomat the redrafted proposal. He explained that President Johnson wanted "the simplest, clearest understanding that is possible." He told the Panamanian envoy that the American president did not want "complicated language which might stand in the way of getting an agreement through the Senate at some later time." Did the Panamanian ambassador catch the implication of those words? We do not know. But clearly the only agreement that would require Senate approval would be a new treaty or a revision of the existing one. Then, as the steely eyed Vermonter could do with great effect, he leaned back, looked hard at Moreno, and said that the United States had no "fall-back position," that it would bargain no more, that this (the proposition Moreno held in his hands) was it. "If this doesn't work," Bunker said in his quiet way, "we think it best to wait until after the elections." He referred to the Panama voting in May and the U.S. election in November. There would be no more haggling, no more playing with words. Take this proposal, he was saying, or we'll get together in seven or eight months. We can wait.

The new proposal was short and simple. Panama and the United States would agree to reestablish diplomatic relations promptly. They would designate "without delay" special ambassadors "with sufficient powers to seek the prompt elimination of the causes of conflict between the two countries without limitations or preconditions of any kind." Bunker explained that the formula itself and the attitude he had described to Moreno had the full backing of President Johnson.

Moreno said he would relay the proposal immediately, as well as the context Bunker had provided. When his message reached Panama, President Chiari realized he had to fish or cut bait. Bunker's meaning was unmistakable. Chiari called his foreign minister and other advisers into session, and the debate raged long into the night. Panama's president was under multiple pressures. His chosen successor, Marco Robles, was losing ground. Arnulfo Arias, the principal opposition candidate, was ignoring the *yanquis* and directing his fire almost exclusively at the Chiari regime, blaming it for the confusion and a deteriorating economy. Meanwhile, pressures from the business community had grown.

One other factor was beginning to influence opinion in Panama's inner circles. In February, the Department of Defense sent a memo to President Johnson urging intensive study be given to building a sea-level canal between the Pacific and the Caribbean. Word was leaking in Washington that the solution to the Panama crisis might be to build a new canal. That word, which reached Panamanian ears quickly, sent chills through the hearts of Panama's politicians and businessmen. If a new canal were built elsewhere, Panama could become what it had been a century and a half before—a rather poverty-stricken backwater.

By the next day, Panama had decided to accept the U.S. offer. Further procrastination could only harm, not help. Chiari and his colleagues had played the game to the point of diminishing returns. They sent word to Moreno and he passed the decision quietly to the U.S. authorities. When he received the news, Lyndon Johnson's first move was to get on the phone to Robert Anderson in New York. He said that the things they had talked about a few days earlier were now coming to a climax. He needed a special envoy to begin working out a settlement with Panama. Would his friend Bob Anderson take on the chore? The president would be deeply grateful. The former treasury secretary said he would—under certain conditions. He reminded the president that he had extensive business interests and that he could not simply abandon them. He would take on the task, he said, if most of the negotiating could be done in New York rather than Washington or Panama. Anderson also wanted to be sure he would have access to the president—with no middlemen—any time he felt it was necessary. President Johnson agreed to these conditions, and Anderson accepted the assignment. It was an arrangement that would cause significant problems with both the State and Defense departments later. But for the moment, it gave Lyndon Johnson what he wanted—a distinguished name, and a Republican as well, who would carry the burden of an unpopular line of policy.

The Panamanians had only one last-minute suggestion. They proposed that President Johnson's statement of March 21 and President Chiari's response to it of March 24 be attached to the final agreement. That was done, and the deal was cut. It was April 3, 1964.

The president called his new diplomatic representative to tell him the deal was completed and that announcement of his appointment would be made in a few hours. Anderson said he would be happy to take on this new assignment as long as his previous conditions were met. It was an arrogant approach, but Johnson accepted it. It riled him, but the affair had gone on too long and was too near a conclusion to change course.

The president then called President Chiari. He told the Panamanian president he had selected Robert Anderson to be his special representative to work out differences between the two countries. He said he had also picked Jack Hood Vaughn to be ambassador to Panama. He would not make that public, of course, until the Chiari government had formally accepted the nomination.

"Now," Johnson told Chiari, "our two countries can sit down together without limitations or preconditions of any kind, and as friends try to find the proper and fair answer."

"That is the way to do it," Chiari replied, "and I hope we can get together on that."

Johnson went immediately into a meeting of the National Security Council. He explained what had happened on the Panama front. Then, as was his fashion, he went around the table to make sure all present were in agreement. The secretaries of state and defense and the others concurred heartily with what the president had decided. Then the president invited top officials of the OAS to join him in the Cabinet Room. A small press contingent was also invited in. And leaders of the Congress were there as well.

The president explained what had happened. He defined the agreement that had been reached. He reported on his talk with President Chiari. He also announced that Robert Anderson would be his representative in negotiations. After describing the basic agreement, the president looked around the room—at the Latin American diplomats, the congressmen, and the members of his executive team—and said:

> So, gentlemen, let us approach our search for a solution with the openness and the generosity of those who seek only the strengthening of friendship. Let us meet as sovereign nations, as allies, and as equal partners in the inter-American system.
>
> Panama can be confident, as we are confident, that we each desire an agreement which protects the interests and recognizes the needs of both our nations.

A painful chapter had ended; the deadlock of months had been broken. President Johnson told his special envoy, Bob Anderson, he thought the differences could be worked out in a couple of months. It would take considerably longer than that, but the president's decision had moved the issue rapidly ahead. For the first time in more than fifty years, it seemed that new, more modern rules would be written for a game that was old and tired.

CHAPTER 5

The Orphan Treaties

"The age before us is an age of larger, faster ships. It is an age of friendly partnership among the nations concerned with the traffic between the oceans. This new age requires new arrangements."

—President Lyndon B. Johnson (at the White House), December 18, 1964

PRESIDENT Johnson was feeling chipper. It was one of those warm, shining days that make spring in Washington a delight for all but the jaded. The cherry blossoms along the Tidal Basin were getting ready to burst and, by their presence, convince all the tired bureaucrats, lawmakers, and lobbyists that winter really was behind. It was April 4, the day after the president had announced that the twelve-week-old crisis in Panama had ended. Privately, Lyndon Johnson was relieved that the first real test of his ability to cope with a tough foreign policy problem had ended, and that he had passed. His mark, as the old schoolteacher in him knew, was not just a "gentlemanly C." The commentators and diplomats were giving him an A—some an A+.

In Panama, there was a similar spirit of satisfaction. If all the sighs of relief there could have been harnessed, they would have driven a sailboat across the Bay of Panama. The political outlook for Marco Robles, the government party's standard-bearer, brightened significantly. Panama's bankers and investors became bullish overnight as their worst nightmare in decades suddenly disappeared. Radical students were still mightily unhappy, of course, but their daily sojourns to the Presidential Palace ended. The Panamanian people believed that a new day was dawning, and they were happy to push out of sight anything that revived the bitterness and worry of the months before.

Once the joint agreement was reached, the wheels of revived diplomacy began to turn. President Johnson's representative, Robert B. Anderson, went to Panama to get things moving. The president had told him he hoped the whole affair could be wrapped up "within two or three months," and the new negotiator was letting no grass grow under his feet. The grass would come later.

Anderson's initial impact on the Panamanians was considerable. They knew he had been Eisenhower's secretary of the navy and later deputy secretary of defense. More important, he had been secretary of the treasury during the last four years of the Eisenhower administration. In that position, Anderson had played a significant role in supporting the Inter-American Development Bank, which sophisticated Panamanians regarded as the most significant development in U.S.–Latin American relations in decades. Millions of dollars were flowing through the bank into development programs in most countries of Central and South America—among them Panama. Knowing that background, more than one Panamanian official who met Anderson on his maiden visit told the touring American they thought he was someone they could talk to, someone who would give them a sympathetic hearing.

On a personal level, some Panamanians found Anderson warm and understanding; others described him as austere, detached, even forbidding. One who met him at the time said: "He seemed more like a New Englander than a Texan." That reaction was understandable, but superficial. Robert Anderson was the epitome of the self-made man. He was the son of a poor farmer and, from his earliest years, helped scratch a living from a small spread south of Fort Worth. He never had a chance to go to high school. Most of his early learning came from books borrowed from a neighbor. He gained admission to tiny Weatherford College by taking a special exam, which he passed with flying colors. Then he went on to law school at the University of Texas. From there, he moved to positions of ever-increasing responsibility—legislator, assistant attorney general, state tax commissioner. In the late 1930s and 1940s, his law practice in Fort Worth flourished, as did his business interests. He became a Republican and was summoned to Washington in 1953 as secretary of the navy. He nearly succeeded Richard Nixon as the vice-presidential candidate on the Eisenhower ticket in 1956.

By the time Anderson went to Panama, he was nearing his fifty-fourth birthday. But he was separated by more than years from his birthplace in Burleson. By the mid-1960s, Anderson was more accustomed to the board rooms of Manhattan and the seats of power in Washington than he was to the Hill Country or the Red River Valley. Or so it seemed to many Panamanians. He impressed them as a cool, detached, highly organized man who rarely relaxed, one who was all business and impatient of distractions. Despite that, the one-time farm boy from Texas had a deeper appreciation of Panama's poverty and its underdog role than most Panamanians ever imagined.

Anderson made the diplomatic rounds in Panama. At the Foreign Ministry, he met with Minister Galileo Solís. He drove through the crowded streets of downtown Panama City to the *presidencia* to visit President

Chiari. With both men he emphasized President Johnson's sincere desire to erase the differences that had been dividing the two countries. The Panamanian leaders told Anderson of their hope that the errors and distortions of 1903 would be corrected quickly. Anderson also met his Panamanian counterpart for the negotiations, Jorge E. Illueca, the well-known lawyer and intellectual who, as president of Panama's Bar Association, had asked the International Commission of Jurists to investigate the January riots. Illueca was a passionate patriot with leftist political inclinations.

Anderson also spent time in the Canal Zone talking with Zone Governor Fleming, General O'Meara, and others. The president's representative was inundated with appeals from Zonians to seek payment of their claims for property lost during the rioting. In Anderson's recollection, that was their paramount concern. They had, he said, "a minimum interest in what took place between the United States and Panama." Like many visitors to Panama, Anderson was impressed by the blinders that limited the political vision of most Zonians.

After his tour of the isthmus, Anderson reported back to President Johnson. He had found the Panamanians he met both intelligent and reasonable and he concluded that he could do business with them. He arranged an appointment for Ambassador Illueca, who would soon be coming to Washington. The tall, curly-haired Panamanian envoy arrived in the U.S. capital the evening of May 4. On May 7, he went to the White House to present his credentials to a warmly welcoming president. The two had a short but cordial visit, then the negotiators went off to New York to go to work. Lyndon Johnson pushed Panama onto the back burner of his attention.

Anderson's base of operations was the headquarters of his business in the massive, modern skyscraper at One Rockefeller Plaza in midtown Manhattan. He helped arrange for an office in that same citadel of the capitalist world for his left-wing counterpart from Panama and for Illueca's fellow negotiators, Dr. Eloy Benedetti, a Foreign Ministry legal specialist, and Dr. Gustavo Tejeda Mora, who advised Illueca on economic matters. Anderson's chief assistants were Sterling J. Cottrell and Robert Newbegin, career Foreign Service officers with considerable experience in Latin America. The Americans continued to live in Washington and work out of the State Department, but they became familiar figures on the airline shuttle to New York as they traveled to Manhattan to brief the ambassador and to attend meetings with the Panamanians once or twice a week.

The New York sessions began with considerable optimism on both sides. The Panamanians believed they had a commitment from the Americans to work out all differences—and for Illueca and his team, that meant a new treaty. Anderson and the U.S. side saw it quite differently. Their goal was to eliminate "sources of friction" between the two countries with un-

derstanding and major concessions *short* of a treaty. Anderson thought
those principal areas of concern could be resolved quickly. At an early session with his staff, he spoke of wrapping it up in three months. Cottrell, a
hard-bitten veteran of Latin American politics who knew Panama, told his
boss: "It'll be closer to three years." Anderson thought he was just being
cynical.

With those conflicting views dominating the thinking of the two diplomatic teams, the nagging problem of "discuss" vs. "negotiate" raised its
head again. More important, both countries were in the midst of major
political change. Three days after Illueca met President Johnson, Panamanian voters went to the polls to pick a new president. It took nineteen days
for the votes to be counted and for Marco Robles to be declared the victor—amid allegations by the opposition of vote stealing and widespread
corruption. In any case, by the time Illueca and Anderson got down to
serious talk, Panama's president-designate was busy shaping his new administration in preparation for his inauguration on October 1. It was the
worst possible time for a diplomatic mission in New York to get coherent
instructions from a home government that was in flux.

In Washington, the Panama talks received only cursory attention. The
president was leading the fight for the most massive program of domestic
legislation ever undertaken in our history over so short a time. It involved
civil rights, aid to education, assistance to the elderly, reduction of taxes,
and a dozen other major issues. He was also coping with complex and
troublesome foreign problems—fighting on Cyprus, Cuban meddling in
Venezuela, growing conflict in Vietnam.

The summer of 1964 was also an active political season in the United
States. It was an election year. Senator Barry Goldwater was the front-
runner for the Republicans. But Henry Cabot Lodge had returned from
Vietnam to battle for the nomination. Nelson Rockefeller was in the running, as was Gov. William Scranton of Pennsylvania. On the Democratic
side, Lyndon Johnson bided his time. He never said he was a candidate,
though everyone knew he was and that no one could compete. Politics
dominated that long summer in Washington and in the country. The Panama talks could have been held in an igloo on the Arctic Circle for all the
attention they received from government or press.

Political realities in both countries made the New York sessions a holding action. Neither party had fully developed staff work or carefully analyzed and approved positions. Anderson and Illueca were like boxers in the
first round—feeling the opponent out, seeing how good his reflexes were.
And so they feinted and parried through the summer.

At their first session following the Fourth of July holiday, Illueca tried
to get agreement on an agenda. Not surprisingly, his proposal focused on

those things Panama considered paramount: elimination of "the foreign colony" in Panama's heartland, recognition of Panamanian sovereignty over all its territory, an end to U.S. activities not associated with operating the canal, increased economic benefits to Panama from the busy seaway, Panamanian participation in canal administration, a termination date for all the concessions made in 1903 and since. Anderson and his colleagues saw *that* agenda, correctly, as a formula for an entirely new treaty. They pointed out, too, that it did not address any of the things that the United States thought were most important—a continued dominant voice for the United States in running the canal, measures for adequate protection, some form of continued U.S. legal jurisdiction over its citizens in the Zone. The Panamanian agenda was rejected.

At the end of that sometimes acrimonious session, the United States engaged in a form of psychological warfare. Anderson had invited Army Secretary Stephen Ailes and his principal assistant on Panama, Deputy Under Secretary Harry McPherson, to New York. After the negotiating session, the two visitors briefed the Panamanian delegates on the sea-level canal option. It was getting attention in Congress at the time and plans for a comprehensive study were moving ahead. The briefing was a not so subtle reminder to the Panamanians that the United States was seriously thinking of replacing the old canal with a wider, deeper one at sea level. More than that, it made evident that Washington was not wedded to Panama as the site for a new canal, but that Colombia, Costa Rica, and Nicaragua were being considered as well. A chill settled over the Panamanian delegation when they considered that the canal—over which they sought increased responsibility and from which they anticipated higher revenues—might within a few years become no more than a tourist attraction with as little utility as the pyramids.

In Panama, the scene was changing politically. Marco Robles, having squeaked by to victory in the May elections, was organizing his new team. The man he approached to take over the crucial portfolio of Foreign Affairs was Fernando Eleta, the prosperous and astute businessman, *bon vivant*, and world traveler who had made the fortuitous financial deal with Franco Spain that permitted Panama to survive the postriot crisis. When Robles approached Eleta with his proposal, the graduate of Stanford and MIT told the president-to-be there were things he needed to know before accepting the demanding post. As Eleta later told me: "I wanted to find out whether you people were willing to deal objectively and reasonably with us, or whether this was to be simply a test of strength." If it was to be an exercise in emotion and patriotism, nothing more, he was not interested. If he judged it could be orderly, systematic, and rational, he would take it on. Most men, offered the post of foreign minister in their government, jump at the chance without looking too hard at what is required. Eleta was the kind of rare pragmatist who wanted to know the rules before he took a hand.

To get his answers, Eleta went to Washington in August 1964. He had arranged an appointment with Tom Mann, whom Eleta had met when the Texan was U.S. ambassador to Mexico. After the initial pleasantries, Eleta put his cards on the table. He explained that he was considering whether he should accept the Foreign Ministry position. Then he leaned forward and told Mann: "Look, Tom, kindly tell me, very sincerely, in this process of negotiation, what are your nonnegotiable positions?" It was the kind of question raised in diplomatic exchanges only when the men involved are confident and realistic, and when they detest beating around the bush. That is the kind of man Eleta was, and Mann as well.

"Well, Fernando," Mann responded, "I wasn't sure exactly what you wanted to ask. But knowing you, I imagined this would be your general approach. So I have the answer. I have it not only from me, but from my superiors." Then he laid down what was to be the basic U.S. position over the next round of talks: "We only wish to be able to exercise, during a reasonable period of time, effective control over the administration of the canal and the right to defend it appropriately."

Eleta realized that any arrangement on the future of the Panama Canal would have to provide for some continued U.S. responsibility for administration. No other alternative had a remote chance of getting through the Congress. He also knew that continued U.S. protection of the waterway was an essential ingredient. He noted that Mann, significantly, had not mentioned any time frame, had not used words like *forever* or *in perpetuity*. The time element was central to Panama's perceptions. He also realized instantly that Mann had not raised any of the issues that were fundamental for Panama—increased participation in running the canal, a fairer share of economic returns, and, most important, Panama's rights of sovereignty over what for sixty years had been the Canal Zone.

All those things and more passed quickly through his mind. He looked at Mann and said: "Tom, I think I can live with your 'nonnegotiables.' Obviously we would prefer a prompt transfer of the Canal Zone to Panama. But that is unrealistic. We will need a period of transition." Then he told Mann: "You are now talking to the foreign minister of Panama." Eleta flew home to tell Robles that he was prepared to accept the key post in the new president's cabinet.

The Eleta appointment set off sparks within the Panamanian negotiating team. The new foreign minister was a man of considerable dignity and *amour propre*. He saw, quite correctly, that working out a new arrangement with the United States would be the central business of the Robles government. That made it his primary task as foreign minister and he had no intention of delegating the authority to others. Illueca, chief negotiator under Chiari, was a man of equal self-esteem. He felt strongly that responsibility for working out a new treaty should be his. As a compromise, he was offered the title of *vocero* (spokesman) of the treaty-making effort, but he refused indignantly. The political differences between Illueca, the romantic revolutionary, and Eleta, the businessman-aristocrat, were considerable, and that hardened the lines between them. Illueca flew to Panama at the end of September. When all efforts at mediation failed, Illueca submitted his resignation as a treaty negotiator on November 17. His colleagues, Tejeda Mora and Benedetti, quickly resigned in sympathy. Panamanian Ambassador Miguel Moreno had left Washington and government service in early September. The stage was set for a new cast to take over.

Clearly the quarterback of the new team would be Eleta. But he and Robles needed a group of professionals to handle the detailed negotiations with Robert Anderson and his U.S. colleagues. As ambassador to Washington, they selected Ricardo Manuel Arias Espinosa, a former president of the Republic. He had taken power in 1954 in the wake of the assassination of President José Antonio Remón—in a complicated and controversial set of political maneuvers (including the mysterious role of an alleged Mafia gunman). Arias was well connected in Washington, knew his way about Congress, and got on famously at Burning Tree Country Club (he was one of Panama's best golfers).

For the complicated negotiating job, Robles and Eleta picked two highly competent and experienced men. One was Roberto Alemán, a noted and extremely prosperous lawyer. "Chato" Alemán attended the National University before he went to Louisiana State for his doctor of laws degree. A short, wiry, energetic man, he had a mind as crisp and controlled as the 5-iron shots he used to dismay his golfing partners at the Panama Golf Club.

His co-negotiator (and spokesman for the team) was Díogenes de la Rosa, an older, more relaxed lawyer and a former ambassador to Venezuela. In his early years, de la Rosa had been something of a firebrand and supporter of revolutionary causes. With maturity, and broad exposure to the world, much of his extremist ardor cooled. But he remained a dedicated nationalist and a man who believed his country deserved a better break in its dealings with the United States. Guillermo Chapman, an able young economist, joined the team as a consultant on such things as tolls policy, canal management, and other technical matters.

There were changes on the American side as well. President Johnson and Ambassador Anderson selected John N. Irwin II to be the deputy negotiator. Irwin was a New York lawyer, a partner in the powerful firm of Patterson, Belknap, and Webb. He had had a previous tour in government as assistant secretary of defense for international security affairs. Later, under President Nixon, he would become under secretary of state and then ambassador to France. A quiet, competent, and dedicated man, Irwin carried the heaviest load of negotiating with the Panamanians during those years—together with his professional diplomatic colleague, Robert Woodward, a veteran in Latin American affairs.

Diplomatic talks aimed at a new arrangement between Panama and the United States were beginning to move. But the other element in the equation was moving, too. Lyndon Johnson had always seen the Panama problem as a two-sided affair. One part was doing something positive about Panamanian grievances that caused periodic eruptions in our affairs. The other part was to arrange to dig a new canal at sea level, a waterway that would accommodate the largest ships in the world and be much less vulnerable in wartime. The president had urged that the possibility be studied thoroughly, and had proposed legislation to that effect. Congress considered the matter through the summer and the two houses finally approved Public Law 88-609, which the president signed into law on September 22, 1964. The bill established the Atlantic-Pacific Interoceanic Canal Study Commission. The new commission was to investigate the feasibility of a sea-level canal and report back to the president. Three matters dominated its agenda: what was the best route for such a canal? what was the best method of construction? how much would it cost? The commission had a 1968 deadline for its work, and the initial appropriation was $17.5 million.

The administration planned on a governmental commission made up of the secretaries of state and defense and the chairman of the Atomic Energy Commission. The choice clearly pointed in the direction the president thought the findings would go. There had been much discussion in Washington over previous years concerning the feasibility of digging a canal with nuclear explosions. Dr. Edwin Teller, who had helped develop the hydrogen bomb, was an enthusiastic advocate. So was Dr. Gerald Johnson, Defense Secretary McNamara's adviser on atomic energy. Memos by them and other specialists helped persuade McNamara and, in turn, the president that nuclear excavation not only was practicable but also would be vastly less expensive than conventional means. That was a time when citizens and governments were much less sensitive than they later became regarding the effects of nuclear fallout.

One imposing barrier stood in the way of nuclear excavation: the Limited Test Ban Treaty with the Soviet Union. It had gone into effect in October 1963, one month before President Kennedy's murder, and it prohibited nuclear testing in the atmosphere, in space, or underwater. Any nuclear explosion that put radioactive material into the atmosphere would have violated the treaty. But some people in Washington thought the Soviets might agree to an exception for canal excavation in Central America.

They believed the Russians were eager to use nuclear power themselves in some major development projects in Siberia. Actually, the notion of a nuclear trade-off was a political dreamworld. It was beaten back in Washington long before it could be tried with the Russians.

The nemesis of the government commission proviso was Rep. Daniel Flood of Pennsylvania, known to some House colleagues and members of the press as "the Congressman from the Canal Zone." Anything to do with the Panama Canal was dear to the heart of the legislator from Wilkes-Barre. When the Interoceanic Canal Commission bill was before the House Merchant Marine and Fisheries Committee, its courtly chairman, Herbert C. Bonner of North Carolina, invited Flood to attend. He not only attended, but asked to address the committee. "Gentlemen, colleagues," he began, his waxed moustache quivering, "having the army investigate building a sea-level canal is like having the devil investigate hell." Then, with sweeping gestures and Shakespearian language, he tore into the proposal with fury. He wanted, and the House should want, he said, a commission not of bureaucrats but of civilians—businessmen, engineers, retired military men, and the like. By the time he finished, an exhausted committee agreed with him. That is what went into the final legislation—a commission of five civilians with *no* representation from the government. Flood's reputation as the staunchest defender of the old canal remained untarnished.

When Congress eliminated the governmental commission, the president had to adjust. He feared that a two-pronged effort—reaching an accommodation with Panama and studying a possible new canal—would produce conflicts. That was one reason he wanted Rusk and McNamara to handle the sea-level investigation. To make the best of Congress' action, he decided to put the two functions under one person responsible to him. He summoned treaty negotiator Anderson to the Oval Office. "Bob," the president said, "I think that if I give the sea-level canal study to one group, and negotiations on the Panama Canal to another, we may find areas of confusion. So I think you ought to head up both groups." Anderson agreed to take on both tasks, asking only that he have some voice in picking the other members. Johnson assured him he would have it.

Talks on the canal were moving ahead between the Americans and the Panamanians. The new representatives from the isthmus quickly made clear that a patchwork approach, a little more of this and less of that, would not satisfy their people. One thing, above all else, became obvious to Anderson and the U.S. negotiators: Panama could not continue to live with the 1903 treaty. Its terms were onerous; the fact that it was to continue forever was politically impossible. There would have to be a new approach. If not, there could be no deal.

By that time, one of the largest obstacles to rational change in the U.S.-

Panama relationship had been overcome. The quadrennial presidential sweepstakes—which always inhibits a moderate approach to most problems—had ended in both countries. Marco Robles took office in Panama on October 1. A month later, on November 3, 1964, Lyndon Johnson was elected president with the largest percentage of the popular vote in American history. Both leaders could put narrow concerns aside and consider the larger interests of their nations.

Anderson mulled over what he had been hearing from the Panamanians during recent months. He discussed it with his staff. Their conclusion: nothing short of a major revision offered any hope of a solution. He asked for an appointment with the newly elected president and went to see him on December 2. As they sat in the Oval Office, the president in his comfortable rocking chair and Anderson on the beige couch to his right, the two men discussed the Panama problem. Anderson told the president he was utterly convinced the old arrangement—imposed on Panama in 1903 when that small country was totally vulnerable, when its national survival depended on U.S. goodwill—had outlived its usefulness. The only real solution, he told his fellow Texan, would be a completely fresh treaty, one that eliminated the most onerous provisions of the Hay–Bunau-Varilla pact. That meant getting rid of perpetuity, he said. The new treaty would have to provide for a fixed termination date. Anderson promised to try to set that date as far in the future as he could, within reason. But that there must be a final date was as clear as a midsummer Texas sky.

There should also be a separate arrangement giving the United States the right to dig a new sea-level canal if it wished to do so, Anderson said. That met one of Johnson's prime requirements for a new deal with Panama. He saw a sea-level canal as a way to pull all the rotten teeth produced by the one-sided pact that Bunau-Varilla had written. Finally, Anderson said, there should be another part of the package guaranteeing the United States the right to continue to defend the canal as long as it was in operation—and to protect a new canal if one were dug. "That, Mr. President, will give us what I think we really need," he concluded.

The president told Anderson he had given him a lot to consider. He understood the arguments and was sympathetic to them, but he wanted to think it over. Privately, the president was delighted with Anderson's report. It gave him the kind of challenge he relished. It had a history-making aura about it, the kind of thing Lyndon Johnson found hard to resist. Digging a sea-level canal appealed to him almost as much as the idea of putting a man on the moon. And the political challenge, as formidable as anything one could imagine, was something only a connoisseur of congressional infighting like Johnson could really appreciate and anticipate. Having just emerged the victor in a hard-fought national campaign, Lyndon Johnson was looking for new worlds to conquer. The Panama Canal issue—which had engaged all his twentieth-century predecessors except Harding, Coolidge, and Hoover—was a likely candidate for his attention.

Once Anderson had spelled out his views, President Johnson took the bit in his teeth. He discussed it with Secretary of State Rusk and with McNamara at Defense. He used the phone to ask the advice of countless old friends in Congress. He summoned Gen. Earle G. Wheeler, chairman of the Joint Chiefs of Staff, laid out the proposition, and told him to sound out his colleagues on the JCS. He called former President Harry Truman in Independence, Missouri, and discussed all the pros and cons. One by one, he covered all the bases. It was a vintage Johnson performance. Nothing was left to chance. As he moved toward his momentous announcement, there was one unchecked name on his list, former President Dwight D. Eisenhower.

Eisenhower was on a train headed west, escaping the snow of Gettysburg to get to the sun of Palm Springs where he could play golf. Johnson believed Eisenhower's views would be crucial. He was not only a former president but also a respected military figure. If the former Allied commander in Europe during our biggest war was on his side, Johnson thought, he would not worry too much about lesser disgruntled generals and admirals who might speak out against his proposal.

Johnson called in John McCone, director of the Central Intelligence Agency, and explained what he wanted done. A phone call was not good enough, he said. He wanted the former president to read the details of what he had in mind. McCone took the paper the president handed him and drove to his headquarters in Langley, Virginia. There he called in one of his principal officers and gave him instructions. The agent took off for Chicago on the next plane. In the Windy City, he located the west-bound train and climbed aboard the special car used by the former president. He gave Eisenhower the paper from President Johnson. Ike read it, thought about it, and called McCone. He told the CIA director he had studied the president's proposal. "My approval is complete," he said. McCone asked if Eisenhower had any objection to the president's using his name publicly in making his planned announcement. "It's perfectly all right with me," Eisenhower replied. The last and crucial piece in the mosaic was in place and President Johnson was ready to move.

On the afternoon of December 18, 1964, at about 4:00 P.M., the White House press corps was alerted to a special announcement. They were told the president would meet them in the White House theater within the hour. At 4:45 P.M., the president walked to the podium before the assembled reporters.

> This Government [the president began] has completed an intensive review of policy toward the present and future of the Panama Canal. On the basis of this review, I have reached two decisions.

First, I have decided that the United States should press forward with Panama and other interested governments in plans and preparations for a sea-level canal in this area.

Second, I have decided to propose to the Government of Panama the negotiation of an entirely new treaty on the existing Panama Canal.

Then he revealed the careful political groundwork laid over the previous two weeks. His decisions, he said, had the unanimous approval of the secretaries of state and defense and of the Joint Chiefs of Staff. They also had the full support of former Presidents Truman and Eisenhower. He said he had reported his decision to the leadership in the Congress where "in most instances" they had been sympathetically received.

The president explained that more than three hundred ships then afloat, or nearing completion in the world's shipyards, could not get through the canal when fully loaded. And many of those—including all modern U.S. aircraft carriers—could not transit at all. It was time, he said, to plan in earnest for a sea-level canal that would be "more modern, more economical, and . . . far easier to defend." He mentioned the study Congress had approved, and he said he had asked Secretary Rusk to begin talks with the governments whose territories provided the likely routes—Panama, Colombia, Nicaragua, and Costa Rica.

Earlier that day, he had told President Robles that his administration was ready to negotiate a new treaty. "In such a treaty," he said, "we must retain the rights which are necessary for the effective operation and the protection of the canal, and the administration of the areas that are necessary for these purposes."

"Such a treaty would replace the treaty of 1903 and its amendments," Johnson explained to the press. "It should recognize the sovereignty of Panama. It should provide for its own termination when a sea-level canal comes into operation. It should provide for effective discharge of our common responsibilities for hemispheric defense." Speaking with great conviction, the president concluded: "These changes are necessary not because of failure but because of success; not because of backwardness but because of progress. The age before us is an age of larger, faster ships. It is an age of friendly partnership among the nations concerned with the traffic between the oceans. This new age requires new arrangements."

When the president finished, the assembled reporters let him take three or four steps toward the exit, then they broke for the rear doors. There was a mad scramble for the nearest telephones. Those without urgent deadlines had the luxury of moving to their typewriters instead. Within minutes, the story of the historic turning point was clattering into newspaper offices and radio stations around the world.

The news created the greatest stir in Panama, naturally. It was received with jubilation by the government, by business circles, by all the powers in the society, and by average citizens as well. It seemed that more than sixty years of frustration were about to end. It was the long-awaited new deal, so often promised and never dealt. On that day, if Lyndon Johnson had walked down Panama City's Central Avenue, he would have been hailed as the greatest man in the world, received the keys of the city, and found himself knee-deep in flowers. He would have loved it—and deserved it.

The president's decisions on Panama were formally codified by National Security Assistant McGeorge Bundy and his staff in National Security Action Memorandum (NSAM) #323. It went out to the bureaucracy on January 8, 1965, and provided the marching orders for the negotiators and for all departments of the government concerned with the Panama problems.

In Panama, one year had passed since rioting exploded in Panama City and Colón. Those who had used violence, and promoted it for political purposes, had not forgotten. Plans were afoot to celebrate those events and to generate a revival, but the Robles government was in no mood to sit by and watch any repetition. Its predecessor government had been embarrassed, even humbled, by the insistent demands of a shouting mob. The newly installed administration was determined not to suffer the same ignominy. On January 12, 1965, hundreds of students and others gathered downtown and began to march toward the American Embassy. When they reached Cinco de Mayo Plaza, the mob found itself confronting armed troops of the National Guard. The Guard tried persuasion to encourage the crowd to disperse. But appeals to reason produced only louder shouting, and soon rocks began to fly, hitting some soldiers.

The order was given: don gas masks. That done, canisters of tear gas were lobbed in front of the mob. As the acrid fumes spread through the crowd, they fell back and soon were running away from the scene. The avenue and surrounding streets were cleared, though some store windows and a few cars suffered as the retreating rioters vented their frustration on the innocent. It was the last gasp of the extremists. Even a dozen years later, however, as the second week of January approached, there was a sense of apprehension in the Panama air. The ninth of January is still celebrated as the Day of the Martyrs, a national holiday. Today, it is far more reverent than riotous.

Even before the president made his momentous announcement, the new team in Panama was gearing up for renewed talks with the *yanquis*. One of the first things newly installed Foreign Minister Eleta did reflected his engineering background and pragmatic approach. He flew to New York to consult an old friend, a roommate at MIT. Nelson Slater was a senior partner in a well-known engineering firm that had conducted surveys for many major toll highways in the eastern United States. Eleta called Slater and invited him to dinner. After cocktails and reminiscences, Eleta put his cards on the table.

"Look, Nelson," he said, "I have been made minister of foreign affairs for Panama. I've got to initiate this whole process of negotiating a treaty over the canal. So the first thing I want to know is what the hell I'm talking about."

He said that, to his way of thinking, a canal was little more than a toll road. Slater agreed that a waterway and a highway were not all that different. If the premises are basically the same, Eleta said, how do you calculate tolls? Slater explained: if it is feasible to build a high-speed highway between points A and B, you have to figure out how much people would save by using the new route rather than an old, longer route. Then you calculate how much it would cost to build the new road. The tolls should produce between two-thirds and three-fourths of the savings the users would enjoy. If that kind of return can pay for the road over a reasonable time, you have a viable proposition. Costs for building were immaterial in the case of the canal, he said, because it was already built. What the dinner conversation did was to give the Panamanian diplomat a totally new way of looking at the toll structure of the canal—one his government had not used before. The approach that came out of that talk in Manhattan provided the basic outlook for Panamanian negotiators for the next decade. It caused considerable heartburn for American negotiators who, for political and historical reasons, sought always to keep tolls on the Panama Canal as low as possible—whether it made economic sense or not.

Eleta returned to Panama excited about his new approach to a problem that had plagued his predecessors for years. Panamanian negotiators and diplomats for half a century had approached their difficulties with the United States from a juridical, legalistic, and emotional viewpoint. They never looked hard at dollars and cents—except for rather general appeals for a "better deal" for Panama.

There still were unanswered questions. How did one learn how much was saved by using the canal rather than some other route? Eleta began to dig deeper. He found that calculations by U.S. sources indicated that shippers using the Panama Canal were saving between $1.3 and $1.5 billion a year. But which countries and which commodities were the prime beneficiaries of that windfall? No serious studies had been made. The word passed through business channels and the diplomatic underground that Panama wanted a detailed report of the monetary benefits of the canal.

The news drifted to Western Europe and beyond, but it reached Mexico City early on. A report of Panama's problem arrived at the desk of a shrewd Soviet diplomat in the Mexican capital. Others who heard of Panama's concern ignored it. Not Moscow's envoy Vladimir Vazikin. The Soviets had been following the Panama controversy with close attention. Obviously, it was the kind of situation they thought might be turned to their advantage if they played their cards right, and if the United States made enough mistakes. Vazikin checked with the Kremlin, then went to Panama. A meeting of the United Nations Economic Commission for Latin America provided a convenient cover for his purposes. From his suite in the El Panamá Hotel, Vazikin called for an appointment with the foreign minister. He had met Eleta at U.N. headquarters in New York and the two engineers had many common interests.

Vazikin went to Eleta's home in La Cresta, an affluent residential area of Panama City, not far from the American ambassador's residence. There, in the small but cozy den where Eleta did much of his thinking and entertaining, the two men had a vodka and talked of the canal. Eleta laid out Panama's problem in general terms, and the Russian made an offer.

"Fernando," he said, "I can personally commit my government officially, right now, to make any number of studies you wish. We can do it through third countries, Switzerland, for example, so that our name does not appear too obviously. And we would do it for nothing."

By then, in the easy camaraderie of a soft Panamanian dusk, it had become "Fernando" and "Vladimir."

"Vladimir," Eleta replied, "I don't think that would go very well with the United States. The source is going to have to come out sooner or later. But let me talk with my president, and I will let you know tomorrow."

Eleta knew the answer would have to be no. He was sophisticated enough to understand what problems acceptance could have produced. Such a study would have given the Soviets a degree of specialized knowledge about canal operations they perhaps did not have. More to the point, it would have given them a line into the highest levels of the Panamanian government, one they would have used to considerable advantage. In any case, as Eleta foresaw—and as he recommended—the Soviet offer was rejected.

Moscow was not the only capital interested in what was happening in Panama. Another of Eleta's neighbors in La Cresta was Lionel Vasse, the intelligent, suave ambassador of France. He, too, had heard of Panama's need and he dropped by to see the foreign minister. Sitting in the same chair the Soviet envoy had occupied a few days earlier, and with a chilled Chablis in hand, the French diplomat said: "Fernando, I understand the Panamanian government is in need of certain basic studies on the canal—its operations, structure, income potential, and the like."

"Well, that's true, Lionel," Eleta replied. "We are very much interested in such a study."

"I anticipated your interest," Vasse said, "and I communicated with my government before coming here. I am authorized to tell you that the

French government would be not only willing but highly desirous of carrying out such a study. You must remember that we built Suez, and that it was de Lesseps who started building this canal. So we are very much interested. As far as the price is concerned, you put your own price." (A considerably more elegant approach than Moscow's offer to do it free.)

Eleta thanked Vasse for France's offer and said he would give it every consideration. But as a shrewd observer of the international scene, Eleta knew that French help to Panama would be only slightly more welcome in Washington than assistance from Moscow. France in 1964 was de Gaulle, and the estrangement between Paris and Washington was already far advanced, a condition that would lead to France's withdrawal from the military side of NATO in less than two years. The French offer, like the Soviet's, was rejected with thanks.

A solution finally occurred to the Panamanians. The future of the canal and its toll structure were of obvious importance to the entire world of commerce. Every nation whose ships transited the canal would be concerned; all who bought goods that passed through Panama would have an interest. They were all in one place—at the United Nations. By coincidence, Panamanian Roberto Huertematte was then one of the under secretaries of the U.N. Through his good offices, Panama received a $250,000 grant to help defray the costs of the study.

In his search for a reputable organization to do the survey, Eleta went first to his undergraduate alma mater, Stanford, and discussed the proposal with officials at the Stanford Research Institute. But the U.S. government had already contracted with them for a similar study. He then went to his other school, Massachusetts Institute of Technology, for advice. Friends there strongly recommended the Arthur D. Little Company, a consulting and accounting firm with a worldwide reputation. Terms of reference were worked out to assure the study was as objective as possible, without reference to political factors or other conditions. The Stanford survey was to be conducted under the same general rules. The Panamanians were especially cautious. They did not want their investigation of tolls and related matters cast aside or disparaged later because they had worked from premises different from those of the U.S. study.*

Preliminary sessions between the negotiating teams were largely "get acquainted" gatherings. They were still working at Rockefeller Plaza in deference to Anderson's wish to devote most of his time to personal inter-

---

*The outcome of this resort to technical studies was rather bizarre. The Stanford Research Institute and the Arthur D. Little Co. took more than a year to complete their work. The results were given to the negotiating teams at a joint session in the General Dynamics Building in New York in 1966. Both demonstrated that Panama Canal tolls were far too low, that they could be raised at least 125 percent without affecting traffic. That meant revenues could expand and Panama's share could be boosted sharply. It was the point the Panamanians

ests. But by January 25, they were down to serious business. On that day, the Panamanian delegation presented a proposed agenda for the talks. It revived demands originally made by Panama in the 1955 treaty talks: recognition of Panama's sovereignty over all its territory, including the Canal Zone; restricting U.S. actions to those actually needed to operate and protect the canal; assurances that Panama would receive a fair economic return for the continued use of its geographic position. Panama also wanted to end the concept of perpetuity, put a final date on U.S. rights, and create a new system of administration giving Panama and the United States joint responsibility for canal operations. With that beginning, the State Department was able to report to President Johnson on February 12 that "this week, negotiations between Panama and the United States began in earnest between Special Ambassadors de la Rosa and Anderson in New York."

Thus, as spring rolled around and Washingtonians began to look for dogwood blossoms in Rock Creek Park, new administrations were well emplaced in the U.S. and Panamanian capitals. New negotiators had begun their work. Technical studies for both sides had been launched. The stage seemed finally set. The only missing element was the proposed sea-level canal commission whose approval President Johnson had nursed through the Congress months before.

For reasons that remain obscure, the president dawdled over appointment of the new commission. He had approved the legislation in September 1964, and had announced a new policy on Panama in December. But he did not get around to naming the sea-level canal study commission until the middle of April 1965. It was an able group when finally unveiled. Outstanding among the members was Dr. Milton Eisenhower. Raymond A. Hill, a civil engineer of international repute, had spent fifty years in the development of water resources and was a recognized authority on the planning, design, and construction of hydraulic structures. Brig. Gen. Kenneth E. Fields (Retired) had an outstanding record in the U.S. Army's Corps of Engineers. He was an executive on the Manhattan Project in World War II, the enterprise that produced the first atomic bomb. He had also been general manager of the Atomic Energy Commission. The final member, and vice-chairman of the commission, was Robert G. Storey. He was 71 years old at the time of appointment and, like Anderson, was a Texas lawyer of the old school. His participation in the exercise was minimal.

As the negotiators began to shape a new arrangement, it became appar-

---

wished to make. When Ambassador Anderson saw the way the wind was blowing, he called a halt before the presentation was completed. "Well, that's enough," he said. "Any questions?" There were none. As they walked to the elevators, he told Eleta the U.S. government was not prepared to accept either study. It was the kind of preemptive move large nations often make. Eleta understood great power politics. Nonetheless, the final treaty drafts accepted the fact that Panama should get much more than it had been receiving. Eleta had made his point. Anderson dodged it in public, accepted it in private.

ent that one treaty to cover everything the two sides were discussing would be an unwieldy document. Anderson flew to Washington and met with the president on May 6 to explain the difficulty. One treaty was good enough in 1903, he said, but not in today's world. He described the many issues raised by the Panamanians, and the multitude of elements the United States wanted to have included. To put it all into one package would be, in effect, putting apples and peanuts and ice cream into the same bag. Johnson saw the point, and agreed. He told Anderson to negotiate three treaties simultaneously: one on the existing Panama Canal; another on a sea-level canal; the third on U.S. military bases and defense rights. Anderson flew back to New York and informed the Panamanians that the three-sided approach they had been discussing had the president's OK. The diplomats moved forward on that basis.

From the time the Panama Canal opened in 1914, Panamanians had been disgruntled because not one of their countrymen ever held any position of significance in the operation of the waterway. If one looked at the ascending steps in the canal hierarchy, there was a steady drop in the number of dark-skinned personnel and in Spanish names. At the upper levels of the Canal Company and the Zone government, there were none. That struck Panamanians as both unfair and unenlightened.

That same attitude had prevailed among U.S. private businesses in the early part of the century. But by the 1960s, all the major U.S. corporations and banks had hired or promoted Panamanians to positions of the highest responsibility. The Chase Manhattan Bank, National City Bank, IBM, Xerox, Sears Roebuck, Texaco, and most other companies had Panamanians at the top levels of management. Even small U.S. businesses relied heavily on Panamanian administrative talent to conduct their affairs. The result was smoother relations with the people and the government of Panama. But the Canal Zone remained a bastion of white supremacy and U.S. domination. Any good management consultant or perceptive sociologist could have foretold that it could not last. But the Zonians and the Merchant Marine and Fisheries Committee of the House of Representatives were not looking for good advice. They wanted to preserve the status quo, an attitude that had helped greatly to generate the rioting of 1959 and 1964.

The Panamanians had listed joint operation of the canal on the agenda they proposed in late January, and during the next months they pushed the notion hard. We both have a deep interest in the canal, they would say, why don't we operate it together? In any negotiation, one requirement is to distinguish between what the other side says for effect and what is fundamental to its position. In this case, it took the Americans about four months to realize that joint operation was basic to Panama, not merely a bargaining chip.

The problem went beyond mere recognition of negotiating priorities.

The U.S. negotiators' marching orders, contained in NSAM #323, called for continued American operation of the canal until it was replaced by a sea-level waterway. Accommodation of Panama's wishes required a change in instructions. Anderson and his deputy, John Irwin, went to the White House to discuss the contentious issue with the president on June 23.

When they were shown into the Cabinet Room, they found the top echelon of the foreign policy apparatus. Secretary Rusk was there together with Tom Mann and Jack Vaughn. Defense Secretary McNamara and Army Secretary Ailes represented the Pentagon. McGeorge Bundy, the national security adviser, was present as well. The president asked Anderson to lay out the problem.

The former treasury secretary recalled the terms of NSAM #323. Then he outlined the Panamanians' case as they had presented it time and time again. If the Panama Canal was really a joint enterprise, as everyone liked to claim, they said, we should make it more than a symbolic partnership. The Panamanians insisted their country had as deep an interest as did the United States in seeing that the canal continued to operate efficiently. But unless some Panamanians were involved in management of the canal, no one in their country was going to feel that the reality reflected the rhetoric.

Anderson made the case forcefully. The discussion spread around the table as Johnson called on one then another of his advisers. All the pros and cons were aired. The advantages of moving ahead with Panama in order to get a reasonable settlement were clear to most of those in the room. They thought the primary disadvantage would be the political storm that might erupt on the Hill against joint operation.

The president grasped the nettle. He told Anderson and Irwin they could explore "some form of joint U.S.-Panama management of the canal." But as a prudent politician, he instructed them to make no commitments until there had been "full consultation with the Congress." He gave orders that the consultation should begin "next week." At the same meeting, the advisers recommended and the president approved a $3.5 million "soft loan" (long term, low interest) for road construction in Panama. It had several purposes, as most such items of generosity do: to assure the Robles government of Washington's goodwill; to provide visible evidence to the Panamanian people that we had their interests in mind; to help blunt opposition criticism of the treaty talks; and to give Panama's economy a much needed, though small, shot in the arm.

Consultations with Congress began, as the president had instructed. Anderson and Irwin and others wore out considerable shoe leather along congressional hallways over the next month or more. They encountered general understanding in many offices. But they also ran into far heavier opposition than they had anticipated. Criticism was particularly vehement on the House side, as they had expected; but few on the Senate side were ready to throw their hats in the air, either. Having exhausted all the positive arguments they could muster, Anderson and Irwin had to admit defeat. They decided there was only one hope and that was the "master persuader" himself. They wrote an eleven-page memo to the president on September 2 reporting on the negotiations to date and the various ideas they had developed for some kind of joint management of the canal. They also provided a rundown on the results of their safaris through the congressional jungle. Summing up the pros and cons of joint administration, they defined the key disadvantage: "A significant number of Senators and Representatives will oppose strongly a real partnership with Panama. They will consider it a 'giveaway' and a weakening of our historic position of strength in Central America."

The negotiators' memo was blunt in its appeal for presidential help. They wrote: "It is doubtful that anyone but you can persuade the leaders of Congress to accept these changes."

The president went quietly to work. For days, his green phone was rarely at rest. At every meeting, every reception, every dinner, he could be seen in earnest conversation with his old congressional friends. Meantime, Anderson and Irwin and their team were continuing their rounds. Slowly but perceptively, the mood was changing.

Two weeks later, Anderson wrote another memo to the president reporting on his soundings on the Hill. A remarkable reversal had taken place. The list of Democratic senators favorably disposed was lengthy. Only Dick Russell of Georgia was holding out—as he would to the very end. Among Republicans, Anderson had approval from a distinguished list—above all Everett Dirksen, who had been so adamant a year before. Bourke Hickenlooper was reluctant but nodding yes. George Aiken, Leverett Saltonstall, Thomas Kuchel, and others were aboard. The main opponents were John Tower of Texas and Strom Thurmond of South Carolina. Their opposition would persist for a decade, and more. Many representatives were consulted as well and a majority favored the president's position. The fervent holdouts were Daniel Flood, naturally, Leonor K. Sullivan, and Armistead Selden—all three firmly wedded to the status quo. It was a quite amazing change in mood. One man was responsible. He just smiled as he read the head count.*

About that time, word reached President Johnson that Robles, Panama's chief executive, was having trouble. Personal bitterness over changes in the Panamanian negotiating team the year before persisted. The Na-

---

*One knowledgeable observer who commented on Lyndon Johnson's foreign policy called his performance on the Panama issue "a political work of art." See Philip Geyelin, *Lyndon B. Johnson and the World.*

tional Assembly was about to reconvene, and it appeared the treaty talks would become a target for Robles' opposition. When Johnson learned of the trouble, he decided to lend his Panamanian colleague a helping hand. He also wanted to inform the American public, to let them know what was happening and condition them for changes he considered inevitable.

The two presidents exchanged views through diplomatic channels and agreed that a joint declaration would serve useful purposes in both countries. On September 24, 1965, Presidents Johnson and Robles met separately with the press. The American president made his statement in the White House theater. He said he was pleased to be able to announce that day that "areas of agreement have been successfully reached." He praised his own negotiators, Anderson and Irwin, and thanked Ambassadors Arias, de la Rosa, and Alemán, who spoke for Panama.

"They have proved again," he said, "the truth of our deepest conviction—that nations can resolve their differences honorably and reasonably, without violence and conflict."

He revealed that the two countries were "negotiating separately a new and modern treaty to replace the 1903 treaty and its amendments, a base rights and status of forces agreement, and a treaty under which there might be constructed across Panama a new sea-level canal." It was the first public revelation that there would be three treaties, not one.

Johnson also prepared the way for the news that there would be joint operation of the canal. "The purpose," he said, "is to ensure that Panama will share with the United States responsibility in the administration, management, and the operations of the canal as may be provided in the treaty."

He then went to the heart of the matter when he said:

> The areas of agreement reached are the following:
> 1. The 1903 Treaty will be abrogated.
> 2. The new treaty will effectively recognize Panama's sovereignty over the area of the present Canal Zone.
> 3. The new treaty will terminate after a specified number of years, or on or about the date of the opening of the sea-level canal, whichever occurs first . . .

In one stroke, he had met head-on the three main points of irritation among all Panamanians—the evils of the 1903 treaty, which they felt had been imposed on them; recognition of their sovereignty over all their territory; and the hated "perpetuity" clause.

He covered other matters as well—the goal of integrating the canal area into the Panamanian Republic, fair treatment for canal employees of all nationalities, requirements for adequate defense of the existing and any future canal. But the key message was in those first three paragraphs.

In about fifteen minutes, President Johnson had turned history around. The old game was over and new rules were being written. The reaction in the United States was highly favorable. Editorials around the country hailed the vision and fairness of the new approach to a long-standing problem.

In Panama, the reaction was even stronger. Until then, the negotiations had been kept under wraps. At an early negotiating session in New York, Ambassador Anderson had appealed for total confidentiality in the treaty talks. Neither side, he suggested, should make detailed notes or release any public statements. The Panamanians had agreed. As a result, when Robles and Johnson made their statements, it was the first time the Panamanian people learned that the 1903 treaty was to be erased, that their country's sovereignty over all its territory was to be recognized, and that the gringos were not going to be in Panama forever in their favored position. It muted the political opposition and gave Robles welcome breathing space.

The American and Panamanian negotiators went back to work. Earlier, about the time the Interoceanic Canal Study Commission was appointed, Anderson had decided to move the treaty conversations to Washington. He finally realized that the previous arrangement was extremely inconvenient for the Panamanians and for his own people. He had come to understand, too, that the treaty talks involved a wider variety of interests than he had originally conceived. The Pentagon, especially the Department of the Army, had a tremendous stake in the canal and its future. The Joint Chiefs of Staff had strong views on protection of the canal, on its strategic use in wartime, and on the U.S. bases there. The Atomic Energy Commission was involved in studies of a new canal. The State Department was concerned with the foreign policy implications of both of Anderson's enterprises—the new treaties and the sea-level study. Finally, Congress had to be kept informed and key members had to be consulted regularly. So Washington became the venue for the two-sided exercise. The treaty negotiators were given comfortable offices on the fourth floor of the State Department. The sea-level study group had space in the Pentagon. Anderson continued to live in New York but commuted to Washington when he was needed. John Irwin was handling most of the negotiating sessions on the treaties. Col. John Sheffey was leading the sea-level study as staff director.

For the remainder of 1965, throughout 1966, and into 1967, the painstaking work went on. The negotiators met once or twice a week, usually at the Embassy of Panama in Washington, but often at the State Department. They haggled, argued, debated, stood fast, or conceded, looking constantly for compromises that would satisfy both parties. In short, it was the excruciating business of hammering out a treaty between two parties who began with quite different views of what was good for each of them, what was desirable, and what was absolutely necessary.

Treaty making is much like labor negotiations or selling a house. The one necessary ingredient is the desire of the parties to come to some final agreement. If that is present, there is hope for, but no assurance of, a settlement. Without it, negotiation becomes a fruitless exercise. In the case of the 1965–1967 treaty talks between the United States and Panama, there was a desire on both sides to reach an accommodation. But both parties had some stiff-necked opposition within their constituencies.

In Panama, that opposition had a strongly political coloration. At one extreme, the Communists and the passionate ideologues did not really want a solution—except as reflected in their favorite cry, "Yankee, Go Home!" They had fed for many years on the problem and did not want it to go away. There was something glamorous to them in marching down the streets, stopping traffic, gathering in front of embassies, and shouting their imprecations—maybe even tearing down a flag and burning it.

At the other end of the spectrum were the ultraconservatives. They rather liked things just the way they were. They had wealth and fine houses. They were honored guests at the governor's dinner parties. They hobnobbed with the generals and the colonels, toured the canal on the yacht *Las Cruces* when distinguished visitors were in town, and complained to their American friends about the low level of Panamanian culture and politics. As for the canal, it had run beautifully all those years; why rock the boat?

The vast majority of Panamanians were in the middle ground—some rich, some poor, educated and illiterate, many schooled abroad and among the most sophisticated people in the world. They were businessmen and soldiers, doctors and lawyers and workmen. But all shared a burning hope: that their little country would stand on its own feet, be master in its own house. Many were strongly pro-American in their regard for democratic values and economic power and technological expertise. But they were Panamanians first and they wanted their country to achieve at long last its full rights.

At the Washington end of the equation, President Johnson and Ambassador Anderson had different but comparable problems. The biggest one was the Pentagon. There is something about many generals and admirals that ties them irrevocably to the last war. What they see and live through as young fighting men makes an indelible impression. In the mid-1960s, when one talked of the Panama Canal, eyes in the Pentagon lit up with memories of World War II and Korea. They saw the ships passing through, the vessels laden with tanks and equipment, troopships headed for Europe and the Pacific. Others remembered a pleasant two-year tour in "the Zone." My God, they said, we don't want to give all that up! Even the Joint Chiefs of Staff, broader-gauged men with a good sense of politics and the modern world, had their hands full keeping their own troops in line on Panama.

The other major pocket of resistance was on Capitol Hill. The Thurmonds, Towers, and Russells were outspoken in their opposition to any change—except perhaps to give Panama a bit more money "to quiet them down." On the House side, Dan Flood and his cohorts were in violent and vocal opposition to anything that smacked of a better deal for Panama. Using the rhetoric and appealing to the emotions of the 1950s, they saw "Communist conspiracy" in any move to meet Panamanian aspirations. In twenty years, historians will probably see it as a comic aberration. In the mid-1960s it was a political fact that a president and his administration had to deal with.

As the Washington talks dragged on through early 1967, both teams of negotiators had their hands full. They were coping with the immediate problems of treaty making—hammering out agreements on one point after another, giving a little here, demanding a little there. All the time, they had to face, and counter as best they could, the sniping and criticism that hit them from fellow countrymen.

Originally, Lyndon Johnson had hoped the whole Panama affair could be wrapped up "in a few months." That hope went aglimmering. Then he told Anderson he wanted to have it out of the way before the mid-term elections in November 1966. That deadline also passed without results. By early 1967, he was beginning to wonder if any end was in sight. President Robles was suffering much the same anxiety in Panama City. He was looking ahead to national elections the following year. But the maneuvering and the political dealing attendant on that election had already begun. In April 1967 the two leaders had a chance to talk it over and compare notes.

That month, there was a gathering of the presidents of all the members of the OAS in Punta del Este, Uruguay. The agenda for the plenary sessions was weighted heavily on economic problems, including a possible common market for Latin America. But between the full-dress meetings, President Johnson took time to meet individually with each of his fellow chief executives. He and Marco Robles exchanged views on the treaty talks and found a large stretch of common ground. Both wanted to finish the job quickly, and they decided to push their negotiators hard and to get the unfinished business completed in the next month or two if possible. Their decision was quickly conveyed to the teams in Washington, and, like good soldiers, the negotiators responded. By the third week in June their task was completed. The three treaties were finished, ready for the approval of "higher authority."

On June 20, 1967, Foreign Minister Eleta flew to New York. The negotiating teams of both countries went to Manhattan about the same time. The next day, they gathered in Robert Anderson's office to put the finishing touches on their work of more than two years. They had deliberately picked New York for the meeting to avoid attracting attention from the press. Eleta and Anderson initialed a statement that was to be attached to the three treaties. It said that the representatives of Panama and the United

States "will recommend these drafts to their respective governments for their final approval."

As they were putting their initials on the package of treaties, Anderson urged Eleta to join with him in an announcement that they had achieved success and completed their arduous assignment. Eleta and his colleagues explained that would be impossible. They had to go back and report to their president and consult with key figures in their own government. Otherwise, they said, word would spread quickly that the treaty had been negotiated in the United States and, like the infamous 1903 treaty, had been "imposed" on them by Washington. They wanted to explain the treaties and their key provisions before there was any announcement. Anderson reluctantly bowed to their demand.

Eleta and his team took the next plane for Panama with the treaty drafts safely locked in the foreign minister's briefcase. Anderson flew to Washington and went to the White House to report to the president. "Here they are," he told Johnson in the Oval Office, handing over the three documents and the joint agreement he and the Panamanians had just initialed. "But I'm worried, because if the details leak out to the press before you send it up to Congress, we're in trouble." The former majority leader in the Senate knew perfectly well what Anderson meant. No one realized better what a huge difference it makes to senatorial egos if they hear something personally from the president or one of his principal advisers before they read about it in the press. President Johnson immediately began making calls to lay the groundwork on the Hill for an understanding reaction.

Eleta landed at Tocumen airport and went directly to the Presidential Palace to report to President Robles. In the next days there were meetings of the cabinet and sessions with the large body of advisers known as the National Council on Foreign Relations. By June 25, Panama was ready to move and messages went back and forth between the Foreign Ministry and Panama's Embassy in Washington, and between the U.S. Embassy and the State Department. On June 26, the two countries issued a joint statement. Presidents Johnson and Robles announced that their negotiators had reached agreement on the form and content of new treaties relating to the present canal and a possible new sea-level canal in the future.

"When approved by the two Presidents, arrangements will be made for signature," the statement continued. "The treaties will then be presented to each country's legislative body for consideration in accordance with their respective constitutional processes."

In a few days, what the president and Ambassador Anderson had feared might happen did. Johnson had just begun the task of cultivating the congressional garden when texts of the proposed treaties appeared, with great hoopla, in the *Chicago Tribune*—obviously supplied by someone who did not like the treaties and wanted to undercut the president and the effort to reach a new accommodation with tiny Panama. Not many members of Congress read the *Tribune*, but reprints of the treaty texts appeared almost miraculously all over the Capitol. The antitreaty forces were working overtime and their efforts produced the expectable furor.*

The principal treaty, "Concerning the Panama Canal," was an extremely long and detailed document of 41 articles.† Its key provisions were:

1. Abrogation of the 1903 treaty—the long-hoped-for goal of all Panamanians.

2. Joint administration of the canal by the United States and Panama. The chief operating officers would be a director general and a deputy director general, one an American and the other Panamanian. There was to be a Board of Directors of nine members, five Americans and four Panamanians.

3. The Canal Zone, as a political entity, would disappear. There would, however, be a Canal Area encompassing those facilities and land and water areas deemed necessary for the operation of the canal. The canal administration could have its own public utilities, fire and police departments, schools, hospitals, libraries, and countless other nonoperational facilities. Retail stores and recreational facilities would be turned over to Panamanians in five years.

4. One major innovation was a new judicial system. The U.S. District Court would be eliminated. The new court in the Canal Area was to be composed of eight judges—two principal judges and six associate judges. One principal and three associates would be named by the president of Panama, the other four by the U.S. president. The court's jurisdiction was limited to the Canal Area, and to a restricted list of crimes.

5. Another significant change was the provision for payments from canal revenues. Panama was to get seventeen cents a long ton of transiting traffic, increasing one cent a year up to twenty-two cents. The United States would receive eight cents a ton, increasing over two years to ten cents. Any excess revenue, after operating costs had been paid, was to be divided evenly between the two countries. The larger payments to Panama reflected the common understanding that the country where the canal was located had been underpaid for more than fifty years.

6. The new canal treaty was to expire on December 31, 1999. If a sea-level canal were completed earlier, the treaty would end one year after the

---

*Texts of the treaties as they appeared in the *Tribune* were reprinted in the *Congressional Record* of July 17, 21, 27, 1967.

†The treaty text tells us something about the inflation of modern diplomacy. The 1903 treaty contained 26 articles and occupied 9 pages. The 1967 version had 41 articles, filled 72 pages, and that did not include 30 additional pages of annexes and proposed exchanges of notes on particular issues.

new canal started operating. If a new canal were started but not finished, the treaty would end one year after the canal opened, but no later than December 31, 2009. That ended the hated "perpetuity" provision of the 1903 treaty.

There were countless other provisions—affirming the neutrality of the canal, setting forth employment policies, arranging for transfer of unused land or facilities in the future, providing for arbitration, and similar details. But the six provisions listed above were the heart of the treaty. Each was the product of almost interminable argument among the negotiators, and each represented a major break with the past.

The second pact was the "Treaty on the Defense of the Panama Canal and of Its Neutrality." It made defense a joint responsibility of the United States and Panama. A Joint Committee of military men would be responsible for assuring that the treaty provisions were carried out in a mutually agreeable fashion. The treaty gave the United States military bases and training areas without cost. Arrangements for U.S. military personnel were similar to those in Status of Forces Agreements with other countries.

The duration clause provided that the defense treaty would expire five years after the Panama Canal Treaty, that is, at the end of 2004 A.D. unless a sea-level canal were built or abuilding by that time. If the United States dug a new canal, the defense treaty would continue until the treaty covering the new waterway expired. That could have continued the defense arrangement until the year 2067. Many Panamanians thought that was close to "perpetuity."

The third part of the tripartite deal was the treaty "Concerning a Sea Level Canal Connecting the Atlantic and Pacific Oceans." That gave the United States the right to build a new waterway in Panama if the decision was made within twenty years. Once Washington notified Panama it would undertake that massive engineering task, construction had to begin in five years. And after such a canal was created, the treaty would run for sixty years.

At that time, U.S. thinking about a sea-level canal centered on nuclear excavation. That approach—with memories of Hiroshima and Nagasaki still fresh—sent shivers down the spines of many Panamanians. And the dispute nearly destroyed the entire treaty. Panama insisted that it have a veto right over use of nuclear devices in building a canal. The U.S. negotiators, pressured heavily by Pentagon officials, resisted. Anderson himself was sympathetic to the Panamanians' concerns. He finally took the matter to former President Eisenhower in Gettysburg and won his backing. Only when the former NATO commander weighed in on the issue did the resistance of the Pentagon generals collapse.

Arrangements for a possible sea-level canal followed closely those worked out for the Panama Canal itself. There was also provision for additional board members from other countries that might help finance the sea-level project.

Lyndon Johnson was eager to wrap up the deal with Panama. He knew the rancor and bitterness had gone on far too long, and realized that, while tension continued in Panama, possibilities for violence were ever present. But he also knew that the original trouble over the canal had begun sixty-five years before because of a miscalculation in Washington. Theodore Roosevelt thought he had a firm deal with Colombia allowing the United States to build a canal in Panama. When the Colombian National Assembly unexpectedly rejected that treaty, Roosevelt exploded, with the consequences we have seen. Lyndon Johnson wanted no repetition of that experience. So he determined not to act on the new treaties until he was certain they had the approval of the government in Panama. The treaties remained at the Department of State, and Washington waited for Panama to make the first move.

On the isthmus, Robles was having his troubles. Election of the next president was ten months away, but the maneuvering that attended that political exercise started early. In Panama, politics was a way of life for most of the community, especially among the oligarchy and the business community. Personal prestige, if not power, and economic advantage were the golden rings sought by all. In 1967, the machinations were thriving by the time the canal treaties were completed. What Robles and his political cohorts had seen as the triumph of his administration was becoming an albatross around his and his party's necks.

Details of the treaties were well known to all informed Panamanians. The texts had been excerpted in at least one major newspaper, and reprints from the *Chicago Tribune* had circulated widely around town. The treaties went to the National Council on Foreign Relations for discussion and that put them into the mainstream of political controversy in the country.

Arnulfo Arias was running again for the presidency and his family controlled powerful segments of the Panamanian press and several radio stations. The Arias-dominated media launched a strong campaign against the new treaties, claiming they gave Panama too little, the United States too much. The drumbeat of criticism increased in volume and began to scare all the politicians in the Assembly who were running for re-election.

Robles was frozen into immobility. The opposition controlled a majority in the Assembly and the president became convinced that if he presented the treaties they would be rejected. More than that, they would be used as ammunition against him and his party.

Criticism of the treaties and the political use being made of them sealed their fate. Robles concluded they had no chance, so he did not fight for them. He did not even present them to the National Assembly. One observer, who knew the treaty business as well as anyone alive, said: "He did not defend what could have been the major work of his administration. He just let events run and did nothing."

In May 1968, Arnulfo Arias was elected president for the third time, and by a large majority. Government officials scurried around trying to find some hidden votes that might salvage the campaign of their candidate, David Samudio. But the margin was too great to overcome. The Arias election killed any chance of the treaties that year.

In Washington, hope for a new arrangement with Panama died as well. It would have been folly to assume that a Congress facing a national election in six months would have had the courage to act on so controversial a move. Moreover, President Johnson, the only person who could have shepherded the treaties through the Senate obstacle course, had already declared he would not be a candidate for another term.

And so the treaties of 1967, three years in gestation, abandoned by both parents, became orphans of history and were soon forgotten.

CHAPTER 6

Coup and Countercoup

"It is better to keep the wolf out of the fold than to trust to drawing his teeth and claws after he shall have entered."

—Thomas Jefferson, *Writings*

ON May 12, 1968, the people of Panama elected Arnulfo Arias as their president—for the third time. With their votes, they bade farewell to political tranquility, as many probably suspected. Why, then, did they do it? The answer lies in the psyche of the Panamanian body politic, and in the character of the man called El Caudillo by his followers, and El Hombre by the common folk.

Panama is rich in characters. But none in the modern era was more enigmatic, controversial, charismatic than Arnulfo Arias. His life was the stuff of which totally unbelievable novels are written. And anecdotes generated by overactive imaginations were so widely believed they became part of the legend, and therefore part of the political reality.

Arias was born in 1901, the second son of a mestizo farmer in Coclé, one of Panama's least developed provinces. He had four prime assets: a lively intelligence; a strong physique; an ability to attract admirers, male and female; and a successful and generous older brother. That brother, Harmodio, had led the way out of the wilderness of Coclé into the more exciting world of the capital city and beyond. He attended Cambridge and returned to Panama with a law degree. He soon became a successful lawyer, married into an oligarch family, and established a prosperous and powerful newspaper chain.

When Arnulfo was ready for advanced education, Harmodio was able to support him. Arias attended the University of Chicago and received a medical degree from Harvard. Back in Panama, he began his medical practice, spending time each week attending the sick in the *barrios*. As his name spread among the people, Arnulfo turned more and more to politics, which was his true love. He joined a group called Acción Comunal (Common Action), in which his brother was a key figure. U.S. diplomats mistakenly thought the organization was linked to the communist movement. In fact, it was strongly anticommunist. It was also emphatically anti-United States, nationalistic, and xenophobic. By 1930, it had become bitterly opposed to the political domination of the traditional politicians, especially the Liberal Party.

On the second day of 1931, Acción Comunal carried out an armed coup against President Florencio Arosemena. An armed band led by Arnulfo crept into the Presidential Palace—reportedly through windows Arias himself had opened in the course of a lively New Year's Eve party the night before. They killed four guards and took Arosemena prisoner. When hoped-for rescue by U.S. Marines never materialized, the president resigned. Harmodio Arias took over as provisional president until the legal successor, Vice President Ricardo Alfaro, returned from Washington. Arias exacted one promise before turning over the reins of government—that the next elections, in 1932, would be honest. Alfaro, an honorable man, kept that pledge and Harmodio was legally elected president the following year.

Seeing his brother in the presidency strengthened Arnulfo's conviction that leadership of Panama was his own destiny. However, electoral law prohibited his succeeding a blood relative. He set about preparing himself in other ways. Named by his brother ambassador to France and then to Italy, Arnulfo went to Europe. In Rome, he saw a great deal of Mussolini, the *duce* of Italian fascism. He visited Germany and had a meeting with Adolf Hitler in 1937. In both Italy and Germany, Arias saw the vague political theories of his younger days converted into action. Apparently he liked what he saw. He returned to Panama in 1938 seemingly convinced that fascism was the wave of the future.

Arias landed running. He took over the Partido Revolucionario Nacional (National Revolutionary Party), which his brother had organized during his presidency. Arnulfo converted it into a personal political machine and made himself its candidate for president in 1940. His opponent was the distinguished diplomat and former President Ricardo Alfaro. Arias clearly had a majority of the people in his camp, but he never fully trusted the masses. To make sure of his success, he did what Hitler and Mussolini had done—sent goon squads into the streets to harass and intimidate Alfaro's followers. The bullyboy tactics of his opponent so sickened Alfaro that he withdrew from the race and his supporters declared a boycott of the balloting. The result was an overwhelming victory for Arnulfo Arias. At age 39, he had realized his dream: to be president.

In his inaugural address in October 1940, Arias left no doubt about the direction he intended to move. He told a shocked National Assembly:

"The words democracy, liberty, liberalism, are so bandied about nowadays that they have no meaning. . . . The demagogic concept that all men are free and equal is biologically without foundation."

The intended course of the new leader took shape in his words: "The concept of liberty as an inalienable and unlimited right of the individual must give way to the more modern concept of liberty conditioned by the social exigencies of the community."

Similarly, the sanctity of private property had to give way to a "more modern and advanced concept" that gave property "a social function." Even the family, that cornerstone of life and social order in Panama, had to be regulated, Arias insisted, so that education of children could be handled efficiently. The echoes of the Third Reich were loud and clear.

Within a month, President Arias had written a new constitution. It increased the presidential term from four years to six, and gave the government authority to set up state-run monopolies and to expropriate private property. The new national code prohibited the immigration of Negroes, Chinese, and Japanese. Any black citizens who did not speak Spanish—many descendants of those who dug the canal continued to speak English at home—were stripped of their citizenship. Those concepts and more were bundled together into an unwieldy doctrine that Arias labeled Panameñismo, "Panama for the Panamanians."

Jewish, Indian, and Chinese merchants found their customers dwindling and they were harassed by Arias' street gangs. Under the mounting pressure, many sold out—often to friends and followers of the president. Some forty thousand blacks were deprived of their citizenship at one stroke of the Arias pen. There were no concentration camps, but the new leader spoke openly of sterilizing those who had come to Panama from the West Indies. Public schoolteachers, workers at the fish and vegetable markets, even barbers were put into uniforms. The new president even tried to appropriate the newspapers controlled by his own brother—who had not attended his inauguration.

American journalist John Gunther, in Panama gathering material for his best seller *Inside Latin America*, met Arias and described him as "suave, confident, vivid, and ambitious." He also said Panama's ruler was "the only Latin American head of state who has avowed emotional sympathies with totalitarianism."* When he returned to the United States, the writer met with a study group on Latin America at the Council on Foreign Relations in New York. Gunther told the assembled scholars and specialists: "Panama has the closest thing to a totalitarian government—Paraguay ex-

---

* See John Gunther, *Inside Latin America*.

cepted—that is to be found in the Western Hemisphere. It is ruled by a Harvard-trained neurotic."*

War in Europe heightened concerns in Washington about the safety of the Panama Canal. After Hitler's invasion of Poland, the U.S. government arranged with private Panamanians to lease a large tract of land at Río Hato, sixty miles southwest of Panama City, to build a new air base. Next, Washington demanded ten scattered sites in the Republic, ostensibly for aerial tracking stations; it wanted 999-year leases. Panamanians said that was "forever." They also objected to a dozen miniature "canal zones" scattered across their country. The United States, acting more in the image of Theodore Roosevelt than of Franklin D. Roosevelt, occupied some of the sites and began construction. The Panamanians seethed, but did nothing. An eminent scholar who studied the period commented: "Legally the action was questionable; politically it was irresponsible."†

When Arias took power, negotiation of bases became more difficult. By late 1940, the U.S. military wanted one hundred sites instead of the original ten. Panamanians took a dim view of so large a grant of territory and rights to another country, and there was no doubt the U.S. demands were excessive. But in Washington, Roosevelt, Hull, and Stimson had a quite different view. Hitler's panzer divisions had swept through Poland. In 1940, they cut through the Low Countries to the channel ports and occupied most of France. How long could Britain hold out? Only the United States stood between a seemingly invincible Germany and the rich targets of the Western Hemisphere. With that perspective, they had small patience for an apparently pro-Hitler leader in Panama haggling about minor base rights that would protect his own country as well as his neighbors.

Arias saw it as more than haggling. He wanted the best bargain he could get; he also wanted to demonstrate he was an effective leader. His economic demands would have given a huge profit to his treasury. He refused to consider the onerous 999-year term, and he insisted on $25 million in economic assistance. He demanded the paltry fee for the Río Hato base ($2,400 a year) be raised to $30 million. Finally, in support of his program to "purify" the racial structure, Arias asked the United States to return to their West Indian homelands the thousands of blacks who had been brought in to help dig the canal and who had stayed. They were not, in Arias' eyes, "real Panamanians." The reaction in the U.S. capital was predictably one of outrage.

---

* See Records of Meetings, VI, Council on Foreign Relations, New York, for the report of Gunther's meeting on March 13, 1941.
† See Walter LeFeber, *The Panama Canal*. This is an extremely useful volume for anyone interested in U.S.-Panama relations in this century.

In Panama, there was a strong but quite differently focused anti-Arias sentiment. Established families that had dominated Panamanian politics were livid at being out of power. They were furious about threats to confiscate their properties if they refused to contribute to Arias' coffers. Teachers and shopkeepers hated the uniforms they were required to wear. Intellectuals were offended by the president's racial doctrines. The press rebelled against government-imposed controls. Government workers cursed the 10 percent kickbacks they had to donate to the Panameñistas. Arias was weakening the National Guard and maneuvering to control the police force. Every significant group in the society seemed to have major complaints against the new president.

Talk of a possible coup spread around town, but before all the bitterness and frustration could be focused into concrete action, Arias made a fatal mistake. It was the first of many major errors that would alternate with success in the life of the strangely tragic man. Typically, it involved a woman.

On October 7, 1941, President Arias traveled incognito to Cuba. He told friends he was going for medical treatment, but, in fact, his then-favorite mistress was in Havana. It proved to be an expensive rendezvous. Word spread quickly that El Hombre had left the country and had ignored legal requirement of getting the Assembly's permission in advance. One of Arias' own cabinet ministers and a disgruntled senior officer in the National Guard approached the U.S. ambassador. If there were a move against Arias, they asked, how would the United States react? Ambassador Edwin Wilson told his visitors that, under the Good Neighbor policy, the United States was not involving itself in the internal affairs of others. The Panamanians interpreted him as meaning the United States would not interfere, and they acted accordingly.

The minister of government and justice, Ricardo de la Guardia, organized an eager multitude and the streets of downtown Panama City were soon filled with people shouting, "Down with Arnulfo." The first vice-president was found ineligible to succeed; the second in line resigned; the third was out of the country. The leadership mantle went to de la Guardia, who was backed by the oligarchy, the National Guard, and many Panamanians who objected to Arias' despotism. Arnulfo, after his romantic but costly interlude in Havana, went into exile in Argentina.

From his sanctuary in Buenos Aires, Arias kept in close touch with his followers and made sure his political machine remained intact. When he returned to Panama after World War II, he resumed his pursuit of power as though nothing had happened. In 1947, he tried to stage a coup but failed. In 1948, he ran again for president. By all accounts, he won handily, but the oligarchs who hated him were determined to deny him victory. The

Electoral Commission, which they dominated, held an emergency session, declared thousands of Arias votes invalid, and proclaimed an aging Domingo Díaz the winner. When Díaz died ten months later, and political chaos was a real threat, the National Guard made a secret deal with Arias and he was declared the "real" winner of the 1948 election.

Restored to power, Arias quickly proved that the mistakes of the past and even the pain of exile had taught him nothing. He closed down opposition newspapers, deprived unions of their legal rights, and ensured National Guard opposition by setting up his own secret police. In May 1951, he took the final, fatal step by announcing his intention to dissolve the National Assembly, suspend the Supreme Court, and abolish the constitution. Panamanians by the thousands poured into the streets and violent riots erupted. Ten Panamanians were killed by Arias' personal guard in front of the *presidencia*.

That convinced the Guard commander, Col. José Antonio Remón, that Arias had to go. He sent two loyal officers to the Heron Palace to inform the raging president. Both were killed, one allegedly by Arias himself. Arias was arrested and impeached, and spent ten months in jail.

Seventeen years later he would prove that Ben Jonson was right: "Memory, of all the powers of the mind, is the most delicate and frail." Arias tried again.

During the 1950s and 1960s, the political scene in Panama underwent a convulsion. An elite of privilege, wealth, and education that had ruled so long was displaying incredible imperviousness to reform. More than that, they were fighting savagely among themselves to protect narrow personal interests. The real winds of change that began to blow strongly with the election of the military President Remón in 1952 seemed to pass over the oligarchy without ruffling many hairs. The popularity of Arnulfo Arias was attributed by them to his charisma, his oratory, his magnetism. They blithely ignored the social issues he raised and the appeal they had for many Panamanians—issues like corruption in government, economic stagnation, rising unemployment, and other painful matters.

The old-line politicians paid little attention to the fact that modern medicine was saving ever more babies from premature death and was extending the life span of older citizens. The problem was not that the birth rate was high—it always had been—but that the "life rate" was going up. And little or nothing was being done to assure that those added mouths would be fed, the added hands gainfully employed. One key element in sound economic growth, the production of food, was virtually ignored. Huge landholdings were devoted to cattle, bananas, and sugar. But the tiny acreage of the average farmer was barely enough to provide subsistence for a family. Farming methods were primitive. There were few roads in the countryside, no marketing system worth the name. The result: a small but fertile country that should have been exporting food to poorer neighbors was buying food abroad.

On paper, Panama's economic development looked healthy enough. Economic growth was almost 8 percent a year in the 1960s and per capita growth was the highest in Latin America. But statistics often belie reality. In fact, one-third of that income was going to 5 percent of the population. Unemployment in the mid-1960s was high. Half the work force was on the farm and earning $100 a year or less.

When Marco Robles took office in 1964, he recognized the worst problems and tried to do something about them. He had little choice. Panama's credit standing in world money markets had dropped alarmingly. With the dollar as the national currency, there could be no recourse to the printing press for additional funds. Economists from the Agency for International Development (AID) worked closely with their Panamanian counterparts to flesh out a recovery program that came to be known as "Plan Robles." During that period, the United States extended grants and credits of about $65 million to Panama, mainly to promote rural development. Part of the goal was to increase food production. Another part was to slow the growing tide of immigration from farms to cities, which was swelling the ranks of the unemployed.

An essential *quid* for the *quo* of financial assistance was the requirement that Panama enforce an effective tax system. Robles concluded that his government had no other option. He was supported by David Samudio, the minister of finance, who would carry the Liberal Party banner in 1968. To Samudio fell the burden of enforcing tax reform. By all accounts, he did it with fairness and energy, far too much energy for the peace of mind of many wealthy landowners and other beneficiaries of the old system. One group particularly outraged by the new taxes was the handful of Panamanian sugar barons. When the sugar industry was established in the late 1920s and early 1930s, sugar producers were exempt from taxation to encourage investment. But the exemption was carried over from one administration to another, and had come to be taken for granted. When Samudio enforced the revised tax code against the emperors of sugar, he created a political storm. The Chiari family controlled much of Panama's sugar production and the leader of the clan was Roberto Chiari, Robles' predecessor in the presidency. Chiari broke with Robles and Samudio, formed his own Independent Liberal Party, and joined the coalition backing Arnulfo Arias for president. It was Arias who had made Chiari's final months in office a misery, but sugar was thicker than old loyalties.

Like Chiari, many large landowners, wealthy merchants, real estate developers, and the like found the newly imposed taxes onerous. The political benefits to Arias were quickly apparent. Under the leadership of his

Panameñista Party, he gathered a coalition of Chiari's Liberals, the remnants of Colonel Remón's old National Patriotic Coalition (CPN), the Republicans, and others. As election time approached, Samudio was left with the old Liberals, the Agrarian Labor Party, the Progressives, and a few others.

On May 12, 1968, Panamanian voters trudged to the polls. The vote counting lasted interminably, or so it seemed. It was a time, traditionally, when those who controlled the electoral machinery could find enough votes here, and lose enough there, to swing any close election. In this case, the results were not close enough to allow for the usual hanky-panky. On May 30, the board of elections announced that Arias had won with more than 175,000 votes to Samudio's 134,000. The final seal of approval was the announcement by the commander of the National Guard, Gen. Bolívar Vallarino, that he supported the announced results. Everyone in Panama knew Vallarino cordially disliked Arias.

It was a hectic summer in Panama. In the weeks while the nation waited for the results, there were minor riots in most major cities. The National Guard had its hands full trying to keep the peace in Panama City and Colón, in Veraguas and David. Most overt violence ended with the announcement of the election results, but uneasiness and concern filled the air. Many Panamanians suddenly realized what they had done, and were asking themselves and their friends: what will Arnulfo do this time?

The institution where tension was highest was the National Guard. Every officer in that military/police force knew directly, or had heard endlessly, what Arnulfo had tried to do to the Guard in 1941 and again in 1951. They knew of his attempt to send Colonel Remón abroad. They knew he had tried to establish his own secret police. They feared the worst this third time around. At *guardia* headquarters in the El Chorrillo area downtown, at the officers' club at Tocumen, in Santiago and David and the other provincial detachments, worried military men discussed little else than what might happen to them and their superiors come October when Arias was inaugurated.

One night in August, the phone rang in the study where Fernando Eleta was sitting reading. The former foreign minister was relieved to be away from the official duties that had occupied his life for four years. But he shared the concerns of many fellow countrymen about what a new Arias administration would do—to Panama and to him. The phone broke his train of thought and he picked up the receiver. General Vallarino was on the other end. Would Eleta come immediately to National Guard Headquarters? It was urgent. Eleta said he would.

At the military headquarters building, he was ushered into the commander's office. Waiting were Vallarino and three of his senior officers; Lt. Col. Omar Torrijos Herrera, secretary of the General Staff; Maj. Boris

Martínez, commander of the garrison in Chiriquí province; and Maj. Amado Sanjur. All were in combat uniforms and armed. Vallarino did most of the talking. He asked Eleta if he and his friends would help them mount a coup against the incoming president to prevent him from taking power. Vallarino said they had evidence that Arias fully intended to break up the National Guard and to put men loyal to himself in all key positions in the military. Vallarino explained that one reason they were appealing to Eleta was because they knew he and his family would be targets once Arias had power in his hands. One thing Arias had learned during years of political machinations was the importance of the media. Eleta owned one of Panama's two television networks and several radio stations. They would be natural prey.

Eleta admitted later that he was sorely tempted. He was certain that, as president, Arnulfo Arias would try to destroy him economically. He also felt that, with Arias out of the way, there would be a good chance to get approval for the Panama Canal Treaties, on which he and his colleagues had labored so hard for so long. But he also had profound doubts about the wisdom of a military coup. As a man dedicated to the democratic political path, he was concerned about what the ousting of a legally elected chief executive might do to his country's political reputation, and to its future. He asked for time to think it over, and suggested calling Roberto Alemán, the well-known lawyer who had served as his adviser and negotiator of the 1967 treaties. Alemán had just spent several years in Washington, and he knew the U.S. government and many key officials personally. If there were a coup, he argued, someone like Alemán would have to explain it persuasively to Washington.

"Chato" Alemán arrived at the *commandancia* and he and Eleta went off to a nearby office to consult. The prospect, they agreed, was highly enticing. They would likely occupy high office if they went along. They would be able to push through the treaties on which they had both worked tirelessly. They would also be doing a service to their country by ending the political career of Arnulfo Arias, whom both regarded as an undemocratic demagogue. Then they considered the negative side of the coin. It meant upsetting the democratic process in the country they both loved. Eleta and Alemán were sophisticated men and they did not look at Panamanian democracy through rose-colored glasses. Compared with the United States, or Britain, or France, or even neighboring Costa Rica, Panama did not have strong or deeply sunk democratic roots. They knew the political system was fragile, often unjust, and that it had been abused repeatedly. Still, it was a democratic government with all its faults, but many of its virtues. They concluded it was worth trying to save.

They went back to Vallarino's office to tell the pacing general and his nervous lieutenants that they could not agree to the proposed action. They argued that the National Guard was not prepared to take the responsibility of government. A coup would disrupt the continuity of democratic government. Moreover, the two civilians insisted, Arnulfo had shown in the past how erratic he could be. Surely he would make enough mistakes again to provide legal grounds for his removal. Alemán and Eleta found Major Martínez the hardest to convince, the most determined to go ahead with the coup. Arias may make serious mistakes, Martínez said, hammering the table in front of him, but by that time we may not even be here. We may be living underground, or in Miami, who knows? But Vallarino was persuaded and the others joined him reluctantly.

The August plot was over; the plotting was not. The National Guard leadership had many friends and informants inside the Arias camp. Through August and September, they received ever more disturbing reports of what was ahead. All significant positions in the military structure would be occupied by pro-Arias men. That included such key slots as the main provincial detachments, the unit at Tocumen airport, and, above all, the Presidential Guard, which protected the chief of state and the *presidencia*. Some leading officers, especially Torrijos and Martínez, were to be assigned minor posts, then quietly separated from the service.

Plotting inside the Guard ranks was being done by a group known as the "Combo." Its members occupied most of the powerful positions below the very top level of command. Among their number: Torrijos and Martínez; Maj. Federico Boyd, who commanded the Tocumen Garrison; Maj. Humberto Ramos, military commander in Veraguas province; Maj. Ramiro Silvera, deputy chief of the important transport division; Maj. Juan Bernal, then commander of the Presidential Guard; Capt. Juan Maléndez, Martínez' deputy in Chiriquí. Other officers were attached to the "Combo" and their names figured importantly in the record of the coming years: Maj. Florencio Flores, Capt. Rubén Paredes, Maj. Amado Sanjur, Capt. Cecilio Fisher, Capt. Roberto Díaz Herrera, and an obscure 1st Lt. in Chiriquí named Manuel Antonio Noriega.

By late September, the disgruntled officers had completed new plans for a preemptive move against Arias. They intended to seize the president-elect and convince him either to withdraw from politics on any pretext he chose, or to go into exile. General Vallarino persuaded his officer corps to relax and give him a chance to "work things out" with Arias. A meeting was arranged in the home of Juan Galindo, a candidate for president against Arias in 1964. Vallarino told Arias about the explosive mood of his senior officers and many of their subordinates. He urged the soon-to-be chief of state to drop or at least soften his plans to decimate the officer corps of the Guard. The wily Arias said he would take Vallarino's warning to heart. Meantime, he had another matter he wished to raise. The general had been in the military for a long time, he said, and it was nearly time for his retirement. Arias wished to reward his long service by giving him a prestigious but not too demanding post, one where his long experience would serve the country well. Would Vallarino agree to become Panama's military attaché in its most important overseas post, Washington? Using all the arguments they could muster, the president-elect and Galindo urged Vallarino to accept. They noted, among other things, that U.S. military assistance to Panama would be negotiated through his new office. Vallarino was skeptical but finally agreed to the deal. He returned to his home where Martínez, Torrijos, and the others were nervously waiting for him. Vallarino told the members of the "Combo" they could relax, nothing drastic was going to happen. He had Arias' word for it. The coup planners agreed to set aside their immediate plans, but their suspicions of Vallarino increased from that day on.

On October 1, 1968, Arnulfo Arias was inaugurated as president of Panama for the third time. By then he was 67 years old, but he was still magnetic, still full of fire. In his inaugural address, he demanded immediate return of the Panama Canal Zone to Panamanian jurisdiction. American businessmen and diplomats, who had been talking for the past year about "the new Arnulfo," were flabbergasted. How could he do this to us, they asked. The answer was incredibly simple: he was doing what he had always done, confound his friends and enemies alike.

The new president's second act was to move ahead with his long-developed plan for gutting the National Guard. He had made his deal with Vallarino. The commandant would step down as leader of the Guard and become attaché in Washington. The number-two man in the Guard, Col. José María Pinilla, was to be retired. The third-ranking officer, Col. Bolívar Urrutia, would become Guard commandant. Major Bernal, in charge of the Presidential Guard, would be ousted. Lieutenant Colonel Torrijos was to be sent to tiny El Salvador as military attaché; once there, he would be dropped from the Guard's ranks. Major Martínez, the other officer Arias feared most, was to be similarly disposed of in an obscure post.

When word of the planned changes spread through the *commandancia* and onward to the scattered detachments around the country, there was dismay. The news consternated most those directly affected, the members of the "Combo." Martínez was a raging bull. Torrijos was equally furious. But they had plenty of company. The plans for action against Arias advanced apace. Vallarino and Urrutia had been cleverly taken care of by El Hombre. Pinilla was apparently too weak in influence to be seriously regarded. The ox that was being gored was that of the powerful second echelon of the National Guard. There were secret meetings, cryptic phone calls to the countryside, clandestine gatherings in bars and private homes.

Colonel Urrutia, the man slated to take the top post in the Guard, was distraught because of the new developments. His personal future, at least in the short run, was assured. Nonetheless, he came under heavy pressure from his fellow officers to protect the institution that had been his life. In his agonized state of mind, he approached the chief of the Military Group in the U.S. Embassy and revealed his anxiety. It was October 9. Urrutia told the American colonel that President Arias was not living up to his promises to the National Guard. In fact, the Guard was convinced Arias was planning to destroy it to all intents and purposes. He laid out in detail for the American the plan to send Torrijos and Martínez to minor posts, then remove them from the ranks. Other key changes were also spelled out. Urrutia asked to see the U.S. ambassador. The U.S. Military Group commander promised to do what he could; in any case he would report Urrutia's concern in detail. He promptly did so.

Ambassador Charles Adair, an experienced veteran in the intricacies of Latin American politics, told Washington what was happening. Adair recommended that his government make clear its support for constitutional processes; that it tell the Guard it intended to remain neutral in the current fracas, as it had during the election campaign. He would urge the National Guard to consider the good of the country first rather than any advantage for individuals in deciding what to do. Finally, the United States should encourage its Panamanian friends to do all possible to resolve their problems by peaceful means.

The trouble with that kind of normally sound, judicious advice was that it did not comprehend the mood of the forces involved. A Martínez or a Torrijos who was about to have his career destroyed, about to be forced into exile abroad, was not likely to view his problem in philosophical terms. Moreover, the United States was dealing with men who had considerable influence, who saw the institution that had been their life on the verge of being destroyed, and who had, above all, guns to support their convictions.

The ambassador's advice was accepted by Washington. A military coup in Peru less than a week before had made everyone edgy. They did not want another on their hands. The ambassador was told to do all he prudently could to avoid a coup on the isthmus. Washington also suggested that he remind the Panamanian military that a coup could make it vastly more difficult for the United States to maintain the military assistance Panama felt it needed. The official reaction was relayed to a senior Guard officer at a social affair that night. He reported to his colleagues the next morning at a secret session of Guard leaders.

The report that went back to the American Embassy was that the Guard had reluctantly accepted its recommendation. The embassy told Washington: "Present indications are that the latest National Guard crisis has abated." The ambassador and the governor of the Canal Zone, Walter Leber, then departed for Washington for a meeting of the Panama Canal

Company Board of Directors. The Canal Zone government, the Southern Command, the U.S. Embassy, and the Central Intelligence Agency did not know what was happening behind their backs.

Ten years later, General Torrijos explained part of that intelligence failure. A U.S. agent had been assigned to *guardia* headquarters as a military liaison officer. When the crisis between the Guard and the incoming president developed, the officer spent almost full time with Omar Torrijos. "He was with me," Torrijos said, "it seemed like from the time I woke up until I went to sleep." The U.S. officer knew Torrijos as a man who liked to drink, liked to party. And he was quite right. "But he didn't really study my character," Torrijos said later. "Seven days before anything important, I don't drink anything, don't even take an aspirin, so I can concentrate." When the American suggested they have a drink, Torrijos made sure he got only ginger ale, while the U.S. agent had scotch.

After October 1, Torrijos told the American he was being assigned to El Salvador. They went to the airline office together where Torrijos bought tickets for himself and his family. They went to a farewell party where Torrijos' *guardia* colleagues were bidding a fond and tearful farewell to their brother officer, and giving him bon voyage gifts. All the time, Torrijos was in touch with his fellow plotters, carefully making plans for the ouster of the new president. Reports to the U.S. Army and the embassy were that the military men were knuckling under to Arias' program for castrating the Guard.

Meantime, the American community was welcoming the new president and his administration with open arms. Governor Leber gave an extravagant party for Arias on the Canal Company's ship *Cristóbal*. There was music and champagne and dancing, a real "wingding," as one participant described it. Panamanians claimed it cost more than $100,000, but that was probably exaggerated. In any case, it did not lighten the hearts or raise the opinion of the men in the National Guard who feared they were about to be professionally destroyed. Panamanians who hated Arias and liked the United States wondered at the gullibility of their erstwhile friends. Supporters of Arias were equally amazed at the skill with which their leader could apparently bamboozle those he was about to do in. Arias delighted in the festivities, drank his champagne, and smiled his inscrutable smile.

October 11, 1968, was a gray, humid day typical of the rainy season. President Arias was enjoying his newly achieved powers, keeping secretaries busy with dictation, summoning cabinet members for reports. At noon, at the *guardia* detachment in Panamá Viejo (Old Panama), there was a farewell party for General Vallarino, who was stepping down as *guardia* commandant. Every top officer in the National Guard was there. So were the leading officers of the U.S. Southern Command. Also invited were the military attachés of foreign embassies. One of those present was

Maj. Gen. Chester L. Johnson, the commander of U.S. Army forces in the Canal Zone. He recalled that, while the party was for General Vallarino, the other Panamanian officers paid little heed to their departing commander. They spent most of their time talking quietly to one another. Now and then, one would leave the reception room and would be seen at the telephone.

Demetrio B. Lakas, an engineer, was at that moment at the headquarters of the transit police listening to the radio. Lakas, a reserve captain in the Guard and a close friend of Torrijos, heard the announcement that President Arias had just appointed an officer named Duque, who had been born and raised in Argentina, to be commander of the Presidential Guard. It was one more development the Guard officers had feared. Lakas called Torrijos at Panamá Viejo and gave him the news. The two men arranged to meet as soon as the lunch for Vallarino ended.

Lakas jumped in his car and drove at high speed out Vía Domingo Díaz to Tocumen airport. When lunch was over, Torrijos sped to the airport as well. The meeting place was the National Guard detachment near the airport, where Maj. Federico Boyd was in charge. They were joined by Major Martínez, who was returning to his headquarters in Chiriquí province. Torrijos addressed the officers. He told them the time had come for action, but he wanted everything handled with care and with no chance for slip-ups. Martínez, always more fiery than Torrijos, argued for immediate action. Torrijos explained there were chances for grave mistakes if they moved too fast. They had waited a long time for this day, he said. All the careful planning they had done could fall apart if they acted on emotion. The officers sided with Torrijos, who was, after all, the senior officer present. Martínez flew to Chiriquí in a black mood. He was not persuaded Torrijos would have the courage to act when the time came. That time, it had been decided, would be 9 o'clock that night.

Torrijos, Boyd, and Lakas stayed together by agreement. No one at the garrison would make any phone calls. If any of them received an incoming call, even from his wife, he would act as though nothing had happened. At 6:00 P.M., the three men got in their cars and drove into town to Guard headquarters, less than two miles from the *presidencia*. All leaves had been canceled, loyal troop units were on alert. Everyone was holding his breath. How would the United States react? Would they send troops from the Zone to resist the coup? Would Arias be tipped off and have his own guards waiting with machine guns to protect him?

In fact, the new president was blissfully unaware anything was amiss. At the hour the "Combo" leaders were assembling clandestinely at the *comandancia*, checking their weapons and monitoring the communications networks, the carefree president was on his way to a party at the Agewood Inn on the Trans-Isthmian Highway. At a few minutes after 8:00 P.M., one of the president's aides reported they had received an indication of trouble in David, the capital of Chiriquí province. Arias told those around him they should not worry; it was nothing he could not settle with one phone call. He did not bother to make the call. He had other plans, he said. He was going to the movies. Accompanied by a beautiful young lady—as was his custom—he drove to the Iris Theater.

What had come to him as a vague rumor from Chiriquí was much more than that. It was, in fact, the beginning of the end of one of the shorter administrations in Panamanian history. The excitable Major Martínez had returned to his headquarters that afternoon determined not to wait too long. He was fearful Torrijos and the other dissidents in Panama City would get cold feet at the last minute. He decided to advance the timetable. Martínez called in all the officers loyal to him and gave them their orders. Enlisted men were told to stand by with their weapons; they were not told why. At exactly 8:00 P.M., one hour before the predetermined time for the coup, the wheels of the anti-Arias plot began to turn. Local politicians loyal to the president were picked up at their homes and placed under arrest. 1st Lt. Manuel Noriega took a large detachment of soldiers and occupied every radio station in the provincial capital. They seized the local telephone station as well. Within twenty minutes, communications with the national capital were severed, except for the military phone and radio links controlled by the dissidents. Major Martínez and his followers had effective control of the country's largest, most prosperous province. There was no turning back. Martínez had forced Torrijos' hand.

Lakas went to the communications center in *guardia* headquarters to tell the personnel there to keep everything normal. While there, he heard the first report of Martínez' premature action. Lakas reported immediately to Torrijos, Boyd, and the others. The air was blue with strong language. Torrijos and his co-conspirators were afraid the early attack in David would alert Arias and his cohorts, give them time to prepare counter-measures. They were relieved when they got on the radio to the squad that had been tracking Arias and found the president was still in the movie house. To the men in the military headquarters, each minute felt like an hour. After what seemed an eternity, the big clock on the wall arrived at 9:00 P.M., H-hour. The die was cast.

A footnote to that critical moment: The U.S. "liaison" officer assigned to Torrijos had been hovering around through the evening but had been excluded from any of the operational talk. At 9 o'clock, when he saw troops moving out of the headquarters building into the city, he grabbed Torrijos and said: "What's going on?" Omar replied: "A coup d'état, stupid." The American said he had to make a phone call. "Like hell you will," Torrijos replied. He put his American friend in a room, gave him a bottle of whiskey, and put a guard on the door. U.S. authorities got their reports of events from other sources.

When the order "go" came down, troops in jeeps and trucks moved out of the headquarters; others swept into the capital from Tocumen. The *presidencia* was surrounded by soldiers. No sign of resistance came from the Presidential Guard inside, to the great relief of the besiegers. All the main intersections in downtown Panama City—especially those that provided access to the *presidencia*—were sealed off.

At a few minutes after 9:00 P.M., an aide tapped President Arias on the shoulder and whispered that there was trouble downtown. Troops were in the streets. They were having trouble contacting *guardia* headquarters. Arias walked out of the theater to his car. He went first to his mother's home on Balboa Avenue. There he changed clothes and returned to his car to go to his official residence. Every route was closed off. The reports he was getting by radio were ominous and he began to panic. He knew the vast majority of *guardia* officers hated him as bitterly as he hated them. He considered going to one of the radio stations to appeal to the masses to support him, but he found they, too, were in the hands of the National Guard. What could he do? Arias was a strong man on the political stump. He loved to picture himself as a powerful leader, one who never hesitated to speak out against the strong, the militarists, the economic interests, the United States. But in that moment of crisis, he had no stomach for confronting his attackers. He wended his way through the back streets of Panama, found an entrance into the Panama Canal Zone, and threw himself on the mercy of the gringos. The man who had reviled the United States for thirty years begged the Americans to help restore him to power. The American authorities told him to calm down, that they would report what had happened to Washington. Meantime, they would provide him with sanctuary and personal protection, nothing more.

In an hour, the crisis was over. The president had fled to the Canal Zone; no opposition appeared. Units of the National Guard all remained loyal to their commanders. No shots had been fired; no lives lost. It was an end, and a beginning. Members of the "Combo" congratulated each other for their success against Arias. But they were not relaxing. More than one was asking, "What do we do now?" Torrijos and Martínez and their colleagues were looking for good advice. They realized they had carried out the coup in efficient military fashion, but they had not thought too much of the follow-up. They were calling people around town whom they thought they could trust, or who could give good counsel. One they sought out was Fernando Eleta, whom they had approached in the near coup of August.

At about 11 o'clock that night, two lieutenants from the National Guard appeared at his door. They were dressed in fatigues and were carrying sub-machine guns. "You are cordially invited by Colonel Torrijos to join him at the National Guard," one of them said. Eleta tried to decline, claiming his wife was not well. The officers were insistent.

"We are terribly sorry, but we are in a hurry," the senior lieutenant said. "And you are very cordially invited, sir. So, please, let's go."

At the *commandancia*, Eleta was escorted to an office where Torrijos, Martínez (who had flown in from David), and others were waiting. They wasted no time. "Look," they told the diplomat-businessman, "you did not participate in what now we had to do ourselves. Dr. Arias is no longer president. We have taken over the government." Eleta made no comment.

Torrijos then asked where Fernando's brother and business partner Carlos was. Eleta explained that he and his wife were, at that moment, at Tocumen airport about to leave for Mexico. Torrijos made a quick phone call. The plane was stopped as it taxied to the end of the runway, and Carlos Eleta and his wife were escorted back to the airport building. Carlos soon joined Fernando at *guardia* headquarters. There was a lengthy discussion of individuals who might serve a new government well—such men as Nicky Barletta, who became director of economic planning in the new government; Roberto Alemán, who became ambassador to Washington; and others.

The Eleta brothers raised a crucial point with the military men. The president had been ousted; they recognized that. But why break all conti-nuity? Why not try to preserve the established legal order as much as possi-ble? In other words, why not ask Vice President Raul Arango to take over as head of the government? Torrijos and his colleagues agreed to try. Car-los Eleta called Arango's wife and learned the vice-president had followed Arias into the Canal Zone, fearful he would be arrested. He entreated Señora Arango to help convince her husband to return to Panama and take over the presidency. She called her husband but urged him not to accept. Lakas called him on behalf of Torrijos and the Guard. Lakas recalled Arango trying to dissuade him and Torrijos from going ahead with their program. "It would be a shame for young men like you to get shot and killed," Arango said. He seemed convinced the U.S. Army would move against the rebels; at least he wanted to frighten the coup makers with that prospect.

The effort to build a civilian government continued, but no approach seemed to work. Those connected with the government felt certain Arias would return to power, probably with U.S. support, and they would be signing their own death warrants if they cooperated with usurpers. Jimmy Lakas summed it up: "It wasn't a revolution at that point. But nobody wanted to join us. They said we were crazy, that they were going to kill us all. So everybody was afraid. He [Arias] had convinced most of the decent people of Panama not to join us because the Americans were going to walk in and take over. So, then, we had nothing left but to go on our own."

The search for a civilian government went on through the night. But, by dawn, the dissident leaders had given up. They felt they were pariahs, not to the Arnulfistas alone, but to many other civilian politicians. At noon, on October 12, they announced the new government would be led by a two-man junta, Cols. José Pinilla and Bolívar Urrutia. It was a bow to institutional orthodoxy and military precedence. Until the day before, Pinilla and Urrutia had been the second- and third-ranking officers in the Guard hierarchy. But Urrutia had been held under detention briefly until the coup succeeded, and Pinilla was kept totally ignorant of what was going on. Still another figurehead was Col. Aristides Hassan, who became the senior officer in the Guard when his fellow officers were elevated to the junta. His tenure was brief, however, and within a few months—just enough to arrange a graceful retirement—Torrijos became commandant of the *guardia* and Martínez became chief of staff.

The reaction in Washington was predictable. Secretary of State Dean Rusk, normally one of the wisest and most temperate of statesmen, expressed amazement that a democratically elected head of government should be ousted by force. Official relations were suspended for a time. There had, of course, been any number of abrupt changes of government in Latin America over the previous decade. In fact, we had welcomed one such change not too long before in Brazil. In Panama, where the United States had such a special interest and so many available sources of information, the most amazing thing was U.S. surprise.

The new rulers of Panama were feeling their way in a totally unknown environment. They were also trying desperately to send signals to Washington, most of which went unacknowledged. Our suspension of relations made it all the harder. Nonetheless, the new junta made clear that its intention was to stay in power only a short time and to arrange democratic elections as soon as practicable. That signal went unheeded. It should have been picked up, and encouraged quickly. With the U.S. Embassy temporarily out of business, there was no clear channel through which such encouragement could move. In the eyes of the new rulers of Panama, military men all, there was only one available and logical line of communication, the soldier-to-soldier route. Colonel Torrijos contacted an American he respected, General Johnson, and arranged a meeting in the latter's house. It almost turned into a disaster.

While they waited for the Panamanians to arrive, Johnson and a few trusted aides had martinis and discussed the situation. Torrijos was late. When he arrived at the guard post at Fort Amador with his small entourage, the trouble began. Their entry had not been carefully prepared, and the U.S. guards, on alert since the night before, were tired and edgy. They halted the Panamanians with raised guns. That made Torrijos, who had hardly slept for forty-eight hours, suspicious and angry. The standoff was finally eased and Torrijos went to the general's house, but he went in a foul humor. There was no question his mood colored his reaction to, and memory of, what followed. On the other hand, General Johnson had his own mood. He was meeting the man who held real power in a new government, but he had no firm instructions as to what he should do or say. He was on his own in a diplomatic quagmire.

Torrijos recalled Johnson urging him to give up power and reinstate Arnulfo Arias. Johnson recalled encouraging Torrijos to move as quickly as possible to civilian rule and constitutional norms. Torrijos remembered feeling threatened (there were armed Americans in the room). Johnson thought he was being friendly and merely trying to find out the state of play. The American general left the room on several occasions. Torrijos thought he was consulting the Pentagon and perhaps getting orders to use force against the new government. Johnson explained later that he might have gone to the phone to check on other matters in his command; or he may simply have gone to the washroom. Torrijos later convinced himself that Arnulfo Arias was possibly in the next room and that the American officer had been consulting him. Johnson insisted Arias was never in his home, that night or any other. Given the electric tension that was in the air, it was less important what was true than what the two men thought was true—especially a nervous young Panamanian officer who was deeply suspicious of almost everyone and everything.

As the goblin of possible kidnapping swirled in his head, Torrijos became increasingly tense. His impression was that Johnson had orders to intervene and that he wanted the Guard leaders to step down and restore Arias to power. No such decision had been taken. Nonetheless, that was what Torrijos believed. In his excited state, he took advantage of one of Johnson's absences to leave the house. He jumped into his car and sped to the exit gate at Fort Amador, headed north back to Panama City. Torrijos told me he was stopped again at the gate by a couple of men in civilian clothes and carrying machine guns. He grabbed his own Thompson submachine gun and told those facing him: "Come ahead, you sons of bitches." They were convinced he meant business, and he was allowed to leave. He returned to his headquarters in a fury. He got on the phone, contacted U.S. headquarters, and informed them that, if Arnulfo Arias came into Panama with their support, he was going to "burn the Canal Zone." No one recalled ever getting such a call, but the memory was burned so deeply in Torrijos' mind that there was surely more than a grain of truth in it.

The next days were frenetic. Pinilla and Urrutia sat in the seats of power but were powerless. Torrijos and Martínez were working desperately to create a government. They did not do badly under the circumstances. A number of highly capable men joined their ranks. Carlos López-Guevara, an outstanding international lawyer, became minister of foreign affairs. Eduardo Morgan, another successful lawyer, took the post of minister of government and justice. Nicolás Ardito Barletta, a leading economist, led the Directorate of Economic Planning. Henry Ford, a well-known businessman, became minister of finance. Demetrio Lakas headed the Social Security system, one of the most important elements of government. Torrijos, Martínez, and Company were doing well.

Arnulfo Arias sat in the Zone, occupying a house a few hundred yards from the governor's mansion. He was doing everything he could to win allegiance to his cause, but he was having great difficulty. His radio network had been effectively cut off by the National Guard. One clandestine station continued to air his appeals, but it had limited range and few listeners. He was on the phone constantly, trying to persuade anyone who would talk with him that the battle was far from over. He would be returning, and they had better not burn their bridges, he warned. He told Panamanians the U.S. military forces would soon be moving in his support. He told American authorities he had a large cache of arms in the interior if he could only get to it. He also told them he had the promise of arms from Spain. He asked to be transported in an army helicopter to his coffee plantation in the interior. That proposal went to Washington and was rejected. He asked to be transferred to Costa Rica but that, too, was turned down. No one could miss the fact that no Latin American country was offering the deposed president asylum or hospitality. Arias had made few friends in the hemisphere.

The ousted politician became an embarrassment. He was clearly not going to regain power in Panama. The longer he stayed in the Canal Zone, the more it appeared the United States was siding with an erratic and irascible old man and ignoring reality.

Treaty negotiator Robert Anderson had met Arias soon after the latter was elected in May 1968. When it became clear he would not be returning to the Presidential Palace, Anderson talked with him on the phone. He urged Arias not to use the Canal Zone, or a platform in the United States, to try to inject our country into the dispute. Another who spoke with Arias during those hectic days was Sol Linowitz, then U.S. ambassador to the OAS. He, too, urged the Panamanian to leave the Zone.

Arias tried one more ploy. He suggested that a helicopter fly him north and then, "by navigational error," land him in Costa Rica. The proposal went to Secretary Rusk. The secretary ruled that Washington could not intrude in that fashion into Panama's affairs. The plan was scratched. But the proud, egotistical politician refused to listen to reason. He turned down an offer from the Grace Line to carry him to New York in style on one of its luxury liners. He refused an offer of asylum from Spain. He refused to ask Costa Rica for refuge, even after other countries had paved the way for acceptance by San José.

After one final conversation with Ambassador Anderson, Arias went to see Governor Leber. He explained he had decided to leave because he felt that would help prevent bloodshed in Panama. It was typical Arias dramatization; there was no likelihood of bloodshed in his behalf, but it saved face. Leber arranged to transport Arias and three of his principal advisers aboard a U.S. military plane. It left Howard Air Force Base in the Zone at 11:00 A.M. on October 21. It reached Washington the next morning after a stopover in Florida.

In the U.S. capital, Arias went immediately to the Panamanian Embassy and took it over. He insisted he was the rightful leader of the country. He held out in the embassy for more than a week, before moving to a hotel. Arias tried everything he could to win support—appeals to the OAS, frequent press conferences. The Latin American governments and diplomats turned a deaf ear. Reporters tired quickly of harangues and self-righteous lectures. Arias was used to manipulating a controlled press; he found it difficult to deal with reporters who were free to pursue the truth. After a time, he left Washington in frustration and moved to Miami to wait for his next chance. He would stay in the citrus belt for ten years before making his next foray into the political arena. But he never gave up his ambitions and he tried to become involved in the American political scene as an adviser. His favorite clients were conservative politicians like Ronald Reagan who, he hoped, could be used for his purposes.

On November 13, 1968, the U.S. government announced that it was restoring diplomatic relations with Panama. It gave as the main reason "the publicly declared intention of the Panamanian Government to hold elections, to return to constitutional government, to respect human rights, and to observe Panama's international obligations." With diplomatic relations revived, and with Arias out of the way, the new leaders of Panama were able to concentrate on their immediate problems—building a government and pursuing the goals that first impelled them to get into politics. The most compelling reason for that involvement, of course, was survival, raw and unvarnished. If Arias had stayed in power, Torrijos and Martínez would have been forced to leave the ranks. In ousting Arias, they were protecting themselves, their careers, their families. Nevertheless, the two men had political dreams, strong ideas of what would be good for their country. Once in power, they pursued those dreams.

Torrijos had been advised that it was important for the new government to explain its policies and future intentions to as wide an audience as possible, especially in the United States. He took the advice seriously and put a team of specialists to work on the project. The finished product, the new regime's statement of principles, appeared in the *New York Times* annual review of Latin America on January 20, 1969. One part of the two-page declaration was the manifesto the new revolutionary government issued shortly after it assumed power; the second and largest segment was the special report Torrijos had ordered; a third section described the advantages of foreign investment in Panama. One of the regime's basic principles was "total repudiation of Communism and all other extremist ideologies." Panama's economic policy was a ringing endorsement of the free enterprise system. It promised strenuous efforts to improve the lot of Panama's poor and underprivileged, and it asserted that the country's development programs "identify completely with the philosophy of the Alliance for Progress" launched by President Kennedy. It was, in short, an unmistakable appeal for help, cooperation, and friendship from the United States. If it had been seized upon, and if Washington had moved quickly to help meet Panama's more urgent economic needs, U.S. influence would have soared. It also would have had a powerful lever with which to encourage the neophyte government in Panama City to proceed in a democratic direction, and to move quickly toward new elections and establishment of civilian government. Unfortunately, the Torrijos White Paper received little attention from an incoming Nixon administration that had other priorities.

Torrijos and Martínez formed an unlikely partnership. They shared much, which was what had brought them together. Both were career military men. Both came from unpretentious beginnings. Both felt a fearsome loyalty to the National Guard and to their people. The two were overwhelmingly ambitious and proud men. Each saw himself as a kind of savior of the downtrodden, a defender of the true values of his people. There was a messianic streak in the two young officers.

But there were deep differences between them, too. Martínez was a highly organized man, a man of charts and graphs and tables of organization. Those who knew him considered him painfully honest, disciplined, unbending toward those who did not meet his standards. One Panamanian described Martínez as a "monk," detached, unfeeling, strict. But he was also a man who enjoyed dominating others, controlling them, punishing them for their mistakes. One acquaintance said Martínez got pleasure from putting sinners in jail.

Torrijos, in contrast, was not highly organized, hated meetings, despised detail. A cabinet session focused on a complicated economic problem could drive him to distraction. No one who knew Omar Torrijos would ever describe him as disciplined or organized. He loved to drink and carouse. He liked to be with people who had foibles or weaknesses. It made them easier to control, to be sure. But it also made them, in his eyes, more human. He had a deep suspicion of anyone who did not like to drink or enjoy being with women. He used both as criteria for measuring manhood. At the same time, Torrijos was not a man of cruelty. He had an amazing respect for life and for most institutions. He hated manifestations of basic weakness, like terrorism or assassination. At heart, he was a romantic. He wanted to do good and he didn't want to hurt anyone in the process. When painful things had to be done, he turned them over to others and looked away.

Without drifting into psychological interpretations, it seemed obvious that conflict between Martínez and Torrijos was inevitable. They were atop the power structure and both harbored overweening ambitions. It took some time, however, for the feud to mature. In the beginning, Torrijos and Martínez worked together against common foes. There was a noticeable shift in power from the figurehead junta and the appointed civilian government to the leadership of the National Guard. Increasingly, it was the *commandancia* not the *presidencia* that really mattered. During the first week of January, five appointed ministers, in office less than three months, resigned. Soon after, the Guard rounded up a number of civilian politicians who had been openly critical of military rule. Almost immediately, the banks reported a dramatic drop in savings accounts as nervous Panamanians shifted their capital overseas.

That alarmed the military leaders. Torrijos and Martínez arranged meetings with bankers, businessmen, civic leaders. They went on television together. Their repeated assurances finally calmed things down and ended the run on the banks. But though they appeared shoulder-to-shoulder during the minicrisis, the strains between the two colonels were increasing. Astute political observers in Panama were convinced Martínez was planning to get rid of Torrijos and occupy the summit of power alone.

In March, Boris Martínez decided the time had come, and he marched out into a figurative main street ready to draw down on his boss. He went before a national television audience to present a new economic program. Providing the backdrop for his performance were half a dozen uniformed officers of the Guard. Martínez proclaimed a new program of land reform to benefit Panama's poor farmers. He also announced that the military government was going to provide more comprehensive health care for the people.

Torrijos had not been consulted and the TV appearance surprised him. He read the handwriting on the wall. For once, he did not hesitate but moved into action immediately. He gathered loyal officers around—and in the middle and lower ranks he had far more supporters than Martínez could muster. The chief of staff and those who had backed him found themselves in protective custody. In a short time, Boris Martínez and three of his leading supporters were on a plane headed for Washington. Martínez, as a face-saving gesture, had been named Panama's representative on the Inter-American Defense Board, a largely ceremonial body and a traditional dumping ground for military men whose home governments preferred to have them as far from their native lands as possible. The disgruntled Martínez left the plane in Miami and promptly got together with his old nemesis, Arnulfo Arias. Together, they hoped to plan and carry out Torrijos' downfall.

Torrijos thought his country's sagging economy was his biggest problem. In fact it was not sagging. The gross national product had increased sharply in 1969. The problem was that Torrijos wanted to do so much, had promised so much, and national revenues were inadequate to support his ambitious programs. Even a trebling of GNP would not have made possible all the low-cost houses, the improved schools, the better health facilities that Torrijos wanted to provide. And so, as the year wore on, he felt increasing frustration and diminished patience for his subordinates, who were doing the best they could. He did not know it, but his biggest threat was not economic at all, and it was closer to him than he ever imagined.

One-man rule always creates jealousy and discontent. It produces some men who think they can only accomplish their goals through the goodwill and sponsorship of the leader. It produces others who believe their dreams will only come true if they get rid of him. Torrijos was surrounded by both types. He naïvely believed the removal of Colonel Martínez and his supporters had eliminated the second type. He was wrong. His intelligence service was much less thorough than it later became. In any case, when his problems became more troublesome than he could bear—as they did periodically for that emotional, high-strung man—he decided to go to Mexico to get away from all the vexations. It was mid-December 1969.

Jimmy Lakas recalled the events vividly. The head of Social Security had heard rumors that a coup was being prepared. Lakas gave the information to Torrijos, but the general passed it off as gossip. His G-2 had checked and told him it was a lie not worth his attention. When Torrijos gave Lakas that reaction, the general's friend said: "Okay. Then you go and I'll stay." Torrijos wouldn't hear of it. He wanted his old buddy with him. And off they went on the morning of December 15—Torrijos, Lakas, Maj. Rubén Paredes, and a small entourage—determined to have a good time in Mexico.

Lakas went to inspect some low-cost housing developments. The Mexicans were building units for $2,000 each and Lakas wanted to see how they did it so something similar could be done in Panama. Torrijos and a few friends went to the race track to watch the Caribbean Classic.

In Panama, a new coup was unfolding. Three colonels who had helped Torrijos dispose of the troublesome Martínez had decided to take things into their own hands and form a new government. They were Amado Sanjur, Ramiro Silvera, and Luis Nentzen Franco. They gave three reasons for their rebellion. First, they noted that Torrijos had made a statement a few weeks earlier supporting the idea of compulsory unionism. That prompted wide speculation in Panama that Torrijos was paving the way for a Perón-like system with himself as leader of the Panamanian "shirtless ones." Second, Torrijos had recently appointed some Communists or extreme leftists to government posts and the dissident colonels pictured him as "soft on communism." Finally, they charged that the general was accumulating too much power in his own hands and that Panama was headed for dictatorship.

Sanjur, Silvera, and Franco had strong backing from elements in the Panamanian oligarchy who wanted desperately to see Torrijos ousted and an end to military rule. It was also widely believed in Panama, not totally without reason, that the rebellious colonels had been encouraged by some individuals in the American community. I uncovered no evidence there was an American plot to remove Torrijos from power, certainly not at responsible policy levels. But some intelligence agents may have given the power-hungry young colonels the impression that a move against Torrijos would not be unwelcome. My suspicion is that something of the sort almost certainly happened, and later events fed that suspicion. Seen through Panamanian eyes, especially the eyes of an Omar Torrijos, one would assume it was true.

Once the rebel colonels thought they had things under control in Panama, with key communications channels in their hands and the nearby *guardia* units apparently loyal to them, they called Panama's ambassador in Mexico City. They instructed the ambassador to get in touch with Torrijos and give him a number to call. The diplomat called the general's suite, got Lakas, and passed on the message from Panama. Lakas awakened Torrijos, who made the call. Sanjur told Torrijos what had happened and that he should not return to Panama. The connection was broken. Meanwhile, the ambassador had called Fernando Eleta, who had gone to Mexico to race a filly in the Classic, and asked him to go to Torrijos' suite immediately. Eleta woke his wife, Graziela, and told her of the call. "Something has happened in Panama," he said, "and I just don't know when I'll see you." He gave his wife her passport, plane ticket, and money and told her to stay where she was and not to open the door to anyone. Then he left.

When Eleta reached the general's suite, he found total chaos. Torrijos was a man gone mad. He was throwing everything in the room that was movable. He was shouting at the top of his voice. "It's impossible," he yelled, "for Silvera and Sanjur to do this to me." He was trying frantically to get through on the phone to Panama, but the rebels controlled the telephone lines and no calls from overseas were being accepted. Lakas was trying to arrange for a plane to get them back to Panama but with no success. By that time it was early in the morning and almost nothing was open in Mexico City. Torrijos was close to apoplexy.

Eleta thought quickly and put a call through to Washington to the IN-TERCOMSA (International Communications Satellite) central exchange. He was a member of the board. He asked the operator to connect him with David, in Chiriquí province. The commanding officer there was a major loyal to Torrijos, Manuel Noriega. In a minute, Torrijos and Noriega were talking, and planning the general's return. Meantime, the problem of how to get him to Chiriquí remained. The quick-minded Eleta looked in the yellow pages and found an air charter company. The night watchman answered the phone and gave him the name of the chief pilot. Eleta called the flyer out of a sound sleep and explained there was an emergency. The general's mother was dying in Panama, he said, and he had to get back immediately. They had to have a plane. The pilot agreed but explained he could not fly all the way without refueling. That's all right, Eleta answered, stop anywhere you must for fuel. It was arranged.

Eleta walked into the next room and told Torrijos: "Omar, you have a plane." Torrijos was overwhelmed, and suddenly cheerful. He and his friends rushed downstairs and took two taxis to the airport. They climbed aboard the plane—Torrijos, Lakas, Paredes, and a couple of aides. They flew from Mexico to El Salvador. By then it was midday. In San Salvador, they located an American pilot who had flown many crop-dusting missions over the banana plantations of Panama. He knew the territory, and the airport at David, as well as any man alive. It was a lucky coincidence. He agreed to complete the journey. His plane was even smaller than the one that had flown them from Mexico. Lakas, a courageous man in almost any circumstance, hated to fly. The smaller the plane, the more he hated it. He insisted on remaining in San Salvador and making his way to Panama aboard a larger aircraft. Torrijos and Paredes and the pilot took off. It was late in the day.

By the time they reached David, darkness had fallen. The airport in those days had no landing lights, but the resourceful Noriega had lined up jeeps and trucks along the runway. When he heard the twin engines of the plane overhead, he ordered the drivers to turn on their headlights. The illumination marked the landing strip. The American pilot made one pass to get his bearings, then brought the plane in for a perfect landing. Omar Torrijos was back in Panama. He clasped Noriega in an *abrazo* and they moved to the headquarters building. Radio contact was made with Panama City and they passed the word: Torrijos is here and will be returning to the capital soon. Torrijos took a short nap, then set off for Panama City. He took most of the Chiriquí garrison with him, about nine hundred men.

They moved eastward, by jeep and car and truck. They passed through Omar Torrijos' hometown of Santiago, and what started as a military march became a festival. Men, women, and children joined the caravan. Then on through Penonomé where more troops and more civilians added their numbers to the parade. The rebels had warned they would stop any effort to enter the capital city at the Thatcher Ferry Bridge. But when Torrijos and his huge throng reached the span across the canal, no resistance was offered. They entered the city. Troops loyal to Torrijos arrested Silvera, Sanjur, and their cohorts and put them in jail. Omar Torrijos was once again master of Panama.

What happened later gave credence to the rumors that Americans had supported the unsuccessful coup. Sanjur, Silvera, and the others who had organized the coup were held in the Cárcel Modelo, Panama City's jail, a highly secure detention facility. One guard was drugged. The cell was opened. The rebellious colonels escaped and appeared in the Canal Zone. The escape required ingenuity, modern techniques, and the cooperation of people inside and outside the jail. That Panamanians had cooperated was obvious; that some American specialists assisted the escape was equally apparent. Silvera and Sanjur and some of the others ended up in Miami, together with previous exiles.

Pinilla and Urrutia, the two figurehead leaders of the military junta, were deposed. On December 19, 1969, a new president was inaugurated: Demetrio B. Lakas, the rugged engineer who had warned Torrijos of a possible coup, then joined him on the trip to Mexico—against his better judgment. Torrijos had decided he needed someone he could trust without reservation sitting in the *presidencia*. Lakas was his man. A new era was beginning in Panama, and it began with Omar Torrijos feeling a resentment and a suspicion of the United States that he had never felt so deeply before.

CHAPTER 7

Ships That Pass

"Ships that pass in the night, and speak each other in
   passing,
Only a signal shown and a distant voice in the
   darkness . . ."

—Henry W. Longfellow, *Tales of a Wayside Inn*

DIPLOMACY is like a ship under sail. On some days, the sky is clear
and a strong breeze fills the canvas. On others, waves smash over the gun-
wales and a wise skipper runs for the nearest haven. But the worst times are
when sails hang limp with only an occasional flapping sound, the kind an
expiring fish makes on a hot deck. That kind of sea is called the doldrums.
That is where the vessel of U.S.-Panama relations was in early 1970.

If anyone had asked President Richard Nixon what his foreign policy
priorities were at that time, Panama would not have been on the list.
Nixon was concerned with bigger game. He was searching for a way to get
the United States out of Vietnam without seeming to be surrendering or
running away. The idea of a summit meeting with Soviet leaders intrigued
him. At the same time, he was considering ways to counter Soviet power,
including opening a dialogue with the Chinese Communists. The ever-
present threat of a new outbreak of violence in the Middle East also
weighed heavily in his calculations.

That panorama of great power politics left little room for developments
south of the border. In the first place, neither Nixon nor most of those
around him felt any great concern about Latin America. Nixon's only major contact with that part of the world, his 1958 tour as vice-president, had
been a huge embarrassment to him and to President Eisenhower. If, in
1970, President Nixon thought about Latin America at all, his focus was on
the threatened rise to power in Chile of Salvador Allende, and on accumulating evidence that the Soviets were developing a nuclear submarine base
at the Cuban port of Cienfuegos. In his reports to the Congress on U.S.
foreign policy in 1970 and 1971, Panama figured not at all, and in 1972 the
issue of the canal and its future merited only a single sentence.

In the U.S. foreign policy establishment, Latin America was accorded only glancing attention. Henry Kissinger, Nixon's principal foreign policy adviser, had little interest in Latin America or the Caribbean except for Cuba and Chile. Secretary of State William P. Rogers, out-maneuvered by Kissinger in the race for foreign policy dominance, had to focus on Europe and the Middle East in a losing battle to stay even. Career experts who knew Latin America was vital for U.S. interests tried, against overwhelming odds, to draw attention to places like Panama and Brazil and Argentina, and even neighboring Mexico. But it was an uphill, largely losing battle. The high rollers were at another table.

Charles Meyer, a savvy ex-vice-president of Sears Roebuck, was assistant secretary of state for Latin American affairs. He had lived long in Latin America and knew it well. Kissinger's deputy for Latin America, career Foreign Service officer Viron P. Vaky, was one of the most knowledgeable practitioners of diplomacy in a Latin American setting. They and others kept trying to promote some interest in our near neighborhood.

In Panama, the effort to get a new treaty was stalled for quite different reasons. General Torrijos, having barely survived the attempt to unseat him, was convinced the effort had been aided and abetted, if not planned, by Americans. Consequently, he was very wary of Washington and its representatives. Moreover, he was under subtle pressure by the United States to revive the 1967 treaties and approve them. That he did not want to do. First, because he thought they were bad treaties. They envisaged a special Canal Area that he saw as just a smaller and disguised Canal Zone. The 1967 pacts also permitted the continued presence of U.S. military forces in Panama well into the twenty-first century. For the Panamanian general, those two provisions alone were enough to make the treaties unpalatable.

There was a second reason, highly political and deeply emotional, for Torrijos' opposition to the 1967 treaties. The designers and negotiators of the pacts were prominent members of old Panamanian families and leading members of the Union Club. They represented a class and style that Torrijos and his followers had made a principal target of excoriation. Torrijos believed he could never approve treaties that they had produced.

To meet his problem, Torrijos used a technique widely practiced by leaders who wish to stall. He appointed a study group to analyze the treaties and report back to him and his government. To make sure he got the kind of report he wanted, Torrijos loaded the deck. As his analysts, he picked three former officials who harbored feelings of hostility toward the United States and had been privately critical of the 1967 pacts. The outcome by that trio was foreordained.

The report, submitted to Torrijos on August 5, 1970, found the 1967 treaties to be not merely bad but atrocious. Everything was wrong with them. They gave Panama much too little; gave the Americans far too much. They lasted too long. They did not return full Panamanian jurisdiction. In short, it said, they were flawed documents that provided no basis for renewed negotiations. Torrijos and Company accepted the study report and informed the United States of its conclusions—that the 1967 treaties were unacceptable and could not even be the starting point for new talks.

When they saw how things were going in Panama, some experts in Washington became concerned. If the 1967 effort was at a dead end, and if nothing were done to ameliorate legitimate Panamanian grievances, the predictable outcome would be deepening frustration and an eventual renewal of violence, perhaps worse than in 1964. Assistant Secretary Meyer, a thoughtful and compassionate man who wanted U.S.–Latin American relations put on a sounder footing, led the search for a new approach. He had able assistance from one of his principal deputies, Robert Hurwitch, a Foreign Service veteran who shared Meyer's concern as well as his compassion. Their conclusion: somehow the dialogue with Panama must be put back on the track. If not, there would be deep trouble ahead.

Charlie Meyer conveyed that view to the secretary of state. Rogers by that time was a disillusioned and frustrated man. His old friend Richard Nixon had kept him on the sidelines of foreign policy actions and decisions. The Washington power brokers, the press corps, and the foreign embassies realized it was Nixon and Kissinger who were deciding and acting. Rogers and his department were seen as little more than observers and minor participants in the foreign policy game.

Nonetheless, when he heard the warnings about Panama, Rogers decided to try to help. A gathering of the OAS in Washington provided the opportunity. The assemblage of foreign ministers from the hemisphere included Juan Antonio Tack from Panama. A sensitive, moody, often dour man, Tony Tack was no great admirer of the huge power to the north. He found Paris considerably more congenial than Washington. But he was a historian and his sense of history, both of his own country's long struggle and of relations between small and great powers, persuaded him that some kind of new arrangement with the Colossus was imperative for Panama's future.

When Secretary Rogers took him aside at an OAS reception, Tack was disposed to listen attentively. Rogers recalled the tragic events of 1964 when blood had been shed because of massive misunderstanding. He regretted that the 1967 treaties had not been approved. But we cannot, he said, leave it at that. He told Tack the United States was interested in reviving a dialogue between them. Washington wanted to find a formula that would be fair for both countries. Tack told the secretary there was equal goodwill on Panama's part. He would report their conversation immediately to higher authority. Wheels that had been locked began to turn again.

The next step in the diplomatic minuet was one of those accidental events that often affect relations between countries—and later are interpreted as part of a well-thought-out plan. The central figure was Demetrio B. Lakas.

Torrijos had picked his old friend to head the civilian government after the failed coup in December 1969. Many diplomats, writers, and analysts devoted vast time to understanding Torrijos while regarding Lakas as inconsequential. In fact, President Lakas represented essential parts of modern Panama that had to be understood to comprehend the whole. He and like-minded men were the balance wheel that prevented the Torrijos revolution from swinging wildly to the left.

Lakas was the son of Greek immigrants. Jimmy, as he came to be known, was born in the Caribbean port of Colón in 1926. He grew up speaking Greek at home, picked up Spanish on the dusty, crowded streets of the port, and then learned English once he began school. Young Lakas, tough, sports-minded, full of adventure, did not always fit the pattern his father and mother had in mind. But he had an inherent intelligence that saw him through. He went to high school in the Canal Zone, and that gave him an insight into American thinking and reacting that no amount of theory could ever provide.

When he finished high school, Lakas went north for his higher education, first to Texas Wesleyan University and then to Texas Tech. He gathered degrees in engineering, architecture, and business administration. He also came to know the United States as few outsiders ever do. Running a tractor on a windswept piece of land in north Texas and getting to know the folks who lived and worked there influenced Lakas' judgment. He decided that freedom and competition were better for his Panama than any alternative he saw or knew about. But he had his hands full trying to convey what he felt to fellow countrymen who were deeply cynical about "the democratic way." Lakas based himself on the world he knew. Those who differed with him were, for the most part, theoreticians who dreamed about what could be. That conflict was crucial in the 1970s, and after.

The physical side of Jimmy Lakas had an impact on all who met him. He was over six feet tall and weighed about 260 pounds. He looked like a lineman in the National Football League. Actually, in his college days, when he was slim and fast, he played basketball more than football. He had huge shoulders, massive arms, and hands that could crush a beer can into scrap metal. He elicited deference, even physical fear, from many with whom he came in contact. It was apparent that if Lakas lost his temper he could inflict serious damage. Normally, however, he was a genial and friendly man, generous with friends, thoughtful of anyone who went to him with personal troubles. But he kept a Thompson submachine gun at his bedside, together with other assorted armaments. Anyone who doubted he would use them if he had to would have been a fool.

On the final weekend of October 1970, President Lakas was in Lubbock, Texas, the honored guest at homecoming celebrations of his alma mater, Texas Tech. On Saturday afternoon he was slated to crown the homecoming queen. Then, with the university president and other dignitaries, he planned to watch the Red Raiders on the gridiron. A call from the White House interrupted the joviality.

President Nixon was giving a state dinner that evening to celebrate the twenty-fifth anniversary of the United Nations. Many chiefs of government who had attended ceremonies in New York had already returned home. When word reached the Oval Office that Panama's president was in Texas, Nixon insisted he be invited. It would help fill out the list of distinguished guests. By that time, it had been trimmed down to Emperor Haile Selassie of Ethiopia, Archbishop Makarios of Cyprus, Nicaragua's Anastasio Somoza, José Figueras of Costa Rica, and a few others. Lakas felt he had no choice but to accept. With apologies to his friends in Lubbock, he took off for Washington. When Nixon greeted the Panamanian president, he thanked him for making the long trip from Texas and said he would like to meet with him the next day.

The following morning, Lakas walked with Nixon out to the Rose Garden for what had been scheduled as a fifteen-minute session. The big, prematurely gray Panamanian and a cheerful, friendly Nixon began to talk over coffee. Nixon asked Lakas about conditions in Latin America. Together they conducted a *tour d'horizon* of the hemisphere, from Mexico to Argentina.

When the talk turned to Panama, Lakas told Nixon that emotions were heating up among his countrymen. They had tried negotiations in 1965–1967 but they produced treaties Panama could not accept. They preserved, on a reduced scale, the hated "government within a government" that was the Canal Zone. Nixon assured Lakas something could be done about that. He insisted on continued U.S. responsibility for defense of the canal, but he thought other issues—a larger Panamanian voice in canal operations, a better break for Panamanian business in the Canal Area, equality of treatment for American and Panamanian employees—could all be handled fairly. If it were up to you and me, he told Lakas, I'm sure we could work it out in six months. With that, they shook hands and parted. The fifteen-minute session had lasted fifty.

Lakas was elated. Ambassador José Antonio de la Ossa took notes and prepared a memorandum for the Foreign Ministry. Lakas took the first plane back to Panama and rushed to meet his friend Omar Torrijos. He summed up his visit with Nixon by saying: "I have succeeded." He then quoted Nixon's statement that a treaty could be worked out in six months. The Americans want to keep their right to protect the canal, Lakas said, but they seem ready to give up the Zone as a political entity.

Torrijos congratulated his friend. Lakas' trip had disproved one of the rumors then prevalent in the Panama cafés—that the United States would never deal with the Torrijos regime because it was only a "provisional government." Torrijos made sure the outcome of the Lakas visit to the White House became common knowledge in Panama's political circles. Nonetheless, Torrijos remained skeptical of U.S. intentions. He began consulting a wide circle of friends, and some nonfriends, whose judgment he respected. The consensus was that he should certainly explore Washington's attitude. The only way to do it was to begin negotiations.

A Pentagon decision in early 1971 greatly strengthened sentiment toward negotiations in Panama. The Joint Chiefs of Staff, prodded by Gen. William Westmoreland, the army chief, had decided they could protect the canal without the extensive military superstructure of the Southern Command. The defense mission would go to the U.S. Atlantic Command in Norfolk, Virginia. The four-star commander in Panama, his two-star deputies, and their considerable staffs would be moved out. Most of the actual troop strength would remain in place, but the large and highly visible command structure—a longtime irritant to many Panamanians—would disappear from the scene. The Panamanians were delighted, but some key members of the U.S. Congress were outraged. In the end, the disestablishment of SOUTHCOM never took place. Conservative politicians on Capitol Hill, encouraged by old-line admirals, put it in a deep pigeonhole, and kept it there.

Having decided to try new treaty talks, Torrijos told Foreign Minister Tony Tack to prepare a basic paper to guide Panama's efforts. Then he turned his attention to assembling a negotiating team. He decided that the leader would be José Antonio de la Ossa, Panama's ambassador in Washington. He was a banker (National City Bank of New York) and a tough-minded, cynical, worldly Panamanian. He was used to judging quickly the merits and demerits of loan applications and investment proposals. What better qualification for a negotiator, Torrijos thought. De la Ossa also knew Washington well and the complicated, often convoluted, way of politics in that strange capital. Torrijos and de la Ossa were not close friends, but the ambassador was one of the sizable group of sophisticated and experienced men whom the general was able to draw into his government, not because of personal loyalty but because of their patriotism.

The second negotiator was Fernando Manfredo, who had made an outstanding record at the University of Panama, taking an honors degree in economics. He also had studied business at several American universities, was an active and successful entrepreneur, and a leader in the Panamanian Association of Business Executives. Manfredo was one of a new generation of businessmen who believed that Panama not only should advance economically through free enterprise but also that society could only do that by improving the lot of all its people. His feeling that his fellow countrymen deserved a better break in life gave him a strong link to Torrijos.

Manfredo asked what he and the others should try to obtain from the negotiations, but Torrijos declined to give any orders. He said the Panamanian team should go to Washington and listen to what the United States had to propose. It is possible they may offer us more than we are expecting, Torrijos said. If I gave you detailed instructions, we might ask for less than we can get.

Nonetheless, Torrijos remained bearish about what the talks could bring. "I am totally convinced that Panama will never be able to achieve its objectives through negotiations," Manfredo recalled him saying. "In my opinion, one generation—our generation—is going to have to sacrifice itself so that later generations can live in freedom." It was a feeling deep within Torrijos, and I heard him use those same words several times in the years ahead. Nevertheless, he was willing to give the peaceful path every chance.

A few days after meeting with Manfredo, Torrijos called Carlos López-Guevara. "Fello, are you going out tonight?" the general asked. The lawyer said he had nothing planned. "Good. Please wait for me." Torrijos said he would come after he had opened the annual fair at Chorrera.

López-Guevara wondered what Torrijos had in mind. He had served briefly as foreign minister following the 1968 coup, but had resigned three months later, denouncing the National Guard's "disrespect for the authority of the civilian ministers." He remained personally friendly with Torrijos, however. His sister Flor was married to Torrijos' brother Moises, and family connections are a powerful link in Latin American society.

When the general arrived, he said: "Look, Fello, we have been talking with the Americans and we are ready to start negotiating with them. We have prepared a basic document. I want you to be a member of the team."

"I would never refuse a task like this," López-Guevara answered. The third member of the Panamanian team was on board.

Over the years, U.S.-Panamanian treaty talks were a diplomatic roller coaster. Each hopeful sign was followed inevitably by discouragement. Then something else would happen to arouse optimism. The 1971 revival was no exception. Lakas' talk with Nixon created measured hope. That was reinforced by the rumored elimination of SOUTHCOM. So the Panamanians were in excellent spirits when they welcomed Ambassador Anderson to Panama in April 1971. The president and the general greeted him warmly and they had a pleasant lunch at the *presidencia*. After dessert, Torrijos asked Anderson if he was really prepared to negotiate an end of the Panama Canal Zone. Everyone was smiling.

"Well, not really," Anderson replied. "I'm here to see how we vary, alter, change, modify the agreements which were entered into in 1967."

There was, Anderson recalled, absolute silence in the room. The smiles disappeared. Lakas rose from his chair, excused himself, and walked out. He went to his office and stared at the wall. He told me later he could not believe his ears. The president of the United States had told him he was ready to end the special structure of the Canal Zone. Now, the U.S. negotiator was talking as though that conversation in the White House had never occurred. Lakas felt he was being double-crossed. He had also lost face in front of his friend Omar. Lakas went back to the session with a heavy heart in time to say good-bye to the visiting American.

Then he and Torrijos talked it over. "Something is all mixed up," Lakas told his friend. "I told you what Nixon said, exactly as he said it. Maybe the Americans are just playing games with us. The president was straightforward. Now the negotiator is being tough. Maybe it's a tactic." Torrijos agreed that might be true; nothing the Americans did would surprise him. However much of a shock the conversation with Anderson had been, Torrijos and Lakas decided to go ahead with their plans. Perhaps the negotiators could sort it out in Washington.

A few days later, Anderson wrote to Ambassador de la Ossa. He asked the Panamanian envoy to thank his government for the many courtesies shown him and Mrs. Anderson on their visit. Then, mixing courtesy with business, he described the U.S. position for the new negotiations. It was a harder line than Anderson and his colleagues had followed four years earlier. The United States, he wrote, "will require control of canal operations and the right to defend the canal in any circumstances." He did not say for how long. The U.S. right to expand the existing canal or to build a new canal would have to be specified. In return, the United States would make "important adjustments" in jurisdiction in the Canal Zone. But clearly those adjustments would not extend to what the Panamanians were seeking, namely, legal control over all their own territory. Anderson made it chillingly clear that the United States would insist on keeping jurisdiction over any matters that might affect its canal responsibilities. A good lawyer could make that reservation cover almost any action.

The final blow to Panama's aspirations came in the fourth item on Anderson's list. "The new treaty relationship," he wrote, "should be without a fixed termination date but subject to periodic review and change by mutual agreement." For almost seventy years, the Panamanian people and government had been complaining about "perpetuity" in the 1903 treaty.

In the 1967 drafts, Anderson himself had abandoned the idea of a canal treaty that ran forever. Now he was back with terminology the Frenchman Bunau-Varilla would have appreciated.

Finally, the U.S. negotiator said that Washington was prepared to find ways to "create additional revenue and other economic benefits for Panama." It smelled strongly of a payoff. That was the approach some members of Congress thought was *the* solution: just pay the Panamanians more and they will quiet down. It ignored Panamanian hopes and pride, reflecting a kind of "every nation has its price" attitude.

Despite the Anderson letter, Torrijos' growing pessimism, and the accumulating evidence that negotiations would not satisfy Panama's basic goals, the decision was made to proceed. Anti-American elements were certain the treaty talks would be so disillusioning on the isthmus that their work would be made easy. Pro-American forces hoped that in the course of quiet discussions Washington's position would change favorably. On April 21, the Panamanian government announced its new negotiating team—de la Ossa, López-Guevara, and Manfredo. The negotiators began to prepare for the task ahead.

On June 28, the three Panamanians went to the White House to present their credentials as special ambassadors and treaty negotiators. They met with President Nixon in the small room next to the Oval Office. Nixon told the Panamanians the treaty was a highly sensitive problem. He reminded them the executive branch not only had to deal with Panama, but had to negotiate as well with the Pentagon, the bureaucracy, the Senate, and the Congress as a whole. The positions of many agencies and groups had to be taken into account, the president insisted. "It will do no good to get a treaty with the executive," he said, "if it will not receive the blessing of these others."

The Panamanians replied politely that their job was to get a treaty with the executive. They could do nothing about the Congress or the Pentagon; that was an internal affair of the United States. The Panamanian negotiators privately doubted that the possible opposition the president had mentioned was important. Their experience with legislative bodies, in their country and elsewhere, was that if there were powerful executive leadership legislative approval would be taken care of.

The next day, June 29, 1971, the new round of treaty negotiations began. At the Diplomatic Entrance on C Street, the Panamanians were welcomed by a Foreign Service officer and escorted to Ambassador Anderson's office. Anderson and his deputy, businessman John Mundt, greeted them. Then they sat down at the long conference table—Anderson at the head, the Panamanians on one side, and Mundt and Richard Finn, a Foreign Service officer and lawyer, on the other. It was 10:00 A.M.

Anderson began by saying the U.S. position was flexible. But he insisted on two key points—U.S. rights to operate and to defend the canal. On legal jurisdiction, he said the United States wanted to go "as far as we can go." But, he quickly added, it was impossible for the United States to move "from 100 to 0" on the matter. It became clear that what he meant was that Panama would have legal control only over non-Americans and, in some cases, not even over them. Americans would continue to be subject to U.S. law and U.S. courts. The U.S. agency that operated the canal would also continue to handle such things as the water supply, electric power, sanitation, fire fighting, hospitals, housing, and schools. Even management of grocery stores, bowling alleys, and theaters would not pass to Panamanian control for five or ten years. A U.S. police force would continue to operate but, said Anderson, some system of "joint police functions" might be worked out.

"For us," Anderson concluded, "this is a major, giant step."

The Panamanians did not think so. They were stunned.

"I feel greatly disappointed by your words, Ambassador Anderson," said de la Ossa. "What you have said changes almost nothing in the traditional position of the United States. . . . Your proposal does not resolve the causes of conflict that have come to affect our relations and, indeed, your plan does not take into consideration either the spirit or the letter of the mandate contained in the resolution adopted by the OAS [in April 1964]. Actually, your words nullify our aspirations."

De la Ossa was clearly furious. López-Guevara intervened. "I would like to know, Ambassador Anderson, why the United States needs to retain jurisdictional powers in the canal," he said.

Anderson's reply was that canal employees could not be considered "ordinary citizens." They were, he said, employees of the U.S. government and controlled by "special regulations." What he meant was unclear. Except for diplomatic personnel, most U.S. government employees working abroad are subject to the same laws and regulations as American businessmen and other foreigners in the country concerned.

López-Guevara raised another question. Why, he asked, when the United States signed a treaty in 1870 with Colombia for construction of a canal in Panama did it agree it would not have jurisdiction over either territory or people? Why does the United States now, in the twentieth century, not accept what it accepted in 1870? *

---

* He referred to the Sánchez-Arosemena-Hulburn Treaty, which was never ratified. He might also have mentioned that, in the treaty with Colombia in 1846 and the proposed Hay-Herran Treaty of 1903, the United States specifically guaranteed Colombian sovereignty on the isthmus.

Anderson's only answer was that "we have to be realists." He doubted that anything less than he had proposed would be accepted by the U.S. government. He reminded the Panamanians they were dealing not just with the negotiators but, as Nixon had said, with many agencies and elements in the U.S. government.

Fernando Manfredo took his turn. He said he was "greatly disappointed" by what Anderson had said because it had, as its goal, the satisfying of crass internal political requirements. Those domestic needs contradicted the foreign policy of the United States, he argued, which had condemned colonies and colonial systems in the modern world. The Panamanian people were demanding recovery of jurisdictional rights over their own territory and he and his colleagues were seeking a peaceful path to that end. Then Manfredo introduced a somber note that reflected the thinking of General Torrijos.

"I am very worried," the businessman said, "that, if it is not successfully resolved by means of negotiations, then the Panamanian people will do it by other means." He said he and his colleagues could not accept a system of colonial rule in Panama "in order to satisfy the interests of certain politicians in the United States."

The mood was grim and López-Guevara tried to smooth the ruffled feathers. "Panama," he said, "has the greatest desire that the transfer of jurisdiction from the United States to Panama not create any chaos. For that reason, I think that transfer ought to be done in a gradual way."

That helped. Panama was not insisting everything be done on Day One of the treaty. It coincided with Anderson's earlier statement that "things cannot move from 100 to 0 in a day." There was, of course, no agreement on what "gradual" meant. Anderson grabbed at the carrot that had been offered. Suppose, he said, transfer of jurisdiction were handled in five-year stages; some things handed over to Panama in the first five years, other things during the next five, and so on "until the jurisdiction of the United States disappeared entirely in, say, 25 years."

Ambassador de la Ossa focused on the central point of Panama's position. The fundamental thing, he said, was that the treaty must write "finis" to perpetuity; the treaty must have a final date. Anderson suggested the treaty might be "open-ended as long as it is satisfactory to both countries." López-Guevara thought it would be acceptable to Panama if a new treaty lasted until the year 1990 and, after that date, either party could renounce it by giving the other advance notice of one year. Anderson, to the surprise of those around the table, said he thought what the Panamanian lawyer had said was "reasonable." The Panamanians were delighted. Then Anderson added: "We can agree that the unilateral right of renunciation can be stipulated after the period that had been agreed to." The smiles faded. The "period that had been agreed to" could be a very long time.

With that, the negotiators agreed to a recess. By 2:20 P.M. they were back at the conference table. Only Ambassador Anderson was missing. Mundt explained the ambassador had some urgent business to attend to, but would join them later. The Panamanians were surprised, somewhat miffed, but said nothing. The discussion resumed where it had left off.

The visitors asked a pointed question: What does control over crimes like robbery, murder, theft, fraud, and the like have to do with running and protecting a canal? They got no answer. Mundt changed the subject.

They turned to the vexed question of land. The dichotomy was clear: the United States was wondering which small parcels of the Zone it could return to Panama for economic use; Panama was considering how much of its territory the United States really needed to operate and defend the canal. Both were assuming the land was theirs to dispose of, and both were calculating how they could give the other as little as possible.

The question of compensation to Panama came up at the end of the session. Anderson tried to rule out any direct payment to Panama from the U.S. Treasury. No session of Congress could commit the next or succeeding sessions, he pointed out. The Panamanians found that peculiar reasoning. The United States, they argued, had in fact been paying Panama an annual fee since 1913—first the munificent sum of $250,000, raised to $450,000 in 1936, and then to $1.9 million in 1955.

Manfredo tried to put the matter of tolls and payments into perspective. He cited testimony presented to the Armed Services Committee of the Senate in 1950. It claimed that savings to the United States, based on ship transits in World War II alone, had been $1.5 billion. Panama, the site of the canal, felt it deserved a larger share of the massive savings enjoyed by the shippers of the world.

With that, the meeting broke up. There were friendly handshakes and an agreement to meet the next week.

As de la Ossa and his colleagues rode back to the Panamanian Embassy, they discussed the day's session. The United States had taken a harder line than they had expected. The list of things the Americans wanted to hang onto was long and, in some respects, insulting, they thought. But López-Guevara pointed out that Anderson had seemed to agree to a phased transfer of powers. If there were phases, there had to be a final phase, and that meant a termination date, which Panama had to have. It would be their job in future meetings to try to pin him down.

The Americans conducted the same kind of post mortem in Anderson's office. They had found the Panamanians somewhat more testy than expected. They had also been surprised at the detail the Panamanian negotiators had at their command on specific questions. But they thought it had been a useful session. Their biggest problem would be to give the Panamanians a better understanding of political verities in Washington. They had to realize that the struggle on Capitol Hill would be much more difficult than they imagined.

The talks went on through the summer and into the fall, sometimes twice a week, more often once. The U.S. side was trying to retain as many rights as possible and to drag out any final solution as long as it could. Uppermost in the minds of Anderson and Mundt was the difficulty the administration would have in getting *any* treaty through the Senate, let alone one that made sweeping concessions to Panama. The Panamanian negotiators were trying to nail down specifics. When will the treaty end? How much of the Canal Zone land do you really need to run the canal? What does jurisdiction over crimes have to do with running a waterway?

There was a fundamental but carefully concealed reason for the failure of the U.S. negotiators to answer questions that were central to the whole exercise. From the time President Nixon entered the White House in January 1969, he never met or talked with his Panama treaty negotiator, Ambassador Anderson. Nor did Anderson ever meet face-to-face with Henry Kissinger. There was a chasm between the White House and the Panama talks that never was bridged during the Anderson years. It was an incredible way to do business. For the president, the Panama negotiations were a political complication. He knew any fair settlement would have only a small constituency in the American body politic. Any change would encounter opposition in the Pentagon. He had been on Capitol Hill long enough to know the resistance a treaty would meet there. He had given his word to try to solve the problem, but he was not enthusiastic. Kissinger took his lead from his boss, and Anderson's repeated requests for meetings or for decisions went unanswered.

Something else explained the Nixon-Anderson estrangement. In 1956, President Eisenhower had become disillusioned with his vice-president and was casting about for alternatives. Eisenhower had developed great admiration for Bob Anderson when the Texas lawyer served as his secretary of the navy and deputy secretary of defense. The president quietly offered Anderson the Number Two spot on the ticket, and the Texan agreed to make himself available. Republican Party professionals rebelled. They convinced Eisenhower that Anderson would not be a strong vote getter and that it would be a political mistake to drop Nixon. The president finally withdrew his proposal, with apologies, and later made Anderson his secretary of the treasury.

Nixon heard about his near unseating, of course, and he never forgot or forgave Anderson. When Nixon became president, additional salt was poured into the old wound. When a new president takes office, all ambassadors and other high-level, noncareer officials submit their resignations. It gives the new chief executive the opportunity to replace or reappoint them. The custom is not just a matter of courtesy; it is good management.

Any representative of the president, one who makes recommendations to him and is responsible for carrying out his policies, should be selected, or personally approved, by the president himself. When the new administration began in January 1969, Anderson was the only individual at that level of responsibility who did not submit his resignation. How he could have expected, under those circumstances, to be effective on a foreign policy problem under Nixon passes all understanding.

The Panamanians were unaware of that background. As they talked in their rooms at the Watergate Hotel, or conferred at their embassy, they puzzled over Anderson's inability to get quicker responses from the White House. They never imagined that the only communication between the U.S. negotiators and the Oval Office was through memos—many of which were never answered.

The Panamanian team was plagued by similar problems. Time and time again, the Americans tried to get Panamanian answers to specific questions. They begged de la Ossa and the others to put their views into writing to which the U.S. side could react. The Panamanians dodged and ducked. The American team thought the Panamanians were simply disorganized and had a different sense of time and urgency.

In fact, the Panamanians were having the same difficulty as the Americans—no one was answering their mail. Torrijos had set the tone in March when the negotiators asked for marching orders. He preferred they follow a "listening brief," as the lawyers say. All well and good at the outset; but as time passed, the Panamanian diplomats found themselves unable to answer specific questions or to react to American initiatives.

At some point in diplomatic talks, representatives of both sides have to be able to say: yes, we'll accept that; or no, that is impossible. In the 1971–72 sessions in Washington, Panama's envoys never had that kind of mandate. They had to deal in generalities that were safe—a treaty with a fixed date; recognition that Panama was sovereign over all its territory; a better economic return. When more specific questions were raised, they begged Panama City for guidance, and waited in vain for answers.

Some of those involved in treaty affairs in Panama did not want an agreement, any agreement, with the Americans. Continuing strife between the United States and Panama served their purposes admirably. There was also an element of fear—fear for individual reputations and political futures. For every Panamanian, Bunau-Varilla, the Frenchman who worked out the 1903 treaty, was one of the great villains of all time. It was a recurring nightmare for Panamanian politicians that they might unwittingly join the French engineer on the historical blacklist. Their fellow citizens who agreed to treaty revisions in 1936 and 1955 had been criticized for not getting more. The able Panamanians who worked out new treaties in 1967 had been attacked even more strongly.

Against that background, any politician was going to be wary of reaching agreement with the *yanquis*. A man like Foreign Minister Tack, inclined by nature to caution and preoccupied with the judgment history would make of his role, could not become overnight a maker of swift decisions or a taker of risks. Nor was anyone around him likely to encourage the foreign minister in that direction.

Neither team realized what was happening inside the other's councils. Each knew its own problems and tried to conceal the embarrassing reality. They were what Longfellow described: "ships that pass in the night." Now and then, a light showed briefly across the intervening water. A signal was sent and received. But in truth they were vessels bound on different courses.

In the middle of the inconclusive talks in the summer of 1971, the United States short-circuited the negotiations and tried direct diplomacy. The idea was to put pressure on Torrijos in order to break the stalemate. A secret cable went to U.S. Ambassador Robert Sayre instructing him to pass a message to the Panamanian leader. Sayre made the appointment and met Torrijos the afternoon of July 29 in the general's suite at the El Panamá Hotel.

In Torrijos' words, "the ambassador told me categorically that President Nixon was not going to accept a new treaty that had a date of duration." Nixon claimed the U.S. Congress would not approve it. Torrijos glared at the U.S. envoy and told him he was "horrified" by the Nixon message. He said that, "if our people were informed of this position, it could be the detonator that could launch the Panamanian masses into trying to recover by force what we have not been able to achieve by negotiations." Torrijos said the "forever" element in the 1903 pact was "the principal cause of conflict" between the two countries. If he did not stand fast on that issue, the Panamanian people, especially the students, would feel he had betrayed them, and they would be right.

Sayre tried to soften the blow. He said the word "perpetuity" could be eliminated but without setting a specific date. Torrijos tried to be conciliatory as well. What we want is a good treaty, he said. To the extent that it was favorable to Panama, duration could be somewhat later. But he never budged from the position that there had to be a final date. Sayre wisely suggested it might be best to put the whole duration question aside and work on other problems.

After his talk with the ambassador, Torrijos did something unusual for him. He dictated a detailed memo for his foreign minister. He used it to put into concrete what he had been telling his advisers and any Americans who would listen.

"It is good to record, Mr. Minister," Torrijos wrote, "that it is an irrevocable decision of the people and the Government of Panama to put an end to the perpetuity contained in the 'unnegotiated' Treaty of 1903 . . ."

The general also informed the minister that "the Treaty that is being negotiated will be submitted to the direct approval of the Panamanian people by means of a plebiscite." It was evident, he wrote, that any treaty that lasted forever would be rejected decisively. He concluded with a stern directive to his foreign policy chief: "If there is no agreement on this point, it is imperative to put an end to the current negotiations."

It began as a political power play. The United States would draw on its biggest gun (the president) and simply tell Torrijos he could not have what he wanted. And that, one can almost hear the geopoliticians argue, will put an end to that. But it didn't. Torrijos adroitly turned it around. We cannot have another treaty that continues forever, he said flatly. If that is the price of agreement, we will stop talking and look for other means to solve the problem. When that prospect emerged in reports in Washington's in-boxes, the policy architects went back to the drawing board. One has to wonder why such a maladroit effort was ever undertaken. Certainly it violated a fundamental maxim of Nixon-Kissinger orthodoxy: if you are going to make a threat, be sure you have the will to carry it out.

The Panamanian delegates went home early in August. At the first meeting after their return, on August 12, they quoted extensively from the general's memo. "As you see," said Ambassador de la Ossa, "we cannot return to Panama with a treaty that maintains perpetuity." Mundt said he had talked with American military officials, and "they have told me they cannot foresee when the canal will cease to be important to our national security." Then he added the political clincher: "And they are in a position to control the votes necessary to block ratification."

The Panamanians listened to the strategic argument and its political concomitant with stony faces. López-Guevara exploded the "national security" balloon with a one-sentence needle: "The canal has no defense without the friendship of the Panamanian people." That was something U.S. military leaders understood perfectly well in Europe and Japan and other important areas. But they never seemed to comprehend the lesson in Latin America. Only when more perceptive men occupied the top military positions would that blind spot be eliminated. In 1971–72, the military men concerned with Panama gave the impression they had charged up San Juan Hill with Teddy Roosevelt. Obviously they had never read *Measure for Measure*: "O, it is excellent to have a giant's strength; but it is tyrannous to use it like a giant."

Having thrown down the gauntlet to Torrijos, the Nixon foreign policy operators quietly retrieved it. Drafts of a new approach to Panama were prepared in the bureaucratic mill. After the usual winnowing process, an agreed version went to Dr. Kissinger and he won the president's approval. On September 13, the president's adviser signed National Security Decision Memorandum (NSDM) #131. It said the United States was "willing to consider the possibility of a termination formula." The president wanted as long a term as the negotiators could extract, but he was ready to settle for fifty years. If the canal were expanded, or a new canal dug, the United States would need a longer term—as much as another fifty years. At least the new rules gave Ambassador Anderson and his team a fixed term with which to negotiate.

The new NSDM was the first guidance the American negotiators had received from the White House since the talks began in June. Anderson made the most of it. The next day he surprised the Panamanians by appearing at the scheduled gathering in his office. It was only the second time in nine weeks that he had taken part.

"Gentlemen," he said, "let me start this meeting by telling you that one of the principal problems that we have encountered in our discussions is whether we could agree on some formula that would succeed in putting an end to the perpetuity stipulated in the 1903 treaty." The Panamanians leaned forward in their seats. "My delegation," Anderson went on, "is now in a position to discuss the development of such a formula, under certain conditions that we believe you will find acceptable."

It was what the Panamanians had been waiting for all summer. But before any euphoria could set in, Anderson brought the proceedings down to earth. He told the Panamanians any changes in the canal area would be "relatively slow." He emphasized that the United States would require defense rights throughout the treaty period. On the treaty period itself, the American negotiator dampened Panamanian hopes even more: "I would not be sincere and precise," he said, "if I failed to tell you that we are thinking of a very long period of time." He provided no details.

The last in that series of negotiating sessions occurred two days later. Ambassador Mundt handed over a couple of position papers and the Panamanians explained that they were going home for consultations and would return in ten days or so.

On October 1, Manfredo and López-Guevara went to the *presidencia* to report to the top level of their government. The issue that received the most attention was the termination date, how long the treaty would run. Manfredo told Torrijos, Lakas, and the others that it was clear the U.S. treaty makers wanted either "a very long period of time or an open date." The reason, as explained by Ambassador Anderson, was that no one could say how long the canal would continue to be vital for U.S. security.

Torrijos' reaction surprised those present. "The duration of the treaty is not what is important," the general said. "What matters is the content of the treaty itself. That is what is really important. If we have a good treaty, I don't mind if we have a fairly long period of duration. Of course, we would all like to have the treaty end soon." In saying duration was not im-

portant, the leader of the Panamanian revolution was certainly not thinking of fifty years. Nonetheless, his basic outlook—that what the treaty gave
his country was more important than how long it took—remained consistent over the years.

Manfredo and López-Guevara returned to Washington moderately encouraged by Torrijos' attitude. They were less happy with the continuing
lack of specific instructions from the Foreign Ministry on other matters.
The evening of their return, they went to the embassy for a powwow with
Noni de la Ossa. The three men concluded that without firm instructions
from home they were blocked from taking any initiatives. Perhaps it would
be better to concentrate on the work of the subcommittees that had
evolved over the previous months. As the Americans made specific proposals, they could pass them along to Panama City and, one by one, force
their own government to make decisions. So they hoped.

The U.S. negotiating team was thinking along the same line. They had
tried futilely for four months to pin the Panamanians down on issues. Possibly the only way to do it, they thought, would be to get into the nuts and
bolts of individual treaty problems. Early in the October sessions, those
trains of thought converged. It was agreed to begin to draft language
jointly on individual treaty articles.

As the negotiations entered that more intensive and more technical
stage, a new player joined the American team. Mike Kozak was a young
lawyer, not long out of the University of California. He was bright and
hard working, but he retained a magnificent sense of humor, especially
about the bureaucratic world in which he suddenly found himself. He was
also a skilled mechanic. When the frustrations of treaty making frayed everyone's nerves, Mike would go home and rebuild a carburetor or reline
the brakes on his old Bentley.

The day he walked into the department in Foggy Bottom for the first
time, Kozak was put to work in minutes. He had barely found his desk
when a senior official told him: "Get down to this meeting. We're starting
new talks with Panama and we need someone to cover it."

"What's Panama?" the new lawyer asked with a grin.

"Go down and figure it out for yourself," he was told. And he went. It
was the beginning of an affiliation with isthmian affairs that would occupy
most of the fledgling attorney's life for the next seven years. Before the
week was out, he knew more about the Panamanian problem than he
imagined he would ever want to know.

That same week, General Torrijos nearly scuttled the whole shaky process. October 11 was the third anniversary of his revolution. A massive celebration was planned in the Plaza Cinco de Mayo. A huge crowd jammed
into the vast open square, many bused in from rural areas to assure a large
attendance, and most of the farm workers carried machetes in their belts.

Another large segment of the crowd came from Chorrillo and other poor barrios in the city.

When Torrijos appeared in his glistening white dress uniform, a great cheer went up. He played on the crowd's emotions like Segovia on a Spanish guitar, appealing to prejudices and to patriotism. The crowd alternately cheered the general and jeered the targets he raised. The performance served many interests. It reminded his domestic critics that he had the people with him. It was a skillful technique for taking the people's minds off their worsening economy. He diverted attention from pressing internal problems by focusing on the Canal Zone and the frustrations of the past sixty-eight years.

"What people," he asked the crowd, "can bear the humiliation of seeing a foreign flag planted in the very heart of its nation?" Shouts of "Omar! Omar! Omar!" filled the air. Farmers waved their machetes.

He said that, if Panama's aspirations were not soon met, the anger of the people might spill over into an attack on the Zone. In that case, he said, he would have no choice but to lead his people.

"If we have to die," he shouted, "we will die."

A roar went up. Parts of the crowd began moving down the street. Some officials worried that an assault on the Zone might take place there and then. But uniformed members of the National Guard stationed on the fringes of the mob dissuaded them from any such rashness. Musicians began to play traditional Panamanian music, and the people began to dance and laugh. The moment passed.

Torrijos' emotional outburst had surprisingly little impact in Washington. But there was a passionate reaction among residents in the Canal Zone. They flooded congressional offices with letters calling attention to the general's threats, and some of his stronger words found their way into the *Congressional Record*. But for the most part Washington remained cool. Nonetheless, it was a near thing. If a few hundred people had forced their way into the Zone, it could have been 1964 over again.

The U.S. team began to prepare specific parts of a possible treaty package. By October 21, they had produced a seven-part document covering the principal treaty issues: duration, expansion of canal capacity, lands, defense, jurisdiction, rights of the two parties, and compensation to Panama. The Americans gave the drafts to the Panamanians and the two teams began to work over the various segments. There was interminable haggling and nitpicking. It was a lawyer's dream, or nightmare, depending on your vantage point.

Even without clear guidance from the Panamanian capital, the artful negotiators from the isthmus produced proposals on a surprising number of topics. By mid-November, they had passed to their American counterparts a treaty preamble, an article on abrogation of past treaties, an essaylike offering of "fundamental principles and objectives," and papers on at least ten other subjects, from canal administration to police operations. It was additional grist for the negotiating mill.

The process of dealing with individual problems, one at a time and in detail, slowly began to narrow the differences between the two delegations. U.S. arguments, repeated ad nauseum, began to affect the thinking of the Panamanian diplomats. Similarly, Panama's more emotional but deeply felt attitudes gradually impressed the Americans. Each side was absorbing from the other a growing sense of what was and was not possible. At that point, in late November and early December of 1971, the negotiating ships of Panama and the United States were closest together in space and communication. For a few brief weeks, the signals were getting through. All too soon, the fog settled in once more, and the messages grew more faint.

On December 11, Ambassadors Mundt and de la Ossa met to summarize what had been done and what remained to be done. It was clear from their memo that the gaps between the two countries remained wide and deep. It specified finally what the United States meant when Anderson spoke of a "very long time." Washington demanded a treaty that would last for fifty years. If the canal were expanded, the treaty would run for eighty-five years; if a sea-level canal were dug, the treaty period would be ninety years. Panama was still asking for a twenty-year treaty, with a possible thirty-year extension if a new canal were dug. The rest of the memo covered the main treaty issues, on which significant differences remained. On the money issue, the memo said nothing about Panama's position. The American treaty makers, then and later, seemed not to understand that, for the Panamanians, it was like agreeing on a dowry before considering whether the prospective bride and groom really liked each other.

On the thirteenth and fourteenth, the two delegations met for year-end sessions in Mundt's office. They went over the joint memo item by item. From the outset, the Panamanians insisted that nothing, in fact, had been "agreed." All items in the memo had to be referred to higher authority in their government. The Americans said they understood.

A new representative joined the U.S. negotiating team during the December meetings. David Ward, a Chicago lawyer, had been under secretary of the army. Because of the army's responsibility for canal operations, Ward had been following the treaty discussions closely from his Pentagon office. He had also been involved in the return of Okinawa to Japanese control, so he was no stranger to the issues involved.

John Mundt was leaving to become director of Washington State's community college program. Long a determined optimist, Mundt had concluded by then that the Panama treaty talks were not suddenly going to produce results. President Nixon was concentrating on winning reelection, and he and his political tacticians saw no advantage in a Panama settlement for the achievement of that goal. Henry Kissinger was focused on China, the Middle East, and détente. His only interest in Panama at that stage was to assure it did not rock the boat.

After December 14, the Panama treaty talks went into a long recess. Manfredo and López-Guevara were preparing to go home for the Christmas holidays, but before they left, they and de la Ossa wrote a five-page summary of the Washington talks. Unlike most reports of its kind, the December 16 memo was a model of brevity. It told what had happened and described the principal issues. It provided what the negotiators foresaw as the configuration of an eventual treaty, a three-part package. Then, after concise diplomatic reporting, the Panamanian negotiators committed a strategic error. In a final paragraph called "Taking Decisions," they placed the blame for failure to move further and faster on officials in Panama City.

"We consider it necessary to state that our work cannot advance if we do not receive from the top leadership of the National Government precise and adequate instructions in order to solve the disagreements that impede progress to the final stage of the negotiating process," they wrote. "In effect, we have gone as far as we can in the absence of precise instructions to enter into, or refuse to enter into, exchanges that will lead to the text of a treaty."

They were absolutely correct, of course. They had received no specific instructions on key treaty issues for more than six months. They could never propose anything they knew their government would back. Their only weapons were experience and intelligence, which they used at every meeting. But treaties are arranged between governments, not between men. A negotiator who relies solely on his own instinct and perceptions of what is good and bad for his country can find himself at the end of a very long and sagging limb. De la Ossa, Manfredo, and López-Guevara had seen the limb sawed behind the negotiators in 1967. They refused to put themselves in the same position. Hence the memo, which they carried to Panama on December 20.

The next day they went to the *presidencia*. López-Guevara and Manfredo gave a detailed report on the treaty talks—what the United States had proposed, how they had reacted, what the outstanding issues were. They made recommendations on how Panama should respond to the unresolved questions. They also handed over copies of the memo they had brought from Washington. The two negotiators left feeling they had covered the ground thoroughly and that, for the first time since the treaty talks began, the leaders in Panama really knew what was at stake and the main problems that had to be resolved.

Soon, the two men began to get disquieting reports from friends and acquaintances. While they were in the United States trying to get a treaty for Panama, others had been working against that goal on the homefront. There was no coordination, no unity of purpose in the circles around Torrijos.

One of the more influential voices at the time was that of Rómulo Escobar Bethancourt, rector of the University of Panama. Escobar was an extremely clever lawyer. He was also a leftist and a former member of the Communist Party.* During the 1950s and 1960s, he had a successful law practice and served as legal adviser to several government agencies. When Torrijos came to power, Escobar filled several influential posts—member of the Electoral Tribunal and minister of labor. In April 1971, Torrijos picked the intellectual leftist to be rector of the university. Torrijos shrewdly concluded that a man with Escobar's background would be more successful in controlling the passionate revolutionary groups that dominated the university campus than would a more moderate academician.

During that period, Escobar spoke out often on the treaty issue. One of his main themes was that any agreement should put an end to the U.S. military presence in Panama. Stirred by Escobar and politicians of like mind, the students delighted in painting the walls near the university with the slogan ¡Panama Sí; Bases No! At the time, the negotiators, Torrijos, and everyone who had looked seriously at the treaty question knew that to demand an immediate end to the U.S. military presence was to assure there would be no treaty of any kind.

Public voices like Escobar's were creating a climate in Panamanian society that made the negotiators' task incredibly more difficult. That, however, was not the most formidable danger they faced. It came from individuals inside the foreign policy machinery of their own government. The dawning came slowly for them, but when it came, it was with sudden thunder.

The New Year festivities, always a riotous time in Panama, had ended. Manfredo and López-Guevara were summoned to the *presidencia* for a session with the cabinet council on January 6, 1972. President Lakas and Vice President Arturo Sucre were present along with General Torrijos. Members of the cabinet, most of them outside the treaty business entirely, were there, and wondering what was happening. Officers of the National Guard General Staff, the real custodians of power, also attended. Everyone was superficially friendly, but there was an unnatural tension in the room. To-

---

*He was expelled from the Party in 1949, at the age of 22. He had received a scholarship to the University of São Paulo in Brazil. On his way, he stopped in Venezuela where he delivered an emotional, procommunist speech. The Venezuelans deported him back to Panama. It turned out that he had not told the Party leadership about his scholarship; nor had he asked for approval to go to Brazil. He was thrown out of the Party for lack of discipline.

rrijos looked grim, and most of the others took their cue from him. He asked the negotiators to give a rundown on the treaty.

Manfredo began and focused immediately on the kind of phased transition proposed by the Americans. The United States suggests a treaty of fifty years, he said. But during those years, many things would be happening. The American police would gradually be removed. Panama would acquire full jurisdiction. After five years, A and B would happen; after ten, C, D, and E; and so on. Panama would regain some land areas immediately; others would be transferred over time. The negotiators also mentioned the option for the United States to build a sea-level canal. That, the two diplomats explained, was a prime condition imposed by the U.S. side. It was necessary if the Senate was to approve the treaty.

To the surprise of everyone, and to the utter amazement of the two negotiators, Torrijos himself took the floor and delivered a blistering attack on the proposals he had just heard. "You are acting like a bunch of *pipinitos* [fortune-tellers]," he said icily. "You are talking about what will happen in five years, in ten years, in fifteen or twenty-five. You are naïve, very naïve."

Panama had long experience with the United States, the general went on. He said the Americans had made many pledges to Panama and had regularly broken them. They would never comply with the long list of promises the negotiators had outlined. Everyone was shaken, most of all the two temporary diplomats who had clearly walked into a lion's den.

Manfredo and López-Guevara tried to defend themselves. We are telling you what the Americans proposed, not what we agreed to, they said. Foreign Minister Tack joined the assault. You should have walked out when some of these things were first presented, he said. How could you sit by and listen when such outrageous things were being proposed. The innuendo was unavoidable: the Panamanian team in Washington was inept and spineless.

The session finally broke up in disorder. Manfredo and López-Guevara walked out of the old white building on the waterfront in a daze. They were hopelessly downcast and ready to throw in the towel. They were also disgusted at the way their colleagues were playing the bureaucratic game. Above all, they were disappointed in Torrijos. How could a man, who only ten days before had been friendly and cordial, turn so abruptly into an antagonist?

It had to be their memo. They had been blunt in accusing officialdom of providing no guidance, no instructions, no policy. The foreign minister and his advisers had taken it as a personal affront. Their response had been to get to Torrijos and turn him against the whole treaty-making effort and those who were conducting it. It was bureaucratic in-fighting of the most vicious sort, and the wounds inflicted that day had not completely healed ten years later.

However, men with the courage to write the outspoken memo of December 16 were not the type to run for cover after one battle. Manfredo became more furious the more he thought of the disastrous session with the cabinet. He analyzed the treaty scene in his own mind, then sat down on January 11 and wrote to General Torrijos. He was sending his thoughts, he wrote, to "the Panamanian with the greatest responsibility in these moments" for determining Panama's future. He had concluded that the best course for their country was to reach a reasonable accommodation with the United States, one that eliminated the worst features of the treaty of 1903. It would provide for gradual additional changes that would lead to Panama's real freedom. He reminded Torrijos that those who opposed any new treaty were actually defending the treaty of 1903 because that would continue to operate. Of that alternative, Manfredo wrote "each day that passes with the Treaty of 1903 in effect, with the consent of the Panamanians themselves, is an act of treason against the fatherland."

In contrast with the unthinking extremists and self-appointed keepers of the patriotic flame, Manfredo and those like him were looking for solutions not for slogans. He toted up the pluses and minuses of each issue: what Panama would get; what would come later; what was in it for the United States. It was a masterful summation of the state of the negotiations, put in a manner Torrijos surely had not seen before. Manfredo took some cuts at the Foreign Ministry advisers, naturally. He regarded them as negativists who made a vocation of looking for traps and hidden meanings in everything that passed across the negotiating table. But he did not try to defend himself or his colleagues as the best or only answer.

"If it is thought that the present negotiators do not have the capacity or ability to extract the maximum possible," he wrote, "then change us. Although I have not yet talked with my colleagues, I am sure they will support me when I affirm that the three of us are ready to make way for whoever can do it better." *

If there were fireworks in the consultations in Panama, the opposite was true in Washington. Ambassador Anderson had lost most of his enthusiasm for the whole project. Mundt had returned to Seattle. Dave Ward was new to the diplomatic scene and was making the transition from army administration to negotiating. Efforts to get the Defense Department to moderate its position ran into stiff resistance. And in White House circles, there was only a glacial silence when Panama was raised.

---

* Carlos López-Guevara wrote a similar, even longer and more detailed memorandum when he arrived in Washington a few weeks later. It was called "Reflections at a Historic Moment for Panama." Anyone wanting to know what feelings were among thinking Panamanians during that period could do no better than to read the Manfredo letter and the López-Guevara memorandum. Those and other background materials will be on file in my papers in the Lyndon Baines Johnson Library in Austin, Texas.

There were men of goodwill on both sides who truly wanted to "end the causes of conflict between the two parties," as the frequently used phrase had it. But they were not in positions of power. The essential will to succeed was missing and, without that will at high levels in government, diplomatic ventures rarely prosper. The talks went on but they were visibly slowing and beginning to wobble, like a top that has lost its momentum.

In January, when the Panamanians returned to Washington, almost the first word the Americans received was that Díogenes de la Rosa had been assigned as a full member of the negotiating team. De la Rosa had been an adviser in the detailed talks before Christmas, but his addition to the first team made the Americans wonder if further changes were in the cards.

The next hint was not long in coming. In mid-March, Foreign Minister Tack sent Jorge Illueca, one of his principal advisers, to Washington. He was one of the group around Tack who were hypercritical of the negotiators in Washington. He met with de la Ossa, López-Guevara, Manfredo, and de la Rosa and with them attended the next meeting at the State Department on March 21. Illueca dominated the proceedings and the meeting was largely a dialogue between him and David Ward. There was a harshness and a lack of mutual understanding in the meeting that impressed everyone at the table. Illueca objected strongly to the memorandum Mundt and de la Ossa had worked on in December. He insisted nothing in the memo had been agreed upon by his government. The Americans knew that perfectly well; so did the Panamanians. Both sides regarded the paper as a working document to be argued about, refined, and clarified. But the Americans got the clear impression that Panama was backing away from everything that had been discussed. They also wondered if they were looking at the new chief of the Panama negotiating team. Illueca's presence had badly undercut the designated negotiators from Panama.

To make matters worse, Illueca set up a secret meeting at the State Department three days later. He went alone and talked with Ward and several colleagues. They gave him a portfolio of six documents—starting with the letter Ambassador Anderson had written to de la Ossa in April 1971 and ending with a U.S. draft of a possible canal treaty dated November 9, 1971. Illueca shipped the documents to Panama with a covering memo to Minister Tack. He treated the documents as though they were a bonanza he had suddenly discovered. In fact, each had been previously reported in full by the regular negotiating team. It is unclear why Illueca, with no charter as a treaty negotiator, should have sought a private session with U.S. officials without the knowledge of his own ambassador. It is equally unclear why the U.S. negotiating team received him behind the backs of the Panamanians with whom they had been trying to develop links of trust and confidence for almost a year. On the Panamanian side, it was more of the bureaucratic in-fighting that had commenced the previous year. On the

American side, it seems to have been a gross miscalculation of individuals and political forces.

It took the Panamanians no time to discover what had happened. Ambassador de la Ossa, an immensely proud man with a very short fuse, hit the ceiling figuratively, and pounded the desk literally. On April 6, he penned a blistering letter of resignation and took the next plane to Panama. Manfredo and López-Guevara followed soon after. They talked to Torrijos and to President Lakas, and did everything they could to calm de la Ossa down, though they shared his sentiments totally. They simply believed the ambassador was too valuable an asset for Panama to lose. The upshot was that President Lakas refused to accept de la Ossa's resignation and urged him to return to Washington and continue to lead the negotiating team.

The tempest blew over, but it was increasingly apparent to all concerned that bets on a treaty in 1972 should be 1,000 to 1, or more. In mid-July, Ambassador Manfredo, in Panama for consultation, had breakfast with U.S. Ambassador Sayre. The U.S. envoy told him quite bluntly that there was no possibility of a treaty that year. The truth was, said Sayre, no one in Washington was interested in the canal issue.

Within weeks, President Nixon convinced the Panamanian government that Sayre's estimate was correct. The president nominated Frank Bow, a conservative Republican Congressman from Ohio, to succeed Sayre as ambassador. Bow, 70 years old, had been in Congress for twenty years. He decided to retire because of failing health, and after barely winning reelection in 1970. The Ohio Republican had built a reputation as a hardworking, if colorless, legislator. He was known as a staunch supporter of his demagogic colleague Dan Flood on anything to do with Panama. Moreover, Bow had never lived or worked in a foreign country, spoke no Spanish or any foreign language. He knew little of the history or the economic problems of Latin America. Bow was confirmed by the Senate but died of a heart attack before he could go to Panama. Still, his appointment further convinced Torrijos and those around him that the Nixon White House really did not want an agreement with Panama.

The desultory negotiations dragged on. Both sides were talking, but neither side was listening. Increasingly, the representatives of the two countries were speaking for the record, not to achieve results. In October, Ambassador de la Ossa was appointed minister of housing. The same month, Manfredo was renamed minister of commerce and industry. It was said that both would continue as treaty negotiators, but that was in footnotes of very small print. For all intents and purposes, the 1971–72 chapter of the Panama Canal treaty negotiations was over.

Omar Torrijos had by that time decided the only way to get U.S. attention was to move the issue into the international arena. Panama's representative at the United Nations, the skillful and effective Aquilino Boyd, was already at work trying to organize a meeting of the U.N. Security Council in Panama. The canal problem would be part of the council's agenda. Torrijos was also consulting his neighboring chiefs of government—Alfonso López Michelsen of Colombia; Carlos Andrés Pérez, Venezuela's leader; and Daniel Oduber Quiros, who led democratic Costa Rica. Torrijos was enlisting their support for Panama's cause, and they were responding positively. He was also casting about for other backers, and finding some support, in Peru, in Cuba, elsewhere. The next phase was taking shape rapidly.

The last gasp of the 1972 treaty talks came in December. The wobbling top finally fell over. Strangely, the American team seemed blissfully ignorant of what was in store. They took off for Panama on December 1 in a good mood, not wildly optimistic but hopeful. The full team was aboard the Pan American clipper that day: Ambassador Anderson, John Mundt in from Seattle, David Ward, Col. John Sheffey. For the first time, the State Department had a formal observer for the proceedings: S. Morey Bell, a career Foreign Service officer, had been named as Panama country director the previous March. It was the first time a line officer in the State Department's Bureau for Latin American Affairs had been permitted to take part, even from the sidelines, in the treaty business. Until then, the only State Department participants were lawyers.

The afternoon of December 2, the American delegation drove to the Panamanian Foreign Ministry. They walked around the big fountain that dominates the ministry's entrance, went up the curving stairway, and were greeted at the entrance by the chief of protocol. Up one more flight of steps, then to the right, and they entered the Salón Amarillo (the Yellow Hall). A large conference table filled the center of the chamber.

There were cordial greetings, handshakes, and jokes. Then the delegations took their seats, and the serious business began. The warmth of the greeting quickly disappeared. Foreign Minister Tack delivered a stiff official welcome, then turned the floor over to Jorge Illueca. What followed had the Americans aghast. It was a long and highly critical attack on virtually everything the Americans had done in Panama for sixty-nine years. Obviously, Illueca was acting under orders, but there was no question he relished the assignment. When he was finished, Minister Tack took over. He was no less critical. All the righteous indignation that Panamanians had felt for decades spilled out in his words. The Americans were too stunned to respond. They left the ministry, boarded their sedans, and drove to their hotel.

Anderson was livid. "This whole effort is lost," he told his staff. "These people will never see reason. We can't even communicate with them." He was all in favor of going to the airport and catching the next plane home. His staff prevailed on him not to and Anderson reluctantly acquiesced.

The next day, they returned to the Yellow Hall. It was no better than the day before. The Panamanians introduced a position paper. It was harder than anything they had talked about in the past eighteen months. It moved away from everything the Americans thought had been tentatively agreed in the negotiations. Moreover, it was delivered in biting language by the foreign minister. Tack concluded with an ultimatum: if the United States could not accept what he had proposed in its entirety, he said, there was little point in continuing this phase of the negotiations.

Anderson had talked little during the two days. He asked a few questions, interposed a few modest objections. Now he spoke up for the first time. The Panamanian position he had just heard was not a negotiable position from the United States' viewpoint, he said. The Panamanians had described their position as nonnegotiable. Under the circumstances, he said, he was in full agreement. "There is no point in continuing," he concluded.

Almost as though on cue, a tray of champagne appeared carried aloft by a waiter. Everyone had a sip. There was not even a farewell toast, an unusual omission at such affairs. The Americans returned to their hotel. The next day, they flew to Washington with the taste of ashes.

Nine days later, Jorge Illueca addressed a gathering at the University of Panama. He spoke for some five hours and laid out in detail all the positions the United States had advanced at the negotiating table. He provided no background as to why those positions were taken or what the Americans' reasoning was. He merely stated each U.S. stand, then tore it to shreds with all the emotion of sixty-nine years of frustration and bitterness. It was a flagrant violation of fundamental diplomatic courtesy and a breach of good faith. It assured that a long time would pass before American and Panamanian diplomats could sit down together and try to reason out their differences.

But at that point, Omar Torrijos and the Panamanian government were looking elsewhere. They had decided that Washington would never pay close attention to Panama and its demands unless world public opinion helped force that result. That opinion was their next target.

CHAPTER 8

On the World Stage

"The good opinion of mankind, like the lever of Archimedes, with the given fulcrum, moves the world."

—Thomas Jefferson, *Writings*

Sᴇᴠᴇʀᴀʟ years later, sitting in Omar Torrijos' bedroom, I asked him about the 1971–72 treaty talks. It struck me that there had been few political leaders I knew of who held court or managed affairs from their beds. Churchill was one; Henry VIII was another; Lyndon Johnson also, but only occasionally. For most politicians, the bedroom was a place for sleep not for politics. But the Panamanian general loved his huge bedroom in the house on Fiftieth Street, and he used it as a lounge and salon as well as for its other purposes. He loved to take off his shoes, lean back against the pillows, puff on a long Cuban cigar, and laugh and joke with his friends. The inevitable scotch-and-soda was in easy reach on the bedside table. So was the remote control switch that enabled him to turn on the TV and watch the latest news. Lolling on the king-size bed, he was relaxed—but only with those he knew and trusted. Strangers were never asked to the general's sanctum.

I was curious about the 1971–72 phase of the treaty story because I had seen it from afar. What did the general remember?

"We were both fooling ourselves," he said, "the Americans and the Panamanians. We were lying to ourselves. We both were just buying time." He drew on the Havana stogy and blew smoke into the air.

"I gather the American position was pretty hard at first," I said. "No final date, and military bases forever."

"Yes," he said, "but that was good for me because I was winning time. We were preparing our response in case there wasn't any response [from the U.S. side]."

I wondered if, when he spoke of "response," the general was thinking of the kind of violent action that had been in the air on the third anniversary of his coup, at the big celebration in the Plaza Cinco de Mayo. He said he had something else in mind.

"I was winning time to make the problem international," he told me. He was persuaded that as long as the matter involved only the United States and Panama "the Americans would not give it importance." The general said he based his strategy on "a very simple principle." That was: "to resolve a problem, the first thing you have to do is *make* it a problem." He was persuaded the only way to do that was to move the issue to the center of the world stage. Quiet diplomatic talks in Washington or Panama would never put the spotlight on the Canal Zone issue, never attract the kind of attention the general and every other Panamanian thought it deserved.

The general's strategy began to take shape in late 1971. The chief of staff for the effort was Foreign Minister Tack. The "general" in command of the field forces was Panama's U.N. representative, the adept Aquilino Boyd. Except for them, a few top leaders in the National Guard, and a handful of the general's cronies, the strategy was closely held. But its existence helped explain the explosive meeting at the *presidencia* in early January 1972.* By that time, Torrijos was convinced the two negotiating teams were talking past each other. The Americans were hanging tough and doing nothing to solve the real causes of trouble. Torrijos decided that perhaps the world community could accomplish what Panama had never succeeded in doing (except for the rioting of 1964). That was to attract and hold Washington's attention.

The opening round in the campaign had an unlikely setting: the ancient city of Addis Ababa. The worldly U.N. diplomats had somehow been enticed into holding a meeting of the Security Council in the Ethiopian capital in January 1972. It was the first session of the council away from its New York headquarters since a gathering in Paris twenty years earlier. There was, to be sure, heated resistance from many to meeting in a dusty and remote capital in Africa. But heavy lobbying by the African nations, with strong assists from friendly allies in the developing world, finally persuaded the council members to take the plunge. Such a gathering, many came to believe, would at least demonstrate the world body's interest in Africa as well as in the problems and people of the southern half of the globe.

Unfortunately, the agenda did not address issues like poverty and hunger that begged for solution or amelioration. Rather it was a political agenda focused on colonialism and racial discrimination. It provided a field day for the Soviet Union, Communist China, and others to lash out

---

*See pp. 168–169.

against the regimes in South Africa, Rhodesia, and the Portuguese colonies. The United States and Britain came in for their share of calumny because of their alleged support of those regimes.

The setting and the subject were made-to-order for Panama's Ambassador Boyd. When his turn to speak arrived, he delivered a long exposition of the parallel between colonialism in Africa and the American "occupation" of the Panama Canal Zone. He ranged over seventy years of history, pointing out the importation of black workers from the Caribbean to dig the canal and their inferior status. He emphasized the notorious "gold" and "silver" payrolls long used to cover black and white differentiation by the Canal Company. Finally, aiming to attract the particular attention of the Security Council, the Panamanian delegate said: "The danger of a violent confrontation between Panamanians and North Americans grows every day."

Boyd's emotional speech took the U.S. representative by surprise. George Bush, a businessman and former congressman from Texas, had not expected that kind of onslaught on that subject. Nor had his staff anticipated a Panamanian broadside in Addis Ababa. Bush did the best he could with a bad situation. He pointed out, rather icily and quite correctly, that the Panama Canal Zone was not on the council's agenda. His colleague from Panama was clearly out of order, he said. In any case, he added: "The subject is not analogous to colonialism in Africa, which is based on racism and deliberate policies of denying the rights of self-determination and repressing basic human rights. There is no valid comparison."

Boyd had the last word. When Bush concluded, the Panamanian jumped to his feet in rebuttal. His final remark—which won a certain celebrity for him over the years—was: "To condemn colonialism, any rostrum at any time is appropriate." There was applause in the conference hall in Addis Ababa. The Panamanian offensive on the world scene had begun.

Back in the more congenial clime of U.N. headquarters on the East River, Boyd went quietly to work. At luncheons, over drinks in the late afternoon, at dinner parties with his colleagues in New York, the Panamanian diplomat pushed his cause. He pictured the Addis Ababa session as a great success. It highlighted as nothing else could, he would say, the council's interest in Africa and its attention to the problems of that continent. Now, he would insinuate, we need to do the same for Latin America. He was shrewd enough not to focus on his own country and its problems. It was the vast, important, largely ignored area of Latin America that now needed the kind of attention Africa had received.

First, he built a solid base of support among his Latin American colleagues. None would dispute Boyd's basic thesis: our part of the world needs more attention. From that hemispheric base, Boyd expanded his campaign to other parts of the developing world. He reminded the Africans how enthusiastically he had supported their demand for a Security Council meeting in Addis. He assiduously cultivated fellow members from South Asia and the Middle East. He was tireless, determined, and effective.

In Panama, Torrijos was also quietly working to buttress the strategy. He flew secretly to Bogotá, to Caracas, to San José. He met with Colombia's López Michelsen and discussed Panama's plight. He did the same in Venezuela with Andrés Pérez. He conferred frequently with Costa Rica's Daniel Oduber. "We could not go and ask for solidarity of the world," Torrijos told me, "if we didn't have the solidarity of our neighbors." He set out to win that unity, and succeeded admirably.

I first became involved in the matter just as the Panamanian campaign to internationalize the issue was taking shape. On March 22, 1971, the Lyndon Baines Johnson Library was opened formally, and President Nixon—and a large segment of the U.S. government—had flown to Austin to mark the occasion and to honor the ex-president. Johnson asked the president to let me accompany the official party back to the capital so I could take care of some business on his behalf. One of those tasks was to check details in the Johnson memoirs with officials from his administration and others who lived in the Washington area.

One of the names on my list was Henry Kissinger. Nixon's foreign policy adviser was one of several unofficial envoys who had tried in the 1960s to open a channel for peace talks with the North Vietnamese. I wanted to be sure the account of Kissinger's activities in Paris was accurate.* When I saw him sitting opposite me on *Air Force One*, I pulled from my briefcase the chapter on Vietnam events in 1967 and handed it to him. Kissinger read it rapidly and returned it. The account, he said, was quite accurate as far as his own involvement was concerned. He said he found the rest of the chapter fascinating because it contained things he had not previously known.

We had a good visit, exchanging views on Vietnam, Lyndon Johnson, and presidential libraries. As I was about to return to my seat, Kissinger asked me about my plans for the future. Would I be interested in returning to Washington to work again on foreign policy? I told him I could not leave until President Johnson's book was completed. Once that happened, I would be happy to get back to foreign affairs. I would, of course, have to talk it over with President Johnson. We left it at that.

I had almost forgotten the exchange when I received a call from the White House early in 1972 asking me to come to Washington to meet with Kissinger. When I walked into his office in the West Wing, the president's assistant recalled our earlier talk and asked if I was still interested. When I

*The incident is recounted in Lyndon Baines Johnson, *The Vantage Point*, pp. 266–268.

said I was, he told me he would like me to take over the Latin American account on his staff. I had studied Spanish and Latin American history in college, but that had been a long time ago. I told him I knew a great deal more about the Far East and Eastern Europe than about the vast area to the south.

"I realize that," he said. "But I want someone who understands politics and economics, and has absolutely no prejudices or preconceived notions about Latin America. I think one of our troubles has been that everyone who works on it has been doing it for too many years. We need fresh eyes, and new ideas."

"Well," I said, "it sounds fascinating. I'll have a lot to learn, but I like that. The only thing I ask is that I be the one to tell President Johnson. He doesn't like surprises, especially from his own staff."

I returned to Texas and talked immediately with the president. He did not want me to leave, he said (he never liked people on his personal staff to leave him), but he understood and would back me.

"I know," he told me, "that your main interest is foreign policy. And I admit there isn't much foreign policy in Austin these days." We parted as close friends, and for that I was profoundly grateful. The man, larger than life, probably the greatest political tactician in our country's history, often brilliant, often his own worst enemy, taught me more about people and politics than anyone in my life. Someday his fellow countrymen will come to understand that great American, will realize what he tried to do, and why. But first the trivia and the trash will have to be washed away. With modern presidents, that takes a bit of time.

On March 10, 1972, President Nixon announced my appointment to the National Security Council staff. I was back in the Old Executive Office Building, surely the most gracious edifice in Washington. At one time, it was the headquarters of the Departments of State, War, and Navy. How we handled all our foreign policy and military affairs under one roof challenges the imagination. When you walked down its marble corridors, or shunned the elevator and descended via the graceful curving stairways, it was hard to escape feeling that you might run into Cordell Hull or Henry Stimson or even John Hay. All those wonderful ghosts disappeared quickly when you looked out the window and saw modern-day bureaucrats hurrying in white shorts to the tennis court on the South Lawn.

My job was to advise Kissinger and, through him, the president on the vagaries of Latin America. Where to begin? I had spent too many years in the newspaper business to imagine I could discover reality in books, or staff studies, or memos. They helped greatly, but I never thought I knew much about any country or people without seeing them myself. My first act was to write a memo to Henry telling him I needed to see Latin America with my own eyes. With his OK, I packed my bags.

Obviously, I could go to only a few countries on that first swing through the hemisphere. After consulting friends in the State Department and old Latin American hands in the press corps, I worked out an itinerary that would take me to countries that would surely be of prime interest in the years ahead. During the next weeks, I visited Brazil, Argentina, Chile, Panama, and Mexico. At each stop, I conferred with our ambassadors and their principal officers and with officials in the governments concerned. I also made it a point to meet as many people outside government as I could and to draw on the knowledge of veteran foreign correspondents who had spent years covering Latin America.

Back at my desk in Washington, I wrote a full report on the trip for Kissinger. I described the moods and the problems I had encountered. The central theme of the memo was that we would do better in dealing with that infinitely varied part of the world if we moved away for a time from the search for some "grand design" in our relations with Latin America. There was, I believed, no meaningful umbrella that would cover our interests in countries as different as Brazil and Haiti, or Argentina and El Salvador. I thought we would be better off to isolate specific, measurable problems and solve them with individual countries. If we did that, I suggested, we would find that our relations were improving and that, in the end, we would have a Latin America policy. I listed some of the conflicts I thought we should address immediately. One was the vexed problem of the salinity of the Colorado River, which was slowly poisoning the Mexicali Valley, and U.S.-Mexican relations as well. Another was the need to put U.S.-Panamanian affairs on a modern footing. Still another was the continuing, and embittering, "tuna war" between the United States and the nations of the west coast of South America, especially Peru and Ecuador. If we tackled those problems and a few others, one by one, and solved them, we were likely to awaken one fine morning and discover that our relations with Latin America had moved to a higher and better plateau. That was the gist of my message.

I was encouraged when Kissinger said he agreed with my approach. He told me to go forward with the agenda I had outlined. Problem Number One was the water dispute with Mexico. I worked long and hard with my friend José Juan de Olloqui, Mexico's ambassador in Washington. He was talking with his specialists, and I with those on the U.S. side. I arranged meetings between Mexico's Foreign Minister Emilio Rabasa and Kissinger. Finally, I proposed that we begin formal negotiations and that the U.S. representative be the distinguished former Attorney General Herbert Brownell. Kissinger agreed and took the nomination to Nixon, who gave his enthusiastic approval.

The only word for Brownell's performance was "inspired." In a relatively short time, as modern diplomacy is measured, Brownell had hammered out an agreement with the Mexicans. There was expectable and vocal political resistance, especially from the congressmen of Colorado and Arizona. The fertilizer that was helping the crops of the Colorado River states flourish was killing the crops in Mexico. By the time the Colorado water reached Mexico, the chemical nutrients were gone; only the killing salt remained. In the past, politicians of the Rocky Mountain states had been powerful enough to frustrate any fair settlement. This time, reason prevailed. Enough congressional support was mustered, not easily and not quickly, but eventually, to back justice as opposed to expediency.

By the time the cold winds began to blow along Pennsylvania Avenue, I was ready to turn to Problem Number Two, Panama. As I began to look seriously at complications on the isthmus, I had a stroke of luck. There was then present in Washington a gifted and perceptive Panamanian, Nicolás Ardito Barletta, one of the top economists in Latin America. When General Torrijos took power, he made Barletta director of his office for economic planning. In those early months of turmoil, Nicky worked out the blueprint for what became the essential economic elements of the "Torrijos revolution," things like better distribution of wealth, an effective tax program, and measures to give the alienated elements in Panamanian society a larger stake and better services. Bureaucratic infighting and other considerations caused Barletta to leave Panama in 1971 to join the economic section of the OAS.

Talking one day with Walter Sedwitz, executive secretary of the OAS division for economic and social affairs, we discussed Panama. Walter said: "If you're interested in Panama, you ought to get to know Nicky Barletta of my staff. He knows more about that country than almost anyone I know." Within a few days, Nicky and I met and my real education on Panama began. I had talked with many American specialists and had read countless documents and reports, but much of what I learned was less valuable than the insights Barletta was able to provide. He knew the economic problems as few men could. More than that, he had a remarkable sense of history and politics. Above all, I had the feeling in talking with him that I was hearing an authentic voice of Panamanian patriotism, fierce at times but always reasonable. Gradually, what had happened in that small country over the years began to sink in and to become real for me.

Near the end of November 1972, another Panamanian moved onto the Washington scene. Nicolás González-Revilla, age 27, had been appointed Panama's ambassador to the United States. When the cable came from Panama asking for U.S. agreement to his appointment, there was total confusion mixed with amazement. No one in Washington knew who he was. A quick check showed he had graduated from the University of Georgia only four years before. He had worked in the Panama branch of the National City Bank briefly, then had started his own economic consulting firm. He had never occupied any governmental position, had never been connected with diplomacy in any way. He was, our sources indicated, a recent addition to the Torrijos clique, one of the many young men of wealth and position drawn to the military reformer. Beyond that, he was a mystery. Years later, Nico told me that Torrijos' rationale was: "If you do badly, there's nothing we can lose, because we have nothing to start with."

The first time I met the new ambassador was a cold evening in November 1972. Nicky Barletta was a friend of González-Revilla and thought we should get to know each other. When the long hours in the office had ended, the three of us met in the lounge of the Sheraton Carlton Hotel on Sixteenth Street. We had a long and useful talk that covered a wide variety of subjects—relations between our countries, the stalled treaty talks, what a new ambassador should and should not do. I told the young envoy he could count on me for help and advice any time he wanted them. In the following months, I kept that promise, suggesting things he should do, people he should know, explaining the political atmosphere in Washington that would, in the long run, make a settlement possible or destroy it. He, in turn, helped broaden my understanding of Panama and the currents that moved that small but fascinating society. It was a mutually beneficial association and Nico and I became friends as well as official colleagues.

One other contact with Panamanians stands out in my memory of that period. I had a call from the Panamanian Embassy asking if I would meet with two Panamanians who were in town. I agreed and they came to my office on December 5. One was Guillermo de St. Malo Arias, about 30, a businessman, scion of two distinguished Panamanian families. His companion was Álvaro González, the same age and a promising architect. Both were members of the talented group of young men who belonged to Panama's upper crust yet were drawn to the Torrijos government because of its populist approach, its pledge to improve the lot of the underprivileged in that rigidly tiered society. All were fiercely patriotic and determined that the many wrongs of the past be righted. They were, in short, good Panamanian nationalists. At the same time, most of them were sophisticated and worldly-wise. They had studied abroad and knew the United States and Europe well. They were, for the most part, convinced that private enterprise, initiative, the free play of market forces, and competition offered the best hope for Panama's economic growth and well-being. In siding with the Torrijos revolution, they created severe strains within their own families and their own class. To some in the older generation, they were traitors to their lineage. That older generation did not comprehend that these young men were, in fact, the best guarantee for the survival of that lineage and its fundamental values.

I welcomed the visitors to my high-ceilinged place of work, ordered up some coffee, and we began to talk. I quickly perceived they were serious young men with a mission. First off, they wanted me to know that General Torrijos was an authentic reflection of the feelings of Panama. Without saying it bluntly, they were telling me that the opinion prevalent in some Washington circles—that Torrijos was a passing phenomenon with a narrow power base—was mistaken. Panama had to create "the consciousness of a sovereign nation," St. Malo said, and it might be necessary to give up their lives to demonstrate that necessity. González insisted that Torrijos, for the last four years, had tried to create an identity of purpose among poor farmers, students, and the underprivileged in the cities. For the first time, those groups, which represented by far the national majority, were beginning to favor force as the best way to demonstrate their dedication to the crusade for sovereignty.

I thought my guests should know that I believed a solution had to be found for the Panama problem. If not, it was going to be disastrous for both countries. I told them many Americans realized that simply holding on to the past was no answer. I rather shocked them when I said that, in my opinion, if the search for an answer continued in the tedious way it had over the past several years, "the final solution might come in the year 1990 with a canal filled with dead bodies." St. Malo told me years later that when he heard that he realized there were Americans who understood what the real stakes were. The pessimism he and González had felt began to diminish.

I reminded St. Malo and González that, while the issue generated a passionate response in their country, there was also a high level of emotion in the United States, especially in the Congress. There was a mixture of patriotic, economic, and political reactions that had to be recognized and dealt with. To ignore them was to make any treaty impossible. Then I raised an idea that had been in my mind for some time.

"Look," I said, "I've heard all the theoretical arguments. I know the issues. I think what I need is to go to Panama, very quietly, with no fanfare. I want to see the problem at first hand. I need to meet and talk with General Torrijos and others. I know what the attitude of my own government is. But I have to look at this thing through Panamanian eyes. Unless I do that, I don't think I'll ever be able to recommend a way to get out of this box."

They jumped at my suggestion. "That's a great idea," St. Malo said. "I'll have to get Dr. Kissinger's approval," I reminded them, "but I'm sure he'll agree. You go back to Panama and check it out with the general. If he thinks it's convenient, I'll do it." When they left my office, the two Panamanians were in a cheerful mood.

That same day, I wrote a memo for Al Haig, Kissinger's deputy. It mainly concerned NSC operations and possible ways to make them more effective. But in the section "Regional Problems," I wrote: "The single most difficult problem we face [in Latin America] in the immediate future concerns Panama and the negotiating of a new canal treaty." I suggested we take a "totally fresh look" at all the complex questions involved—what were the real security factors, what was the function of the Canal Zone in the last quarter of the twentieth century, how should we handle relations with Torrijos, and a host of other matters that needed study and decision. Haig called me a few days later and said he and Kissinger agreed that a fresh look at Panama was in order. They wanted me to go to work on it.*

Within weeks, early in January 1973, Panama launched Phase Two of its campaign to internationalize the canal problem. The Panamanian delegation at the United Nations informed Secretary General Kurt Waldheim that it planned to invite the Security Council to meet on the isthmus in March. Aquilino Boyd, working behind the scenes, had already lined up a majority of the council's fifteen members in support of his ploy. He was far too clever to propose a meeting devoted solely to Panama's problem with the United States, though that is obviously what he wanted. The formally declared purpose of the council session would be to consider "problems of colonialism and dangers to peace in Latin America."

George Bush, the U.S. representative, with an able assist from Sir Colin Crowe of Great Britain, fought manfully against the proposal. Sir Colin opposed the whole idea of moving the Security Council about the globe, taking it away from its records, its communications, its home base. Bush argued that it was not the function of the council to intervene in bilateral problems not on its agenda. He also cited the danger of holding council meetings where local pressures from public opinion could affect the deliberations.

The effort was futile. The council deck was stacked in Panama's favor. The Soviet Union, Communist China, France, and the other council members, most of them from the developing world, sided with Panama. The council decided to assemble in Panama City on March 15 for six days of meetings. Torrijos' scheme was proceeding nicely.

In some ways, the events at the United Nations made my planned trip to Panama more timely. Kissinger agreed. So I took off at mid-morning on February 9. It had been freezing in Washington. The 90-degree heat on the tarmac at Tocumen airport was a shock, but a pleasant one. Ambassador González-Revilla was there to greet me. An aide took my passport and baggage check, and Nico and I climbed aboard a National Guard helicopter. The ambassador told me we were flying to the general's beachside house at Farrallon along the Pacific shore.

It was the eve of Torrijos' forty-fourth birthday, and he was celebrating

---

*The main reason for the sudden shift in White House attitude was President Nixon's sweeping victory in the 1972 election. That erased inhibitions that had blocked any initiative on Panama and other problems during the previous year.

early. A handful of friends were with him, including Rory González, a businessman from Chiriquí province and a trusted aide and confidant. Others dropped in with gifts and good wishes throughout the evening. It gave me a chance to meet the general's inner circle and to see how he handled them. He was in a relaxed and cheerful mood, though he said he didn't much like the idea of being 44. I told him about Jack Benny, who never passed 39, and he laughed. There was no serious talk; it was just a get-acquainted session, a breaking of the ice. I had the feeling Torrijos was sizing me up, just as I was getting impressions of the young leader of a young country. He went to bed rather early, about 11 o'clock, which was his custom. I stayed up late talking with Nico and Rory, learning more about their boss and their country.

We were up early the next morning, had a quick breakfast, and climbed aboard the general's helicopter. He was wearing the outfit most Americans had seen in pictures of the Panamanian leader—green fatigue pants and shirt, canvas-and-leather combat boots, a green campaign hat with both brims raised at the sides. He wore a webbed military belt with a holstered .45 automatic on one hip and a canteen on the other. It was his everyday uniform, the one he liked best. His only decoration was the insignia of his rank, the golden branches on his collar.

The next two days were a whirlwind. In and out of helicopters, sedans, jeeps, walking through the streets of towns and villages, listening to farmers and shopkeepers and ranchers. Torrijos was "doing his thing." He was far happier in the countryside than in the capital city, much more at ease with rural folk than with cabinet ministers or foreign visitors. That was one reason he did it so much, because he liked it. He was also convinced that only in that way could he truly feel the pulse of his people, find out what they were thinking, what their worries and complaints were. There was no question that Torrijos knew more about what was happening in his country outside the urban areas than did anyone else in his government. It was also true that the general spent more time with his people than did any political leader in the hemisphere, probably in the world. It was one reason why his people admired him, why he could count on *campesino* support in any crisis—as the rebels had discovered to their regret in 1969.

Through it all, I tagged along, not as a foreign guest or VIP singled out for special treatment, but simply as another member of the general's party. I had told Billy St. Malo I wanted to see Panama through Panamanian eyes. Torrijos was making sure I did just that. Perhaps more to the point, it was simply Torrijos' way. He tended to forget he had guests and his handling of them caused more than a few to label him discourteous. Those visitors forgot that the soldier tramping down a dusty street in a remote village was the head of a government who had more important things on his mind than the comfort of visiting firemen. His attitude toward visitors was pretty much that of most field-grade officers in a military unit: if the troops have water and are fed, they will get along.

It was a priceless opportunity to see the leader of a revolution in action. When he met a farmer, he listened. He asked about crops and animals and marketing. He was constantly ordering members of his staff to write things down—this village needs a small bridge; that farmer needs seed; let's have this road fixed; there is no health clinic within fifteen miles. Ministers and aides dutifully noted the problems. It would be well for them if Torrijos did not hear the same complaint the next time he visited that village. It was government at the grass roots and in its simplest dimension. It was the kind of government Omar Torrijos liked best and handled most effectively.

At the end of a long and tiring day, we ended up in the town of Las Tablas on the Azuero Peninsula. Our quarters were in what was going to be a motel. The furniture was meager (a cot and a chair only in most rooms). The walls were bare. A single light bulb hanging from a ceiling cord provided the only light. After washing up, we gathered outside around a long table at one side of a concrete floor that served for fiestas and Saturday night dancing. The sky was the only ceiling. There we ate chicken soup, rice, beans, bread, a chunk of meat, and luscious fresh fruit. Then, as the rum and whiskey made the rounds, Torrijos held court for the local elders. I remember the hottest issue was whether the town should have a slaughterhouse. It had been debated for a long time. The owners of the nearest such establishment, some forty-five miles away, insisted there was not enough business to support two slaughterhouses in the area. The good farmers of Las Tablas insisted they were wrong. At one point, Torrijos introduced me to the group as a "slaughterhouse economist from Washington." I told them, in good bureaucratic form, that I needed to know much more before making a decision. But my first impression was that the town really did need a slaughterhouse and I thought they would support it energetically. That brought a round of applause. Torrijos laughed and said he had to agree with "the specialist." I retired to my preferred obscurity.

The talk went on for several hours. As the level fell in the Carta Blanca and Johnny Walker bottles, the noise around the table rose correspondingly. Economic problems were replaced by earthier topics. The city fathers continued to lay their problems and their ideas before the general, but with jokes and good humor. Torrijos joked back but made clear their complaints would be dealt with.

The dialogue impressed me. Here was a general who commanded the only real power in the country. He was the leader of their government. Yet those men, mostly farmers and small-town officials, had no hesitation about speaking up, no reluctance to complain about things the government was not doing, or was doing badly. It was my first exposure to something I came to respect increasingly over the years: the candor and courage of ordinary Panamanians in the face of authority. They might be long-suffering, but they were not docile.

The next day was more of the same. We were up early, had a Spartan breakfast, and were in the helicopter before 8 o'clock. More villages, more town meetings, more farms and farmers. Wherever he went, Torrijos showed a special concern for schools and pupils and teachers. If the general had any one overriding social preoccupation it was with education. It stemmed naturally from his heritage. His mother was a schoolteacher; his father, both a teacher and a school administrator. All his brothers and sisters had received good educations and several made teaching their life work. Only Omar of the eleven children did not pursue any higher education, choosing, instead, a military career. But his respect for learning was deep. So was his love for children.

Whether they were talking about their books or their school garden or their physical exercises, the youngsters responded to Omar as to a friendly older brother or uncle. It was more than baby kissing in the traditional political sense. The man truly cared about the young, about their problems, their opportunities, and their future. More than just caring, he had done more for primary education in Panama than any other political leader in the country's history. So had he done more for health care in the remote countryside than was ever done, or even tried, before.

By evening of that second day, we returned to Panama City, dusty and tired. My notebook was crammed, my mind even more so, with a congeries of impressions and information and vignettes. I had what I had come for—a firsthand impression of Panama itself and of its people and its leader. I had learned, contrary to Panamanian propaganda, that the Panama Canal was not a burning issue for the people who lived fifty or two hundred miles away. They were far more concerned with the weather and crops, markets and prices, roads and schools and health care. In fact, they seemed rather proud the canal was in their country. They also recognized it as a source of economic benefits. The one thing that bothered them universally had nothing to do with the canal itself. It was the existence in their country of a strip of territory that was under foreign control. They wanted to change that. They believed it should have been changed long ago. For the most part, they seemed to like Americans as people, but they could not accept an American colony in the heart of their small country.

The next morning, the general and I had a long and useful talk. We met on the open porch of the house on Fiftieth Street. It overlooked the pool in back of the house and had brightly upholstered, comfortable summer furniture. A fan kept the air moving. The general was wearing the dress uniform of the day. A small green plastic rectangle over his right pocket bore his name. He looked rested and alert.

I thanked him for permitting me to travel with him and to see his country with my own eyes. He asked for my impressions and I gave them. We then turned to the major business: the canal treaties and relations between our countries. I told Torrijos I had been studying the problem and its long background. I had talked at length with a fair number of Panamanians. I said I was convinced that a solution, a fair solution, was desirable for both our countries. I told him I was certain that Dr. Kissinger and President Nixon would be receptive to a reasonable approach to the problem.

"Jorden," the general said, "I hope you are right. You know there have been many disappointments in the past. Every time we've seemed to be moving forward, something has come up to set us back. I would like to believe what you say about a new approach. But I have to be skeptical— not about goodwill but about the willingness to really move ahead. I don't think the United States will ever face this thing until there is some outside pressure that gets its attention."

He was talking about the coming meeting of the United Nations Security Council. At that point, U.S. policy was to try to prevent the meeting if possible. With the date set and preparations going forward, it seemed to me that was a pipe dream. It was more important to keep the U.N. sessions from doing serious harm. Meetings that featured outrageous charges against our country would do serious injury to the approach I saw taking shape.

"General," I said, "I understand how you and your government feel. You want to put the spotlight of world attention on the Panama problem. You think that if the world, or a significant part of the world, sides with your cause, it will force the United States to pay attention. I want to suggest it may work the other way. Right now, I think there's a readiness in Washington to take a fresh look at this whole matter. Certainly I want to get a new approach started. I think Henry Kissinger is inclined that way. And my impression is that the president might be favorably disposed as well . . . It may be that what we need is new negotiators on both sides, a new point of view, a totally fresh approach, and people who are ready to give this problem the high priority it deserves."

Torrijos took it all in. He looked pensive. "That's good," he said. "I hope it's true."

"Look, General," I responded, "you know who I am; you know my job. I'm only a cog in the machinery. In the end, it's only the president who can approve a new course. All I can tell you, in all candor, is that this is the way I think things are moving. On the other hand, if this U.N. meeting goes forward, and if it becomes a donnybrook, a lot of name calling and the like, I have to tell you honestly that it's going to set us back badly. It's just going to make a lot of people mad, people we need if there's ever to be a reasonable solution."

"I understand what you're saying," he answered. "But we've got to do what we can to bring this thing to the world's attention. And people in Washington have to understand as well. If we don't make some noise, then things will just go on as they have for far too long. The purpose is not to insult your country; it is to wake them up."

"I see your point, General," I said. "But please remember that waking people up and slapping them in the face are two very different things."

"I know that," he said quickly. "And what you have said has made me think. If we both work at it maybe we can do better. Meantime, please understand that we have to do what we have to do."

"Yes, I know," I said. "But please always remember that my country, too, will have to do what it has to do. I only hope that in the process we don't get so far apart that a rational and peaceful and sensible approach becomes impossible."

"I have the same hope," he said. We both stood up and shook hands. I had the feeling we understood each other very well indeed. Torrijos told me some years later that he got the strong impression from that meeting that things might be turning in the right way at last. He had gone too far along the Security Council path to turn back, he said. But my words about a new attitude, a new negotiating approach, and new people gave him a degree of modest hope he had not felt before.

I have a picture of that long meeting on the porch in Panama signed by Torrijos. He wrote: "To a friend as a memento of a change in attitude in the coexistence of our two countries." That change of attitude was clearly on its way. But there were hurdles, some of them fairly high, that had to be passed before it arrived.

By March 15, the machinery of the United Nations Security Council was in place in Panama City. Some 150 staff members—stenographers, interpreters, messengers, communications specialists, drivers, security men, many others—had gathered like the chorus in a Verdi opera, each to do his or her assigned task so the stars, the permanent representatives, could work smoothly and efficiently. The better hotels were jammed, even some of the lesser-known hostelries. The $92,000 budgeted for the extravaganza was flowing on schedule, pleasing greatly the innkeepers, waiters, cab drivers, and others who shared in the small bonanza that had come their way.

Ambassadors whose nations belonged to the council played host to their representatives. Those without an embassy in Panama, including the envoys from Moscow and Peking, were provided comfortable suites in the

El Panamá and Continental hotels. Headquarters for the international gathering and the site of the plenary meetings was the Legislative Palace located in the center of the city, one block from the Canal Zone. It had been the meeting place for the National Assembly until that body was disbanded by the revolution in 1968. Across the street from the conference site, three stories of the facing buildings were covered by a huge sign in five languages. The U.N. delegates, on entering or leaving, could not miss its message: "What country of the world can bear the humiliation of a foreign flag piercing its heart?"

George Bush had left the U.N. post the month before to head the Republican National Committee. His replacement was John Scali, a veteran newspaperman who had worked for many years for the Associated Press and then the American Broadcasting Company. Scali had joined the White House staff in 1971 as a special adviser to President Nixon on foreign policy. A correspondent in Washington for more than twenty-five years, the ex-reporter was no stranger to the diplomatic scene. But he was about to learn, as many of us have over the years, that there is a vast difference between reporting on world affairs and dealing with them firsthand. The Panama meetings would be Scali's baptism in the ways of the United Nations world. The water in the baptismal font was very chilly.

The single item listed for the meeting was "consideration of measures for the maintenance and strengthening of international peace and security in Latin America in conformity with the provisions and principles of the Charter." It was a broad, almost meaningless, phrase that is all too common in international bodies. When he read the wording, one diplomat commented: "This looks like a meeting in search of an agenda." In fact, the wording was merely a smoke screen. Everyone knew the central issue would be the continuing failure of the United States and Panama to reach some kind of reasonable settlement of their differences. They also knew that the name of the game was propaganda warfare, not serious political discussion.

A few days before the U.N. sessions began, a reporter asked General Torrijos what he expected from the international assemblage. "I want the moral backing of the world," he answered, "and, especially, I want the people of the United States to know how we feel about the canal. The Americans are very decent people and when they realize what is happening here, they will feel a sense of shame, just as they did during the Vietnam war."

That same day, an American diplomat said: "One of the reservations about the United Nations in the United States is the feeling that too often it has been used as a platform to attack us. If the proceedings are too vigorous, violent, and fiery, it could backfire on Panama."

The two statements set the parameters for the coming meetings. Panama wanted to rally world opinion and attract Washington's attention. The

United States wanted to make sure the rhetoric did not get out of hand and create new problems.

When the day of the opening session arrived, all was in readiness. The hall had been cleaned from top to bottom, the carpets vacuumed, the conference table polished to a high sheen. The delegates' earphones had been checked; the booths for the interpreters were spotless. Even the outside of the building was carefully prepared, the large glass windows polished, the concrete walks swept. It was, after all, the most important international gathering Panama had hosted since President Eisenhower and his fellow chiefs of government from the Western Hemisphere had assembled there in 1956. Before that, the only thing to compare with it was the gathering summoned by Simón Bolívar, the Liberator, of all the Latin American states that had recently broken their colonial ties with Spain. That was in 1826.

As leader of the host government, Omar Torrijos took the rostrum. It was the first time he had addressed a multinational body, and he was understandably nervous. His customary uniform had been doffed for the occasion, and he was wearing a dark business suit. Witnesses told me there was no great anticipation among the diplomats. They expected the head of government would express the usual formal welcome. They assumed the "fireworks" would come later, from Panama's foreign minister or its U.N. representative. They were quite wrong.

After welcoming the diplomats and expressing the hope their visit would be pleasant, the young general launched a diplomatic broadside. Panama and its people, he said, have suffered seventy years of indignity. He claimed that the United States had created "a colony in the heart of my country." We live in a world where colonies are being freed, not kept, he said. He lashed out at the notion that any arrangements between sovereign countries should be written to last "forever." Panama had the right to exploit her own geographic position, he insisted, and it would never be "another star on the flag of the United States." There was "a new conscience" among the peoples of Latin America. If ignored, it would force those people "to carry out violent changes."

The oration lasted more than half an hour. Most of the diplomats were surprised and the Russians, Chinese, Cubans, Peruvians, and others were doubtless enjoying the discomfiture of the American delegation. But the U.S. representative refused to be goaded into attacking the host country. Ambassador Scali sat quietly in his chair foregoing his right to respond. It had been decided in Washington to avoid doing anything that would turn the council meetings into a battle. Instead of engaging in acrimonious debate, the U.S. delegation would work behind the scenes to get a council resolution that it could live with.

It was a trying introduction to the U.N. stage for Scali. Following developments closely from Washington, I knew he must be seething. John was an emotional, proud, and intense man with a temper that bureaucrats around the capital had come to know well over the years. When he was working on a news story, woe be to any official who tried to mislead him or falsely plead ignorance. They quickly felt the cutting edge of his fine Italian indignation. For such a man, it was incredibly difficult to sit quietly while his country was criticized. When I spoke with him on the phone, I sensed what he was going through and sympathized.

However, before that first day had ended, Scali had a chance to vent some of his frustration. The Cubans were not members of the council at the time but their foreign minister, Raul Roa, attended nevertheless. With the usual courtesy shown any U.N. member with an interest in the subject under discussion (the subject *was* Latin America), the council allowed Roa to speak. He delivered a fiery speech, strongly supporting Panama's grievances. He then went on to lambast the United States for its "economic imperialism" and "nuclear blackmail." It was nothing the Cubans had not said many times over the years. But it so irritated Scali that he used his right of reply. The voice from Havana, he said, was "the voice of venom." Let us not listen to these "counsels of hate," he told the council. Given the level of cynicism that prevailed in U.N. circles, it was doubtful Roa's intemperate outburst, or Scali's cutting rebuttal, affected most people in the hall in any way. At least it served to lower the head of steam the U.S. envoy had built up during the long day. In an editorial that morning, the *New York Times* had called the Panama session a "costly and questionable propaganda exercise." That is certainly what it looked like.

The second day, Friday the sixteenth, was given over to speechmaking by the other council members. In most cases, they provided moral support for Panama's position, especially that it have sovereignty over all its territory. The British, in the person of Sir Colin Crowe, tried to foster some moderation in the debate. He reminded the council that the matter was, after all, an issue between two members of the world body and that they had been busy in bilateral talks trying to find an answer. He advised against any heavy-handed outside interference.

The real action was going on behind the scenes. Everyone recognized it was inevitable that some kind of a resolution would come out of the meetings. Those most concerned were the Americans and the Panamanians, a fact the other delegations readily accepted. So while the talk dragged on seemingly without end in the Legislative Palace, Ambassador Scali and his team were busy trying to work out a formula that would satisfy Panama while doing no injury to the U.S. position. They were in regular contact with the Panamanian side, headed by Foreign Minister Tack. The United States wanted the Security Council to recognize that the problem was a bilateral one between Panama and the United States. The U.S. government would have no difficulty accepting a council recommendation that the two parties press ahead to an early settlement—one that recognized Panama's aspirations as well as U.S. responsibilities.

Over the weekend, the Americans and Panamanians worked separately to find a formula. The other delegations and the U.N. staff were able to relax. Many toured the Panama Canal. Others picked up bargains in the tax-free shops. And in the evenings, diplomats from New York were seen winning and losing sizable amounts at the roulette and dice tables in the government-run casinos.

On Monday, Panama and Peru introduced a long resolution. It was a well-drafted statement, given its purpose, which was to state the Panamanian case on every significant point. It had, in fact, been drafted in the Panamanian Foreign Ministry. In its second paragraph, the draft resolution noted "the disposition shown by the Governments of Panama and the United States to conclude the following agreements," and went on to list all the points Panama wanted included in a treaty. The United States had not agreed to half of them. Moreover, the one-sided document made no reference to any U.S. rights, requirements, or responsibilities. When the text arrived in Washington, all concerned agreed it was patently unacceptable. Scali and his team had assumed as much, but quickly were left in no doubt. That word immediately went to the Panamanians and other key delegations.

When news of Washington's emphatic disapproval of the Panama-Peru draft circulated, it was back to the drawing board. As he walked out of the Monday morning session at the Legislative Palace, Ambassador Scali was immediately surrounded by eager reporters wondering what was happening. "We expect to be negotiating all day, and perhaps into the night," he said. His expectations were realized. The U.S. delegation worked well past midnight, consulting with Washington and going back and forth with the Panamanians.

At the Tuesday meeting, Scali took the floor to explain the U.S. position. A veteran television reporter, he was not awed by the bright lights and whirring cameras that focused on him. He said the United States, no less than other countries, supported Panama's just aspirations. He noted that U.S. treaty negotiators had already recognized that the 1903 treaty should be replaced by a new and modern arrangement. His government had also accepted the fact that any new pact should have a fixed termination date. "Those who attack the 1903 treaty are attacking a phantom foe, a nonexistent enemy," he said emphatically. But he left no doubt that U.S. interests also had to be considered. "We believe it is necessary that the United States continue to be responsible for the operation and defense of the canal for an additional, specific period of time." It was an excellent, hard-hitting statement of the U.S. position, and it had an impact. Panama was thrown on the defensive for the first time in five days.

If the ambassador had left it right there, it would have been a "strike" in bowlers' parlance. But he went on, and thereby put some pins back in place. He concluded with a detailed statement of how much the United States had done for Panama and Latin America over the years—with loans and grants, with technical and military assistance, with aid to education, health, and agriculture. It was all quite true. But whoever drafted the statement was no psychologist. Governments and people do not enjoy being reminded that they have been the recipients of charity, however well intentioned. And other governments are not pleased to be exposed, even indirectly, as having been less than generous with their poorer, less advantaged neighbors. In any case, the self-congratulatory paragraphs were extraneous to what was being debated. They diminished the force of the ambassador's otherwise eloquent statement of the U.S. position.

Just how well Scali had scored was clear from what followed. Panama's Foreign Minister Tack almost leaped to the floor. He claimed that there had been no true negotiations between the two countries. (Dozens of people who had been involved in treaty talks for the previous eight years must have winced!) The United States was only interested in "maintaining the status quo," the minister said. Washington's real goal was "to perpetuate the colonial enclave." Ignoring what Scali had said about the agreement to replace the 1903 treaty, Tack demanded that that treaty had to be abrogated. After more in that vein, he lashed out at Scali's "public inventory" of U.S. generosity. The fact was, he said, that Panama was subsidizing the United States because the North Americans were the main beneficiaries of the canal and its low tolls. He charged that the United States was interested in Latin America mainly as a source of low-cost raw materials and cheap labor.

At the end of that heated exchange, a new Panama-Peru resolution was introduced, backed by Guinea, India, Indonesia, Kenya, Sudan, and Yugoslavia. The list of Panama's "just demands" was considerably shortened. It was in most respects a great improvement. I believed, as did many of my colleagues in Washington and Panama, that it was something we could live with *if* we could get in a phrase recognizing that the United States had interests and rights that must be considered in any Panama settlement. The effort to make that change went on through that evening and into the next morning.

A phrase recognizing U.S. responsibilities was almost accepted by Panama. That would have made it possible for the American delegation to vote for the resolution. I was on the phone with Scali several times that Thursday morning and relayed his reports to Lt. Gen. Brent Scowcroft, Al

Haig's replacement in the White House. While the Washington-Panama phone line worked overtime, a plan was hatched at the top level of the Panamanian government. Torrijos told me later that, after consulting with University Rector Escobar and other advisers, he decided Panama's cause might be better served if the United States opposed the resolution. That, they concluded, might attract even more world attention than unanimous approval of a more balanced statement. At the crucial moment, the Panamanians refused to go along with the compromise phrase.

Scali passed that news directly to Scowcroft. Kissinger's deputy had been keeping President Nixon informed of developments and knew his thinking. When it was clear Panama would not accept any balancing wording, Scowcroft told Scali he should vote against the resolution.

"That means a veto," the ambassador said.

"I know that," the air force general replied. The call ended.

Scali was sitting in the ambassador's office with his colleagues and gave them the news. Someone asked if he was sure Scowcroft and the White House intended to go that far. They should understand it meant the isolation of the United States in the council. Scali got back on the phone and raised Scowcroft again. He reminded him it would be only the third U.S. veto in U.N. history. Kissinger's deputy said curtly he knew that, but the decision stood. The phone went dead.

While those frantic phone calls were being made, the time arrived for the Security Council to go into session. Scali and his colleagues were still trying for a last-minute solution. They sent Morey Bell to the council chamber to hold the fort. Bell recalled racing through the streets of Panama with a police escort to get to the Legislative Palace. He was to occupy the U.S. seat so that the council could convene and rumors would not spread that the Americans were boycotting the meeting. Bell walked down the aisle and sat nervously between the British and Yugoslav ambassadors.

Sir Colin Crowe, the experienced British diplomat, turned to Bell and said: "Young man, I assume you don't know what to do."

"You are absolutely right," Bell answered.

"Not to worry," the Briton reassured him. "I'll tell you what to do, more or less."

The Yugoslav ambassador leaned toward Bell and asked what he was going to do.

"How do I know?" he recalls saying. "Ask my colleague on the right. He's going to tell me what to do."

Fortunately for Bell, the business of the council at that point was routine.

Back at the embassy, Scali and the others were getting ready to leave for the council chamber. A call came through for the U.N. ambassador from Colonel Noriega, Torrijos' G-2. He told Scali he had a message from his government. "If you are going to veto the resolution, you better do it at the airport," he said ominously. Scali exploded. He told the Panamanian he was going to cast his vote in the council chamber in front of everyone.

Torrijos later explained the phone call was a bit of psychological warfare. The Panamanians wanted to put pressure on Scali to make sure he would veto. They had no intention of allowing any harm to come to him. The Panamanians did not realize that, on a matter of that importance, the feelings of the ambassador were not significant. The decision on a veto is made at the top level of government. But years later, the Panamanians still thought that the veiled threat pushed the U.S. ambassador into casting the veto. Torrijos later apologized to Scali and said the incident was a "misunderstanding."

At the council meeting, Morey Bell was ready to hide under his chair. From mundane matters, the council had turned its attention to the resolution and voting was to begin. Bell was about to plead with his British neighbor to please find some way to delay things. As he turned, he saw out of the corner of his eye the figure of Ambassador Scali in the doorway. The U.S. representative walked quickly down the aisle and Bell vacated the chair "with a great deal of pleasure." When the chairman asked for votes in favor of the pro-Panama resolution, thirteen hands were raised. When he called for those opposed, there was only one, that of the U.S. ambassador. Britain abstained. Immediately there were boos and catcalls from the audience. People stood and shouted their disapproval. The atmosphere, as one witness said, was "really bad." But soon order was restored and the proceedings continued.

The story of the U.S. veto at the United Nations was on most front pages the next day. If a milder resolution had been unanimously approved, one can fairly assume the story would have been on page 3 or 13. The Panamanians wanted front-page coverage, and they got it. The U.S. delegation flew back to Washington the next day in a sour, disgruntled mood. The Panamanians had a very large party, and Torrijos' popularity had never been higher.

Panama's elation did not endure for long. Some relished the fact that their country had won support from the Security Council. Others were delighted to see the United States almost isolated in the world body. But many Panamanians began to see the affair as a Pyrrhic victory. They had savored their moment of triumph on the international scene, but what would happen next? They began to realize that victories by ballot are seldom lasting—unless they put a person into office or commit governments to act or to spend money. Once the Panama meetings ended, delegates from India and Indonesia, Kenya and Yugoslavia, and all the others, returned to New York and resumed their normal schedule. That meant focusing on the questions, large and small, that most concerned their home governments. Panama found it was not on any of their lists.

In Washington, the reaction to the U.N. excursion into Latin America was one part outrage, one part frustration, and one part disappointment. There was in that stew a soupçon of satisfaction as well. Enemies of any treaty with Panama thought the upstart on the isthmus had given them welcome ammunition. They saw the whole rumpus as a devious plot, probably engineered by Castro and backed by Moscow and Peking. Since that group included few, or no, admirers of the United Nations, it also gave them a chance to rail against that body and its "insult" to the United States.

Others, who wanted to develop some kind of more modern relationship with Panama, were totally frustrated. They believed the Security Council and the veto had derailed hope for progress for the foreseeable future. One friend in the State Department told me: "We're not going to be able to sit down with the Panamanians and talk seriously for a couple of years." He and others reckoned the White House would be so furious at its seeming humiliation that the Panama issue would go into the deep freeze for a long time. That sentiment was expressed by the *New York Times* in an editorial two days after the Panama meetings. "However justified many of Panama's claims against the United States may be," the *Times* editorialized, "the abortive session in Panama City probably delayed a just Canal settlement and almost certainly damaged the Security Council as well."

My feelings were mixed. I had told General Torrijos six weeks earlier that a Security Council meeting on the issue would set back efforts to find a solution. I felt we were ready to move forward faster than most Panamanians realized. At the same time, I had to admit their tactic had aroused attention in the capital that had not been there before. I heard in the White House mess that President Nixon was irritated, but I doubted it really affected him. The Watergate scandal was gaining momentum each day and the president's attention was focused on that overriding problem. I suspected that if he gave Panama any thought at all it would have been to regard it as just another wave in the storm that was buffeting him.

Henry Kissinger's view was different. Somewhat removed from the domestic hurricane of Watergate, he could look at Panama with better perspective than the embattled man in the Oval Office. He recognized that he had largely ignored Latin America and had given Panama only fleeting attention. But the embarrassment of the Security Council meeting, the fact it was held inside the hemisphere we had always regarded as beyond outside influence, sounded an alarm loud enough to get Henry's attention. His geopolitical mind recognized that an explosion on our own doorstep, while it might be contained, would not add luster to U.S. prestige or improve Washington's ability to cope effectively with larger issues. It would have done for us about what an outburst of violence and a general strike in Eastern Europe would have done for Brezhnev.

I wrote several memos at the time trying to put the U.N. meeting in Panama into perspective. We should not, I argued, let hurt feelings and embarrassment divert our attention from the real world and the real problem. Policy based on pique was certain to be bad policy. Panama had considerable justice on its side; we had obvious interests that had to be protected. Somehow we had to find a way to bring those divergent goals together. It would require the right men with the right attitude, and with the full backing of their governments. Surely those were not impossible conditions. No reactions came back, which was par for the course in those unusual White House days.

One of the better ways to get policy guidance in the Nixon-Kissinger years, as in most administrations, was to write something for public use— a speech or part of it, a public statement, a report or policy statement. If it were used, you knew what policy was, at least for the moment. If it were changed, you took careful note of the changes. If it were scrubbed, your reading of the signals had probably been wrong.

Within days of the U.N. gathering in Panama City, members of the NSC staff were hard at work on drafts for the president's report to the Congress on foreign policy. I was responsible for the section on Latin America. I talked at length with my two remarkably perceptive colleagues who shared with me the burdens of the Latin American account. One was Serban Vallimarescu, a veteran Foreign Service information officer who had lived for many years in Latin America, spoke fluent Spanish, and understood the Latin American mind better than many Latin Americans. The other was Mary Brownell, who had studied and observed the Americas and the Caribbean with the kind of intellect and rare sensitivity few people are blessed with. After absorbing their many ideas and suggestions, I sat down and drafted thirty pages on the hemisphere. In part, I simply recounted what had happened in the troubled area to our south. Other parts suggested what should be done.

Despite all the extended nit picking and editorial suggestions that such drafts must pass through, most of the ideas survived remarkably well. The full report was, of course, the president's. He had read it, changed it where he wished, and signed it. Kissinger, too, had read every word in the long document that had countless authors, including himself. The report, which went to Congress on May 3, 1973, took a swipe, naturally, at the recently concluded U.N. meeting:

There has been an unfortunate tendency among some governments, in some organizations, to make forums for cooperation into arenas of confrontation. This phenomenon was evident at the recent meeting of the UN Security Council in Panama.

More important was what the president said about Panama itself. In the section on current problems, he told the Congress:

> Another important unresolved problem concerns the Panama Canal and the surrounding Zone. U.S. operation of the Canal and our presence in Panama are governed by the terms of a treaty drafted in 1903. The world has changed radically during the 70 years this treaty has been in effect. Latin America has changed. Panama has changed. And the terms of our relationship should reflect those changes in a reasonable way.
>
> For the past nine years, efforts to work out a new treaty acceptable to both parties have failed. That failure has put considerable strain on our relations with Panama. It is time for both parties to take a fresh look at this problem and to develop a new relationship between us—one that will guarantee continued effective operation of the Canal while meeting Panama's legitimate aspirations.

What President Nixon was saying—to the dismay of some strong supporters on Capitol Hill—was that, despite the unfortunate U.N. meeting, the United States was ready to go forward with Panama in the search for a new relationship. The most notable thing about the Nixon statement was its timing. By the date it was issued, the Watergate affair was the subject of consuming interest in the Congress and on the front pages. The harassed president needed all the friends he could muster to help stave off the ever-deepening investigation. Yet he risked alienating some members of the Senate and the House who were rigidly opposed to any change in Panama. It took a good deal of political courage, assuming that he read it carefully and affirmed it consciously.

The Nixon statement had an immediate impact. Members of Congress and individuals in the executive branch who were persuaded the time was more than ripe for a new deal for our small neighbor took heart from the president's call for "a fresh look." Other people, including a number of "Rough Riders" in the Pentagon, were dismayed. They thought the Security Council debacle had put the final nail in the coffin of treaty revision. In Panamanian circles, where the Nixon statement circulated rapidly, there was considerable satisfaction. Many thoughtful Panamanians had feared the U.N. "adventure" might have put peaceful change on ice for a long time. In that case, they knew that internal pressures would build up and the potential for violence would mount accordingly. The Communists, who loved the status quo because it suited them admirably, were amazed that a conservative leader like Nixon could be flexible on the issue. Once again, ultraconservatives in the United States and extremists in Panama were following a parallel course.

Just as it seemed events were beginning to take a more rational course, the whole structure was shaken by another tremor. In its issue of June 11, 1973, *Newsweek* magazine reported there had been a plot to kill General Torrijos in 1971. The journal said that the talkative White House lawyer, John Dean III, had told "investigators" about the plan. According to the printed account, some "low level" officials in the White House, that is, the notorious White House "Plumbers," had discussed assassinating the Panamanian leader. Their reasons were that the Panamanians had been "uncooperative" in treaty negotiations and they suspected some Panamanian officials had been involved in the world traffic in drugs. E. Howard Hunt, Jr., the ringleader of the Watergate burglars, had assigned a team to do the job, according to the magazine, and they had gotten as far as Mexico City before the murder mission was aborted.

When the report reached Panama City, Torrijos and those around him were infuriated. Even eight years later, when Torrijos talked of this strange affair, his hands clenched into fists and his eyes flashed his rage. Himself a conspirator by nature, the general assumed from the first moment that the story was true. What he did not believe, then or later, was that such an exercise could be launched without the approval of higher officials in the government. It took considerable time, and much persuasion, to bring Torrijos back to earth and convince him the story, even if true, did not represent U.S. policy and that people in Washington were as flabbergasted as he was.

In Washington, we were moving ahead slowly, considering the next steps. One would be the selection of a new negotiating team. It was apparent to those involved, including, I think, Bob Anderson himself, that the Texas businessman had gone as far as he could in the treaty business. He had worked out excellent treaties in 1965–1967, but they were a dead issue. He did not have any burning drive to get a new arrangement. Moreover, he clearly was not on the same wavelength as the White House.

I had given the problem considerable thought and came to the conclusion that any successful treaty-making effort called for a man with a cool head, patience, experience, and considerable prestige—especially in the Congress and the Pentagon. I dredged up a dozen possibilities in my mind, and discarded them. Finally, one day at lunch with my friend Vallimarescu, an inspiration hit me. "I've got it," I said. "Got what?" he wondered. "The right man for the Panama talks," I said. "My old friend Ellsworth Bunker. He's smart; he has experience; he has always gotten on well with the military; he's respected on the Hill. I think he'd be perfect. And he'll be coming out of Saigon soon."

That afternoon, I wrote a memo for Kissinger passing along the idea. He took it from there. Not long afterward, I learned that a colleague in the State Department had independently come to the same conclusion. He gave the suggestion to Secretary of State Rogers. Precisely how Kissinger and Rogers got together on the move is not clear. It was Rogers who called Bunker after he had returned from his long and demanding years in South Vietnam to ask if he would consider taking on the Panama treaty problem. Bunker agreed—provided he could get a much needed rest in his beloved Vermont.

Before long, the story was creeping onto the Washington grapevine. On June 30, a small item appeared on page 14 of the *New York Times*; the headline: "Bunker Is Expected to Get Panama-Negotiations Post." Meantime, Bob Anderson had heard the same rumors others had. He asked his military assistant, Colonel Sheffey, to check it out. Sheffey called Al Haig, who had returned to the White House, and asked if it were true that they wanted Anderson to resign. Sheffey recalled that "Haig very courteously said 'yes, we mean it.'" Anderson promptly sat down and wrote his resignation. On July 2, it was announced at San Clemente that the president had that day accepted the resignation "with the deepest regret."

Coincidentally, it appeared that treaty discussions were about to be put back on the tracks. The impetus came from a surprising source. At a meeting of the OAS foreign ministers in Buenos Aires in late June, Panama's Foreign Minister Tack handed Secretary Rogers a letter. The gist of it was that Panama thought there should be a renewal of efforts to work out a new treaty. He listed a number of principles Panama felt should guide the work of the negotiators and provide the basis for an agreement.

On July 3, the State Department spokesman told reporters at the daily briefing: "We have received a letter from Panamanian Foreign Minister Juan Antonio Tack inviting our negotiating team to Panama to continue treaty negotiations. We are studying the invitation and will respond shortly."

The Panama roller coaster was on the upgrade. A new phase had begun, with the initiative from Panama City and with a new U.S. negotiator about to take the helm.

CHAPTER 9

The Kissinger Principles

"Loyalty to petrified opinion never yet broke a chain or
freed a human soul."

—Mark Twain (inscription in the Hall of Fame)

P ANAMA was riding high after the United Nations meeting. Its apparent "victory" on the world stage created a sense of euphoria on the isthmus
and there was a strong temptation to enjoy it as long as possible. The lure
was especially potent for those who had charted the strategy and carried it
out so successfully—General Torrijos, Foreign Minister Tack, and Ambassador Boyd. Fortunately for Panama, its young leader was not given to rejoicing too long over yesterday's victories. However enthusiastically he
might celebrate with exuberant cronies, however much of the grape he
might imbibe, Omar Torrijos was an early riser. And in those cruel morn-
ings, when he walked miles to erase the pain and dispel the poison, the real
world was with him. He might not always like it; but he recognized it. He
was wise enough to know that any politician who basks too long in the
sunshine of yesterday's success risks a severe burn. He himself had been
singed by those rays more than once.

Even as the Security Council diplomats were settling back into their familiar routines in New York, Torrijos and a few colleagues were looking at
the real world around them. What they saw was disquieting. The high economic growth rates of the 1960s were declining. The real estate boom was
collapsing—in part because of a government decision to restrict luxury construction in favor of low-cost housing. Torrijos' efforts to make life on the
farm more attractive by building roads and schools and installing health
clinics had some modest success. But it was overwhelmed by the drastic
plunge in world sugar prices, a prime money crop in much of Panama. To
pay for all the sharp increases in social services for its people, Panama was
borrowing heavily in world money markets. Its per capita foreign debt ri-
valed that of the biggest and most prosperous countries in Latin America.

Domestic prices were in an inflationary spiral, jumping 10 percent in 1972.

Almost the only bright spot on the economic front was the existence of a large and growing banking center on the isthmus. Drawn by the most liberal banking law in the hemisphere, more than fifty foreign banks had established headquarters in Panama by 1973. Total deposits were $1.5 billion and it was estimated that the banks were putting between $80 million and $100 million into local investments and loans annually. The keystones of the burgeoning banking industry were the American banks—Chase Manhattan, National City, Bank of America, and others. It was one thing to insult Uncle Sam and drive a hard bargain on treaty matters. But Torrijos and his advisers knew that, if they went too far, pushed too hard, and thereby alienated the foreign business community, it would be Panama that suffered most. A huge deposit of copper had just been surveyed in the remote mountains of Chiriquí province and Torrijos hoped to see that resource exploited for the benefit of his people. That would take hundreds of millions of dollars. Where would those dollars come from? Surely not from a banking community that saw Panama as unstable and irrational.

Not that economic concerns dominated the thinking and the decisions of Omar Torrijos and his followers. But the economic facts of life were a balance wheel that in part governed the pace and intensity of psychological and patriotic passions. When he looked hard at all the facts, Torrijos concluded that it was time to do some fence mending. After the United Nations meeting, there had been a deafening silence from Washington. The Americans were bitter and sulking. If there was to be a new start, it clearly was going to have to come from the Panamanian side. But some kind of spark was needed to ignite it. The Nixon message to Congress—with its mention of a "fresh look"—provided that spark.

Until that moment in early May 1973, there had been considerable pessimism on the Panamanian scene, especially among those who believed good relations with the United States were necessary to their country's well-being. Torrijos and others told me they were greatly encouraged when they read the U.S. president's words in their newspapers on May 4. Absorbing the positive reaction of his cohorts, Torrijos called in Foreign Minister Tack. "Tony," he told his scholarly, emotional minister, "you've been critical of past treaty talks and past negotiators. Now I want you to take charge. Let's see what you can do." They discussed the U.S. president's statement and decided it might serve as the peg for a new effort.

For the next several days, Tack thought of little else. He talked with friends he trusted. At night, he sat in the book-lined study of his modest home, drank quantities of Johnny Walker, paced up and down, and thought some more. What to say? And to whom? It was the agony all men face who confront historic moments and who must speak for their countries. It was especially excruciating for Tack whose much-loved discipline was history. He kept thinking of the problem, then thinking of the way it would read in the history books.

Finally, a solution took shape. The inspiration came from the Nixon statement that had been the starting point. Tack had read, and re-read it. All of a sudden it was clear. The U.S. president had written that his policy toward Latin America was based on five principles, including "respect for national identity and national dignity." Tack decided that was the answer: a set of principles. For nine years, the talks with the United States had dragged on, constantly getting bogged down in one detail after another—how much land would be controlled by which country, who would run the courts, what rules would govern the presence of the U.S. military forces, who would issue license plates, and all the other technicalities. "We're beginning the house with the roof," he thought. We should begin with principles, then fit the details into that framework.

Tack sat at his desk and scribbled rapidly. He knew well what the "causes of conflict" were. He had lived with them from boyhood. As a man and a politician, he had talked of them often enough. As a Panamanian he felt he knew what their solution should be. His pen flowed quickly over the paper. When he was done, he had written eight principles. Those, he thought, are the foundation stones of any real treaty. If we get them, a new page in history will be written.

Tack's "basic principles" were:

1. The 1903 treaty must be abrogated.

2. A new treaty must have a fixed termination date.

3. U.S. jurisdiction in any part of Panama should end.

4. The United States could use land and water areas necessary to operate and maintain the canal and to protect vital installations.

5. Panama must receive "a just and equitable share" in canal benefits.

6. U.S. government activities should be limited to operating, maintaining, and protecting the canal.

7. Military activities could be only those "expressly stipulated in the treaty."

8. The United States would have the right to build a sea-level canal if (a) the U.S. decision was made within "a reasonable period," (b) Panama retained full jurisdiction in the new canal area, and (c) a sea-level canal treaty also had a fixed final date.

Tack took his "principles" to Torrijos the next day and won the general's approval. Then the question was how best to convey them to the Americans. A perfect opportunity materialized with an invitation from the government of Argentina to the foreign minister to attend the inauguration of its new president, Héctor Campora, during the last week of May. Secretary of State William P. Rogers would head the U.S. delegation. Tack immediately accepted the Argentine invitation, then sat down and wrote a nine-page letter to Rogers.

He recalled their meeting in Washington at the OAS session in 1970, which prepared the way for the 1971–72 treaty talks. Tack also outlined some of the main events of those futile discussions, and the reasons for their futility as he saw them. Then, turning positive, he mentioned President Nixon's report to the Congress of May 3. He cited with hearty approval the president's call for "a fresh look" at the Panama problem.* "The concepts of the president of the United States," Tack wrote, "certainly reflect a very clear historical awareness of the significance of the profound political, economic, and social changes which characterize the present era." Then he listed his eight principles. Tack concluded by inviting U.S. negotiators to come to Panama "as soon as possible." He hoped they would arrive with "specific instructions" that would make it possible to agree on the principles and get on with a treaty that would settle the differences that had divided the two countries for so long.

Tack met with Rogers in the latter's suite at the ornate Plaza Hotel in Buenos Aires on May 24 and handed over his letter to the U.S. secretary of state. Rogers promised to give it immediate and careful attention.

The Panamanian minister's letter was by all odds the most comprehensive document on the canal problem to emerge from that government in six years. It was lucid, carefully reasoned, persuasive. Above all, it offered a specific course of action—agreement on broad principles to be fleshed out later with specifics. Most of the handful of officials who read Tack's message found it impressive. We were also surprised. Based on the experiences of 1971–72, most Americans dealing with Panama had concluded that the foreign minister was a self-righteous and negative-minded man, one who found it easy to criticize others but not to produce anything constructive. His detailed letter to Rogers called for a reassessment of the man.

What Tack did not realize was that his bid for a renewal of negotiations could hardly have reached the city on the Potomac at a worse time. It was widely known in Washington's inner circles that the man to whom Tack delivered his proposal, Secretary Rogers, was not long for the bureaucratic world. As it turned out, he was back at his New York law firm long before the summer was out. His departure was only one of many during those tumultuous months. In an amazingly brief time, the United States lost its vice-president to enforced resignation and had three secretaries of defense, two attorneys general, and two secretaries in each of five other departments. To be sure, Rogers reported to President Nixon on Tack's message. But when the president and the secretary met in the Oval Office the morn-

*The two paragraphs quoted on p. 199 were the same as those cited by Tack in his message to Rogers.

ing of May 29, they had much more urgent matters to discuss than a diplomatic initiative from the isthmus of Panama. The roof was falling in and a beleaguered president was unable to focus on anything unconnected with the survival of his tottering administration. In the summer of 1973, a time of bureaucratic musical chairs and of profound indecision at the top level of the government, it would have been futile for anyone to draw attention to the innovative message that had come from Panama. It went into the files to await a more propitious time.

Actually, that time came much faster than I or my fellow workers in the diplomatic vineyard had thought possible. By the beginning of July, Bob Anderson had resigned as treaty negotiator. My old friend Ellsworth Bunker was named to succeed him. In August, the president announced that Henry Kissinger would replace Rogers as secretary of state. The Senate confirmed Bunker's appointment on September 13 and Kissinger's eight days later. Suddenly, a new team was in place and it was ready to confront the problem on the isthmus.

What made Kissinger willing to face reality in Panama? In two years in the White House working on Latin America, I never felt that he had any real interest in that part of the world, that he understood the area, or that he wanted to. His preoccupation was always with the bigger game, relations between the NATO world and Moscow, the opening to China, the delicate balance in the Middle East. Henry Kissinger's world moved on an east-west axis. In staff meetings, when questions of Africa or Latin America or South Asia came up, an almost perceptible glaze covered his eyes. He heard the words, but he rarely appreciated the music. His mind moved in other spheres.

But, with time, that perspective began to change. Great power politics, which shaped the 1950s and 1960s, was no longer adequate in coping with rising, assertive, ambitious, hungry, demanding peoples and nations from Thailand to Tierra del Fuego. Kissinger never liked that harsh fact, but he came to accept it. By 1973, he understood there was an important north-south dimension in world affairs, though he still continued to view the problems and the potential conflicts there in terms of their possible impact on greater power relations.

Panama was a small cog indeed in the machinery of world affairs for Kissinger. Nonetheless, he was wise enough to recommend, and to win President Nixon's approval for, a "fresh look" at the canal issue in early 1973. But I believe that what really made Kissinger understand he was sitting on a potential powder keg was the U.N. Security Council meeting in early 1973. It was, after all, a gathering not of the Western Hemisphere but of the world. Votes against the United States came not only from Panama and Peru but also from the Soviet Union and China and even France. That was enough to awaken any geopolitician. Bangladesh and Cambodia were on the other side of town; Panama was in the backyard. Kissinger saw the danger and acted. A bemused president, focused on survival, was brought along more by acquiescence than by strong conviction at that point.

Kissinger's selection of Bunker to carry out a new effort with Panama was well conceived, and he had no trouble selling the appointment to Nixon. Bunker had just returned from six long years as ambassador in Vietnam. With that service came a high level of respect from the military services, crucial to any Panama settlement. He had had extensive diplomatic experience in demanding posts. He had dealt with seemingly intractable problems like the West Irian settlement with Indonesia. Before entering the diplomatic world, Bunker had had a long and successful career in business. His many years in Washington and overseas had won widespread esteem from the denizens of Capitol Hill. Nixon and Kissinger realized that any settlement with Panama would require strong backing from the military and from the Congress. Few men had support in those quarters equal to that of Ellsworth Bunker. He seemed, and was, a natural. The tall, white-haired, Yale graduate was 79 at the time of his appointment. Men twenty years his junior could only envy his vigor, enthusiasm, acuity, and common sense.

Bunker's entry onto the Panama treaty scene tells much about the man and about his method of approaching a complicated problem. He made no demands for access to the president or even to the secretary of state. He did not insist on a large staff, or indeed any staff. He had an office on the seventh floor of the State Department, a phone, and a good secretary. That was all he required. He was quite prepared to work with the foreign policy machinery that was in place; he felt no need to create his own autonomous apparatus. Anyone who saw how Bunker was operating recognized he was a man who did not confuse perquisites with power.

One Monday in late September 1973, Bunker went to the State Department, ambled down the long corridor on the seventh floor to his office, and walked in. His secretary, Cecilia Lucas, was at her desk and he told her, "I guess we better get to work." Over the next weeks, he spent many hours with Bob Hurwitch, the deputy assistant secretary of state who was the principal action officer in the department for Central America and Panama. He spent even more time with S. Morey Bell, the Panama director who devoted full time to affairs on the isthmus. Together, Hurwitch and Bell, plus negotiator Dave Ward and Colonel Sheffey, brought the new ambassador-at-large "up to speed," as they say in Washington. They filled him in on people and problems, and the rugged course the treaty talks had taken over the years. They gave him files and loose-leaf notebooks filled with background data. I called on the ambassador during that period. His desk was piled high with papers and he sat behind them with a frustrated look in his eyes. "How is it going?" I asked. "Well, I'm learning a lot, Bill," he said.

"But I'm ready to get to the real thing." Bunker was wise enough to know that paperwork was necessary but that it was only a shadow of reality.

Once he had mastered the essential elements of the Panama question, Bunker began to move out. His experience in Vietnam and his reading of the Panama record told him the Defense Department would be a key factor in any solution. If military men were convinced a settlement was possible that did not weaken their ability to protect the canal, a treaty would be conceivable. If they felt it would jeopardize that task, chances for an accord were near zero. Bunker recognized that hard fact. Over the next weeks, a black State Department sedan crossed often over the Memorial Bridge and pulled up at the River Entrance to the Pentagon with a slim, white-haired passenger. Bunker was making his rounds. He called on Defense Secretary James Schlesinger and found the top civilian in the Pentagon only vaguely aware of the Panama issue, and inclined to think any change would be a bad one. He encountered a similar negative reaction from another political appointee, Secretary of the Army Howard "Bo" Callaway.

Bunker's reception from top-level men in uniform was considerably more cordial than from civilian officials, who were more attuned to political advantages and the next election than to military reality. Gen. Creighton W. Abrams was then chief of staff of the U.S. Army. He had commanded U.S. forces in Vietnam when Bunker was ambassador. The tribulations of Saigon forged links of trust and friendship between Bunker and Abrams that no petty squabbles in the Washington bureaucracy could possibly sunder. When Bunker explained what he was doing, Abrams assured his old friend that he could rely on a fair, honest, and unemotional judgment from the U.S. Army. Bunker expected and wanted nothing more.

Bunker got the same reaction from the top man in the air force. Gen. George S. Brown, a fighter pilot in World War II, was a tough, outspoken airman who had done everything the U.S. Air Force offered, from fighters to transports to training. I knew him when he was director of operations for the Fifth Air Force during the Korean War. During Bunker's tenure in Saigon, Brown had led the Seventh Air Force. They, too, had become friends with a deep mutual respect for each other's integrity and candor. Brown gave Bunker the same assurance Abrams had: let me know what kind of a settlement you think is right and I'll give you an honest reaction. As we shall see, Brown's support for a rational and just settlement proved absolutely crucial when the final crunch came.

The third member of the military triumvirate whose views Bunker sought was the chief of naval operations, Adm. Elmo R. Zumwalt, Jr. Graduated with distinction from the Naval Academy in 1942, he rose steadily from ensign to admiral on the basis of high intelligence, hard work, dedication, and—like his colleagues in the army and air force—

plenty of guts. During Bunker's Saigon service, Zumwalt was, from 1968 to 1970, commander of U.S. naval forces in Vietnam. The two men got to know each other during those days and established the same kind of mutual regard that Bunker and the other military commanders shared. Zumwalt told Bunker much the same thing Abrams and Brown had: let me see what you propose to do about Panama, and you can be sure I'll give you my honest judgment, and my support if I agree with what you produce. All three military leaders recognized that some kind of readjustment in U.S. involvement on the isthmus was probably overdue.

The principal dissident voice among the military high command was that of Adm. Thomas H. Moorer, then chairman of the Joint Chiefs of Staff. Moorer was older and more conservative than the individual service chiefs. In many respects, he typified the top echelon of his service, more bound by tradition, less receptive to change. As a veteran of Pacific and Atlantic operations in World War II, Moorer recalled well what an advantage the Panama Canal had been to our massive supply effort then, and in the Korean War and Vietnam as well. The waterway was also an invaluable link in the chain of world commerce which the navy might at any time have to defend. What was baffling in the thinking of traditional navy men like Moorer, when they argued the "strategic importance" of the Panama Canal, was that they knew the big carriers that provided their main strike force could not pass through the canal. Moreover, every military planner I had known in the last thirty years admitted that, in case of a major war, we had to assume the Panama Canal would not be available to us. That was why the navy developed a Pacific Fleet and an Atlantic Fleet. They had to be able to function separately. If, in a world conflict, the Panama Canal were of great advantage to us, it would by the same token be a great disadvantage to our enemy. One missile from a submarine in the Caribbean could take it out.

In any case, the "vital strategic value" of the Panama Canal was a myth, the product of nostalgia. It would disappear in the first week, perhaps the first hours, of a nuclear war. What of the usefulness of the canal in the case of a limited war? The advantages of the canal were apparent. It was a hugely beneficial line of transport from the Pacific to the Caribbean. As in the past, it continued to make the movement of matériel, troops, and ships significantly shorter, cheaper, faster. But it was like a bridge or a road or a military base on foreign soil. Its utility for us was governed in considerable part by its surroundings, most particularly by the attitude of the local citizenry. In a hostile atmosphere, the waterway could have quickly become inoperable.

Within ten days of his swearing-in, Henry Kissinger went to New York to attend the opening sessions of the United Nations, his first as secretary of state. One feature of such international gatherings is a series of bilateral

meetings—usually arranged weeks in advance—in which the foreign minister of Country X gets together with his counterpart from Country Y to
discuss common problems. It is often an effective way for diplomats to re-
new acquaintances and even to solve some problems. The "bilateral merry-
go-round" is a particularly onerous chore for the U.S. secretary of state
because every head of delegation, and there are more than 150, wants to see
the top diplomat of the United States. No matter if there are no problems
to discuss. It is enough that newspapers in the minister's capital carry a
story the next day that he has met with the foreign policy chief of the
United States—and then of the Soviet Union, and China. For the most
part, it is a charade about which diplomats laugh over scotch-and-soda in
the lounge. But to refuse to play one's part is to inflict insult and to court
unnecessary problems in the future when votes are needed, or concessions
sought.

There are bilaterals when something can be accomplished. Kissinger's
meeting with the Panamanians was one such occurrence. Foreign Minister
Tack was accompanied by Ambassador Boyd and his envoy in Washington,
Nicolás González-Revilla. Kissinger had invited Bunker to the meeting
and he introduced the newly designated treaty negotiator to the Panamanians. "I want you to know, Mr. Minister," Kissinger told Tack, "that Ambassador Bunker never finishes anything in less than four years." Everyone
joined in the laughter. "I'm very serious," Kissinger said with a wide grin.
"My friend Ambassador Bunker is interested in job security." That ludicrous notion brought new guffaws, none heartier than from Bunker.
The secretary turned to Ambassador Boyd at that point and said: "Mr.
Ambassador, I would like to know your point of view on this matter. As I
understand it, you have been giving us a hard time in the United Nations
on this issue."

I leaned forward to catch Boyd's response. I had not met him before but
had followed closely his activities at the United Nations. Like many others,
I had concluded from his speeches that Boyd was profoundly anti-
American. That attitude may have colored my reports on the ambassador's
statements and his lobbying efforts in international circles, and probably
contributed to Kissinger's question. I was curious to see how this "ogre"
would reply to the secretary's query.

"Well, Mr. Secretary," he said smoothly, "we have been waiting for a
brilliant mind like yours to solve this problem which has been going on for
generations. What I have been doing on my side is only to bring to the
attention of public opinion the problems, the complex problems, that we
have to solve in order to be successful in these negotiations." The meticulously dressed diplomat recalled a talk he had had with Kissinger's predecessor, Dean Rusk, five years earlier regarding the 1967 treaties and their
failure. Boyd had argued that any treaty would fail unless public opinion

was behind it. He quoted Rusk as saying: "I agree with you, Ambassador Boyd. A treaty of this importance must have public opinion in support if it is to be accepted by the people of Panama and of the United States."

"So, Dr. Kissinger," Boyd continued suavely, "what I have been doing is to promote national and international public opinion in favor of a fair and equitable understanding between the United States and Panama."

Kissinger knew when he had been bested and he laughed heartily. So did everyone else. As I walked to the elevator with the Panamanian delegation, I complimented Boyd on his statement. From that day on, I saw the man through different eyes. He was not working overtime to attack our country, but to defend his own. And he was doing it with great skill, even though his rhetoric was sometimes excessively caustic.

Back in Washington after the United Nations interlude, Bunker resumed his rounds of the bureaucracy. He visited with old friends on Capitol Hill and touched bases with others in the government. Finally, late in October, Bunker decided his next step would be a visit to Panama. He had seen the problem from the Washington perspective. It was essential that he know how the Panamanians regarded all the key issues and that serious talks begin. The obvious starting point was the set of principles Minister Tack had given to Secretary Rogers five months earlier. Lawyers and political officers had analyzed the list and had produced a counterproposal, eliminating some of the difficulties created by Tack's wording. But the project had a low priority and the results were accumulating dust in a filing cabinet. Bunker asked for the document, read it, and instructed departmental officers to work it over and polish a response. Bunker still had no official staff as such. The man who worked most closely with him and became his de facto assistant was Morey Bell. Morey had a quick mind and was adroit at drafting.

When the rewrite job was finished, Bell took it to Bunker. As the Foreign Service adviser recalls it, he and the veteran diplomat "stared at it for some days" and discussed it with colleagues. Bunker then decided to circulate it inside the government to see what reaction he got. When I read the draft principles, it seemed to me they were a perfectly good counterproposal. I suggested no significant changes, knowing full well the wording would be revised in the negotiations. But the Pentagon showed no such restraint. The Department of the Army, the Office of International Security Affairs (ISA), the Defense Department's legal counsel, and many others bombarded Bunker with memos. Almost every phrase was questioned; new wording was suggested for each principle; legal briefs were advanced explaining why this or that principle would adversely affect some vital national interest.

Bunker was wise enough in the ways of government to appreciate the old dictum "when you can't fight it, bury it in paper." He sensed immediately what was happening. If he took seriously all the proposed changes, and redid the principles to reflect them, he would only be subjected to a second wave of additional changes. He called Secretary Schlesinger and told him: "Look, I am going to Panama, you know. And I'm going to take a piece of paper with me, and it's going to be called 'principles.' We have read everything your people have written about it and we've taken all that into account. We've made a lot of changes on that basis. But now I have a paper and this is what I'm going to go with. I'll send it to you right away. But please, no more changes." Schlesinger was shrewd enough to recognize a superior bureaucrat in action. "Mr. Ambassador," he responded, "you have a job to do. You are the president's representative. I think you should go ahead with what you want." When word passed through the Pentagon that the secretary had not opposed Bunker's venture, there was considerable frustration. The bureaucrats had hoped to block the diplomatic effort with one objection piled on another. Their boss had cut the ground from under that scheme.

Bunker flew to Panama on November 26 accompanied by Bell and his secretary, Cecilia Lucas. It was dark by the time the big jet taxied to a stop at Tocumen airport, one of the busiest terminals in Latin America. Waiting to greet the visitors were Foreign Minister Tack, Ambassador González-Revilla, and half the press corps of Panama City. The other passengers marched off to the customs and immigration area in semiconfusion. They had not known that the tall, white-haired gentleman on their flight was a celebrity. They kept asking each other: "Who is he?" No one seemed to know. In a few years, Bunker's "recognition level" would be considerably higher.

In front of a dozen microphones, Bunker read his short arrival statement. He said little more than that he was glad to be in Panama and looked forward to meeting with representatives of that government. Then, while reporters tried to push additional questions on him—"What's the real reason for your trip?" and the like—Bunker and his hosts moved across the tarmac to a waiting plane and climbed aboard. They took off and in twenty minutes had landed on the island of Contadora. The island, now a major resort area in Panama, is part of the Pearl Islands group lying south of Panama City. In 1973, the island was in the early stages of development.

Bunker was given the use of a comfortable home owned by an American businessman, Frank Zeimetz, one of the first to buy land and build on the developing island. The house was on a two-lane dirt road, five minutes from the airstrip. An open patio at the back of the house looked over a quiet cove and small private beach. Bunker, who had loved the sea from childhood, was entranced by the setting.

After they had unpacked and changed clothes, Bunker and Bell were driven to a large, thatch-roofed restaurant and clubhouse that was the center of the island's social life. It was near the end of the runway, but on a beautiful stretch of beach used by both residents and visitors. Sailboats and motor cruisers were anchored in the lagoon.

Foreign Minister Tack and Ambassador González-Revilla, dressed in *guayaberas*,* the customary informal dress for Panamanian men, were waiting for the visitors. Many Contadora "regulars" were on hand and were introduced to the American diplomats. Among them were Gabriel Lewis Galindo, the businessman who had bought Contadora and was developing it into a resort community; his wife, Nita; Jaime Arias Calderón, Yale graduate and successful lawyer; and his wife, Mirella. The restaurant was crowded and the atmosphere was festive. A four-piece combo was playing in the corner; people were dancing, enjoying themselves thoroughly. And none more than the tall, Yankee ambassador in his beige summer suit and Brooks Brothers tie. He had those nearest him doubled up with laughter at his stories of sharp-witted Vermont farmers and visiting city folk.

By 11 o'clock, everyone was overfed and thoroughly happy. Bunker complimented the chef, thanked his hosts repeatedly, and made his way through the crowd saying good-night. He and Tack had talked and laughed together but never even mentioned any serious treaty questions. It broke the ice nicely. Bunker and Bell returned to the Zeimetz house for a good night's rest. A soldier from the National Guard walked the perimeter of the property so the visitors could sleep without worry. Another was on the beach below.

The next morning, the Panamanians had a surprise for Bunker. They had heard from American friends that the U.S. diplomat loved the sea and boats. When he looked out the picture window from the breakfast table, the ambassador saw an obviously powerful cabin cruiser at anchor. He wondered whose it was. When the Panamanians appeared, they asked if he had seen the boat. He had and "it's a beauty," he said. They walked down the long, steep path to the beach, got into a small boat and rode out to the cruiser. Tack explained the boat was President Lakas' and that he had sent it over for Bunker's use. It was called the *Maruquel* and its powerful engines enabled it to outrun almost anything in those waters.

The diplomats spent most of the day cruising around the Pearl Islands where Spanish explorers four hundred years before had found a treasure in pearls, which gave the islands their name. They passed a lazy afternoon, talking of Panama's history, and Bunker's early years as a sugar merchant, and foreign capitals they had known, and how Tony Tack the historian had

---

*A *guayabera* is a shirt, usually made of cotton, worn outside the trousers. It has four pockets, an open collar, and either short or long sleeves. Some have narrow vertical pleats from the shoulders to the hem; others are decorated with elaborate embroidery work.

become Tack the diplomat. They mentioned their families, and their schools, everything except their most urgent business. It was done with the tacit understanding that they were establishing a new and different mood from the formal approach that had foundered twice before. Bunker and Tack both told me they were thinking: perhaps if we get to know these people as human beings first, we will get further when we actually sit down to deal with serious business. The evidence on both sides suggests they were quite right.

When they got back to shore that afternoon, there was a call for the Panamanian negotiators from General Torrijos. The head of the government had been pacing up and down wondering what was happening. It had been almost twenty-four hours since Ambassador Bunker had arrived. Torrijos was surprised when González-Revilla told him: "Well, chief, we are just fooling around, getting to know each other." Torrijos couldn't believe it. Then he thought for a minute, smiled to himself, and told Nico: "Just keep on doing that. That's good." He got the point immediately.

While Nico was talking with Torrijos, Bunker took the foreign minister aside. He had decided it was time to begin work. He told Tack: "Look, Tony, we have brought some papers with us. They look like your principles, but they aren't exactly the same. We changed them here and there. Would you like to have a look at them?" Tack said he would. Bunker thereupon handed him the revised principles that had been written in Washington. Tack stuffed them in his pocket, said good-bye, and went to his quarters. He was staying at the home of Dr. Benjamin Boyd, Panama's best-known ophthalmologist, who lived next door to the Zeimetz house.

Tack and González-Revilla worked late that night with the telephone as the third member of their team. They spoke with Torrijos. Tack consulted a few of his closest advisers on technical points as they went along. They made a list of things that gave them trouble, another list of those that seemed to create no problems.

The next morning, the two sides held their first official meeting. They gathered in the glass-enclosed den at the house of Gabriel Lewis, a magnificent residence atop a rocky promontory facing north toward Panama. Tack and González-Revilla represented Panama; Bunker and Bell, the United States. Jorge Carrasco, an intelligent, rotund journalist, anchorman on one of the principal evening TV news programs, served as interpreter. It seemed a strange choice. But Carrasco's English was excellent and he was sworn to total secrecy by the general. To my knowledge, the separation between the confidential diplomatic talks and Carrasco's profession was never violated in four long years.

The foreign minister said he had read the U.S. proposal and that it was "not bad." They then discussed the proposed principles one by one. Bunker explained why he had changed the wording of Tack's original suggestions. On point number one, for example, Tack had written: "The 1903 treaty must be abrogated. The two countries are willing to conclude an entirely new interoceanic canal treaty." Bunker explained that the United States could not agree to abrogate the old treaty and only then try to write a new treaty. If the old treaty were eliminated, he said, and there was no new arrangement to take its place, there would be total chaos regarding the canal and the Canal Zone. The two concepts had to be irrevocably linked. At another point in the discussion, Tack argued that it was not only the 1903 treaty that was involved but also the various revisions and amendments to that pact that had been adopted over the years. It made no sense to abrogate the 1903 treaty and leave in place later amendments. Each side saw the other's points and finally, after endless haggling, the first principle was developed: "The treaty of 1903 and its amendments will be abrogated by the conclusion of an entirely new interoceanic canal treaty."

For the next five days discussion of the principles continued, but at a leisurely, tropical pace. It had been agreed early on that the chief negotiators did not have to confront each other every day or at every session. Both sides felt there was a distinct advantage in keeping the top negotiators apart from the infighting that is a necessary part of any technical talks. Nico and Morey did most of the arguing and debating; Bunker and Tack appeared when there was a roadblock or when a compromise was needed. By December 2, all eight principles had been discussed thoroughly and there was a considerable body of agreement. They were still at loggerheads, however, on several key points. One was the formula that would permit the United States to build a sea-level canal. Another was the way U.S. defense rights would be described. The third concerned economic benefits for Panama.

Bunker concluded after a week that they had gone as far as they usefully could. He was convinced he should consult with officials in Washington before advancing further. On December 3, he and Tack issued a joint statement which described the week-long conference as "a significant effort" toward developing a "just and equitable agreement." Then Bunker flew back to Washington for consultations with the home team.

He went to see the secretary of state and Kissinger asked him how things were going. "Well, the foreign minister told me that our proposal was 'not bad,'" Bunker answered. "I can't tell exactly what he means, but that is what he said. So I'm going to pursue it on that basis." "Fine," Kissinger said. "Go ahead and pursue." When Bunker raised some details that had arisen in the Contadora talks, it was quickly clear Kissinger did not wish to get into them. The secretary told the veteran diplomat that he had been picked to work on the Panama problem because he was experienced and he was trusted. He should, therefore, go ahead and do what he thought was good for the United States and fair to Panama. It was an unusually broad charter, one that Kissinger rarely granted to any diplomat. He gave Bunker one parting suggestion: "If you get into trouble with Defense, or with the president, come to me." Bunker was delighted. He had the kind of backing for his new assignment that ambassadors dream of but rarely receive.

Bunker went to the Pentagon to tell officials there about his week-long talks and to explain the issues that were still pending. He touched base with a few old friends on Capitol Hill to make sure the Congress was not left out of the proceedings. Morey Bell flew back to Panama to continue the detailed work and reported daily to Bunker. Return cables carried the ambassador's instructions to his assistant. By early January, the job was virtually completed. Bunker returned to Panama on January 6 to work out with Tack a few final touches. He returned to Washington the next day with the completed principles in hand.

It was a historic document, providing the blueprint to shape a new bilateral partnership. It was one of those rare occasions when two governments agree to build a new relationship, then proceed to develop the conditions the new agreement has to meet. True, it reflected the spirit and the letter of the Johnson-Chiari understanding of ten years earlier. But it went well beyond that rather terse statement of intent and put considerable flesh on the bones of the concept of 1964.

The main features of the new agreement were the decision to write a new treaty to replace that of 1903 and to give it a fixed termination date; ending U.S. jurisdiction in the Canal Zone "promptly"; recognition of the U.S. right to use the lands, waters, and airspace required to operate and protect the canal; recognition of Panama's right to "a just and equitable share" of canal profits; agreement that Panama would participate in both the administration of the canal and its defense; an understanding that the two countries would work out an agreement on expanding canal capacity (which could mean a sea-level canal or a third set of locks).*

Back in Washington, Bunker went immediately to see Kissinger. In the secretary's huge, paneled office, the smiling Vermonter handed over the final version of the principles. Kissinger had read the cables from Panama and knew in general what was in the agreement, but he read the wording of a couple of the more sensitive points, then grunted approval. He told Bunker he had done an excellent job and that he was confident the president would approve the agreement. In that case, Bunker said, all Kissinger would have to do was initial the final version. "But that," the ambassador

---

*Texts of Foreign Minister Tack's original list of principles and of the final agreement are in Appendix A. Comparison of the two shows clearly what the negotiations of November 1973–January 1974 were all about.

said, "should really be done in Panama. I hope you will go down and do it there." Kissinger bridled. "I'm not going to do it," he said. He explained he did not like tropical countries. "Oh, but this will be a great thing," Bunker explained, "a great thing for you." Kissinger's interest perked up. "A great thing?" he asked. "A diplomatic triumph," Bunker insisted. "Well, perhaps the staff can look it over and make a recommendation," the secretary granted. The old New England angler had planted the bait nicely, and the big fish was eyeing it with interest.

Back in his office, Bunker dictated letters to go with copies of the new set of principles. He sent them off to the secretary of defense, the secretary of the army, the Joint Chiefs of Staff, and other interested officials and offices. The critical comments came in a flood in a few days. Why had the right to build a sea-level canal not been nailed down firmly? What was meant by "Panamanian participation" in defense of the canal? Why did we make political concessions to Panama, and agree to pay them more as well? To anyone who had followed the Panama issue, the complaints were totally predictable. They were a rehash of all the arguments that had been used for a decade by opponents of a new arrangement with Panama. Bunker expected no less. But with Kissinger's backing assured, he let the criticisms from the Pentagon flow off his back. He had heard it all before, many times, and he had made up his mind that, if there were to be a new agreement worked out under his direction, it would be truly new and just and forward looking.

Once the principles for a new understanding with Panama had been established, I began to disengage from the National Security Council. My understanding with Kissinger when I joined his team was that I would work about two years on the staff and then go on to more direct operational responsibilities. When we discussed it in December, he recalled our understanding and said it made sense for me to take over the embassy in Panama. He realized no one, except Bunker and those working directly on treaty affairs, had followed developments in Panama as closely.

Unknown to me, the "club" that is the career Foreign Service was busily angling to get the Panama post for one of its own. That service operates very much like a trade union, the graduates of the military academies, or the academic cliques that dominate appointments and promotions at universities. Anyone who "belongs"—and in the Foreign Service, that means joining up in your early twenties as a vice-consul—is to be preferred over any outsider. At that point, I had spent thirteen years in the foreign policy machinery of government but was, nonetheless, an outsider. The U.S. Foreign Service judges the appointment of an "outsider" on the basis of "The Principle of the Dangerous Precedent." That, as its wise author pointed out, is as follows: "Every public action which is not customary either is wrong or, if it is right, is a dangerous precedent. It follows that nothing should ever be done for the first time."*

I was surprised to receive one morning a message that I had been nominated to be ambassador to Costa Rica and that another man was slated for Panama. It was unfathomable. Not that I had any but the warmest feelings about Costa Rica. It was a delightful, prosperous, and beautiful country. But I knew that the firing line over the next years was going to be in Panama, and I had stayed in government to help solve problems, not to be comfortable. I had Kissinger's word regarding my next assignment, and I made sure the mix-up was called to his attention. The secretary of state reversed his bureaucracy and on January 16, 1974, the White House announced that President Nixon had nominated me to be ambassador to Panama. I appeared before the Senate Foreign Relations Committee on February 5 and was confirmed by the full Senate three days later. I began reading Panamanian history, reviewing my Spanish, and otherwise preparing for the tasks ahead.

Meantime, Kissinger had reconsidered his snap judgment not to take a personal role in approving the principles. Ego played a part, as Bunker had accurately sensed. Kissinger had never shrunk from the limelight or avoided events that were certain to put him on the front pages or television screens. His sense of history played another part. He realized that the agreement on principles was a dramatic turning point in U.S. relations with Panama and, thereby, with the developing world. Moreover, as an academic, deeply stung by the hatred and verbal barbs from students and former colleagues because of his role in Vietnam and Southeast Asia, Kissinger doubtless saw an opportunity to help right the balance of judgment by being generous and just toward a small, weak country that was restive under American domination.

There was another factor. Kissinger had managed to work himself into something of a diplomatic corner at the time and a trip to Panama promised to ease his problem. At the U.N. meeting in October, Kissinger gave a luncheon for all Latin American foreign ministers. Warmed by the evident good-fellowship in the room, Kissinger had waxed eloquent and proposed a "new dialogue" among those who called the Western Hemisphere home. It was a nice touch, warmly applauded, and certainly approved by all who hoped to see an improvement in U.S. dealings with Latin America. The trouble came when the Latin American diplomats reacted more seriously and faster than Kissinger had expected.

In the wake of Kissinger's dramatic initiative, twenty-three foreign ministers gathered in Bogotá, Colombia, six weeks later. In a two-day session,

*F. M. Cornford, *Microcosmographia Academica*.

they hammered out a prospective agenda for the "new dialogue." At the end of November, Colombia's Foreign Minister Alfredo Vásquez Carrizosa met with Kissinger and presented the list. It was spare and reflected Latin America's main complaints and problems, largely economic matters. But high on the agenda was "solution of the Panama Canal question." Kissinger agreed with Carrizosa to talk about all those items at a hemispheric gathering in Mexico in mid-February.

Faced with the prospect of that assembly at Tlatelolco, Mexico, Kissinger concluded that his participation in solving one of the main items on the agenda would be useful. It would disarm his Latin American colleagues and demonstrate U.S. goodwill in one stroke. Hence the decision to go to Panama two weeks before the meeting in Mexico.

The morning of February 7, 1974, Secretary Kissinger, Ambassador Bunker, a small group of senators and congressmen with an interest in Latin America, and various assistants, staff people, and technicians assembled at Andrews Air Force Base in the Maryland countryside. They climbed aboard the well-appointed Boeing 707 of the presidential fleet and soon were airborne to Panama.

The big air force jet landed at Tocumen airport in Panama at noon, within thirty seconds of its planned time. In an unusual gesture, General Torrijos was at the airport to greet the visiting Americans. The motorcade formed up at planeside and Torrijos, Kissinger, and Foreign Minister Tack occupied the first limousine. Bunker followed with U.S. Ambassador Bob Sayre. Then came senators, congressmen, and the others. The U.S. Secret Service and special agents of the Panamanian National Guard led and followed the first car with its distinguished occupants.

Many Panamanians lined the streets as the motorcade entered the city, and the crowds thickened perceptibly as the line of cars reached the heart of town. Schools were in recess and boys and girls swelled the throng assembled to welcome the American statesman. To reporters who traveled in the caravan in a press bus, the crowd seemed friendly but not overly demonstrative. Perhaps there was some confusion as to just what the "principles" meant. They were not a new treaty, that was clear. What, then, were they? At least there was enough indecision about the matter to inject a certain wariness into the general attitude.

There was a notable absence of the posters and banners that usually proliferate on such occasions. One movie theater had filled its marquee with "Welcome Mr. Kissinger." But it was the only one of its kind. In the shopping district and around the Presidential Palace, leftist students waved hand-painted signs proclaiming "Sovereignty, Yes; Colonialism, No" and "One Country under One Flag" and similar slogans. The police kept the politically active students well away from the official party.

The motorcade went through the narrow streets of the old city and pulled to a stop in front of the rugged but graceful old building that is Panama's Presidential Palace. Built in 1673, after English pirate Henry Morgan had destroyed the original city of Panama, it once served as a storehouse for the gold and other treasure moving from Peru to Spain. The building was thoroughly reconstructed in 1922 to serve as both the official office and the residence of Panama's presidents.

Torrijos, Kissinger, and Tack walked up the front steps of the *presidencia*, and passed through the twin lines of the Presidential Guard standing at stiff attention. Before them was the graceful vestibule, known as the Andalusian Patio, marble-covered, with a large fountain in the center, and open to the sky. Kissinger was surprised, as all visitors are, to find himself walking around stately white herons that populate the patio.

Kissinger was warmly welcomed to the *presidencia* and to Panama by President Demetrio B. Lakas. They met in the president's modest office on the second floor. The secretary conveyed President Nixon's best regards and good wishes and Lakas recalled his cordial meeting with the president three and a half years earlier. When those pleasantries were concluded, the president led his guests out of the office, around the open court, and into the formal reception room of the *presidencia*, known as the Salon de Amarillo (Yellow Hall). There, the other dignitaries were waiting: Torrijos and high-ranking officials of his government, Ambassador Bunker, and the other members of Kissinger's official party.

At a signal, the golden yellow draperies at one end of the Yellow Hall were drawn aside exposing the entrance to the State Dining Room. Lakas and Torrijos led Kissinger through the doorway to the elaborate buffet. As they ate, the three men exchanged jokes and banter.

From the Presidential Palace, the Torrijos-Kissinger entourage went along the narrow, one-way street next to the Panamanian White House, back through the crowded, shop-filled streets jammed with friendly, curious watchers. As they recognized Torrijos and Kissinger, the people waved and shouted greetings. To the dismay of the Secret Service men and Panamanian security, Torrijos rolled down the windows of the limousine so that he and his visitor could wave back, and even shake a few outthrust hands. They finally arrived at the Legislative Palace in the heart of the city, about one hundred yards from the Canal Zone border. It was an area where the rioting of 1964 had been most fierce. It was also the site of the U.N. Security Council meeting one year before. The festivities that day would be markedly different from the confrontation of 1973.

The greeting Kissinger received from the street crowds had been friendly but temperate. Inside the Legislative Palace, it was unrestrained. Assembled there were the leaders of the Torrijos government, ministers and heads of agencies, officers of the National Guard, and the resident diplomatic corps. There was also a sizable group of leading citizens—businessmen, lawyers, doctors, engineers, teachers. They were people who *did* know what the "principles" meant and who saw them as a chart for their country's passage into a more promising future. They were also sophisticates who recognized Kissinger as the leading practitioner of foreign policy on the world scene at that time. His name and face were almost as well known as those of Nixon himself. When Kissinger appeared at the front of the hall, they gave him a standing ovation. The secretary beamed with pleasure and waved to his new admirers. They clapped louder still.

The actual ceremony was relatively brief. The text of the eight principles was read, first in Spanish, then in English. There was scattered applause and some cheering after each principle had been read. But the entire audience stood and clapped wildly when the words of Principle Number Four reached them: "The Panamanian territory in which the canal is situated shall be returned to the jurisdiction of the Republic of Panama." Once the reading was completed, Kissinger and Foreign Minister Tack set to work initialing each page of the several copies of the document. Morey Bell, who was acting as protocol officer and assisting the secretary with the signing, recalls that Kissinger was in high spirits. At one point, pen in hand, the peripatetic statesman asked, "What am I signing?" Bell said it was the Panama agreement. "Oh, yes. Panama," he said with a grin.

When the applause died down after the signing ceremony, Foreign Minister Tack went to the podium. He hailed the day's event as a momentous one in the history of the two countries, an important break with the past. But he reminded the Americans present that the Torrijos government looked on the principles as a bill of rights for its people and not as a historic abstraction. "Our sole responsibility at this moment," he said pointedly, "is to the Panamanian people, who have been claiming justice for seventy years, so that the sovereign rights which legitimately belong to them be restored."

Kissinger, in his response, took the diplomatic high road. "We meet today to embark on a new adventure together," he began. "Our purpose is to begin replacing an old treaty and to move toward a new relationship. In the past, our negotiations would have been determined by relative strength. Today we have come together in an act of reconciliation." But even as he spoke in generous terms, the secretary wanted to focus Panamanian attention on the real world. He told them the United States wanted "to restore Panama's territorial sovereignty while preserving the interests of the United States and its participation in what is for us an indispensable international waterway."

His particular turn of mind, perhaps his long academic background, seemed to compel Kissinger to look always for the broader implications, the general lessons, of every experience. Then, too, he was doubtless thinking of the three-day meeting he would have two weeks later in Mexico with the foreign ministers of all of Latin America. Whatever the reasons, he was not content to let the accord with Panama stand by itself as the impressive historic achievement that it was. Somehow it had to be more. So he dwelt at considerable length on its significance for the entire area. He spoke of the new agreement as "an example of what we mean by the spirit of community in the Western Hemisphere." He said that he and President Nixon were "now fully committed to a major effort to build a vital Western Hemisphere community." That was empty rhetoric, as Kissinger must have realized, knowing the president's precarious situation at the time. Nixon had no intention, or capability, of building a new community in the hemisphere or anyplace else at that juncture.

What was real, and possible, in the situation was the building of a new relationship with Panama. Kissinger knew that, and returned to it at the end of his remarks. "In the president's name," he said, "I hereby commit the United States to complete the negotiation successfully and as quickly as possible."

The audience stood once again and cheered the secretary's words. Kissinger squeezed Tack's shoulder in a friendly gesture. Then he patted the back of the veteran diplomat, Ellsworth Bunker, whose skill and persistence had made the principles come to fruition.

As they left the headquarters of the defunct National Assembly, with the applause and cheers still ringing in their ears, Torrijos and Kissinger had a chance to see the depth and venom of the extremist opposition to any deal with the United States. In a nearby parking area, demonstrating students were in the process of smashing up five cars. The general had given permission to the left-wing Federation of Revolutionary Students to demonstrate, but he had not sanctioned any violence. While National Guardsmen moved in on foot and motorcycles to push the students back and stop the incident, an embarrassed Torrijos hustled his American guest into the waiting limousine and they roared off to the accompaniment of squealing tires. Kissinger may not have even noticed the fracas, but Torrijos did. They sped through the streets, still crowded with curious and waving bystanders, to the general's sanctuary on Fiftieth Street.

Years later, as we talked in the same house, I asked Torrijos about his private session with Kissinger. He said there had been nothing eventful. "The first thing I did," he told me, "was to point out the nearest bathroom and I went to another. People who make schedules never seem to think of the basics." Then, as they sat together in the glass-enclosed porch, Kissinger asked Torrijos what he really thought of the eight principles. The Panamanian leader told his visitor they were just fine. "If you back up what you said in those eight points," he said, "there's no problem." Torrijos thought Kissinger was waiting for him to ask for something more—additional pledges, guarantees, or added assistance. "But there wasn't anything more to ask for," Torrijos said. "Many times not to say anything is one way of saying a lot." The general was content with the new design that had been approved that day. Kissinger was equally content, though he knew he would run into criticism at home from some elements in the Pentagon and from the conservative side of Congress.

The two men walked together across the street to the house of Gene Gerard, the head of the Panama branch of National City Bank of New York. The rest of the official party, American and Panamanian, had assembled there for a celebration. The air was filled with laughter and impromptu toasts, with clinking glasses and ribald humor. The escape valve had been opened by the new agreement signed that day, and the confined steam of tension and long frustration was leaking harmlessly into the soft Panamanian evening. In other parts of town, those who never wanted any agreement with the hated gringos were drinking as much, or more, but there was no joy in it. For them, the event was less like dangerous steam escaping than it was air leaking from a tire, leaving it flat. And in more exclusive parts of the city, in Altos de Golf and La Cresta, men of an earlier regime drank their scotch-and-soda and cursed an agreement that by rights should have been theirs.

On Fiftieth Street, the partying had gone on long enough for Kissinger to glance at his watch and look meaningfully at one of his aides. The signal passed quickly. Good-byes and *abrazos* were exchanged, and the American party walked out and boarded the waiting cars. Led by National Guard motorcycles, they raced down Fiftieth Street, through the ruins of Old Panama, up Fiftieth Anniversary Drive, to the highway that led to Tocumen airport. The National Guard escort led them directly to planeside and Kissinger and his party quickly climbed aboard for the trip back to Washington. Five hours later, at midnight, the pilot lowered the landing gear and flaps, and the big plane glided to a smooth landing at Andrews Air Force Base.

As he drove into the capital city that night, Bunker relived the amazing day in his mind. Then he thought: what's next? Where do we go from here? No answers came immediately to mind. He dozed off as the black sedan drove through quiet streets.

CHAPTER 10

New Envoy to the Isthmus

"Tell the truth."

—Sir Henry Wotton [when asked how to confound a diplomatic adversary], ca. 1612

THE green Braniff jetliner was flying south over Cuba. The captain's voice came over the aircraft intercom: "If you look out the windows on the right side, you'll see a bay on the south side of the island. It's called the Bay of Pigs and that's where the unsuccessful invasion of Cuba took place in 1961." It looked like any other jungle-fringed inlet on a tropical coastline. It was hard to imagine that, thirteen years before, that tiny body of water and the swampy land around it had been the scene of events that dominated the front pages of every newspaper in the world. I wondered if anyone aboard had been down there during the ill-fated invasion. If so, how different would be their reactions from those of the tourists who craned their necks to catch a glimpse of history from seven miles up.

My own thoughts were far away from the Bay of Pigs. Crossing the southern coast of Cuba meant we were about two hours from Panama, and that was where my mind was. It was April 8, 1974, and I was about to assume responsibility for running the U.S. Embassy and for representing our country in that small republic. No one had to tell me I was taking over at a critical time. One year before, during my visit to the isthmus, General Torrijos had explained that Panamanian patience was growing thin and that he had his hands full trying to keep the radical elements under control. They want guns, he had told me, so they can go into the Canal Zone and make their point. Allowing for the general's sense of drama, I knew from many sources that he was not exaggerating all that much. After ten years of fruitless treaty talks, the potential for violence was nearer the surface than most outsiders realized.

I knew, too, that Torrijos and his young government were under pressures. Panama's economy was less than sparkling. Wealthy Panamanians, still mistrustful of the inexperienced military man who ran the country, were more inclined to invest their capital in Florida or California, in Mexico or Venezuela, than in their homeland. Bankers were looking with increasingly harder eyes at applications for loans for economic development projects. Unemployment was high. Farmers, still the largest segment of the population, were having trouble borrowing money for seed and fertilizer. Meantime, prices for their crops were depressed. New graduates of the university and high schools were having great trouble finding jobs, especially the kinds of jobs they thought their hard-won educations merited. So there was deep discontent in many sectors—and all of them were demanding that the government help them out. It was a natural temptation for the government to try to divert that discontent away from itself and direct it elsewhere. The long-standing dispute with the United States over the treaty of 1903 and the "colony" that was the Canal Zone was an obvious target for that diversion. An ambassador, as the personification of government policy, could expect to find himself in the bull's-eye of that target.

At least the short-term auguries seemed favorable. The entrance of Ellsworth Bunker on the treaty-making scene had brought a marked change in atmosphere. Deliberately, patiently, he had set out to create a mood of relaxed informality and mutual confidence in U.S.-Panama negotiations. The Panamanians were responding in kind, and that was no mean feat. Until late 1973, Panama's foreign minister, Tony Tack, had been regarded by most Americans as a withdrawn, thin-skinned, intellectual superpatriot. He was all of those. Yet, in the glow of the "Bunker treatment," even Tony was beginning to relax, unwind, even laugh. Torrijos, a most informal and antiprotocol kind of leader, was delighted with what was even then being called the "Spirit of Contadora." It had already produced an agreement on principles, which was a major step toward a new treaty.

In addition to the principles, a milestone in the treaty-making process, the visit of Secretary Kissinger to Panama to affirm them had a salutary effect on Panamanian opinion. If the busiest statesman in the world could take time to visit Panama, they told themselves, the U.S. government must truly be serious about this endeavor. My arrival as ambassador reinforced that notion for some Panamanians because my job as Kissinger's assistant for Latin American affairs had by then been widely publicized in the local press. All in all, I concluded, the timing of our arrival in Panama was about as auspicious as could have been hoped. I could not know that that judgment, formed on the flight from Miami, would be tested sharply in less than two weeks.

As the "Fasten Seat Belts" sign flashed on and the big jet began its final approach to Panama's Tocumen airport, I glanced quickly through the arrival statement I had written, then stuffed it in my pocket. I grabbed my wife's hand and said: "Let's wish each other luck. I have a feeling we're going to need a lot of it." She smiled and said: "You're wearing your green necktie. That's all the luck you need." We were laughing as the wheels met the runway.

The plane taxied to the front of the airport entrance and parked. The first person aboard, behind the Braniff manager, was Ambassador José Manuel Watson, chief of protocol for the Panamanian Foreign Ministry. Watson welcomed us warmly to his country and led us out of the aircraft and down the mobile stairway. Waiting at the bottom of the steps were the principal officers of the U.S. Mission and their wives—Gordon Daniels, the tall, mustachioed officer who had been directing the embassy's business since the departure of my predecessor, Bob Sayre, a month before, and his wife, Helen; Mel Niswander, the public affairs officer, and his wife, Norma; Alex Firfer, director of the U.S. AID program, and his lively Amy; and an old friend, Yale Newman, the information officer, who was there to see that I did right by the press, and vice versa. We walked into the airport building, turned right into the Diplomatic Lounge, and there we confronted bedlam.

The lounge was jammed with people and half of them seemed to have cameras. Everyone was talking at once. A few members of the embassy staff were there and we shook hands, but I knew I would never remember their names because we barely heard them. Finally, my wife and I found ourselves seated on a couch at the end of the room facing the hot floodlights and the lenses of several score of movie and still cameras. I made my arrival statement. It was quite brief. After all, what can you say when you have only been in a country for twenty minutes. Moreover, I was there to carry out policy, not to make it. But there were two things I wanted to get across in that initial appearance and I wove them into the matrix of pleasantries. At one point, I said: "It is my conviction that Panamanians and Americans in the 1970s do not have the time—or the energy—or the resources—to waste on sterile arguments. As we look into the future, we and our other neighbors face many urgent problems of food and energy, problems of economic development, problems of developing and adapting new technology, problems of social progress and improving the quality of life for all men and women." I wanted to remind the Panamanians that the canal and its associated problems, however important, were less significant in the long run than other matters that faced us all. On the waterway and the revived effort to get a treaty, I suggested that any new arrangement "should permit us to get on with the business of operating and, if need be, defending an enterprise that is critically important to us both—and to the entire world. We need to get on with that business as friends, as partners, who badly need each other." I felt strongly that the United States and so small a country as Panama could in fact be real partners. It was the central theme of every major statement I made in my tenure on the isthmus.

When I finished, the reporters tried to press me with questions. I asked them to hold their fire and be patient. I explained that, technically, I could conduct no public business until I had presented my credentials to their president. They understood and backed off. We shook a few more hands, then walked through the main part of the terminal to our waiting cars. There I met for the first time Juan Lee, the ambassador's driver, who would be my constant companion and friend for the next four years. With him was José González, a handsome, wiry, tough ex-soldier who would ride shotgun and protect my wife and me from physical attack, and often just inconvenience, for the same period. José and another good bodyguard, Víctor Urrutia, worked alternate days to fend off any would-be assassins, or even pickpockets.

Following the rigid, if often archaic, rules of protocol, I rode into town with Chargé Gordon Daniels; Mili followed in the second car with Gordon's wife, Helen. During the 35-minute ride, first through countryside, then past the slums of Paraiso and San Miguelito, and on into Panama City itself, Gordon filled me in on the immediate agenda—plans for meeting the foreign minister and then the president, the scheduled receptions to meet the embassy family, Americans and Panamanians, some staffing problems, and the like. While listening to Gordon, I kept glancing out the window to see the people, the kinds of stores they had, the way they traveled, all the trivia that a reporter automatically looks for and absorbs almost unconsciously.

We turned right on Vía España past the graceful El Carmen Cathedral, then right again up the hill to La Cresta, one of the more exclusive residential areas in Panama City. Forty years before, some unknown but farsighted administrative officer had managed to acquire the most desirable piece of land in the neighborhood for the American Embassy. The residence was built just before World War II. It was a solid, well-constructed building that carried its years well. Its architect had been a traditionalist with an affection for the rectangle. As a result, the residence in Panama had little of the old-world charm of its counterparts in many capitals. Still, in its setting of tall trees and carefully tended shrubs, the two-story beige house looked strong and solid, as it was.

We drove through the open, wrought-iron gate, around the curving driveway, and pulled to a stop under the porte-cochere. We walked through the big oak doors at the entrance and into the spacious entry hall of the residence. I had sent a message earlier urging the officers of the embassy not to make the long trip to the airport but to meet us at the residence. They and their spouses were waiting, and gave us a warm and friendly welcome. We also were introduced to the Panamanian staff who kept the household running smoothly.

After toasts were drunk and the latest gossip exchanged, after we had brought each other up to date on the doings of common friends, the staff said good-bye and went to their homes. Mili and I had some chicken salad, good Panamanian coffee, and a variety of fresh tropical fruit. We walked up the long marble stairway to our private quarters to unpack and begin to settle into our new home. It was the end of a memorable day, and the beginning of a new life.

I recall that first week in Panama as a blur of activity. The first morning, I went to the venerable old building on Avenida Balboa and met with the heads of the several main sections of the embassy—Administrative, Consular, Economic, and Political—and with the chiefs of the related agencies that operate under the ambassador's direction—the U.S. Information Service (now USICA), the AID program, the CIA, and the Military Group. Collectively, they make up what is called the Country Team. We met every week during the years I was in Panama. I used that first session to get better acquainted with the principal officers with whom I would be working and on whom I would rely heavily in the months ahead. Second, I wanted to give them an indication of how I believed the embassy should function and to learn what they thought were our main problems. Third, it gave them a chance to size me up and begin to know their new boss.

My first impression was that I had luckily inherited a first-class team. There were no notably weak links, and there were some strong ones, indeed. I doubt, for example, that there have been many AID directors anywhere better than the late Alex Firfer. John Blacken, head of the Political Section, was and is one of the best Foreign Service officers I have known in more than thirty years of exposure to U.S. operations overseas. Blaine Tueller, chief of the Consular Section, a quiet, controlled man, solved more problems involving American citizens on a foreign shore in a month than most people encounter in a lifetime. There were some Bs as well as As, to be sure; but, thankfully, we had no Ds.

I mention the embassy staff and its composition primarily to underline that, while the large task of making a new treaty was proceeding, the business of the United States went on day by day in Panama, as it does in all our foreign posts. We had an obligation to keep Washington regularly informed of what was happening in Panama politically and economically. Our commercial interests had to be protected. Our military concerns and our relations with Panama's National Guard required constant attention. Our citizens who got into trouble, or who lost their passports and money, or who merely needed guidance on where to go and what to see, had to be taken care of. Senators and congressmen, whether on serious congressional business or merely junketeering, required special attention. Each week seemed to produce a new group of visitors—from the latest class at the National War College to a gathering of traveling bankers from New England to a tour group on a cruise ship. Many visitors seemed to think that the U.S. Embassy's main function was to serve as a kind of personal tourist service. We tried to accommodate them all cheerfully and to make their way easier. But it was a time-consuming process that used up a great deal of energy and taxpayers' money.

A few words about the U.S. Foreign Service. I have been part of or have observed closely countless groups of people in many places over the years—representatives of the press and the military services, businessmen, missionaries, criminals, tourists, diplomats, legislators. I have known my share of autocrats and revolutionaries, college professors and dropouts. I have known no group who collectively surpassed the men and women of the Foreign Service in intelligence, ability, dedication, or sense of national service. My impression is that the American people do not have the foggiest idea of what a resource they have working for them overseas. Few things rile me more than to read some ill-informed editorial writer or hear some pompous congressman referring to "the striped-pants boys" or the "cookie pushers" or, sneeringly, "the diplomats." I would dearly love to see those same supercilious commentators trying to get a drunken American out of jail at 3:00 A.M., or helping to feed the starving people in a remote province, or discovering what was happening politically in an alien society and forecasting what was likely to happen next. The job of the Foreign Service is to implement the foreign policy of the United States as laid down by the president, the secretary of state, and, increasingly, the Congress. Sometimes a policy is enlightened; sometimes it is terrible. Regardless, it is carried out as ordered by these anonymous and hard-working folk, from Tokyo to Tehran to Timbuktu. They merit considerable understanding and support, not the thoughtless brickbats so often tossed their way. For without them, we would have no policy at all.

Once I got to know the Foreign Service team with which I would be working, I moved out to cover the other important bases. I called on Foreign Minister Tack to give him a copy of my credentials and to request an audience with the president. That would formalize my representation of the United States in his country. I also called on the governor of the Canal Zone, Dave Parker, a major general in the U.S. Corps of Engineers. The tall, thin, balding, pipe-smoking, articulate man who headed both the Panama Canal Company and the Canal Zone government impressed me greatly. Obviously he knew the canal operation inside out. More than that, he was able to look at the political factors surrounding the U.S. presence in Panama with understanding and historical perspective. That, I was soon to learn, was rare indeed among those who looked out at Panama from the lofty heights of Ancon Hill. Dave and his charming wife, Betty, quickly became our friends, confidants, and golfing partners, but also staunch allies in the effort to move U.S.-Panama relations into the last quarter of the twentieth century. His was a particularly demanding assignment because he was dealing with a constituency, the employees of the Canal Company and the residents of the Zone, who were deeply entrenched and determined to hang on to all the privileges and prerogatives they had come to assume were the natural way of life. A lesser man than Parker would not have even tried to wean them from their heavy dependence on the past. And even his best efforts were never greatly successful. At least he tried to open the door to better understanding and, in the doing, nudged his fellow Americans several steps forward into the real if hard world.

I devoted considerable time in those early days getting to know the third branch of the official U.S. family in Panama, the commanders and principal officers of the military services. Capably led by army Gen. William B. Rosson, the U.S. Southern Command was responsible for protecting the Panama Canal and for dealing with the armed services of all the countries in the Western Hemisphere. In this latter role, SOUTHCOM had an important diplomatic as well as military function since in many Latin American countries the leaders of governments and of national armed forces were one and the same. Rosson and his component commanders— Maj. Gen. Arthur Salisbury of the air force; Maj. Gen. George Mabry, commander of army forces; and Rear Adm. Robert Blount, who led the small navy detachment—spent a considerable amount of time on the road visiting with their service counterparts throughout the hemisphere. I always thought that this aspect of their jobs was badly underestimated in Washington, especially in the State Department, and that the contacts they had could have been used to far greater advantage in promoting U.S. interests. As I got to know them, I developed a high regard for Rosson and his fellow commanders, not merely because of their proven capacity in the martial arts but because, with few exceptions, they had a good sense of history and of international politics. To be sure, an officer rarely reaches two-star rank and above in any of the services without an acute understanding of politics.

The beginning of my official tour of duty in Panama came on April 17, 1974, nine days after our arrival. That morning I presented my credentials as ambassador to President Lakas. I was delighted that the wheels of protocol were moving so quickly. I remembered vividly having to placate many irate Latin American ambassadors who arrived in Washington only to cool their heels for weeks, sometimes months, before an appointment could be arranged for them at the White House.

An ambassador's presentation of his letter of credence to the head of the host government is the act by which he becomes an ambassador in fact. Until that moment, he cannot perform any official action, cannot sign any note or letter to the local government, nor have any official contact with other diplomats. Until then, he exists only as a nominee or designate. To many, the presentation of credentials must seem an archaic ceremony from an earlier, perhaps more graceful, time when diplomats represented their sovereigns in the courts of other sovereigns. In the last half of the twentieth century, it may appear to be a rather meaningless procedure. After all, an ambassador arriving in Washington presents his credentials to the president, then rarely if ever sees him again—unless his own head of state pays an official visit. We may yet reach the point, God forbid, when a newly arrived envoy inserts an appropriately stamped piece of plastic into a designated machine and thereupon joins the list of approved diplomats on a computer printout. I hope that respecters of tradition will be able to fend off indefinitely that kind of ultimate triumph of the utilitarians. But who knows? Especially in a time when a handful of primitives in the once proud kingdom of Persia can savage all the norms of civilized behavior, violate every canon of diplomatic immunity—and be met with little more than a whimper from the governments of once proud nations.

On the morning of April 17, I dressed in the uniform designated for such ceremonies—a dark business suit, white shirt, gray cravat. (In many capitals, the approved costume includes striped pants and morning coat—hence the overworked cliché about "the striped-pants set.") At 9:30 A.M., an official car of the Foreign Ministry drove up to the residence with its sole passenger, Ambassador Watson, the chief of protocol. I joined him and we drove out the gate, down the hill of La Cresta, and through the crowded streets of the city. Behind us were cars carrying the principal officers of the U.S. Embassy; ahead was a motorcycle escort carving a path through the traffic with wailing sirens. We pulled to a stop in front of the *presidencia*. Out of the car, up the steps, through an honor guard standing at stiff attention, we walked around the ambling herons in the courtyard, then up the marble stairway to the second floor. We stopped outside the reception hall, the Salon de Amarillo, so the embassy contingent could take their places in line. Then we walked into the salon, turned left, and stopped.

At the far end of the room stood President Lakas. He was dressed as I was—dark suit, white shirt, gray tie—but across his chest was the flaming red sash of presidential office. To his left was Vice President Arturo Sucre, and to his right, acting Foreign Minister Carlos Ozores. Following the dictates of protocol, I bowed to the president, then walked down the length of the hall, stopped in front of him, and bowed again. Then I handed him the official documents that I had brought from Washington. "Mr. President," I said, "I have the honor to present to you my official credentials as ambassador of the United States of America. I look forward to working closely with you and the representatives of your government in sustaining and improving close relations between our two governments."

Lakas accepted the documents (one was the official recall of my predecessor; the other a letter from President Nixon designating me as ambassador with his "full trust and confidence"). He smiled broadly and replied: "Mr. Ambassador, I accept these credentials and welcome you as ambassador of the United States to the Republic of Panama." He put out his huge hand and I shook it warmly. Lakas motioned me to a chair next to his large, ornate presidential chair, its high back crowned by the coat of arms of Panama.

When we were seated, he leaned over and said: "We used to serve champagne at these occasions, but I decided that coffee was more Panamanian. I hope you don't mind." "Mr. President," I replied, "I don't really like champagne, especially at this hour. Coffee is much better." So began a relationship and a friendship that would enable our two countries to weather more storms than I could possibly have imagined on that April morning. The first test came within twenty-four hours.

The day after I had presented credentials, I was in the Canal Zone visiting with the various staff chiefs of the Southern Command. Shortly after noon, a call came to the embassy from the State Department asking if we knew anything about an American tuna boat called *Raffaello* that had been seized by the Panamanians. The department had received an urgent call to that effect from the Tuna Boat Association in California. Chargé Daniels told the officer on the Panama Desk we would look into it immediately. Then he called me at SOUTHCOM headquarters and passed on the Department's inquiry. I told Daniels to call Col. Tom Austin, head of our Military Group, and ask him to find out what he could from his police contacts. I suggested Daniels get Alex Firfer, chief of the AID Mission, to make inquiries through people in the fishing industry. Finally, he should reach Blaine Tueller, chief of our Consular Section, the normal office any American in trouble with the local authorities would call. If anyone on a U.S. boat had been arrested, Blaine could find out in a hurry through officials at the police station. "Get the wheels moving," I said, "and I'll be back as soon as possible." I canceled the remainder of my appointments and rode back to the embassy.

By the time I was back at my office on Avenida Balboa, the staff had pieced together most of the picture. The *Raffaello* had been fishing for tuna well within Panama's declared 200-mile limit, at approximately 97 miles, to be exact. It had come into port to seek medical care for one of the sailors who had taken ill (appendicitis, as I recall). Once inshore, the tuna boat had been taken into custody by a patrol craft of the Panamanian National Guard. The Guard had been watching the *Raffaello* and other tuna boats and knew they were fishing inside Panama's territorial waters. The sick sailor was sent to the hospital; the captain was arrested, then released on his own recognizance; the boat was sequestered. When we reached the captain, he was comfortably ensconced in a local hotel. His first thought had not been to contact the U.S. Embassy but to call his company in San

Diego. The skipper's interest was in getting his ship back. His company's interest was in protecting the catch of tuna in the hold. They both automatically assumed that the best way to protect their interests was to turn to Washington rather than trying to deal sensibly with local authorities. (I have always found it strange that some of the most vocal defenders of "free enterprise" and laissez faire economy are the first to turn to the federal authorities when they run into trouble, at home or abroad.) *

My interest in this affair was, first, to assure that the captain and any Americans in his crew were treated fairly and in accordance with the law. Second, I wanted to make sure that the boat and its valuable cargo were not the objects of unreasonable seizure. Finally, I wanted to settle the entire affair as quickly and as amicably as possible. I knew full well that an incident of that kind, if allowed to drag on in time, could easily become a cause célèbre and lead to a souring of relations between the two countries. Enemies of a new treaty and of improved relations between the United States and Panama were certain to seize on that kind of issue and blow it all out of proportion. At a time when it was national policy to create improved understanding, that outcome was the last thing we needed.

With all of that in mind, I called President Lakas and asked if I could see him. His cordial invitation only the day before to "come see me if there are any serious problems" was fresh in my mind. He generously agreed to see me immediately, so I drove straight to the *presidencia*. A security guard met me and led me through the marble-floored patio and down a narrow corridor to a small elevator.[†] It took us to the third floor where President Lakas did most of his work. The massive chief executive, wearing a white *guayabera*, greeted me warmly, squashing my hand in his big fist. He sat in his usual chair at the head of the conference table that was the central feature of his working quarters. His large collection of phones, radios, CBs, and other paraphernalia was within easy reach. He motioned me to sit at his right facing the full-length glass windows that look out over Panama Bay.

"What's up, Mr. Ambassador?" he asked. I told him I was there about the *Raffaello*. He had heard about it, of course, but knew few details. "Let

---

*The central issue here was the 200-mile limit on territorial waters claimed by Panama and many other countries. The U.S. Congress and American fishing interests found that limit unreasonable and unacceptable. Later, when the United States expanded its own territorial waters, the same U.S. Congress and the same fishing companies were among the first to demand strict enforcement against "poachers" from Japan, Norway, the Soviet Union, and other maritime nations. As I have said, much in politics depends on whose ox is being gored, or whose waters are being fished.

†The elevator was installed in 1934 by the United States in preparation for the visit of President Franklin Roosevelt. It enabled the crippled president to get to and from meetings and receptions with his host, President Harmodio Arias.

me check," he said, grabbing the red phone, his direct line to National Guard headquarters. He told the officer at the other end what he wanted to know, then listened carefully. He made a few noncommittal grunts, and with a final "correcto" he hung up. He told me the evidence seemed clear that the *Raffaello* had been fishing well within Panamanian waters. It was only the latest in a long series of such incursions. No self-respecting country, he explained, could just sit by and let this kind of thing go on and on without enforcing its own laws. They had to fine the boat and they were going to confiscate the catch. Otherwise, he said, these large fishing boats from overseas were going to come in closer and closer, strip the waters of valuable seafood, and go home and sell it—leaving not one penny behind for the people whose waters these were.

I could have gone into a long diplomatic song-and-dance about the 200-mile limit and its disputed validity in the eyes of international law. I could have talked at length about the difference between migratory species like tuna and the more common forms of seafood like the red snapper and mackerel and shrimp that abound in Panama's waters. I considered, and rejected, the idea of raising the International Tuna Convention. I realized instinctively that I was dealing with a practical and straightforward man, one who was more interested in solutions than in chewing bones of controversy. As president, he was suddenly faced with a problem that had been thrown his way by an eager patrol boat crew with no advance knowledge or planning.

Instead of all the technical and legalistic arguments that could have been dredged up, I asked this practical man a practical question: "What are you going to do with all those fish, Mr. President?" He looked surprised. "Well, I guess we'll give them to the poor who don't have enough to eat," he said. "Mr. President," I said, "if you and I go out fishing and catch a mess of mackerel, it's easy enough to give away what we don't need to folks who do need them and who'll eat them in hours. But here we're talking about tons, many tons, of fish. There's no machinery for unloading them; no facilities for storing them; no way to keep them refrigerated. Before they could get to families that need them, they would be rotting and the smell would cover half of downtown Panama. You'd be handing out sickness, not good food." He looked at me hard, then looked out the window. He turned back and said: "You're probably right. What can we do?" Suddenly, we were no longer president and ambassador but simply two men staring at a problem and looking for an answer that would satisfy both countries' interests.

I explained that the tuna boat incident had the potential for disrupting other, more important business. We were in the middle of negotiating a new treaty and building a relationship based on mutual trust and cooperation. Those who do not want that kind of relationship, I argued, will surely use this affair to try to prove that Panama is out to harass the United States, or that the United States disregards Panamanian rights. The longer it drags on, I said, the more it will be blown out of proportion. Lakas agreed. Only then, when we were well on the way to working out a solution, did I remind the president that there were elements in U.S. law that could affect anything we did. One was a provision in the U.S. Foreign Military Sales Act that prohibited any sales or credits of a military nature to any country for one year if that country seized or fined a U.S. vessel for fishing outside a 12-mile limit. Another was a clause in the Fisherman's Protective Act. It provided that U.S. fishing boat owners who paid a fine to a foreign government for fishing in territorial waters outside the 12-mile limit would be reimbursed by the U.S. Treasury. The U.S. government then had to deduct the amount of the fine from any military or economic aid provided the country in question. In both laws, however, there was provision for a waiver of any penalty if the president found that it was "important to the security of the United States" (under the Military Sales Act) or was "in the national interest" (under the Fisherman's Protective Act). In the first law, a waiver was also authorized if the United States received "reasonable assurances from the country involved that future violations will not occur."*

Lakas understood perfectly the implications of what I had said. We agreed that creating a major incident would serve no useful purpose, for them or for us. At the same time, national pride was involved and a fine would have to be imposed. But the catch (worth about $300,000) would not be confiscated. Lakas also assured me that seizure of the *Raffaello* had not been planned in advance, nor was it the beginning of a new, stricter policy of enforcement on Panama's part. I thanked the president for his time and his assurances and drove back to the embassy to inform Washington.

With my report in hand, the State Department contacted the *Raffaello*'s owners in San Diego. They were happy to get off so lightly and readily agreed to pay the fine. They knew, of course, that they would be compensated in full by the U.S. Treasury. The next day, the agent for the fishing company paid the fine, the captain was released from custody in a downtown hotel, and the *Raffaello* sailed for home in the late afternoon. What could have been a source of major friction, if allowed to continue, had been quickly excised. That, at least, was the judgment in Washington

---

*These laws are good examples of the way special interests get the Congress to approve legislation that protects them regardless of the overall effect on U.S. policy or our relations with other nations. The tuna companies could refuse to buy fishing licenses knowing that if their boats were seized or they were fined by the authorities in Peru or Ecuador or Panama, or any other country, they would be reimbursed by the U.S. taxpayer. What their actions did to American relations with those countries was of little or no concern to them.

where calls were already coming in from Capitol Hill about "this tuna boat those people have grabbed." Two days later, I received a thoughtful cable from the department which began: "The Department wishes to commend the Ambassador for his successful efforts in obtaining release of the *Raffaello* and preventing confiscation of its catch. These efforts reduced the magnitude of a problem the repercussions of which could have affected adversely the state of our bilateral and negotiating relationships with Panama."

I have described the *Raffaello* affair in some detail because it was the first real crisis I faced in my new post and therefore lives vividly in my memory. But more to the point, it is a reminder that from 1974 until 1978, incidents of this kind kept cropping up with painful regularity. Many or most of them, if misunderstood or mishandled by any of the parties concerned, could easily have ended the negotiation of a new treaty. In some cases, as we shall see, that was not only a possibility but undoubtedly the intention of some of the participants in those many incidents. As I think back on the whole process, it seems something close to miraculous that the treaty-making enterprise did not founder on at least one of those reefs that emerged suddenly in our path. There were, to be sure, some very close calls.

The *Raffaello* incident illustrates, as well, the deliberate division of labor we had adopted in regard to the Panama problem. Before I left for the isthmus, Ambassador Bunker and I had discussed how we would proceed. He asked me if I wished to take an active role in the negotiations, a course he told me he would welcome. I told him I felt the two functions should be kept separate, at least in the short term. His assignment was to work out a new treaty relationship. Mine was to keep U.S.-Panama relations on an even keel and, insofar as possible, to help sustain an atmosphere in which the negotiations could proceed smoothly. I felt certain that was going to require all the time, energy, and imagination I could muster. Frankly, I was much more pessimistic than some of my colleagues in the State Department in my estimate of the time that would likely be needed to accomplish a new treaty. And I knew that, as time passed, tempers would shorten and patience would wear thin. Maintaining a mood of trust and confidence was going to demand increasing effort on our part to overcome the inevitable frustrations on both sides.

At the same time, I had to be fully informed of what was happening at the negotiating table. Bunker and I both realized that, when he was away from Panama, I would be dealing with the Panamanians on treaty matters, answering their questions, clarifying our proposals, trying to bridge the gap between their ideas and ours. There emerged from this understanding a very smooth and effective working partnership. He and his deputies kept me fully briefed on every development on the treaty-making front. I regularly supplied them with background and information on Panamanian attitudes, sensitivities, likely reactions. It worked exceedingly well, though anyone who has watched at first hand the relations between resident ambassadors and special envoys knows how rare that is. All too often, conflicting personalities and incompatible temperaments interfere with the larger business at hand. Between two old friends engaged in the search for an agreement in Panama, it was never a problem. We had more important things to occupy us.

CHAPTER 11

Treaty Making on a Tropic Isle

> "'The question is,' said Alice, 'whether you can make words
> mean so many different things.' 'The question is,' said
> Humpty Dumpty, 'which is to be master—that's all.'"
>
> —Lewis Carroll, *Through the Looking-Glass*

CONTADORA is a small gem of an island located in the Pacific south-east of Panama City. From the air, it looks something like a green elephant rolling on its side in a deep-blue sea. The gash across its midsection is a small airstrip. The Hotel Contadora and its splendid beach are on a cove formed by the elephant's trunk and forelegs. Several times a day, the reliable Otters of the Perlas Airline fly to and from the mainland with their cargo of tourists from Frankfurt and Milan and London. Followers of Izaac Walton are drawn by one of the richest fishing grounds in the world in pursuit of marlin and sailfish and the elusive dorado. Many wealthy Panamanians have homes there and retreat to the island for weekends and holidays.

All in all, an unlikely setting for the exercise of modern diplomacy. Yet it was on the island of Contadora—which took its name from its "counting-house" background in the sixteenth century when its pearls went into the treasury of Spanish kings—that much of the negotiating of the Panama Canal treaties took place. When the treaty talks moved into their new phase in 1973, Gen. Omar Torrijos picked Contadora as an ideal place to hold them. He was thoroughly disillusioned by the meager results of traditional approaches. He reasoned that if the talks could be more relaxed, more informal, they might move faster. If his representatives and the Americans were working together away from the glare of publicity and media pressures, they might avoid some of the rigidities of the past. He realized that positions taken publicly were vastly more difficult to alter or walk away from than those advanced in private across a coffee table or during a walk along the beach.

Torrijos' notion fitted perfectly with the ideas Ellsworth Bunker brought to the business of making treaties. The Vermonter's long experience working with peoples as different as Italians and Indians, his success in negotiating the West Irian agreement with Indonesia, his many years in Saigon dealing with the proud and sensitive Nguyen Van Thieu, all had convinced him that privacy is better, and mutual trust is essential, in diplomacy. He liked to compare his approach with that used in the Vietnam peace talks in Paris: "they turned out to be just propaganda exercises until the secret discussions could be arranged."

The morning after Secretary Kissinger's whirlwind passage through Panama City, Bunker's deputy, Morey Bell, and lawyer Mike Kozak had flown back to the island. The Panamanian deputy negotiator, Ambassador González-Revilla, was to meet them on Contadora to lay the groundwork for the next phase. Bell and Kozak waited through the day, but no Panamanians appeared. They were still celebrating the Kissinger visit and apparently forgot the two Americans waiting on the island. Late the following morning, a National Guard plane landed on Contadora with General Torrijos, Ambassador González-Revilla, and a few friends. Reportedly all hands, except the pilot, were in "a rather poor state." Action had temporarily succumbed to revelry. Only on the afternoon of the third day did the deputy negotiators finally get together—on the veranda of the Zeimetz house—to begin looking at the problems that faced them in the wake of the agreement on principles.

Panama's leisurely approach to the new Contadora meetings was the result, in part, of an amazing misapprehension. The reason Kissinger had been so warmly welcomed, and the cause of the ensuing three-day festival, was the mistaken notion that the Tack-Kissinger Principles represented "nine-tenths of a treaty." On the afternoon of February 10, the Panamanians began to discover how wrong they were.

Now that the principles have been worked out, Bell began, we have to decide the main issues that must be negotiated. González-Revilla said the main issues had been settled; the details should not be too hard to agree on and write up. Bell insisted it was much more complicated than Nico seemed to think. It was true, he said, that Principle Number One ("The treaty of 1903 and its amendments will be abrogated by the conclusion of an entirely new interoceanic canal treaty") needed no elaboration. But each of the other seven principles required agreements by the two parties; their terms would have to be defined. González-Revilla had by then a sinking feeling inside. The euphoria of the previous days was fading fast.

Bell went on. Look at the second principle, he said. It required an end to perpetuity ("The new treaty concerning the lock canal shall have a fixed termination date"). But what will that termination date be? Panama wants a short duration, he said; but the U.S. side is under instructions to demand a much longer time.* González-Revilla, Minister Tack, General Torrijos, and their colleagues all assumed that when Kissinger accepted the principle of a fixed termination date he was, at the same time, acceding to Panama's chosen date. There was no basis for that blithe assumption, as Bell's exposition made clear.

The painful recital continued. Bell went through the remaining principles. He noted pointedly that all but one contained a phrase "in accordance with terms specified in the treaty" or something similar. In other words, the Tack-Kissinger Principles were fine, as principles, but each dealt with issues of importance on which there was as yet no common understanding, to say nothing of agreement. González-Revilla listened in stunned amazement. As the truth sank in, he realized that the wild excitement he and his fellow countrymen had felt as a result of the Kissinger visit had been a dream. Even several years later, looking back on this and a few subsequent meetings on Contadora, González-Revilla would describe them as "one of the worst moments in the history of Panama."

"We were sure, and everybody here was convinced, that the treaty was a matter of sitting down and writing it down," he said, "because we had agreement in principle. It was incredible how you saw the eight principles and how we saw them."

Allowing for the ambassador's hyperbole, it was nevertheless a time of testing for Panamanian optimism. The next day, González-Revilla tried to nudge things back on course (at least on what the Panamanians *thought* was the course). He delivered a Torrijos message obviously intended for the U.S. secretary of state. Kissinger's visit, the general wrote, had "restored my faith in the intent of the United States to modernize its relationship with Panama promptly and equitably." Torrijos said he felt that way even though Kissinger had "thrown a few little stones at Panama" in his signing ceremony talk. He had, for example, emphasized "the vital interests of the United States" but had made no mention of a termination date for a new treaty. "Panama acknowledges receipt of the little stones," Torrijos wrote, "and states that it caught them with understanding." It was an obvious attempt to revive the good atmosphere that attended the secretary's visit. It was also intended to move the U.S. side away from the hard line it seemed to be taking in the deputies' conversations.

The Torrijos gambit failed. The Panamanians were trying to substitute a "good atmosphere" for the down-to-earth business of treaty negotiation. Bell's approach was rigid not because it was his nature or his wish, quite

---

*The Bunker team was still operating under presidential orders to get a treaty that would last no less than fifty years—with an additional thirty to fifty years if a sea-level canal were dug or if the existing canal were expanded. Panama had been insisting on a treaty that lasted until the end of the century at most.

the contrary. But the U.S. deputy was functioning within narrow parameters. Bunker and his team still were working from guidelines prepared by the Nixon-Kissinger White House three years earlier. Moreover, once the Tack-Kissinger Principles were publicized, the latent opposition to *any* treaty with Panama began to mobilize its forces.

Typical of the opponents was Congressman John Murphy of New York. A member of the Panama Canal Subcommittee, Murphy was a West Point graduate and an intimate friend of Nicaraguan dictator Anastasio Somoza. The day after Kissinger affirmed the treaty principles, Murphy made an impassioned speech in the House. The United States, he insisted, should not even consider turning over a vital waterway to "an unstable government" that he claimed "might be overthrown tomorrow."* He alleged there were serious plots to unseat Torrijos. Murphy even advanced the preposterous theory that Torrijos had offered the presidency to Arnulfo Arias, the man he had ousted as president six years before. I later learned that Torrijos knew about the inept coup planning and that he had reason to believe Murphy's friend Somoza was one of the moving forces behind it.

The same day Murphy made his bizarre allegations in the House, a like-minded member of the Senate was making a similar appeal. Republican Sen. Strom Thurmond of South Carolina bitterly opposed any change on the Panama scene. Referring to the Tack-Kissinger Principles, Thurmond told his colleagues: "There is nothing of consequence left to negotiate once we surrender our rights, even if only in principle." He claimed that the Tack-Kissinger agreement was "a pseudotreaty which will cause grave harm to United States interests, not only in Latin America but also in the world."

Bell, sitting on Contadora and trying to bring the Panamanians to a realistic view of treaty problems, was aware of the noisome opposition. The Murphy-Thurmond barrage had occupied three columns in the *New York Times* the day before his first meeting with González-Revilla. But acting on instructions from Ambassador Bunker, the deputy negotiator went ahead with what later came to be known as the "defining the issues" process. Once the initial shock wore off, Ambassador González-Revilla began to appreciate that there were indeed problems that had to be faced and settled if there ever was going to be a treaty. Those early Contadora talks were an exercise in education and clarification rather than in serious treaty making. They were, nonetheless, essential because at that point neither the Panamanians nor the Americans had crossed the psychological or political thresholds that would make a new treaty possible.

---

*Seven years later, General Torrijos was still a potent figure in Panamanian politics while Congressman Murphy had been ousted from his seat by the voters of Staten Island following allegations of bribe-taking in the Abscam scandal.

At that juncture, we began getting hints from knowledgeable sources of friction inside the Panamanian camp. The contending factions were led by the chief negotiator, Foreign Minister Tack, and his deputy, González-Revilla. Tack's supporters were older members of the foreign policy establishment and politicians, lawyers, and academics. Nico's backers were young businessmen, technocrats, and relatives from upper-crust families who had been attracted to the Torrijos "revolution." The younger diplomat had one ace of trumps, his close association with the general.

The rivalry stemmed more from personality than from policy. Tack was twelve years Nico's senior. He had been a delegate to the OAS when his deputy was just finishing high school. Moreover, Tack had no voice in selecting González-Revilla for the Washington assignment, the most prestigious post in the entire Panamanian foreign service. The foreign minister undoubtedly resented the many nights and weekends that Nico spent in the company of Torrijos and his closest cronies partying and discussing Panamanian politics. Among the Tack clique, González-Revilla was regarded as immature, flamboyant, inexperienced.

On the other hand, Nico saw himself as a future leader of his country. Like most Panamanians of the privileged class, he grew up thinking the presidency might well be within his grasp. He saw the ambassadorship as a major advance toward that goal. Tack and the traditionalists around him were an obstacle to that ambition. After he arrived in Washington as ambassador, Nico encountered endless delays and obstruction whenever he suggested any changes in personnel, organization, or budgeting. Somehow his letters and telegrams on embassy affairs disappeared in the bottomless in-baskets of the Foreign Ministry. He blamed Tack and those around him for making things more difficult.

The talks between Morey Bell and Nico helped bring the Panamanian feud to a head. When what looked like a hard U.S. line emerged from the Contadora conversations, González-Revilla was criticized for failing to oppose it more vigorously. It was the same tactic Foreign Ministry officials had used against the Panamanian negotiators in Washington in 1971–72. González-Revilla explained, quite correctly, that Bell and Kozak were not presenting negotiating positions; rather they were explaining the history and past controversies that surrounded key treaty issues. They were also urging the Panamanian side to understand why certain matters were particularly sensitive in Washington, especially in the Pentagon and Congress. With those arguments and, more important, with Torrijos' support, the young ambassador was able to fend off, though not stop, the sniping of his critics.

The deputies' talks on Contadora continued for a week. González-Revilla and Bell resumed their work twelve days later in Washington. By late March, they decided another Contadora round was in order. It was part of an evolving pattern—we meet in our house, then we meet in your house. Part of the purpose was to give the Panamanian people regular evidence—in the form of periodic visits by the negotiators—that there was progress on the treaty front. It was an old technique. If official representatives are meeting, it is assumed something must be happening. Often, that is totally illusory.

That does not mean the meetings between the deputy negotiators served no purpose. At the least, they provided an invaluable educational base for what lay ahead. Neither Nico nor Morey had been in the 1971–72 negotiations. Mike Kozak, who was Bell's right hand through those months, had witnessed the earlier effort at treaty making and knew precisely what the positions had been. He was also able to explain legal fine points which politically oriented negotiators might overlook or consider trivial.

When, for example, talks turned to Principle Number Three ("Termination of United States jurisdiction over Panamanian territory shall take place promptly in accordance with terms specified in the treaty"), both sides could argue long into the night about what "promptly" meant. But Kozak raised a more basic question. What, he asked Morey and Nico, do you mean by "jurisdiction." Does it mean *all* police and legal authority? Or, does it mean all such authority unrelated to the canal and its operations? He recalled the interminable haggling in 1971 about that very question. He pointed out that many Americans, particularly those connected with canal operations, felt that the right to operate the waterway meant, necessarily, the right to protect it, and to arrest and punish any who tried to endanger canal installations. Where did legal jurisdiction end and effective canal operation begin? It was a kind of Socratic dialogue in which Kozak's questions forced Bell and González-Revilla to think more deeply about all the issues inherent in the principles. Their answers led on to new, more complicated questions—and to more re-thinking.

Bell and Kozak flew to Panama on March 25, for the third round of deputies' talk. John Blacken, chief of our Political Section, met the visitors at the airport and took them to his home. He had a dinner for the principal officers of the embassy so that Bell could update them on the talks. Step Two of the arrangement was for Nico to go to Blacken's house at about 10:00 P.M. so the two deputies could plan their work for the week ahead. That brought the first glitch in the program. Nico did not show up. The Americans went to bed, puzzled but not thinking much about the breach of etiquette. Panamanians in the Torrijos regime were not notorious followers of Emily Post.

The next morning, Bell and Kozak flew to Contadora, went to the Zeimetz house, and began thinking about the coming sessions. Kozak had a new project that occupied his time. In addition to being an expert auto mechanic, he was also a ham radio operator. Having suffered the pain of trying to use the island's tenuous telephone link at the airport office, Mike decided a radio would help solve the communications problem. That first day, he spent hours setting up the small transmitter he had brought, stringing aerial, and testing his rig. He finally got it operating tolerably well. In the months and years ahead, Kozak's radio would be an invaluable connection to the outside—especially to the embassy in Panama City and, through phone patches, to almost any part of the world.*

Tuesday passed, and still no Nico. Wednesday brought nothing more— no Panamanians, no message. By that time, Bell was thoroughly puzzled and irritated. He sent a message to Ambassador Bunker explaining what was happening, or rather *not* happening, and asking authority to tell the Panamanians that unless the talks resumed, full-scale negotiations could not be expected soon. Bunker approved. We passed the word in strong terms to an officer of the *guardia* who was close to Torrijos, and to another official who was an intimate of President Lakas. By the next afternoon, word came back that someone from the Panamanian side would appear the following day.

On Friday, both Tack and González-Revilla appeared at the Zeimetz house. Sources in the Panamanian camp later explained what had happened. Tack, as minister and chief negotiator, believed he should be dealing only with his counterpart, Ambassador Bunker. But the rivalry between him and Nico was then so deep that he did not want the young ambassador contacting the Americans alone. It was a standoff and left Bell and Kozak alone on Contadora twiddling their thumbs. Only the threat of a possible breakdown in the talks ended the impasse, but the exchanges over those next few days were notably unrelaxed.

One thing that finally helped induce the Panamanians to put aside internal dissension was a news item from Washington. Senator Thurmond planned to introduce a resolution opposing any relinquishment of sovereignty over the Canal Zone. The Thurmond resolution, written jointly with Democrat Sen. John McClellan of Arkansas (whose daughter worked in the Canal Zone), had thirty-two co-sponsors, and eventually thirty-five, enough to block any treaty. It was a strong rejection of the principles approved by Secretary Kissinger the previous month. To be sure, some senators who signed the Thurmond initiative would later repudiate their action, saying they had "not read it very carefully" or that they "just wanted to do a favor for old Strom." Nonetheless, when the so-called Thurmond

---

*Some Panamanians jumped to the conclusion that a lawyer working for the State Department who was also a radio technician had to be an undercover agent of the CIA. It took some time to dispel that erroneous notion.

Resolution went to the Senate floor on March 29, it shook treaty partisans badly both in Washington and in Panama City.

On the weekend, Bunker arrived and went immediately to the island. His presence, plus his genial manner and unfailing courtesy with the Panamanians, helped greatly to smooth things over. He had several long sessions with Tack, and they agreed that the work of the deputies had been extremely helpful—but that it had gone about as far as it usefully could. Bell and González-Revilla had by that time accumulated a detailed list of all of the issues, large and small, that would have to be dealt with in a treaty. It was time, the chief negotiators agreed, to move from lists and mutual education to the major problems confronting them. By the time Bunker and Bell left for Washington, tensions within the Panamanian camp seemed to have eased.

The foreign minister's mood was further improved when he went to Washington two weeks later for a gathering of top diplomats of the hemisphere. Ambassador Bunker saw to it that his Panamanian counterpart received more than the normal courtesies. A call on the president was out of the question because Nixon was in the midst of his fight for survival. But on April 15, Bunker took Tack to call on Vice President Gerald Ford. The session in the vice-president's office in the Old Executive Office Building was exceedingly cordial. Ford had not followed the talks with Panama in detail, but he supported the basic goal: a closer and more modern relationship. When a question was raised about the canal's vulnerability to outside interference, Tack told Ford: "I believe that for the United States the best security for the canal is to have friends on both sides of it." The vice-president agreed heartily. "It would be a very, very unstable condition from our point of view," he said, "if things were otherwise."

Ford realized better than most that a new treaty would have rough sledding among his old colleagues in the Congress, and he wanted to be sure Panama's foreign minister understood that. As they were parting, Ford told Tack: "Let me be clear, Mr. Minister. I believe the majority of our people basically want a solution to this problem. However, they of course do not know all of the details, and many of those details are extremely difficult. So the task ahead is going to be arduous." Shaking the vice-president's hand, Tack told him that he realized that was true. He hoped that Ford understood it was going to be difficult in Panama as well.

Two days later, Tack and the other foreign ministers from the hemisphere began a series of meetings with Kissinger. It was a "love feast" similar to the sessions in Tlatelolco two months earlier. No solutions were found to the troublesome questions of trade and market access and exchanges of technology that dominated the agenda. But the atmosphere was good; Kissinger was his inimitable, ironic self; and the visitors were delighted. To be sure, the more cynical among them wondered when the "dialogue" would begin to produce answers to the crushing problems their countries faced. Only on the question of Panama was there agreement, but that did not make the hearts of diplomats from Argentina or Brazil or Mexico beat noticeably faster.

A few days after the foreign ministers' conclave, Tack and Bunker met in the latter's office in the State Department. By that time, Tack's somewhat bruised ego had been revived wonderfully by the elixir of Bunker's solicitude and by association with his fellow ministers. When Bunker suggested that the preparatory work already begun on Contadora should continue, Tack readily agreed. He also accepted Bunker's recommendation that the task be carried out by the deputy negotiators. Bunker and Tack agreed to get together in Panama at the end of May to review what their deputies had done and to plan the next steps.

With accord in hand, the tall Vermonter and his stocky, dark-haired fellow negotiator walked down the long seventh-floor corridor at State for the pièce de résistance on Bunker's menu for Tack—a private meeting with Kissinger. It was not a long visit, only about twenty-five minutes, but it was friendly and laced with humor. Kissinger reassured Tack that achievement of a workable and just treaty was an important goal of U.S. policy. He joked that perhaps one reason for the slow progress was that Bunker had fallen in love with the island of Contadora and did not want things to move any faster. Tack left the large paneled office laughing and in excellent spirits.

After talking with Bunker, Tack understood better what the real purpose of the Bell–González-Revilla sessions was. More important, his sojourn in Washington reinforced in Tack's mind the awareness that he was, in Washington's eyes, the minister, the chief negotiator, the representative of central authority in Panama without whom a treaty could not be developed. With that assurance, Tack flew back to Panama in a relaxed and amiable mood.

But if pressures within the Panamanian camp were subsiding, they were building on the American side. Despite his good relations with top-ranking men in the armed forces, Ambassador Bunker was having constant problems with the Pentagon as an institution. When the State Department sent a proposal on any canal-related issue to Defense, it was farmed out to a dozen offices that had an interest. Then the specialists, and the special interests, would go to work, putting every paragraph under the microscope and dissecting every phrase or, more often, applying a meat axe. Back would go the collection of comments, generally adding up to: "this is an outrageous proposal for the following reasons . . ." Bunker read every word, then did what he thought was right. But he knew that, in the long run, State and Defense would have to be on the same wavelength, certainly when the administration went to the Hill with a treaty.

On the trip back to Washington after their moderately disastrous sessions with the Panamanians in March, Bell and Kozak threshed over this touchy subject. Bell, as a career Foreign Service officer, was inclined to think of it as a matter of bureaucratic infighting. What were the pressure points? How could his establishment, State, bend another piece of the bureaucracy, Defense, to its will? Kozak was more pragmatic. As a good lawyer, he was less concerned with whether one department or another won a battle than with the long-range outcome, the final adjudication of a complex problem. What's the best way, he asked, to get from where we are to where we want to go?

Kozak had considerably more experience than Bell in working with the military. On the Braniff flight, he argued that State always had more success when it dealt with the Pentagon on an informal basis rather than in the traditional bureaucratic way. Why not establish an advisory group made up of State and Defense specialists, he suggested. The core of his idea: get State and Defense working together on ideas for the negotiations before, not after, formal proposals were made. Bell, though a traditionalist in many ways, had a lively intelligence and recognized a good idea when he heard one. On the second leg of their flight, from Miami to Washington, he and Kozak refined the notion. By the time they landed at National Airport, Bell had drafted a memo in his mind. The next morning, he put it on paper and sent it to Bunker. Soon after, Bunker sent the new proposal to the Pentagon.

Fortunately for the whole enterprise, Bunker's proposal went to one of the sager, most politically experienced men in the huge five-sided building across the Potomac. Henry "Barney" Koren was then deputy undersecretary of the army. Koren had served in the army in World War II and rose to the rank of colonel. As a career Foreign Service officer, he advanced to be ambassador to the Congo. He had experience in intelligence and as a White House staffer, and had been a civilian adviser in Vietnam. In short, he had a breadth of background shared by few individuals in government service. That varied experience, plus a first-class mind, enabled Koren to see the Panama issue as a multifaceted and complex problem with profound political, commercial, psychological, and military implications. Careful study led him to conclude that significant but balanced change was necessary.

Koren enthusiastically supported Bunker's proposal for a small, multi-agency "think tank" to back up the negotiating effort with fresh ideas and careful analyses. He sold the idea to other key officials in the Defense establishment. On May 10, he sent a memo to Bunker nominating the Defense Department representatives on the Support Group. Koren picked Col. Ben Walten from his own office as one member. Col. Trevor "Ted" Swett, Jr., had been working on the Panama problem in the Office of International Security Affairs. Col. Evan L. Parker represented the Joint Chiefs of Staff. Capt. Jeffrey H. Smith, a bright young military lawyer, was seconded from the staff of the army's judge advocate general and assigned to Koren's office.

At the State Department, there had been a change in the Bunker team. Col. John Sheffey, a holdover from the Anderson days, had clashed with Morey Bell on substance and temperamentally, and had resigned. His replacement was Col. Richard Wyrough, who retired from the army to join Bunker's staff as military adviser. A disciplined, organized man, good at administration, he became indispensable to Bell, who had little patience for day-to-day detail and the trivia of operations. Before long, Wyrough was made deputy director for Panamanian Affairs as well. In that capacity, he headed up the new Defense-State Negotiations Support Group. Joining him were Mike Kozak and Richard Howard, an able Foreign Service officer who had been working on the Panama problem for some time.

The basic idea, made clear at the first session of the Support Group, was that none of the participants was there to represent his department or agency or office. Rather they had been included because they were knowledgeable, experienced individuals who knew a good deal about the problem. The purpose was not, as Wyrough specified at the outset, to get precleared positions on individual questions; it was to encourage a group of savvy individuals to let their minds run free on any given subject and to come up with recommendations they thought might work. Each member was guaranteed anonymity. No one had to sign off on any proposal in his own name or for his parent organization. Their purpose was to take an issue, any issue; strip it down to its essentials; then recommend how it could best be handled. The final product went only to Ambassador Bunker, at times with a suggested line of action, more often with several options among which he could choose.

The genius of that approach was threefold. First, it assembled some of the better minds in Washington on the Panama problem and gave them the luxury of thinking freely and in a confidential atmosphere about what could and should be done. Second, it reassured high officials in the Pentagon that their interests were being protected and their views were being heard because their own men were part of the mechanism. It fitted admirably the dictum laid down by a shrewd member of Congress who once advised a president: "If you want us in on the landing, you better have us in on the takeoff."

Perhaps most important of all, the method eased the road to decisions and action as nothing had in the long, often tortuous path of negotiations during the previous decade. Once Bunker decided how he wanted to handle a given problem with the Panamanians, he would prepare a memo to that effect for the Pentagon, with the usual request for comments and reactions. It would go to the secretary of defense. Then it was farmed out, in turn, to the departments and agencies with a special interest—the Department of the Army, the Joint Chiefs of Staff, the Office of International Security Affairs, and others. In those entities, Bunker's proposal was sent to the most expert officer on board. Generally, those "most knowledgeable" officers were members of the Negotiations Support Group or close associates. If they had not originated the idea themselves, they had supported it, or knew precisely why it was being advanced in preference to other actions. As a result, responses from the Pentagon began to speed up significantly. More than that, concurrences became more frequent, and reservations increasingly minor.

Bunker and Tack had agreed to meet in late May and address the major issues, but that proved an impossible deadline. Bunker was heavily engaged at the time with Secretary Kissinger in the latter's search for an accommodation in the Middle East. Moreover, the deputies, Bell and González-Revilla, had not completed the preliminary work that would make a full-dress meeting fruitful. By the end of June, both obstacles had been cleared away. Bunker was able to escape from the secretary's always whirling diplomatic carousel and get back to his primary assignment, Panama. And Morey and Nico had by then gone as far as they could with the advance work. With approval from their superiors, they had worked out agreements on a number of questions. Unresolved matters were listed in orderly fashion for decision by the chief negotiators. The stage was set for the first act in the real negotiation of a new Panama treaty. It was June 26, 1974.

The mutually agreed subject for that first major round in the Bunker era was Principle Number Six of the Tack-Kissinger agreement. It provided that Panama would participate in the administration of the Panama Canal. It also committed Panama to give the United States the rights necessary to "operate, maintain, protect, and defend the canal." It was certainly not the most burning issue for Panama. Tack and his colleagues were far more interested in things like treaty duration and jurisdiction. Nor did it top the U.S. list of concerns, which focused on defense and possible expansion. For that very reason, because it was not the most critical issue, or even the second or third, for either side, both parties decided it was a good place to start. And so it proved to be.*

---

*There are contrary philosophies of negotiations. One has it that, if one settles the "gut issues" first, everything else falls quickly into place. The other argues that, if you settle simpler questions first, the "gut issues" become more tractable. In the case of the Panama problem,

The mood on Contadora for the first substantive round was exceptionally good. Tack's visit to Washington and his talks with Ford and Kissinger had improved the atmosphere notably. Bunker was delighted to be back on his favorite tropic isle and away from the Kissinger shuttle. The warmth of the island, the salt air, the sea-level pressure, all eased wonderfully his inner ear problem. So the talks between Tack and Bunker went smoothly. Morey and Nico had done their work well and comparatively few wrinkles needed pressing by the chief negotiators. The main elements of agreement were that the United States would have primary responsibility for operating the Panama Canal during the lifetime of the new treaty and that Panamanian participation would increase steadily in running the canal and formulating overall policy. The Panamanians would have preferred, of course, an arrangement that was 50-50 from the outset. But Tack and his colleagues knew their country did not have the trained specialists to take over half, or even many, of the technical tasks that kept the canal operating—pilots, for example, or hydraulic engineers, dredging experts, and others. The new agreement provided for recruitment and training programs so that Panamanians could develop those skills over time. The underlying assumption was that by the time the treaty expired Panama would have all the engineers and other specialists needed for continued smooth operation of the waterway.

Ten days after he returned to Washington, Ambassador Bunker went to the Pentagon to brief top-level Defense Department officials on treaty developments. They met in the office of Defense Secretary James Schlesinger, the strong-willed, pipe-smoking economist who earlier had headed the Atomic Energy Commission and, briefly, the Central Intelligence Agency. Secretary of the Army Howard "Bo" Callaway, a Georgia Republican and one-term member of Congress, attended. So did the newly installed chairman of the Joint Chiefs of Staff, air force Gen. George Brown, along with the chiefs of the four military services.

Schlesinger was late for his own briefing. After Bunker was well into his account, the self-important secretary entered the office, made no apologies for his tardiness, and signaled the senior diplomat to continue. To others in the room, the secretary seemed abstracted. His eyes roved restlessly around the room and to his desk. Loose socks kept slipping down his legs and he bent over periodically to pull them up.

Bunker reminded the Defense chiefs that the commitment to negotiate a new treaty was ten years old, made first by President Johnson "after con-

---

the second course of action, Bunker's choice, was demonstrably the correct one. But everything depends on the issue, the adversary, the time, the place, the history, and a dozen other factors. That is why diplomacy is an art, not a science.

sulting with former President Truman and General Eisenhower," and that President Nixon had renewed the pledge. Bunker told them he felt it was time to negotiate seriously because "time is running out." He doubted that the United States "can or would want to be the only country in the world exercising extraterritoriality on the soil of another country."

We could, if we were so determined, maintain our privileged position in Panama, he said, but "we would have to do so in an increasingly hostile atmosphere of confrontation." Eventually, he warned, we would find ourselves engaging in hostilities with a friendly people on their soil. "I believe the American people would find such a position unacceptable," he said, "as would the countries of Latin America and, indeed, the rest of the world." The problem was "to give Panama the sovereignty it desires, while keeping the control we need" for an extended period.

Bunker then reviewed the negotiations to date—working out the set of eight principles, identifying the key issues, and the beginning of substantive talks in late June which produced the first "Threshold Agreement." The ambassador pointedly noted that each of those steps had been taken "only after consultation and agreement with the Department of Defense." He made clear that that kind of cooperative effort was a fixed part of his negotiating plan. As a good team player, Bunker told the Defense group he would be looking to them for advice and help in developing positions in the months ahead, and in selling those positions to Congress. He surprised his listeners by telling them that his goal for completing a draft treaty was "early 1975." No one in the room had realized the target date was so near except the ambassador himself.

When Bunker finished, Schlesinger did not thank him or even use his name. He brusquely read off the first of several prepared questions: "Why should we jeopardize our national security by giving up our vital sovereignty?" The tone was that of a jaded professor addressing a freshman at exam time. Bunker, who was Schlesinger's senior by thirty-five years, found rudeness unacceptable and aggressive egotism offensive. He sat looking straight ahead as though nothing had been said. An aide worried that the ambassador had drawn a blank or had not heard. Then he realized that the elderly Vermonter was simply not going to respond to impertinent quizzing. The silence deepened. General Brown finally jumped in to ease the moment. "Mr. Secretary, I think there are some good reasons for that," he said. "Ambassador Bunker, could you fill us in?" Bunker then responded graciously and fully to the question.

Schlesinger was intelligent but insensitive. The same procedure was repeated several times. Either he missed the point, or cared nothing for the feelings of others. He finally left the briefing without a word of thanks or farewell. He had proved to all present that the consensus in official Washington and in the press was firmly based: that the secretary of defense was probably the most arrogant, self-centered, opinionated individual in the capital city.

When he had left, the others asked a few more questions, congratulated Bunker on his presentation, and promised to be as helpful as they could. As time passed, Bunker would realize how solid some of those promises were—and how shallow the others.

Bunker's meeting with the leaders of the defense establishment was timely because the next item on the negotiating agenda was "protection and defense of the canal." It was something Bunker believed he had to nail down early and unequivocally. Unless he had Panamanian agreement that the United States would have an unquestioned right to protect the waterway throughout the term of the treaty, he knew that any new pact could never win approval. He had no doubt of that, but if he had, his meeting at the Pentagon would have dispelled it. Clearly it was a sine qua non for any new arrangement. Fortunately, it was not something that required grinding effort on Bunker's part. After ten years of negotiating with the Americans, the Panamanians could recite the arguments for defense almost as well as we could. They might haggle about minor items, and they did; but on the central issue—the right of the United States to defend the Panama Canal for as long as it operated it—there was no Panamanian demurrer.

Morey Bell and Mike Kozak arrived in Panama for the next go-around on July 12. They took over the guest wing in the embassy residence and the next days were filled with preparations for the upcoming substantive round. They met regularly with González-Revilla, sometimes in the residence study, sometimes at his house. In two weeks, the essentials of an agreement on defense had been hammered out for approval by the chief negotiators. Morey and Mike returned to Washington, then came back with Bunker on August 5 for the plenary sessions on Contadora.

The agreement achieved over the next week provided that protection of the Panama Canal would be the joint responsibility of both countries. But in a critical sentence it gave the United States "primary responsibility" for defense until the treaty ended. It also anticipated a Status of Forces Agreement to govern U.S. forces in Panama.

There was argument on most sentences, naturally, because the presence of foreign troops is sensitive for all governments. The existence of some personnel and training facilities totally unrelated to protection of the canal was especially touchy for the Panamanians. Two things in particular came close to wrecking the Contadora talks. One was the matter of "residual defense"—the right of the United States to continue to defend the canal *after* the treaty expired. Bell had introduced that idea in his talks with González-Revilla. He reasoned it was something Defense would want and that it should be recognized early. Bell had calculated Defense Department attitudes with great accuracy; he had not foreseen the violence of the Panamanian reaction. When González-Revilla reported the proposal to Minister Tack and the treaty advisers, a small mushroom cloud rose up over the Foreign Ministry building. When the matter came up later between Bunker and Tack, the atmosphere was sulphurous. Tack's point, vehemently made, was that "residual defense" is another way of saying "perpetuity." "You're asking for the right to keep troops in our country forever," he told Bunker. "That's what we've been trying to get rid of for seventy years."

When it was clear there could be no agreement, Bunker proposed putting it aside for the moment. It was agreed to cover the point with a phrase that U.S. defense rights would lapse with the treaty "unless the two parties agree otherwise through negotiations to be held five years before the expiration of the treaty."

The other sensitive issue concerned the neutrality of the canal. The United States wanted neutrality guaranteed by the two partners. Panama wanted broader underwriting, an international guarantee through the United Nations. That prompted sharp debate inside the U.S. camp. Bell favored the international approach. Kozak argued, correctly as it turned out, that the Defense Department would oppose international guarantees. Bunker's view was colored by his recent experience in the Middle East peace effort. "Look," he finally said, "we're trying to get the Russians and everybody else to join us in guaranteeing peace in the Middle East. There's no reason we can't have everybody guarantee the neutrality of the canal." But he did not accept U.N. involvement. The final version said the two parties would ensure the neutrality of the canal and would "make efforts that such neutrality is recognized and guaranteed by all nations." With that, the agreement on canal defense was locked up.

The vital talks on Contadora took place while the U.S. government was passing through its worst constitutional crisis in more than a hundred years. Vice President Spiro Agnew had resigned under a dark cloud. Throughout 1974, President Nixon was the target of exposés in the press and of repeated congressional investigations. By August, it was clear that Nixon's only choice was to resign or face impeachment by the Congress. On August 9, the embattled chief executive wrote out his resignation and turned the presidency over to Vice President Gerald Ford.

If Nixon's resignation surprised the American people, it stunned many foreigners and their governments. However used to abrupt changes in their own regimes (some were; some were not), most people considered the administration in Washington an example of extraordinary stability. When news of Nixon's action flew around the world, cabinets gathered to assess the meaning. The Panamanians were more concerned than most. After all, they were engaged in negotiating a major change in relations with Washington and they were relying on a pledge from Nixon to see that process through. My phone rang constantly that morning and I kept reassuring Panamanians that we expected no major change in our principal business. But they needed more. Fortunately, it was not long in coming.

In the middle of one of the many phone calls, Bob Ribera, head of our communications section, brought in an "Eyes Only" message from the secretary of state. It was a letter for Minister Tack which Kissinger wanted delivered immediately. The secretary wrote that he assumed Tack knew of the change in the U.S. presidency. He wanted to assure Panama that "this will not affect in any way the negotiations" for a new treaty. He informed Tack that President Ford had asked him to continue as secretary of state and that he had accepted. "One of my highest priorities as I continue in my responsibilities," he wrote, "will be to press ahead with the negotiations in order to conclude a new treaty promptly." He asked Tack to convey the substance of his message to President Lakas and General Torrijos "so that they also will have no doubts whatsoever about our continued adherence to our commitment."

We arranged an immediate flight to Contadora and one of my political officers delivered the letter to Ambassador Bunker so he could hand it to Tack immediately. The Panamanian minister read the letter with obvious satisfaction and immediately called Lakas and Torrijos to relay the reassurance from Washington. Word that the Ford administration intended to continue negotiating a treaty moved swiftly through the Panamanian information underground, and soon it was common knowledge. The uneasiness of the morning hours had dissipated by sundown.

A few days after Bunker returned to Washington, we had a sample of what student radicalism, Panama-style, could mean. A controversy had been raging through the summer among Panama and other major producers of bananas in Latin America. Torrijos, pushed by some advisers into an ill-advised effort to set up a producers' cartel, a kind of "banana OPEC," was trying to form a united front of banana exporting countries. Torrijos' scheme was to get the major growers of bananas, principally Costa Rica, Guatemala, Honduras, and, above all, Ecuador, to impose a uniform export tax on every box of bananas. The tax was to make up for the losses suffered because of the skyrocketing cost of imported oil. Needless to say, the Torrijos plan quickly ran aground. The main producers and purchasers of bananas, United Brands and Del Monte, patiently explained the difference between oil and bananas. Automobiles, trucks, airplanes, power plants, manufacturers, all needed oil to operate. But everyone could do without a banana on his morning cereal. Torrijos won scattered support from his Central American neighbors. But the Ecuadorians, the world's largest producers of bananas, refused to go along.

The whole rather incredible exercise came to be known as the "Banana War." (Why "war" I never understood, except that it provided the kind of shorthand beloved of headline writers.) On the afternoon of April 14, 1974, the "Banana War" came to Avenida Balboa and the U.S. Embassy. We knew gangs of students had been moving through the streets shouting their support of Panama's "Banana War" and their hatred of United Brands. But it had little to do with the embassy. The U.S. government had taken no position, made no statements on the issue. We reckoned without the imagination of activist students to convert almost any issue into an anti-American campaign.

They marched down Avenida Balboa eight abreast with hand-painted signs denouncing "multinational villains" and "imperialist swine" who refused to pay a fair tax on bananas. We stood at the windows to watch them pass by. But they didn't. Instead, they massed in front of the embassy, shouted their slogans, vile and otherwise, and jeered in unison as their leaders directed. Anyone who has lived through a riot knows what a depressing sight it is to see otherwise rational people, especially students, turn into unthinking robots at the instigation of organized cheerleaders with bullhorns.

Suddenly I heard a window crash somewhere on the first floor. Then another, and another. I told my security officer, Billy Hughes, to pass the word for everyone to stay away from all outside windows and gather on the inner corridors. We had locked the big oak doors at the front of the building and called in a few extra Marine guards. But those were our only precautions for the unexpected assault. I had Col. Tom Austin, the head of our Military Group, contact the National Guard and tell them we had a riot on our hands. "Tell them to get someone over here to stop this stupidity," I said. Tom went to the phone. Meantime, one pane of glass after another was crashing into the offices at the front of the building.

When they saw there was no reaction, the mob moved down the two side streets along the wings of the U-shaped building. Windows began to crash there, too. By that time, I was seething—at the stupidity and cowardice of the rampaging students, and at the failure of the government to react to the violence. I walked into my office, which was a shambles, grabbed the phone, and called the president. Lakas answered his direct line.

"Mr. President," I said, trying to remain as restrained as possible, "I don't know if anyone has told you, but this embassy is being attacked by a mob and no one is doing anything about it."

"I heard there was some trouble," he said, "but I don't know what it's all about."

"I don't know what it's all about either," I told him. "All I know is that a bunch of students with placards complaining about the 'Banana War' are all around my embassy and they're busting every window in sight. Can't you send a detachment of the National Guard to stop it?"

As we talked, stones kept coming through the windows. I held out the phone to make sure he could hear what it sounded like.

"Look, Mr. Ambassador," he said (he was being official; he usually called me Bill), "let me see what I can do. Meantime, please stay cool."

"Mr. President," I said, "I'm cool. Don't worry about that. But there's a brick the size of a grapefruit on the desk in front of me and the floor is covered with stones and broken glass. And if these bastards come into my embassy, some people are going to get killed. So I would just ask that you act as soon as you can. Otherwise, let's just forget about good relations and treaties and all that baloney. And please tell Omar [Torrijos] what I said."

"Hold on, Bill," he said. "I'll get someone there right away."

"Thank you, Mr. President," I said. "I appreciate that."

In five minutes, a platoon of National Guardsmen in battle dress arrived at the rear of the embassy. Then another platoon showed up. They fanned out around the building and began to move the students away ever so slowly. But when a couple of the soldiers were hit by flying rocks, they took an increased interest in their job and became more aggressive. When the shouting students saw that the Guard meant business, they ran to escape the rifle butts and billyclubs that the Guard was finally using.

Fortunately, no one in the embassy was injured in the melee and I gave thanks for that. But when we took an inventory, we found that more than two hundred panes of glass had been broken, venetian blinds had been shredded, draperies ripped, and there was damage to typewriters and other office equipment that had been in range of the student-thrown missiles. I had the Administrative Section tote up the damages, get estimates for repairs, and give me a bill for the total. In any capital, the host government is responsible for the safety and property of foreign embassies. When it fails to provide reasonable protection from a civil disturbance, the local government pays the bill, or should. When I had the list of the destruction and the repair estimate, I sent it with a stiff note of protest to the Foreign Ministry. I also called on my friend, an embarrassed President Lakas, and gave him a copy. He expressed great regret that the nasty incident had occurred. In a matter of hours, I received payment in full for all the damages.

The next time I saw General Torrijos, he complained mildly about the language I had used with Lakas in the midst of the rioting at the embassy. But he said he "forgave" me because we were friends. I told him I did not seek "forgiveness" because I had said exactly what I felt. "You know, General," I told him, "I'm sure that if you were in your office and someone started throwing bricks through your windows, you'd use language a lot stronger than I did." He laughed and agreed I was right. We left it there and went on to other business. That "other business" was a major change in Panamanian foreign policy, one that could have a serious impact on the whole treaty-making effort. I had learned that Panama planned to reopen relations with Cuba.

The flirtation with Castro had begun two and a half years earlier with

U.S. encouragement. In December 1971, the Cubans seized a small Miami-based freighter, the *Lyla Express*, off their coast. Ten days later, a Cuban gunboat attacked a sister ship, the *Johnny Express*, in Bahamian waters far from the Cuban mainland. Captain José Villa, an American citizen of Cuban origin, and two crewmen were wounded. The gunboat took the injured men to Havana and a second vessel escorted the *Johnny Express* to Mariel, a harbor west of the Cuban capital.

The attack was denounced in Washington as "an unconscionable act" and we asked the Swiss Embassy to insist on Captain Villa's release. The demand fell on deaf ears. Radio Havana called the vessels "pirate ships" and claimed they had engaged in "counterrevolutionary actions." Captain Villa's distraught wife camped out on President Nixon's doorstep in Key Biscayne and when he heard her tearful story, the president promised to do everything possible to get her husband released.

The Swiss connection was tried again but to no avail. Then someone in Washington remembered that the two ships sailed under the Panamanian flag. Perhaps authorities in Panama City could help secure release of the boats and their crews. Pushed hard by the Americans to lend a hand, General Torrijos sent University Rector Escobar, a man with excellent left-wing credentials, to Havana to see what might be done. He and Castro talked for hours and established excellent rapport. But Villa remained in jail, and the rapidly rusting boats stayed at the pier in Mariel.

I first became involved in the affair when a plaintive letter to the president from Mrs. Villa was sent to me in the NSC for recommendations. I read into the matter and concluded that while Panama's Escobar might be a brilliant man, he was accomplishing nothing. I went to see Ambassador González-Revilla and urged him to contact General Torrijos with my personal appeal to get Captain Villa out of his Cuban jail. Omar responded by sending his tough-minded, realistic intelligence chief, Col. Manuel Noriega, to talk with Fidel Castro. The result, as I had hoped, was that the two ships were released to Panama (they almost sank on the trip across the Caribbean) and Captain Villa was put in their custody with the face-saving proviso that he be tried for espionage. There was, of course, no way an American citizen could be tried by a Panamanian court for espionage against another country. Villa went to Panama, his wife was allowed to visit him, and finally, after incredible quantities of red tape were slashed, he was released.

Thus, Panama's links to Castro commenced in 1971 at the request of the U.S. government. By 1974, Torrijos was ready to use that connection as a trump card in the treaty game. He decided to jolt the U.S. side, and the "shock" was the recognition of Castro. The purpose was to force the Americans either to reevaluate the Panama issue or to break off the talks.

Through the summer, the Panamanian general had been in close touch with neighbors—Presidents Oduber of Costa Rica, Pérez of Venezuela, and López Michelsen of Colombia. Torrijos had persuaded them that, despite the Tack-Kissinger Principles, the Americans were taking the same old hard line. The gringos need a reminder, Torrijos argued, that Latin Americans have minds of their own as well as pride and independence. He also pointed out that Washington was making noises about "regularizing" its relations with Cuba. A real nightmare for most Latin American leaders was that the United States would recognize Cuba first and unilaterally. Torrijos shrewdly played on that fear. The four countries began to plan joint recognition of Castro.

When word reached Washington about what was afoot, the search began for ways to forestall the Latin American initiative. William Mailliard, the newly appointed ambassador to the OAS, was sent to Costa Rica, Venezuela, and Colombia to dissuade them from any sudden move in Castro's direction. The central argument Mailliard used was that the decisions to isolate Cuba in 1962 and 1964 had been collective actions by all the American states in the OAS. Any reversal should similarly be a collective move. The obvious, but unstated, corollary was that Washington would take a dim view of any moves in that direction without our participation. As a result of Mailliard's intervention, the governments in Bogotá, Caracas, and San José pulled back from their understanding with Torrijos.

I went to see Torrijos about the opening to Cuba with considerable reluctance. He knew we were busy trying to block his play. Afflicted with a conspiratorial mind himself, Torrijos could only read "anti-Torrijos plot" into what we were doing. I knew Omar Torrijos well enough to sense that trying to isolate him on this issue would likely only stiffen his back.

I was right. As we talked, it was clear that Omar had made up his mind. When I used the central argument—that breaking relations with Cuba had been a collective decision in the OAS, and that reversing that course should also be joint—Torrijos reminded me that Mexico had never broken relations with Havana and that Argentina and Peru had recently restored relations with Castro.

"And frankly I am not sure that your country, if it considers it to be an advantage, will not act alone when the time comes," he said. I told him I had reason to believe the United States would not act alone on this matter, but his eyes and the shrug of his shoulders told me he remained skeptical. I then tossed on the table the argument that had most influenced my own thinking, and that I hoped would affect his.

"If this were another country," I said, "it might make only a little difference. But it is Panama, and that gives it special meaning in Washington. We're in the middle of working out a new relationship. People who don't want that relationship keep claiming you are a Communist and that a deal with you will just open the doors of the canal to Fidel Castro. If you move now to establish relations with Cuba, it's going to strengthen those allegations and make our job harder."

Torrijos took a long drink of scotch, and looked at me hard.

"You're probably right, Bill," he said. "It's going to make things more difficult. But I think the time has come when tough decisions have to be made. Your people have to understand that we are independent, that we have minds of our own, and that we can go in more than one direction. The only kind of friends worth having are those that stand on their own feet, not those who kneel before you to your face, and curse you behind your back."

I knew then that the die was cast. I thanked the general for his time, asked him to think over what I had said, and promised to report his reaction. As he walked me to the door, he urged me not to take it too seriously. "It will all turn out for the best," he said, "if everybody stays calm and works for what is important in the long run."

Until then, I had not realized how frustrated Torrijos was with the treaty talks. He made only passing references to the "slow pace" and to the "hard line" we were following. But it was enough to expose his internal struggles and to reflect the pressures he was feeling. Clearly, he looked on the opening to Cuba as a way to shake Washington out of its lethargy. But it meant more than that to him. It would reinforce the independence of his regime in the eyes of his own people. It would burnish his image in the opinion of other Latin American leaders and governments. It would win support for Panama's cause from the Nonaligned World, where Cuba was very active. More than that, it would greatly placate the leftists and the emotional students whose anger had recently been demonstrated in the attack on the U.S. Embassy. In other words, Torrijos, like most politicians, had several irons in the fire at the same time.

In mid-August, Torrijos met with President Lakas and members of the General Staff of the National Guard. The general told them what he planned to do, and why. Lakas and the colonels, most of them strongly anticommunist, raised some hard questions—about the impact in Washington, the likely consequences for the treaty talks, the effect on political stability inside Panama. Torrijos responded with typical rhetoric, emotion, and Veraguan parables. In the end, it boiled down to simple questions: Do you trust me? Are you with me? Lakas and the military men who had supported Torrijos from the night of the coup in 1968 had little choice but to go along with the *jefe*—and hope for the best. Privately, most of them had deep reservations.

Torrijos was a pragmatist not an ideologue. Though he had carried off the talk with Lakas and the colonels with great élan, he suddenly realized he had unleashed a tiger. That night, he had to face some more hard questions. What good does it do to satisfy the leftists and calm down the students, he asked himself, if I alienate all the bankers and businessmen, the lawyers and contractors, and investors? We already have enough problems. Am I making them worse? The possibility of political glory and economic chaos loomed in front of him. He went to bed in a foul mood.

Part of the political genius of Torrijos was the ability to see a problem, look immediately for a solution, then give the impression that that was what he was thinking all the time. Having recognized the trap he had set for himself in the Cuba ploy, he charted a path around it, then acted as if it were part of his strategy from the beginning.

The day after his session with Lakas and the colonels, Torrijos began to plan the next step. He knew it would be a disaster to send a delegation to Cuba headed by a leftist. That would give entirely the wrong signal to Washington and to Panama. Nor could he go himself. At that stage, he had to preserve a certain distance. Tack might have been a logical choice, but that surely would have affected the treaty talks with Bunker. His final selection was brilliant. He called his minister of economic planning, Nicolás Ardito Barletta, and asked him to head the delegation to Havana. As one of the best economists in the hemisphere, he would be acceptable to the Cubans. He was known and respected in Washington. He was recognized in the business community as a staunch advocate of the free enterprise system. And even the most radical students had to respect his qualities of mind and his academic credentials.

Torrijos appealed to Nicky's patriotism and won him over. Torrijos meantime put Rory González to work assembling a group of cattlemen and merchants from his home province of Chiriquí, the most conservative area in the country. He asked Gabriel Lewis and other business leaders to join the exercise. The left wing was represented by Rómulo Escobar Bethancourt, Adolfo Ahumada, and a few others. Representatives of the trade unions were invited. There was a large press contingent. It was a well-balanced group that would help ease some of the inevitable concern of many in Panama that Omar Torrijos was abruptly turning to the Left. It would also counteract some of the heartburn in Washington—if anyone took the trouble to look at the makeup of the Panamanian delegation.

On August 21, Barletta and his huge delegation departed for Havana. In typical fashion, Torrijos had given no firm orders, or even suggestions, as to what to do or not to do. He merely said he had confidence in Barletta's judgment. The only useful suggestion Barletta got was from President Lakas. "Why don't you mention, at some point, that Panama and Cuba follow parallel paths toward their goals?" he proposed. "That would sound nice." The shrewd engineer was thinking of everyone who had studied plane geometry and knew parallel lines never meet. Barletta worked the "parallel lines" theme into his major speech in Havana. After four days—

filled with meetings and receptions, with visits to farms and schools and hospitals, with all the rigors of protocol and many parties—the Barletta group returned to Panama. Soon, Cuba had established an embassy in Panama City and Panama had opened one in Havana.

Strangely, the change in the Pan American scene attracted little media attention in the United States. But if Panama's initiative toward Cuba escaped the attention of editors, the same was not true in the government. The State Department was irritated and Secretary Kissinger was reported to be furious. Officials in the Pentagon who wanted to preserve U.S. bases and defense rights indefinitely saw the move toward Havana as new justification for their stand. And on Capitol Hill, opponents of any new arrangement with Panama were reading Panama's move as confirmation of their charge that Torrijos was pro-Castro.

Instead of negotiating a treaty, Ambassador Bunker found himself answering phone calls from congressmen and replying to angry letters. I was going through the same in Panama City. Friends in the business community drew me aside to ask, "What does it mean?" The local grapevine was filled with rumors of communist plotting and dire developments. I explained that Omar Torrijos was a shrewd politician, that he was trying to get our attention, and he was succeeding admirably. But most people were looking for deeper meanings with dreadful implications. I realized it would take time for that miasma to dissipate. Meantime, the idea of negotiating a treaty went into the deep freeze.

The chill began to get to Torrijos. Like the elation following Panama's "victory" at the U.N. Security Council meeting, the huzzahs and parties that followed Cuban recognition died quickly. I reduced embassy contacts with the Panama government to the necessary minimum. Development loans and other programs were delayed for further study. Foreign banks, nervous about Panama's rapprochement with Cuba, were taking a closer look at official loan applications. In Washington, Panama dropped from sight as a matter of concern.

By October, it had become clear to even the most skeptical officials in State and Defense that Omar Torrijos had no intention of moving any closer to Cuba than he already had. Indeed, he was busy paying unusual attention to Panamanian and foreign businessmen and bankers. Having secured his left wing with his Cuba move, he set about shoring up his tattered right. In Washington, Bunker was quietly making preparations for the next round. The main topic would be the touchy one of jurisdiction, and Bunker was readying some surprises for his Panamanian opposite number.

In late October, Ellsworth called me on the secure phone. He had worked out some new positions and he wanted to discuss them. He said he also wanted my assessment of Panamanian attitudes and the atmosphere he could expect when he met them. He asked if I could come to Washington. I told him I would be there the next day. I arrived at National Airport on Friday evening, and the ambassador and I spent most of Saturday morning together in his office at State.

He asked about the current mood in Panama and I reviewed the bidding since Cuban recognition. Despite the flap the gesture toward Havana had caused, I could guarantee that he would be welcomed back warmly. Torrijos wanted to get on with the business of writing a treaty as much as we did, perhaps more. "He would be happy if it were finished tomorrow," I told Bunker. Then he told me about the moves he planned to make with Tack the following week. I told my friend that the Panamanians would not only be pleased, they would be overjoyed.

"But you understand, Bill, that we're going to have to have language in the treaty that gives us primary responsibility for operating and defending the canal as long as the treaty lasts," he said with a question in his voice. I told him I thought we had that in the understandings worked out in April and August. "Yes, but those are just tentative agreements," he said. "They don't have final approval."

"Don't worry, Ellsworth," I told him, "we'll get it. Be sure, we'll get it."

Another point was the Status of Forces Agreement to cover our military personnel. I said I had talked at length with the Panamanians about that requirement and I was certain they understood it was a necessity.

"Yes, but we would like to have the civilians in the canal operation covered by the same understanding," he explained.

"That's a different matter," I said. "The first thing they'll ask is whether nonmilitary U.S. civilians are covered by our agreements in places like Germany, Japan, and other countries. When we tell them no, they'll say there's no reason to have it in Panama."

"Well, we've got to try," Bunker said. "The Canal Company folks want it badly, and they have support from some people on the Hill."

"All we can do is give it a go," I said. "But my reading of the Panamanians tells me not to bet very much on our getting that one." He nodded. "I'll just try my best," he said.

The third and final round of the 1974 treaty talks began on Contadora on October 28. Bunker and Tack, Bell and González-Revilla gathered that morning to discuss the "threshold agreement" on jurisdiction. Minutes into the session, Bunker dropped his bombshell. It concerned a central, and highly emotional, question: how long would the transfer of authority from the United States to Panama require? Bunker reminded the Panamanians that they had demanded a transition period of no more than five years. The U.S. side had been arguing for no less than fifteen years.

"I am prepared to offer," Bunker said in his severest tone, "that in no instance shall the period exceed five years. If we can turn over jurisdiction to Panama more rapidly than in five years, we shall do so. I believe in some cases we can do it in three years, or less."

He added that he was ready to propose disestablishment of "the agency known as the Canal Zone Government" as soon as the treaty went into force.

Tack was stunned. González-Revilla could not believe what he had heard. Both sat looking at Bunker in amazement. Bell swore that he saw tears in Tack's eyes. The foreign minister asked for a recess. "We are emotionally unprepared to continue," he said. He and his deputy walked out the door and went to their rooms. Bunker and Bell returned to the Zeimetz house to wait for further word.

After about an hour, there was a knock on the door. It was Ambassador González-Revilla. He sat down on the couch and looked at Morey and Mike. Bunker had gone to the beach.

Nico gulped the drink he had been given, and smiled. "Look, you've broken the back of the negotiations," he told the Americans. "This is the treaty." Morey said he hoped the ambassador wasn't kidding. "No, no. I mean it," Nico said. "There will be a lot of crap after this, but you have just given us a treaty." That is what he and Tack and Torrijos (they had just called the general) believed, he said. "There's still work to do, but the back is broken."

"I'll drink to that," Morey said. Glasses were raised and clinked, and the contents disappeared. Everybody was laughing.

Two hours later, the negotiating teams were back together in the study at Gabriel Lewis' house. They began going over the draft agreement on jurisdiction line by line, paragraph by paragraph. There were still differences, still some haggling, but there was an entirely different spirit in the exchanges. There was good humor on both sides, and jokes flew back and forth.

The next day, Bunker unveiled his second surprise. He informed Torrijos that the Board of Directors of the Panama Canal Company had decided a few days earlier to establish the position of counselor to the president of the company for Panama–United States relations. A distinguished Panamanian would be appointed to the new post. Torrijos told Bunker he was delighted with the U.S. initiative. He saw it as "significant evidence" of the U.S. desire to move toward a new relationship with his country. Within weeks, Torrijos told me he intended to nominate his friend and adviser Gabriel Lewis to occupy this precedent-setting position in the Canal Company's hierarchy.

After a few more days of negotiating—with some sailing and excellent seafood dinners worked into the schedule—the understanding on jurisdiction was completed. On November 7, Bunker and Tack initialed all three "threshold agreements."

That evening, Bunker sent a message to Secretary Kissinger. He reported that he had made a package proposal of the three understandings, that the Panamanians had accepted it, and that he and Tack had affixed their initials.

"I believe it is now fair to say that a treaty is in sight," Bunker told the secretary. He reported that Torrijos had told him that "the United States has broken the back of the treaty problem." Then, with customary Vermont reserve, Bunker added: "Perhaps they are overstating the case, but I am hopeful."

CHAPTER 12

Struggle behind the Scenes

"The essence of a free government consists in an effectual
control of rivalries."

—John Adams, *Discourses on Davila*

O N the Zeimetz patio that November morning, after Bunker and
Tack had initialed the "threshold" agreements, the optimism was palpable.
The hopeful tone the Panamanians had sounded produced something
barely short of euphoria in the American camp. Morey Bell exuded high
spirits. Mike Kozak, cheerful even in adversity, shared his colleague's mood.
Even Bunker, the most restrained of men, was enjoying the moment thoroughly. When I suggested that some of the unresolved problems were
going to be tougher to settle than we might think, I was accused of excessive pessimism. Bell joked that I was still mad at the Panamanians because
of the attack on the embassy.

"I wish it were that simple," I told him. "The fact is I think we're going
to have more trouble in Washington than we are with the Panamanians.
But we'll see. I hope I'm wrong."

When I flew back to the mainland, I carried Bunker's report to Kissinger and sent it off as soon as I arrived at the embassy. It reflected the
morning's optimistic mood, and was more hopeful than I felt. A year in
Panama, and three years watching treaty moves closely, had conditioned
me to expect periods of hope to be succeeded quickly by disappointments.
"It's just not going to be this easy," I told myself as I handed the cable over
to the communicator.

Bunker informed the secretary of state that he and Tack had worked out
a negotiating schedule they hoped would produce a treaty by March. Admittedly, that was optimistic, he said, but it was "possible." Bunker was
working on the assumption that the sooner a treaty could go to the Senate
for approval in 1975, the more likely it would not become an issue in the
1976 election. Of the "four remaining issues to be negotiated," Bunker and
Bell had calculated that two "should not be difficult"—how much the

United States paid Panama for use of its territory for canal purposes and how much land was to be returned to Panama from the Canal Zone.* Bunker judged the other two issues to be quite difficult. One was how long the new treaty should last; the other was whether the United States would continue to press for an option to build a sea-level canal. The ambassador warned Kissinger that he would probably have to ask for "some relaxation of the existing presidential guidance in order to handle them."

One reason for Bunker's upbeat approach was the fact that the next phase of treaty talks was, in fact, already on track. The night before the chief negotiators approved the three general accords, the American team had delivered to the Panamanians a draft of a proposed Status of Forces Agreement (SOFA) combined with a Base Rights Agreement. They provided the rules under which U.S. military forces would operate in Panama under a treaty. It was the kind of agreement we have wherever American troops are stationed abroad—in the United Kingdom, West Germany, Japan, Korea, and dozens of other countries. A SOFA governs what military personnel and their dependents can or cannot do legally, and what their obligations are to the host country. It determines their tax status, their right to import goods, procedures for licensing cars and boats. Most important, a SOFA specifies those crimes over which the U.S. military retains jurisdiction and those that fall under control of the host government. It is in every sense a treaty of crucial importance to both parties and involves both the retention and the waiver of basic sovereign rights. A SOFA is as important to a military establishment as the tax code is to the business community.

I strongly favored putting the SOFA high on the treaty agenda. It had the advantage of being a specialized piece of business with fixed parameters and, therefore, was much less apt to generate long flights of rhetoric by either side. It seemed to me, too, that the subject would have considerable appeal to the Panamanians. They had been railing for years against the unilateral actions of the U.S. military; at last they would have some say in what could and could not be done. Moreover, the Panamanians could hardly object on grounds of national pride or sovereignty when some of the strongest and most advanced nations in the world had such pacts with the United States. Finally, negotiating a SOFA would bring the Pentagon into an active role in the treaty-making process and that involvement was essential to the success of the whole exercise.

Planning for a SOFA began in the early fall. In October, the army's Barney Koren informed Bunker that the Defense Department's representative in the SOFA talks would be Philip Barringer, director of the Office of

---

*Both issues would be bitterly contested in the negotiations and each came close to causing a break in the treaty talks.

Foreign Military Rights Affairs. Barringer was a lawyer and a veteran of the Pentagon's bureaucracy, the most experienced man in the U.S. government on matters of base rights and status of forces agreements. His vast knowledge and background were invaluable in developing a viable SOFA with Panama. Joining him on the U.S. SOFA team were Lt. Cmdr. Neil Johnson from the legal staff of SOUTHCOM; Jeff Smith, the army lawyer who did outstanding work on the State-Defense treaty advisory group; and Mike Kozak of State.

On the Panamanian side, the SOFA talks brought the debut on the treaty scene of Rómulo Escobar Bethancourt, rector of the University of Panama and one of the most colorful and controversial figures on the isthmus. Then 47 years old, Escobar had spent most of his life as a passionate advocate of revolutionary causes while making a good living as a lawyer for corporate clients and governmental agencies. As a student at the National Institute, he had become enamored of leftist causes. By the time he earned his law degree from the University of Panama, Escobar was an active member of the Peoples Democratic Party (the Communist Party). In 1951, when he was 24 years old, he was jailed briefly for publicly insulting President Arnulfo Arias. By then he had been tossed out of the Party for insubordination.

By the time he was 45, Escobar had written a small library of anti-American articles and had delivered countless speeches with an anti-gringo theme. Yet he knew virtually nothing about the United States, as he readily admitted. Like many of his fellow countrymen, he had created in his mind a stereotype of Americans based on isolated exposure to a small number of Zonians and, more important, the often distorted rumors of excessive behavior by Americans that had spiced coffeehouse and barside conversations and student meetings in Panama for more than seventy years.

His first trip to the United States, in 1972, was an eye-opener for the Panamanian Marxist. As a guest of the National Academy of Sciences, he visited the University of Kansas and lectured at the University of New Mexico. He was amazed to find himself and his wife being invited into many American homes for quiet family dinners. He was even more nonplussed to discover how frank the conversation was and how eager people seemed to be to learn something about Latin America. Those friendly folks just did not fit the picture that years of propaganda and emotional distortion had firmly fixed in his mind.

Torrijos' selection of Rómulo to represent Panama in the SOFA talks was deliberate and shrewd. The general knew that generations of Panamanians had been taught that the U.S. military presence in their country was "illegal." It was not, of course. The 1903 treaty specified that the Canal Zone could be used not only to build a canal but also to protect it. But most Americans, if they were candid, recognized that many military activities undertaken in the Zone over the years had only a remote connection, or none at all, with defense of the waterway. In any case, the presence of U.S. forces and bases inside Panama was a matter of considerable political sensitivity for the Panamanians. Torrijos concluded that, if a leftist like Rómulo could work out a SOFA with the Americans, Panama's Marxists and activist students would not likely oppose it. He was also confident that the veteran lawyer would look carefully at every comma and footnote and that he would resist any outrageous concessions. For reasons of politics and protocol, and so that his team would not be hopelessly outmanned, Torrijos instructed Ambassador González-Revilla to head Panama's SOFA team though Escobar's was clearly the dominant voice on matters of substance.

The SOFA draft that the Bunker group turned over to the Panamanians in November was a hastily concocted document, what is known in the trade as "a cut-and-paste job." It pulled together all the most favorable segments of other SOFA's worked out through the years. The presumption on the U.S. side, arrogant but perhaps natural, was that we knew all there was to know about SOFA's and the Panamanians knew nothing. Since we had this kind of arrangement with dozens of other countries, what was there to argue about? That was not the way the Panamanians saw it. An agreement on bases and military personnel in their country was touchy. They were not prepared to sign off on the first proposal that came their way.

When Escobar arrived in Washington to discuss the SOFA in December, he immediately let it be known he was there to negotiate, not sign blank checks. That created some consternation in the State Department and the Pentagon. What is there to discuss, they asked each other. This is a perfectly straightforward, uncomplicated agreement like countless others around the world. The irate consensus seemed to be: "If Panama doesn't want this, they don't want a treaty."

The balm of reason came from Mike Kozak. "Look," he told his colleagues, "a negotiation is a negotiation. They haven't said they don't accept the general principles, but they want to play with the language and stuff. We've got to do it." That commonsense approach carried the day and the SOFA talks began.

At the first meeting, held at the Panamanian Embassy, Escobar took the Americans aback by presenting a Panamanian draft of a SOFA. It was the last thing the U.S. lawyers expected. But they gulped hard and said they would study it. It followed the U.S. format but dealt with each problem from a Panamanian perspective. It was filled with problems and unacceptable language, but the U.S. lawyers handled it with skill. Instead of tossing it out as impossible, their first inclination, they went over it carefully and prepared a rebuttal brief. At the next meeting, they explained which points created problems—and why—and which could be accommodated. The

Americans undertook to prepare a totally new draft, one that would take full account of the Panamanian version.

At that stage, the "greening" of Rómulo Escobar had barely begun. The Americans found him filled with suspicion and mistrust. He was also ready to make a speech at the drop of a controversy—about Panama's long oppression at the hands of the gringos, about the injustice of unilateral interpretations of the old treaty, about little Panama's being drawn unwillingly into outside conflicts, and the like. At an early meeting, Escobar pulled Kozak aside and told him he was "too young to be a fascist" and that he really shouldn't get drawn into "defending U.S. imperialism." It was vintage Escobar drawn from the accumulated clichés of a lifetime of Marxist activism. In the months ahead, ever so gradually, the layers of stilted rhetoric fell away from Escobar's presentations. He put the outmoded baggage of youthful prejudice behind him, and became a tough-minded and thorough, but rational and perceptive, negotiator. Eventually, he came to understand American thinking and U.S. political realities better than some of his colleagues who had spent far more time in our country.

Discussion of the SOFA continued through much of December with the meetings being rotated—one session at the Pentagon, the next at the State Department, then at Panama's embassy. After the Christmas and New Year's break, the talks resumed on the island of Contadora. By that time drafts on individual articles were passing quickly back and forth between the two teams on every relevant subject—from the flying of national flags to the approved uses of defense sites. One by one, differences were reduced, then eliminated. But one issue seemed impervious to solution. It had to do with the continued use by the U.S. military of certain facilities (a couple of pipelines, some communications sites, trash disposal areas, electric power transformers, and the like) that were outside the base areas themselves. Drawing on legal phrasing from previous SOFA's, the U.S. drafters had demanded that Panama agree that "the United States has a right to enjoy and to continue to enjoy" use of those facilities. Every time the subject came up, Rómulo dug in his heels and said it was impossible. The Americans kept insisting with equal vehemence that they had to have the right to maintain and use the facilities.

Finally, Kozak took Escobar aside and said: "Look, Rómulo, we have to have these things. Tell me what the problem is."

"My problem," Rómulo replied, "is that we know you're going to screw us. But do you have to put it down in black and white in the agreement?"

It turned out that "enjoy and continue to enjoy" had been translated into Spanish with a biblical or Elizabethan flavor that suggested the pleasuring of a man by a woman. When the two sides realized what the hangup was, they roared with laughter—and changed the wording. From then on, the phrase became a leitmotif of humor among the negotiators. When any-one celebrated a birthday, he was likely to get a card hoping he would "en-joy and continue to enjoy" all the pleasures of life.

In February, the SOFA talks moved back to Washington. The Panama-nian side was augmented by two more lawyers. One was Jaime Arias, a Yale graduate and Tulane-trained attorney, a partner in one of Panama's best law firms. The other was Adolfo Ahumada, like Escobar the son of a poor black family, a man with a brilliant mind, a rebel, a Marxist, and soon to be named minister of labor. Arias was picked because he understood U.S. thinking and American law and could draft quickly and accurately in Spanish and English. Ahumada was selected for his sensitivity to Panama-nian political trends as well as his legal talent. Moreover, Torrijos expected that he, like Escobar, would be invaluable in persuading the left wing that any agreement reached was a just one. No one on the left could question Escobar's or Ahumada's credentials.

Most of the February SOFA meetings were held in the Pentagon. It was convenient because of the ready access to maps, technical data, and ex-pertise at the home base of the most interested party, the U.S. military. Strangely, it was a matter of Panamanian choice as well.

"When I'm in the Pentagon, I can smell the power," Rómulo liked to say. "And it helps me think these Americans are really serious."

An interesting social and psychological phenomenon emerged in the SOFA discussions, and it would be repeated later. Panamanians of wealth who had been educated abroad felt at a certain disadvantage in the Panama of Omar Torrijos, in a government that had labeled itself a "revolution." There were times when such men felt compelled to demonstrate that they were more revolutionary than the revolutionaries, and more anti-American than even the most fervent Marxist. In their own councils and in confront-ing us, they sometimes resorted to more violent language and extreme viewpoints than did the confirmed leftists. Men like Escobar and Ahu-mada had no need to prove themselves in that fashion. Thus, they were usually able to deal with matters of substance in a more pragmatic way and as good horse traders.

One incident illustrates the point. The flying of national flags was a con-tentious issue during the SOFA talks. Initially, each side thought that only its banner should wave over the U.S. bases. They finally agreed that the two flags should fly together and that the banner of Panama, as the host country, should be in the place of honor. The U.S. side drafted language that said the Panamanian flag "will fly *over* the defense sites" together with the U.S. flag. Jimmy Arias found that unacceptable. He said that both the 1967 draft treaty and the Spanish Bases Agreement had said that "defense sites will be *under* the flag of Panama (or Spain)." By then, Phil Barringer and the other Americans were growing tired of Arias' suspicions and his demanding manner. The U.S. expert, in an uncharacteristic show of anger, stayed with his original position and claimed the "under" phrasing was demeaning since it implied "subordination" to Panama. Arias was equally irate. If the U.S. side would not use language it had accepted before, it proved the Americans were "not in good faith" and the talks should be terminated.

Most reasonable people would say that whether flags were over the bases or the bases were under the flags made no real difference. But the spurs of patriotism and ego do strange things to men's judgment. More than once, recesses were called so Ahumada could take Arias aside and calm him down, and Smith and Kozak could do the same with Barringer. The dispute was deferred, and later settled quietly without trumpets or cymbals.

Months later, at a party at the Panamanian Embassy, Ahumada recalled the sharp arguments. "You know, I think the problem was that they're both Ivy League lawyers [Arias from Yale, Barringer from Princeton]," he said. "Those damned Ivy League lawyers are the most inflexible, stubborn bastards you'd ever want to find." Then, with deliberate irony, he added: "On the other hand, we graduates of Lumumba University* are taught to be very flexible."

By mid-February, most of the SOFA problems had been ironed out but there were still eight or ten contentious issues outstanding. They were a strange bag of apples and oranges, or perhaps grapefruit and raisins would be more accurate. For example, the Americans were arguing hard for the right of U.S. military forces to move freely throughout Panamanian territory—a significant right but a necessary one if those forces were to be able to do their job of protecting the canal. By contrast, the Panamanians were insisting that American military personnel who had cars or boats should buy Panamanian licenses. Dealt with in isolation, each issue had become a bone of contention at the negotiating table. What was needed, clearly, was compromise on both sides.

On a quiet Sunday, when the formal talks were in abeyance, a formula was finally developed. A few negotiators gathered by prearrangement at the Panamanian Embassy. Over Bloody Marys and coffee they listed the remaining, unresolved problems. Then the bargaining began. The Panamanians first wanted to know which of the issues were ones on which the United States was ready to make some concession. "That's the whole trouble," an American said. "You are asking for concessions but you're not giv-

---

*Lumumba University was established in Moscow in the 1960s. Named for Patrice Lumumba, the late Marxist leader of the Congo, it is a training ground for budding revolutionaries from the Third World. It has also been the scene of more than one anti-Soviet outburst on the part of Third World students who claimed they were treated as pawns and second-rate citizens.

ing on anything. What we need is a package deal where we *both* give in on some things." One of the Panamanians said: "Okay, that's fair enough." And so they went to work.

Through the rest of the morning and into the afternoon the haggling went on. You need A and we need B; let's both concede. You need the right to travel freely outside your bases, admitted the Panamanians, but we have to insist that your people with cars buy our license plates. On it went until a deal was struck. The final agreement was that the package of compromises would be put on the table as a Panamanian proposal, mainly because the U.S. team felt that until that point they had been making most of the suggestions, and most of the concessions. The Panamanians agreed.

The next morning, at a meeting in the State Department, González-Revilla and Escobar announced that they wanted to make a presentation. "We said we wanted to get this wrapped up by tomorrow and we're prepared to do it," Nico said. "There are hard decisions to be made, but we are ready to propose a package." They then listed all the remaining issues and what they were prepared to do about each one. A recess was called. The American team went into the hall to consult. One who had been at the private Sunday session looked at the others and asked: "How does that sound to you?" "It's great," said one. "We can buy that," said another. It was unanimous. They went back to the conference room and told the Panamanians that the package was acceptable. Jimmy Arias and Jeff Smith were asked to put the agreement into treaty language. A few weeks later, on Contadora, Ellsworth Bunker and Tony Tack initialed the SOFA agreement, the first detailed and formal accord of the new treaty. The techniques used to achieve it and the spirit that prevailed at the long, sometimes rancorous but generally friendly sessions would henceforth be cited by both sides as an example of "what we need to do and the way we should do it."

While the SOFA discussions were proceeding, there were other issues on the negotiators' agenda and they were being handled by other people and in quite different ways. One was the matter of compensation: how much Panama would receive under the new treaty. Almost everyone recognized that payments to the Panamanian government for use of one of the most strategically located pieces of real estate in the world had been grossly inadequate from the very beginning. Under the original treaty, the United States began paying Panama in 1913 the princely sum of $250,000 a year. That was revised in 1936 to $430,000, largely because of the devaluation of the dollar. In 1955, the annuity was boosted again, but only to $1.9 million (later upped to $2.3 million). Thus, in more than sixty years, we had paid Panama, in whose territory the canal had operated all that time, only about 30 percent more than we paid the defunct French canal company in one year for its rights.

The matter of appropriate compensation was discussed during the drafting of the Tack-Kissinger Principles in early 1974, but the talk never went beyond generalities. It was, however, sufficiently on the minds of both sides that Principle Number Five said: "The Republic of Panama shall have a just and equitable share of the benefits derived from the operation of the canal in its territory." To develop specific proposals on just payment, Torrijos asked Planning Minister Barletta to head a commission on compensation. The group included representatives of key government ministries as well as a few nongovernmental advisers of high quality.

On the U.S. side, planning was much more informal. Ambassador Bunker relied mainly on Morey Bell, who had some experience as an economic officer. Bell, in turn, consulted specialists in the Bureau of Economic Affairs, the embassy, and the Panama Canal Company. When he asked my advice, I said it was clear we were going to have to give Panama considerably more than we had been, but it was going to have to come from canal earnings. After all, we had been undercharging ships and cargo for decades and the time had come to reduce that subsidy of shippers and exporters from all over the world. If tolls were raised, Panama's slice of the action could be considerable. But I ended with a warning: "We can't make a deal to eventually turn over the canal to Panama and, at the same time, appear to be paying them from our own treasury for the privilege. Congress would scream bloody murder, and rightly so, and a treaty would never go through—not on that basis."

Bell prepared a memo for Bunker in December 1974, and it focused on three elements: sharply increased payments to Panama to be drawn from increased tolls; a modest economic development program ($5–$10 million annually) for perhaps the first five years under the new treaty; and perhaps $1 million a year to help beef up Panama's National Guard and help it assume a growing role in defense of the canal. Bunker floated the general formula with the Panamanians in January.

To say the U.S. approach to compensation disappointed the Panamanians would be like saying that the eruption of Vesuvius disturbed afternoon naps in Pompeii. They were flabbergasted. At the next meeting, Barletta presented Panama's case. He argued that Panama had never been adequately compensated for use of its territory for a canal that saved billions of dollars for trading nations that otherwise would have had to use alternate routes (the same case Eleta had used so effectively ten years before). He questioned the logic of a toll system that charged the same for a ton of coal and a ton of television sets. He also called attention to the fact that Panama had been the site of valuable military bases for decades for which it had received not one cent. He contrasted that with the huge benefits provided other countries (e.g., Spain, Thailand, Turkey, the Philippines) for such privileges. Barletta did not say what Panama thought fair payment would be, but it was clear the proposal the U.S. side had offered was not in its ballpark.

Faced with that stalemate, General Torrijos abruptly removed the subject from the agenda. One evening at the general's house, someone brought up the subject of payments under a treaty. Until that moment, Torrijos had been in a jovial mood. Suddenly his manner changed. He roughed up his hair with stiff fingers, and his eyes turned cold. "Look," he said, "I think we should stop talking about money. If we get what's fair, people are going to say we bought a treaty with our souls. If we make any concessions—and I know we're going to have to make some—everyone will claim it's because we're going to get millions of dollars. The hell with that. Let's settle all the other issues. Then we can talk about what the gringos will pay us for using our territory." The compensation issue was moved abruptly from the back burner to the deep freeze. It was hardly mentioned again for the next two years.

The other subject being pursued was the matter of land areas the United States would need to run the canal effectively. The Tack-Kissinger Principles recognized that Panama would regain full sovereignty over its territory, but they also provided that Panama would grant the United States "the right to use the lands, waters, and airspace which may be necessary for the operation, maintenance, protection, and defense of the canal and the transit of ships." That provision, which appeared so simple on the surface, produced by far the most complicated, technically difficult task for the treaty negotiators. It also generated, on both sides, a degree of emotion easily missed in the cold print of the final arrangement.

To handle Panama's side of the complicated issue, called by the negotiators "Lands and Waters," General Torrijos picked an old and trusted friend, Edwin Fábrega Velarde. Torrijos and Fábrega had grown up in Santiago, the capital of Veraguas province. They were classmates from the fourth grade on. In fact, they became classmates because they had so much in common: both were bright and both were troublemakers. The two boys, both from solidly conservative families, loved to play tricks on their teachers and helped create minor chaos in the classroom. In the fourth grade, they and twenty other similarly inclined youngsters were put in one classroom with a young, athletic, and stern teacher who tolerated no nonsense. The in-school shenanigans dropped off immediately, but not the extracurricular high jinks.

After high school, the careers of the two sons of Santiago diverged. Omar went to the military academy in El Salvador. Fábrega became an outstanding student at the University of Panama, earning a degree in architecture. Later he received a master's degree in city planning from the University of California. When he returned from the United States, Fábrega joined the Office of Planning in the *presidencia*. On one of his many inspection trips in that job, he barely survived a plane crash in which the pilot was killed and Fábrega sustained serious injuries. After his recovery, he established a successful contracting firm with a fellow architect, Ernest de Diego.

When Omar Torrijos took power in 1968, one of the first people he considered for a major position was his old friend. At 6:00 A.M. the morning after the coup, Torrijos called Fábrega to ask him to head the Directorate of Planning. The busy architect explained he had just concluded several major contracts and he had heavy commitments to those who had invested in his company. Fábrega recommended Nicky Barletta for the planning post, a suggestion that Torrijos accepted and that proved to be greatly advantageous for his government.

Six months later, Fábrega agreed to become rector of the University of Panama. During his brief tenure, he moved the university along the path of academic excellence. If he had stayed in place, and if his standards had prevailed, the University of Panama might have become one of the jewels in the crown of Latin American higher education. Instead, within two years, he was made minister of public works, and under his successor the university resumed its traditional role as a hotbed of political activism although some departments successfully demanded high standards.

About the same time he became part of Panama's treaty team, Fábrega was made top man in Panama's Institute of Hydraulic Resources and Electrification. He was one of the most competent, mature, and reasonable men I knew in my years in Panama.

In the early stages of the Lands and Waters talks, no one on the U.S. side could compete with Fábrega on the technical questions involved—piers and powerlines, water supply and sewage disposal, roads and dredging and repair facilities. It was not that experts were not available; rather it was an error in tactics and basic approach. Morey Bell believed all aspects of treaty negotiating should be directly, and tightly, controlled by the chief negotiator. Thus, everything was channeled through Bell to Bunker. Nervously jealous of his prerogatives as deputy negotiator, Morey opposed any independent bases of influence. The notion of setting up autonomous, high-level teams to deal with the major treaty issues was anathema.

Beyond that, Bell viewed Lands and Waters as more of a political problem than a technical or military one. He thought that if the will to get a treaty was strong on both sides, as he believed it was, then reasonable men could readily agree on whether a piece of real estate or a dock or a dredge was essential to the efficient operation of the canal. In an ideal world, he would have been correct; in the real world, his assessment was far off the mark.

When Bell asked if John Blacken, my principal political officer, could head up the U.S. team on Lands and Waters, I agreed. Blacken had a better understanding of the Panamanians than any officer on my staff. He was also a tough-minded, realistic man and I knew he would catch on quickly to practical and technical requirements. What I did not know was the depth of feeling inside the Pentagon regarding the question of lands to be kept or returned to Panamá. It took about a month to realize that things were not going as we had hoped. It should have been obvious that the dismantling of military bases or facilities under Pentagon control should be handled by the military itself. To do otherwise was to court resistance unnecessarily. Not that the military forces and the Canal Company were not consulted. They were, regularly and in detail. But they felt they were sitting on the sidelines when final decisions were made.

Bunker and Bell finally presented their Lands and Waters proposal in mid-January. They offered to return some 202,000 acres of the Canal Zone to Panamanian control. That sounded generous, but it was, in fact, less than 60 percent of the total area under U.S. control. The Panamanians were surprised and disappointed, but they concluded it was merely an opening gambit. Three days later, they made a counterproposal. It went as far in reducing U.S. holdings as the U.S. plan had gone in keeping everything possible. Plotted on a map and colored red, the U.S. proposal looked like an only slightly reduced Canal Zone. Similarly plotted and colored, the Panamanian proposal looked like little more than the canal itself. Among the negotiators, the U.S. plan got the nickname the "Giant" and the Panamanian counteroffer was called the "Snake."

Then the bargaining began. One of the U.S. negotiators took Escobar aside and said: "My God, Rómulo, your position is outrageous. We can't operate the canal with nothing but water."

"Of course not," he responded. "You just don't understand our position." He explained that Panama wanted to regard large areas as regions of "joint use." In fact, they would be used almost exclusively for canal operations, he granted. But, referring to the map the U.S. side had presented, he argued that Panama had to oppose anything that looked like a continued, though smaller, Canal Zone. As Escobar explained his ideas in more detail during the meetings, most of the Americans realized that he was suggesting an approach that could accommodate the Giant and the Snake. At a meeting in late February, following one of Rómulo's detailed expositions, a colonel from the Joint Chiefs who had taken a very hard line said that the Panamanian position had been a "real advance." "For the first time," he said, "I'm confident we can have a real bargain here." Based on Escobar's approach to the matter, the U.S. support group drafted a revised Lands and Waters position, one that took into account the innovative notion of areas of joint use (which really meant U.S. use).

During February, Bell took an increasingly active role in the Lands and

Waters discussions but without the background that would have made his interventions useful. To spur the working group to faster action, he spoke threateningly of moving the issue from the "technical" level to the "political." Everyone interpreted that to mean bringing it under his direct control. That upset the technical people from Defense and they reported what was happening to their chiefs. The latter were already nervous about surrendering one of the Pentagon's major bargaining chips before they knew how other elements in the treaty package were going to be handled. The groundwork was laid for.a large-scale revolt.

Before he left for Panama on March 6, Ambassador Bunker asked the support group to forward the new Lands and Waters proposal to the Pentagon for its approval. While he was in Panama signing the SOFA, the Pentagon rebellion occurred. The Defense bosses instructed their people on the Treaty Support Group to disapprove the Lands and Waters proposal they had helped formulate. It was the beginning of a bitter confrontation between the State and Defense departments, one that lasted all summer. It largely destroyed the effectiveness of the support group, which had been such an invaluable asset. The Panamanians never knew how bitter the conflict was within the American camp. They did realize that, beginning in March, serious treaty discussions came to a virtual standstill.

Throughout 1974, Ambassador Bunker carefully avoided the question of treaty duration. He was still operating under the Nixon guidance of 1971, which authorized a termination date, but not sooner than fifty years. Bunker had been in the negotiations less than a month before he realized that goal was unattainable. So he bided his time, waiting for the right moment to seek new guidelines.

By early 1975, Bunker felt the time had come. Before he went to Panama in March, he sent a memo to the Defense Department outlining his thinking and suggesting the United States open its mind to the possibility of a much shorter treaty, one that might end by the beginning of the twenty-first century (as we had agreed in 1967). He also proposed that insistence on exclusive rights to build a sea-level canal be downgraded and made more palatable. By that time, a sea-level waterway had lost most of the attraction it held in the 1960s—mainly because nuclear excavation had become unthinkable and the cost of conventional digging was approaching the prohibitive.

While Bunker was on Contadora, a cable arrived informing him the Defense Department agreed with duration to the end of the century for a canal treaty. But it also told him the military wanted to stick with fifty years for defense rights. Bunker's immediate reaction was: "Let's accept it. At least it gives us enough flexibility to go in and make a new proposal." He knew the Panamanians would never accept fifty years for defense rights, but he felt he could whittle that down over time. Meantime, a new offer on duration—if only for canal operations—would preserve the momentum of the talks.

Bell had other ideas. He thought Defense's insistence on fifty years, plus its backing away from the formula for Lands and Waters, reflected a conscious effort by the Pentagon to undercut the whole treaty-making effort. He felt it was time for a showdown between State and Defense on those issues. He was persuaded that, when it came, Secretary Kissinger would overwhelm any Pentagon resistance.

There were at least three serious miscalculations in Bell's recommendation to slug it out with Defense. One was the assumption that the secretary of state shared the negotiators' enthusiasm for a fair and early settlement with Panama. (Kissinger was far more concerned with the Soviet Union, the Middle East, and the evolving relationship with China than with Panama. On those big items, he needed Pentagon cooperation.) Another error was the notion that the threat of the Kissinger whip would easily cow the Pentagon brass into submission. The third mistake was the failure to realize that senior Pentagon civilians were viewing the Panama issue in strictly political terms, and saw it as a disadvantage to President Ford in his bid for reelection in 1976. The diplomatic impulse to do what was right ran into the political impulse to put off what might be embarrassing.

Nonetheless, Bell charged ahead in the drive to get new presidential guidance. He drafted a memo proposing the negotiators be authorized to fall back to twenty-five years for defense rights, if a longer period was unattainable. He included a suggestion that the president tell Defense the negotiators could turn over any land and water areas they considered appropriate. After heated argument within State, especially between Bell and Kozak, the deputy negotiator dropped the strongly worded paragraph on Lands and Waters and the completed memo went to Defense for comments. The Pentagon leaders repeated their agreement to have a twenty-five–year term for canal operations but they still wanted fifty years for defense rights. They were willing to compromise on forty years, but only if strenuous negotiating demonstrated fifty was impossible.

Knowing that Panama would never accept fifty years, or even forty, Bell decided—and convinced Bunker—that it was time to lay all the cards on the table and get a firm White House decision. On the second go-around, Bell's draft instructions for White House approval included not only allowing the negotiators to accept a twenty-five–year term for defense rights, but also giving the treaty team the right to decide which land and water areas should be retained for canal operations and defense. That memo, especially the paragraph on Lands and Waters, set off one of the most intense bureaucratic fights of the 1970s. Pentagon officials, military and civilian alike, were outraged, as was the hierarchy of the Panama Canal Company.

They thought it preposterous that State Department negotiators would solely determine which territories and facilities were needed to run and protect the canal. The ensuing verbal battle and memo barrage continued for five months, leaving tempers frayed and old friends barely speaking to each other.

In part, it was a phony argument. John Blacken and his team were consulting closely with specialists in the Canal Zone and in SOUTHCOM on every significant Lands and Waters issue. They had ample opportunity at every point to weigh in and make their views known. What rankled was not that they were kept in the dark, but that the final decisions would not be theirs under the proposed new guidance. Some generals and admirals, and a few highly placed civilians as well, who opposed a new treaty but who lacked the courage to flatly say so, used the bureaucratic fight as a means to undercut what was, and had been for a dozen years, the stated policy of their government. They used what I have always thought of as the "termite approach" to policy—to gnaw away at the underpinnings of a position they did not like, but secretly, in the dark, in small bites, and with the hope of never being discovered.

Another factor was at work in the struggle. It was the personality and working style of Deputy Negotiator Bell. A man of high intelligence and tremendous ego, he managed to convey to Pentagon counterparts an attitude of arrogance, even disdain. They became convinced he did not like them and never consulted them except when he had to. They knew that in Washington and on Contadora, Bell met frequently for hours at a time with Ambassador González-Revilla. They never received reports of those sessions. As often happens, lack of information led to doubts and distrust. Bell came to be regarded in Pentagon circles as a "soft" negotiator, one who moved too quickly to "fall-back" positions before basic stands were fully expounded and defended. It was not clear to what extent Ambassador Bunker was aware of the intramural feuding and backbiting going on around him. Bunker preserved an Old World aloofness toward personality clashes as well as the output of Washington's rumor mills. However, when a solution was presented to him after the infighting had gone on for months, he snapped at it.

When the SOFA was signed in March, Bunker and those around him had hoped final treaties could be worked out by June, but the clash between State and Defense destroyed that hope. The Panamanians, meanwhile, had no clear idea what was happening. They only knew that top-level talks with the Americans had stopped abruptly and that the only contacts were sporadic and nonsubstantive.

Meantime, Torrijos was determined to continue his program of internationalizing the issue and keeping the spotlight of world attention on Panama's "just cause." The next step in that plan was a carefully staged meeting between the general and the leaders of Panama's nearest neighbors. For three days, beginning March 22, the Panamanian leader played host on the island of Contadora to his friends the presidents of Colombia, Costa Rica, and Venezuela. After their friendly gathering they issued a joint statement, known as the "Declaration of Panama." It called on all governments in Latin America to step up support for Panama's effort to get a new treaty, and urged the United States to reach a new accord that would "eliminate the causes of conflict" between the two countries. The Latin American leaders took Washington to task for moving too slowly in the negotiations.

It was an unusual step. Heads of Latin American governments had not found it easy, traditionally, to reach full accord on international issues and to publish their stand, especially away from the protective screen of the OAS. Strangely, the unique exercise in regional diplomacy attracted almost no attention in the United States. The *New York Times*, for example, gave it only six paragraphs on page 24. In frustration, and to counter what they regarded as editorial misjudgment, the four governments published the text of their declaration as a paid advertisement in many major dailies on April 10. That attracted some notice in Washington and at the United Nations.

On their last day on Contadora, the presidents took another unusual step to ensure that their views would get a hearing at the top level of the U.S. government. They composed a joint letter to President Ford, which, like their public declaration, expressed sympathy for Panama's "legitimate" desire to retain full sovereignty over all its territory. But with Ford, the three presidents were more specific than in their public statement. They expressed concern about two issues, duration and the presence of U.S. military forces. On the former, López, Oduber, and Pérez argued it would be unfair and unnecessary for the treaty to extend beyond the end of the century. Regarding U.S. forces, they recognized the need to protect the canal but suggested some military installations adjacent to Panama's two major cities of Panamá and Colón could quickly be vacated. That would influence Panamanian opinion favorably, they said, and help ease tensions.

Ford took almost three months to answer the presidents' letter, an amazing delay in a White House that insisted that letters from Congress be answered in three days and that citizens get a reply in no more than a week. The long silence testified eloquently to the confusion then prevailing inside the U.S. government on the Panama question. When he finally did answer, in mid-June, Ford merely acknowledged the concerns expressed by the Latin presidents and repeated his administration's commitment to seek an accommodation of Panamanian and American interests.

The next opportunity for internationalizing the issue came at the annual meeting of OAS foreign ministers in Washington in May. Kissinger, using all his powers of persuasion, convinced the Panamanians not to use the

OAS gathering for a confrontation. He argued that a public face-off would play into the hands of treaty foes and only make his and Ambassador Bunker's task more difficult. With Panama's agreement, he read a joint statement to the OAS delegates on May 10. It said there had been "significant advances" in the past year but that some fundamental problems—especially duration and the use of lands and waters—remained to be settled. Kissinger told his fellow ministers that "the need for a new treaty is clear" and that he was convinced it was "imperative to achieve real and visible progress in the subjects to be negotiated." He stated that both governments were "bending their best efforts to that end," though he knew, as did many diplomats in the room, that the chief negotiators had not met for two months.

Soothed by Kissinger's assurances, the assembled ministers approved an innocuous resolution. They noted favorably the report on "progress made" and expressed hope that "a prompt and successful conclusion will be reached in the negotiations." It was probably the least they could do—and the most they could do—under the circumstances. The truth was that at that moment, in the minds of most foreign ministers, the readjustment of relations with Cuba had a much higher priority than did the U.S.-Panama dispute—at least as long as the latter appeared to threaten no open break.

Another thing that paved the way for a smooth passage through the OAS meeting was a speech the secretary of state had made two months before in Houston, Texas. It was the most detailed statement on U.S. policy toward Latin America that Kissinger had ever undertaken. On Panama, he was especially forthcoming. He said, in part:

> The United States understands that a treaty negotiated in 1903 does not meet the requirements of 1975. We are ready to acknowledge that it is reasonable for Panama to exercise jurisdiction over its territory and to participate in the operation and defense of the canal. We are prepared to modify arrangements which conflict with Panamanian dignity and self-respect.
>
> In turn we will expect Panama to understand our perspective—that the efficient, fair, and secure operation of the canal is a vital economic and security interest of the United States; that a new treaty must provide for the operation and defense of the canal by the United States for an extended period of time; and that a new treaty must protect the legitimate interests of our citizens and property in Panama.

That helped greatly to put the Panama problem in perspective. But what captured the attention of the press was what Kissinger said in the same speech about Cuba. Jerry O'Leary of the *Washington Star* captured the essence in his lead sentence: "Secretary of State Henry A. Kissinger yesterday signaled a turn toward resumption of normal relations with

Cuba." Other papers agreed on the key element in Kissinger's remarks. The *Washington Post* headlined its account: "U.S. Eyes Cuban Detente," and the *New York Times* reported: "Kissinger Makes Overture to Cuba." If one looked for any reference to Panama, he would have found it only in a paragraph, sometimes two, halfway through the stories. On Diplomat Row, of course, the full text of the secretary's speech was read with close attention. The Houston pronouncement, by design, prevented any major fireworks at the OAS meeting in May.

Kissinger's talk in Houston and a Bunker speech in Seattle soon after broke the logjam of official silence that had helped obscure what the treaty talks with Panama were all about. Members of Congress who were attracted temperamentally and intellectually to modernizing U.S. relations with Latin America suddenly had some cogent arguments to use when talking with their colleagues, and in answering mail from home. But the number so affected was still relatively small; antitreaty forces still held sway on Capitol Hill.

That was never more apparent than on the afternoon of June 26. On the floor of the House of Representatives, a desultory debate was underway over a \$7.2 billion appropriations bill to fund activities of the State, Justice, and Commerce departments for the next fifteen months. In the midst of the droning proceedings, Republican Gene Snyder of Kentucky was recognized to propose an amendment. The ultraconservative congressman (the National Association of Businessmen gave him a rating of 100 in 1974 while the AFL-CIO's Committee on Political Education gave him a 9) offered an amendment to the money bill that would have prohibited the use of any funds "to negotiate the surrender or relinquishment of United States rights in the Panama Canal Zone." Snyder had developed a unique theory that the United States was in serious danger from a vicious viselike movement that would press it from north and south. The northern jaw was represented by the Quebec Liberation Front, which was set on grabbing the St. Lawrence Seaway. The southern jaw was the Torrijos regime, which wanted to seize the Panama Canal. In that Snyderian nightmare, the man who held the handle on the vise was none other than Fidel Castro, and the bearded one was about to squeeze us unmercifully.

In his presentation to the House, the legislator from Kentucky also argued that U.S. sovereignty over the Panama Canal Zone was "as legitimate as our owning New York City." Apparently, the Kentucky congressman had not read the treaty of 1903 or the statements of Theodore Roosevelt and William Howard Taft or the many court decisions of six decades that made clear that the Canal Zone was not like New York City or Alaska or anyplace else. Nonetheless, the Snyder amendment was approved 246 to 164. Thereby, the House of Representatives, in its wisdom, sought to destroy the constitutional power of the president to make treaties, one of his few specifically stated prerogatives under the law of the land.

Several things helped explain the House vote on the Snyder amendment. On the simplest plane, the words Snyder used had a superficially patriotic sound. Congressmen with other things on their minds felt they could not go wrong in supporting "U.S. sovereignty." More than that, the U.S. government was still painfully conscious of the Watergate fiasco. The power pendulum had swung away from the White House and toward Capitol Hill. Profoundly aware of that swing, many members of Congress took childish delight in further humbling the executive branch and thereby, they thought, enhancing their own authority. It was the latest manifestation of a power struggle between the executive and legislative branches that was as old as the country itself.

Another historical battle was evident in the unstatesmanlike maneuvering. It was the ever-present jockeying for power and prestige between the House and the Senate. The Founding Fathers made the president responsible for negotiating treaties. They also provided a brake on his actions by requiring that the Senate give its advice and consent to such arrangements by a two-thirds vote. From the earliest days of the Republic, that assignment of authority in foreign affairs had given members of the House a massive inferiority complex and they regularly sought ways to right the apparent imbalance.

In Panama, surrounded by the real world, knowing we were sitting on a powderkeg, aware constantly that the central question we faced was whether we were going to have a canal that was open or one that was closed, I read congressional discussions with amazement. It seemed to me that many debaters on the Hill would have been quite at home in a medieval monastery arguing about how many angels could dance on the head of a needle.

While the House was thrashing about trying to influence the Panama treaty, the Senate had not resigned itself to a backseat. Republican Strom Thurmond revived his resolution of the previous year opposing any surrender of U.S. rights or property in the Canal Zone. He rounded up thirty-eight co-signers. As in the 1974 exercise, a number of sponsors admitted later they had not read carefully what Thurmond was proposing, or they felt it did not matter too much at that stage. Protreaty forces in the upper house began to wake up only when word went around that Harry Byrd of Virginia, the Senate's only Independent, planned to introduce a carbon copy of the Snyder amendment cutting off funds for negotiations.

The congressional liaison office at State concluded it was "hopeless" to try to beat the Byrd amendment. They reckoned without Ellsworth Bunker. The stubborn Vermonter went up to the Hill every working day for two weeks and talked with more than seventy senators. He took along a lawyer to make the legal and constitutional case, but it was Bunker's arguments that carried the day. He explained the Senate would have a shot at any treaty that was negotiated. The Byrd amendment would deprive senators of their right to approve or reject treaties, as it would deprive the president of the right to negotiate them. Bunker also pointed out, with tongue in cheek, that though he was dedicated to the negotiations, he was not so altruistic that he would pay for them out of his own pocket.

Bunker persuaded Sen. John Pastore of Rhode Island (a co-sponsor of the Thurmond resolution) to become floor leader for the administration against the Byrd amendment. Minnesota's Hubert Humphrey and Wyoming's Gale McGee rallied the liberal and moderate forces—and even some conservatives—who thought it was absurd to tell any president he could not talk with another country about a new arrangement. When Byrd realized his proposal could not win, he pulled it back.

The expected fight developed in the conference committee that took up the appropriations bill. Senate conferees refused to accept the Snyder amendment. A compromise was worked out but the House opposed it—but only by six votes. Back it went to another conference. New wording was written. More important, the amendment was reduced to a "sense of the Congress" declaration. With that face-saving formula, the appropriations bill went through both houses. More important, the right of the president of the United States to discuss new treaty arrangements with other countries was successfully defended, but it had been a very narrow thing.

Through all those hectic months, while elements in Congress tried to scuttle the work of a decade, we had to try to keep U.S.-Panama relations afloat. I was certain that if hope went down the drain we were going to face a situation far more serious than all but a handful of people in Washington realized. I knew the top leadership in our country—the president, the secretary of state, the more thoughtful members of Congress—truly wanted a modernized relationship with Panama for a simple reason: it would be good for us. But they were being whipsawed in Congress, and by emotional, highly vocal, and well-organized pressure groups. As the summer wore on, one harsh reality threw all else into shadow. President Ford was running for reelection, and the Panama issue was a political liability. The White House knew it; Ford's political followers in the Pentagon spoke of it increasingly; Republicans in Congress grew more nervous as each day passed.

Americans who knew little of Panama and thought of Torrijos as a "dictator" underestimated or did not realize the heat the man was enduring from factions in his own country. It came from both those who wanted a new treaty (and therefore faster action) and those who opposed a treaty (and therefore advocated breaking off the talks). I sometimes felt that Omar exaggerated the strength of the internal forces at work on him, but that was to be expected. Nonetheless, sources inside and outside his government were unanimous in their insistence that criticism of Torrijos was great and growing. The man was sitting on a boiler and the pressure was rising dangerously fast.

At that juncture, while the U.S. government was at war with itself and while internal pressures were building against Torrijos, I was asked by Bill Rogers, then assistant secretary of state for inter-American affairs, to make an assessment of the Panama situation. Rogers wanted to know how Panama would react to three possible developments: (*a*) if there were no treaty; (*b*) if we finished a treaty but did not submit it to the Senate; (*c*) if we submitted a treaty but the Senate delayed action on it. I closed my door, sat down at the typewriter, and began to hammer out an answer. An embassy officer was flying to Washington that afternoon, and I wanted him to carry my response to Rogers.

In a three-page letter, I gave Bill my assessment of the three possibilities he had raised. I also tried to convey some of the emotions that were swirling around the treaty issue on the isthmus. I particularly wanted him to have a realistic appreciation of Torrijos and of the forces beating on the man at that moment. Of Torrijos, faced with a "no treaty option," I wrote: "However much he might want to hold back the storm and moderate reactions, he would very soon have to decide whether he was going to use violence to resist his own people, or to lead the nationalist wave that would sweep across Panama City and Colón. Given his temperament and his deep-seated wish to make an indelible mark on the history of his country, Torrijos will not turn against his own people—even if he thinks in his heart they are wrong."

After giving Rogers a detailed estimate of each of the possibilities he had raised, I summed up my views as follows: ". . . if we fail to get a treaty, the sands rapidly run out and we face confrontation, demonstrations and probably worse. With a treaty in hand that is not submitted to the Congress, I reckon we get 6 or 8 months, during which I believe there are things we can do to further extend the deadline. If we got a treaty, put it into the Senate and that body—in its wisdom—decided to hold off on any action, I think the leadership here can neutralize and channel the extremists' threats and activities until early 1977. If nothing happens then, batten down the hatches, fasten the seatbelts, and stay away from outside windows."

One thing that provided modest light in an otherwise gloomy tunnel was the fact that Torrijos' grasp of internal problems at the Washington end had expanded greatly. As I told Bill Rogers: ". . . I see evidence that Torrijos has come to understand much better than ever before the intricacies of U.S. politics and the complicated interplay of forces that is at work. We have pushed hard to convey these 'facts of life' over the past many months here. And our negotiators have done a superb job of conveying same in their many informal talks with Panamanian counterparts . . ."

But that did not mean the Panamanian leader was ready to abandon his basic game plan. I had warned Rogers: "There is strong sentiment here behind the view that we North Americans only react and pay attention to problems when there is friction, embarrassment, and pressure from world opinion. Right or wrong, they will act on that assumption." Bearing out that forecast, Torrijos flew to Mexico in early July for a meeting with President Luis Echeverría in Agua Azul. After their session, the Mexican leader issued a statement urging the United States to abandon its hold over the Canal Zone. The ambitious, leftist Mexican politician told the press: "Latin America is impatient because it recognizes the sovereignty of Panama" over its territory, including the Zone.

Two days later, the incoming and retiring secretaries general of the OAS, Alejandro Orfila of Argentina and Galo Plaza of Ecuador, called on the United States to resolve the Panama problem as soon as possible, and with respect for Panama's sovereignty.

Those gestures of Latin American support did not go unnoticed on the seventh floor of the State Department. The day Torrijos left for Mexico, Secretary Kissinger sent a letter to the Panamanian leader. He assured the general that he had not abandoned the search for a solution to differences over the canal. He described the Snyder amendment as "a tribute to the success of what you and I have been and are trying to achieve." "I want you to know," he told Torrijos, "that in spite of these things, I am still engaged in the search for a final and just solution to this problem and the establishment of a new and more modern relationship between our two countries." Parts of the Kissinger letter were released to the Panamanian press on July 8 in an obvious effort to calm Panamanian opinion in the face of the highly publicized gestures of opposition in the Congress.

By then, the acrimonious fight between State and Defense had been going on since Washington had its last snow. The trans-Potomac conflict made the infighting that had occurred within the Panamanian team the year before look like a Sunday school picnic. Members of the once efficient and close-knit Negotiations Support Group had cut their contacts as though they represented unfriendly powers. For the secretaries, Schlesinger and Kissinger, it developed into a struggle between two of the largest egos in the capital city. Any retreat, any compromise, began to seem impossible. As usually happens in that kind of dogfight in the bureaucracy, leaks to the press were used as a weapon. Charges and countercharges seeped through the cocktail circuit and into print: "State wants to give away the canal,"

"Teddy Roosevelt is still alive in the Pentagon," "The U.S. negotiators aren't 'tough' enough," and so on and on.

The way the whole thing was being talked and written about gave the impression that the central fight was over how long the United States would keep the Panama Canal. It was not the issue at all; that had been settled in March. What was being debated was whether the United States would retain the right to defend the canal *after* it stopped operating it and, if so, for how long. Far more rancorous was an issue that was never mentioned in the thousands of words written then or in later reports. That vexed question was: What land and water areas would the United States keep as long as it operated the canal? And even more bureaucratically explosive: Who would determine what to give up and what to hold?

There was an attempt to get an agreed position at a meeting of the National Security Council in July, but it was unsuccessful. Both sides were standing fast on their proposals. Rumors spread quickly through Washington that Kissinger had tried to use the meeting to put pressure on the Defense Department. The secretary emphatically denied it. "Defense was not leaned on," he later told a reporter. "Before that they just didn't have a position." That was hardly accurate. Defense's attitude was clear, if rigid.

Two officials who stayed above the unseemly backbiting and haggling were Ellsworth Bunker and Barney Koren, the principal action officer for Panama affairs in the Pentagon. Both were experienced, level-headed men who had long since developed the ability to see the war beyond the immediate battle. Bunker and Koren were convinced a reasonable treaty would be of tremendous advantage to the United States. Both were appalled to see it moving ever closer to the maelstrom of domestic politics.

Two others who kept their heads and perspective were the young lawyers who had been instrumental in making the Support Group function effectively: Mike Kozak in the State Department's granite block on C Street and Jeff Smith in the huge five-sided building in nearby Arlington. Through the long months of interdepartmental bickering, the two managed to preserve not only friendship but also communication. One day in July, Smith called Kozak and there was urgency in his voice.

"Mr. Koren is very concerned that the negotiations are going to go down the tube if this fight continues much longer," he said. "And he doesn't think we need that. He would like a signal from Ambassador Bunker. If Bunker would be willing to compromise on the issue, he [Koren] will stick his neck out and use his contacts here to try to get people to lay back a little bit and get this thing resolved before there's any more blood spilled."

Kozak said he would check it out right away. He tried to call Morey Bell, but the deputy negotiator was ill and unavailable. Kozak took the bull by the horns, rode the elevator to the seventh floor, and went in to talk with Ambassador Bunker. He reported what Smith had told him.

"Well, for heaven's sake, of course," was Bunker's reaction. "I never wanted to go to the mat on this anyway, as you know. I was wrong to have gotten talked into it. Let's cut it off. Go back and work with them and see what kind of a deal you can come up with."

Kozak warned the elder statesman that it would probably not be too good from the negotiator's standpoint. "Right now," Bunker said, "keeping the negotiations going is more important than internal bureaucratic decisions. So let's get it over with."

Kozak went to the Pentagon and he and Smith worked out a formula that would at least move things back to where they had been in March. Bunker accepted their approach, and Koren made the Pentagon rounds selling the package to his colleagues. That prepared the way for a crucial meeting of the National Security Council on August 9. President Ford met in the Cabinet Room with the vice-president, the secretaries of state and defense, the director of CIA, chairman of the Joint Chiefs of Staff, and a few other key advisers. The battle lines appeared relatively unchanged. President Ford, impatient with the continuing fight between two of his principal departments and concerned about reports of growing Panamanian restiveness, instructed everyone concerned to review their positions, compromise their differences, and get back to him quickly with an agreed stand.

One decision made at the meeting was that the treaty talks should be revived promptly. A priority cable was on my desk the next morning asking me to inform Torrijos that the United States wanted to resume negotiations and that Ambassador Bunker planned to come to Panama in early September. The general was in the countryside, but I arranged to see him late in the day. Knowing how sharp the differences had been between State and Defense, I had no illusion that all the issues had been resolved. But I assumed there had been enough of a shift to justify Bunker's decision to revive the talks. The very fact of renewed negotiations was a relief after the painful months of trying to hold things together with little more than tape and baling wire. The general heard my news with as much pleasure as I had in delivering it. "That's good, very good," he said. "Maybe now we'll be able to move ahead."

"I hope so," I told him, "but I don't think we should expect any miracles. You're still going to have to be patient."

Of the August 9 meeting in the White House, one Defense official said: "We were asked to go back and scrub our arguments very hard and to be as forthcoming as we could be. We found a little more give." Nonetheless, all the "scrubbing" and reviewing and compromising produced a negotiation position much closer to Defense's obstinately held stand than to what

Bunker wanted and Kissinger had argued for in the NSC. National Security Decision Memorandum #302 was signed by President Ford on August 18, 1975, and went to the secretaries of state and defense as a presidential directive.

The major revision in the marching orders was the authorization for Bunker to make separate arrangements on duration for canal operations and defense. In the former case, he had authority to agree on a date "not earlier than December 31, 1999." For the first time, Bunker was freed from the unrealistic demand to get a treaty that would last for fifty years.

The orders on defense were considerably more rigid. Bunker was told to try to get defense rights for fifty years; if that proved impossible, he was authorized to "recede to no less than 40 years." He was also instructed to try to get the Panamanians to accept "a right in principle" for U.S. participation in canal defense even after the treaty expired. Anyone with the remotest understanding of Panamanian attitudes should have known that Bunker was being asked to do the impossible. The walls of downtown Panama City were plastered with signs: "Bases No!" and "Yanqui Go Home!" It would be tough enough to get an arrangement for a continued U.S. military presence for another generation. If Torrijos had accepted it for an additional fifty years, I am certain he would have been forced into exile—if he escaped being shot.

On a new or bigger canal, Bunker was instructed to try to get the longest possible period for a U.S. option to expand canal capacity. Failing that, he was to seek a Panamanian commitment that (*a*) no new canal would be built in Panama unless the United States was given the first chance to build it; (*b*) no country except Panama or the United States would be responsible for operating and defending a new canal; and (*c*) neutrality applicable to the existing canal would apply to any new canal. Those provisions were little more than an insurance policy. The United States, at that time, had no intention of building a sea-level canal, but it wanted to make sure no one else did. If changing technology and the demands of world commerce made a sea-level canal feasible and desirable by the end of the century, Washington wanted a protected option.

On the matter of Lands and Waters, the Defense Department won the day hands down. The negotiators could not select the areas or facilities to be kept and those to be transferred to Panama. Instead, Bunker was told to try to get Panama to accept the offer he had made in January. If he found it necessary to sweeten the pot to win Panamanian agreement, he was allowed to add a few additional areas—some piers in Cristóbal, jungle areas around Gatun Lake, a small portion of the Fort Sherman training area, and the like. When he saw the add-ons, one of the treaty negotiators called them "piddling little concessions, just junk."

Someone in the White House had realized that the offer outlined in

NSDM #302 probably would not win Panamanian agreement. An important sentence was added to the instructions: "If agreement is not possible on the basis of these offers, the United States negotiators should request further instructions from the President." That left the door open for early revision of the orders.

Activity in the political arena at the time probably affected treaty strategy more than negotiating decisions did. Gerald Ford had occupied the Oval Office only a year, but he had decided to run for a full term. By the summer of 1975, it was apparent he would have opposition. California's Gov. Ronald Reagan had been running hard since he left the state house in Sacramento. John Connally, former governor of Texas and Nixon's treasury secretary, was drumming up support among selected Republican audiences. Both were highly critical of Ford's effort to get a reasonable treaty with Panama. On the Democrat side, former Alabama Gov. George Wallace was conducting an active speaking campaign. Though he had been shot and partially paralyzed in 1972, Wallace had not given up hope of gaining the White House.

All three politicians were appealing to conservative constituencies. Each was slipping the Panama issue into his speeches and using it as a symbol of American retreat and weakness. It was a time when the American conscience was still badly bruised by the defeat in Vietnam. At the Veterans of Foreign Wars convention in Los Angeles on August 18, for example, both Reagan and Wallace spoke out against the "weak wills in Washington" that had "lost in Vietnam." Reagan was particularly emphatic in his attacks on eventually turning over the Panama Canal to Panama. "That nation exists only because of us," he said. He sounded like a French politician speaking of the young United States at the end of the eighteenth century.

Nonetheless, Reagan, Connally, and Wallace were scoring points, and President Ford and his political supporters recognized it. They were also aware that a sizable if amorphous "Panama Canal lobby" was taking shape based on various conservative political action groups, including an active faction in the Canal Zone. In the fall of 1975, the *New York Times* estimated the size of the antitreaty lobby at 100,000 people. By siding with the Pentagon in its tough stand on canal defense, Ford was protecting his political flank. His advisers were urging him not to go too far too fast on Panama lest he open the way for a successful attack by the right wing of his own party. It was the classic political dilemma: do you stand fast and fight for what you consider right, and possibly lose all? Or do you trim sails, retain power, then try to do what is right? Politicians and statesmen had been fighting that battle with themselves for several thousand years.

The developing political fracas was reflected in NSDM #302. In addition to providing Bunker with guidance on specific issues, the White House directive asked him to get Panama's agreement to keep the treaty talks confidential "so that the Panama Canal issue will not be injected into the domestic political process in the United States in 1976." The same directive told the State and Defense departments to consult regularly with the Congress and to start "to build support for a new treaty."

While Americans were fighting amongst themselves, and their president was puzzling over how to respond to the conflicting demands of good policy and skillful politics, Panama was pursuing its own line. The next step in Torrijos' campaign of internationalizing the issue was for Panama to join the Organization of Non-Aligned Countries. If ever an international group was misnamed, that surely was it. In its earliest years, under the tutelage of its founders, Tito of Yugoslavia, Nehru of India, and Sukarno of Indonesia, it had some tenuous claim to the title. But by the 1970s it had been infiltrated and gradually transformed into an anti-American, anti-European, anti-Israel, anti-democratic gaggle of countries that never found fault with the Soviet Union. With countries like Cuba and Vietnam taking leading roles in its activities, claims to "nonalignment" were absurd.

When I heard of Panama's plans, I went through all the counterarguments with Torrijos. He listened patiently and was disturbed by some of the background I gave him. He was most perturbed when I explained how violently anti-Israel the nonaligned group had become. Torrijos' wife was Jewish; he had a profound respect for Israel's progress under adversity and its ability to survive in a sea of antagonism; he also depended heavily on the support of the talented, wealthy, and active Jewish community in Panama. But by then, the die was cast. Torrijos explained he was not allying himself with all the extremist positions the nonaligned had adopted in the past. But he insisted that he needed the support of as much of the world community as possible for Panama and its cause. The nonaligned were another resource in his struggle.

I knew it was a losing battle. Still, I was obliged to fire one last volley. "Aren't you concerned that in doing this you are going to alienate a lot of Americans who see this nonaligned group as no more than a communist front?" I asked him.

"Look, Bill," he said, "the ones who get mad will be the ones who already don't like us. And maybe the others will think a little more and work a little harder to find a good answer. That's all I want."

In August, Foreign Minister Tack and his staff flew to Lima, Peru, for the meeting of the Non-Aligned, which lasted from the twenty-fifth through the thirtieth. The final pronouncement attacked U.S. "colonialism" and defended Panama's "legitimate cause." Panama took its distance from the anti-Zionist rantings of the final communiqué.

The impact of the Non-Aligned gathering was minimal in Washington. August is a time when residents, including members of Congress, are more interested in swimming pools and long weekends than in foreign policy.

Henry Kissinger was in the Middle East trying to work out a Sinai agreement, and if the press and U.S. officials were paying attention to anything outside our borders, it was to that troubled area.

While the effect on the U.S. government of Panama's joining the Non-Aligned was considerably less than Torrijos had expected, I was never able to convince him of that. The reason was that, on the final day of the gathering in Peru, I received a cable from Washington asking me to tell the general that several high administration officials wished to come to Panama to talk with him. I could not tell him that the warning I had sent to Bill Rogers about what would happen in Panama if there were no treaty had much to do with the coming visit. I simply told Torrijos that Deputy Secretary of Defense William Clements; Gen. George Brown, the chairman of the Joint Chiefs of Staff; and Assistant Secretary of State Rogers planned a one-day trip to the isthmus, and their main purpose was to talk with him. When I told him it had nothing to do with Lima, he just laughed and said he would be delighted to meet the visitors. He suggested they come on Tuesday, September 2, and I sent that word to Washington.

On the appointed day, Brown, Clements, and Rogers arrived at Howard Air Force Base. I met them and we transferred to a U.S. Army helicopter for the twenty-minute flight to Contadora. Cars were waiting for us on the island and we drove to the home of Gabriel Lewis. The meeting site was the large, glass-enclosed, air-conditioned sitting room where many of the treaty discussions had taken place during the previous twenty-two months.

I had not been able to give Torrijos any precise purpose for this sudden trip by our country's top soldier, the No. 2 man in the Pentagon, and the State Department's principal officer on Latin America. Panama's leader was taking no chances in case something momentous was afoot. Waiting with him were President Lakas, Foreign Minister Tack, and most of the members of the General Staff of his National Guard. The political, diplomatic, and military fronts were covered.

Torrijos was wearing his usual summer uniform, khaki pants and shirt adorned by the gold-leaf insignia of his rank and a black plastic name tag. The colonels followed their leaders sartorially, as in all things, even down to the shiny black Cordovan shoes. President Lakas and Minister Tack wore white, long-sleeved *guayaberas*. Clements, Rogers, and I were in light-weight summer suits. General Brown stood out from the rest of us in his well-pressed air force blues, with seven rows of "fruit salad" over his left pocket, and the four stars of his rank gleaming from each shoulder tab.

After the introductions were over, we settled into the available chairs and sofas. Torrijos welcomed his visitors warmly. Then, like a good tactician, he took the lead. He said he wanted his guests to know what the real situation was in his country. He recalled seventy years of frustration and inequality. He spoke of the new wave of hope that swept across the isthmus with the visit of Henry Kissinger and the agreement on the eight principles. Then, he said, the treaty talks bogged down in details and petty haggling; the spirit of the principles seemed to have been forgotten. There had not been any talks for almost six months. His people were running out of patience; they could see no results. He was doing everything he could to keep emotions from exploding, he said, "but frankly, gentlemen, I don't know how long that can continue."

Clements thanked Torrijos for his candid description of the mood. He said that we Americans understood the impatience and the desire to move ahead. We shared the wish to make progress. But he called on Torrijos, Lakas, and the others to understand our problems. President Ford would soon be actively running for a full term and he had to get his party's nomination. Clements said he was sure the Panamanians understood that the treaty issue was not a popular one in the United States. They had already seen evidence of the opposition in the Congress. Public opinion was highly vocal on the matter and largely opposed to any change. It was going to take time to change that. Meantime, we hoped nothing would be done to make our job more difficult.

Torrijos said he understood the argument Clements had made and he had sympathy for it. But he asked us to look at things from his viewpoint for a change. Every time we have run into a tough problem in the treaty talks over the past ten years, he said, your people always ask *us* to be patient, ask us to understand your political problem, talk about the Congress and public opinion. "What I am saying is that *we* have political problems, too," he said. "My people have emotions and feelings just as yours do. And if a government here doesn't give the people what they want, it can't last forever either."

General Brown said he appreciated what Torrijos was saying and he was sympathetic to it. "We all tend to look at any problem from our own point of view," he said. "What we have to do is try to see it through the other fellow's eyes."

The talk went on in that vein for quite a long time. Some of us interjected a thought here, an idea there. But for the most part, the conversation settled down to a discussion between Torrijos and Brown. The decisive moment came when Brown looked Torrijos in the eye and said: "General, you have my word as a soldier that we will work for a fair and just treaty. We are going to have problems, but I'm sure we can do it. But we can't do it quickly. I am asking you to be patient a little longer and keep things under control here until we can move ahead. Then, I assure you, we'll move." No dates were mentioned; no deadlines were set. But everyone in the room knew what was involved—the 1976 campaign, and President Ford's primary struggle.

Torrijos said he would do his best to carry out his side of the bargain. That did not mean, he added, that there would not be times of tension and even some things people in Washington might not understand. But he wanted Brown and Clements and Rogers to know that he was trusting them and that they could trust him. "We have come this far," he said, "and we can go a little farther. But please not too long. Our patience will not last forever."

Then came the farewells and we walked to the cars. Everyone in the room that day knew that a key barrier had been crossed. What made it special was the pledge made, and the pledge offered in return, by two members of the military fraternity. There is a special quality in relations between the members of that order that is often stronger than promises made between politicians or diplomats or businessmen. At least it exists between men of honor who take pledges seriously. Generals Brown and Torrijos were such men. Brown had promised to do everything possible to get a treaty; Torrijos had promised to keep the lid on in Panama until men of goodwill in Washington could fulfill their pledge.

In the helicopter, Brown and Clements asked Rogers and me to draft a short statement that would cover the day's events. The wind was whipping through the Huey because both side doors were open. I pulled out a notebook and pen and Rogers and I went to work. We wanted it short, and we wanted it clear. It took five minutes. General Brown read it to the press when we got to Panama. He explained that he and the other visitors had enjoyed "a very frank and useful meeting" with General Torrijos and the Panamanian leaders. Then came the crucial sentence: "I assured General Torrijos that the Joint Chiefs and the Department of Defense were committed to working out a new treaty and that we fully support Ambassador Bunker's efforts."

It was a major turning point in the treaty-making business. For the first time, the Defense Department and the U.S. military leadership were on the public record in support of a new treaty. It was significant enough for the *New York Times* to headline its account: "A New Panama Canal Treaty Is Now Supported by Pentagon."

Let it be said for the record that from that day on, through the long negotiations, and through the fight before the Senate, Gen. George Brown proved himself a man of his word, a man of honor, a soldier-statesman. Without him, there would have been no Panama Treaties.

For six long months, the State and Defense departments had been at war with each other. The Brown-Clements visit to Panama effectively ended that battle and brought the Pentagon directly into the treaty talks.

CHAPTER 13

The Political Ingredient

"An election is coming. Universal peace is declared, and the foxes have a sincere interest in prolonging the lives of the poultry."

—George Eliot, *Felix Holt*

THERE is a saying in Panama during the rainy season: "If the sky is clear, just wait a minute." That morning in September 1975, the sky was blue and unclouded. Ambassador Bunker and his team had come to Panama a week before to resume the treaty negotiations. In the midst of the revived talks, Bunker's deputy, Morey Bell, was called to Washington by the sudden, ultimately fatal, illness of his father. Bunker and Mike Kozak came into the capital to continue discussions with the Panamanians and to carry out some earlier commitments Bell had made—a meeting with Zone residents, a briefing of the embassy staff, and similar chores.

When I left for the office early that morning, I found Bunker relaxing on the second-floor balcony, reading the morning paper over his second coffee and waiting for Mike Kozak to join him for a quick shopping trip before a scheduled meeting with the foreign minister. We met again later in the day to review the session with Minister Tack, and Bunker and Kozak then flew back to Contadora.

That evening when I got home, I barely had time to greet my wife and take off my coat and tie when the phone rang. It was Alex Firfer, our former AID director, who was handling information problems in Washington for the treaty negotiators. He wondered if I had heard anything from Florida, and I told him I had not.

"Well, we may have a bit of a problem," he said. Alex explained that Secretary Kissinger had made a speech that day to the Southern Governors Conference at Disney World. In the question period, Gov. George Wallace of Alabama had asked the secretary: "After the unfortunate conclusion of the Vietnam war, do you feel the United States can now afford to give up control of the Panama Canal?"

Aware of the political storm then beginning to swirl around the Panama issue, Kissinger's reaction was to defend the Ford administration with a "tough" response. He told Wallace and the governors: "The United States must maintain the right, unilaterally, to defend the Panama Canal for an indefinite future, or for a long future. On the other hand, the United States can ease some of the other conditions in the Canal Zone."

I groaned when I heard the words, and Alex said, "Yeah, I know." Anyone exposed to the treaty talks over the years should have known the explosive content of words like "unilaterally" and "indefinite future." It was precisely those features of the 1903 treaty—the one-sided nature of U.S. rights and their continuation for all time—that had aroused Panamanian bitterness for so many years. It was surprising to have them used by one who prided himself on a highly developed sensitivity to nuances in political vocabulary.

Kissinger seemed to realize he had committed a political gaffe and tried to remedy it. He said that one choice for the United States would be to risk "a Vietnam-type situation" in which it had to use military force to protect its interests in the canal against resistance from Panama and most of Latin America. Kissinger thought it preferable to work out an arrangement "in which our defense interests can be maintained for many decades and our operating interests can also be maintained for several decades, and thereby defuse the immediate situation." It was a fair try, but it was his first statement, not the elaboration, that drew wire-service attention and was even then spilling out of the ticker machines into newspaper offices in Panama.

I called Ambassador Bunker because he might be the first one hit with questions about the secretary's remarks, but Bunker and his staff had gone to dinner and there was no phone at the seaside restaurant. I then called Bill Rogers in Washington to find out what he knew. He realized there was a flap about Kissinger's statement but he had no details. He said he would check it out and get back to me.

While I waited for Rogers, Bunker called. I told the ambassador what had happened and gave him a rough summary of what Kissinger had said.

"What could he have had in mind?" the ambassador wondered.

"I don't know," I told him. "Of course he was in the middle of a highly political meeting."

Minutes later, Rogers called to say he still did not have a transcript but that what he had was not good. We agreed something had to be done to limit the damage and that the best way to do it was to have Bunker give the Panamanians some kind of clarification before he left the next day. Rogers and I then composed a statement for Bunker. It cited what Kissinger had said, then went on to describe "what he really meant."

I called Contadora, told Bunker what we had done, then dictated the statement to Mike Kozak. Bunker wisely realized that repeating Kissinger's words would only cause additional pain to the Panamanians. He took them out and emphasized what the secretary had in mind. I sent the Bunker revisions to Washington and they were quickly approved.

The next morning, as he was about to leave for Washington, Bunker handed Tack a personal message. It said, in part:

> It has been learned that some statements made Tuesday in Florida by the Secretary were distorted and misinterpreted in some press reports. As we both know, we are working toward a situation in which the defense of the Panama Canal will be a joint operation in which the Panamanian National Guard will play an important role . . .
>
> What I am sure the Secretary meant was that our country could not renounce our right to defend the canal from foreign enemies until we have achieved with Panama effective agreements for the canal's defense. Up to now, the course of our negotiations has been in this direction, and nothing has changed in this respect.

The Bunker message helped, but only a little. By the time he got it, Tack had already been collared by reporters and he told them that if Kissinger's statement reflected the U.S. position "then we simply have to think of stopping the negotiations." Torrijos was incensed, and he ordered the foreign minister to put out a full report on the treaty discussions. That order was carried out three days later. The Ministry White Paper was filled with errors and exaggerations tilted in Panama's favor. One thing that the report emphasized heavily was the U.S. demand for a fifty-year term for defense rights plus authority to continue protecting the canal indefinitely. Needless to say, those disclosures set off fireworks in Panama City, especially among leftist students.

The day after Bunker left, there was a brief strike by bus and taxi drivers to protest the Kissinger statement. On Saturday and Sunday, all Panamanian papers were filled with the text of the Foreign Ministry report and comments on it. On Monday morning, buses, taxis, and crowds of people effectively closed off most entrances into the Canal Zone. Angry protest meetings were held on the grounds of the university and at many high schools. It was clear that the government was encouraging them, or at least looking the other way—and that was encouragement enough.

When I got to the office Tuesday morning, the atmosphere in the city was tense. Student groups were roaming the streets with banners. The activity seemed sporadic but I was certain it would not remain so. The Administrative Section contacted all employees who had not yet come to work and told them to take the day off. We instructed most of the other employees to go home immediately. I called the Southern Command and they helped us beef up the small Marine guard detachment. Left on board were a handful of senior officers, the Military Group, and the Marine guards. We had plans for what we would do if trouble came, but we hoped there would be no real confrontation. If attacked by force, we would have resisted with appropriate countermeasures, but I hoped Panamanian authorities would intervene before it reached that point.

As I suspected, the scattered demonstrations gradually coalesced and word came that a large crowd was converging on the embassy. Down Avenida Balboa they marched by the hundreds, shouting, waving banners, stopping traffic. A few organizers with electric bullhorns led the cheers: "Panama, Sí; Bases, No" and "Yankee Go Home" and "Down with the Zone." They filled the street in front of the embassy, they hung their hand-painted banners on the gates and on the hedge along the sidewalk, and the shouting went on and on. A dozen entered the grounds to get at the flag-pole, but that morning a couple of our Marines had loosened the halyard from its normal mooring at the base and had lashed it halfway to the top. There was no way to get at it without climbing the tall pole. Several rioters tried that but slipped back down. Someone produced a hacksaw, but the ten-inch steel column was far too tough to cut. More frustration.

Then the rocks and bricks began to fly. One after another, the windows of the embassy cracked and broke. Bottles filled with paint were thrown against the face of the building. A few Molotov cocktails crashed against the front but their worst damage was to plants at the base of the building. One smashed through a window and was quickly doused by a Marine with a fire extinguisher.

I called Torrijos but was told he was out of town. President Lakas was at a meeting. Our Military Group, headed then by Col. Paul Coroneos, contacted the National Guard repeatedly and gave them progress reports on the demonstration with pointed reminders of their obligation to protect foreign embassies. After the ruckus had continued for nearly an hour, a detachment of Guardsmen finally appeared at the rear of the embassy and deployed along the adjacent streets. Inside the embassy, we had noticed that the shouts of the demonstrators were directed not only at us Americans but also at the Torrijos government for negotiating with the gringos. When the Panamanian soldiers appeared, part of the crowd's venom was turned on them and the students began to throw rocks and bottles at the *guardia* as well as at the embassy. That turned the soldiers against the crowd and they began to use both rifle butts and tear gas to dispel the unruly mob. Before long, the streets were clear and traffic along the waterfront boulevard slowly resumed its normal pace.

I went to my desk and typed a note to the Foreign Ministry protesting the incident itself and the "inadequate protection afforded the Embassy by the National Guard." Soon after I sent it, I had a call from President Lakas asking me to come to his office. He told me he regretted the whole affair and was glad no one had been seriously hurt. I told him I appreciated his feelings and shared his thankfulness.

"But why, Mr. President," I asked him, "did it take the *guardia* so long to respond when they knew we were in trouble?"

"Maybe, Bill, it was better to have them take out their bad feelings on you instead of trying to march into the Canal Zone and get shot," he said. He had a point.

The next day, the Foreign Ministry sent a note expressing regret over the incident. I also received payment for all the damage that was done. It was enough to send about thirty students through the university for a year; instead, it went to the glass manufacturers and repairmen.

Kissinger's badly phrased statement in Orlando and the resulting sourness in Panama attracted little notice in Washington. The foreign policy machinery of the United States and the press that followed its moves were fully occupied with President Ford's forthcoming visit to China, deepening trouble in Angola, and a Middle East that seemed perpetually on the verge of explosion.

While official and popular attention was directed elsewhere, there was at least one positive development on the Panama treaty scene. When General Brown and Deputy Secretary Clements returned from the isthmus, they did some serious assessing. Despite the temporary pause to accommodate U.S. political needs, it appeared certain that treaty negotiations would proceed, however haltingly. It also struck them that the Panama talks were the only major exercise in U.S. negotiations in which the Department of Defense was playing no direct, top-level role. They decided to correct that oversight.

In early October, General Brown called retired Lt. Gen. Welborn "Tom" Dolvin at his home in Virginia. He explained that he was looking for "a retired army general who doesn't know anything about Panama." He told Dolvin that it was clear the Defense Department needed high-level representation on the Bunker team. "We want someone who will not be part of the problem," Brown explained, "but, hopefully, can be part of the solution." Explaining his earlier remark, Brown told Dolvin he thought anyone who had served previously in Panama would almost certainly have preconceived notions of what could or should be done. Brown wanted someone to look at the problem with fresh eyes. Dolvin later said: "It's the only time in my life I've ever been hired based on absolute ignorance."

Dolvin brought to his new task considerable experience that would prove invaluable. In Europe, he had worked closely with German authorities on problems that required overcoming many fixed ideas and misunderstandings. Even more applicable to the Panama problem was

Dolvin's major role in arranging the return of Okinawa to Japanese jurisdiction. In both assignments, he developed the ability to see problems through the eyes of those across the table.

Dolvin had many other qualities that fitted him admirably for the unorthodox style of the Panama negotiations. He caught on quickly and grasped treaty complications without long indoctrination. He was a pragmatist who liked to see things for himself before jumping to conclusions. Before long, he knew more about some of the docks and housing areas and warehouses than did those who were responsible for them. He had known and admired Ambassador Bunker in Saigon, so there was no awkward personal adjustment. To be sure, Dolvin had a stubborn streak that caused him occasionally to dig in his heels and resist suggested changes, but he usually had good reasons and as often as not he was right. More than once, by standing fast he saved Bunker and the other negotiators from mistakes. One other quality that helped him and his colleagues through many tribulations was a splendid sense of humor. He loved good jokes and could tell them by the hour. That approach to life helped greatly when things got rough, as they often did.

Dolvin was given two jobs. One of his "hats" was as co-chairman of the Defense Department's Negotiations Working Group. In that slot, with an office in the Pentagon, he had direct access to the deputy secretary and to the chairman of the Joint Chiefs. His other "hat" was as deputy negotiator working under Ambassador Bunker on defense-related matters. His appointment was announced on October 30, 1975. A few days later, he arrived on the isthmus for his first exposure to the mysterious world of Panama and the Canal Zone. Except for a long talk in my office and a working lunch at the residence, Tom spent his entire time in the Zone, getting acquainted with the territory and visiting with Commander-in-Chief of Southern Command Lt. Gen. Denis P. McAuliffe, Canal Zone Gov. Harold Parfitt, and key members of their staffs. The word passed quickly through both organizations that the Panama treaty negotiations had entered a new phase. It was no longer a State Department exercise, but a joint State-Defense effort. Many Zonians regarded the State Department as vulnerable game; now they had to deal with the Pentagon as well. It was disheartening for treaty enemies.

The only adverse reaction to the Dolvin appointment was within the negotiating team itself. For two years, Morey Bell had been *the* deputy negotiator and had become happily adjusted to the influence and perquisites of his position. He jealously guarded his monopoly of access to the chief negotiator. When he heard of the Dolvin appointment, he was momentarily upset, taking it, understandably but quite unfairly, as a derogation of his role and as implied criticism of the work he had done. I talked with him, as did a few other friends, and convinced him he was taking far too narrow a view. There was no question that the addition of a distinguished soldier to the negotiating team was going to strengthen the whole effort. Bell was far too bright not to see the logic of the argument and he quickly shoved aside his personal pique. Bunker worked his two capable deputies in joint harness with consummate skill.

The addition of Dolvin produced several distinct pluses. Communications between State and Defense improved several hundred percent. The Pentagon brass had confidence as never before that their views were being transmitted to Bunker in an unvarnished, soldierly way. For his part, the ambassador had a clear channel to the Defense hierarchy through which to convey his problems and some sense of the labyrinth of Panamanian psychology and emotion. On the isthmus, the fact that a lieutenant general had joined the treaty team gave Phil McAuliffe and SOUTHCOM assurance that their mission, protecting the waterway and the Americans around it, would be carefully considered. On the Panamanian side, in a government where real power rested in military hands, the addition of an experienced soldier to the U.S. team was a signal that the Americans were increasingly serious.

A fair number of people who worked in the Zone realized that some kind of new arrangement was inevitable, and even desirable. Others tried to stay above the dispute and went about their work, trusting their government would not do them in. But there was a hard core of emotional, sometimes irrational, fanatics in the Zone for whom any change would be for the worse. They thought that what was good in the days of Warren G. Harding was good forever. They did not know Panama, but they did not like Panama. They did not know Panamanians, but they were willing to write them off as incompetent and inefficient, at best, if not violent Marxists. Many spoke no Spanish, rarely visited Panama, took their vacations in the United States, and in general were about as parochial as a farmer from Montana or Mississippi who never went to the county seat.

But they were Americans and they did work on the canal or in the services surrounding it. Their jobs and their way of life were involved in any process of change that might come. Therefore, it became clear that we badly needed some form of dialogue with those hard-core opponents of any treaty. We needed to understand their fears, why they felt that any change threatened their well-being. And we needed to look for steps that might allay their worst anxieties. They, on the other hand, had to begin to understand why six presidents of the United States had concluded that a change in relations with Panama was overdue—and why it would be good for us as well as for our Panamanian neighbors.

In 1974 and 1975, we arranged meetings for Ambassador Bunker and members of the negotiating team to talk with representative Zonians, officials of civic councils, officers of unions, other community leaders. But this had severe limitations. Bunker believed strongly, and correctly, that in any negotiation it is unwise to lay out your positions in public. Once you or the other side does that you tend to get locked into that stand and it becomes doubly hard, sometimes impossible, to change. Successful negotiation is necessarily the art of give and take. When you go public, maneuverability diminishes. In those sessions, the ambassador was explaining his job in terms of general objectives, laced with reassurances that the rights of canal workers would be protected. In his audience were people who wanted things laid out in black and white. He was preoccupied with overall treaty aims—duration, defense arrangements, jurisdictional problems, compensation. His listeners wanted to know about job security, pensions, union rights, retirement, and the many other things that worried them: police patrols, schools, taxes. In truth, most of those concerns had not been dealt with in the treaty talks at that stage and there was no way for anyone to answer the Zonians' questions with the specificity they thought was their due. When they did not get the clear answers they sought, the Zonians used the necessary vagueness to "prove" that they were being "sold out." After sitting through a few of those sessions, I concluded they were doing little good. Bunker could not tell them what they wanted to hear; they refused to understand that larger problems had to be dealt with before their more narrow concerns.

Despite the obvious difficulties, it was clear that we had to have some kind of information program within the Canal Zone. The spokesman we chose for that effort was John Blacken, the capable chief of the embassy's Political Section. Beginning in the fall of 1974, with a talk before the Navy League chapter, Blacken had spoken on treaty problems to many small groups, military and civilian, in the Zone. He knew the issues as well as anyone on the negotiating team; he also understood the Panamanian scene better than most.

As a result of the many small sessions with Zonians, Blacken was pressured to address a larger group. One member of the Balboa Civic Council explained: "There are a lot of people here who want to hear somebody speak on this, not just through us. They want to be there in person and hear you and ask questions." A kind of town meeting was arranged in the Balboa High School auditorium on the evening of September 16, 1975. By 7:30 P.M., the hall was jammed and several hundred people were crowded around the building to listen through a public address system. The press turned out in force expecting a lively confrontation and ABC and CBS camera crews were on the scene as were at least ten reporters from U.S. publications.

The antitreaty forces showed up in strength and arrived early so they could fill most of the seats at the front of the hall. Blacken began speaking at the appointed hour and he talked for about thirty minutes. He was interrupted half a dozen times by boos and shouts and had to stop and wait for the disturbances to die down. The fanatics in the front of the hall were not there to listen or learn, to share ideas or get information. They were there to protest their government's policy and damn it as a subversive plot.

During the question period, Blacken fielded the audience's inquiries calmly and with as much information as was available. But most of those who spoke from the floor did not want to ask but to talk. William Drummond, a Canal Zone policeman who had gained notoriety as a rabid foe of any treaty, delivered a long, impassioned statement. "Did you know," he shouted, "that there is an outfit in New York which is a communist front organization and has produced all of the recent secretaries of state?" He said that Ambassador Bunker and Secretary Kissinger were both members. The organization he was assailing was the Council on Foreign Relations, a distinguished assemblage of scholars, businessmen, lawyers, military officers, journalists, and current and former government officials, all linked by a common interest in the world about us and a concern for U.S. policy to deal with that world.* I doubted seriously that Drummond could have distinguished among the Council on Foreign Relations, the National Council of Churches, or the City Council of Akron, Ohio. What he lacked in information he made up in vehemence.

The full flavor of the meeting came through in the last statement of the evening, made by the wife of a canal employee. "Mr. Blacken," she said, "I noticed when you came in this evening you were wearing a pink shirt. But as the evening has gone on, it's gotten redder and redder." Blacken just looked at her in amazement, shrugged, and walked from the podium. There was no good answer to the irrational.

The gathering in Balboa had been a trial for Blacken, but it helped promote the cause of a reasonable treaty. Many Zonians, the thoughtful ones, walked out of the auditorium that night with some ideas they had not heard before. They were also bothered by the extremism of some of their fellow Zonians. Reporters from major publications and TV networks left with a new appreciation of the emotional, often illogical, quality of Zonian opposition. The reports on the TV news and in the press the next day conveyed the impression clearly. It came across as something closer to a Ku Klux Klan rally than to a town meeting.

There was one other modest plus. Sitting in one of the back rows in the Balboa auditorium that night were a few Panamanians, among them Carlos López-Guevara, a member of the negotiating team, and Juan Antonio Stagg, Panama's consul general in New York. Over the years, U.S. nego-

*The council was an offspring of the Institute of International Affairs, founded in 1919, by such "radicals" as Col. Edward House, President Wilson's chief of staff; Herbert Hoover; Christian Herter; and scholar Charles Seymour, later president of Yale.

tiators had tried to explain that the U.S. government had a serious problem with the Zonians. After Blacken's ordeal in Balboa, one of the Panamanians said: "We always thought you were exaggerating. Now we understand. It's not just a logical problem; it's an emotional problem." From that day forward, when we spoke of passion versus reason, the Panamanian side understood as never before.

The September meetings on Contadora produced no real progress in the treaty effort. Ambassador Bunker had proposed a treaty package of four parts: a pact on the future of the canal, another pact on canal neutrality, a treaty on canal defense, and the already-agreed Status of Forces Agreement. Bunker offered a canal treaty that would last twenty-five years and embraced earlier agreements on canal administration and jurisdiction. The pact would have given the United States the exclusive right to expand canal capacity during the twenty-five years. It also provided U.S. canal employees the same rights the military had under the SOFA. Bunker included a payments package offering Panama twenty-seven cents for every ton of cargo that went through the waterway—an estimated $35 million a year.

The second treaty would have made Panama and the United States the guarantors of the canal's neutrality for the life of the waterway. It also provided that only the two countries could operate the canal or maintain military forces in Panama, unless both agreed otherwise. The defense treaty was to be a fifty-year pact, and there was a provision that at least three years before it expired the two countries would make arrangements for continued U.S. participation in canal defense in the posttreaty period.

It surprised no one when the Panamanians turned down the package on the final day. In a commentary passed to Bunker, Tack accused the United States of preserving "perpetuity" under guise of a defense treaty that would keep U.S. troops in Panama forever. He reminded the Americans that Kissinger had agreed in 1974 that "the concept of perpetuity will be eliminated." Tack suggested that "the end of the century" would be an appropriate final date for any treaty. The Panamanians also complained about the slow pace and wondered if the talks could not be speeded up. The Panamanian paper was given to Bunker the morning after Kissinger's talk in Orlando. Three days later, they published its main elements.

Panama's disclosure caused the usually unflappable Bunker to pen a caustic note to Tony Tack. The Panamanian action, Bunker wrote, "appears to be a distinct departure from what I took to be our agreement to carry on our discussions on a basis of confidentiality and 'no surprises.' I must confess that we were greatly surprised by the extent of the Panamanian disclosures." Panama's rush into print also raised the question, Bunker wrote, "whether we can continue to carry on our talks in the same spirit of frankness, 'give and take,' and relaxation that has characterized them up to now—and which has been so productive." The protracted treaty talks were beginning to frazzle nerves and test patience in both camps.

The next few weeks were quiet on the Panama front. But there were straws in the political wind that told the prescient observer that Panama would continue to be a burr under the president's reelection saddle. In a TV interview in Knoxville in early October, Ford assured listeners he would never accept any treaty that "would hurt the national security of the United States." Two weeks later, speaking in Philadelphia, undeclared candidate Reagan got his loudest applause when he insisted the United States retain sovereignty in the Canal Zone. Reagan repeated his message the next day in New Haven, over the weekend in New York, and then in Minnesota and New Mexico. He said later he did not realize Panama was an issue before the New Hampshire primary, but presumably his aides were noting which statements stirred applause and which fell flat. Reagan himself was sufficiently attracted to the Panama problem to hold a secret meeting in Florida in early November with deposed President Arnulfo Arias, the man whose anti-American posturing had given Franklin Roosevelt and the U.S. military so many headaches thirty-five years earlier. Arias clearly hoped that a friend in the White House would help restore him to the Presidential Palace in Panama City. What Reagan had to gain by associating with an exiled politician who had demonstrated xenophobic and racist inclinations was hard to fathom. But the candidate's later derogatory statements about Torrijos and the Panamanian government derived in part from that clandestine session with Arias and the written material that followed.

Both sides were under heavy and conflicting pressures during this period. In Washington, President Ford, Secretary Kissinger, Ambassador Bunker, and most who had any connection with Panama knew that time was rapidly running out for the old, one-sided treaty, and they wanted to reach an accommodation before there was an explosion. At the same time, the steady rumblings on Capitol Hill were a constant reminder that the issue was politically incendiary. As the year wound down, the political rhetoric of Reagan and Wallace was arousing empathy among voters. Ford's advisers, including top-level political appointees in government (like Deputy Secretary Clements and Army Secretary Callaway), were urging that the Panama issue be muffled, at least until Ford had sewed up the nomination. The problem was to keep the wheels turning, to keep the Panamanians mollified, but to move in ways that would not thrust the Panama issue into the political hopper or the headlines.

On the isthmus, extreme leftists who did not want a settlement were pushing hard for a rupture in the negotiations. Others were confident that the longer Panama stalled the more concessions it could wring from the

Americans. Still other advisers, sensitive to the increasing frustration of their fellow countrymen, were urging Torrijos to try for the earliest possible settlement. Bankers and businessmen, acutely aware of their country's economic plight, saw a new treaty as the path to short-run salvation. They argued it would bring increased revenue from the canal and, more important, would create a new climate of confidence among overseas investors. Meantime, the average Panamanian was growing more cynical and apathetic. "The government keeps promising there will be a new treaty in a month or two," a young office worker told a visiting reporter, "but nothing happens. I don't have any faith in the negotiations. I don't think the Americans will ever leave Panama."

After the inconclusive and sometimes acrimonious sessions of September, Ambassador Bunker would have been happy to see a long delay. Obviously we were far apart on key questions and he believed the passage of time would help melt resistance on both sides. But the Panamanians were in no mood to welcome a long gap. Growing disillusionment among the people plus economic pressures forced Torrijos and his cohorts to "prove" that the treaty was still high on the national agenda. Every time I ran into a member of the Panamanian negotiating team, I heard the same question: "When will we have the next round of talks?" We knew such a meeting would serve a public relations purpose more than a serious negotiating end. Still, you do not live long in the political arena without understanding that public relations may at times be as important as policy itself. Finally, reluctantly, Bunker and his team flew to Panama on November 12. His departure passed unnoticed in Washington. In Panama, his arrival was front-page news. The Panamanian government was telling its people that the effort to get a new deal was still very much alive.

The sessions on Contadora beginning on November 13 were a series of probings and clarifications based on the U.S. proposal of September. What do you mean by "neutrality"? How can the United States claim the right to defend the canal after the treaty period? Didn't we agree that "perpetuity" was finished? Why can't civilian employees have the same rights as military personnel? Panama was still insisting there be a formal international guarantee of the canal's neutrality through the United Nations. Bunker reminded them they had agreed at the end of 1974 that the United States and Panama would be the basic guarantors of neutrality while others could endorse it if they wished.

There was a particularly prickly session on November 20. Tack complained that the American position remained unchanged on everything essential. He gave Bunker a paper in which Panama alleged the U.S. position "offers no possible basis for negotiation." It accused the Americans of departing from the principles agreed upon by Kissinger. The meeting ended with sour feelings on both sides.

That day, Spain's dictator Francisco Franco died after a long illness. Governments throughout the world designated representatives to attend the funeral of the man who had controlled Spain's destiny for forty years. Panama's selection to attend the rites in Madrid was Foreign Minister Tack. He flew to the Spanish capital that night without a word to Bunker. We knew nothing of it until we read the newspapers the next morning. Bunker was left to wonder when, or whether, his counterpart would return to the negotiations he had so abruptly abandoned.

No doubt it was a calculated insult. There were many ways Tack could have explained and apologized for his temporary absence. He did nothing. I concluded that the Panamanians, having seen the rigidity of the U.S. stand, became frustrated, had a few drinks, and in an emotional moment decided that a break in the talks was inevitable. But they did not want to bear the onus themselves. They wanted Bunker to walk out—then they could blame him. The U.S. negotiator, a wise and patient man, buried his personal irritation and refused the bait. He saw the plot as a kind of "I'll show you" outburst common to grade school playgrounds, not to the world of diplomacy. He went sailing, walked the beach, read his books— and waited for the Panamanians to recover from their tantrum. Five days later, the squall had passed and Tack was back on Bunker's patio ready to resume.

The American side knew, of course, that the Panamanian rudeness was symptomatic of genuine frustration. The heart of the matter was the continued U.S. insistence on the right to defend the canal—therefore to maintain military bases—for at least another fifty years, and longer if possible. Two things about it were particularly hateful to the Panamanians. First, for those dealing with the problem, men in their forties and fifties, another fifty years was "forever." Torrijos and his colleagues thought Kissinger and the U.S. government had agreed to do away with that. Second, the demand made no sense militarily. In an age of missiles and nuclear weapons, the so-called bases in Panama would be as effective as bows and arrows. Against a threat of sabotage of the waterway, by far the best defense was the goodwill and cooperation of the Panamanian people and their National Guard. So, Panamanians asked themselves, why does the United States need bases and military forces here except to use against us if we "get out of line"? That feeling was gradually poisoning the atmosphere for an enterprise that aimed at creating a "new relationship of trust and cooperation."

Bunker understood perfectly well. He knew the hard-line stand he was being asked to push reflected not military reality but domestic politics. He was also convinced that, unless he could keep treaty negotiations afloat until U.S. policy was once again based on reason instead of emotion, we faced a possible disaster—sabotage, killing, even the closing of the canal—

and all of it totally avoidable. He decided the only thing he could do was to press to the outer limits of the instructions he had received from the president.

On November 25, Bunker told Tack, in his most austere manner, that he had reviewed the total negotiating spectrum and that he was prepared to make major adjustments. We have proposed a defense arrangement of fifty years, he said, and I am ready now to accept forty years. We offered to terminate our operational rights in the canal after twenty-five years; we will now agree to a termination date of December 31, 1999. Finally Bunker said he was no longer asking for a Panamanian commitment to accept a U.S. role in canal defense beyond the treaty's life. Instead, he suggested a clause in the new pact in which the two sides would agree to work out long-range security arrangements before the defense agreement expired. He had gone as far as he could, Bunker told the Panamanian minister. Now it was Panama's turn to look hard at its own position and make some adjustments. Bunker and his team flew back to a chilly Washington and the Panamanian team commenced a thorough review of all positions.

The November round was General Dolvin's introduction to the intricate game of treaty making. It was almost his farewell, as well. The morning after the U.S. team returned to Washington, Deputy Secretary Clements called Dolvin to his office. Why in the name of heaven, he wanted to know, did you give in on defense rights? He was talking about "residual defense"—the right to keep U.S. troops in Panama after a treaty. Dolvin explained that Ambassador Bunker felt Panama would never accept it and there was no point in holding out. Clements said coldly that Dolvin had been added to the negotiating team to protect Defense Department interests, not give them away. It was an angry session and Dolvin was completely unprepared for the scathing attack. In part, he found Clements' manner overbearing and offensive. But he felt, too, that he had been sandbagged by the other negotiators, who had failed to explain to him the sensitivity of the issue.

In truth, I think no one on the U.S. team, including Bunker, fully realized how sensitive the matter was in the Pentagon's inner ring. Obviously, it was something Defense wanted, as they "want" as much as possible in any defense arrangements. But anyone with modest exposure to the Panama problem knew that long-term continuance of U.S. military force on the isthmus was something Panamanians would never accept. Moreover, the instructions from the president had been written in very permissive terms. The negotiators were advised that "they should also make efforts to obtain a right in principle for the United States to participate in Canal defense, including a limited military presence in Panama" after the treaty expired. Bunker knew, as Clements did not, how many efforts had been made to get the Panamanians to agree to that idea. The Vermonter had been trying for a year, with different words, to bring his opposite number around. He had run into a dead end every time. In abandoning it in November, he was giving up the unobtainable.

When he learned of the trouble his decision had caused his new deputy, Bunker contacted Clements immediately. He explained patiently why what the deputy secretary wanted was not in the cards, that it was impossible for Panama. But Bunker added that he believed the essential that the United States required—the right to defend the canal against any serious attack in the future—could probably be worked out as part of the neutrality treaty in which the two countries would agree that the canal must be kept out of unfriendly hands. That was the beginning of the approach that eventually solved the problem and made a treaty possible. Clements was mollified though clearly still nervous about anything that jeopardized President Ford's political position.

The Panamanian team, led by Minister Tack, flew to Washington on December 17 for a secret round of talks. They later told me they made the flight to a snow-swept Washington in high spirits and considerable optimism, prepared to stay as long as necessary to get a treaty. Part of their exuberant mood stemmed from Bunker's acceptance of the end of the century as the termination date for a canal treaty. Another part came from our dropping the demand for "residual defense." They felt that if the Americans were willing to take one more step, to accept a defense treaty with the same duration as the pact on canal operations, they would have a viable agreement. The Panamanians were so optimistic because they saw the final step as a relatively minor one. Surely, they thought, the Americans are smart enough to know that keeping a relative handful of troops in our country for another forty years is meaningless in terms of real defense.

As a matter of fact, the December round was doomed from the outset. Ambassador Bunker was in no position to grant what the Panamanians sought. His instructions made forty years for defense the *minimum* he could discuss, and it was perfectly clear to him that any request for a change in those orders would have caused a political earthquake within the U.S. administration. The White House was already walking on eggs because of the increasingly strident Reagan attacks. Ford supporters, like Clements in Defense, would have been greatly pleased if the whole Panama problem had simply disappeared. Even Kissinger, who truly wanted a treaty, had passed the word to Bunker to stay away from sensitive treaty issues for the time being, especially the matter of duration.

The political shackles on Bunker were tight and unyielding. What made the situation doubly difficult was the fact that no member of the Panamanian team really understood U.S. politics. There was no one on the Panamanian side with whom the veteran ambassador could sit down quietly and discuss our electoral mysteries. My feeling was that the only two men in positions of power in Panama who might really appreciate what we were going through were General Torrijos and President Lakas. I talked with both of them during those days before Christmas and they both understood what the central problem was. They did not like it; but they understood it. To what extent they shared with their colleagues in the government the chilling central fact—that nothing was going to happen on the treaty until the U.S. election was over—I did not know.

With the Panama treaty talks in the U.S. political refrigerator, General Torrijos decided to continue his program of internationalizing the issue. He was persuaded that, if he just sat quietly and waited for the Americans to move, he might wait for a long time. He also had to remind his own constituency regularly that he was not simply dangling from Washington's string. Torrijos had a standing invitation from Fidel Castro to visit Cuba ever since the two countries reestablished relations in August 1974. The Cubans had pushed Torrijos several times and each time he had put them off. The slowdown in negotiations in 1975 persuaded him the time had come to play the Cuban card.

When I learned that Torrijos had decided to go to Havana, I went to see him. I had no illusions about getting him to alter his plan. I knew his mind was made up, and to have tried to divert him from this basic strategy would only have diminished our credibility. The concern of the U.S. government was not that General Torrijos had decided to visit Cuba; rather it was what he might do or say while there that could exacerbate our relations. Sitting on the porch on Fiftieth Street, I told Omar that I could see only two possible results of his trip to Cuba: it would either slow the treaty talks considerably or it would blow them entirely out of the water.

"The treaty talks couldn't be slowed much more than they have been," he said laconically. "You were there when I talked with General Brown. You and I knew nothing serious is going to happen until your elections are over."

He was right, of course, but I tried to make a distinction between slow and slower. I agreed we were not progressing on some of the big questions but insisted we were moving ahead on several secondary issues. "And that means," I argued, "that once we get the green light, we can move all the faster to the end of the road."

He took a slug of scotch and began pacing the room.

"Look," he said, "I don't want the talks to stop. They help. They keep the show going. But on the big things, we know that when you want to move, when you are ready to move, then things will move. Not before. Meantime, I have my own problems. I can't just sit and wait for Ford. You guys think only your political problems are important. My people are jumping on me every time I go out the door. 'Where is the treaty you promised?' they ask. What can I tell them?"

I told him he had a good point. It was much harder, however, for people sitting in Washington facing a tough election campaign to be always fair and statesmanlike. Paraphrasing a favorite remark from Samuel Johnson, I told the general: "Nothing concentrates a man's mind more on his own problems than the possibility of his early political extinction."*

He liked that and laughed for the first time. "It's true," he said. "I've been through it."

The general asked what I meant earlier when I talked of "blowing the talks out of the water." There was no need to recite the history of U.S.-Cuba relations over the past fifteen years. What I was talking about, I said, were two recent Cuban actions that had aroused particular animosity in my country. In September, Castro had hosted a conference of Marxists who were working for the independence of Puerto Rico, a U.S. commonwealth.

"The status of Puerto Rico is none of Castro's business," I said. "It is the business of the people of Puerto Rico." I reminded Torrijos that in the last plebiscite held on the island, 99 percent of its people had voted either to keep commonwealth standing or to become a new state in the United States.

"Anything you say, General, that might appear to ally you with Castro on the Puerto Rico question will, I can assure you, put an end to our search for a treaty," I said.

That made sense to him. "What happens there is the business of the Puerto Ricans," he said. "It has nothing to do with Panama."

The other problem I raised was Angola. In October, Castro had sent the first detachment of Cuban troops to that African country to fight in the civil war. They were helping the Popular Movement for the Liberation of Angola, backed by the Soviet Union. The use of Cuban mercenaries in Angola had stirred frenzied debate in the U.S. government. There was no coherent policy to oppose the Cuban ploy, and opinions were sharply divided between the White House and the Congress, but no one in Washington was happy about the situation.

I told the general any statement on his part that seemed to support Cuban intervention in Africa would stir up a hornet's nest. His critics were already trying to pin the "communist" label on Torrijos, and support for the Angolan adventure would only solidify that impression. The general told me he did not know what Castro was doing in Angola. He thought it was an incredible mistake, certainly one that could not help the Cuban people in any way. Later, Panama's representative at the United Nations sharply criticized Cuba's adventure on the African continent.

---

*Dr. Johnson's statement was: "Depend upon it, Sir, when a man knows he is to be hanged in a fortnight, it concentrates his mind wonderfully."

If Torrijos had any doubts about what I had told him, they were erased within a week by a visitor from Washington. Sen. Jacob Javits of New York was on a study tour of Latin America over the New Year's holiday and he stopped in Panama the day before Torrijos' departure for Havana. On the ride in from the airport, and during a working lunch, I brought Javits up-to-date on the general situation and the Torrijos trip to Cuba.

Soon after, I took the New York senator to see the general. It was good, straight talk between two experienced practitioners of the political art. Torrijos, the emotional soldier, the nationalist, the romantic revolutionary, laid out in detail his country's case for a fair and just treaty. Javits, the shrewd politician, the hard-headed lawyer, a lifelong defender of the harassed and abused, listened sympathetically. Then he quietly explained why it could not all be done overnight, even though it must be done eventually. Near the end, Javits told the general he understood the reasons for his trip to Cuba but he reminded the Panamanian leader that while he was in Havana his words would be read carefully in Washington by those of goodwill and of ill. Anything that even hinted at possible military ties between Cuba and Panama would sound the death knell for any treaty, he said. Any word of approval by the Panamanian leader of Cuba's Angolan adventure would similarly sidetrack our serious business.

Torrijos knew Javits' reputation for candor, and he realized the New York senator was one of the more influential members of the U.S. Congress. He told him his advice was "loud and clear" and that he would remember it. His visit to Cuba, which began the next day, proved he had.

The Castro regime gave Torrijos a lavish welcome at José Martí Airport on January 10. Hundreds of Young Pioneers in white shirts and red kerchiefs had been assembled to shout greetings to the visitor. The bearded Cuban leader, in his customary green fatigues, gave the Panamanian general a warm *abrazo* when he stepped down from the plane. Thousands of citizens waved flags and cheered from their nearby assembly areas. An honor guard stood at attention and a military band played the national anthems of the two countries. Strangely, none of the banners made any reference to the Panama Canal or the negotiations. The largest sign said: "Long Live the Friendship of the Panamanian and Cuban Peoples." The anti-American manifestations that would have been normal on such an occasion had been carefully shelved.

Torrijos planned his visit to the communist island with the same finesse he had used seventeen months earlier in arranging to reopen relations. He took with him a huge entourage representing every important segment of Panamanian society—government, business, labor, students, farmers, the military, the Church, the professions. He even took a group of folk dancers and musicians as a symbol of cultural exchange. The general did not want anyone in Washington, or in Panama, to say he had gone to Havana with a small clique of leftists to curry favor with Castro. Hence the representative makeup of his company, which numbered about two hundred people.

Several things were notable in the Torrijos visit to Cuba. One was that the Cuban dictator advised Torrijos, both privately and in public, to be patient in his negotiations with the United States. Many analysts in Washington had expected that Castro would push for quick action, possibly even the use of violent demonstrations. Instead, in Havana and later in Santiago de Cuba, his theme was "time is on your side." Perhaps he was sharp enough to know that, if he had pushed Torrijos toward violence, the Panamanian leader was prepared to tell him he would consider using force on the canal issue when Castro used force to regain the naval base at Guantánamo.

One minor incident during the Panamanian visit to Havana told much about Torrijos' outlook toward the trip, what he wished to get from it and what he did *not* want. During one of the breaks in the formal schedule, the Panamanian general was talking with Raul Castro, Fidel's brother and minister of defense. The wily Raul maneuvered Omar into position in front of a large hammer-and-sickle banner and ordered the official photographer to take some pictures. When the photos were taken, Torrijos turned around and immediately realized what had happened. One witness told me the angry Panamanian leader clenched his fist and took a swing at Raul. Several others reported that Torrijos stomped out of the room and locked himself in his quarters. It took a long time for him to calm down and he did so only after Cuban apologies for the "misunderstanding." At his request, the Cubans destroyed the offensive pictures.

The final noteworthy event occurred at the end of Torrijos' trip. At the airport, as he was about to depart, the Panamanian general had a press conference. He thanked his host and the friendly people of Cuba. He praised the progress made in improving the standard of living and in providing services for the people. But his parting comment was that the Cuban system might be well and good for the Cuban people, but that it was not an appropriate solution for Panama's problems. With that, he climbed aboard the jet plane and left for home. No other political leader ever had the audacity to tell the Cubans directly that their system was not the best or the most appropriate for other peoples in other circumstances.

When Torrijos got back to Panama City, he found his advisers in an uproar. During the Supreme Leader's absence, a group of Panamanian businessmen had met in the provincial capital of David and held an anti-Torrijos rally. They vigorously attacked the general and his government for a broad range of sins. Torrijos' trip to Cuba was used to "prove" that he was procommunist. Concessions made to the United States in the treaty negotiations, on the other hand, "proved" that he was too soft with the gringos. The ranchers and businessmen lashed out at the government's economic policy, which they complained was stifling free enterprise. Large landowners grumbled about the seizure of some of their property for distribution to peasants. Lack of freedom of the press was a common, and justifiable, growl. It was a long litany of complaints, many soundly based, some marginal, and a few grossly exaggerated.

Two of Torrijos' ministers were in David when the gathering was held and they were outraged at some of the things that were said. The minister of agriculture, Col. Rubén Paredes, was especially incensed by what he took as a personal attack on him. A close friend and ally of Torrijos, Paredes prided himself on his vigorous anticommunism and, in truth, he had done a great deal to rid his ministry of many leftists put in place by his predecessor. When Torrijos returned from Havana, Paredes and others filed a strong indictment of the David "plotters." Their protest was as intemperate, and as inaccurate, as the emotional outburst in Chiriquí's capital city had been.

After long and impassioned debate in government circles, ten ringleaders of the David assembly were rounded up and sent into exile. There were no indictments or judicial hearings; the whole thing was accomplished by executive fiat. Many saw it, correctly, I believe, as a victory for leftists in the Torrijos camp. It was a gross and insupportable violation of the civil rights of the men who were summarily ousted from their country, and for many Panamanians the action created bitter feelings against the regime. Certainly it retarded economic advances in a major way. The incident remained a festering sore in government-business relations for the next year and a half—until the exiles were allowed to return to their homeland. It was probably the worst mistake in political judgment Omar Torrijos ever made.

To preserve some balance, both internally and externally, the Panamanian government combined the exile of the businessmen with that of three Marxist agitators. Nonetheless, to anyone raised in the tradition of guarantees and protections that insulate the individual from the arbitrary acts of government, the performance was callous and dictatorial. As Torrijos and his supporters saw it, those prosperous men, with large assets to draw on, were considerably more comfortable in exile in Miami and Caracas and Mexico City than they would have been serving time on the prison island of Coiba. The exiles felt they had broken no laws and if tried would have been freed by a jury of their peers.

The next round of treaty talks began on Contadora on February 2. By that time, both sides knew that the increasingly contentious political campaign in the United States, and the widening split in the Republican camp, made an early Panama settlement impossible. Bunker and his team were under instructions not to make any waves that could affect the upcoming primary battles. The Panamanians by then sensed the mood on the U.S.

side quite well and had developed a growing sophistication as regards American politics.

Strangely enough, the February round on Contadora, from which neither side expected significant results, proved to be one of the turning points in the search for a new U.S.-Panama treaty. What happened was that in those sessions, with both parties totally relaxed, a new method for confronting issues emerged. It began with General Dolvin. He had been working with the Panamanians and with Americans in the Zone on the Lands and Waters problem. Instead of simply presenting rigid positions, he found he made better progress by posing theoretical questions: "What would happen if we did A or B?" "What if this small piece of land were turned over; would it affect canal operations?" "What if we gave you A? Would you then give us X?" It worked well and he was getting better insights into Panamanian and Zonian thinking that way than by focusing on narrow problems, a building here, a pier there, or an unused piece of real estate.

He told Bunker he thought the same approach would pay dividends in the overall discussions, and the ambassador decided it was worth a try. It came to be known in treaty talk circles by the name Dolvin had given it: the "what if" approach.

Starting slowly, with considerable nervousness on both sides, the "what if" method began to open up new ideas, new approaches. Both sides began to talk more openly, knowing that everything said could be disavowed. That was the method used from then until the end of 1976. One of the negotiators told me: "We discussed all kinds of different formulas which everybody then retreated from at the end of the meeting. But it gave us a good idea of what their bottom line was, and I think vice versa. From that point on, I think we all knew what it was going to take. It was a question of having the political will to do it."

At the beginning of 1976, no more than a handful of citizens in any American community could have located the Panama Canal on a map. By the end of the summer, one would have thought that reaching a new relationship with the tiny country of Panama threatened the emasculation of the United States and the end of its position as a great power. That so many otherwise intelligent people could be so manipulated by misinformation, emotional slogans, and demagoguery is a sobering realization. It nearly deprived a relatively popular, thoroughly decent, incumbent president of the nomination of his own party; it also probably helped defeat him in November.

The anti-Panama campaign by President Ford's chief rival, former Governor Reagan of California, began in the fall of 1975 with brief references to the issue. By the time the snow was melting in New Hampshire and candidate Reagan was walking through the slush of Manchester and smaller towns, he was regularly introducing his simplistic version of the Panama question and getting warm applause. When the votes were counted on February 24, political reporters, pollsters, analysts of all kinds, and Reagan himself were amazed to learn that Ford had won by only about 1,500 votes. The former actor and his advisers concluded there was gold in the Panama question.

Early in the campaign, Reagan had pledged he would make no direct attacks on the president. New Hampshire changed that. Looking at the narrow margin of votes in the Granite State, the Californian's advisers urged him to emphasize his differences with Ford. Reagan accepted the advice. In Florida, only days after the New Hampshire primary, Reagan was attacking the Republican president with gusto. The vigorous 65-year-old politician lashed out at Ford on a broad front—at the president's choices of cabinet officers, at Ford's lack of experience as an executive, and at the administration's policy on the Panama Canal.

Citing an unspecified "report published in Latin America," the candidate told an audience in Winter Haven, Florida, that the U.S. government had "secretly accepted a compromise formula in which Panama would be given sovereignty over the canal." He went on to attack another favorite target of politicians on the hustings. "If these reports are true," Reagan said, "it means that the American people have been deceived by a State Department preoccupied by secrecy."

It was political demagoguery of the worst sort. Most national politicians knew it had been U.S. policy for twelve years to reach a new understanding with Panama and that the agreement would recognize Panama's sovereignty over all its territory. The policy was made even more explicit when Secretary Kissinger signed the Tack-Kissinger Principles in early 1974. That accord was on the front pages of newspapers across the land and on every TV news program. It produced thousands of words in the *Congressional Record*. So much for "secrecy."

Why President Ford, fighting for his political life, did not jump on the issue and use it to prove how misinformed his opponent was and how badly he was misleading the American people was a mystery. Kissinger and a few others in the administration thought the president should grab the nettle and face Reagan down. Instead, he waffled, kept Bunker under wraps, and hoped the issue would go away. It very nearly toppled him within his own party. Ford could never bring himself to meet directly the challenge that Reagan raised that day in Winter Haven—and repeated interminably thereafter—when he said: "When it comes to the canal, we bought it, we paid for it, it's ours, and we should tell Torrijos and company that we are going to keep it."

What under a Harry Truman or a Lyndon Johnson would have brought a roar from the White House produced only a whimper, two days later, from the State Department. A spokesman was quoted as saying: "It is just not true that the United States and Panama have arrived at a secret agreement." That appeared at the bottom of page 34 in the *New York Times*, and almost nowhere else.

With that, President Ford turned the Panama issue over to Reagan. In the remainder of the Florida campaign, he concentrated on Cuba and other issues, branding Castro as "an outlaw," defending his record on national defense. When the ballots were counted on March 9, Ford had won in anti-Castro Florida with 53 percent to Reagan's 47 percent. It was a victory, but hardly one an incumbent president could celebrate. Ford was considerably happier about his win in Illinois a week later where he took almost 60 percent of the Republican vote in the state where Reagan was born.

The challenger's breakthrough came in North Carolina in late March. At that point, Ford had won all five primaries and there was talk in Reagan's camp of throwing in the towel and returning to California to wait for 1980. Defying the polls and the pundits, the Republican voters of North Carolina gave Reagan a 53–47 percent edge. In the scramble for explanations, most analysts concluded that what had made the difference was a thirty-minute taped speech by the ex-actor broadcast on fifteen of North Carolina's seventeen TV stations a few nights before the vote. An NBC poll found that 75 percent of the late deciders had gone for Reagan over Ford.

Within days the ex-governor was running in high gear once again. In a talk to supporters in Virginia, he attacked the Ford administration strongly, concentrating his fire on Ford's failure to "keep America strong," Kissinger's alleged willingness to "negotiate the best deal he can for us, in second place," the Panama treaty negotiations, and a call for a "quarantine" of Cuba. A few nights later, on national television, Reagan delivered another technically flawless political speech, using the material that had proved most effective in the campaign.

"The only trouble with it," *New York Times* columnist James Reston commented, "was that it was studded with vague half-truths, wildly misleading charges, and simplistic policies which even he wouldn't dare follow if he ever had the bad luck to get into the White House." Among other things, Reagan had quoted Henry Kissinger as saying: "My job as secretary of state is to negotiate the most acceptable second-place position available." The difficulty, as with so many of the candidate's "quotations," was that Kissinger had never said it. The State Department called the Reagan quotes "a total and irresponsible fabrication."

President Ford won the Republican primary in Wisconsin handily in April. But the real shoot-out was ahead, in Texas on May 1, and both candidates knew it. They campaigned energetically, visited all the main cities (and many smaller ones), and spent vast amounts of money. Part of the

explanation for the large expenditure of energy and funds was the obvious
political weight of Texas. But it was more than that. The Ford camp believed that if they could beat Reagan in Texas the Californian's campaign
would be finished. Conversely, the Reaganites were convinced that if their
champion defeated the president it would prove the viability of his candidacy and he would have a chance to go to Kansas City a winner.

While the political contenders were squaring off in Texas, the treaty negotiators were jolted by a surprise announcement. The Panamanian government disclosed on April 1 that Foreign Minister Tack had resigned. The
abrupt departure of Panama's principal negotiator stirred considerable
speculation. Was Panama losing interest in the treaty talks? Did it portend
a shift to a harder line, or perhaps a softer line? President Lakas, who accepted Tack's resignation, had no explanation for the sudden move. Torrijos was as puzzled as anyone else. Tack went into hiding and was unavailable. Those of us who had seen him fairly regularly in the preceding months
had found him increasingly moody, even depressed at times. But there was
no hint he was about to leave the treaty-making scene.

Some years later, Tack told me he believed a change of negotiators was
necessary if the talks were to move faster. He admitted there were elements
in the U.S. position that he personally could not accept. At the same time,
he believed strongly that a new treaty was necessary for both countries and
that it might be easier to reach that goal if someone with more flexibility
were doing the negotiating.

Tack's resignation was no less a surprise than was the choice of his successor: Aquilino Boyd, Panama's longtime representative to the United
Nations and a former minister. The news of Boyd's appointment perplexed
him as much as anyone. On the evening of April 1, Boyd had just returned
to his apartment from his U.N. office when the phone rang. Boyd's son in
Panama said: "Papa, the television says you have been appointed foreign
minister. Why didn't you tell us?" Boyd was amazed. "That can't be possible," he told Aquilino, Jr. "I talked to Torrijos only a few days ago about
my speech on Angola and he didn't mention anything to me." "Well," the
young man told his father, "the television says it's true."

The puzzled ambassador called Torrijos and reported what he had just
heard from his son.

"Yes, that's right," Torrijos said. "You deserve the job. You have earned
it, and I want you to be here with me. When can you come to Panama?"
Boyd said it would only take him two or three days to make the necessary
arrangements. The ambassador walked from the phone shaking his head
and gave the unexpected news to his wife, Dora. They began organizing
their move that night.

What bothered Washington about the sudden shift was the reputation
Boyd had made in the United Nations over the years as an anti-American

spokesman and a constant thorn in the side of U.S. policy makers. Because of that concern, I asked to see Boyd as soon as he took office. I wanted to find out if his appointment signified any major change in Panama's basic position. He recalled our meeting in these words: "I remember that you, my good friend, as ambassador of the United States, came to visit me in a very blunt manner. It was one of the first conversations we had. You told me, 'Well, Aquilino, do you think that Panama is really interested in these negotiations for a new canal treaty?' And I told you: 'Bill, I would not have accepted this job if I were not convinced that Panama wants, in good faith, a new Panama Canal treaty with the United States as soon as possible.'" Boyd also recalled: "As time went by, you remember, Bill, that I started pressing you because I considered that President Ford was dragging his feet on the negotiations because of the election—and because of the great pressure that Ronald Reagan was giving him for the nomination of the Republican Party."

The news for Ford out of Texas was bad, and it got a little worse each day. Reagan had taken the initiative and the president was reduced to counterpunching. Everywhere Ford went, he was bombarded with questions about his foreign policy, including Panama. The Reagan campaign strategists made sure that at every Ford appearance someone was present to throw the barbed questions. "Why are we falling behind the Russians?" "Why does Kissinger accept our being Number Two?" "Why are you giving away our Panama Canal?" One reporter covering the campaign wrote: "Ronald Reagan's campaign issues tracked the President across the Lone Star State today with the relentlessness of a Texas Ranger."

Under the pressure, the president became increasingly defensive, less sure of himself. In Dallas, when pushed on the Panama question, Ford replied: "The United States will never give up its defense rights to the Panama Canal and will never give up its operational rights as far as Panama is concerned." In one ill-considered phrase, the president had moved U.S. policy back to the days of Teddy Roosevelt. He certainly had not described the course he himself had approved eight months earlier. The next day, the White House press office issued an embarrassed disclaimer, admitting that the president's remarks in Dallas were "lacking in precision and detail." What the president meant, the press spokesman explained, was that the United States would retain operation and defense rights for the duration of a new treaty.

Watching this comedy, which was nearing tragedy, the *New York Times* was moved to comment: "Is Mr. Ford so frightened of the Reagan candidacy that he felt it necessary to respond to this cheap shot [Reagan's charge of a "giveaway"] by appearing to back off from an entirely honorable and essential policy on the Panamanian problem?" After describing the fallacies in the Reagan position and the reasons for the change in policy, the *Times* concluded: "This attitude, adopted by President Nixon and, presumably, by Mr. Ford, need be no political liability if the President understood it well enough to explain it to the American people as the absolute prerequisite for a viable United States policy toward Latin America."

Ford never made a serious attempt to explain why revision of the 1903 treaty made good sense in 1976. He could have used the issue to demonstrate his leadership and courage, as well as the jingoism and shortsightedness of his opponent. Instead, he chose to try to frighten his listeners by claiming Reagan's approach would lead to guerrilla warfare and a possible blood bath. Many Americans, still smarting from the defeat in Vietnam, were not psychologically prepared to listen to implied threats that the same thing might happen again. That approach by Ford, and by Kissinger as well, was not likely to appeal to most Americans, and certainly not to Texans. Whoever was advising the president was feeling the pulse of the American people with very thick mittens.

Nonetheless, to suggest that Panama was *the* decisive issue in the Texas primary would be a considerable distortion. In fact, on the eve of the primary vote, a number of astute political observers in the Lone Star State were describing the Panama question to out-of-state reporters as a "nonissue." Far more important for Texans was a controversy over the price of oil and gas. Congress passed a bill in late 1975 that allowed only modest and very gradual increases in fuel prices. Instead of vetoing the bill, as supporters in Texas advised, Ford signed it on the ground it was "better than nothing." Vice President Rockefeller had warned Ford of the negative reaction he could expect in oil- and gas-producing states if he signed the bill. Rockefeller later said: "He did [sign it], and he lost the election."

The votes were counted on May 1 and Reagan won in every district and captured two-thirds of the Republican ballots. One major newspaper called it "the worst trouncing ever suffered by an incumbent in a presidential primary." While Texas was not typical of the rest of the country, Reagan had proved himself a viable candidate. From then on, President Ford was "running scared" and any hopes for an early Panama treaty were dead.

Reagan's victory in Texas caused several Republican leaders to spring to Ford's defense. The day after the Texas vote, Sen. Barry Goldwater told reporters he thought Reagan did not understand the Panama issue and suggested he stop talking about it. "I have supported Ford's position," the Arizona senator said, "and I think Reagan would, too, if he knew more about it." The same day, Rockefeller told questioners on ABC's "Issues and Answers" he thought Reagan was "totally deceptive in the way he is raising the issues." On Panama, the vice-president said: "Mr. Reagan is telling the American people things that are not true. He says that we had the same sovereign rights over Panama that we had over Louisiana. That is factual misrepresentation." The criticisms from his own party had no apparent effect; California's ex-governor had discovered a popular issue and he was determined to keep hammering away at it.

As the Texas primary was reaching a climax, my hands were full trying to prevent a flare-up in Panama. Torrijos had agreed with General Brown to stay in a holding pattern until fall, but Reagan's inflammatory rhetoric was clearly getting under the Panamanian leader's skin. During a visit to Jamaica in late April, he told reporters he thought the presidential candidates in the United States were treating the Panama issue irresponsibly. He said that "one candidate [obviously Reagan] gives the impression Muhammad Ali is writing his material." Then, two days before Texas voters went to the polls, Panamanian authorities claimed to have uncovered a plot by Florida-based exiles to seize the Cuban and Spanish embassies in Panama and to hold diplomats for ransom. The plot was frustrated by the arrest of one of the alleged terrorists. Candidate Reagan was said to have given "moral support" to the Panamanian exiles. Was there such a plot? Certainly, my colleague, Spanish Ambassador Rafael Gómez-Jordana, believed it on the basis of evidence he had seen. But there was no credible link between the plotters and candidate Reagan.

There were four meetings of the negotiators on Contadora, beginning on May 3. Their most useful purpose was to introduce the new Panamanian negotiator, Aquilino Boyd, to the complexities of the treaty issues. They also allowed Bunker and Boyd to get to know each other better and to size each other up as diplomatic operators. In terms of the real business at hand, no progress was made, nor could it be. The Texas primary had cast a dark cloud over the proceedings. I called Bunker with the results the morning after he had arrived. He listened quietly and thanked me. A member of the staff who was in the room told me later that the ambassador put down the phone and looked out the window. Then he said simply: "I think I'll go for a swim."

The Reagan sweep made members of the U.S. team wonder if a treaty would ever be possible. Congressional and popular opposition looked extremely potent at that moment. Rumors out of Washington that Secretary Kissinger might be asked to resign—because of a speech he had made on ending white rule in Rhodesia, which inflamed the conservatives—did not improve the atmosphere on Contadora. It turned even darker the first Tuesday in May when Reagan won primaries in Indiana, Alabama, and Georgia. Republican leaders told Ford that Kissinger had hurt him by allowing the Panama talks to resume at the beginning of one of the busiest primary weeks in the year.

As the issue of Panama gained prominence, it became both a political and operational headache for the men responsible for the nation's military security. First, they had to decide how a new treaty would affect their respective missions of protecting American lives, property, and national interests—whether in Panama itself or elsewhere. Would a new arrangement make their jobs easier or harder. They had to be prepared to cope with a variety of situations that might arise if a treaty were not completed, or if it were rejected.

Periodically, the chairman of the Joint Chiefs of Staff presides over a conclave of all top officers of major U.S. commands throughout the world. The gatherings are unpublicized and protected by the best security possible. Such a conference was held in mid-May 1976 at MacDill Air Force Base in Florida, then the headquarters of the Readiness Command (RED-COM). At that meeting, the problem of Panama occupied the best minds of the U.S. armed forces.

Lt. Gen. Denis P. (Phil) McAuliffe, the commander-in-chief of the Southern Command in Panama, briefed his colleagues on the situation and on the military aspects of the emerging treaties. McAuliffe had in his command at the time a force of about 9,500 troops, the main combat element being an infantry brigade. The air force contingent was about 2,500 strong, equipped mainly with helicopters and light planes plus a few C-130 transports and four A-7s. The navy element was little more than a command-and-control unit with a modest logistic capability for servicing navy ships. McAuliffe described for his colleagues his plans for using his modest force to cope with minor threats to the Canal Zone—rioting on the borders, small incursions, and the like. The host and moderator of the conference, General Brown, JCS chairman, asked the key question: "What kind of a force are you going to need in Panama if fighting breaks out because this treaty has not been approved?"

That set off a long discussion among the commanders who would have had to act if real trouble developed—McAuliffe, Gen. Jack Hennessy of REDCOM, Adm. Isaac Kidd commanding the Atlantic Fleet, and others. They estimated that, if the threat came from small guerrilla units attempting infiltration, the command would need an additional 6,000 to 8,000 men, mostly army. A larger threat, conducted by well-trained guerrillas together with terrorist gangs and backed by the National Guard, would have required a counterforce of an additional 30,000 to 36,000 troops. In other words, they were considering a divisional force plus tactical air and naval backing. In what is called a "worst case" scenario—that is, with much of the population back of the effort, with an all-out insurgency under way, and with possible third-country assistance—U.S. military leaders calculated they would need a three-division force: a corps, with large support elements—100,000 men at arms in tiny Panama. Those were the best military estimates of what might be needed if Congress turned down a treaty and an embittered Panamanian populace reacted as it was likely to, or as it could. Pentagon authorities shared the figures with many members of

Congress and with key committees. They did not reach the public, however, and did not influence an increasingly emotional popular opinion. Candidate Reagan kept saying, "It's ours and we should keep it." He never talked about the price Americans might have to pay to carry out his policy. But military leaders who, with their troops, would have to do the paying had it very much in mind.

After four straight primary losses, the Ford camp was in disarray. The president seemed unable to cope effectively with his challenger's campaign of oversimplifications, catch phrases, and patriotic slogans. The strategy developed by Ford campaign planners was to have their candidate follow a "presidential" high road stressing his experience and statesmanlike goals. Others acting as surrogates would take on the thankless but necessary task of hammering away at California's ex-governor as irresponsible, extreme, and probably unelectable.

In Nebraska, the instrument chosen for the pro-Ford, anti-Reagan crusade was an unlikely but powerful one. Republican Senator Goldwater, the GOP candidate in 1964, had been making highly critical remarks about Reagan's candidacy. The Ford people gathered them together in hard-hitting, one-minute commercials that went out over forty-five radio stations across Nebraska two days before the primary election. The heart of Goldwater's message on the Panama question was: "I know Ronald Reagan's public statements concerning the Panama Canal contained gross factual errors. I also know his statements on the Panama issue could needlessly lead this country into open military conflict. He has clearly represented himself in an irresponsible manner on an issue which could affect the nation's security."

The media blitz featuring the Arizona senator failed in its purpose. Reagan won the Nebraska primary with 55 percent of the Republican votes. The only solace in the president's campaign headquarters was that Ford won 57 percent of the vote in West Virginia that same day. Goldwater, stung by a flood of critical mail, some of it accusing him of being a Communist, begged the Ford people to stop using the tapes of his news conference in the campaign. They did so. That pleased the Reagan supporters greatly. But many others who had long admired the Arizona senator's candor and courage were disappointed by his retreat for cover when the political heat was turned up.

On the Panama treaty front, not much was happening because not much could happen. Mention of the subject in Washington stirred about the same reaction as the ringing of a leper's bell in a medieval village. Between early May and late October, there were no meetings between Ambassador Bunker and Minister Boyd and sessions of the deputies were without substance. The only real action was the work of General Dolvin and Edwin Fábrega and their technical assistants on Lands and Waters problems. Slowly, persistently, they hacked away at the differences that divided the two teams trying to bridge the gap between the "Snake" and the "Giant." It was demanding work and not very glamorous, but it was essential to any final settlement, as both sides realized. Without the Dolvin-Fábrega enterprise of 1976, the final treaties would have required several additional months of negotiation.

Panama's next chance for international exposure came in June at a meeting of the OAS General Assembly in Santiago, Chile. Kissinger was there as were Panama's Boyd and the foreign ministers of the other twenty-three member nations. The Panama question was by then a fixed part of the OAS agenda, though most participants were far more interested in other matters—winning trade preferences in the U.S. market, upping the prices of commodities, encouraging the flow of technology into Latin America. Kissinger and Boyd had trouble working out a joint statement. The American diplomat favored keeping it general; the Panamanian wanted much more detail. Bill Rogers, who had been promoted to under secretary of state for economic affairs, put his negotiating skills to work and developed a compromise. The joint statement, read by Boyd to the assembled ministers, reported "significant progress" in the treaty talks (a good example of diplomatic license) and promised "a most serious effort to achieve such a treaty as promptly as possible." Boyd's demand for realism was reflected in one paragraph that admitted differences remained on some "important issues." The ministers listened politely, but outside the sessions they spent more time discussing the U.S. primaries than they did Panama. Reagan had just won California, as expected, but Ford took Ohio with 55 percent of the Republican votes. Like their counterparts around the world, the diplomats in Santiago were wondering what the U.S. election would mean to their countries.

In the heat of the seesaw battle between Ford and Reagan, outsiders were virtually ignoring what was happening on the other side of the political fence. While the president and his challenger were slugging it out week after week, a man who had begun in New Hampshire known best as "Jimmy Who?" was racking up one victory after another on the Democratic ticket. By June, it was clear that Jimmy Carter, the former governor of Georgia who had been quietly campaigning for two years, was so far ahead no one was likely to catch him. Only very late did overseas observers begin to pay attention to the relatively unknown candidate from the Deep South.

Panamanians kept asking what I thought of the Georgia governor and what his views were on Panama. I could not help them because I had never met Carter and if he had said anything about Panama, I had missed it. Finally, in the *New York Times* of June 24, I found long excerpts from a speech Carter had made to the Foreign Policy Association. One question thrown at him concerned U.S.-Panama negotiations and his answer was revealing. First, he did not try to duck the question, as Ford had been doing for weeks. Second, he showed in a dozen sentences that he had read far more of the history of the dispute than had Reagan. He said, for example: "I think the American people have lost sight of the fact that the early agreement signed in the 1900's under the aegis of President Theodore Roosevelt spelled out that Panama should have sovereignty over the Panama Canal Zone, that we should have control as though we had sovereignty, that we should have limited arms and troop placements there, that there should be an adequate payment to Panama for the use of the canal."

There was more truth and history in that one sentence than in anything Ford or Reagan had said in months. Ford wanted the right thing, but was unprepared to explain it or fight for it. Reagan was filling the air with slogans and misinformation in an appeal to emotion. To be sure, Carter made his own appeal to electoral sensitivities when he said: "I would never give up full control of the Panama Canal as long as it had any contribution to make to our own national security." But he went on to say he would "look with favor" on a sharing of control, on possibly reducing the size of the U.S. military establishment in Panama, and on increasing payments to Panama for the use of its territory. He was talking about real problems and my estimate of the man from Plains went up sharply.

By the time the Democrats went to their convention in New York City in July, it was clear no one could deny Carter the nomination. He selected Walter F. (Fritz) Mondale of Minnesota as his running mate. A Hubert Humphrey follower, Mondale added strength to the ticket, including the kind of geographic balance the Georgia governor needed.

One month later, the Republicans assembled in Kansas City. President Ford and Governor Reagan had waged a vicious campaign that went down to the wire, and even as the delegates gathered in Boss Pendergast's old hometown, the outcome was unclear. Neither candidate had enough committed delegates to assure victory and the infighting was intense. The trend finally became clear when Ford forces began winning one fight after another in the Republican platform committee. When the time came for nominating a presidential candidate, Ford won on the first ballot. Some analysts later concluded that Reagan probably lost the nomination in July when he announced that his running mate would be a liberal Northerner, Sen. Richard Schweiker of Pennsylvania. Ford wisely kept still about a running mate. Only when his party's nomination was safely his did the president announce his choice, Sen. Robert Dole of Kansas. Carter had made a bow to a liberal wing of his party; Ford's gesture was to GOP conservatives.

While the Republicans were meeting in the American heartland, Panama's General Torrijos was half a world away, in Colombo, Sri Lanka, beating the propaganda drums for his country's cause. Called Ceylon in the days of the British raj, the newly renamed republic was the host in 1976 to the conference of nonaligned nations. In reality, the Panamanian leader's trip to the Indian Ocean was a contrived political charade. The astute general had learned enough of world politics by then to know that the backing of the Nonaligned World plus one dollar would buy him a good cigar. Meantime, the Panamanian economy was suffering greatly from the drain of higher fuel costs and the shrinking of foreign investment. Prices were going up, people were finding jobs hard to get, and the blame was being put on Torrijos and his government. The general calculated that pictures of him hobnobbing with Tito, Castro, and Madam Bandaranaike would help take Panamanian minds off their immediate troubles—that plus the kind of ringing endorsement of Panama's "just cause" that he sought and received from the so-called nonaligned.

The Torrijos trip to Sri Lanka was like a loose bandage wrapped around a broken arm. Panamanian discontent with the recession would not go away regardless of a sideshow in far-off Colombo. Two weeks after the general returned, the government announced a two-cent increase in the price of a pound of rice and a similar boost for milk. It was the last centimeter in a fuse that had been sputtering for months. Angry meetings were held at high schools and the university. Before long, columns of students were marching along the main thoroughfares carrying rudely printed posters and shouting antigovernment slogans. It was not entirely coincidental that the day, September 10, was the third anniversary of the coup in which Chile's Marxist President Salvador Allende died. When the demonstrators began breaking store windows and creating other damage, the National Guard moved in with minimum force and ordered them to disband. The government issued an order banning future unauthorized demonstrations.

Four days later, students took to the streets again, ignoring the government's edict. The violence was even greater and the damage to property much higher. Dozens of store windows were smashed and some streets were impassable because utility poles had been toppled across them. Torrijos' patience was exhausted and the National Guard waded into the crowds with hard rubber truncheons. In some areas, they used tear gas. No serious casualties were reported, but several ringleaders were arrested and all high schools were closed. The government said it was shutting the schools "because of the infiltration of delinquents and extremist civilian elements into the student movement."

That sounded suspiciously like the beginning of a search for scapegoats. Within twenty-four hours, it was clear that was what it was. The morning of September 17, Foreign Minister Boyd invited me to his office and there handed me a strong protest note alleging that Americans had led the rioting and that there was a U.S. plot to "destabilize" his government. The charges were totally unexpected but I told the minister I was certain there was no basis for them and would investigate immediately. As for the "destabilization" charge, I told him it was absurd. Back at the office, I launched a full-scale investigation and we soon had the essential facts in hand.

The three "secret agents" who supposedly tried to upset the Panamanian government were: an 18-year-old private in the U.S. Army who had gone downtown for a beer, found himself in the middle of a mob, and was arrested; a 29-year-old native Costa Rican, a naturalized Panamanian, who worked as a check-out clerk at an air force retail store; a 20-year-old Panamanian who had a stolen identity card in his possession when arrested. Surely one of the most remarkable collections of "conspirators" ever assembled in a nonexistent "plot," as I told an embarrassed foreign minister the next morning.

The diplomatic note I handed him was couched in more restrained language. But the hard facts were also included. It was clear the poor minister had been given misleading information and had been asked to make a "federal case" of it. No purpose would have been served by rubbing salt in his wounds. He thanked me for the information, and the "U.S. conspiracy" allegations disappeared from the Panamanian press.

Political circles in Panama quickly decided the whole thing was a poor joke fostered by the government. Even leftist students who were in the vanguard of the antigovernment demonstrations handed out leaflets describing the charges against the United States as "a government campaign to confuse the masses." Meantime, revolutionary students were refusing to call off their protests. Trouble erupted again on September 20 when university students tried to march from their campus to the center of the city. They were blocked by platoons of National Guardsmen in battle dress and at least one hundred of the demonstrators were arrested. Fearful of the combat-ready troops and of the tear gas they were throwing, many students scampered through back alleys to get to their homes or to take refuge with friends. Others retreated to the university grounds.

By midafternoon, the soldiers had pulled back out of sight. The students set up barricades on roads leading into the university grounds and burned a government sedan they found parked on the premises. In the early evening, with some students still rampaging, the National Guard returned, blocked all entrances to the campus, and arrested another fifty students. At that point, the embattled rector of the university, Eligio Salas, a dedicated leftist, ordered an indefinite suspension of all classes at the university. That, plus the fear engendered by the Guard's tough tactics, finally put an end to the largest and longest antigovernment manifestation of the Torrijos era.

In the United States, Panama's troubles made no dent on public awareness. What dominated the eyes and ears of the American people was the
Ford-Carter contest for the presidency. One of the climactic points of the
campaign came on October 6 in a face-to-face debate between the two candidates on national television. It was an encounter probably best remembered as the occasion when President Ford announced there was "no Soviet domination" of Eastern Europe. Near the end, one panelist asked the
candidates about Panama. Would they be prepared "to sign a treaty which
at a fixed date yielded administrative and economic control of the Canal
Zone and shared defense which, as I understand it, is the position the
United States took in 1974?"

Carter noted that President Ford had seemed to back away from his
own earlier position on Panama when Ronald Reagan made it an issue in
Florida. He then gave his own opinion:

> I believe that we could share more fully responsibilities for the Panama
> Canal Zone with Panama. I would be willing to continue to raise the payment
> for shipment of goods through the Panama Canal Zone. I might even be
> willing to reduce to some degree our military emplacements in the Panama
> Canal Zone. But I would not relinquish practical control of the Panama Canal
> Zone any time in the foreseeable future.

He never explained, and the reporter had no chance to ask, what he meant
by "practical control."

To the same question, Ford said:

> The United States must and will maintain complete access to the Panama
> Canal. The United States must maintain a defense capability of the Panama
> Canal. And the United States will maintain our national security interests in
> the Panama Canal.
> The negotiations for the Panama Canal started under President Johnson
> and have continued up to the present time. I believe those negotiations should
> continue. But there are certain guidelines that must be followed, and I've just
> defined them.

Ford's answer set forth the basic U.S. objectives—free access to the canal and adequate protection for the waterway, with national security interests underlined. Carter's view, in contrast, seemed closer to the Reagan
position than to the platform his own party had adopted in July. The Panama plank worked out at the Democratic Convention had promised "support for a new Panama Canal treaty which insures the interests of the
United States in that waterway, recognizes the principles already agreed
upon, takes into account the interests of the Canal work force, and which
will have wide hemispheric support." There was a glaring difference between that and keeping "practical control" for the "foreseeable future."

One had to remember, of course, that the Georgia politician's first priority was winning approval from the American people. At that moment, less than a month before the election, talking tough must have seemed more expedient than talking sense.

Carter's statement caused a small storm in Panama. Asked about the debate that evening, General Torrijos said: "The superficial manner in which the most explosive topic in U.S. relations with Latin America was broached constitutes a great irresponsibility toward the American people." He said Ford was proud that no young Americans were fighting anywhere in the world, but he reminded him that troops of the Southern Command in Panama were "sleeping lightly with their boots on and rifles and canteens ready." As for Carter's statement that he would "never give up complete control" of the Canal Zone, Torrijos said he wanted to tell the candidate that "the word 'never' is a word that has been erased from the political dictionary."

Foreign Minister Boyd, in New York for the U.N. General Assembly, watched the debate on television and soon after had a call from an angry Torrijos. The general read the statement he had just made and instructed Boyd to pass it on to the Americans. When he met Kissinger at the latter's suite in the Waldorf Towers the next morning, he handed over the Torrijos statement. Boyd later described Kissinger's mood in that meeting as a mixture of irritation and frustration. Apparently the secretary of state felt the debate had been a disaster for Ford. Kissinger's reaction was surely caused more by what the president had said about Eastern Europe and about the Arab boycott of U.S. firms than by his remarks about Panama.

The principal result of the Boyd-Kissinger meeting was a decision to send Ambassador Bunker back to Panama soon to resume treaty talks. That gave a clear signal that, despite the election frenzy, the United States intended to pursue a new and rational arrangement with Panama. Kissinger told Boyd, however, that such sensitive matters as treaty duration would have to wait until after the election.

Two weeks before the election, I drove to Tocumen airport to welcome Ambassador Bunker and his colleagues to Panama for the thirteenth time. Driving to the airport, I kept wondering why the negotiating team was coming. There was no change in the U.S. position, so the Panamanians were bound to be disappointed. At the same time, any publicity attending a Bunker visit would do President Ford no good just before the election. The whole exercise was one of futility—and possibly something worse if the Panamanians were expecting anything significant.

At the first meeting, on October 21, it was clear to everyone that nothing would be accomplished. Most of the time was taken by a long exposition by Minister Boyd of what he called "a new compromise." The Americans found it little more than a restatement of Panama's position five months before. At the second meeting, Bunker argued for providing the Zonians with the same privileges and rights to be given the U.S. military. The third meeting was given over to a new Lands and Waters proposal worked out by General Dolvin and Edwin Fábrega. The climax of the session was a presentation on compensation given by Minister Boyd in which he insisted that Panama should get a much larger annual royalty, a percentage of income from tolls, and a lump sum payment to compensate the country for the inequities it had suffered for seventy years, in other words "reparations." The U.S. reaction was mixed. Everyone realized annual payments to Panama had been far less than they should have been. Nor was there any resistance to giving Panama a percentage of the tolls paid by ships that used the canal. But the idea of paying Panama for "inequities of the past," whether real or imagined, was politically impossible for the United States.

While the negotiators haggled on Contadora, an explosion was building within the Panamanian government. An hour after the first session, Panama's leadership circle knew the revived negotiations promised little or no forward movement. That unleashed a major controversy within the Torrijos entourage, an outpouring of emotions and frustration that had been building for months. To understand what was happening one had to appreciate the psyche of the central figure, Omar Torrijos.

The general from Veraguas was a moody, introspective, emotional man. He had tremendous ambitions, for himself and for his small country. After some years in power, he began to see himself not merely as the national leader of Panama but as a key figure in the destiny of his region, of all Central America. He suffered a strange mixture of drives and desires. At one moment, he could criticize his most dedicated followers with snide remarks and insults. The next moment, he could shed real tears when he talked of the poverty of his people and their right to have a better life.

Beyond the peccadillos and occasional pettiness, Torrijos was a man of deep patriotism. One of his favorite slogans was: "I don't want to go into history; I want to go into the Zone." But in fact he did want to go into history, and he wanted to be enshrined there as one who left his country better and stronger than when he took power. One key to leaving it better was to rewrite the rules laid down in 1903 by the United States and a Frenchman that left Panama divided by a foreign enclave and constantly subject to the whim of external power.

From the time he seized control in 1968, Torrijos vacillated regularly between force and diplomacy as the preferred route to his goal. At times he felt convinced that negotiation was the fastest and best road to his target. Two crests of that wave were the Kissinger visit to Panama in 1974 and his talk with Gen. George Brown in 1975. But there were other times when the general became darkly pessimistic, when he felt sure that only some kind of shock treatment would wake up the powers in Washington and, in turn, the American people to the fact that a change had to be made. It was in that mood that he opened relations with Castro, joined the nonaligned movement, and went to Havana in person. But those were diplomatic gestures. Having lived through the political explosion of 1964 as a troop commander in the riot-torn city of Colón, Torrijos often felt that only violence, real violence, would shake the Americans out of their comfortable dedication to the status quo. He spoke to me often, in moments of frustration, about "the other road" or "the other alternative." By that he meant force, confrontation, and bloodshed. In his blackest hours, I am sure Omar believed that only another 1964—magnified tenfold—would wake up the gringos and make them finally realize that colonialism, even the benign version practiced in the Canal Zone, was dead.

One thing made Torrijos no different from most men of great power, whether despots or democrats. There were those around him always ready to cater to his moods, to urge him on, to tell him how right he was in even the most outrageous statements. Some of them felt that by catching him in a receptive mood, when he was particularly angry or bitter, they could push him in the direction they wanted to see him go. On the question of a new treaty with the United States, several in his closest circle believed it was the wisest course for their country. Others strongly opposed any accommodation with the "devils" from North America. In October 1976, the latter caught Torrijos in a particularly vulnerable mood and went to work.

Many things created the Panamanian leader's humor at that moment. He had just suffered the strongest display of opposition to his regime in its eight-year history. That it came from those Torrijos relied on most for support, the youth, worsened his temper. His trip to Sri Lanka had had no visible effect on Washington or anyone else. He had listened to the TV debate between Ford and Carter and he felt both candidates had dealt with Panama in cavalier fashion. He was particularly upset by Carter's reference to "never" giving up "practical control" of the Zone. Then Bunker had come down with absolutely nothing new to move the treaty discussion forward. Torrijos' main foreign policy goal seemed to be fading; his economy was in chaos; his people were increasingly critical. The sense of panic became palpable. And all that time, people who did not want a treaty were working on him, slyly, insidiously, appealing to his courage, his manhood. One could almost hear them saying: "We must teach these bastards a lesson." At some point during that week, Torrijos bent under the pressure and decided to take forceful action.

It came to our attention in an unorthodox way. The evening of the last Bunker-Boyd session on Contadora, Gabriel Lewis gave a party for the two delegations in his beautiful hilltop home looking out over the Bay of Panama. It was a relaxed occasion with much good food and lots to drink.

One of the guests, Rómulo Escobar, was doing more than his share of depleting the Lewises' liquor stock. Half way through the evening, Rómulo went for a nap in one of the guest bedrooms. The party went on and finally the American guests returned to their quarters, Bunker, Bell, and Dolvin to their villa, the others to the Contadora Hotel. No one felt like sleeping and a game of water tag in the hotel pool seemed a good outlet for their restlessness.

While most of the Americans thrashed through the water trying to catch each other or avoid being caught, two of the team were sitting quietly at one end of the pool making disparaging remarks but enjoying the spectacle. One was Mike Kozak, a key member of the team from the beginning of the Bunker era; the other was Gerri Chester, an attractive, marvelously intelligent, and sensible lawyer, who had joined the treaty team in early 1975.

With feet dangling in the water, while their colleagues churned up the pool at the other end, Kozak and Chester were talking about the session just ended and what might come next. At that point, they looked up to see Rómulo wending his way in their direction. Revived by his nap, the Panamanian lawyer had returned to the hotel and was on his way to bed. He saw the Americans and walked over for a visit.

Rómulo was in a grim mood, more serious than Kozak and Chester had ever seen him. He began by saying that the negotiations were dead, that they were going nowhere. As a result, the Panamanian side had decided to "take more direct action," as he put it. In the time he had known them, the Panamanian lawyer had come to like and respect the two U.S. legal officers. He seemed to be advising them more as a fond uncle than as an adversary. "I know that you have tried very hard," he said. "But now I would advise you to get out of this. I think there is no good left in this for reasonable people. Somebody on your side is going to have to take the blame, and I hope it won't be you."

Kozak and Chester tried to reason with Escobar. "Let's give it a chance and be a little patient," they said. The U.S. election was not far off, and they believed things would look better once that was over. They reminded Rómulo that statements in recent months were campaign rhetoric, generally very different from real policy. Whether Ford or Carter was elected, they argued, the new president would look at the Panama problem much more realistically than he could in the heat of a campaign.

That might be true, Escobar granted, but it was too late. "The decision has already been made," he said, "and we are going to have to act directly." Kozak reminded him that using force would not succeed, that the army brigade and the Marines in the Zone were well trained, disciplined, and tough. Any resort to force would be met and beaten back. Rómulo nodded; he knew that perfectly well. The two Americans had the feeling that it was a moment of great sadness, of regret, for this man who had spent most of his adult life as a rebel and yet who had come in the past two years to believe that a negotiated settlement, a settlement of law and reason, was finally possible.

"I know that when we go this way, you will react and that you will occupy our country," Rómulo said. "It means the end of Torrijos and of me and of many others. We are finished. But we have to do it. It has been decided. I hope you will get out in time."

Then he wandered off to his room, his shoulders bent, deep in thought, wondering, no doubt, what the future held for him, for his family, for the country he loved. The fanatics had pushed Torrijos to the wall and there seemed no way out for Escobar and those who thought like him.

He left behind two very puzzled and deeply concerned Americans at the edge of the Contadora pool. "What was that all about?" Mike asked. He and Gerri reconstructed it word-by-word. Was it as real as it had sounded? Or was it a tactic? They thought back to the negotiating sessions of the past few days and remembered that the hard-line stand taken by Minister Boyd had sounded more like something designed to be published than a serious negotiating position. It might be part of a careful ploy, they thought, to force a break and blame the United States. That would be for others to decide. They then wrote a detailed memorandum of the menacing conversation.

I read their report the next morning. It was the beginning of the worst fortnight I spent in Panama. Rómulo was as close to Torrijos as almost any Panamanian and he was totally loyal to the general. If Rómulo said decisions had been taken, they had been taken; if he said there would be violence, there would be violence—unless someone or something intervened. I racked my brain for a candidate, but nothing came to mind. I decided I would have to wait, see how the cards fell, and play whatever was in my hand. Two days after the last meeting on Contadora, Bunker and his team flew back to Washington. When I got back to the embassy, I met with the key officers of the Country Team.

I told them there were signs we were in for a rough passage, but there was no way of knowing what form the trouble would take, or when it might happen. I suggested they fan out around town, dig out everything they could about what was happening, tap all their contacts, report every rumor. I also asked them to be particularly careful about personal security. If real trouble broke, any one of them could become a target. There was no way of knowing at that point whether we faced only the product of frustration or something much deeper and of greater consequence.

While we focused on Panama and possible trouble from that source, the next tremor came from the Canal Zone. The day after Bunker's departure, Canal Zone policeman William Drummond filed a civil suit in the U.S.

district court demanding a halt to treaty negotiations. Naming President Ford, Secretary Kissinger, and Ambassador Bunker as co-defendants, Drummond complained his constitutional rights were being violated by pursuit of a new treaty with Panama, namely his rights to "life, liberty, and property" under the Fifth Amendment. He was the same man who, at the open forum in the Zone the year before, had described the Council on Foreign Relations as a communist front. He was one of that group of Zonians who believed any change in their privileges was a blow to the foundations of the Republic. Federal Judge Crowe took Drummond's application under advisement, and gave the defendants sixty days to respond.

Three days later, in the small hours of Sunday morning, a homemade bomb severely damaged Drummond's car parked in front of his house in the Corozal housing area of the Canal Zone. Another car parked nearby received some damage as did the front of Drummond's house. There were no witnesses and the police could find no one who had seen any unknown persons or strange cars in the area. The battery-and-clock mechanism provided no clues as to who might have made and planted the device. The identifiable ingredients were of U.S. origin. By midmorning, news of the bombing had spread through the Canal Zone and Panama. Most residents of the Zone were sure that Panamanians had planted the bomb to frighten Drummond, a leader in the antitreaty campaign. On the other hand, many Panamanians were equally certain that Zonians had arranged the bomb explosion to cast blame on Panama and to influence our national election two days later.

A good case could be made for either theory. We reported the essential facts to Washington, relayed the two prevalent hypotheses, and pointed out there was insufficient evidence to prove anything.

That night, there was another explosion in the Zone. It was in the parking lot of the hospital in Coco Solo, south of the city of Colón and close to the Trans-Isthmian Highway. It did considerable damage to the outside of the building, broke several windows, and damaged some cars, but there were no personal injuries. The next evening, another bomb went off close to a housing area in the Zone. Apparently the device was thrown from a car passing along the highway that led to the Thatcher Ferry Bridge. Again, there was physical damage, mainly broken glass, but no injuries.

It seemed that Rómulo's forecast of "direct action" was becoming fact. One incident could have been a coincidence; three explosions in forty-eight hours could only be a deliberate campaign. The purpose was evident: to convince us that if the peaceful road were abandoned the alternative was the use of force. There was probably a secondary goal, that is, to convince residents of the Zone that they were vulnerable and that their vitriolic and anti-Panamanian attitudes violated Panamanian pride and would be countered. If that was a purpose, it was succeeding. I had never seen the Zone in such a state of nerves.

It was less important to me to know why and how the bombing exercise had been launched than it was to end it as quickly as possible. Unless the Panamanian government had a death wish, the use of random explosives was idiotic. To that point, there seemed to be a deliberate effort to avoid human casualties. But I knew it was only a matter of time until some "accident" occurred—a man walking his dog at night in the wrong field, a car parked in an unaccustomed place, an excessive charge that caused more damage than planned. I had seen enough of explosives and human error over the years to know that luck was perishable.

But what could be done? Whatever my suspicions at that juncture, I had no evidence that the perpetrator or responsible group was Panamanian. What I did was pass the word quickly and emphatically through every available channel that the use of explosives was madness, that it would end any chance for a reasonable solution in the foreseeable future, and that those who suffered most would be the Panamanian people. All senior officers in the embassy relayed that message to every contact they could reach.

Tuesday November 2 was election day. The embassy had a huge election-night party at the El Panamá Hotel, complete with a massive board of states to record the votes as they came in, a dozen TV monitors carrying the results, and even wire service tickers for those interested in details. There were bowls of Ford and Carter buttons at the entrance so the guests could display their personal preferences. The turnout was enormous—most of the American community in Panama City; the entire diplomatic corps; a large number of Panamanians from the business community and from the government, too. Gov. Hal Parfitt and his wife, Pat, were there, but few others from the Zone.

By midnight it was apparent Jimmy Carter would be the next president of the United States. Antitreaty people who had read his campaign statements were delighted. The protreaty forces, who had counted on Ford's strong commitment to a new agreement, went home disappointed. I myself had become skeptical over the years about statements made in the heat of a close campaign. On the way home that night, I told Mili: "Once Carter is in the White House and has a chance to look at this thing carefully, he'll probably come to the same conclusion every other president has for the past twenty years."

During the next few days, I began to receive disturbing reports from intelligence sources. They indicated that a few members of the National Guard knew more about the recent bombing incidents than they could have learned from skimpy press accounts. Later reports suggested that a few Guardsmen not only knew about but might also have taken part in the exercise. We knew that several members of the Guard had received training in demolitions and explosives, some from us, some from other countries.

We had no evidence that linked Torrijos himself or any members of the General Staff with the incidents. It was possible that lower-echelon personnel had decided to be "patriots" and that they had acted without direct orders from above. It was not entirely incredible that a group outside the Guard, hoping to derail the treaty effort, had undertaken this foolhardy action and had drawn on a few friends in the Guard for advice and cooperation. I had to accept both scenarios as possibilities, however remote. Nonetheless, the reports I had received called for a reaction and Washington instructed me to take it up with "appropriate Panamanian authorities."

Normally, when an ambassador has a problem to raise with the host government, he goes to the foreign minister. He does have the right in matters of great importance or delicacy to ask to see the head of the government. In this case, the situation was of the utmost sensitivity. Second, it involved the National Guard, and Torrijos was not only the chief of the "Revolutionary Government" but also commandant of the National Guard. Finally, I believed that, in the alleged plot to "destabilize the government" by "intelligence agents," the police had given the foreign minister misleading and even erroneous information. I had no doubt they would do the same in this case. To see Minister Boyd on this matter would only have embarrassed him, frustrated me, and produced no quick solution. Therefore, I asked to see General Torrijos.

I gave no reason for my visit, but it was immediately apparent he knew precisely what it was. I realized that as soon as I received his message that he would see me in his office at *guardia* headquarters. It was a first. For two and a half years, on the many occasions when Omar and I met, it was invariably at his beach house in Farallon, his retreat on Fiftieth Street, or at the houses of mutual friends. Also, we almost always met late in the afternoon or early evening so we could share a glass or two, relax, and talk over whatever was happening. For Omar to suggest a meeting in his National Guard office at 10 o'clock in the morning meant only one thing: he was expecting trouble.

I took Ray Gonzalez, my deputy, to the session. Ray's Spanish was fluent and I wanted total precision in this discussion. I also wanted a witness so there was later no misunderstanding about what was said. When we walked into Torrijos' rather Spartan office, he appeared agitated, distracted, and colder than I had ever seen him. With him (his witness) was Lt. Col. Roberto Díaz Herrera, executive secretary of the General Staff and the general's cousin.

I told Torrijos I had come on very serious business. I reminded him of the recent bombing incidents. "It is painful and unpleasant for me to tell you that I have received certain information in recent days that indicates some members of the Panamanian National Guard knew of these incidents in advance, and some of them may have taken a direct role in them," I said. He was looking at me with frozen, angry eyes, but he said nothing. I said I realized it might be possible this was done without direct orders or even the knowledge of the top level of the Guard. I urged him to look into it and, more important, to make sure it did not happen again. If there was any repetition, I could only warn that it would have the most profound and negative effect on relations between our countries.

I reminded the general how far we had traveled on the road to a treaty, and how close I thought we then were. All of that, I said, would be destroyed if this kind of terrorism were to continue for another day. I ended by telling him what he knew perfectly well, that I spoke as a friend of Panama who wanted to see the closest and best relations possible between our countries and peoples.

The only sound in the room was the drumming of Torrijos' fingers on his desk. Then the general said that the charges I had made were unprecedented. If I were not a friend, he would walk out then and there. He asked what proof I had. "Show me the proof, and you can be sure I'll do something about it right away," he said.

It was what I had expected, what I would have said if the positions had been reversed. Obviously he wanted to know how much we knew, and where it came from. If there was a leak in his own organization, he wanted to close it off. I told him that obviously I could not disclose how or from whom I had received the information I had given him. Whether it was 100 percent accurate, or something less than that, I believed it was basically true, otherwise I would not have come to see him.

He insisted it was not true, could not be true. This kind of thing could not happen without his knowing about it. But he promised to look into it immediately, if only to assure himself that it could not have happened. I thanked him and Ray and I left. It was the most painful session I ever had with Omar, and neither of us ever forgot it. But pain is one of the ingredients of policy. What really mattered was that from that day forward there was never another incident of violence or terrorism in the Canal Zone until I left Panama.

Through November, there was a wholesale review of Panama's position. By then, I think Torrijos realized that those who had been pushing him in the direction of violence had really been prescribing disaster—for Panama, for his government, and for him. Voices of reason in the general's inner circle began to have an impact. I suspect that other influences were at work during those critical weeks—possibly President Lakas and key members of the General Staff, possibly businessmen and bankers, possibly the heads of other governments, and probably all of them—to persuade Torrijos to stay calm and avoid any irrevocable actions or final judgments. One thing that may have helped improve the atmosphere was the noises coming from the Carter camp, assurances that the new administration wanted to take a fresh and unprejudiced look at the Panama problem. It was clear early on that the new secretary of state would be Cyrus Vance, and I repeated endlessly to my Panamanian contacts that he was a man of high intelligence, great wisdom, courage, and fairness. He would look at the Panama issue, I assured them, with understanding and with a sense of history.

Whatever the reasons, and they were varied, the mood of confrontation dissipated and Minister Boyd made ready to go to Washington. His main purpose was to assure that the new administration picked up where the old was leaving off. He arrived in the capital on December 1 in a temperature that was about fifty degrees lower than the one he left behind.

One part of his mission was to set at rest any fears people in Washington may have felt about the recent bombings in the Zone. After three weeks of waiting for the "proof" he had asked me for, I think Torrijos decided either that we were not going to produce anything or that it was less than convincing. Whichever it was, he felt free to take the offensive. The day before Boyd left for Washington, Torrijos gave him a letter addressed to Secretary Kissinger. In it, the general repeated the allegations I had made in our talk three weeks earlier. He then told Kissinger that he had conducted a "full investigation" and had found there was "no evidence that such an accusation is well founded." He noted that I had refused to provide any evidence. He said he talked the matter over with the presidents of Colombia and Costa Rica, and that he was writing "to warn you that it is not with threats that you will gain our support and continued vigilance," which were the canal's best defenses. Torrijos said further that he did not plan to publish his "indignation and displeasure in the face of this rash accusation" for fear it would inflame his people and arouse the students of Panama to "angry and vigorous protests."

It was a well-crafted letter, written, I felt sure, by the foreign minister himself, redolent of the flavor of United Nations confrontation and old-school diplomacy. What neither Torrijos nor Boyd seemed to understand was that we wanted to kill this issue forthwith and make sure it was never repeated. The Torrijos letter only helped keep it alive. A few weeks later, when some unknown antitreaty bureaucrat violated the law by leaking the report of alleged Panamanian complicity in the bombing to columnist Jack Anderson, the Panamanian Embassy's reaction was to release the text of Torrijos' letter to Kissinger. It was amateur night on Embassy Row.

Boyd's campaign to set at rest the bombing charges included a luncheon at the Panamanian Embassy with CIA Director George Bush. The two had known each other in New York when Bush served as our U.N. ambassador. To bolster his case, Boyd asked Torrijos to send a representative of the Panamanian National Guard to join him at the lunch. Torrijos chose Colonel Noriega, the chief of intelligence, for the assignment. Noriega dutifully denied any complicity of the Guard in setting off explosives, argued that Panama had nothing to gain by such actions, and insisted that the technology used was not part of the Guard's expertise. Bush listened courteously, never said what he really thought, and moved on to other matters. He was telling the Panamanians as subtly as he could: let's drop this subject—as long as it does not happen again.

At his meeting with Kissinger, Boyd pressed the secretary to explain to the incoming administration that the only thing that really stood between the two countries on a new arrangement was the question of duration of a new treaty. Kissinger promised to do it. But when Boyd asked the outgoing secretary what he thought a fair time period would be, Kissinger demurred. He explained that the Ford administration had lost the election "and the people in the next administration might think that I was trying to influence their thinking." The one concrete result of the Kissinger-Boyd meeting was the decision, cleared with Vance, to send Ambassador Bunker to Panama for another negotiation round during the interregnum. The purpose was to give the Panamanian public fresh evidence that the treaty-making process was not dead, as they had reason to fear it might be. It was also a form of subtle pressure on the incoming administration not to abandon a foreign policy effort that had been going on for a dozen years.

Bunker and his group flew to Panama on December 13 and met with their Panamanian counterparts for three days (December 15–17). Most of the time was spent in sessions of the several working groups, primarily the Lands and Waters teams. Kissinger had told Boyd once again that there could be no serious discussion of key issues like duration and defense. Some minor progress was made, but it was obviously a cosmetic session— to signal to public and political opinion on both sides that the search for a new treaty was continuing. A joint communiqué claiming "modest progress" was issued before Bunker and his staff returned to Washington in time for Christmas.

Early in January 1977, Alejandro Orfila, the Argentine diplomat who was secretary general of the OAS, stopped in Panama on a journey to Latin America. Minister Boyd gave a dinner in his honor at the El Panamá Hotel. Over coffee, the energetic Orfila told Boyd he had "great news" for him. The day before, Orfila had lunched with Cy Vance, the secretary of state-designate, and the New York lawyer had told him the new Carter administration wanted to find a solution to the festering problem of Panama, which had become increasingly dangerous for everybody. Vance told Orfila that the first invitation to a foreign diplomat to visit Washington would go to Panama's Foreign Minister Boyd so they could discuss what the next steps should be.

A new cast was taking over in Washington. The Panamanian foreign minister was packing his bags to travel north. The stage was set for the next act in the long-running drama of Panama treaty making.

CHAPTER 14

A Bitter Pill to Swallow

"Life cannot subsist in society but by reciprocal
concessions."

—Samuel Johnson, *Letter to Boswell*

As a candidate, Jimmy Carter had said he would not give up "practical control of the Panama Canal Zone any time in the foreseeable future." By the time he moved into the Executive Mansion on Pennsylvania Avenue, he had decided a settlement in Panama should have high priority. What had caused the Georgia politician to make such a distinct shift in his outlook and his policy?

Once elected, Carter enjoyed the luxury that comes to successful political seekers, a chance to study more deeply the matters he soon would have to address frontally. On Panama, the thirty-ninth president-to-be had that chance after November 2. One of the first things he learned was that his choice for secretary of state, Cyrus Vance, knew a great deal about the Panama problem and that Vance favored continuing negotiations for a new arrangement. "The United States cannot renege on commitments," Vance had told *Newsweek* magazine in early December, referring to the Nixon-Ford-Kissinger pledge to work out a new deal with Panama.

Then, in mid-December, the commission on United States–Latin American Relations released its long report on the Western Hemisphere. The commission, headed by lawyer-businessman Sol Linowitz, made early completion of a treaty with Panama its primary recommendation. A copy of the report went to Secretary-Designate Vance on December 14, with a copy for President-Elect Carter. Over the Christmas holidays, the hard-working Carter read the report. When he met the press on St. Simons Island two days after Christmas, Carter told the reporters he was giving high priority to the Panama problem, which he thought "ought to be resolved quite rapidly."

It was a quite remarkable change for U.S. leadership. For decades, newly elected presidents had focused on the East-West aspects of foreign policy—on the "Cold War" and détente, on NATO allies and communist adversaries. Suddenly, a president was putting a spotlight on a North-South problem, modernization of our relations with Panama.

Even before the inauguration, word filtered through the foreign policy bureaucracy that the new leader wanted action on Panama. The Carter transition teams working in the State Department and the Pentagon asked for position papers on all the issues that played some part in the Panama problem. The diplomats, military men, and lawyers who had been dealing with Panama compiled a massive report on the background of each question, and possible options for dealing with them. It went to the new president's staff and to the soon-to-be secretaries of state and defense.

By the time Jimmy Carter took the oath of office in front of the Capitol on a chilly January 20, the wheels of U.S. policy toward Panama were turning. The first foreign policy order of the Carter administration was issued the morning after the inaugural festivities. Presidential Review Memorandum #1 directed the new Policy Review Committee, chaired by the secretary of state, to make a survey of "our interests and objectives with regard to concluding new canal treaties with Panama." Addressed to the vice-president, the secretaries of state and defense, and other top officials, it ordered an analysis of "our present interests and objectives" in reaching a new agreement with Panama. The military were to assess the security implications of the several treaty options. In all, seven specific subjects were to be studied and the results packaged in a report "no longer than 30 pages."

In fact, most of the studying and analyzing had already been completed—including a report on Panama's internal political and economic situation, which we provided from the embassy. There was an amusing error in that first Carter order. It reflected the confusion that sweeps through the White House on the new administration's first day in place. The PRM was dated January 21; it demanded that the report be ready by January 20. That must have been the shortest deadline in history.

Before the inauguration, when the new administration was being organized, Cy Vance sought to enlist Sol Linowitz, one of the top international lawyers in Washington, as a key member of his new team in Foggy Bottom. The two were old friends who had shared responsibilities in many public and private enterprises. Linowitz, a partner in Coudert Brothers, did not want to abandon his law practice or resign his directorships in several influential corporations, which would have been necessary if he took on any full-time assignment in the department. Vance then pointed out that "one of the things we're going to have to get into is Panama." Would Linowitz consider taking that on as a short-term responsibility, no more than six months? Linowitz agreed to consider it.

After talking with the president-elect, Vance called Linowitz a week later and they met again. The secretary-designate said he and Carter really wanted the former chairman of the Xerox Corporation to take on the Panama task. What some in the White House were thinking at the time was that Linowitz would replace Ellsworth Bunker as the Panama Treaty negotiator. But Linowitz, a friend and admirer of Bunker—he called him "one of our true giants in diplomacy"—spiked that notion immediately. He would consider an assignment, he told Vance, but "only if Ambassador Bunker wants me to do it." In other words, he would serve as co-negotiator but would not consider replacing his old friend. Vance accepted that; Bunker welcomed the idea warmly; the White House approved. Washington had a new Panama Treaty team.

The review of Panama policy ordered by the president on January 21 was held six days later. I went to Washington to take part. It was the first time I had been back in the White House since I had left for Panama almost three years before. The change in atmosphere was striking. Three-piece suits had been replaced by slacks and sweaters. Haircuts were two or three inches longer than before. And it appeared that the average age of the White House staff had dropped about twenty years.

Gathered in the Situation Room in the basement of the West Wing that Thursday morning were the foreign policy and national security leaders of the Carter administration. Secretary of State Vance presided. Next to him sat Dr. Harold Brown, the new secretary of defense, a physicist who had served as secretary of the air force under President Johnson, then as president of the prestigious California Institute of Technology. At his side was Gen. George Brown, the chairman of the Joint Chiefs of Staff, in his blue air force uniform. Also at the table was the new presidential assistant for national security affairs, Dr. Zbigniew Brzezinski, the Polish-born scholar who had taught international affairs at Harvard and Columbia. Treaty Negotiators Bunker and Linowitz were at the table, as was Andrew Young, the Georgia civil rights leader who had been named U.S. representative to the United Nations.

The rest of us were there because we were working on either Panama or Latin American affairs. Terry Todman, my fellow ambassador in neighboring Costa Rica, was the new assistant secretary for Latin American affairs. Retired Lt. Gen. Tom Dolvin, a deputy to Ambassador Bunker since 1975, accompanied General Brown. Bill Hyland and Bob Pastor attended from Brzezinski's staff, Hyland a veteran of the NSC and Pastor a recent Harvard Ph.D. who had directed the Linowitz commission's study of Latin America.

After the first few minutes, it was clear a consensus had already developed among the leaders of the new administration. Vance early on raised a crucial question: Should the new administration reaffirm the eight principles for a new Panama treaty adopted in 1974 by Secretary Kissinger and Foreign Minister Tack? Everyone at the table said "yes." Brzezinski suggested that thought be given to ways to inform public opinion on the Panama issue and win domestic support. The conferees thought it would be good for the president to mention the problem in a "fireside chat" (which he was then considering) or in his State of the Union message. There was also support for the suggestion that State and Defense coordinate efforts to win backing in the Congress for a new arrangement. But the idea of a national information campaign was rejected as premature.

At one point, Secretary Vance turned to me and asked what I thought. I told him my views were very simple: "I believe a new treaty can be negotiated. I'm sure it will be greatly to the good of the United States. And if we get a treaty, I'm sure it will work—because it will be to the advantage of us both to make it work."

The committee members decided negotiations with Panama should be resumed during the second week in February. The main purpose of the revived talks would be to find out if Panama was willing to accept "fundamental U.S. requirements" (meaning the right to continue protecting the canal even after it was turned over to Panama) in return for a basic treaty that would run to the end of the century. Secretary Brown said a formula under which the two governments would protect and defend the canal and assure its neutrality would be acceptable to him and the U.S. military if—a large *if*—Panama would agree not to dispute the right of the United States to exercise that responsibility unilaterally.

The committee gave Bunker and Linowitz their marching orders. They were to determine what kind of package Panama would accept. Would a formula as discussed at the White House meeting be acceptable? Assuming it was, the men sitting in the Situation Room that day wanted to run a fast track—complete a treaty by June, get the president's approval in July, send it to the Senate in August. Having watched the painful process of treaty talks over the past years, I walked out of the Situation Room thinking how refreshing it was to encounter the optimism of the newly enlisted. I hoped they would prove to be right, but I had the feeling that, except for Ellsworth Bunker, Tom Dolvin, and me, no one in that windowless room fully appreciated how difficult it was going to be.

Three days after the White House meeting, Panamanian Foreign Minister Boyd took his nation's case to Washington in person. At the invitation of Secretary Vance, he was the first high official of any country to be welcomed by the new administration. But before he left for Washington, Boyd attended a critically important meeting with General Torrijos and the members of the General Staff of the National Guard. They gathered in a conference room in the gloomy, almost prisonlike headquarters building in the run-down area of Chorrillo.

The contrast between the participants was marked. Boyd, 55 years old, the suave, prosperous scion of one of Panama's old families, wore his customary well-tailored business suit. Graduated from an American college and trained in law at the University of Havana, Boyd was worldly, sophisticated, a man with an ironic sense of humor. Service as his country's permanent representative at the United Nations for fourteen years had made him thoroughly at home in the diplomatic world. Torrijos and his colonels were considerably younger than Boyd. All had been educated in military schools, mostly in Latin America. None had lived abroad except for military training.

Torrijos began the session rather abruptly by saying: "Your guidelines for this visit to Washington are that you should discuss the duration of the treaty to the year 2000. You should not talk about the kind of guarantees the North Americans are demanding for the neutrality of the canal." A prudent man would have said, "I understand," and followed orders. But Boyd, for all his intelligence and experience, was not noted for his prudence. If he thought something was wrong, he was likely to say so. He knew that Torrijos and others were still thinking of a guarantee of canal neutrality through some kind of vague assurance from the United Nations. Boyd realized that was unacceptable to the United States. Moreover, his long years of working the political corridors at the United Nations left no doubt in his mind that it would not work. He had already told Torrijos as much, clearly without too much effect.

Boyd thought it important that the other colonels, the men who wielded real power in Panama, hear firsthand what was at stake and why a U.N.-backed guarantee was not viable. He plunged ahead, knowing it would not please the *jefe de gobierno*. He explained the rules of the U.N. Security Council, which gave each of the five Great Power members the right to veto any proposal. For that reason, he told Panama's military leaders, the United States will never accept a U.N. guarantee of the canal's neutrality.

Nonetheless, Boyd argued, if we are to successfully conclude a treaty, we are going to have to provide the United States with some "proper guarantees" for the canal's protection. He hastily added he did not mean a U.S. right to keep military bases in Panama forever. Nor did he mean a right to intervene in Panama's internal affairs. But some kind of protection must be assured, he said, for Panama as well as for the country that built the canal and those that use it. Boyd raised an argument he thought the military men before him would readily understand.

"What would happen in the future," he asked, "if Colombia turned communist and, with its army of 200,000 [more than twenty times larger than Panama's], decided to take over the canal because they claimed Panama was not fulfilling its commitments to Colombia? What would we do?"

He thought it was clear that Panama should work out "proper safeguards" with the United States, and he believed it could be done in a treaty of friendship and cooperation. Boyd buttressed his argument by noting that Cuba, with one of the strongest military forces in Latin America, might one day launch an incursion into Panama. "What kind of safeguard would we have," he asked, "if we do not have a bilateral agreement with the United States?"

When he finished, there was no debate and the session ended abruptly. Boyd had delivered a valuable lesson in international politics for the unsophisticated men of the General Staff. He may also have built the toboggan for his own rapid slide from power. Boyd later confessed that, as he walked from that meeting, "I realized that I was losing my usefulness."

Despite his premonitions, Boyd flew to Washington in good spirits. It pleased him that the foreign minister of his tiny country should be helping inaugurate a new American president's foreign policy and that he was that man. Late Monday morning, January 31, Boyd and five colleagues drove up to the diplomatic entrance of the State Department. The minister's party was composed of three ambassadors—Nicolás González-Revilla, envoy to the United States; Jorge Illueca, who had replaced Boyd at the United Nations; and Nander Pitty, Panama's representative to the OAS. Also with him were Rómulo Escobar Bethancourt and Edwin Fábrega, leading members of Panama's treaty team. The group was welcomed at the door and escorted to Secretary Vance's office on the seventh floor.

Waiting with the secretary in his spacious, paneled office was his newly named deputy, Warren Christopher, a successful lawyer from California. Ambassador Bunker and his new partner, Sol Linowitz, were there along with Terry Todman, State's new chief of Latin American affairs. I completed the U.S. group.

We sat in a circle while Vance and Boyd carried the burden of conversation. The Panamanian minister expostulated at length on his favorite theme—the iniquities of the 1903 treaty and the urgent need for a new arrangement that had a fixed, and not too distant, end. The burden of Boyd's argument was that if we could agree on a treaty that lasted no longer than the year 2000 all other matters would fall into place. The new secretary of state told his visitor the United States was prepared to consider a treaty that ended on a fixed date. At the same time, we had to provide for safety of the canal and a guarantee of unhampered access by world commerce.

Boyd told Vance he was delighted the secretary accepted the idea of a new treaty that would eliminate the hated "perpetuity" of 1903. Did that mean he also endorsed the other basic principles agreed to in 1974 by his predecessor, Henry Kissinger? Yes, Vance said. He had read the earlier understanding carefully and was prepared to reaffirm the eight principles as a proper basis for a new pact. After a brief discussion of the Tack-Kissinger agreement, we adjourned for lunch.

Vance led the way to his private elevator and we rode up to the eighth floor. As we ate, the secretary said he was pleased to inform the Panamanians that Sol Linowitz would be joining Ellsworth Bunker on the U.S. negotiating team. The appointment had not yet been announced, but he wanted them to know in advance. Later, over dessert, Vance reminded Boyd again that the Carter administration wanted a just treaty with Panama, but that our main consideration was assuring that the waterway would remain secure and open. Boyd said he understood.

Vance accompanied his guests to the main lobby of the department where a large press contingent was waiting, microphones and cameras poised. Vance made the appropriate remarks about his visitors, then publicly reaffirmed that the principles of the 1974 agreement would provide the basis for a new agreement. Boyd followed with fulsome thanks to the secretary and his delight that Vance had accepted the idea of a new treaty that had a termination date. He waxed so eloquent and hit such an optimistic note that Vance felt obliged to step in and remind all present that many tough questions remained unresolved, including the requirements of security. Boyd agreed that was a problem but one he thought could be worked out satisfactorily. Later, meeting with reporters, Boyd suggested that Panama might consider some kind of bilateral guarantee of the canal's neutrality. It was another nail in the coffin of Boyd's diplomatic career.

Two days later, Boyd and some of his group went to Capitol Hill for breakfast as guests of the Senate Foreign Relations Committee. Senators Hubert Humphrey and Jacob Javits were the hosts. Ten other senators were present, both Democrats and Republicans. It was an unstructured meeting and talk flowed freely around the large square table in a private Senate dining room. Most of the questions tossed at Boyd related to the 1903 treaty and why it needed to be replaced. Hubert Humphrey walked in late and declared: "Anyone who plans a meeting before 9 o'clock in the morning is uncivilized, gentlemen." He was his familiar ebullient self, but already diminished by the disease that would kill him all too soon.

The questioning went on and Boyd was handling himself well. Someone asked Rómulo Escobar a question and he delivered a brilliant, if lengthy, recital of the agonies of the U.S.-Panama relationship. My neighbor, Iowa's Dick Clark, asked me a question about Panamanian politics and I was quietly replying when I noticed Humphrey looking our way. "Let's hear what our ambassador in Panama thinks about all this," he said. I could have declined on diplomatic grounds; or I could have offered a noncommittal answer. But those were serious men looking for honest answers, not evasions.

"Senator," I said, "I've thought of very little else for the past three years. If I thought a new treaty was a bad idea, I would say so—even in front of our Panamanian friends here. But it's not. The old arrangement of 1903 has outlived its usefulness. As you've heard today, Panama will not long continue to accept it. I think we owe it to ourselves and to them to find a better way. And I'm confident that way can be found—good for us, good for them, and good for our relations in the neighborhood. But it has to be fair, and balanced, and just. What we have now is none of those things."

Humphrey smiled and thanked me. I was sure he had already made up his own mind that a new deal for Panama was the right thing to do. Soon after, we broke up, the senators to go to their offices, the rest of us heading downtown to work. I rode from the Hill with Minister Boyd. He was enthusiastic about the session and about his visit. "It really is going well," he said. I agreed but I had the uneasy feeling that the minister might be figuring in too many news stories, personalizing the treaty business too much. I told him as much. "Look, Aquilino," I said, "it's none of my business, I know, but as a friend let me ask if maybe you aren't getting too far out in front and getting too much publicity. There are a lot of jealous people in Panama."

His look told me he thought I was being presumptuous. "I understand what you are saying, Bill," he said, "but I know what I'm doing. We have to get this story out so people will know what's happening, why there is a problem."

"You're probably right," I told him. "Anyway, it's not my affair. Forgive the unsolicited advice." He laughed. By then, we were in front of the State Department and I jumped out. The minister went on to his embassy where he had another appointment with several reporters.

When I went to Washington in January, I did not know whether I would be returning to Panama to stay or to pack my bags. Like all ambassadors, I had submitted my resignation to the new president so he could pick his own envoys. But during the luncheon for Boyd, Secretary Vance had taken me aside to tell me he had discussed the matter with President Carter and that they wanted me to continue to deal with Panama during the treaty-making process. Vance gave the same news to Minister Boyd, explaining that he and I had "worked together in the past on many important problems" and that I had his full support. That endorsement strengthened my hand in dealing with the Panamanian government in the months ahead.

Boyd returned to Panama elated with the success of his mission to Washington. He was eager to report to Torrijos on his productive talk with Secretary Vance and the warm reception he had received from the senators. The next morning, the first thing he did was to phone Torrijos. A secretary told him the general was not available but would call him back. He waited all day, but no call came. The next day, he phoned the general's office again, with the same result. That evening, Panamanian television carried a statement by the chief of government. He said that, with a new round of treaty talks about to begin, he was changing Panama's approach to the negotiations. Henceforth, Torrijos said, there would be "no permanent front-line negotiators." Panama's representatives would deal with the Americans "as a team." On the matter of the canal's neutrality, the general again said that Panama was disposed to arrange it under the United Nations.

The proud, sensitive minister of foreign affairs was incensed. He had not been given the courtesy of a hearing by the head of his own government. He had not been consulted on the new technique for negotiations. He felt he had been insulted and that his usefulness was at an end. Fuming at the rebuff, he sat down and penned his resignation. Noting that he did not agree with the new approach, he said he was withdrawing because "I do not wish to interfere."

Remembering that his appointment had been announced on television before he had even been consulted, Boyd decided to follow the same path with his farewell. He called in a local TV station and read his resignation statement on camera. He would later say that he had been hired and resigned on television, the only foreign minister who could make that claim. Torrijos accepted the resignation and, to the surprise of nearly everyone, named his youthful ambassador to Washington, Nicolás González-Revilla, to replace Boyd.

Ambassadors Bunker and Linowitz and the entire U.S. negotiating team flew to Panama on February 13. Key officers of the embassy were at Tocumen airport with me to welcome the twelve-member team and, as administrative officer John Hedberg used to say, "to do the necessary"— meaning handling passports, luggage, classified documents, and the many other housekeeping details of diplomatic travel. The new foreign minister and members of Panama's treaty team were on hand to greet the visitors. After a brief arrival statement by Ambassador Bunker, the Bunker-Linowitz entourage climbed aboard a Panamanian helicopter and a fixed-wing plane for the trip to Contadora. Thirty minutes later, they were settling down in their rooms in the newly opened Hotel Contadora.

The Panamanian hosts, to give their guests time to get acclimated to new surroundings and to the sharp change from Washington's blustery February, scheduled nothing for the next day. The "old Contadora hands" enjoyed that kind of leisurely transition. But for Linowitz, an intense, active man who hated too much relaxation, it was the worst possible treatment. He chafed under the inactivity. His mood was not improved by a less than efficient phone system that frustrated his accustomed two dozen daily phone calls to Washington and New York and Paris. That first day of inaction, and several events that followed, sounded the death knell for Contadora as the site for treaty talks.

The first face-to-face meeting of the new round occurred the next morning at 10 o'clock. Bunker and Linowitz met briefly with Rómulo Escobar and Edwin Fábrega to work out technical details—where they would meet, how interpreting would be handled, and the like. The Americans also gave the Panamanians a letter from President Carter for delivery to General Torrijos. In it, Carter expressed his hope that "these negotiations will bear fruit and will result in a treaty which will be fair, reasonable and appropriate in every respect." He said the U.S. side would act in "a cooperative and flexible spirit," and he assured Torrijos that he wanted a treaty that would "satisfactorily meet the proper concerns of both Panama and the United States."

In one sense, the Carter message served a highly useful purpose. When he read it, Torrijos decided the new administration might be serious about getting a new agreement that would change the one-sided history of past decades. But in another sense, the letter almost backfired in the faces of the U.S. delegation, as we shall see.

The first real meeting of what was then being called "the new Contadora round" occurred that afternoon at 4:15 P.M. The meeting place was a pleasant conference room on the second floor of the Hotel Contadora. A long conference table and comfortable chairs filled the center of the room. Large windows occupied the western wall and looked out on a small nine-hole, pitch-and-putt golf course.

The Panamanian team was composed of González-Revilla, the new foreign minister; Rómulo Escobar, the principal negotiator (though his role was still not clear); Edwin Fábrega; Adolfo Ahumada; and Jaime Arias. On the U.S. side were Ambassadors Bunker and Linowitz, Morey Bell, Tom Dolvin, and Dick Wyrough.

González-Revilla welcomed the U.S. representatives to Panama. Bunker responded, then delivered a statement that concentrated on the three central issues of treaty duration, canal neutrality, and posttreaty defense of the waterway. Bunker's statement was couched in general terms but its purpose was apparent: to find out whether Panama would accept U.S. requirements on defense if the United States agreed to a treaty that ended by the year 2000. We also were seeking some sign that the Panamanians would be flexible on other matters that concerned us—the nature of the entity that would run the canal, operating rights for that agency, certain privileges for canal employees, and the like.

At that juncture the two sides were on different wavelengths. Bunker and Linowitz were trying to find out what kind of treaty package Panama might accept so they could then report back to the president and his advisers. The Panamanians, on the other hand, thought the new administration in Washington wanted to move quickly and that the addition of Linowitz to the negotiating team would mean fast decisions and prompt resolution of differences. The Americans were probing treaty possibilities with a foil. The Panamanians were eager to attack the problem with a broadax. The Panamanians read the Carter letter to Torrijos as favoring their approach. But the Bunker statement sounded to the Panamanians like the same hard line they had been hearing for two years. They were devastated. When he gave them a long paper describing the U.S. position on half a dozen issues beyond duration and defense, they hoped it at least would reflect the "flexible spirit" Carter had mentioned. The meeting adjourned with a Panamanian promise to study the U.S. position carefully and to respond the next afternoon.

The Panamanian negotiators flew to General Torrijos' seaside house at Farallon on the Pacific shore. There they went over the Bunker-Linowitz paper paragraph by paragraph. The more they read, the angrier they became. The Americans were asking that Panama and the United States be the sole permanent guarantors of the canal's neutrality. To the Panamanians, that meant keeping the hated "perpetuity" they wanted to eliminate. The U.S. negotiators were also proposing that the two countries agree to a mutual defense agreement before the canal treaty expired. That meant the continued presence of U.S. military forces on Panamanian soil into the indefinite future. The U.S. position on other issues was similarly unbending. They still wanted canal employees to have all the rights and privileges extended to U.S. military personnel. The Americans made a few concessions on Lands and Waters, but they would still hold many areas Panama felt it needed for economic development.

Every sentence brought angry reactions, and as he listened to his advisers, General Torrijos became increasingly aroused. The Panamanian leader was under continuing pressure. The country's economy was not improving; voices of opposition were becoming more strident. One thing that had helped ease tensions somewhat was the high hopes aroused about a possible new treaty. Vance's acceptance of the Tack-Kissinger Principles, the warm reception Minister Boyd had received in Washington, the appointment of Sol Linowitz—all had been played heavily in the Panamanian press. Torrijos now saw those hopes fading and he imagined his people turning against him.

He decided it was best to break off the talks, but he wanted to do it in such a way that the actual rupture would come from the American side. Then, he calculated, he could rally Panamanian opinion by picturing poor Panama as the injured party. When he revealed the "excessive" U.S. demands at the right moment, he was sure the noisy outrage that followed would stifle his critics. Taking their lead from their chief, his advisers set to work to prepare a scathing rebuttal certain, they thought, to force Bunker and Linowitz to walk out in disgust.

The next day, they were still working on it. Jimmy Arias joined them at midday. They showed him their handiwork and explained what they were trying to do. Arias read it and laughed. "Some of these things sound terrible in Spanish," he admitted, "but they are not so bad in English. They might even be proud to be called some of these things." They begged him to redo it in English so the desired message would get across. He sat at the table and began writing.

The meeting was to have begun at 4 o'clock, but Arias' chore took longer than expected. The Panamanians arrived more than two hours late. When the two delegations were assembled, lawyer Arias took the floor. He apologized for their late arrival but said the nature of the document the U.S. side had presented "warrants an introductory comment," which he said he would make in English. He noted that he was making the comments "on behalf of the negotiating team" and after consultation "at all appropriate levels."

"It is our opinion that the document that was presented to us yesterday is lacking in good faith," he began. Bunker and Linowitz were amazed at the rude beginning. They wondered what was happening. If that document represented the U.S. position, Arias continued, "then the previous fourteen meetings of the negotiators could have been replaced by fourteen telegrams."

The bitterness continued to pour forth. Bunker tried to defang it as best he could. A *Time* magazine story some weeks before mentioned that Bunker had a hearing problem. He knew that word had traveled. At one insulting phrase, Bunker interrupted to say, "Sorry, I didn't get that. What did you say?" Arias repeated in a louder voice. Bunker said: "I still don't get it," forcing the nervous Arias to repeat it again.

Arias said the U.S. paper "appears to be a direct warning of a brazen power play."

"Would you say that again, please," said Bunker. Arias raised his voice to comply.

Bunker's interventions broke the flow of the angry harangue, and Arias' composure as well. But it went on. "If the activities preceding this visit [the hopeful noises from Washington] were only for American propaganda purposes," he said, "then they have certainly been achieved, but at an unacceptable cost to our dignity as an independent nation."

The climax of the Arias performance came with his charge that the U.S. government's policy toward "the most reactionary centers of white colonialism" (a reference to Rhodesia) was considerably more liberal than it was toward Panama.

"I heard that," said Bunker, "and I believe we've heard quite enough. I would simply like to say that I will not attempt to respond in detail. This is a serious accusation, one that I think is not merited. We made our proposals in good faith. Our only purpose is to continue negotiations."

Escobar handed over Panama's written reply to the U.S. position and Bunker suggested a recess. The American team walked out on the balcony to confer. They were angry and felt they had been insulted. There was a brief discussion of packing up and going home, but Bunker and Linowitz set that to rest. President Carter was committed to finding an answer and had staked considerable prestige on the issue. If, after all the hoopla, the U.S. delegation came home in two days with everyone angry, it would have been a blow to the new president's foreign policy. If there was a break, the U.S. negotiators decided, Panama could make it and take the responsibility. They returned to the conference table.

By that time, Jimmy Arias had flown back to Panama City. Bunker told the remaining Panamanians of his grave disappointment over the outburst. "We have presented our views," he said, "in order to get your views. We need to go back to the president and tell him the shape of a possible agreement." He said that he and Linowitz hoped the talks could proceed in "a spirit of trust and respect."

Linowitz said he, too, was "disappointed and saddened" by Arias' harsh words. He reminded the Panamanians there were "very strong forces" in opposition to a treaty. "We would not help you," he said, "and we would not be frank and honest if we put before you more convenient terms if they could not, in our judgment, be approved by the Senate." He urged the other side to reread the paper of the previous day, and to study the detailed suggestions Bunker was about to offer on neutrality. "Regard these as proposals from people who want to find a solution," the U.S. lawyer told them. Bunker then read a paper on canal security and posttreaty defense and handed it over to the Panamanians.

After another recess, called by the Panamanians, Escobar concluded by saying: "We will study this document. We will communicate to you our reaction. We are grateful for this document. Thank you very much."

With that, the stormiest session of the entire Panama negotiations ended. The Americans went off to assess the damage and report to Washington. The Panamanians flew to Farallon to tell Torrijos what had happened. There was little joy in either camp.

The next day provided a welcome cooling-off period for both sides. The embassy was hosting a large delegation of congressmen (nine House members and their spouses) plus a sizable group of staff people and officials from the Departments of State and Defense. Since they were there, among other reasons, to learn something about the treaty, I had importuned Bunker and Linowitz to meet with them. The two ambassadors flew in that morning and we had a two-hour briefing in the study at the residence. It was a long and productive session and the congressmen told me later they had learned a great deal. I still remember a moment in the dialogue when one questioner wondered if the Panamanians could ever take over some of the more complicated jobs on the canal, such as piloting. Yvonne Burke, the bright and beautiful congresswoman from California, volunteered the answer. "Gentlemen," she said, "if you gave me twenty years, I could learn to be a pilot—and I'm not even a sailor!"

The following day, the two U.S. negotiators had an informal session with Escobar and Fábrega. The Panamanian mood seemed conciliatory. "I want to say," Escobar began, "that we are sure of your seriousness and concern regarding the search for a solution to our problem." The two sides agreed to form subgroups to study the various issues facing them—the kind of organization that would run the canal, the rights of canal employees, the disposition of land in the Canal Zone. They also agreed that the two most sensitive problems—treaty duration and future defense—would be discussed privately rather than in formal sessions.

For Bunker and Linowitz, the weekend was a dead loss. Escobar flew to Farallon for what he thought was a quick conference with General Torrijos. I soon learned that they and a few close friends had taken the general's plane to Barranquilla in Colombia to celebrate Carnival, the pre-Lenten festival. It looked suspiciously like another calculated insult, but I felt sure it was simply inadvertence and poor judgment. Torrijos wanted to enjoy himself and he wanted his friend Rómulo with him. After all, it was a weekend, wasn't it? The philosophical Bunker was willing to let events take their course, and he went sailing. But for the always active Linowitz, it was a wasted two days. It helped confirm his feeling that Contadora was beautiful, but a poor place for serious work.

By Monday, Rómulo and Torrijos still had not returned from their carousing interlude. The meeting planned for that morning was held in the afternoon with González-Revilla, Fábrega, and Ahumada. Nothing was accomplished, and by that time Linowitz' patience had worn thin. He had a quiet talk with Bunker and they told the Panamanians they saw no point in sitting and waiting for the other side to come to a meeting or not, to come on time or late. "If you are not ready to negotiate seriously," Linowitz told them, "we see no reason for staying."

The next morning Rómulo was back in place, a little the worse for wear, to be sure, but in attendance and in charge. "Now that I have returned," he began, "we can get down to business." But the session was as inconclusive as the earlier meetings. The two sides were still miles apart on the central issue—how the canal might be protected once the canal treaty expired. However the Americans phrased their position, and Linowitz tried half a dozen formulations, the Panamanians turned it down on grounds it violated their sovereignty.

The night before their return to Washington, Bunker and Linowitz met once again with Rómulo and his colleagues. Bunker explained they had to have something to take back to President Carter that would describe what would make a treaty possible. Rómulo promised a document that would reflect Panama's position. He said it would include U.S. responsibility for operating the canal to end in 1990; defense rights terminating in 1999; a short-term security pact to be worked out by 1995 but aimed solely at third-country threats; a unilateral Panamanian guarantee of the canal's neutrality; major U.S. concessions on Lands and Waters. All were unacceptable to the United States. Linowitz told Rómulo he was "shocked" at his unrealistic approach.

The final meeting left Bunker and Linowitz disappointed, even dejected. At dinner that evening, Linowitz told the Panamanians that he was leaving for Washington discouraged about the prospects for any success in the treaty talks. When he returned to his room, he found a message from Rómulo inviting him to breakfast the next day.

In a quiet corner of the hotel that next morning, Linowitz and Escobar met alone for the first time. The Panamanian explained that they knew Linowitz' background, recognized his commitment to Latin America. They believed that the American wanted to find a basis for mutual understanding. But there were many burdens to be overcome, Rómulo said, and Linowitz should not be "shocked" at the fact that it would take time and patience. They were ready to accept Sol's goodwill, he said, but the American was going to have to spend more time on the issues before he could see all of their complexities.

"It's like the story of the psychiatrist," Rómulo said. "He was walking down the street and saw a man with his ear glued to a hole in a fence. 'Poor man,' he said. 'I must help him.' He walked up to the fellow and asked, 'What are you doing?' The fellow said, 'I'm listening.' The psychiatrist said, 'Let me try.' He put his ear to the hole but after a little while he turned to the man and said, 'I don't hear a thing.' The man said: 'You must be crazy. I've been listening for three days and haven't heard anything. And you just got here and expect to hear something!'"

Linowitz roared at the story. Romulo said: "You're like the psychiatrist. You just got here and you want the negotiations finished right away. You are expecting too much. That isn't the way it will happen. It will happen only slowly and if we can find common ground. So please don't go away disappointed."

Linowitz found the breakfast meeting the most encouraging event of the entire week. He left agreeing with Rómulo that "we have made some progress just in coming to know one another." He could never accept the leisurely pace of the old Contadora pattern, but he realized that patience was an essential ingredient in making a treaty with Panama.

As the two men were parting, Escobar handed over a letter to President Carter from General Torrijos. Linowitz went to tell Bunker about his breakfast talk and the two ambassadors read the letter. The Panamanian leader told the president it did not appear to him that the United States truly wanted an agreement. He explained that any treaty that allowed U.S.

military forces in Panama after the year 2000 would be traumatic for Panama. On the other hand, Torrijos wrote, if the American side stopped insisting on a post-2000 military alliance, the Panamanians would look at all other treaty issues differently. Torrijos made the final point that any further concessions by his negotiators would have to meet with reciprocal U.S. concessions, especially in the area of Lands and Waters.

Before leaving for the island's small airstrip, Bunker and Linowitz met briefly with Escobar and Ahumada to approve a short joint communiqué hailing the "useful talks." It was as uninformative as most such documents. Linowitz pulled Escobar aside to tell him that the Torrijos letter raised "very difficult problems." Nonetheless, he said, Escobar could be sure the U.S. team would be guided by "restraint and goodwill." As they shook hands, the Panamanian lawyer smiled and told Linowitz: "Don't forget the psychiatrist. Be patient; be patient."

The last American aboard the plane was Mike Kozak, the State Department lawyer. Rómulo ignored his glum expression, put his arm around the young lawyer's shoulders, and said: "Don't worry. You'll be back here very soon. It's not really as bad as it looks." Rómulo's reassurances to Linowitz and Kozak were shared with the others on the short flight to Tocumen. By the time they climbed aboard their Miami-bound plane, the group was feeling a few degrees better than they had the night before. But the anticipation they had felt ten days earlier had largely dissipated. They concluded, quite correctly, that they and the new president were being tested.

While the Americans flew northward, the Panamanians were also reviewing the just-ended sessions. They came to an almost identical conclusion: the gringos are testing us; they want to learn how much we will give; they want to see if what we are saying is just propaganda, or if we mean it. One of the Panamanian negotiators told me later: "They thought that a treaty that ended in the year 2000 was all we wanted. When they accepted that, they thought we should accept everything else. But that was only one of the problems. There were many others, but they didn't understand that at first."

The conclusions on both sides were strikingly similar. The Panamanians decided to wait for Washington for fear the Americans would think they wanted a treaty at any price. The Americans decided to bide their time lest the Panamanians conclude they were bending under pressure.

The Americans landed on the wind-swept runway at National Airport that Wednesday night and promptly went their separate ways. The next day, Bunker and Linowitz had lunch with Secretary Vance to report on their trip. They admitted that, though they had probed some issues deeply, they had reached no agreements. They told Vance they had concluded that Panama was "testing the United States under a new president." They believed the United States should use the next weeks to urge Panama to show greater flexibility. At the same time, they wanted to avoid any indication they were in a hurry for agreement. Bunker and Linowitz told Vance they thought the United States should solicit advice and support from countries in Latin America. He agreed they should begin planning a trip for that purpose.

The president called Bunker and Linowitz to the Oval Office on March 2. With Carter were Vice President Mondale and National Security Adviser Brzezinski. The president made it clear he was eager to move forward on a Panama solution but he left the method and the timing up to the two negotiators. He did, however, instruct them to brief key members of Congress. They mentioned their plan to contact Latin American leaders to gain their understanding, and Carter approved. They told the president they thought a good way to preserve some momentum in the talks, but to avoid the pressures of publicity, would be to hold a "secret" meeting with the Panamanians—in New York or Miami—to explore next steps.

Back at their adjoining offices in the State Department, Bunker and Linowitz set to work to carry out the president's mandate. They arranged a meeting two days later with House Speaker Thomas P. "Tip" O'Neill of Massachusetts. They asked for appointments with Senate Majority Leader Robert Byrd and Senator Humphrey. A briefing was scheduled for the Latin American Subcommittee of the House International Relations Committee, which would soon be leaving for Panama. They also agreed to meet with the House Merchant Marine and Fisheries Committee in executive session on March 16.

I sent my views on the talks to Bunker and Linowitz in a confidential letter the first week in March. "I think the time is fast approaching," I wrote, "when we must make an all-out push for a treaty. But, if we are to be successful, I strongly believe we will have to rethink our technique for achieving that treaty." I told the ambassadors I was convinced the traditional approach, "coming to Contadora for ten days or two weeks and then returning to Washington, will no longer be effective in the new situation." I urged that the talks be held "outside of Panama" and predicted that in a new round "Torrijos will probably give his subalterns more flexibility on most issues than he did in the latest round."

Almost from the hour the Bunker-Linowitz team took off for Washington, my principal officers and I went to work to persuade the Panamanians that what had happened was not a fair test of either side. We were convinced Torrijos wanted a treaty, if it was a fair one. We were equally certain that the Carter administration wanted a new understanding with Panama. We argued endlessly that the talks on the island had been little more than a shakedown cruise and should be kept in perspective by both sides.

While we were preaching patience and hope in Panama, and our colleagues in Washington were building the necessary political base, the next move was being planned. Ambassador Bunker called to discuss the "secret" meeting he and Linowitz had been considering. It struck me as a useful step and I said so. Bunker asked if I would sound out the Panamanians "at an appropriate level" and see what the reaction was.

I met the general in the house on Fiftieth Street and told him I came to reassure him that my government really did want a new arrangement with Panama and that we wished to move ahead. We believed the next logical step would be to get the negotiators together in a strictly private, unpublicized meeting. "Let them talk about anything they wish to," I said, "without records or press conferences or any of the usual baloney. Let's find out what it takes to make a deal." I assured Torrijos that we were serious and not just playing games. "If you say it's serious and it could do some good," he told me, "then we'll do it. Let me know where and when."

The "secret" session was arranged for March 12 at the Century Club in New York where a private room had been reserved. The Panamanian representatives were Escobar, Fábrega, and a newcomer to the negotiations, Aristides Royo, the 36-year-old minister of education. Royo was a high-strung, intelligent, emotional man, yet one of the most organized Panamanians I had known. He had a doctorate in law from the University of Salamanca in Spain and had done postdoctoral work at the University of Bologna. After working in the Panamanian equivalent of the attorney general's office after his return from Italy, he joined the prestigious law firm of Morgan and Morgan in 1968. Under the new military regime, he helped rewrite Panama's civil and criminal legal codes and later, in 1972, he was a member of the commission that wrote the new constitution. In 1973, he was appointed minister of education, a demanding job in any government, but a special challenge in a country that produced too many college graduates for too few "white collar" jobs.

While the Panamanian negotiators were flying to New York, an urgent cable reached me. It was President Carter's answer to the Torrijos letter of February. The general was out of town, but the foreign minister was going to the interior that evening to meet Torrijos, so I delivered it to him.

It was a long and friendly letter expressing the hope that the two countries would not only conclude a "mutually satisfactory treaty" but also provide "a model" for relations between large and small countries. Carter reminded Torrijos that Panama would be getting several of its long-sought goals: "early transfer of jurisdiction to Panama, increasing participation by Panama in the administration and defense of the canal, and a treaty of fixed duration." In return for those concessions, the president told the general, he had to insist on "an arrangement which allows the United States to meet its responsibility to operate the canal during the treaty's lifetime and which recognizes our security interest in the continuing neutrality of and access to the canal after the termination date of the treaty." Carter put the U.S. case to Torrijos about as succinctly as it could be stated.

When he had read the president's letter, Torrijos asked me to forward his reaction to the White House. He appreciated Carter's courtesy in answering so promptly and he found the president's message "comprehensive and warmly human." It was Torrijos' impression "that the two leaders are clear about the real objectives." But he thought "perhaps the negotiators want their leaders to do their job for them." Torrijos wanted Carter to know that, because both were from rural areas, he thought the president and he were going to establish "a great and profound friendship." "Rural life is basically the same all over the world," Torrijos said, "and it creates a special way of thinking."

It was an unusual exposure of a side of Torrijos that few people realized he possessed. A touch of humor and a reaching out for trust and mutual confidence. The heart of the message was in the one phrase "the two leaders are clear about the real objectives." He was saying he realized what Carter needed from a treaty and that the president knew what he required. He was less sure that the negotiators understood equally well.

Escobar, Fábrega, and Royo flew into New York on Friday night to be in plenty of time for their appointment with the Americans the next day. On Saturday morning, the U.S. deputies, Bell, Dolvin, and Wyrough, flew to New York but a heavy snowstorm forced them to land at Newark instead of LaGuardia. They took a cab to Manhattan and arrived in good time at the Century Club. Bunker and Linowitz took a later plane and by the time they reached New York the blizzard had worsened. They circled in a holding pattern but the plane was ordered to return to Washington. From the terminal, Linowitz called the Century Club, located his guests, and explained what had happened. He asked if they could come to Washington and meet the following day. The Panamanians checked out of their hotel and took the Metroliner to Washington that evening.

The next morning was dismal in Washington. The storm that had hit New York and most of the East Coast the day before was still spreading its misery. The snow had stopped but there was plenty of cold rain and sleet, and the streets were treacherous. Panama then had no ambassador in Washington, but the Panamanians had suggested meeting in the ambassador's residence on McGill Terrace. The place had been unoccupied for a month; there was no staff in residence; and it was almost as cold inside as out. The heating system was not operating and an embassy officer tried to take off the chill by building a fire in the fireplace. It helped, but only a little.

Bunker and Linowitz arrived promptly at 10:00 A.M. and walked into the chilly house. It was so cold, in fact, that they kept their overcoats on for the first couple of hours. Jimmy Arias, the Panamanian lawyer who had jolted the Americans in the February meeting, was in Washington on private business. The Panamanian team had asked him to join them and that did not put Bunker and Linowitz at ease. But he listened quietly and entered the discussions hardly at all.

Escobar opened the meeting with a long (one-hour) exposition of Panama's position. His central point was that any agreement would require serious political decisions on both sides. He recalled that in the gathering on Contadora he and his colleagues had given the Americans a list of things important to Panama. He listed them again—Ancon Hill, the transisthmian railroad, significant areas of land at both ends of the Canal Zone. They were all necessary, he argued, for psychological reasons as well as to help Panama's healthy economic development. It was, as the American diplomats conceded later, an eloquent and persuasive legal brief of the Panamanian position.

When he finished, it was the Americans' turn. Posttreaty defense was our key issue and Sol Linowitz outlined U.S. views. Still wrapped in his overcoat, the U.S. lawyer delivered a persuasive case for the U.S. right to continue to protect the Panama Canal during and after the treaty period. A long discussion followed on how "neutrality" was defined, how and when it might be declared, what the United States meant by "defense rights," and a host of related questions.

It was an extremely useful exposition for the Panamanians of what Americans saw as the minimal conditions for a successful treaty. But if the goal was to make the March 13 meeting a turning point in the negotiating process, our approach was a failure. Linowitz was operating under his basic assumption: "If we can settle the defense issue, everything else will fall into place." He was absolutely right—from the U.S. point of view—but negotiations must encompass at least two points of view. Linowitz made the U.S. case with great skill; we were not listening carefully to the other side.

By one o'clock, everyone was cold, tired, and hungry. Bunker and Linowitz went off to get a warm meal and to thaw out. The Panamanians stayed in the chilly house and devoured the hamburgers and milk an embassy secretary had brought in. At 2:00 P.M., the Americans returned and the discussions resumed.

It was more of the same. The two sides were talking past each other, just as the negotiators had in 1972. Each side was making a good case, but neither was accepting anything the other said. The Panamanian negotiators were not prepared to welcome anything on defense arrangements until some of their needs were satisfied. Whenever they mentioned specifics, like the ports or the railroad, the American answer was "We'll have to consider that further" or "We'll have to consult higher authority on that."

Escobar and Fábrega raised several times the problem of "dismantling the Canal Zone." Bunker asked them: "Why do you talk about dismantling the Zone over time when we have already agreed that, when the treaty enters into force, there will be no more Zone? You can't dismantle something that is no more." But the Panamanians were not thinking of broad concepts. They were looking at a map that showed half the existing Canal Zone continuing under U.S. control. That looked to them suspiciously like a new, if smaller, Zone. Again, the ships were passing in the night, not tying up at the same pier.

By 6:00 P.M., after seven hours of talk, the two sides were no closer to agreement than they had been that morning. The Americans were frustrated at their failure to get Panamanian acceptance of the concept of continuing U.S. defense rights. The Panamanians were equally foiled by the refusal of the U.S. negotiators to talk seriously about what was uppermost in their minds—the territories and facilities then in the Canal Zone that they felt should be transferred to Panama.

On leaving the residence that evening, Bunker and Linowitz urged that negotiations continue at an early date. The Panamanians were noncommittal. They said they would have to consult General Torrijos. When they were alone, Escobar argued strongly that, if the meeting just ended was any indication of what they might expect, it would be better to close off the treaty talks for the time being. The others were of the same mind. They called Torrijos after Royo had compiled a summary of the day-long session, gave their report, and told him how fruitless the talks had been. He told them to return to Panama to consider what the next steps should be. They flew out of Washington early the next morning. Escobar and his colleagues reported to Torrijos the next day and it was decided to stay away from the negotiating table until the United States was ready to give "real answers" to Panama's questions.

During those months, everyone connected with the Panama problem was trying to explain why the treaty-making effort was so bogged down. Panamanians blamed the Americans; Americans said the fault was Panama's. The Panamanians were arguing among themselves about what a treaty had to contain if they were to accept it. Americans were doing the same thing. American public opinion seemed fearful the United States would give away too much. The Panamanian public worried that their government would accept too little. General Torrijos probably described the difficulty of working out a Panama treaty better than anyone. In an interview with Panama City's TV Channel 4 in late March, he was asked why there was still no final solution.

"The problem is," he said, "that there can't be a treaty that completely satisfies the Zonians, the Canal Company, the U.S. armed forces, the ecologists, the Congress, the White House, and Panama. This would be as impossible as meeting the demand of the mythical princess who had very large feet. She called in her shoemaker and ordered him to make her a pair of shoes that were small on the outside and large on the inside."

The day after the secret gathering at the Panamanian Embassy, there was considerable gloom in both camps. The Americans had hoped that at least one or two issues might be settled. The perennial question was revived: do these people really want a treaty? At the Panamanian end, the vexation was just as profound. How can we ever get an agreement, they asked, if all the Americans will talk about is what concerns them?

I was persuaded that both sides were underestimating the value of what they had gone through. To be sure, the session was too short. I wished the Panamanians had stayed another day. Still, as I read the record, there were pluses that were being missed. Sol Linowitz' hammering away at the absolute necessity for U.S. involvement in long-term security had to have made an impression on Panama's negotiators. Until that point, they did not understand what a critical ingredient it was for political success in the United States. Linowitz' tactics made it impossible for them to ignore this central issue. On the other hand, the U.S. negotiators seemed to have missed the point that during those seven hours in the embassy the Panamanians never once said "this is impossible" or "we could never accept anything like that." It was the first time that talk of posttreaty security had met with anything but a flat turndown.

On the other side of the coin, Rómulo's stress on the "courage to make hard political decisions" did not get through to the Americans immediately. What he was saying, as he told me later, was: "What you want means swallowing a bitter pill for us. But you are going to have to swallow some bitter medicine too. We won't get anywhere if one does it and the other doesn't." The bitter pill he spoke of for us was making major concessions on lands and facilities in the Canal Zone. Like the Panamanian reaction to "security," ours was to shove this aside.

The next weeks were a diplomatic marathon for my embassy team. At lunches and receptions, over dinner tables and sitting up with friends until the small hours, we pushed the message hard: Yes, the United States wants a treaty; yes, we understand Panama's priorities; there will be no treaty unless we have a role in protecting the canal, now and in the future; we know there will be no treaty until the Zone becomes part of Panama, in every sense. And the final message: we're closer than you realize.

On April 14, talking to the Permanent Council of the OAS, President Carter said: "I am firmly committed to negotiating in as timely a fashion as possible a new treaty which will take into account Panama's legitimate needs as a sovereign nation and our own interests and yours [the other Latin Americans] in the efficient operation of a neutral Canal, open on a non-discriminatory basis to all users." We made sure that got wide dissemination.

The man with whom I talked at the greatest length on this mix of problems and possibilities was Gabriel Lewis Galindo. During my years in Panama, Gabriel and I had become good friends. He was a prosperous businessman, the principal paper box manufacturer in Central America, the founder and developer of Contadora as a resort area. He was also a friend and adviser of Omar Torrijos. But Gabriel held no official position in the government, so we could talk freely with few bureaucratic inhibitions.

Through late March and early April, Gabriel and I often discussed the key issues—what Panama required, what the United States needed, and how they could be reconciled. We explained, and haggled, and argued. I looked at Panama through his eyes; he saw the United States through mine. What helped tremendously in building understanding was one dominant fact: both of us wanted the same thing—a situation in which Panama and the United States were partners, working together for the good of both.

One afternoon in April, Gabriel called and asked me to drop by his house on the way home. When I got there, he gave me his news. "The general has asked me to go to Washington as Panama's ambassador," he said. "What do you think?" My first reaction was, "It's the best idea Omar has had for some time." Then we began toting up the positive and negative features of such a move. It would mean breaking away from profitable business ventures and turning most of his affairs over to others. He and Nita would be separated from three of their sons whom Gabriel was bringing into his business. On the other hand, another son was in college in Washington and they planned to send their youngest to a prep school in the States, so they would be closer.

Personal considerations aside, what mattered most was that Panama sorely needed a new envoy in Washington (the post had been vacant since February). In view of the upcoming struggle to get a new treaty—and to get it approved by the Senate—it was imperative that the new ambassador be active, imaginative, and personable. He had to understand the importance of the media and be able to win their confidence. The new diplomat would have to present his country's views vigorously and with conviction, at the same time appreciating American views.

By every criterion, Gabriel was better qualified than most candidates for the post. One other factor pushed him strongly toward acceptance. More than thirty years before, his father, Samuel Lewis Arango, had been ambassador to Washington. The son was powerfully drawn to follow in the footsteps of the father he so greatly admired.

As we wound up our talk, I told my friend, "Gabriel, you love your country. This is a chance to serve her in a way most men never get. I think you have to accept."

He looked at the portrait of his father on the living room wall. "I guess you're right," he said, "but you're going to have to help me. You know damn well I'm no diplomat."

I put my arm around his shoulder and told him: "You don't know it yet, but that's the best thing about Omar's idea."

A few days later, I received official notification from the Foreign Ministry of the Panamanian government's intention to name Gabriel as ambassador to the United States. I sent off a cable to the secretary of state reporting the fact as well as Panama's request for formal U.S. agreement to the appointment, as protocol demanded. I added my own strong personal endorsement and urged the approval be handled expeditiously. It was. Within days, I informed the Panamanian government that the Lewis appointment was welcomed in Washington.

Meantime, we had all been working overtime to put the treaty talks back on the track. I talked at length with Foreign Minister González-Revilla, members of Panama's negotiating group, countless advisers, and, eventually, Torrijos. I quoted President Carter's speech to the OAS and assured them that the new administration was deadly serious about getting a new and workable understanding with Panama. I told them that Ellsworth Bunker and Sol Linowitz were dedicated to achieving a fair and balanced agreement and I pointedly reminded them of Linowitz' limited six-month appointment. I discussed the realities of U.S. politics, including the relative strength of a new president to pursue a few chosen objectives, and emphasized with them how fast that influence could dissipate.

Torrijos recalled that the secret session in mid-March had not gone too well. "Why do you think a new round would be better?" he asked. I told him, first, that I did not think the March 13 meeting in Washington had been all that bad. "A lot of ground was covered," I said, "and by the end of one day—only one day—each side had a much better understanding of what was important to the other." I told the general I thought the biggest problem was that each side was so eager to push its own views it wasn't listening carefully enough to what the other side was saying. I argued that both sides could and should be more flexible than they had been in the last two encounters.

"But what makes you think they will be?" he insisted.

"I can't give you any guarantees, General," I told him, "but I've talked with Washington; I've discussed it with Ellsworth and Sol. The clear impression I get is that they want to move forward—and they know that progress depends on compromise. Anyway, I don't think either of us has anything to lose by giving it a try."

He puffed his cigar, ruffled his hair, looked at the ceiling. "OK," he said, "we'll try it again. But damn it all, Bill, tell your people to get moving. There's only so much patience down here. If we don't settle it one way, the quiet way, then we have to think about other ways to get their attention." I didn't have to ask him what that meant.

I relayed the word to Washington that the Panamanians were ready to go ahead with another round of talks. On April 22, State Department sources told the press that the next negotiating session would begin in Washington on May 9.

Torrijos chose that moment for his next foray on the world stage. His purpose, as always, was to keep the Panamanian issue in the limelight and to remind Washington that he had alternatives if they decided a fair settlement was impossible. He went to Tripoli to confer with Libya's dictator, Col. Muammar al-Qaddafi. It was, without a doubt, the most ill-advised of Torrijos' numerous expeditions abroad. Qaddafi was a tough-minded tyrant with a messianic complex, a patron of terrorism from Ireland to Iran. He was anathema to many in the Arab world, especially the Egyptians, Saudis, and Sudanese. He was committed to the destruction of Israel and was a close collaborator of the Soviet Union.

Torrijos and those around him had not done their homework. They had seen Qaddafi as a military leader who, like Torrijos, wanted to improve the lot of his people. But in Panama, the journey backfired badly. Torrijos had no Arab constituency and the trip to Tripoli won plaudits only from the tiny, bloody-minded minority that favored violence as the answer to all questions. What the general did have was a large, influential, and, until then, friendly Jewish constituency. They were up in arms when they heard of his venture to North Africa. When he returned home and found what a hornet's nest he had broken open, the general shoved his Libyan ploy into the deep freeze. Plans for a Libyan bank were quietly buried, along with all mention of his trek to Tripoli.

On May 4, I flew to Washington to consult with Bunker and Linowitz and other members of the negotiating team on the upcoming talks with the Panamanians. I also wanted to smooth the way for Gabriel as he took on his new responsibilities as Panama's ambassador. The morning after I arrived, I went to the State Department for a long session with our treaty negotiators. I gave them a rundown on the then-current situation in Panama, told them of my talk with Torrijos, described what I thought the Panamanians hoped for from the talks about to begin. I told them I thought we could get the Panamanians to accept some kind of mutual guarantee of the canal's security, but only if we made concessions to their priority goal, that is, the transfer of significant pieces of territory and facilities. They said they understood, and I left feeling that chances for progress in the talks were good.

The rest of the morning was taken up with meetings in the department and at noon I went to lunch with Morey Bell. One thing that came through was the fact that Morey was not on the same wavelength with Sol Linowitz. Part of it was temperament. Sol was a driver, an organized man, a lawyer who wanted to get the brief written and the case tried. Morey had a kind of Latin outlook, a nineteenth-century view of diplomacy in which anything done hurriedly was not done well. He set much store on form and loved the sideshows of the diplomatic circus. Sol was only concerned with the center ring.

I spent that afternoon on Capitol Hill talking Panama with Bob Dockery, the competent Latin American specialist on the staff of the Senate Foreign Relations Committee, and with Paul Sarbanes, Maryland's bright, hard-working senator who headed the Latin American subcommittee of the SFRC. It was a pleasure for any U.S. official coming from abroad to talk with people on the Hill who knew their business, were interested, asked solid questions.

I went back to the department, talked to a few people, and suddenly it was 7:30, time to go to National Airport to welcome Panama's new ambassador to our capital city. National Airlines Flight 102 was on time and suddenly I saw Gabriel and Nita walking toward me through the crowd at North Terminal. Warm *abrazos*, words of welcome, and we were on our way to the Panamanian Embassy. We stayed up late talking about this strange capital, how it worked, people Gabriel should get to know, what really mattered and what was trivial. It may have been one of the most detailed briefings any newly arrived ambassador ever received from an ambassador of the host country.

The next day, Lewis took the first of two official steps required before he could actually perform as ambassador. We managed to expedite things and he had his appointment with Acting Secretary Warren Christopher (Secretary Vance was out of the country) in less than twenty-four hours after his arrival—a new record for Foggy Bottom. Morey Bell and I accompanied Lewis to his appointment. Christopher received the new ambassador with considerable warmth, accepted his official documents, and invited us all to sit down. The acting secretary noted the speed with which the newly arrived diplomat had been received and said it reflected the importance the Carter administration placed on Panama and on an early settlement. "I hope," he told Lewis, "that we will have a new treaty before the first snowfall."

Lewis said he had been in Washington the previous year and the first snow had come in October. "Okay," said Christopher, "and I hope we have snow by October this year, too." As we were leaving, the acting secretary explained that President Carter would be traveling to Europe but that Lewis' appointment in the White House would be fixed as soon as possible. The ambassador thanked him for his kindness, and we left.

Thus commenced the work of one of the most imaginative ambassadors ever to alight on the banks of the Potomac. No diplomat from Panama ever had anything close to the impact Lewis had on the Washington scene. No ambassador from any country I know of ever navigated the treacherous waters of diplomacy, congressional relations, and the press in the U.S. capital with more skill.

In the next twenty-four hours, members of the Panamanian negotiating team arrived in Washington. Rómulo Escobar had done most of the talking at the "secret" session in March and we assumed he would be the principal negotiator. Aristides Royo, the minister of education, had also been active in the March session and he accompanied Rómulo to Washington. The third member of the Panamanian trio was Edwin Fábrega, who had devoted most of his attention to the vexed question of Lands and Waters.

Ambassador Lewis had already told General Torrijos that he preferred not to be on the negotiating team. He and I had discussed the matter at some length and I explained to him that when Ambassador Bunker raised the question with me I had told him I thought I could be more useful by staying in the background, giving advice when he asked for it or when I felt it would be useful, and maintaining close contact with the Panamanian government. Lewis reached the same conclusion. As it turned out, we both played active roles in the negotiating process, but in ways that neither of us, nor anyone else, ever foresaw.

What came to be called the "May Round" began at 10:30 A.M. on Monday, May 9, in the conference room of the Panamanian Embassy, next to the ambassador's office. The three Panamanians sat on one side of the long wooden conference table, Escobar in the center. The U.S. team was made up of Ambassadors Bunker and Linowitz, the two deputies, Bell and Dolvin, and Dick Wyrough. With them was a State Department interpreter and a stenotypist to take notes.

Escobar welcomed the Americans "to the Republic of Panama, where you are at this particular moment." He said he spoke "in a spirit of goodwill which must prevail in our negotiations." Escobar then asked the U.S. negotiators to respond to the points that he and his colleagues had advanced in the March 13 meeting.

Ellsworth Bunker thanked the Panamanians for their welcome and for their willingness to come to Washington to resume the talks. He proposed the two teams discuss "all the outstanding issues as a package," arguing that they were all interrelated. If they could agree on all the major problems, they could then decide how to go about writing specific treaty language. If agreement eluded them, then "neither side would be bound by positions which it may take on any one issue."

The nightmare of any negotiator is to make a concession on Item A, which the other side then files away as an accomplished fact without granting any reciprocal concessions on Items B or C. It reminded me of a line I sent from Moscow twenty years before about Soviet negotiations. "Nikita Khrushchev's view of diplomacy," I wrote, "is that 'what's mine is mine and what's yours is negotiable.'" Bunker was getting his caveats in early.

The U.S. statement recognized that Panama placed its highest priority on the question of Lands and Waters. That had been the main subject pushed by Escobar in the March meeting. As Bunker spoke, Panamanian hopes rose that at long last the Americans were focusing on their prime target. But Bunker then pricked the balloon of their expectations. "I should make it clear," he said, "that what you asked for concerning some of these Lands and Waters questions will require the approval of our highest authority." He and his colleagues were not prepared then to give a yes or no answer to any of Panama's territorial questions.

Bunker then reverted to what was the prime U.S. consideration—an arrangement for the canal's permanent neutrality. If the Panamanians would agree to the U.S. proposal, Bunker said, the U.S. side would make "two important concessions": a treaty on canal operations *and* defense would expire on December 31, 1999, and there would be no posttreaty security pact or any U.S. military presence after the treaty ended. Those two "concessions" were welcomed by the Panamanians but they were, in fact, things that Panama had been insisting on for years. They had said repeatedly that without them any treaty would be unthinkable. Moreover, the talks on Contadora in February and in Washington on March 13 had led the Panamanians to assume that the United States would grant those two elements. Hence, the Panamanian negotiators saw them on May 9 not so much as "concessions" as simply acceptance of reality.

Bunker then spelled out the main elements of a treaty on neutrality, and it was the first time the U.S. team had formally proposed it as a separate pact rather than as part of an overall Panama Canal treaty. The first part was a bow to Panamanian pride. It stated: "Panama, as territorial sovereign, declares the Canal to be permanently neutral."

It was the second part of the formula that was the heart of the matter. It had begun to take shape soon after the Policy Review Committee meeting in the White House in late January. Following that session, Bunker and Linowitz met with Secretary Harold Brown and other top Defense officials to discuss the neutrality concept and how it could provide the United States the necessary flexibility to protect the waterway once the canal treaty expired. Everyone concerned was persuaded that an earlier formula, worked out in the Pentagon in 1976,* was too restrictive and badly needed

---

* It was called the "Clements formula," named for then Deputy Secretary of Defense William Clements. It called for consultation between the two parties in case of a threat, and then reliance on a broad spectrum of diplomatic countermeasures, including appeals to the Interna-

revision. The new Pentagon hierarchy wanted to be able to act quickly and unilaterally if a threat to the canal arose.

After those discussions, the negotiators asked State's Legal Adviser's Office to prepare alternative formulations of a neutrality guarantee. Under the leadership of State's capable Mark Feldman, the lawyers consulted with Defense's best legal minds and produced four or five possible solutions. Just before they left for Contadora in February, Bunker and Linowitz sent the legal memo to Defense for clearance. In the Pentagon, the key formula was reduced from two sentences to one and was approved by the top brass. Because the defense secretary and the chairman of the Joint Chiefs had given it their blessing, the formula came to be known as "Brown and Brown."

That, with minor word changes, was what Ambassador Bunker presented to the Panamanians on May 9. It said: "Panama and the United States commit themselves to a regime of neutrality which shall be maintained in order that the Canal shall be secure, free, and open to vessels of commerce and of war of all nations on terms of entire equality so that there shall be no discrimination against any nation or its citizens or subjects concerning the conditions or charges of traffic or otherwise."

The phrasing was altered and tightened in subsequent sessions, and most of the awkwardness of the paragraph was eliminated by judicious editing. Nonetheless, the central concept survived amazingly well and eventually emerged as Article IV of the Neutrality Treaty. It was, in fact, the heart of that agreement.

Responding to Bunker, Panama's Escobar left no doubt that his country, while accepting the general idea of neutrality for the canal, had definite reservations about what it meant. Escobar wanted the American negotiators to understand clearly that "no internal event inside Panama" could be judged a violation of neutrality. If any local incident threatened the functioning of the waterway, he said, it would be "the exclusive responsibility of Panamanian authorities and the Panamanian National Guard" to deal with it. He said Panama never would tolerate any internal disturbance in his country being used as a pretext to introduce U.S. military forces into the country to "protect the canal." This later became a highly contentious issue in the Senate and, at one point, nearly destroyed the whole treaty.

Escobar then dealt with the other subjects raised by Bunker—the organization that would run the canal, the rights of employees, duration, and others. But the one he gave greatest attention to was one Bunker had barely mentioned, Lands and Waters. Escobar reiterated "that this is a problem of vital importance and that we, as we have been stressing so far,

---

tional Court of Justice. Only after the various diplomatic measures had failed would the two countries have been free to resort to economic or military measures to protect the canal.

would like there to be a concrete proposal from the U.S. delegation." He said Panama wanted a statement on this subject from the U.S. team that was "as clear as the one the delegation had made to us on the problem of neutrality."

At that point, the negotiations were turning into a chess game. Escobar knew, of course, that General Dolvin and Edwin Fábrega had worked out a fairly comprehensive package on Lands and Waters, admittedly with a few loose ends. As some Americans saw it, certainly Tom Dolvin, Escobar was revising the rules of the game. In effect, he was telling the U.S. side: "In the neutrality pact, you are asking us for much more than we ever expected to give. In return, you are going to have to provide, in lands and facilities, more than you have expected to give."

The Panamanian negotiator posed several specific questions. Did the United States agree to transfer the ports to Panama? And the railroad? And Ancon Hill? He said he and his colleagues would study carefully the Bunker statement. In return, he begged the Americans "to study the points we have just made and the purpose and intention behind them."

Linowitz responded by asking two detailed questions—one on neutrality, the other on employees. On the first, a long exposition boiled down to one key question: Did Panama accept the language the U.S. had suggested on neutrality as the basis for negotiation or did it wish to change it?

Escobar's answer was short and to the point. The U.S. terminology "goes along the correct path and we can work with it," he said.

The Panamanian then reemphasized the heart of his country's position: "The greater or lesser amount of progress to be made on this task depends on the greater or lesser progress made on the other subject." He could hardly have focused a brighter spotlight on Panama's basic attitude toward the treaty. The Americans either did not absorb the import of the Panamanian lawyer's message, or they chose to ignore it.

Linowitz' second query was whether U.S. canal employees could enjoy the same rights given the U.S. military forces under the Status of Forces Agreement. Escobar's answer was equally pointed: No, they could not. The SOFA was for military personnel, he said, and canal workers were not in the military. What concerned the Panamanians, as Fábrega made clear a few minutes later, was that if the agency that operated the canal was part of the Defense Department, and if SOFA rights were extended to all canal workers, the next step would be to make all military bases and canal operating areas into "Defense Sites." That, they foresaw, would mean nothing less than a new, if somewhat shrunken, Canal Zone—precisely what they sought to eliminate.

While the negotiators were negotiating, I was traveling around town, meeting the appointments an eager State Department always lines up for visiting ambassadors. They had booked visits in State, at the Pentagon, at the White House, and on Capitol Hill. When I got back to the State Department in the late afternoon, Linowitz was out but I talked with Bunker and Bell. They were pleased with the way the morning session had gone. That was relaxing news. I was concerned—as all of us were—that the revived talks might produce another February fiasco, or an inconclusive March 13.

The second meeting of the May Round convened the next day at 3:05 P.M. at the Panamanian Embassy. In many respects, the discussion was a repetition of what had transpired on Monday. It was a good example of intelligent men aiming at a common goal but talking around and past each other. Essentially, both sides were saying the same thing: if you agree to settle what is absolutely crucial to us, then everything else, we are sure, will fall into place.

Royo began with an urgent plea to the U.S. negotiators to give him and his colleagues a clear indication of the U.S. position on Lands and Waters. We talked about this in February, he said, and we talked about it in March, and we talked about it again yesterday. Twice he said that the subject was "very important" to Panama. Escobar followed up, emphasizing the same point. In the process, he gave the Americans two clear signals that exposed the Panamanians' outlook and mood. He spoke of the "reality" of the negotiations, "that is, the reality of a small country negotiating with a great power." He was saying: you are a major power in the world; we are a small and weak nation; you can afford to be considerate.

His second point was that Panama regarded the Lands and Waters issue as a litmus test of U.S. intentions. "To begin our discussions on Lands and Waters," he said, "would allow us to give our government some real information on the shape of the solution toward which we are working, and would allow us to use it as a gauge for the solution of other problems."

In part, the impact of what the Panamanians were saying was undercut by tactics they themselves had used in the previous year. More than once, they had told Dolvin that this area or that facility was "vital" to them. Once transfer was agreed, they became "minor" and other things became "primary." That produced some justifiable cynicism in Dolvin, which was shared by others. However, the fact that the Panamanian case was being made at the chief negotiators' level in May—and that Torrijos was watching every move closely—made a qualitative difference. We were no longer dealing with tactical moves but fundamental Panamanian strategy.

There seemed to be an invisible filter between one side of the conference table and the other. Passing through it, the words of Royo and Escobar lost potency. What mattered to Bunker and Linowitz was not what Panama wanted but what the United States had to have. For three months, their outlook had been dominated by one consideration: without an acceptable security plan for the canal there would be no treaty. They had not yet fully appreciated the other crucial fact: unless Panama's fundamental requirements were met, there also would be no treaty.

The Americans responded by assuring the Panamanians that they understood the importance of the Lands and Waters issue. But, as they had said the day before, some key items were "still subject to the approval of our highest authority, and we have not yet obtained such approval." To help ease the disappointment, Ambassador Bunker told the Panamanians that the railroad, which paralleled the canal route from Balboa to Colón, would be transferred to Panama. He also told them they could have "the top of Ancon Hill."

Instead of leaving it at that, and letting the good effect sink in, the U.S. team undercut its own tactic by immediately introducing the inevitable caveats. In the first place, transfer of the railroad was hardly a surprise. It had been discussed for two years and, by 1977, both sets of negotiators assumed the railroad would go to Panama. The only real questions were how and when. The Americans stressed the limited nature of their generosity by noting that the transfer would be "subject to certain conditions inasmuch as it is an essential link in the operation and defense of the canal." Panama would get the railroad but the United States would have priority use for supplies, equipment, and personnel whenever necessary.

Those limitations were not grossly unfair, or even unexpected. The Panamanians knew perfectly well that in an emergency the railroad might be required to move supplies and personnel to a trouble spot. What irked them was having the obligations of partnership shoved upon them in a way that implied they did not understand what their side of the bargain would be.

"When discussing this question of Lands and Waters," Escobar said with obvious bite, "I think we must begin from one basic premise: that the United States and Panama are not enemies. It is not that the United States wishes to maintain efficient operation of the canal and Panama wishes to obstruct it. . . . Both have the same interest in mind—that the Canal should function as it has to date, or even that the efficiency of its functioning will be improved in the future."

Once the railroad was under Panama's control, he said, regulations would be issued that "transport of equipment and workers related to the operation of the Canal" had priority. If Panamanian passengers and cargo had to be delayed, he said, that would be done.

"All of this is very easy to understand," Escobar said, "if it is understood that we want to work together with the United States."

If the way transfer of the railroad was handled gave some offense, the turnover of the "top of Ancon Hill" cut deeply. To understand why, one had to be part geographer, part poet. Ancon Hill dominates the landscape in Panama City—more than Capitol Hill in Washington, more than the hills of Rome. On a relief map, even more from a plane flying over the city, Ancon stands out as a tree-covered eminence visible from every part of the city. Because it was the largest physical feature in sight, and because it was in the Canal Zone, it became for Panamanians a symbol of their lost territory, a daily reminder that their country was not entirely their country. Hence it became a central theme in sad songs and angry poems. To be able to "walk up Ancon Hill" became the measure of real independence.

Given Panamanian sentiment toward Ancon, talk of turning over only the "top of the hill" was a slap at their pride and hopes. It was like telling Athenians they could have the Parthenon but not the Acropolis. No one on the American side of the table seemed to understand how severely they were rasping Panamanian sensibilities.

The Americans were thinking of practical considerations. There were installations on the slopes of Ancon that they felt had to be kept in U.S. hands—the Canal Company's administration building, Gorgas Hospital, SOUTHCOM's headquarters at Quarry Heights, the governor's house, and other facilities. There were also communications antennas on top of the hill to which we required free access. Given the mind-set in May 1977, the U.S. negotiators felt the only way they would have what they needed was to keep the hill under total control.

The Panamanians were saying: give us Ancon Hill, and you can continue to use anything you really need. "What we are trying to bring to the attention of the distinguished ambassadors," Escobar said, "is that occupation by Panama of any area of the present Canal Zone will never signify any obstruction to the operation and defense of the Canal." He begged the U.S. side to understand that the effective functioning and protection of the canal was as much in Panama's interest as in America's, perhaps more so.

The Americans said they fully intended to take up all the questions the Panamanians had raised "not today, however, because . . . we need clearance on them." Perhaps, in order to speed things up, we can now deal with some issues that are important to us, Bunker suggested, "such as neutrality."

Linowitz was trying to nail down what the U.S. side saw as the essential ingredient of any Panama treaty. He spelled out the formula as follows: "The United States commits itself to participate in the maintenance of the neutrality of the canal in accordance with the regime of neutrality, upon which we both agree, against a threat or attack from any source."

The U.S. government had to be able to say that much on neutrality, he told the Panamanians. There should be no doubt in their minds that we viewed the agreement as an assertion of our right to protect the waterway from a threat "from any source." That was what we meant, and that was the way we would interpret it. Linowitz then made a tactical mistake by recognizing that the Panamanians might not interpret it that way. No one foresaw how crucial the question would later become, and he was trying to provide some flexibility in order to solve a major problem. Within five months, that "flexibility" would create major misunderstandings—with Panama and thus the Congress—and force a rewriting of the treaty's central article.

That was a difference for the future. A more immediate disagreement developed on the spot. Escobar praised Linowitz for his great contributions to moving the neutrality discussion forward so effectively. He had, for example, said Escobar, "understood why the United States could not be the guarantor of neutrality." A slip of the tongue? Possibly, but not very likely. He might have meant to say that Panama, not the United States, should *declare* the canal's neutrality. But making the United States a *guarantor* of neutrality in the waterway was precisely what the Americans wanted, indeed had to have. Bunker and Linowitz looked at their Panamanian colleague in amazement.

Then came a second surprise. Escobar elaborated on Linowitz' willingness "to obviate the necessity to develop a neutrality treaty now." He said he and his colleagues felt the general principles of neutrality arrangement were well enough understood to feel confident it would be worked out "before the end of the Canal treaty."

The Americans could not believe their ears. They jumped in with pointed questions, and the more they pressed for clarification, the more it appeared that Escobar meant what he had said—a neutrality pact could be worked out later. Linowitz and Bunker, for a brief moment, saw the whole enterprise going up in a wisp of smoke.

"I must tell you," said Linowitz, "that, I say candidly, you have now created a very real problem." He had not talked of a neutrality arrangement at some indefinite point in the future. It had to be an integral part of the treaty they were working on. He explained that he and Ambassador Bunker had to be able to tell the president, the Congress, and the American people "that the United States will not be impotent if the Canal is threatened."

To allay Panamanian concerns, he added: "I assure you most sincerely that the United States has no intention of intervening in the internal affairs of Panama." But he added pointedly: "We must be free to make the statement I indicated if we are to obtain approval for this treaty." Moreover, it could not come later but had to be "contemporaneous with the Panama Canal Treaty itself."

There may have been—and several Panamanians later insisted there was—some confusion between a neutrality arrangement and a mutual security pact. Earlier, the U.S. side had talked of a joint defense pact that might be worked out in the final years of a canal treaty. But the neutrality formula was a different concept, and Bunker and Linowitz never talked about it being anything but an essential part of the new treaty arrangement.

It was by then 6:00 P.M. and the Panamanians suggested an adjournment until 3 o'clock the next afternoon. It was agreed to hold the next session in the conference room of the deputy secretary of state, mainly because it offered better facilities for simultaneous translation.

I had gotten back to the State Department late in the afternoon after my round of appointments, including a good talk with Gen. George Brown in his Pentagon office. Brown agreed heartily that the best defense of the Panama Canal was the friendship and cooperation of the Panamanian people and their government. The U.S. role in future protection of the waterway, he told me, could best be handled from U.S. air bases and by the ships, submarines, and fighter aircraft of the Atlantic Fleet. I asked about the small force and scattered bases we had in the Canal Zone. Brown thought we should keep them during a treaty, more for political reasons at home than for real military utility. But what if we don't get a treaty, I asked, and real trouble breaks out? Then we would need four or five times as much as we have there, he told me.

There were some cables from Panama waiting for me and a few phone call reminders. One was from Ambassador Lewis. When I reached him, he asked if I could come to his house, and I told him I would be there as soon as I cleared off my desk.

At the residence, Gabriel was in his shirt sleeves with a tumbler of scotch-and-soda in his hand. We walked to the comfortable family room at the rear of the house. I could see it was going to be a long session so I took off my coat and tie and draped them over a chair.

"What's up, my friend?" I asked him.

"This thing is falling apart," he told me. "These guys have talked to Torrijos and they're going home tomorrow."

"Hell, they just got here," I tried to joke. "And they said they came with orders to get a treaty."

"I know that," he said, "but they just don't think they're getting anywhere. And when they told Omar how things were going, he got mad and ordered them to come home."

"You know, Gabriel, Omar is like a thermometer. He can go from hot to cold in a hurry. Maybe he'll cool off by tomorrow."

"Maybe, but I don't think so," he told me. "He really sounds fed up."

"Well, let's take a look at the thing step by step. Maybe we can find some answer—if it's that much of a mess. What happened today?"

He went through the main points of the meeting. The essentials agreed with the short summary I had received earlier. Naturally, Gabriel was putting a slight Panamanian twist on each ball he tossed out, but I took that into account. From the thousands of words that had been exchanged during the past two days—indeed during the past three months—two central problems stood out. Bunker and Linowitz were pressing the Panamanians hard with their demand for a neutrality treaty. It was bitter medicine for Panamanians because they and their fathers and grandfathers had been objecting to the dominant U.S. role in Panama, and to "perpetuity," for seventy years.

The second point, equally rancorous, was that the United States was not paying attention to the things Panama counted most important. Those "things" were land and facilities. Part of the force behind the Panamanians' views was national pride. The key symbol of that emotional component was Ancon Hill.

The other central element in Panama's attitude was the drive for economic improvement. When Panamanians looked at the Canal Zone, they saw large areas between the Atlantic and Pacific not serving any constructive purpose. Much of that land could be used for housing the growing population of Panama City and Colón; much could provide sites for new small- and medium-size industries. They were especially interested in extensive expansion of the Colón Free Zone. More than three hundred businesses were importing into the duty-free zone everything from pharmaceuticals to electronic equipment for processing and repackaging for shipment to all of Latin America. The gross value of business activity in the Free Zone in 1977 was estimated at more than $1.2 billion. By using adjacent land from the Canal Zone, economists estimated the Free Zone could double its activity and provide several thousand additional jobs, as well as precious foreign exchange. The planners also had ambitious designs for a huge container port near the Free Zone which would act as a transshipment point for products from all over the world. That whole range of interests and expectations was at the heart of Panama's hopes for a new treaty, and the U.S. negotiators were pushing them aside, promising action in the future but not then.

After we covered the economic territory at length, I turned Gabriel's attention to our interests. I assured him the Carter administration honestly wanted a new deal for Panama, and no two men wanted it more than Ellsworth Bunker and Sol Linowitz. But the White House knew, and our negotiators knew even better, that, unless we had an arrangement that permitted the United States to continue to protect the canal indefinitely, there would be no treaty. It was as simple and as hard to digest as that.

He led me through long segments of his country's history, explaining why sensitive nerves were rubbed raw by the kind of commitment we were proposing. In turn, I guided him through the intricacies of congressional politics and the problems of public opinion. I explained there were sensitive nerves on both sides. Finally, I said: "Gabriel, if I were a Panamanian, I'd see and feel exactly what you and other patriotic Panamanians do. But if you were an American, you'd see and feel what I do. Both of us have to look at what's in the long-run best interest of our countries. And we both have to think hard about the price if we fail. You and I don't want to see your young people and mine killing each other. Neither of us wants to see the canal closed. The only ones who would gain by that would be the communists, and who wants to hand them that kind of a gift?"

He and I had talked before about the canal's security and some kind of joint guarantee. I asked if he agreed that a neutrality arrangement along the lines Linowitz had been pushing was absolutely necessary. Without it, I told him, there wasn't a ghost of a chance of Congress approving a treaty.

"I see that," he said. "I don't like it, because we all hoped it wouldn't be necessary. But you've made it clear why it has to be. You have my word, I'll explain it to Omar and Rómulo and Royo. I may get fired, but I'll do it. It's the only way we'll ever get what we need."

It was a courageous decision. Gabriel was refusing to take the easy route, which would have been to remain uninvolved. He believed a treaty was the best thing for both countries, and he was willing to face reality. I knew he would be bucking some individuals who were close to General Torrijos and who tried regularly to prove how "tough" they were by pushing their leader into intransigence. Gabriel was as patriotic and nationalistic as any of them, but he was wiser, less self-serving, and much more realistic.

"While you do that," I told him, "I'll tell Ellsworth and Sol why we have to move on the transfer of lands and facilities. I admit we've been dragging our feet. We've reached the point now, though, where we're both going to have to bite the bullet."

Gabriel raised his glass in a final toast. "Maybe we'll both be fired," he said.

"At least we'll be in good company," I told him.

There was a meeting of the negotiating team at 9 o'clock the next morning and that was an opportunity to convey the essentials of my long discussion with Gabriel. When Bunker asked how things looked, I told him about my meeting with the Panamanian ambassador. I explained the unhappiness in the Panamanian camp at the seeming reluctance to face up to the transfer of lands and facilities. I said it seemed to me the negotiations had to be a two-way street if they were to succeed.

"I feel sure we can get what we need on security," I said, "if we give Panama what it feels it needs for pride, first, and for economic development."

It was handled with restraint and with the focus on pending treaty issues. I hoped it would lead to a serious discussion of strategy and the necessary next steps. But the talk shifted almost immediately to the neutrality formula, how it could be better explained, and how we could get what *we* wanted. It was a perfect example of what the Panamanians had described and what Gabriel had belabored me with the night before. I listened as long as my patience would tolerate, and then decided I had to introduce some harsh reality into those self-deceptive proceedings.

"With all due respect," I said, addressing the ambassadors, "I'm afraid you didn't understand what I was trying to say, or else I said it badly. If we go along the way we have been, we're going to blow any chance for a treaty right out of the water." I said the Panamanians were not happy. "In point of fact, they're furious. They think they've been handled like children. Every time they raise something that matters to them, we tell them they've got to wait, that we don't have the necessary authority. Torrijos is just as frustrated as they are, and he's ordered them to come home."

Everyone in the room was surprised at the vehemence I was using. One member of the team later told me: "You were always very quiet and controlled. When you unleashed the heavy artillery, it really had an effect." Bunker and Linowitz were listening carefully to every word. The others were sitting back quietly, but as I talked I began to notice some heads nodding in agreement. Certainly the news that the general had ordered his negotiators home drew everyone's attention.

"We want a neutrality treaty," I said. "Good—and quite right. But I can tell you that we're not going to get it this way. We're a big country, a power in the world. We're dealing with one of the smallest nations on earth. Because we're strong, we can afford to be generous. And if they see we're being fair with them, then they'll be fair with us. But we have to take the lead."

"Could you explain that, Bill?" Bunker asked.

"Take the railroad, for example, Ellsworth," I said. "They've known for a year at least that they were going to get it and they were happy about that. But then when we agree to turn it over, we put on so many caveats and provisos that it makes it sound like it's still our railroad—that what we need it for is more important than what they need it for. They know damn well there will be conditions on usage. But if we simply agreed to turn it over—and then talked about the conditions two days later in a subcommittee or something, we'd get ten times as much mileage from the move.

"And Ancon Hill," I went on. "That's like a sensitive nerve for them. It's a symbol of their independence and their nationhood. So what do we do? We offer to give them the top of the hill! It's like turning over the steeple without the church. Take my word for it, if we give them the hill they'll let us use anything on it we really need—the hospital, the headquarters building, whatever is essential. They just want the hill painted one color on the map, not a jigsaw puzzle.

"And another big thing is the ports. If we say we're partners, why in the name of heaven can't the Panamanians run the ports in their own country? They won't use them against us. For any country in the world, it would be shameful to have a foreign government running the two major ports in the country."

I looked at Ellsworth and Sol and it was clear they were thinking hard and taking in every word. Around the rest of the room, there was a mixture of expressions—some amazement, some smiles. I had moved forward in my chair and I suddenly realized my hands were clenched. I sat back and relaxed. I had said what I came to say—more, in fact.

"Forgive my candor," I said, "but I had to give you my honest judgment. I'm sure we can get a treaty and it can have in it what we must have. But we'll get more in the long run if we give more in the short run."

Bunker adjourned the meeting and he and Linowitz asked me to stay. When the others were gone, Sol told me: "I think you're right. What's the best way to move?"

I asked where the major bottleneck was. In the Department of Defense, specifically the army, I was told. "Well, then, that's where I'd go and try to get some decisions," I said. "The president said he wants a fair treaty. I doubt the army wants to be responsible for having the bottom drop out of everything. And that's what's going to happen if we don't move."

Sol called Cliff Alexander, the secretary of the army, and arranged a visit within the hour. In Alexander's office, they laid out all the pending Lands and Waters issues and stressed the importance of resolving them quickly. Alexander asked the ambassadors to give him a little time to work things out and promised to be back in touch that day. Linowitz reminded him there was a meeting with the Panamanians scheduled for 3 o'clock that afternoon.

I called Gabriel to tell him I was keeping my half of the bargain. Only then did I learn that he, too, had gone to the Pentagon that morning for a meeting with Secretary Alexander. He had met Cliff at the U.S. Residence during the army secretary's first visit to Panama earlier in the year. Lewis had described the situation on the return of lands, told Alexander how important it was for Panama, and said he had come to deliver an urgent SOS to the secretary. Cliff heard him out and at the end told him, "SOS received."

The next hours were filled with nervous tension for all concerned. Bunker and Linowitz were waiting to hear from Alexander. Ambassador Lewis had tried to put his colleagues in a hopeful mood after his talk with the army secretary, but he remained nervous and kept calling me every hour. I hoped Alexander would cut the Gordian knot; otherwise, there was going to be a shambles. I could see the headlines in my mind's eye: "Panama Treaty Talks Disrupted; Visiting Negotiators Fly Home."

Escobar, Royo, and Fábrega arrived at the State Department with time to spare before the 3:00 P.M. meeting and Bell and Dolvin kept them occupied. At a few minutes before 3 o'clock, the phone in the Bunker-

Linowitz suite rang and everybody jumped. Alexander ran down the list the ambassadors had given him of problem areas, and a secretary took notes on his comments. The key points were typed up and Bunker and Linowitz hurried down the seventh-floor hall to meet the Panamanians.

When the two teams settled around the long table, old pro Bunker opened the session with a calm, detached introduction. One might have thought it was something he had planned to say for days.

"As Ambassador Linowitz and I mentioned at our first meeting," he said, "we would need to have some consultations in connection with the Lands and Waters areas. We were unable to do that until today, but we had some consultations and we would like to make some statements to you about what we are prepared to do."

He then went down the list of the most vexatious problems of territory. "The ports would pass to Panama on entry into force of the treaty," he began. He proposed a joint port authority under which Panama would control all shoreside activities and the joint body that ran the canal would handle traffic along the waterway. The railroad would go to Panama, as he had said two days before, without the detailed reservations used previously. Civilian housing would be jointly managed and it would be turned over to Panama at five-year intervals. Ancon Hill (not just the top) would go to Panama though the United States would control things like the hospital, schools, and a few other key installations. The Albrook airstrip bordering downtown Panama City would be handed over, minus a few military facilities. There were other major transfers of property, including the entire city of Cristóbal at the Caribbean end of the canal.

The Panamanians were stunned. It was something they had hoped to hear, but never really expected. To give themselves time to adjust, they turned the floor over to Architect Fábrega, who had long been working on these matters, and he asked questions about some of the things Bunker had mentioned. It was a way to fill time and to give the others a chance to adjust to what clearly was a totally new ball game.

Minister Royo finally was able to face the changed situation and make a comment. "We have received these proposals made by the United States Delegation, and we would like to express at this point our great appreciation and gratitude in recognition of this presentation. . . . This is the spirit in which Panama has wished to see these negotiations conducted for so long."

Escobar then commented on the U.S. presentation: "We do understand that this is an occasion of an enormous effort made by the United States Delegation to achieve progress in these negotiations, and we are much aware of this and we are appreciative of it, and we would like to say thanks to Ambassadors Bunker and Linowitz who have been working tirelessly on this problem." He said it was "a demonstration on your part of great honesty, a demonstration that you are indeed endeavoring to have our countries resolve this problem."

Linowitz responded: "We are pleased that you appreciate the significance of this presentation by the ambassador, and that you do see this as an indication of our spirit in these negotiations."

He then spoke briefly about the neutrality agreement, but he took the advice of his advisers and merely gave the Panamanians a draft agreement that had been prepared. He asked the Panamanians to "study it and examine it and then let us have your reaction to it."

The mood had suddenly been transformed; the gloom of previous days disappeared. It was Bunker's birthday and Royo, noting that fact, read a poem in tribute to the man and to friendship between the countries. By mutual agreement, technical talk was shoved aside, a tray of champagne was brought in, and everyone toasted the birthday of the senior U.S. negotiator. They agreed to meet again the next day at the same time.

Escobar, Royo, and Fábrega returned to the Panamanian Embassy on a cloud. Ambassador Lewis was waiting in the family room at the rear of the residence, what by then had been dubbed the "loco room" because so many crazy things kept happening there. Escobar told him: "You know the list of things we wanted, Gabriel? It's all been completed. The Americans made a 180-degree change in position." One of the Panamanians later described it as "a moment of great joy for all of us."

Royo went over his notes, and then they called Torrijos to pass on the good news. The general was caught off guard, totally surprised but delighted. When they asked if they should stay in Washington, he told them to return to Panama and give him a full rundown on the new U.S. proposal. "And now," he added, "we have to take a hard look at their neutrality idea." It was agreed that Edwin Fábrega would stay to refine details of the land transfers with Tom Dolvin. Escobar and Royo went to the airport. But instead of flying home in anger and frustration, they made the trip in the happiest frame of mind they had known for three years.

May 16, 1977, was a red-letter day for Ambassador Lewis, the day he presented credentials to the president of the United States. A few days in advance, a protocol officer from State met with the ambassador to brief him on procedure. Since three other ambassadors were presenting credentials that same day, the protocol expert emphasized, everything had to be precisely timed. "When you go into the Oval Office," he said, "you hand the president your credentials, shake hands, and say a few words. The photographers will come in to take a few pictures. You shake hands again, say a few words—just light conversation, the weather, that sort of thing. The photographers file out and you leave. It should take four minutes."

That well-laid, if sterile, plan reckoned without the personality of either Jimmy Carter or Gabriel Lewis. After the presentation of documents and the picture taking, the president and the ambassador were left alone in the office. Lewis began by apologizing for any breach of protocol he may have committed. "After all, Mr. President," he said, "I'm not a diplomat, just a plain businessman." The president laughed. "Well, we're in the same boat," he countered. "I'm just a plain farmer." Lewis, never one to miss a chance to plug his favorite product, explained that he was in the paper box business. "I used to buy all my paper from Oregon," he said, "but since January twentieth I've been buying it in Georgia." Carter enjoyed the joke.

Pleasantries aside, the talk turned to a new Panama treaty and Zbigniew Brzezinski joined the discussion. Carter said he definitely wanted a new treaty, and as soon as possible. He had given Lewis a written statement of his views, and he explained it was not the usual collection of polite words but that it said what he really believed.

"A new treaty must protect the interests of both countries," Carter had written. "Also, the treaty should accommodate your aspirations and serve our needs." The heart of the president's view was in two sentences: "For our part, we need an agreement that grants us the necessary rights to operate, maintain and defend the Canal during the treaty period. In addition, we need an arrangement that provides reasonable assurance that the Canal will remain permanently open to world shipping on a secure and non-discriminatory basis."

The president told the ambassador that a neutrality treaty, as presented by Ambassadors Bunker and Linowitz, was a political necessity if the treaty was to be approved by the Senate. Carter said he was prepared to push ahead quickly to get a treaty and to take the political heat that action would generate. He told Lewis any unnecessary delay would complicate chances for success in the Congress. Lewis promised to convey both the words and the spirit of the president's message to General Torrijos and the government of Panama.

That first meeting established a warm rapport and a level of congeniality that few ambassadors enjoyed with President Carter. It would be sustained through a long and testing summer.

Back at the embassy, Lewis got on the red phone and called Torrijos. He told the general he had enjoyed "a wonderful meeting" with President Carter and he thought it would be a good idea to describe it in person. Torrijos told his ambassador to catch the next plane to Panama. To save time, he sent his Westwind, an Israeli-built executive jet, to pick up the ambassador in Miami. The plane landed on the long runway at the Río Hato military base near Torrijos' beach house at 10:00 P.M.

Waiting with the general at Farallon to hear the ambassador's report were some of his closest advisers. Lewis described his meeting with Carter and read the group the nine-paragraph message the president had given him. For the next three and a half hours, the Torrijos entourage chewed over the Carter-Lewis talk and the latest developments on the negotiating front. Torrijos listened to all the pros and cons, but three things were dominant: the U.S. team had made a major move in the direction of Panama's main goal, "the dismantling of the colonial enclave"; a neutrality treaty was essential to any agreement; speed was essential for President Carter and for Panama. Over breakfast the next morning, Torrijos told the ambassador he wanted him to return to Washington immediately. He had taken what President Carter had told Lewis as a personal message to him (as indeed it was), and he wanted to respond quickly.

"I don't want you to bother the president," Torrijos told Lewis. "But since Brzezinski was at your meeting with the president, I want you to go see him right away and deliver the message." Neither man knew Washington at that point and both were thinking of the free-wheeling Kissinger days when the special assistant for national security affairs had been a principal channel for some diplomats.

A plane picked up the negotiators (Escobar, Royo, and Fábrega) at Tocumen airport, and flew them to Farallon. As he lounged in his favorite hammock, Torrijos outlined what he wanted to tell Carter through Brzezinski. Royo took careful notes. The ambassador later told me that only on the flight to Washington did he suddenly realize that he might have promised more than he could deliver. As soon as he reached his embassy that evening, he called me and Morey Bell and told us his problem. We managed to get Brzezinski to call Lewis and they agreed on a meeting at 8 o'clock the next morning.

The phone woke me from a sound sleep at midnight. It was Gabriel. "Sorry to wake you up, Bill," he said, "but everyone has gone home and I have this meeting with Brzezinski early in the morning and I'm not sure this message from Torrijos says exactly what he wanted to say. Can you help me?"

"OK, my friend," I told him. "Why don't you send your car down and I'll be ready by the time it gets here?"

When I walked into his office, he handed me a copy of the Torrijos message—the original and a rough translation they had worked out. I read it through, then worked over the rough spots in the translation. Then I typed out my rendition of the Torrijos message so the embassy typist, who was coming in early, would have no trouble.

"That is really above and beyond the call of duty," Gabriel said as he looked at the typed copy. "Well, it sure isn't traditional diplomacy," I told him, "but neither of us is very traditional."

The next morning, just before 8 o'clock, Ambassador Lewis rode through the White House gate and got out at the entrance to the West Wing. He was escorted to Brzezinski's office and Lewis thanked the presidential assistant for receiving him. He explained the background of the

Torrijos message and handed it over to the former professor. Brzezinski read it quickly and told Lewis it was "very encouraging" and that the president would be "very happy with your message."

"I was very pleased with President Carter's expressed intention to move ahead with the negotiations and to accept the political problems which may be generated in his country by presentation of a new treaty," Torrijos had written. "I am prepared to do the same in Panama. . . . I share President Carter's feeling that a treaty should be concluded as quickly as possible."

Then came the major breakthrough: "I am fully aware of the importance of the declaration of neutrality of the canal," the Torrijos message said. He added: "We are confident that such neutrality will be useful in peace and in war, that it will be so interpreted by the United States, and that Panama will never be converted into a target of attacks or reprisals in case of military conflicts with other countries."

Torrijos, for the first time, acknowledged in writing the necessity for a neutrality pact—one that would give the United States the right to continue to protect the Panama Canal even after the Canal Treaty itself had expired. That message and what flowed from it made a new Panama Treaty possible.

As he was about to leave, Ambassador Lewis asked how he could contact Brzezinski in case of need. The president's assistant reminded the ambassador that the normal channel for diplomatic discussion should be Secretary Vance. "We don't work as the old system did," he said, underlining the difference between the Carter regime and the Nixon-Kissinger years.

Three hours later, at the negotiating table in the Department of State, the Torrijos decision was made even more specific. It took time, to be sure. Escobar began the session with a lengthy exposition of Panama's desires on Lands and Waters and urged, as Torrijos had in his message to Carter, that everything in the Canal Zone be turned over to Panama except the areas and facilities the new canal management "really and truly needs."

Escobar then turned the floor over to Royo to state Panama's position on neutrality. The minister began by noting what a severe political problem acceptance of the neutrality concept would raise for his country and his government. He also insisted that he and his colleagues would have to prove to their own people that the mutual protection agreement would never produce "an abuse or a misinterpretation by the United States."

Royo then paused and withdrew a paper from the folder in front of him. "I have here a message from General Torrijos which he asked us to deliver to you," he told the Americans. All eyes were riveted on him and the room was completely still. To heighten the drama of the moment, Royo read Torrijos' words slowly, quietly.

"It is understood, and I accept the fact," Torrijos had written, "that by accepting the neutrality formula, I will be attacked by all the jingoistic hounds here and in the Hemisphere. But a Head of State should take decisions and accept their consequences.

"I accept the general concept of neutrality," he continued, "because I am convinced that neither the people nor the armed forces of the United States of America will make an incorrect or unwise use of this authority."

When he finished reading the general's words, Royo paused once more to let their import sink in.

"In other words, gentlemen, distinguished negotiators," he said, "we are very much aware of the significance of the problem of neutrality, and in principle we are accepting it!"

It was not the end of the line by any means. There would be arguments, sometimes extremely rancorous ones, before the last *t*'s were crossed and *i*'s dotted. But with the Torrijos messages to Carter and to the U.S. negotiators, the back of the neutrality issue was broken. From that moment on, it was agreed that the United States and Panama would maintain jointly the neutrality of the Panama Canal—and that meant defending it against any attacker.

At long last, the road to a new Panama treaty was open, potholes and detours notwithstanding.

CHAPTER 15

Generous, Fair, and Appropriate

"It may be that these proposals will be less than you had
expected or wished . . . In my best judgement, the proposals will be generous, fair, and appropriate."

—President Jimmy Carter, letter to General Torrijos,
July 29, 1977

In the austere, colorless conference room on the seventh floor of the
Department of State, there was no physical evidence in mid-May 1977 that
it was the joyful month. The sun could not invade the windowless chamber, and not even a vase of flowers broke the brown-and-beige monotony.
Nonetheless, a spirit of optimism and good cheer was palpable as the
American and Panamanian treaty negotiators gathered there for the fifth
meeting of the May Round.

The warm-up games were behind them and the real season was about to
begin for both teams. At that May 19 meeting, the two sides put the finishing touches to the Neutrality Treaty, and as they neared the end of their
work that afternoon, Panamanian negotiator Rómulo Escobar said: "Well,
gentlemen, as we said at the beginning, we sincerely believe that we have
taken a major step forward. It has not been easy. But I think that this is the
way we should proceed."

That same day, a supplementary negotiating forum began to emerge. It
was an exclusive club of two, my colleague Gabriel Lewis and me. Ambassadors Bunker and Linowitz told me that my intervention the week before
had been crucial and they wanted me to continue working closely with
Gabriel. They recognized that our moving aggressively on territorial questions had opened the way to the Neutrality Treaty. They believed similar
behind-the-scenes diplomacy could be useful on other matters.

The same thought occurred to the Panamanians. Escobar, Royo, and
Fábrega recognized that Gabriel had played a decisive role in breaking the
logjam at the beginning of the May Round. They, too, concluded that continuation of the Lewis-Jorden channel could benefit both sides. They discussed it with General Torrijos and he endorsed the idea. It had the kind of
conspiratorial touch that Torrijos relished. Not that there was any secrecy

within the negotiating teams themselves. But there was just enough of an unorthodox, sub rosa, informal aspect to this approach to give it great appeal to a man who used precisely those techniques in his own political maneuvers.

Gabriel and I developed a work plan that day on a flight to Houston. Panama's President Lakas was in the bustling oil capital for his annual physical checkup, and the ambassador and I flew down to brief him on the latest negotiating developments. On the trip down and back, we talked at length about how we could best support the main negotiating effort.

We agreed quickly on a list of things we would *not* do. Clearly it was not our job to negotiate agreements. We would not try to pin each other down to any specific commitments. We would never have an agenda. And we would never lie to each other. If there were things we could not discuss at any given moment, we would say so and put it off to another day. In fact, that rarely happened.

Gabriel and I both believed we could make our most useful contribution by easing the course of the talks with the grease of candor. After each negotiating session, we would get together privately and go over the main issues. I would explain why the United States was taking the stand it was at the formal sessions. I could point out some of the background, political and historical, that the pressures of time and diplomatic restraint made impossible at the plenary sessions. He did the same for me, often citing some incident in his nation's history that most Americans had never heard of that explained why Escobar and Royo were particularly adamant on a given point. In the process, I received a liberal education in Panamanian history and psychology. Gabriel once told me he thought our sessions gave him "a master's degree in U.S. politics."

In time, we both developed a second sense about what the other side really had to have, what it wanted but could trim down, and what it would eventually drop if it brought a fair return on another issue. Gabriel and I met invariably at night, sometimes for a few hours, often until midnight or later. Then, before the next formal meeting, we could relay to our negotiators what we had gleaned ("They'll fall on their swords over this one" or "I get the feeling they'll retreat from position A if we put what we want in different terms" or "They're just haggling about this for the record, but it doesn't mean all that much to them"). With that background available, the negotiators were able to speed their work considerably. In time, they knew quite well whether they were hitting a solid wall or a patch of smoke.

The only snag in this unique and effective arrangement developed inside the U.S. team in the person of Morey Bell. For three and a half years, beginning in 1973, the central fixture in Morey's official life was his relationship with Ellsworth Bunker. He treasured it and guarded it vigilantly. Anyone who dealt directly with Bunker on Panama was a potential usurper.

Bell once threatened one of his ablest assistants with an official reprimand because he had reported a significant treaty development directly to Bunker without informing Bell first.

I knew that side of Morey, though less well than those who worked with him day in and day out. From a distance, I could look on his foibles with more tolerance perhaps than nearer witnesses. In any case, when the Lewis-Jorden channel was established, I went out of my way to keep Morey informed and, at the outset, made him the main channel for the insights derived from our late-evening sessions. As country director, he was my principal line of communication with the department. Moreover, he was a friend.

It soon became evident, however, that Bell was not playing the game with the forthrightness the new technique demanded. Meetings at which I was supposed to brief the treaty support team were unaccountably canceled, or the times were changed at the last minute. I found that Bunker and Linowitz were not getting all the details I thought they needed, and nuances in my talks with Lewis were being lost in transit. When I realized what was happening, I made it a point to report directly to Bunker and Linowitz. When they were not available, I made sure that Dick Barkley, Bunker's exceptional aide, and Ambler Moss, Linowitz' equally capable assistant, were aware of what I had gleaned. From then on, the unfiltered version of the late-night conversations went directly to the men who needed it.

With the Neutrality Treaty wrapped up, the negotiators turned to the future organization that would operate the Panama Canal. In the jargon that inevitably develops in any protracted bartering, this came to be known as "the entity." For the most part, debate about "the entity" was a political exercise far more than a discussion of administrative techniques and organization. One could well have argued—and some Americans did—that the Panama Canal Company had run the waterway efficiently for sixty-three years. Why not let it continue to do so? The trouble was that the very name of the company was anathema to the Panamanians and it stirred almost as many unpleasant memories as did the name and the concept of the Canal Zone. It had to go.

More was involved, of course, though the U.S. team at first thought that was the main issue. What the Panamanians had in mind for the operating agency was a binational administration that would reflect the notion of partnership. It was the element in the failed treaties of 1967 that the Panamanians most wished to see revived. They visualized a Panama-U.S. canal authority under which everything would be decided jointly—hiring and firing, ship handling, toll policy, purchasing, training, the gamut of activities involved in running a major waterway.

The Americans saw it differently. They realized that "the entity" had to be subject to U.S. government control if a new treaty was to win congressional approval. They also argued that the Tack-Kissinger Principles of 1974, the basis for the new treaty, clearly gave the United States prime responsibility for both operating and defending the canal for the duration of the revised pact. They proposed a U.S. government agency to run the canal. The concession they offered to meet Panama's desire for joint responsibility was an advisory board composed of an equal number of Americans and Panamanians.

That proposal fell on Panamanian ears with a dull thud. Royo argued that an advisory group was a very different thing from the administrative element that would actually run the canal. "We're fully aware of how these advisory boards work," he told the Americans. "They would . . . be providing advice and counsel but they would not have the power to issue orders . . . What's important," he added, "is that high-ranking people—administrative people, highly educated people, policy makers and technical people—can participate in the senior executive ranks of the operation of this canal."

The U.S. team pointed out the problems inherent in a binational canal organization. The Panamanians had already conceded that canal operations would be primarily the responsibility of the United States until the treaty expired. The issue was whether that responsibility would be carried out by majority participation of the executive branch on an international board, or whether Congress would continue to govern "the entity" through legislation. The Panamanians were not asking to have a dominant voice in operations, but they did want to be more than "advisers." As the talk flowed back and forth, Linowitz realized the views of the two sides were not mutually exclusive. At one point he said: "I think we are not that far apart."

Gabriel and I discussed the problem of "the entity" at length in our nightly meetings that week. I explained why the organization that would run the canal had to be a U.S. government agency, probably under the Department of Defense. He understood that. But he also argued vehemently for more than token participation by Panama. "It just isn't fair," he insisted, "that 70 percent of the workers on the canal are Panamanians but not one is in an important executive position. We've been running banks and businesses and law firms and everything else for many, many years. And after all the canal is just another business, right?"

Of course he was right. Recalling the 1967 treaties, I told him: "Maybe the answer, Gabriel, is to have an American as the president or director of the new canal entity and a Panamanian as his vice-president or deputy. That would give you participation at the very top."

He picked it up immediately. "That's a great idea," he said. "You understand what we're talking about."

Bunker and Linowitz were aware of that exchange and it may have been in the back of their minds at the next meeting. After listening to the long speeches, Linowitz broke the logjam, as he so often did. First reminding the Panamanians that the canal administration had to be a U.S. government entity, he said: "Suppose the United States were to receive from the Republic of Panama suggestions of, let's say, two or so members of this administrative entity, which the United States would then appoint to the entity, so that there is Panamanian representation and participation. . . . Does this get at what you think would be appropriate, if we could do it that way?"

The Panamanians immediately asked for a recess. When they returned, they announced they were dropping their idea of a binational public entity and agreed it should be an agency of the U.S. government. Nonetheless, Royo said, there should be "effective participation" by Panama even though "we realize it will be a minority participation because the primary responsibility rests with the United States."

He then went on: "We would like to suggest within this growing participation—this secondary responsibility that rests with Panama during the life of the treaty—that our country should have an assistant director, or deputy director, with the United States, of course, having the post of director."

Royo carried his suggestion one step further. He suggested that ten years before Panama took over responsibility for running the canal, that is, in 1990, the director of the U.S. agency could be a Panamanian. He also proposed a seven-member Board of Directors for the canal enterprise, four Americans and three Panamanians. That would give the United States majority control of policy, but would also give Panama significant representation in management. Linowitz asked several questions to clarify the Panamanian position, and it was then the U.S. team's turn to call for a recess.

When they returned, Linowitz said: "We have only one question that we will have to leave open—but in general the principles are agreeable." The unanswered question was whether it was possible legally to have a non-American heading up an enterprise run by a U.S. government agency. That question was later resolved favorably in discussions with lawyers from State, Defense, and Justice. The format for handling administration of the Panama Canal worked out in the May 20 meeting became part of the final treaty. The only significant change was expansion of the Board of Directors from seven members to nine, five Americans and four Panamanians.

During the next weeks, the two teams met daily and chewed over a variety of contentious issues. All were important but, in the context of a total treaty, none were matters on which a treaty was likely to founder. Once the negotiating teams began haggling about things like payments to be made for public services, guarantees of labor gains, and the disposition of Canal Zone housing, it was clear the long-sought goal of a new treaty was in sight.

That is not to say that the diplomats and lawyers from both sides didn't spend a vast amount of time on the many mundane issues that went into the final product. Discussion of payment to Panama for public and governmental services was a case in point. It began innocently enough on May 24 when Minister Royo took the floor. He was, he said, going to introduce an aspect of the treaty which, "because of an oversight," had not been presented before. "It reads as follows," he said: "The entity will pay the Republic of Panama for the public services or utilities and governmental functions which the latter renders in the area whose use is entailed in [later changed to 'dedicated to'] purposes of the operation and maintenance of the Canal."

That seemingly simple statement set off a long, tiresome, and complicated exchange. There were questions about what kind of services were meant and what was the definition of "governmental functions." There was extensive debate whether the question should be handled as a separate item or as part of the "economic arrangements." The Americans felt it should be part of the overall settlement; the Panamanians wanted to get the principle nailed down—that "the entity" would pay for things like electric power, sewer service, police protection, and the like.

What happened was that the Panamanians suddenly came face-to-face with a harsh reality. For seventy years they had argued that running a police department and a court system, operating a mail service, maintaining stores and recreational facilities, providing housing and water and electricity for employees—none of those things were essential to operating a canal. The Panamanians had insisted that such functions were rightly their responsibility. Now, all of a sudden, they were going to have to assume all the burdens they had so eagerly sought, and they were going to have to finance them. In most communities, public services are supported by the local tax system. But under the Panama treaty, Americans working on the canal would not be paying property or income taxes. In a panic, the Panamanians could see the new treaty making them large consumers of red ink. Hence their eagerness to pin down the principle of payments for services rendered.

Though mildly amused by the corner the Panamanians had painted themselves into, the U.S. negotiators were sympathetic. They recognized that it was only fair for those who would benefit from Panamanian services to pay for them. Sol Linowitz stressed the point that any compensation for services and utilities would have to come from canal revenues. That, in turn, would reduce the fund from which Panama expected its annual payment. Once that consideration was understood, the negotiators accepted the Panamanian principle and agreed to work out details when they considered the economic package.

The last week in May was filled with discussion of technical treaty problems, mainly concerning the rights of canal employees. They included the way Americans would be treated if arrested for criminal violations, their rights to import household goods and automobiles, how Panama would handle visas for new employees, and similar matters. The U.S. negotiators were perpetually concerned that there be no serious diminution of the canal workers' rights and privileges. In part, it was the natural obligation to protect the rights of fellow citizens. In part, too, it was recognition of political reality. The Zonians had a strong constituency among some members of Congress and everything that might affect them was the subject of countless letters, telegrams, and phone calls to congressional offices. Bunker and Linowitz knew the administration would have its hands full getting a treaty through the Senate under the best of circumstances. They were eager not to complicate that task by giving treaty critics additional ammunition.

The meeting of May 27 was adjourned at 12:30 P.M. and Royo concluded it by telling the Americans, "I hope you spend a very nice weekend." The next day, the entire Panamanian team, including Rory González, who had just flown in from Panama, climbed aboard a train at Washington's Union Station and headed north to Philadelphia. In the City of Brotherly Love they were joined by Planning Minister Barletta and Minister of Finance Ernesto Pérez Balladares, who had been in New York signing a commercial loan. In Philadelphia, the large and lively group of Panamanians located the Paoli Local and filled half a car on that Main Line institution. They passed through Ardmore and Bryn Mawr and finally reached their destination, Wayne, Pennsylvania, the site of Valley Forge Military Academy. Rory González' son was to graduate from the academy, the ostensible purpose for the sojourn of a proud father and all his friends.

After a good dinner, the senior Panamanians assembled in the living room of their hotel's presidential suite and turned to the one major, unresolved issue in the treaty talks, economic arrangements. What began as a cold-blooded analysis of economic factors surrounding canal operations quickly turned into a heated political dialogue. Nearly everyone contributed to the recital of grievances going back to 1903 and the despised Hay–Bunau-Varilla Treaty, which gave Panama only $250,000 a year for one of the most strategically placed pieces of real estate in the world.

"How can we put a price tag on all the business lost by Panamanians because they couldn't open stores in the Zone?" one of the participants asked. "And what about all the land—our land—that we haven't been able to use for seventy years?" asked another. Nicky Barletta pointed out that there was another side to the coin—the huge economic advantage the United States had enjoyed through all those years in which Panama did not share. The deliberately low tolls maintained in the canal (they were about the same sixty years after the canal opened) were a direct subsidy to American and other shippers and exporters. The benefit to Panama was zero, or close to it.

Then Aristides Royo, who had studied law in Spain, called attention to the U.S. lease of military bases there and the large benefits that flowed to the Spanish government. Others mentioned Turkey and the Philippines. The proceeds were billions of dollars. The United States had a major military command in Panama as well as several valuable army, air force, and navy installations. For those bases, which the United States had used for decades, Panama received virtually nothing.

The discussion went on, divided between what some thought was fair and others thought was possible. The "fair" amount was several billion dollars. The "possible" was $500 million. They decided to compromise at an even $1 billion as the lump-sum payment they would demand. Rómulo Escobar argued that the round figure might sound too artificial and he suggested they make it $1.020 billion. By that time in the early morning, all hands were feeling no pain, most notably Rómulo, who had a powerful attraction for Scotland's best-known product. If they got what he suggested, he told his colleagues, the added $20 million could be his "retirement fund."

Before turning in, the Panamanians agreed they should begin work immediately on the case they would make in support of their economic proposal. The main burden fell to the man who knew most about economics and the canal's financial status, Minister Barletta. He and Royo, the most abstemious members of the company, began to prepare a report for General Torrijos. Barletta turned his agile mind to the shape of the overall case he would soon have to present to the U.S. negotiators.

On the long trip back to Washington the next day, Ambassador Lewis and the treaty team wondered if there was some way to ease into the economic problem with the American side before making a formal presentation. They discussed several possibilities but nothing satisfied their requirements. Finally, as they neared Washington, Chief Negotiator Escobar ended the discussion. "I'm going to see Sol Linowitz," he said. "I'm going to meet with him alone and tell him how we feel." His abrupt announcement caused surprise, and even some consternation, among his colleagues. First, Rómulo knew less than most of them about canal economics. A second worry was that his English was far from fluent. But everyone realized Rómulo was closer to Omar Torrijos than any of them and, if his mind was made up, that settled the matter.

At the embassy, Lewis called Linowitz and told him Escobar wanted to have an important and very private lunch the next day. Sol was a trifle piqued because it was Memorial Day and he had counted on spending the holiday away from treaty problems. But the approach was unusual, and he felt he had no choice. He told Lewis he would make the necessary arrangements. Linowitz contacted the Panamanian Embassy the next morning to say he would meet Escobar at the Mayflower Hotel dining room at 12:30.

It turned into both a liquid and an emotional luncheon. On that occasion, Rómulo forsook his normal scotch and was belting martinis as though a drought were expected any moment. And all the time he was talking, talking. His English, halting at first, gradually became more fluent.

The heart of Rómulo's message was that he was worried about the economic settlement. Unless a fair deal was struck, he said, the whole treaty could fall apart. He repeated many of the recollections stirred at Wayne over the weekend: the refusal of Zone authorities to permit Panamanians to operate businesses in the canal area, the U.S. monopoly of housing and recreation, foreign control of imports and exports. He talked about the small sums paid to his country during the years of canal operations. And he reminded Linowitz of the massive U.S. outlays to countries like Spain, Turkey, and the Philippines for military bases. All those considerations had to enter into any calculation of Panama's just benefits under a new treaty, Rómulo argued.

Sol listened carefully to Rómulo's long summation of the Panamanian case. He nibbled at a light lunch, asked an occasional question, and was thoroughly impressed with the cogency of his fellow lawyer's presentation. Only when they had finished eating did Rómulo drop his bombshell.

He told the American that over the weekend the entire Panamanian team had discussed the economic problem in detail and had agreed that $1.020 billion was a fair figure to ask as a lump-sum payment. A much larger payment would be thoroughly justified under the circumstances, he said, but he thought Panama could "live with" the amount he had mentioned.

Linowitz was not merely surprised, he was thunderstruck. When the U.S. team discussed the economic side of the treaty, they thought exclusively of annual payments based on canal income. They recognized that Panama had been getting a pittance and that the amount should be sharply increased. But the kind of massive one-time payment Rómulo was talking about never entered into their calculations. When he recovered from the initial shock, Linowitz told Escobar anything even remotely like the figure mentioned was politically impossible. It would create such a storm on Capitol Hill, he said, that the treaty itself would be lost.

"Come now, my dear colleague," said Escobar, "you people spend a billion dollars every afternoon. It wouldn't even be noticed."

"Believe me, my friend, it would be noticed," Linowitz told him, "and it would undercut everything we're trying to do."

It was by then 3 o'clock and the two men left the dining room and moved to the main entrance on Connecticut Avenue. Each promised solemnly to think over what the other had said. It was clear to both that a huge obstacle had emerged.

As that new problem loomed on the treaty horizon, the actual business of writing a canal pact was going on in secret. Mike Kozak walked into his office one morning late in May with an idea that had nagged him for days. He told his colleague Gerri Chester: "I suspect that pretty soon we're going to need a draft treaty. Let's start doing something because, when it breaks, it's going to come awfully fast."

The two lawyers went to work. The Neutrality Treaty was in relatively good shape with only a few clauses still not agreed. The Status of Forces Agreement had been locked up since 1975. They had the Tack-Kissinger Principles and the several "threshold agreements" accepted by the Panamanians over the years. They pulled out the drafts used in 1971 when large chunks of a treaty had been hammered out. They cut and pasted, redrafted, and cribbed liberally from past documents. The first draft of a new Panama Treaty began to take shape.

The day after the Escobar-Linowitz lunch, the negotiators had a long working session and the Panamanians announced that they were going home for consultations. A Council of State meeting was scheduled for June 3, and they had to attend to inform Panama's top officials what was happening in the treaty talks.

Before the Panamanian negotiators left Washington, we had agreed to hold the next round in Panama the week of June 13. No sooner was the Panamanian team headed for Miami than the Bunker-Linowitz group began to have second thoughts about their commitment. Linowitz feared that once the Panamanians got on their home ground they would fall back into the leisurely ways of the past. In Washington, all hands had worked intensively over the previous month, and Sol wanted to maintain that pace. Moreover, the two ambassadors were about to order up a draft treaty and, once that was finished, they knew that key members of the staff would have to work around the clock to get Defense Department concurrence. Another consideration was the need for close consultation with the White House and the Congress. Bunker and Linowitz had been conducting extensive missionary work on the Hill, especially with the Senate, and they knew that lobbying activity was almost as important as negotiating itself. One final consideration was that Linowitz had an eye problem, a threatened detachment of the retina, and he did not want to be far from skilled medical treatment.

When I realized how strongly they felt about keeping the negotiating venue in Washington, I went to work on Gabriel. I explained all the operational reasons for continuing the talks in our capital. The Panamanians had to be concerned about public opinion at home, to be sure, but they did not have a Pentagon or a powerful Congress to worry about. Moreover, practically all the treaty talks from 1973 through 1976 had been in Panama. Simple reciprocity required that we spend more than one month in Washington. I also played shamelessly on Panamanian sympathy by stressing Sol's eye problem. Gabriel passed the message to Panama, and his colleagues graciously went along with our request. They returned to Washington on June 7, a week earlier than scheduled.

A few days before Escobar and Royo and their team came back to Foggy Bottom, Linowitz summoned Kozak to his office. "Listen, can you have a draft treaty for us in a week?" he asked his legal aide. Linowitz expected it would take much longer than that, but he wanted to give it urgency. Kozak, privately thankful for the long hours he and Chester had already devoted to the task, just smiled and said, "Yeah, I think we can." Linowitz was surprised but said nothing.

With the new priority that came from the top, Kozak and Chester went to work in earnest redrafting one article after another. By the evening of June 11 they finished their task. Both remember the date and time vividly because it was at 5:30 P.M. that Gerri told Mike she felt that "something is happening." At one o'clock in the morning, Serana* Chester was born. Kozak would later laugh nervously when he considered his near brush with unplanned midwifery.

On Monday morning, Mike took the Kozak-Chester draft to the seventh floor and delivered it to Bunker and Linowitz. Obviously, there had to be Defense Department concurrence before the document could be handed to the Panamanians. General Dolvin was called in and asked to make a maximum effort to get agreement from the Pentagon in a week. "That's impossible," he told Linowitz. "It will take at least a month." They discussed it at length and Dolvin finally agreed to try to get approval in two weeks. For the next fortnight, Dolvin and Kozak were in the Pentagon every day from early morning until ten or eleven at night, meeting with policy makers and lawyers, cajoling and explaining, until an agreed version finally emerged.

The Americans were delighted that the Escobar-Royo team had decided to return to Washington early, and they assumed it meant moving forward quickly on a treaty. That happy assumption was dispelled fifteen minutes

---

*A contraction of *soberana* meaning "sovereign." Few words were used more often in the lengthy treaty discussions.

into the June 8 meeting. It began smoothly enough with Escobar introducing a new member of the Panamanian team, lawyer Carlos López-Guevara, who had played a central role in the 1971–72 negotiations. Rómulo announced they would soon be joined by still another colleague, veteran Díogenes de la Rosa, an authority on U.S.-Panama relations. Then they got down to work. It was quickly apparent that Rómulo and his colleagues had returned with a satchel full of problems for the Americans.

For example, Bunker and Linowitz thought all the main features of the Neutrality Treaty had been agreed, including the right in times of emergency for U.S. warships to receive "preferential treatment." Now the Panamanians wanted to eliminate that provision because it "violates the principle of neutrality." There had been agreement that the two countries would keep the Panama Canal open to world commerce except for natural disasters or the periodic need for major repairs. The Panamanians wanted to add a clause saying the waterway could be closed if it were losing money. The Americans wanted to be sure the United States had the first option to build a sea-level canal in the future. The Panamanians asked to defer that decision. Finally, Escobar and Royo insisted that Panama name the Panamanians who would serve in high positions on the canal entity. The implication was that, though it was a U.S. agency, the United States would have no voice in choosing Panamanian members of the board or the deputy administrator; it would simply ratify Panama's selections. More important, they insisted such appointees could not be removed from their jobs without Panamanian approval. The U.S. side argued that the right to choose, and to fire, such officials was inherent in its responsibility for running the canal. In addition to those major issues, the Panamanians also wanted to change or delete words in a dozen different places in previous understandings.

The Americans were stunned. They had believed most of those matters had been agreed upon. They were embarrassed because they had reported that fact to Secretary Vance and to the White House. Suddenly they had visions of returning almost to square one and renegotiating things they thought had been locked up.

After hearing them out and asking some pointed questions, Linowitz told the Panamanians bluntly: "I think you ought to know that what you are suggesting is very dangerous. It is your right to do it, of course, but I want you to know how dangerous it is."

At the May 31 meeting he had asked if "the principles as codified in these papers" were satisfactory, and the Panamanians had said they were. "A number of the suggestions you have now made very substantially affect what we thought we were working on and agreed on," he said, "and would require the most extensive reconsideration."

To some extent, the Americans were overreacting to the Panamanian presentation. Looked at individually, each of the proposals or questions Escobar and Company had brought back from Panama could readily have been negotiated out. The really crucial issues were preferential treatment for U.S. warships and the right to remove Panamanian administrators for incompetence or other reasons. The outcome on those two would critically affect Pentagon and congressional reactions, as Bunker and Linowitz knew full well.

The U.S. negotiators had not reckoned with the Panamanians' proclivity to change their minds, and the equal tendency to become ensnarled in words and footnotes. Another problem was the Panamanian presentation itself. Escobar and Royo had put entirely too much on the negotiating plate at one time. Though much that they raised was trivia, they gave the impression of suggesting massive revision. The difficulty would have been considerably less if they had presented one or two items at a time.

When the meeting ended, Bunker and Linowitz walked to their suite and huddled with their advisers. They were genuinely upset and wanted the Panamanians to know it. Their first decision was to cancel the next day's meeting. Then they made an appointment with Cy Vance. Finally, they concluded that the next move should not be a full meeting but a restricted one of the chief negotiators only. Somehow the broken crockery had to be mended.

Escobar and Royo arrived two days later at the State Department and were escorted to Bunker's office. There was a chill in the air as only the silver-haired Vermonter could produce with a look. He began by telling the Panamanians he wanted to express the U.S. side's concern about the papers and proposals the two Panamanians had submitted. They were "very disturbing" because they seemed to withdraw from what had been agreed upon a week earlier. Linowitz said that he and Bunker understood the Panamanians had given assurance of their agreement on basic principles at the May 31 meeting. On that basis, he said, he and Bunker had gone to the president and the secretaries of state and defense to report that agreement. Now they faced a serious situation because the ideas the Panamanians were advancing were "inconsistent with what had been established earlier." They should know that could "jeopardize the negotiations." The Panamanians were jolted by Linowitz' harsh choice of words.

Escobar denied that anything they were saying represented a change in past agreements. Royo ran through their proposals and also denied they deviated from basic principles. Linowitz explained that what concerned him and Bunker was that the Panamanians did not understand that their "small changes" would affect U.S. positions considerably. Panama had agreed that the United States would be in charge of managing the canal during the treaty period, for example. Now they were claiming the United States had to accept anyone Panama nominated for a key post in canal management and could not remove them even if they refused to carry out their duties. That would be "an encroachment on U.S. responsibility," he said. Earlier, the Panamanian negotiators had said they "would" waive jurisdiction on certain crimes committed by Americans during the treaty period. Now, they were proposing that Panama "might" waive jurisdiction. "This is a great difference," he said.

Skipping over what Linowitz had said, Escobar jumped to the question of closing the canal when it was not profitable. "My country would not like to see a situation arise where it would have to put its entire national budget into operating the canal," he said, "when it presumably ought to yield a profit." He had deliberately chosen an issue on which the U.S. negotiators were likely to be reasonable. Then he moved to a more central problem—the preferential passage of U.S. warships through the canal. That clause, he argued, "would destroy effective neutrality." He then launched into a defense of Panama's right to select its citizens who would serve in responsible jobs in operating the canal. He insisted that most things Panama was asking for were designed to make it impossible for the United States later to interpret them unilaterally and to its own advantage, as he claimed it had done over the years.

His long discourse irritated the Americans. "There will never be a treaty," Linowitz said, "if our starting point is going to be mutual suspicion." Escobar said he had cited the examples from the past "only to illustrate why Panama seeks concrete terms on certain issues." Royo assured Bunker and Linowitz there was no "mutual suspicion" but that each side had to recognize that both had to have "a package that will sell" in their respective countries.

Bunker said the talk had been useful but he hoped the concerns expressed by Linowitz were fully understood. Rómulo assured him they were and that he and Royo would report the exchange to Panama. He said he believed "there will probably not be as many difficulties involved as might appear to be the case." On that hopeful note, they agreed to meet again on Monday and to use the weekend to study each other's proposals.

I went into the department the next morning for my usual meeting with the negotiators and the staff. They wanted to wrap up the neutrality agreement but two obvious hurdles stood in the way. One was our desire to get "expeditious passage" for U.S. Navy ships; the other was Panama's demand for a "profitability" clause. They asked me to see what could be done on those matters over the weekend.

Ensconced in the "loco room" at Gabriel's residence, we thrashed over the positions both sides had pressed that week. The ambassador told me that his side was really worried about the commitment to keep the canal open under any and all circumstances. "We don't know what's going to be invented in the next twenty years—huge airplanes or pipelines—that would make the canal obsolete," he said. "We don't want to give our word that we're going to keep the canal open, and then find we're losing millions of dollars to do it." I told him my country would have the same problem over the next twenty-plus years. He argued that the kind of technological advances he was talking about were not likely to come that fast. "Anyway, if you lost a few hundred millions, it would be a drop in the bucket," he said. "For us, it would be a disaster." I assured him we knew that. All we were asking was that, before the waterway was closed because it wasn't making money, we would have a chance to consult together and try to work something out. He explained that asking the United States to keep the canal operating would mean loss of face for his country. We agreed to think about it further.

I shifted to the problem of getting U.S. Navy ships through the canal on a priority basis. He understood that to get a treaty through Congress, we had to have the Pentagon's full support. And to get the generals' and admirals' backing, we had to be able to guarantee that our ships, supplies, and men could get through Panama quickly in an emergency. It was as simple as that, I told him, but essential to any deal we made.

Gabriel dredged up the arguments his negotiators had used, that what we were asking was a "violation of the spirit of neutrality." I said we were not asking anything his country would not share; the priority would be for U.S. *and* Panamanian warships.

"Hell, Bill, we don't have any warships to speak of. You know that," he said.

"Sure I know it," I told him. "But that's today. How about twenty or thirty years from now? Who knows what you'll have? And what your relations are going to be with some of your neighbors?" I told my friend I thought his negotiators were bending over backward to be technically pure and legalistically righteous. I thought they were losing sight of the real world.

"You know, Gabriel, and the whole world knows, that the United States and Panama have a special interest in the canal," I said. "It's in your country. We built it. And together we've operated it for a lot of years. There isn't one country, one government, in the world that's going to question our having some special rights under a treaty made between us. Now is there?"

He chewed on an ice cube, crushing it with his molars. He shook his glass and popped another cube into his mouth. He was thinking hard.

"If you pick up that phone and call Omar right now," I said, "he'll understand what we're saying. Point one: we have to have expedited passage in order to get a treaty. Point two: every country in the world will understand that special privileges go with special responsibilities."

"Message received," he said. "Let me work on it."

The next day, after a family lunch in the embassy, Nita and Mili went off to discuss books and life and the latest gossip from Panama. Gabriel and I retired once more to the "crazy room" to take up where we had left off the night before. The main item on our agenda was the possible closing of the canal if it became unprofitable. I had thought about it overnight and wanted to try out some ideas on my friend.

I understand your worry, I told him, but how serious is it really? All we were asking was that if technological change made the waterway unprofitable we could get together and work something out. I explained that we were worried about some future Panamanian government using "unprofitability" to close down the canal for political reasons.

"That would be like cutting off your leg because you had an attack of gout," he said. He spoke with some feeling as one who had suffered that affliction.

Knowing that one problem was any hint of overdependence on the United States, I asked him why we couldn't involve others. "Suppose we said that if the canal was losing money Panama and the United States and other principal users of the waterway would consult on ways to meet the problem?" I asked. Gabriel thought that approach might have promise. I suggested we raise it with our negotiators and see what they thought.

At that point I wondered aloud if we weren't making a big problem out of nothing. "You know, Gabriel, we're working overtime trying to figure out how we can avoid breaking a promise to keep the canal open if it's losing money," I mused. "If we didn't make the promise we wouldn't have to worry about breaking it. The world knows our countries want to keep the canal open, and that we'll do it if it's humanly possible. Why do we have to say it?"

"But I thought that was part of every treaty we've ever talked about," he said.

"It has been," I said. "But the more I think about it the less reason I find for saying something that's so obvious. If you eliminate the question, you don't have to worry about the answer."

The meeting the next afternoon was smoother than any in the recent weeks. It began with a signing ceremony—all hands endorsing a message to Gerri Chester congratulating her on the birth of her daughter. Then they got down to business and Sol Linowitz took the lead.

His first point concerned Article III, that part which said: "The Canal shall remain open except in cases of *force majeur*, acts of God, or major repairs requiring temporary closure." It was there the Panamanians wanted to insert the idea of "unprofitability" as an additional cause for closing the waterway. Linowitz said the U.S. team proposed the addition of a second sentence: "In the event the continued operation of the Canal should become an economic burden to the nations responsible for Canal operations, the parties shall promptly enter into consultations among themselves and other interested Canal-user nations in order to develop appropriate arrangements with respect to the future of the Canal." That, he explained, made keeping the canal open less of an unalterable commitment and recognized Panama's concern about a possible onerous economic burden.

"There is an alternative suggestion which I also want to make to you," Linowitz said, "and that is simply to remove that whole paragraph from the treaty."

He noted the surprise on the Panamanians' faces and quickly moved on to the second major proposal. He called their attention to another sentence they had discussed previously. It read: "In recognition of the important contributions of the United States of America and of the Republic of Panama to the construction, operation, maintenance, protection and defense of the waterway, vessels of war and auxiliary vessels of those nations shall, notwithstanding any other provisions of this treaty, be entitled to transit the Canal irrespective of their internal operation, means of propulsion, origin, destination, armament, or cargo carried."

That had been put in to assure there would be no future ban on nuclear-powered ships or vessels carrying nuclear weapons. Linowitz suggested adding a sentence: "Such vessels of war and auxiliaries will be entitled to transit the Canal expeditiously in accordance with established precedent." Linowitz said if that language was acceptable, "I think we can live with it, so far as the Defense Department is concerned."

The Panamanians had only one question: what was meant by "in accordance with established precedent"? Did the U.S. team mean procedures adopted unilaterally by the U.S. government over the years? And were the procedures written into the Canal Company rules? None of the Americans could answer but they promised to check it out. What worried the Panamanians was that the "precedent" might apply only to U.S. warships, not to those of other nations. That worry was unfounded.*

Linowitz admitted that the heart of the U.S. proposal was the phrase "entitled to transit the Canal expeditiously." Escobar, Royo, and their colleagues caucused briefly, then said they were ready to accept the U.S. proposal but they suggested dropping the reference to "precedents." In relatively few minutes the troubled question of priority passage for U.S. warships was settled and the principle locked into the new canal treaty.

The negotiators then returned to the matter of keeping the canal open even if it were losing money. After a recess, Royo told the Americans they

---

*The precedent established by the Canal Company was to give priority passage to warships in general, not just those of the United States. During World War II and the Korean and Vietnam conflicts, U.S. naval ships routinely passed through the canal ahead of commercial vessels, but so did the warships of other nations.

were in favor of deleting the entire paragraph listing the reasons the canal might be closed. "We would suppose," Royo said, "that the canal would remain open benefiting world commerce."

Bunker and Linowitz were surprised again. The troublesome issue of "profitability" had suddenly disappeared. The Panamanians had a few technical questions on "territorial waters" and their delineation on maps, but they were quickly disposed of. Royo summed it up: "I think that, with this, there is nothing left. As far as neutrality is concerned, we consider this to be finished." It was June 13 and phase one of the new treaty relationship was completed at last.

That and the two meetings that followed went smoothly. The two teams covered considerable ground, narrowed differences on several issues, and were developing a kind of teamwork rarely achieved in major international negotiations. No one on either side of the conference table realized that a huge thundersquall was forming just over the horizon, one that would threaten to wash out all the goodwill that had developed.

The first storm warning came from an unlikely spot, the island republic of Grenada in the Caribbean. The OAS foreign ministers were meeting on that lovely, remote isle to review developments in the hemisphere. In previous years, Panamanian foreign ministers—first Tack, then Boyd—had agreed with Secretary Kissinger to make a joint report on the status of treaty negotiations. On June 16, we learned that Panama's new foreign minister, the youthful González-Revilla, was refusing to collaborate with Secretary Vance on a joint statement. That seemed peculiar, especially as more progress had been made in the previous two months than in any recent year.

That same day, a second and seemingly unrelated warning sign drew our attention. The *Washington Post* printed a column by Jack Anderson which alleged there was "disturbing evidence" that General Torrijos had made a "secret deal" with Libyan dictator Muammar al-Qaddafi "to give Arab extremists a foothold in the Americas" and to "cooperate with the Arab boycott against the Jews." An elaborate conspiracy theory was woven from a few facts and endless conjecture. The information obviously came from antitreaty sources who regularly sought to use Anderson and other journalists in their campaign to disparage the Torrijos government and thereby undercut any treaty. The same "evidence" also went to two Jewish members of Congress who asked the State Department for clarification.*

Early on the morning of June 17, Ambassador Lewis received an urgent

---

*When nailed down, the "evidence" was a memo signed in Tripoli by an inept official with little authority. It stated that a contractor in Panama had no "ties with Jewish or Zionist firms." It was the same formula used by many Arab countries when arranging contracts with foreign companies. When revealed, it was promptly repudiated, as was the man who signed

call from a thoroughly angry Omar Torrijos. The head of the Panamanian government rattled off a list of complaints and questions. "What is this anti-Semitic campaign?" he began. "What is the campaign on Guatemala?" (Rumors in the U.S. press claimed Panama intended to send military forces to Belize to help defend against a Guatemalan takeover.) "What is the attitude of the political counselor of the U.S. Embassy?" (Torrijos had heard that Elkin Taylor, chief of our Political Section, had met with some Panamanians opposed to the Torrijos regime. That much was true; it was part of his job. But someone had told the general that Taylor was informing those people that "the treaty is completed but Torrijos doesn't want to sign it." That was absurd. Taylor was a careful political observer and too smart to have said anything of the kind.)

Torrijos then raised the case of a deranged U.S. soldier who had gone into Panama City a few days before and shot a policeman at a traffic intersection. The soldier boasted under questioning that he had gone into the capital to assassinate Torrijos. Anti-American members of the general's entourage played up the incident as part of a concerted anti-Torrijos plot.

Torrijos told his ambassador to pass everything he had said to the Panamanian negotiating team. They, in turn, were to relay it to the U.S. negotiators just as he had conveyed it. "And make the Americans understand clearly," he concluded, "that the Panamanian people are a great ocean and the canal is a fish. The ocean can live without the fish, but the fish can't live without the ocean."

An hour and a half later, Torrijos called Lewis again. The general said he wanted the Panamanian negotiators to explain his viewpoint clearly; then he wanted Escobar and the others to come back to Panama. "Don't break off the negotiations," he said, "but make my position clear and say they are going home to consult."

The ambassador said, "Yes, General," and put down the phone. He wiped his brow with a handkerchief, and called the treaty negotiators in to pass along Torrijos' stern words.

When they walked down the seventh-floor corridor that Friday afternoon, Bunker and Linowitz were chatting amiably, wondering if the Panamanians might bring up the Anderson column. They knew the Panamanians had denounced it earlier in the day, and they planned to congratulate them. They had absolutely no notion they were about to run into a buzz saw.

When the Panamanians arrived, they were looking exceedingly grim. It was a sharp change from the warm camaraderie earlier that week. Without

it. Anderson's staff could readily have learned that Israel had several contractors and official advisers in Panama at that moment. To set the canard at rest, the government of Israel declared its confidence in the Torrijos regime a few days later.

preamble or even the normal opening courtesies, Rómulo Escobar took the floor.

What followed was one of the longest, most impassioned statements Rómulo would make in the entire treaty-making exercise. Though he spoke with only occasional reference to the notes before him, his long exposition was superbly organized. It was also biting. He began by telling the Americans they were making "an error of judgment" if, as they seemed to think, "that in negotiating with Panama, the United States is doing our country a favor.

"If we are seated here at a negotiating table with the United States," he said, "it is because since 1903 to the present it has been the absolute, categorical position of the people of Panama that they struggle for national liberation and for the greater improvement and achievement of their independence . . . and that this will be achieved by the true, not fictitious, removal of the colonial enclave held by the United States in the midst of our territory . . ."

Rómulo claimed the U.S. negotiators were offering proposals "directly injurious to our dignity as a nation and our image as a government and our situation as negotiators." He did not question the U.S. right to appoint top canal officials, but he insisted the selection of Panamanians for those positions had to be the exclusive right of Panama's government.

He then ran down the list of complaints Torrijos had made in his phone calls. He described them as part of "a whole international campaign" launched to weaken Panama's position in the treaty talks. Part of that campaign was the malicious rumor that there was "an attitude of discrimination toward or of persecution of people of Jewish origin" in Panama. He said it was "completely and absolutely false" and was being disseminated "in utter bad faith." Panama's relations with Israel were excellent, Rómulo noted, and "exist on a high level of cooperation." He recalled that Panama had voted for establishment of the Jewish state and had opposed the U.N. resolution that equated Zionism with racism.

He repeated the allegation that Political Counselor Taylor had told opposition politicians that the only obstacle to a treaty was Torrijos' refusal to sign. Escobar reached his emotional climax when he spoke of the U.S. soldier who "confessed his true purpose was to assassinate General Torrijos." He said it raised a question whether the United States was negotiating with Panama with one hand and trying to assassinate its leader with the other. He then lashed out at U.S. concepts for an economic settlement.

Rómulo concluded his lengthy diatribe by saying that he and his colleagues were going home the next morning. They would continue the negotiations "if there is a change with regard to these questions." If there was no change, Panama would not be able to continue the talks. He had held the floor for an hour.

The Americans were taken aback by Escobar's vehemence. They were totally unprepared for the sharp break in the smooth-flowing talks of the previous week. They were also insulted by the implications of some of his statements. After a brief pause, the usually imperturbable Ellsworth Bunker responded to the Panamanian's passionate monologue.

"Distinguished Ambassador Escobar," he began, "I would be less than frank if I did not say to you that we have been astonished and surprised at some of your statements. We are not negotiating on the basis that we consider we are doing Panama a favor. The representatives of every country are presumed to look out for their own country's interests. We would not be negotiating with you if we did not think it in the interest of the United States to do so."

He categorically denied there was a campaign to weaken Panama. "There is no such thing," he said. He told the Panamanians that he and Ambassador Linowitz had been prepared to deny the existence of any anti-Semitic moves in Panama.

Bunker turned caustic when he addressed the alleged assassination attempt. "Your comments about the confession of a private, obviously demented, soldier, not a United States citizen, and your attempt to tie that to a government policy are, to me, astonishing," he said icily. "It's beyond my comprehension how your government could attach any importance or credence to that sort of thing."

As for the economic issue, Bunker said it was something he and Linowitz were always ready to discuss "but we are just not here to accept anything that is proposed to us without discussion." He then suggested a recess, and the Panamanians agreed.

After the break, Bunker told the Panamanians that he and Linowitz were "still baffled" by Escobar's statement. Linowitz said the Escobar monologue had been "such a serious departure" from conference norms that they had to ask: "Do you really want the president of the United States to see what you have said?" It was an effort to bring the Panamanians back to normal from what the U.S. negotiators saw as a gross aberration. Royo answered that "we have no objection to having President Carter read the minutes of these meetings and becoming fully aware of the concerns Panama has regarding the present negotiations."

Bunker and Linowitz were worried that the Panamanians might leave the meeting and repeat their accusations to the press. If that happened, there might be a permanent rupture in the treaty talks. When they asked about it, Escobar and Royo assured them they had no intention of going public. What they wanted was a rethinking on the U.S. side, not a public controversy. Then the Panamanians handed over several documents on some outstanding questions and left for their embassy. The Americans walked slowly to Bunker's office to mull over the perplexing development.

When I heard about the near debacle, I jumped in a cab and went to see Gabriel. We needed to know whether the Panamanians were giving us an ultimatum or whether Escobar's performance was part of a Torrijos "shock treatment." I believed it was the latter. I recognized the general's basic skepticism about our intentions, and I knew there were some around him who enjoyed, however irresponsibly, fanning the sparks of irritation. But I was convinced that Torrijos, in his innermost heart, wanted a treaty.

"What the hell is going on?" I asked my friend when he met me at the door. "Look," he said, "Omar is really mad. He thinks you're playing games with us."

"I think he's the one who's playing games," I told him. "When things like this happen, grown men sit down and talk them out. They don't have a tantrum."

"Rómulo was just following orders," he explained.

"I know that, Gabriel," I said, "but he put a lot of garbage on the record. It just wasn't necessary. Who pushed Omar into this mood anyway?"

"Let's go in here," he said, leading the way to his small private office. The Panamanian negotiators were gathered in the "loco room."

We went through the complaints one by one. I told him Torrijos was reacting to the anti-Semitic charge just the way those who had planted it wished. After all, I said, an idiot Panamanian had signed the document. Then some anti-Torrijos, anti-treaty Panamanian had got hold of the paper and passed it along to Jack Anderson. The idea that we would use something like that to embarrass Omar was absurd. "The general's missing the real target," I said.

The alleged assassination was even more incredible. I told Gabriel the soldier in question was a citizen of the Dominican Republic and he was in the U.S. Army in order to get U.S. citizenship. He was a private with little education, and we had learned he had a record of mental instability. He had stolen the gun, was absent without leave, and had shot the policeman in panic. He would be tried and punished. It was insane to think anyone trying to get at Torrijos would use such a pitiful instrument. "More than that," I said, "the suggestion that anyone in our government would consider for a minute an attack on Torrijos is total fantasy. President Carter would be repelled if anyone even hinted at such an action, and so would the rest of us."

As for my political counselor, he was doing his job and doing it well. He was talking with opposition figures, as any good political officer should. But the suggestion that he had blamed Torrijos for the failure to get a treaty was an unadulterated lie. "Someone is trying to poison the well," I told Gabriel, "and Omar should check on who is feeding him misinformation."

Gabriel listened carefully and I could tell he knew I was giving him straight information. He promised to pass along what I had said to Torrijos, but he said he thought Panama still had some legitimate complaints.

"That's right," I said, "but we need to talk them out, not accuse each other of bad faith."

I told him that I frankly believed Panama was right in wanting to select its own people for the canal Board of Directors and the top administrative slots. The problem was semantics, not policy, I told him.

"We're not going to appoint anyone you haven't picked for one of these jobs," I said. "But it is going to be a U.S. agency that runs the canal for the next twenty years or so, and we have to keep the right to appoint them."

"Well, why don't Bunker and Linowitz say that?" he asked.

"They have to be able to tell the Congress that we have the right to appoint and to fire all key personnel, American and Panamanian," I explained.

We agreed that, in the real world, what would happen was that Panama would pick its people and privately tell us who they were. Unless we had strong objections, we would appoint them. If we had an excellent reason for objecting to some nominee, Panama would undoubtedly pick someone else. "It's just like naming an ambassador," I told him. "You pick a candidate and tell the other government privately. Most of the time, there is no question. But if the host finds the candidate objectionable, for whatever reason, the name is withdrawn. I'm sure this will work the same way."

He suggested we get together the next morning and talk over some of the other matters that were roiling the waters. "Why don't you and I get together with Ellsworth and Sol and talk some more?" he proposed. I told him I would raise it with Bunker because I was seeing him that evening, but Sol, I knew, was going to be out of town.

When Bunker and I met with the ambassador the next morning, it was as though the violent storm of the previous day had never happened. We discussed the real issues, while the peripheral matters that had aroused so much passion eighteen hours before were not even mentioned. Lewis obviously wanted to get the train back on the track, and that meant Torrijos' temper tantrum had passed. The general and his ambassador had had a heart-to-heart talk overnight.

Bunker wanted to know what issues were vital for Panama so the negotiations could resume their normal course. Gabriel said he had talked with Panama that morning and it was clear there were two central problems. One was the "lack of interest" on the part of the Americans in considering the economic settlement, which was vital to Panama. The other was the method of selecting Panamanians who would join the canal's administrative hierarchy. Lewis reviewed his country's views on both issues, using the same arguments Escobar and Royo had advanced in recent days, but with considerably less emotion.

Bunker explained once again why it was impossible to ask the Congress to appropriate funds for annual payments to Panama. The annuity would have to come from money generated by the canal itself. Lewis said he thought it was unfair that Panama should receive no compensation for such things as the use of its territory for U.S. military bases. He then quickly asserted that he was not a negotiator and that those things really should be discussed by the specialists. Since the Americans obviously were reluctant to discuss money matters in the treaty format, Lewis suggested the United States organize a high-level group of economic specialists from the State Department, Treasury, and other agencies with financial interests and expertise. They could meet with a Panamanian group headed by Planning Minister Barletta and perhaps together find some solutions. Bunker thought that might work and he promised to take it up with the White House.

It was getting late and we decided to adjourn until Ambassador Linowitz returned and could take part. The four of us met on Monday at the Panamanian Embassy. An understanding was hammered out on the troublesome question of Panamanian participation in the canal administrative machinery. Bunker and Linowitz agreed Panama should name its own people to the Board of Directors. If the United States wished to remove a director, it would consult with Panama first and Panama would pick a replacement unless it felt the removal was unjust. We insisted that the post of deputy administrator and, after 1990, that of administrator were essentially different from the board. The U.S. agency that was running the canal had to be able to fire them if they proved incompetent or for any other good reason. It was agreed, however, that replacements would be nominated by the Panamanian government. When Torrijos received Gabriel's report on our talks, he sent his negotiators back to Washington two days later.

The two teams got back together on Thursday, June 23. It was as though nothing unusual had happened. The Panamanians had gone home for consultation; now they were back at work. Bunker began the session by telling them that the U.S. team had accepted Ambassador Lewis' idea of organizing a group of top-level economic specialists to work with Minister Barletta and his group on the financial aspects of the treaty. It would be headed by Under Secretary of State Richard Cooper. Treasury Under Secretary Anthony Solomon and experts from AID, the Export-Import Bank, and other agencies made up an impressive roster of participants.

Linowitz then led into that day's agenda. At the last meeting, he said, the Panamanians had made several suggestions and proposals and the Americans had promised to study them and reply. "We're now in a position to give you responses on virtually all of the items," he said. He then went through them one by one, paragraph by paragraph.

The American lawyer reviewed the understanding reached with Ambas-

sador Lewis on the selection and removal of Panamanians who would occupy key administrative posts in the new canal entity. Linowitz then
turned to another vexed question, the right of U.S. canal employees to use
military mail service, commissaries, and post exchanges. The U.S. negotiators had tried to get that privilege for the workers for the duration of the
treaty. The Panamanians wanted to eliminate it on the first day. The U.S.
then proposed ten years and the Panamanians agreed to make it three.
Linowitz now suggested a five-year compromise—long enough to allow
U.S. workers to adjust to shopping in Panamanian stores and using the
Panamanian postal service; short enough to ease Panamanian worries
about the smuggling of goods into their economy. The Panamanians accepted the compromise with the proviso that abuse of the privileges could
lead to losing one's job.

One of the Tack-Kissinger Principles was that there should be "increasing participation" by Panamanians in the operation and management of
the waterway. A variety of formulas had been tried but none satisfied both
sides. At the June 23 meeting, Linowitz offered a new approach. He suggested that all U.S. citizens working for the canal when the treaty went
into effect could continue in their jobs until retirement "or termination of
their employment for any other reason." Then, he said, we add this: "The
number of these U.S. employees will be reduced 20 percent within five years
after entry into force of the treaty. These positions shall be filled as required
by Panamanian citizens possessing requisite skills and qualifications."

That met a serious Panamanian concern. Indeed, it was more specific
than they had hoped for. A 20 percent cut in the U.S. work force over five
years was a much better guarantee of increasing Panamanian participation
in canal operations than reliance on some general principle. On the other
hand, the U.S. team felt safe in making the offer because Canal Company
records showed that normal attrition over five years—through retirement,
resignations, firings, ill health, and the like—had produced more than a 20
percent turnover in U.S. personnel.

By the end of the session on June 23, all the essential features of an accord on "the Canal Entity" were agreed upon. There remained some technical problems on arrangements for canal workers—the U.S. Civil Service
system versus Panama's Social Security System, the transfer of some workers from the Canal Company to the U.S. military, and similar matters. In
the interest of speed, it was decided to turn those questions over to a joint
subcommittee on labor affairs. The way was clear to begin work on the
remaining major element in a new treaty, the so-called economic arrangements, the dollars and cents of the deal. Minister Barletta arrived in Washington that night to carry the burden of Panama's case at the negotiating
table. He was accompanied by Rory González, a favorite Torrijos crony
who was leading Panama's drive to exploit its huge copper deposits.

Bunker, Linowitz, and the U.S. negotiating team went to the deputy secretary's conference room on Friday morning to hear Barletta spell out Panama's position on economic arrangements. What they heard was an appeal for economic justice and for a new order in U.S.-Panama relations.

Barletta possessed one of Latin America's finest economic intellects. Unlike many technocrats, he had an uncommon ability to translate cold statistics and raw data into a cogent political case. He could analyze charts and graphs with the best of his colleagues, but within the statistics and tables he saw people—those getting an education and those deprived of it, citizens who got decent health care and those who did not, those who benefited from the creation of wealth and others who were barely getting by, the workers and the jobless. With degrees from two U.S. universities, he knew the American scene and psyche better than most of his compatriots. He was the ideal choice for the nearly impossible task his government had given him.

Barletta developed his case around three main propositions: first, that the treaty gave the United States what it wanted most—an open and efficient canal protected for the lifetime of the waterway; second, that distribution of benefits from the canal had been grossly unfair for sixty-five years; and, third, that modernization was Panama's main goal but it should also be important to its partner, the United States. He developed each theme at considerable length.

Panama had reluctantly accepted what the U.S. side had described as "an absolute and essential element"—the right to protect the canal as long as it operated, Barletta began. That acceptance was "loaded with risk for Panama"—internal political risk because it was unpopular with many Panamanians, external military risk because the partnership could involve Panama inadvertently in any "conflagration" in which the United States was engaged.

The special tie would give the United States military bases in his country for the next twenty-three years, he said. More than that, the Americans would have major communications facilities and one of the best tropical training areas in the world. Surely all those military advantages were worth a reasonable price.

Barletta noted that when people talked of the "investment" in the Panama Canal they thought exclusively of money. Even on that basis, he claimed that the United States had saved $2 billion or more in initial investment by its agreement with Panama instead of having to use longer, more inconvenient routes for the waterway. The real estate in the heart of Panama used in canal construction—"some of our best land for urban and economic development"—was worth "at least half a billion dollars." Panamanian water made canal operations possible (fifty million gallons for each ship passing through). Used for electric power generation instead, it would have given Panama $300 million worth of electricity for homes and industries.

Adding it all up, Barletta concluded that Panama's basic investment in the canal was at least as large, probably greater, than that of the United States.

So much for the investment. What about the benefits? Barletta argued that shipping companies and trading nations had benefited hugely from the Panama Canal, which saved them from using longer, vastly more expensive routes. Those large savings were increased further by U.S. policy, which kept tolls as low as possible and operated the canal at cost. The Panamanian economist calculated the savings to world shippers in 1975 alone at between $500 million and $700 million. More than a third of those savings from cheap transportation went to the United States. He reckoned that, from the time the canal began operating, the U.S. economy had benefited by at least $14 billion. Some analysts put the figure at twice that amount.

The massive benefit to the civilian economy was not the only advantage that flowed to the United States because of the Panama Canal. Barletta calculated the military savings—because of the isthmian bases, the rapid movement of men and matériel between the two oceans, the shortened route for naval vessels, and other factors—at $13 billion, probably considerably more, since 1914.

Barletta's balance sheet revealed a stark comparison: the United States had benefited to the tune of at least $27 billion, perhaps as much as $45 billion, since the canal opened. Panama's benefits he put at $1.1 billion during the same period. He included annuity payments plus wage differentials between Panamanian workers on the canal and in the Republic.

What Barletta's scholarly analysis ignored—and no American pointed out—was a comparison between the Panama of 1977 and the likely conditions on the isthmus if the canal had not been dug there. As a Colombian province, or even as a small, independent country, Panama's standard of living and gross national product would perhaps have been half what they actually were in 1977 if the canal had not gone through their territory. Nonetheless, the canal was in Panama and the massive imbalance in benefits that Barletta underlined was valid.

The economist turned to his country's plans for economic development. The blueprint was multifaceted and imaginative. Panama would expand its already thriving service economy—banking, tourism, legal services, the free port. Commerce and transport could grow with the new international airport, a container port, fish processing, expansion of the Free Zone. Natural resources—wood, copper, meat, fruits, and vegetables—could provide additional jobs and income. The country's investment in hydroelectric power would be expanded to cut dependence on expensive petroleum.

Barletta forecast that those projects and others could give Panama, by the end of the century, a per capita income equal to Belgium's or Israel's. But the program would require massive inputs of capital, and obviously the United States was the logical source. He argued that Americans should provide it as a matter both of justice and of enlightened self-interest. The United States had underpaid Panama for more than sixty years for its contributions to the canal and to U.S. security. He was also saying that the United States should be wise enough to see the value in proving that it really did pay to be a friend and partner of the great power.

Barletta had reached the hard core of his presentation. Panama wanted economic compensation in three forms: a lump-sum payment, a substantial annuity, and a military assistance package to build up Panama's National Guard. The lump-sum Panama proposed was $1.02 billion.

Escobar looked at Linowitz and said: "You remember?" Sol replied: "I remember."

The annuity, to be applied to the development projects Barletta had described, should be $300 million.

Linowitz said: "I remember that, too." Escobar commented, "You have a good memory."

"Only when I'm shocked," said the American.

Barletta said budget assistance for Panama's military should be "around $50 million over a period of years."

Bunker and Linowitz had listened to Barletta's presentation attentively and with considerable admiration. Bunker found it "very impressive" and Linowitz described the statement as "logical, succinct, and persuasive." However, it was politically impossible to include anything even close to what Barletta desired in the Panama treaty. After complimenting the Panamanian minister, Bunker nailed the point down hard. "I think we have made it clear already to Ambassador Escobar," he said, "that what we can do within the treaty is limited; that is, a program such as you described here, whether it is possible at all, certainly is not possible in the treaty itself." He said the U.S. negotiators had arranged for Barletta to meet the following week with the high-level group of U.S. economic specialists to see if some kind of separate assistance program might be developed.

Barletta understood perfectly what the U.S. negotiators were saying. He said Panama was willing to accept putting part of the economic package in the treaty and handling other elements in a separate agreement, an "economic cooperation document or whatever." But he added that the Panamanians "very much would want these two things to be done together, parallel, and at the same time."

Rory González gave another view. "I can assure you," he said, "that it will be almost impossible to tell our people that, yes, we have given the United States perpetuity in neutrality; that, yes, we will only be getting the canal after another twenty-three years; and we will have to spend a lot of money on the armed forces to keep the neutrality for both of us—but then say there was no money. It will never pass."

Linowitz quickly responded, "We have never said, 'No money.'" González said he thought that what the United States considered possible added up to "no money." Royo mentioned the large benefits granted to countries like Greece, Turkey, and Spain for military bases. Bunker punctured that balloon. In those countries, he said, we were getting something we needed, but we were giving nothing but money. In Panama, we were turning over the canal as well as numerous facilities, housing, and other assets. "There is a vast difference," he said, "between the kind of treaty we worked out with a country like Spain and what we are doing with you."

Linowitz poured additional cold water on the lively Panamanian expectations. "It may be," he said, "that, if your insistence is so great that all of this must happen at the same time, it will not be possible for us to work out the terms of a treaty. That might very well be the case, which neither of us wants."

Barletta responded: "We both want the same thing. We want to finish the treaty as quickly as you do."

The Panamanian treaty team believed they could not sell a treaty that lacked clear economic advantages. On the other hand, they consistently exaggerated this element in order to drive the hardest bargain possible. During one of our late-night sessions, I told Ambassador Lewis: "We know this economic deal is important to you. And we are going to do the best we can to meet your needs. But I remember Omar once saying that he was 'not going to make a treaty, or turn one down, because of money.' The time to make a pitch for large-scale economic cooperation is after we have a treaty, after we've proved we're real partners, after the world sees that this deal is really working. Then the bankers and investors—and the U.S. government, too—will see that Panama is a good place to put their money. There's too damn much skepticism right now to do everything you want at one time."

"You have a point," Gabriel admitted.

The money problem moved into the international realm with the visit to Washington in late June of Venezuela's President Carlos Andrés Pérez. On June 29, Bunker and Linowitz went to Blair House to bring him up-to-date over breakfast. They expressed their serious apprehension about the "astronomical figures" the Panamanians had suddenly thrust into the treaty talks. Pérez was noncommittal but seemed sympathetic to their concerns. He promised to relay their worries to the Panamanians and to Torrijos.

Pérez heard the other side of the argument in a secret meeting with the Panamanian negotiators in his suite at the Waldorf Astoria the next evening. When he got back to Caracas, he called Torrijos and reported the essence of his meetings in Washington. He also described the growing argument on compensation to his neighbor and friend President López Michelsen of Colombia. The two Latin American leaders were convinced that Panama was holding up a treaty in order to get as much money as possible. While sympathetic to their small neighbor's needs, they thought it was a serious mistake on Torrijos' part. Their stand was decisive in finally persuading the Panamanians to revise their thinking.

The day the Panamanians went to New York to meet Pérez was my final day in Washington, or so I thought. I told Bunker and Linowitz that I thought I had done all I usefully could. I felt it was time to get back to running my embassy, and Mili and I certainly should be there for the annual Fourth of July celebrations. We took off for Miami with a certain sense of relief, eager to get back to a more normal life.

The morning after their session with Pérez, the Panamanian negotiators asked for a private meeting. Bunker and Linowitz took Escobar and Royo to the quiet old F Street Club. The Panamanians had left their meeting with the Venezuelan leader feeling—as the Americans had two days earlier—that he understood their position, and therefore was on their side. Escobar and Royo made an impassioned plea for acceptance of their economic proposals. Without it, they told the Americans, there could be no agreement. They were returning to Panama the next day for consultations, and they left Bunker and Linowitz with the clear impression they would be in no hurry to return until there was a revision of the U.S. position.

As I was easing back into the routine of accustomed duties, there was a move afoot behind my back to make it a brief hiatus. Only later did I learn that there had been a decline in communication between the U.S. and Panamanian teams when I left Washington. Part of the reason was a lack of rapport between Panama's Ambassador Lewis and Morey Bell. Disparate temperaments, faulty chemistry, whatever, the two men functioned on different wavelengths. The subject came up in a talk between Lewis and Sol Linowitz.

"Look, Sol," Lewis said, "we've established a very informal and good way of working on these things. I know you're running against the clock, that your appointment only runs to a certain date [August 10]. I know you want to move, and one way to do that is to have a good counterpart for me to work with informally, and that counterpart is Bill Jorden." The next day, Linowitz and Bunker were meeting with Lewis on the economic problem. Sol looked at Lewis and said, "Why don't you tell Ellsworth what you told me yesterday about your working relationship with Bill Jorden." Lewis repeated what he had said. "You people want speed," he said. "There's a good way to speed things up. You people meet, and I meet afterward with Bill. Then if something isn't clear to you or it isn't clear to our negotiators,

Bill and I can talk it over and find a better understanding. A lot of things could be solved overnight. Then when you sit down at the negotiating table, my people know what your real problem is even when you don't want to spell it out at the table. And you know what's bothering us. My negotiators accept this as a good way to do business. But it's up to you."

Bunker's reaction was immediate. "We have to get Bill back here," he told Linowitz.

The next day, Bunker called me on the secure phone. Over the scratchy connection came the familiar voice. "Bill, we've been doing some thinking here, and we think it would be good if you could come back for a while," he said. "Don't want to inconvenience you, of course. But your way of working with Gabriel had been a big help to both sides, and Sol and I think we shouldn't lose it." What could I say? The treaty was our biggest piece of business and if I could help . . . "Let me tie up some loose ends here, Ellsworth," I told him, "and I'll be in your office Monday morning." "That's great," he said.

On July 11, at the first meeting after their return from consultations, the Panamanians introduced a new member of their group. He was Lt. Col. Armando Contreras, a member of the General Staff of the National Guard. In presenting him, Escobar said the colonel had come to work especially on the Lands and Waters question and on problems of military coordination under a treaty. The U.S. team took the addition of Contreras as a positive sign. Torrijos would not have assigned one of his top officers to the treaty exercise if he had no intention of reaching an accord. However, we also assumed that the addition of the *guardia* colonel was going to lead to tougher bargaining for General Dolvin, as indeed it did.

Allocation of land for military use and many other questions were still unresolved and occupied much of the negotiators' time. Some concerned the rights of employees. What quantity of household effects could a worker import duty-free? How would visas for entry and exit be handled? Would employees be under U.S. Civil Service or Panamanian Social Security for retirement purposes? Would American workers be subject to Panamanian income tax? Each produced long debates and some heated arguments. One by one, they were settled through compromise and the application of common sense. We made concessions on the items of greatest sensitivity for Panama; they did the same for those we felt strongest about.

But, inevitably, the Panamanians contrived to raise the issue that for them was the most important unresolved problem: compensation. Just as inevitably, the Americans said that Panamanian expectations were far too high. At the July 11 meeting, for example, Royo asked the U.S. side to accept a lump-sum payment to his country as "a matter of principle." Ambassador Linowitz replied sharply: "Mr. Minister, we have said a number of times—and we will repeat it now—that if this treaty is to be approved and ratified, it cannot be tied in with economic arrangements that go beyond what can properly be paid to Panama out of tolls from the canal. You know from President Pérez that President Carter said this to him in unmistakable terms."

The next day, the Panamanians halved their proposal for an annuity—from $300 million to $150 million. They also slashed the lump-sum request from $1.02 billion to $450 million. They did it, they explained, "to show that we are flexible" and to speed conclusion of a final agreement. They realized by then, of course, that their original submission would never be accepted. But even the $150 million seemed exorbitant to us. It was more than the total tolls collected in 1976 (approximately $135 million). The Panamanians assumed that tolls could be increased significantly without adversely affecting traffic volume. Linowitz told them that tolls high enough to pay them $150 million "would shut the Canal." The Panamanians countered with their original contention—that payments should not be confined to tolls alone. They were quite prepared, for example, to include in the total the income tax payments they hoped to collect from U.S. canal workers.

Linowitz was finding it difficult to dredge up new ways to express the unpalatable facts of life. His frustration was evident when he told them on July 12: "You can be as eloquent as you want at this table, but if the position is not going to be one that will be approved by the president and by the Senate, it will avail us nothing. . . . It does not serve you and does not serve us to put the kind of figures you have here suggested and to expect that we can get support for a treaty with those figures. Now that is as blunt as we can be with you."

In the middle of those discussions of economic desires and political realities, a new development threatened to rend the treaty effort. It began innocently enough with an old Washington institution, an off-the-record breakfast at which reporters and a public figure share scrambled eggs and views on a topic of current interest. In this case, the public figure was Sol Linowitz; the reporters, a group regularly assembled by Godfrey Sperling of the *Christian Science Monitor*; the topic, Panama and the new treaties. Linowitz was normally a forthcoming commentator with the press. At this meeting, he felt especially confident because he was dealing with some of the top reporters in Washington and, moreover, he had the protective mantle of the off-the-record rule.*

---

*In an earlier time, "off the record" meant just that—not to be written or disclosed. Its purpose was to provide serious reporters with a bench mark by which to judge other information. It has lost almost all meaning except when used by one source with one honorable reporter.

Linowitz spoke frankly to the Sperling group about the negotiations. He cited Panamanian monetary demands as the most formidable remaining barrier to a treaty. He also described the Neutrality Treaty—with its grant of authority to the United States to use military force to protect the canal. In short, he gave the select group of journalists an accurate but general picture of the state of play. From it, he hoped would come stories over the next weeks that were balanced and fair.

The main difficulty with off-the-record press sessions is that reporters not present work hard to find out what happened—and often succeed. But not having been present, they feel immune from the ground rules. In this case, reporters not at the breakfast quickly learned much of what had been said, combined it with information they had gathered on the Hill and from other sources, and put the story on the news wire. In the first cycle, stories reached newsrooms giving the essentials of the Linowitz talk. The second cycle named Sol as the source for the stories. Then the fat was in the fire.

All that took several hours. Meantime, Bunker and Linowitz had a useful meeting with the Panamanians at the State Department. There followed a working lunch at the Panamanian Embassy at which the talk was even more open and constructive. During lunch, the U.S. negotiators offered to boost the per ton payment that would go to Panama from twenty-seven cents to thirty cents. The experts calculated that would produce an average annual payment of about $53 million over the twenty-plus years of the treaty. The differences between the two sides were gradually narrowing.

By late afternoon, parts of the breakfast story appeared in some evening editions. The wire services moved it into newsrooms around the world, including Panama. It was given significant play in most morning papers. The headline in the *Washington Post* was typical: "Panamanian Demand for $5 Billion Snarls Canal Treaty Talks." One unfortunate feature of the affair was that the figures used in the stories had already been slashed by the Panamanians—the annuity halved and the lump-sum figure reduced even more.

The Panamanians were furious, more so in Panama City than in Washington (where the Torrijos team had learned much about the U.S. press and were actively using it to get their own viewpoints across). On the isthmus, however, it was seen as "a filthy plot," as one official called it, a scheme to discredit and embarrass the Panamanians and weaken their negotiating position. Early Saturday morning, forty-eight hours after the Sperling breakfast, Ambassador Lewis received an angry phone call from Foreign Minister González-Revilla. If this is the way the gringos are going to play, he told Gabriel, we can do the same. They planned to send a high-level team to Washington to hold a press conference, including the TV networks. The minister said they would explain Panama's treaty position, expose the "lies" that had been spread in the press, and accuse the U.S. side of bad faith. He said the authorities in Panama realized it would mean an end to the negotiations for the foreseeable future.

Gabriel called me and explained what had happened. I was appalled by the extreme reaction in Panama. I told him about the violation of the off-the-record rule and explained that much of the material in the news stories had not come from Linowitz at all but from other sources around town. I assured him there was no "plot" and that we were as unhappy about the leak as they were. "Well, what are we going to do about it?" he asked. "We've got to move fast." I told him the best thing would be for Sol himself to explain to the Panamanian negotiators what had happened. He agreed that would help and I went in to see Linowitz.

When he heard how upset the Panamanians were, Sol agreed immediately to meet with them. I called Gabriel and asked him to round up his negotiators. We used the short break to describe the problem to Ellsworth Bunker; then the three of us drove to the embassy. The ambassador had located Royo and López-Guevara, and they were waiting for us.

Linowitz was at his persuasive best as he explained exactly what had happened at the controversial breakfast, and later. He patiently answered all the questions posed by the Panamanians. Finally, he took a step that proved decisive; he gave Royo and López-Guevara a copy of the notes he had used at the breakfast meeting. As they read through them, they realized that the ambassador's talk had really been fairly innocuous and that their compatriots in Panama City were exaggerating the affair far beyond its real importance. After we left the embassy, the Panamanians called Torrijos, described their talk with Linowitz, and successfully killed the plan to have a block-busting news conference.

Monday, July 18, was a red-letter day in the Panama treaty talks. That afternoon, the two negotiating teams discussed for the first time an actual text of the proposed canal pact. The draft in English, prepared by Mike Kozak and Gerri Chester and approved by the Pentagon, had been delivered to the Panamanians five days before. At the meeting on the eighteenth, the text in Spanish was handed across the table. Herbert Hansell attended the meeting as the State Department's principal legal officer. Kozak explained briefly each of the ten articles in the draft and the three attached annexes and the basis on which they were written. The Panamanians raised objections to some of the wording, but in general they found the first detailed treaty draft "quite acceptable," as Royo put it, though they reserved the right to propose changes after more careful study. It was a right they would use to the very end. When I heard of the Panamanians' initial reaction, I reminded some of my colleagues of Yogi Berra's comment on baseball: "The game ain't over 'til it's over!"

I was in the office talking with Ambler Moss, Linowitz' right-hand

man, and Bill Pryce, who had replaced Dick Barkley as Bunker's executive
assistant, when the two ambassadors returned from their session. They
asked me to come in for a talk. They thought the session on the treaty draft
had gone fairly well though lots of hard bargaining remained. What bothered them most was the chasm that still divided the two sides on the economic issues. Several comments at the just-ended meeting persuaded them
the money problem was still uppermost in the minds of the Panamanians,
and they believed the whole effort might founder in that morass.

"They just don't understand, or they refuse to accept, that our charter
doesn't go beyond payment from tolls," Linowitz said. "We've told them
over and over again, and in every way we can think of. It just doesn't seem
to get across." Bunker asked me what we could do to make it clear. "They
seem to have the view that we're rich and they're poor and a few hundred
million just don't matter that much to us," Bunker said. "How can we
make them understand that it isn't a question of money in this case?"

"I suggest that I have a good, heart-to-heart talk with Gabriel and try to
straighten this out," I said. I warned them that I would probably have to
be more outspoken than they would like, and much more specific than
they would approve. But I felt there was no other way. Bunker and Linowitz looked at each other for a moment, then urged me to go ahead. "Do
what you think is right," Ellsworth told me. "And what's necessary," Sol
added.

That night, Gabriel and I had one of our longest and most complicated
sessions. It began about 8 o'clock and ended just before 2:00 A.M. With
countless permutations and combinations, what I told him boiled down to
three core points: (a) "We can get a reasonable treaty"; (b) "with a lot of
hard work and some luck, we can possibly get congressional approval"; (c)
"but we cannot ask the Congress or the American people to pay for the
privilege of turning over the Panama Canal." That did not mean there
would not be clear economic benefits for Panama, I said; there would be. I
then outlined what I thought was a possible economic package. It was
based on what I knew our economic specialists were considering, but I
warned him that it was "strictly unofficial, informal, and no more than an
educated guess."

First, I said, the thirty cents a ton from tolls we had just offered would
give Panama more than $50 million a year. It would increase if use of the
canal grew, as some experts believed it would, especially with the traffic of
Alaskan oil to Gulf and East Coast ports. "So we start," I told Gabriel,
"with more than $1 billion going to Panama under the treaty."

Beyond that, I told him, we would support Panama's low-income housing program with investment guarantees of $70 million or so over a five-
year period. Our Overseas Private Investment Corporation (OPIC) would
guarantee borrowing by Panama's National Finance Corporation (CO-

FINA) up to $20 million. (We were asking for more, but I told him I doubted we would get it.) The biggest item would come from the Export-Import Bank, which would provide loans and loan guarantees to finance U.S. exports to Panama for $150 million to $200 million over a five-year period. Finally, I said I was sure Panama could count on preferred treatment and low-cost loans for the purchase of military equipment for probably $5 million a year for five years, possibly ten. That added up to a package of $265 to $340 million during the first ten years of the treaty.

I realized it was modest compared to what Panama had been asking. But it was really as much as we could then provide. I admitted, too, that it was a package of loans, credits, and guarantees, not hard cash. But obviously it had real cash value, and it gave the Panamanians something they could present to their people as solid economic benefits.

"The big thing, Gabriel," I told him, "is that this is just the beginning. If we get a treaty, and it works well, and your country and mine are working together and making the canal a continuing success, you know damn well that support for Panama's economic development is going to get a friendly hearing in Washington. But it's something that has to be proved and grow. We just can't set the initial price tag too high."

Gabriel said he thought the Panamanians would be disappointed with an economic package of the dimensions I had given. They had been led to believe we would be considerably more forthcoming. I told him I was not trying to negotiate or to cut the cost of the treaty. I was telling him what I thought the final package would be.

It was midnight by then, time to raise the central question. "If I'm right, Gabriel, and the kind of package I've described is the bottom line on this whole bloody question of economic returns, will Torrijos accept a treaty on those terms? And what is the best way to present it to him?"

Gabriel repeated that the Panamanians, and Torrijos, would be bitterly disappointed if what I had described was, in fact, the bottom line for the United States. But if it were, he thought it was imperative the general be informed "in an authoritative and totally credible way."

"That," he said, "can only be a direct message to Omar from President Carter."

I asked him if he would convey such a message. He said he would, of course, but he thought there was a better way. He recommended that the chief negotiators, Escobar and Royo, be made special envoys for the purpose. Reading between the lines, I knew he was right. Escobar and Royo spoke for the radical, leftist elements in Panamanian society. If they were persuaded that huge economic benefits were not in the cards but that a treaty was worthwhile nonetheless, it would make the case easier for Torrijos to digest.

We talked about a possible visit to the White House at which President

Carter could make the case personally with the Panamanian negotiators. At such a meeting, the president could hand over his message to Torrijos and ask the negotiators to deliver it. Gabriel and I agreed that probably only in that way could the shaky treaty effort be salvaged.

The next morning, I gave Bunker and Linowitz a detailed account of our talk. They asked me to write it out so they could share the exchange with Secretary Vance and the White House. I went down to the fourth floor, sat at a typewriter, and put it all in a four-page memo. To the report, I attached a suggested draft of a letter that President Carter might send to Torrijos. It covered all the points that Bunker, Linowitz, and I had agreed the president should stress to the chief of the Panamanian government.

What turned out to be the last meeting of the Panama treaty negotiators in Washington—though neither side realized it at the time—took place on July 20, a hot and muggy Wednesday. By then, Escobar, Royo, and the rest of the Panamanian team had had a chance to pore over the treaty draft we had submitted the week before. They insisted that it contained "new points which have not been discussed," and Royo, with inflated rhetoric, told the Americans: "It is as though we were reopening the negotiations." They announced they were already preparing their own draft and would offer it as a "counterproposal." When that line of attack persisted, Linowitz intervened to tell them there had been no intention to introduce anything new, and there was certainly no desire to "start from scratch." In fact, there really was little new in the U.S. draft. Kozak and Chester had carefully crafted the document to conform with the total negotiating record. The difficulty was that that record went back over many years, whereas Escobar and Royo had only been engaged in the treaty talks for five months. Those few things not yet agreed were put in deliberately to elicit a Panamanian reaction.

That final meeting in Washington brought home to both sides that it was not only the economic issue that remained unresolved. There was a host of unsettled labor problems, though none appeared insoluble. More crucial was the sudden realization that the disposition of Lands and Waters—which negotiators for both teams thought was virtually finished—had actually moved farther from agreement, not closer.

By the middle of June, General Dolvin and Edwin Fábrega had reached a broad understanding on all the main land sites—those that would revert to Panama and those that were necessary for the operation and defense of the canal. That changed markedly when Colonel Contreras joined the Panamanian negotiators in early July. The Americans found him stiff, arrogant, and demanding. He constantly questioned past agreements and regularly made new demands. Tom Dolvin, who had been commanding troops when Contreras was in first grade, found his patience sorely tried. To be fair to the Panamanian colonel, he was in a difficult position. Normally buffered from the rude civilian world by the collegiality of the Panamanian General Staff, Contreras found himself in an unfamiliar diplomatic milieu with no previous experience to guide him. He had the typical "charge" mentality of the young military commander, but he had not yet mastered the arts that distinguish a military politician from a good soldier. His orders, when he went to Washington, were to get the best deal possible for the National Guard, and he pursued that goal without deviation.

His single-minded drive produced demands that altered significantly the arrangement patiently molded by Dolvin and Fábrega. At the July 20 meeting, Dolvin bluntly told the Panamanians: "In all honesty, I should report to you that the latest Panamanian proposals are just unacceptable." Royo and his colleagues were visibly surprised. "Not acceptable?" they asked. Dolvin answered sternly: "Are not acceptable, and will not be really supported." He said the Panamanians had gone to the well of U.S. generosity once too often and "I think that the well is dry." Bunker quickly changed the subject.

At the end of the meeting, it was agreed that the principal negotiators would get together again after the U.S. and Panamanian economic specialists had met. In the meantime, Escobar, Royo, and the others planned to return to Panama to consult with Torrijos, see their families, and relax for a few days. They took off for home the next day, and so did I. It had already been agreed that the wrap-up sessions on the treaty would be held in Panama in early August, so when I went in to say goodbye to Bunker and Linowitz, I told them: "I'll see you in Panama in two weeks."

That same day, President Carter unwittingly introduced a controversial element into the treaty picture. Speaking at a town meeting in Yazoo City, Mississippi, he advocated building a sea-level canal in Panama. "I would say we will need a new Panama Canal," he told his listeners. That bald pronouncement produced some consternation on the isthmus. Several Panamanian friends called that night asking: "If you're going to build a new canal, why do we need a treaty on the old one? What kind of games are you playing?" It took several days of patient explaining to soften the hostile reaction. We told every Panamanian we could reach that the president was talking of a possibility, not a reality; that such a project would require huge outlays of money and it was far from clear the Congress would go along; that it would take years to complete such an ambitious undertaking; and that, even if it were done, Panama would get as much benefit, or more, from a new canal as it was going to get from the old one. Within days, the controversy died.

The meeting between President Carter and the Panamanian negotiators that Gabriel and I had advocated was finally arranged. Escobar and Royo flew to Washington on July 28 and the next morning, at 9:30 A.M., they and Ambassador Lewis walked into the reception room in the West Wing of the White House. They were escorted immediately into the Cabinet Room.

Carter handled the session with sensitivity, praising generously the work the two negotiating teams had already accomplished. But he conveyed two key messages with no ambiguity. One was the need for a speedy conclusion to the treaty talks so the pact could go quickly to the Senate. ("We have to move with great speed, as fast as possible.") His other point was that he could not go beyond the economic benefits then being discussed by the negotiators. ("It would be impossible for me to convince the people and the Congress of the United States that we should pay Panama in some way for taking over control of the canal.") He said he would describe his position in full in a letter he wanted the negotiators to deliver to General Torrijos.

Rómulo Escobar responded with words of warmth and admiration for the spirit with which President Carter was approaching relations with their country. He also had high praise for the ability and understanding of the U.S. negotiators. He said these factors "allow us to feel optimistic about the results of those negotiations." He said General Torrijos had asked them to inform the president of one development: the Panamanian leader and the presidents of Colombia, Costa Rica, Mexico, and Venezuela and the prime minister of Jamaica would meet in Bogotá on August 5. The general planned to give his Latin American neighbors a full report on the treaty talks at that gathering. Rómulo said he had learned from one of the presidents that they planned to organize an assembly of all the heads of state of Latin America to celebrate the conclusion of the Panama treaty. Carter told the Panamanians he would be pleased to take part personally in such a ceremony when the treaty was finished.

After forty-five minutes, and a few more expressions of goodwill and optimism on both sides, the meeting broke up. The Panamanian and American negotiators retired next door to the Roosevelt Room while the letter to General Torrijos was being readied for the president's signature. Royo said he and his colleagues were looking at the date of August 10—the day Linowitz' commission as special ambassador would expire—as the day by which they hoped to complete all work on the treaty. It was unmistakable, if casual, recognition of the vital role the brilliant lawyer had played in bringing the treaties so close to fruition. The Panamanians at the bargaining table had become persuaded that, if a treaty were not finished while Linowitz was aboard, it might never be.

When they received the letter from President Carter, the Panamanian negotiators left immediately for the airport. The president's letter was cordial and he hailed the progress that had been made. But he minced no words on the two unresolved questions, Lands and Waters and the money settlement. On the former, Carter said the United States had made "major concessions" in recent months and "any significant further adjustments would handicap us unacceptably in operating and defending the Canal." On the financial arrangement, Carter said the U.S. proposals were the products of "intensive analysis and an effort to be just and fair." Then came the central message to Panama's leader: "It may be that these proposals will be less than you had expected or wished, but I hope that you will understand that they represent the most that we could undertake to do, based on our consultations with the Congress. In my best judgement, the proposals will be generous, fair, and appropriate."

The president went on to say that, once a treaty was finished, he intended to work closely with Torrijos "on improvement of Panama's economic health and development." He foresaw many opportunities for effective cooperation as the two countries operated and protected the canal together. Carter said he looked forward to signing with Torrijos "a great historic document that will make our countries and our peoples real partners in the adventurous years ahead."

The Carter letter had considerable impact on Torrijos. He was disappointed that the economic arrangements were not more advantageous for Panama, but he believed the president when he said that any larger payments would pose a serious political danger to the fate of the treaty. And he took heart from Carter's pledge to look for ways to help Panama's economic growth in the posttreaty era. Looking back on those events, both American and Panamanian negotiators later concluded that the Carter message to Torrijos at the end of July was the crucial element in solving the last major problem standing in the path of the Panama treaty.

The economic proposals made in the wake of the Carter letter varied little from those I had outlined informally for Ambassador Lewis ten days earlier. Panama would get thirty cents a canal net ton* for vessels passing through the canal. The program for support of Panamanian economic development included $75 million in housing investment guarantees over five years; OPIC underwriting of up to $20 million in loans to Panama's National Finance Corporation; loans, loan guarantees, and insurance of as much as $200 million over a five-year period from the Export-Import Bank to finance U.S. exports to Panama; and repayment guarantees for loans to purchase military equipment and services for up to $50 million over ten years. In addition to the per-ton payment, the United States sweetened the annuity pot by promising to pay Panama $10 million a year from canal

---

*A measurement devised by the Canal Company based on 100 cubic feet of a vessel's earning capacity. The toll rate in 1977 for loaded cargo or passenger vessels was $1.29 a net ton; $1.03 for such vessels in ballast.

revenues. The economists reckoned that could be covered easily by eliminating the nonsensical requirement that the canal operating agency pay the U.S. Treasury annual interest on the original U.S. investment in the canal—an investment repaid many times over to the U.S. economy and government during more than sixty years of canal operations. The United States would also pay for the public services that had been discussed so heatedly.

The Panamanians asked that the thirty-cents-a-ton payment be tied to some kind of inflation index. They feared that thirty cents in 1977 could be worth only fifteen cents in 1987 and even less in future years. The United States eventually agreed to review the payment after five years, and at two-year intervals thereafter, and to link it to the U.S. wholesale price index for manufactured goods. Under that formula, if one assumed an annual rise in the index of 6 percent, the per-ton payment after five years would be forty cents. It was easy to understand why the Panamanians wanted some form of hedge against inflation.

As those economic arrangements were taking shape, Bunker called and asked me to return to Washington. With the Panamanian negotiators out of contact and Torrijos preparing to go to Bogotá, he and Linowitz wanted to make sure that liaison with the Panamanians did not collapse. They thought my working arrangement with Ambassador Lewis was the best way to handle it. So for the umpteenth time I boarded a Braniff jet on August 1 and flew to Miami and thence to Washington.

The treaty-making machinery in Foggy Bottom was in a mixed state. Parts were roaring ahead in overdrive; others were sputtering. The economic team was working on the compensation arrangement and haggling over every percentage point. The Lands and Waters subgroup was fighting over every house and hill. The lawyers were busy rewriting the articles the Panamanian negotiators had objected to. In the midst of all that activity, a long-simmering problem within the U.S. team finally boiled over.

Morey Bell, the capable, temperamental Foreign Service officer who had been Bunker's deputy since 1973, had never accepted the fact that he was playing a secondary role in a new and different ball game. The addition of General Dolvin as a co-equal deputy in 1975 had caused Bell considerable heartburn. The Carter decision to make Sol Linowitz a co-negotiator with Bunker was an even more damaging blow to Morey's ego. Instead of adjusting readily to the new situation, he tended to sulk and try to preserve as much of the "good old days" atmosphere and style as he could. It was a losing struggle, as it had to be, and the chemical reaction between the Panama Desk and the seventh-floor negotiators worsened steadily.

Part of the reason for Bell's declining effectiveness was a series of tragic personal blows that would have devastated the strongest individual. Within about a year, both his mother and father died. Then his wife, Marian, passed away after a long bout with cancer. Those tragedies, coming one after another, were hammerblows that left him alternately depressed and then hyperactive. No individual should have been subjected to such multiple personal torments and be expected to carry on concurrently in one of the most demanding jobs in the State Department. The wise and reasonable course would have been to give Bell another assignment much earlier.

There were other aspects of the sad affair that I did not know and made no effort to learn. The central fact was that Bunker summoned Bell to his office on August 5 and told him, with considerable regret, that he would not be going to Panama with the team. Internal tension and lack of rapport had become a detriment to the larger business at hand. Morey took it well, but there were tears in his eyes when he walked back to his office. The goal he had dreamed of for four years was close at hand, but he would not be part of it. It was an unfortunate ending for one who had contributed so much to the final product. But those familiar with all the circumstances felt the blow was largely self-inflicted. In his solitary moments, I think Morey agreed.

That same day, the first wave of the U.S. treaty team left for Panama. At a small staff meeting the day before, Ambassador Bunker had wondered aloud if it might not be wise to get on with treaty drafting. His casual comment preyed on Mike Kozak's mind through the day. That evening, he called Gerri Chester at home. "I have a funny feeling," he told her, "that maybe we ought to take our suitcases to the office tomorrow. I think they may decide we ought to get down there right away and get to work." Sure enough, at 10 o'clock the next morning, Bunker called in Mike and told him: "Listen, Sol and I were talking and we think you and Gerri ought to get to Panama and start working on this draft because we're way behind on that. We're doing fine on the economics and other things, but we really haven't done anything on the text other than give them our original proposal. Can you work that out with Carlos [López-Guevara]?"

Mike called the Panamanian lawyer to tell him what was in the wind. Then he and Gerri made a dash for the airport. López-Guevara had said he would have to get the foreign minister's approval to go forward with treaty drafting, but he thought there would be no trouble. Frantic phone calls to Eastern Airlines held the Miami-bound flight for five minutes until the two State Department lawyers arrived, out of breath and suitcases in hand.

That afternoon, as I was cleaning off my desk and getting ready to make the same flight the next day, the fateful phone call from Ambassador Lewis jolted me out of happy recollections of a crab-cake lunch with old friends. With that began the unorthodox, even bizarre, events described in Chapter 1. I went to the embassy at Gabriel's request and we then arranged for Bunker and Linowitz to join us to talk about what was happening in Bogotá. It was the first, and probably the last, time that U.S. negotiators would argue over key international treaty provisions with half a dozen heads of government over the long-distance telephone.

The next morning, after a talk with President Carter, Bunker and Lino-witz passed along the U.S. agreement to the sea-level canal option that the Latin American leaders had proposed from Bogotá. I learned of that de-nouement in a phone call from National Airport minutes before Mili and I took off for Panama.

The next day, Sunday, the Bunker-Linowitz team departed from An-drews Air Force Base aboard one of the big jet transports of the presi-dential fleet. We had told the Panamanians to expect the visitors at about 6:00 P.M. It did no damage to U.S. prestige when the wheels of the big jet hit the Tocumen runway at precisely 6:00 P.M.

Once the formalities were taken care of, we drove to the residence. Bunker and Linowitz had called from the airplane to propose a meeting later that night, and the Panamanians had agreed. We had a welcoming cocktail and dinner; then my guests took off for the inaugural session of the final round at the home of Rory González. The Panamanian negotiat-ing team—with the notable exception of Escobar, whose absence was un-explained—were waiting for the Americans. They spent the next two and a half hours reviewing the unresolved questions, listing them more than try-ing to settle any of them. Lands and Waters was at the top of the U.S. list; economic compensation, several labor issues, and the same Lands and Wa-ters question were high on the Panamanian agenda. Bunker and Linowitz found the Panamanians cordial and cooperative, but they detected no ap-parent eagerness to move quickly into the treaty's final lap.

The next morning, the two American diplomats rode to the Holiday Inn on Punta Paitilla and went to the eighth floor where the Panamanians had reserved the Presidential Suite for the final sessions. The chief negotia-tors and their key aides sat around the conference table in the spacious suite and went to work. As agreed the night before, special working groups dispersed to separate rooms to deal with the remaining bones of contention. Tom Dolvin took Edwin Fábrega and Colonel Contreras off to his rooms on the twelfth floor to put the finishing touches to Lands and Waters. Planning Minister Barletta was closeted with Ambler Moss, Lino-witz' deputy, to wrap up the economic package. Dick Wyrough was con-ferring with López-Guevara and Ricardo Fábrega, a top official in Pan-ama's Social Security system, on some of the remaining labor issues. Gerri Chester was working with Dolvin part of the time and occasionally with Escobar and López-Guevara on U.S. business activities in the soon-to-disappear Canal Zone. It was a five-ring circus, with people coming and going from one working session to another, and with the chief negotiators sitting at the big conference table, which had become the center ring, ar-guing about matters great and small.

As the day wore on, some issues were settled but others seemed increasingly intractable. Tom Dolvin ran into stubborn resistance on several matters he thought had long since been settled. Barletta still insisted that the new canal administration pay Panama everything then being expended by the Canal Company for such things as police and fire protection and other governmental services. That was approximately $17 million. Moss argued that it was far too much, that the size of the new canal operating area would be considerably smaller than the old Canal Zone, and that the burden of services obviously would be reduced. By midday, there was little or no light at the end of the several tunnels.

On leaving Washington, Linowitz had promised to keep Presidential Assistant Hamilton Jordan informed of developments at least once a day. That noon, he called Jordan, told him of the continuing differences, and said that he and Bunker were then feeling more than a little pessimistic. Late that afternoon, hopes for an early resolution got another severe jolt.

The Panamanians invited into the conference room the large press corps that was hovering around the meeting site trying to cover the complicated proceedings. In full view of the assembled newsmen, and to a chorus of clicking camera shutters, Royo handed the Americans the long-promised Panamanian version of a treaty text. From a Panamanian viewpoint, it was good public relations. But the U.S. ambassadors found the timing and the technique dismaying. The tardy introduction of a new and different treaty document seemed to confirm that the Panamanians were not ready to reach an early agreement. When they returned to the residence, Linowitz called Jordan and gave an even gloomier forecast for treaty hopes.

There was no joviality around the dinner table that evening. I tried to cheer up my two colleagues, arguing that the late submission of their draft could be simply a ploy by the Panamanians to probe our intentions. "Some of them seem to think that we want a treaty more than they do," I said, "and this might look like a good way to find out." Bunker and Linowitz agreed that might be true, but, if so, it was a poor way to do business. Linowitz said: "It's mighty late in the day to be playing games—if that's what they're doing."

We were discussing the situation over coffee when an embassy officer came in with the hastily completed English text of the treaty draft. We looked at it briefly, then Sol retired to his bedroom to study it. When I knocked on his door at midnight to see if he needed anything, I found him in shirt sleeves, sitting on one bed with copies of our treaty draft and theirs spread all over the other bed. "It really looks terrible," he said, "worse than I thought."

The next morning, when Sol joined us at breakfast, he was more dour than I had ever seen him. He had been up very late, had gone over every article, and had concluded there was not going to be a treaty. "They've changed words; they've changed ideas; they've altered things that were clearly agreed to," he said. Bunker had not read the document, but he trusted Sol's judgment. The two left for the Holiday Inn in a grumpy mood.

As they drove out the gate, with the security follow-car close behind, I told Mili: "Our Panamanian friends are putting too much pressure on those two. If they're not careful, they're going to blow this thing out of the water." Then I went in and called Gabriel.

I told him: "Look, Gabriel, Ellsworth and Sol just left here and they're in a mighty bitter mood. You better tell your folks that this thing is right on the brink. One more push, and it all goes down the tube."

He was surprised. "What brought this on?" he wanted to know.

I told him about the draft we had received the night before. He knew about it, but he had not read it in detail. He said he did not think it was all that bad.

"It wouldn't be bad," I told him, "if we had another six months to argue about it and dissect it. But we don't have that kind of time, as you well know. All I'm saying is: let's not blow it all at the last minute."

In typical Gabriel fashion he said: "Message received loud and clear. Let me check it out."

When the Panamanians arrived for the Tuesday meeting, they were jovial and friendly. During the Washington talks, Torrijos had seen a picture of Linowitz and had told Ambassador Lewis he "looked as if he had sucked a lemon." It came to be a cliché of the treaty discussions. Whenever Linowitz was in a bad mood, someone was sure to say: "Sol has been sucking a lemon." On this day, Rómulo kidded Linowitz, saying he had not only sucked a lemon but had "eaten a dozen."

Sol was in no mood for jokes or banter. He told the Panamanians the U.S. team had been "gravely disappointed" by the treaty draft they had given us. It seemed to go back on many things we thought were agreed. He also pointedly reminded the Panamanians that his tenure as special ambassador was going to end the next day and he would then no longer be available at the negotiating table. He said the talks would go on, of course, but without him. It was a sharp reminder for Escobar, Royo, and the others that the man who had breathed new life into the treaty effort was about to wave good-bye. If they wanted to drag things out, they would do so in his absence.

Linowitz also told the Panamanians that, if he and Bunker went back to Washington with no agreement, the first thing they would recommend to President Carter would be to disclose to the world the terms of the treaty the United States had proposed.

"We are proud of it," he told them, "and we think the United States has acted with a generosity unmatched in human history." He was certain world public opinion would congratulate the United States "for having been so forthcoming." If Panama turned down the treaty at that point, the U.S. government would be "willing to face the world proudly and say: this is what we offered." The Panamanians, having just returned from Bogotá, knew from their talks there that even some of their neighbors thought Panama was getting a fair deal.

The Panamanian negotiators had listened carefully to every word. When Linowitz finished, there was a pause. Then Rómulo asked for a recess. When they resumed, Rómulo defended the Panamanian draft as an expression of Panama's perfect right to state its views on all issues. And he denied emphatically that it was an effort to slow things down. "We are as anxious as you are to reach a fair agreement," he said.*

Just when things seemed to be getting back on the track, there was another outburst. As a good soldier, General Dolvin wanted all the rights of the U.S. military not only nailed down but also doubly guaranteed. One of those rights—which his superiors in the Pentagon had told him to guarantee—was the freedom of U.S. troops to move unhampered anywhere in Panama in case of a threat to the canal. Two things were noteworthy about that right. One, it was especially sensitive for the Panamanians. Second, and more important, the right had, in fact, been provided in the Status of Forces Agreement worked out in 1975. Those two things prompted Dolvin's colleagues to suggest he avoid this delicate matter in the final round. Unfortunately, he ignored their advice.

In the talks on base areas, Dolvin referred several times to the right of U.S. forces to move freely in Panama. Each time, it provoked a negative reaction from Colonel Contreras. The Guard officer had not been involved in the SOFA talks, hence did not know the background. Instead of letting the colonel's Panamanian colleagues explain the facts to him quietly, Dolvin kept insisting that U.S. freedom of movement be spelled out in the full treaty.

Just the night before, a member of the U.S. team had asked the colonel if he smoked. He explained that he did, but only when he was furious. That day at lunch, the U.S. group noted that Contreras was puffing like mad through the meal. When the talks resumed, Contreras took the floor and denounced the idea of giving U.S. forces the right to move freely inside Panama. Dolvin, with an equally short fuse, answered acidly. The noise level rose and sparks were flying across the table.

---

*Two years after those wild sessions in the Holiday Inn, I asked Panama's negotiating chief about Panama's last-minute introduction of a new draft. Escobar laughed and told me: "We tried to present some things that were different, hoping that with the speed-up and all the confusion the Americans would say yes. We thought that at the last minute they might not study everything all that carefully. And we thought: maybe they'll say yes to some things because they're as anxious and as nervous as we are. But they said no."

Everyone was embarrassed and worried. Linowitz turned to Kozak and asked: "What should we do?" The lawyer urged an immediate recess and a talk with Dolvin. Sol took the general aside and told him to drop the subject. He would personally take responsibility for assuring that the rights the Defense Department wanted were not lost. The same thing was occurring at the other end of the room. Rómulo and his colleagues were telling their irate military colleague to "cool it." Linowitz and Escobar then agreed that the angry exchange between the military men would be expunged from the record.

When the session resumed, Adolfo Ahumada, the shrewd labor lawyer who had helped negotiate the SOFA, provided a face-saving out for both sides. He readily admitted that freedom of movement had been accepted in the military agreement. He also explained why it was politically difficult to emphasize the point too much. He argued the whole thing could be handled by a reference in the canal treaty to rights for U.S. forces that would be "governed by the aforesaid agreement." Bunker and Linowitz quickly agreed, and it was done.

The work went on through the afternoon, hard, slogging work that often focused on what outside observers might have called trivia. And emotion continued to play a role on both sides, never as bitter as the Dolvin-Contreras exchange but never absent either. One participant recalled the atmosphere as follows: "We had negotiated all the big problems without any violence. And here we were losing our tempers over whether a couple of houses in Coco Solo would be used by the U.S. military or by Panamanian canal workers. It was hard to believe."

The negotiators had a quick meal that evening, and the haggling went on as darkness settled over the city. When one or another of the treaty makers got up to stretch his legs, what he saw out of the big picture windows of the Presidential Suite was the glow from downtown Panama City, the lights on the shrimping fleet bobbing on the surface of Panama Bay, and, much farther out, the running lights of big freighters and tankers waiting their turn to transit the canal. They were reminders that the real world and the diplomats in their concrete-and-glass aerie were not too far separated.

In the economic subgroup, Ambler Moss continued to insist that the Panamanian demand for $17 million for services was exorbitant. With significantly smaller territory and the obviously lower wage scale in Panama, he argued, the cost would probably be half the amount the Canal Company had paid in the past for such services. The Panamanians knew he was right and finally agreed to a payment of $10 million a year, subject to review every three years when adjustments could be made up or down because of inflation or other changing circumstances.

The grinding, paragraph-by-paragraph debate continued through the long evening. By then, many arguments revolved around petty points and nerves were frazzled on both sides. Perhaps the nadir was reached when the Panamanians tried to put a $3,000 limit on the value of household goods a new canal worker could bring in without duty. Gerri Chester quietly but deftly killed that absurdity when she told Rómulo she had a coffee service that was worth that much alone. The Panamanians retreated in embarrassment. Then came the final bombshell.

During most of the evening, Rómulo had been sitting back and listening while Royo carried the burden as Panamanian spokesman. Just after midnight, however, he leaned forward and addressed the Americans. "Mr. Ambassadors, there is one more thing we have to discuss," he said. "There comes a time in any negotiation when hard decisions have to be made, when political will has to be used. This is that time. What is necessary to finish this treaty is an agreement to limit the size of U.S. military forces in Panama."

Americans who had heard the pitch before groaned inwardly. General Dolvin ground his teeth. Linowitz, who had not debated the issue before, turned to Mike Kozak and asked: "Is this bad?" Mike told him: "Well, if you want to see General Dolvin go up to the top floor without an elevator, all you have to do is say yes." Linowitz said he would like his colleagues to comment on the proposal.

Dick Wyrough, a retired army colonel, normally one of the quietest and most restrained of the negotiators, took the floor. Very calmly, he said: "As you all know, I have been a member of the U.S. military forces for most of my life. And I know that has led to some suspicion of my intentions. But I think by now that you all know that I consider myself to be a friend of Panama. But for you to raise this issue at this time is simply not helpful. And I say that with complete serenity."

Kozak was even more negative. "Rómulo," he said, addressing his fellow lawyer, "you know you raised that two years ago. And you know our position and that it absolutely can't be done. We've told you that many times and we assumed you accepted it because you haven't brought it up since. For you to raise this issue at this time is absolutely outrageous."

Linowitz stood up and so did all the Americans. "I think the usefulness of these negotiations has ended," he said. They picked up their papers and filed out. The Panamanians were stunned—half angry at Linowitz' curtness; half fearful that the long-awaited treaty was disappearing before their eyes.

A good night's sleep and a bit of reflection do wonders for people under mental pressure. When the two negotiating teams assembled Wednesday morning in the spacious conference room, it was as though all the unpleasantness of the previous night had been washed away. Rómulo set the tone by saying: "We think we are going to give Sol a nice going-away present."

They were acutely aware, of course, that that day was Linowitz' last as an ambassador. The business of limiting U.S. troop strength was forgotten, and the two teams began attacking the remaining unresolved issues. One by one, the changes and additions Panama had tried to insert were dropped or moderated. Within two hours, it was clear to both sides that they were on the threshold of an agreement.

The negotiators then began discussing how their accord should be handled with the press. Linowitz, aware that many details remained to be worked out, was concerned that any public statement not be overplayed. We agreed it should not speak of "agreement on a treaty" but rather "agreement in principle." The ambassadors asked me to draft an announcement and coordinate it with the White House. I went to the U.S. control office on the fourteenth floor and quickly wrote out a possible statement.

Meantime, inside the negotiating room, as one problem after another was resolved, at least in outline form, Rómulo gently referred back to the problem he had raised so disastrously at midnight. "I am afraid I did not make our position clear last night with respect to this question of force levels," he said. "We are not insisting on anything. What we would like—and I want to put it in the right way so you understand it this time—is to ask you to realize that this is a very sensitive issue for us politically. We are asking if there is anything you can do in this area. It would be helpful to us. If you could look at it in that spirit, we would appreciate it."

Bunker replied: "Well, if you put it that way, let's see what we can do."

Dolvin and Kozak went to the side of the room and began working with words, while the main table occupied itself with other problems. Mike tried one formula—we would "try to maintain existing force levels"—but Dolvin said, "No, I don't think so." Then Mike tried "endeavor with our best efforts" but that still did not appeal to Dolvin. Kozak finally put down words that won Dolvin's nod. As it emerged in the final text, the formula was: "To the extent possible, consistent with its primary responsibility for the protection and defense of the Panama Canal, the United States of America will endeavor to maintain its armed forces in the Republic of Panama in normal times at a level not in excess of that . . . immediately prior to entry into force of this Treaty." It did not meet all of the Panamanians' hopes, but it was more than they really expected. Rómulo thanked the U.S. team, and they went on to other matters.

When I finished the draft announcement, I showed it to Bunker and Linowitz and they accepted it with minor changes. Then I called Hamilton Jordan and read it to him. He liked it well enough but thought it was tied too closely to the president. (The draft began: "We wish to make a statement on behalf of President Carter.") Jordan suggested the U.S. negotiators speak for themselves as representatives of the United States. I quickly revised the statement as we talked, read it to him, and got his approval. I then went to the eighth floor and handed it to Bunker and Linowitz, assuring them it had White House clearance.

It was then 6 o'clock. All the main issues had been settled, though much detailed work remained in putting the agreements into final treaty language. But the framework of the treaty structure was at last complete. Thirteen long years of haggling had produced what the representatives of both countries judged to be a fair and honorable settlement for both.

The two teams walked out of the suite to the elevators. Linowitz and Barletta were still discussing wording that would give Panama an additional $10 million in annual payments if it were available. We crowded into the elevators and rode to the nineteenth floor where a large assemblage of reporters and photographers had gathered. The room was designed to handle about one hundred people. At least five hundred were crowded into the limited space, and body heat and floodlights raised the temperature well above 100 degrees.

Bunker and Linowitz, Escobar and Royo sat on a couch in the middle of the noisy, overheated room. At least twenty microphones were stacked on the coffee table in front of them. No one seemed to be in charge, and Rómulo finally shouted for quiet. When order was established, the imperturbable Ellsworth Bunker spoke the words that many had waited to hear for so long: "We are deeply gratified to be able to announce that we and our Panamanian colleagues have today reached agreement in principle on the basic elements of a new treaty—and a new relationship between our countries. Our legal specialists will continue working to express promptly those elements in formal treaties."

He concluded with words aimed more at the American people and the U.S. Congress than at the Panamanians: "From the point of view of the United States, we are confident that this treaty will not only protect but strengthen our national security interests. It will also be a strongly positive element in our overall relationship with our Latin American neighbors and preserve our common interest in an open, secure and efficient canal."

Rómulo spoke for the Panamanians, hailing the "historic agreement" as a great step forward in the life of his country. It would, he asserted, bring to an end once and for all "the hateful perpetuity that prevented our country from regaining its full independence." When the speechmaking ended, the smiling negotiators stood and shook hands warmly while the TV cameras whirred, recording the moment. Slowly, we made our way through the press of bodies to the elevators and descended to the lobby. There, another crowd waited, more reporters, tourists, hotel employees. They broke into spontaneous applause as the two American envoys walked to the main entrance. Our cars were waiting and we drove off, preceded by a motorcycle escort that cleared the way.

Our destination was General Torrijos' informal headquarters on Fiftieth

Street. The general, wearing a red sport shirt and khaki trousers, was smiling broadly and received his guests with enthusiasm. Everyone in the room—most of the Panamanian negotiating team, high government officials, close personal friends—was laughing and joking. The Americans were in the same mood. Linowitz told Torrijos that on that day he was smiling, not sucking lemons, and the general roared. He told the Americans he was delighted the negotiations had been completed successfully. He wanted to apologize for anything he had said in the previous months that might have sounded offensive and created unnecessary problems. "Sometimes I get carried away," he said. Linowitz passed along President Carter's best wishes and his gratification with the agreement.

They talked briefly about the struggle ahead in both countries to win approval for the agreements. Torrijos explained that he and Carter had "different customers" and they were going to have to use "different sales pitches." The general said there were "lots of electric currents" that had to be kept under control in his country, and Bunker congratulated him for "keeping the voltage down."

Torrijos was aware that the day's agreement was not the final treaty, and that considerable work remained in drafting actual texts. He said he assumed the lawyers from the two sides would get to work immediately, and Bunker and Linowitz agreed. The general then asked where the final treaties should be signed. His preference was to invite all the presidents of Latin America to Panama for the event. Linowitz said he and Bunker would pass that view along to the president, but they knew no decision had yet been made.

After more banter, we took our leave of the cheerful Panamanians and drove back to the residence. There, Bunker and Linowitz spoke "on background" to a large number of U.S. reporters who had traveled to Panama for the concluding phase of the negotiations. Soon after the reporters left to file their stories, we had a visitor. President Lakas arrived to convey his congratulations personally to the two American negotiators. It was, he said, a great day for Panama and for the United States, and he thanked Bunker and Linowitz for their patience and understanding. "I've waited a long time for the day when our little country and the big United States would be real partners," he said. "I'm glad that day has finally come."

While we were talking with Lakas, a call came through for Sol from the White House. Hamilton Jordan said that President Carter wanted him to call former President Ford, inform him of the agreement, and outline the main elements. We placed the call through the White House switchboard, and in minutes Sol was talking with Ford in Vail, Colorado. After hearing the Linowitz account over the rather fuzzy connection, the ex-president said he wanted to be helpful and that he would be forthcoming. Of course, he wanted to study the text first and "look at some of the details." Linowitz said he and Bunker would happily brief the former president whenever it was convenient.

When the call was completed and Lakas had left, we had a quiet supper, drank a toast to the new agreement, and went to bed exhausted but satisfied. The next morning, we drove to Tocumen airport where the big U.S. Air Force jet was waiting to take the U.S. team back to Washington. We called from the car to ask Mike Kozak and Gerri Chester to be standing by at the foot of the ramp because we had just received word that the Panamanians wanted to do the technical legal work in Panama rather than in Washington. Mike and Gerri were understandably surprised, especially Gerri, who had a two-month-old baby waiting at home. But both said they would do it *if* the Panamanians were serious and ready to get to work. When the Panamanians arrived, a bit frazzled after a long night of revelry, Linowitz took Royo aside and said the U.S. lawyers would stay if the Panamanians were ready to go right to work. Royo assured him they were and that he personally would take an active role. Mike and Gerri retrieved their suitcases and got ready to go back to Panama City. The big jet lumbered slowly down to the end of the runway and then, with the roar of its four big engines filling our ears, was airborne for Washington.

We walked through the airport and got in our car. As we drove toward the city, the whole wild experience filled my mind. We had been too busy the past weeks to even think about the long-range import of what was going on. Now that it was over, it began to sink in. What previous presidents and negotiators had been trying to do for thirteen years had now been done. "I suppose you know that we've just been through a page in history," I told Mili. She nodded. "But does history have to be so wild?" she asked.

CHAPTER 16

Treaties at Last

"Deep within them, what nourished the hopes of Panamanians and fortified their patience throughout these many years was the firm conviction that the people of the United States have no colonialist ambitions, for you were once a colony and fought heroically for your liberty."

—Gen. Omar Torrijos, at the Pan American Union, Washington, D.C., September 7, 1977

As we drove back into Panama City, we noticed that the streets were amazingly free of traffic. Only a few pedestrians ambled along sidewalks that were normally clogged with shoppers. Suddenly I remembered that it was a national holiday. In the exuberance of the previous night, after agreement had been reached, a celebrating Omar Torrijos had decided his fellow countrymen should have a day away from their offices, shops, and classrooms.

It was a wise decision. Word of the momentous agreement had spread quickly and half the town had been up partying most of the night. The other half got little sleep because of the music, laughter, and other festive noises that bombarded them from all sides. Taxis and private cars had roared along the streets with horns blaring until the wee hours. Few Panamanians would have earned their salt at the workbenches or desks of the capital city that day.

For the writers of the new pact, it was a different story. Mike Kozak and Gerri Chester were still skeptical that the firm pledge of an all-out effort, made at planeside, would be honored to the letter. But at 1 o'clock, when they went to the Presidential Suite of the Holiday Inn, they found a distinguished company of Panamanians waiting for them, as promised—Royo, Ahumada, López-Guevara, and de la Rosa. They went to work immediately.

Aboard the air force jet carrying the U.S. negotiators back to Washington, the atmosphere was relaxed and jovial. Bunker and Linowitz were justifiably proud that their efforts had finally produced what four U.S. presidents had said should be done. The hard-working staff shared the exhilaration, and the sense that they had helped write history. Well into the flight, a call came through from the White House. Bill Hyland, a top man on Brzezinski's staff, informed the ambassadors that a helicopter would be waiting to take them to the White House.

When they arrived at Andrews Air Force Base, the president's big Marine helicopter was waiting as promised. Bunker and Linowitz climbed aboard the olive-green-and-white chopper and it carried them to the White House. When they landed on the south lawn, the president was outside waiting for them. Flanking him were Toni Linowitz and Carol Bunker. When personal and official greetings were finished, the two diplomats walked with the president through the Rose Garden and into the Cabinet Room. There they were greeted by Secretary of Defense Brown, Acting Secretary of State Christopher, the Joint Chiefs of Staff, and several members of the White House staff. For an hour and a half, the returned diplomats briefed the president and the others on the central features of the new agreement and answered their questions.

At the end, the waiting press was called in for pictures. President Carter told the reporters he was satisfied with the new treaties and felt sure they were in the best interests of U.S.-Panama relations. The two ambassadors winced when the president noted that the United States would retain the right to protect the canal "in perpetuity"—a word all old treaty hands knew would irritate Panamanian sensitivities. But except for that lapse, the session went well. Bunker and Linowitz drove home thoroughly pleased, with a major diplomatic achievement to their credit.

While everything was happily optimistic and cheerful in Washington, the two American lawyers in Panama were operating under several handicaps. First, they had no specific instructions beyond "get the job done." Second, it had been agreed that morning that the treaty writers would use the Panamanian draft as their basic document. Most of the rough edges of that controversial document had been smoothed off in the final twenty-four hours of negotiations by Bunker and Linowitz, but many differences remained between it and the U.S. draft. More troublesome was the fact that no one at the working level in Washington had received a copy of the Panamanian draft, or even knew the lawyers in Panama were working from it. To compound the confusion, the Panamanians had rearranged the order in which some subjects were dealt with, so Article IV in their version of the treaty, for example, was not necessarily Article IV in the U.S. document.

Much of the trouble stemmed from a breakdown in Washington's bureaucratic command. In the wake of the agreement on principles, most of those involved were either taking a well-deserved break or were busy explaining the treaties. Linowitz' commission as ambassador had ended and he was paying attention to urgent private matters he had pushed aside for months. Though still much involved and working closely with the White House, Sol had vacated his State Department office and was no longer in an operational position. His assistant, Ambler Moss, was preparing to return to the practice of law. Bunker was fully occupied, with Linowitz, in briefing top-level national figures and filling speaking engagements. Morey Bell had left the scene. Dick Wyrough was away from Washington promoting the treaties around the country. Mark Feldman, the splendid international lawyer who was Kozak's boss, was on annual leave. Kozak and Chester were reporting regularly, and begging for guidance and decisions, but no one was answering the mail.

The two lawyers could have taken sanctuary in the time-honored refuge of tremulous Foreign Service officers ("But we have no instructions"). However, they knew that the treaties, despite Washington's temporary silence, had a high priority. They decided to go ahead, use their best judgment, and trust they would make no serious errors. Fortunately, they knew more about the details of the treaty and the negotiating history than most other Americans.

At the opening session in the Holiday Inn, they encountered trouble with the first few articles of the Panamanian draft. They pointed out that some words and phrases were different from the U.S. draft, and from what had been agreed by the negotiators. Royo, head of the Panamanian team, was impatient to get through the drafting job and he thought the Americans were being needlessly picayune. "If we're going to haggle about every word and comma, we'll never get this job done," he said.

Sensing Royo's impatience, the Americans called for a break and Chester suggested a strategy. When they returned to the table, they proposed working first on the implementing agreements instead of the treaties. Royo agreed. The drafters were then operating from a U.S text and the Panamanian lawyers, López-Guevara and de la Rosa, began nitpicking in earnest, making almost every clause the subject of debate. Royo heard a half hour of that and finally exploded. He began to berate his colleagues in stronger language than he had used earlier with the Americans. Kozak and Chester walked out of the room to let the storm blow over.

When they went back, Royo told them: "We have a real problem here. We are as bad at nitpicking as you are." The Americans explained that they had no more desire to haggle over minor details than the Panamanians did. But it was an important treaty and neither side could afford to have the job done badly. "We should not question each other's good faith," Kozak said. "We both want to move quickly so let's make decisions and get them over with, but not argue about whether we should look at an issue and renegotiate it." Royo agreed that was the best way to proceed. From then on, the pace of treaty writing accelerated.

Royo established the mode for those crucial discussions. When he saw a point that was particularly sensitive for Panama, he insisted it be handled according to the Panamanian draft. When the U.S. arguments were compelling, he gave way. He proved himself willing to make decisions and stick by them. More than the other Panamanians, he had his eye on the end of the line. He frequently frustrated them by cutting the debate short when they would have loved to go on and on.

Each day, the U.S. lawyers sent full reports to Washington with the tentative agreements and requests for comments or approval. But the silence from the other end was deafening. The papers were going from State to Defense but lawyers in the Pentagon were not reacting any quicker than Foggy Bottom. One day, in desperation, Kozak got through to the State Department's legal adviser and tried to explain the situation over an especially bad phone connection. The reaction was: "I see. You're tired and need more people."

"No, no," Kozak said. "We're not tired and we don't need more people. We need instructions." But still nothing happened.

Finally, Kozak contacted a colleague in the legal office who had been dealing with defense and told him: "Don't try to write a cable and get it cleared. Just tell me what Phil Barringer [a leading Defense Department lawyer] and the others want." The young man said he had just received a "laundry list" of things Defense thought should be covered and he dictated the main points. Some were sensible; some were impossible. Defense still did not have a clear picture of what Bunker and Linowitz had agreed to in the final week, nor did they have the text being used in Panama.

After a few days, the venue for treaty writing changed. Some of the Panamanians argued they had to be closer to their files and to typists and a Xerox machine. They moved the exercise from the Holiday Inn to a rundown building near the Foreign Ministry where the Panamanian treaty advisors had maintained offices for a year or more. At one point, the ground floor had been occupied by a Chinese restaurant, and from then on many of us referred to "the treaty that was written over the Chinese restaurant."

The tiresome, slogging work continued for ten days. When they had Defense's suggestions in hand, Kozak and Chester went over them carefully and decided which had no chance of success, which were worth trying for, and which they would insist upon. When Royo saw the long list of proposals, he was aghast. "You have that many changes?" he asked, looking at the pile of papers in Chester's hand. "You should be more sympathetic," said Kozak. "We had twice that many but we cut half of them out."

The lack of close supervision from Washington was not because the principal architects of the treaties were taking it easy. Bunker and Linowitz were fully occupied. On Sunday, August 14, for example, the two ambassadors appeared on "Meet the Press" where they were grilled by a panel of newsmen. Soon after sunrise on Tuesday morning, Linowitz flew from Washington with General Brown to Vail, Colorado, where they gave former President Gerald Ford a detailed briefing on the agreements. At the end of the session, Ford announced his unqualified support for the treaties and urged their ratification. Bunker and Brown did the same thing for former Secretary of State Kissinger and he, too, declared the treaties were "in the national interest of the United States." On Wednesday, Bunker and Linowitz appeared before the House Merchant Marine and Fisheries Committee and for four hours answered blunt and often rude questions about the treaties. The committee, headed by ex–West Pointer John Murphy of New York, was loaded with members who had made "defense of our canal" a central plank in their political philosophy. In the flurry of activity on the political front, the two U.S. lawyers in Panama were left on their own.

Piece by piece, paragraph by paragraph, the Panamanian and American drafters molded the treaty details around the framework of the agreed principles. Thanks to Royo's firm hand on the drafting tiller, the journey through treaty details went rather smoothly after the initial squall. There were arguments aplenty, of course, but they no longer centered on trivia. Royo had ruled out nitpicking. Clearly he wanted to get the job done. His handling of the arbitration issue was typical.

This was a subject dear to the heart of López-Guevara, the meticulous international lawyer. He knew that under any contract there would be times when the parties involved would interpret an article or a phrase differently. He insisted that when that happened the dispute should go to an agreed third party, or parties, for decision. The United States, however, had always been reluctant to submit its actions or policies to the binding verdicts of other governments or judges.

Panama raised the issue periodically through the May Round of negotiations. The United States regularly pushed it aside. At the final meeting at the Holiday Inn on August 10, López-Guevara once more tried to force the matter to a decision, and was once more rebuffed. "We can work something out when we are doing the final treaty draft," he was told. That left it up to Kozak and Chester.

At one of their sessions "over the Chinese restaurant," the Americans, at Royo's request, agreed to draft some language on arbitration. The next day, they gave their handiwork to Royo, one paragraph called "Settlement of Disputes." It said that, in case of differences, the two sides would try to work it out together. If that failed, "they may, in appropriate cases, agree to submit the matter to conciliation, mediation, arbitration, or such other procedure for the peaceful settlement of the dispute as they may mutually deem appropriate." It was as beautifully vague as diplomats and lawyers can be when they wish to.

Except for López-Guevara, none of the Panamanians felt it was a burning issue. Royo and the others realized the United States was not going to accept compulsory arbitration, or anything close to it. He glanced at the paragraph while López-Guevara leaned over and tried to read it, too. Royo said quickly, "That's perfect; exactly what we want." He then put it on the table face down and put his hand on it. López-Guevara was saying, "Let me see it." Royo kept his hand in place, and told him, "It's just fine, Carlos. Don't worry." Royo knew that if he had decided to fight the arbitration issue, the two sides would still be arguing a month later.

The laborious work went forward day after day. After the tedious sessions in the ramshackle Panamanian conference room, the lawyers on both sides worked separately into the night, drafting new language, preparing for the next day's negotiation. With manifest dedication on both sides, the Panama treaty and the agreements that would implement it took shape. The central engine that drove things forward on that race to the finish line was Royo's energy and his willingness to make hard decisions on the spot. His performance during those trying days added weight to the case then being made by his friends behind the scenes in Panama that Royo was presidential timber.

On Friday, August 19, a cable finally arrived from Washington with some detailed views from State and Defense—what Kozak and Chester had been begging for for a week. It permitted them, on Saturday, to take a firmer stand on several of the outstanding issues and to iron out last-minute differences. By sundown, the American and Panamanian lawyers had dotted the final *i*'s and inserted the last of the commas. The Panama Canal Treaty was ready to be submitted to the two governments for final approval.

While Kozak and Chester were working on the treaty itself, they assumed that the technical job of compiling the necessary annexes and drawing the maps was being done by the Pentagon. General Dolvin had worked out the agreement and the Defense Department had the technical expertise necessary for that complicated job. Again, the lack of tight central control in Washington produced confusion.

That evening, as Kozak, Chester, and Dick Wyrough (who had come two days before) were celebrating completion of the treaty and its implementing agreement, two high-ranking officers who had worked with Dolvin arrived in Panama. They were Cols. Larry Jackley and George Carroll. The State Department officers were delighted because they thought another section of the treaty picture was ready to be put in place. "Let's see your annexes," one of them said. The answer was: "What annexes?" "You mean you didn't come with the annexes on Lands and Waters?" They had brought lots of papers containing details of the agreement, but no annexes. "My God, we're in trouble," said Kozak. The two officers had come to offer the lawyers technical advice in writing the annexes; no one had said they should be written in Washington.

The five Americans went to a room in the hotel to assess the damage, go over the papers Jackley and Carroll had brought, and decide how to proceed. It was quickly evident that a huge amount of work remained. Most troublesome, it appeared there were as yet no clear agreements with the Panamanians on some points. Instead of just wringing their hands, they attacked the problem. Working from the colonels' papers, they developed a list of annexes that would be necessary and how they would fit into the overall treaty pattern. Then they made a list of all the decisions that were pending, the things that would still have to be settled with the Panamanians. The job took them all night.*

The Americans had planned to return to Washington that Sunday. It was obvious by 2:00 A.M. that that would be impossible. They decided that Wyrough and Chester would stay in Panama with Jackley and Carroll to work with the Panamanians on the annexes. Kozak would fly to Washington to deliver the texts of the treaty and the implementing agreement so those documents could get final approval in the bureaucracy.

Early that Sunday morning, Wyrough, Kozak, and Chester went to see Minister Royo at his home. They explained their predicament, argued that the planned meeting of U.S. and Panamanian specialists would be a waste of time, and asked him to delay it for a few days until the U.S. side sorted out its position. Royo was understanding and agreed. Kozak then went to the airport to catch the Miami-bound plane.

Wyrough formed a task force of the Americans from Washington and a group of specialists from SOUTHCOM and the Canal Company. For the next seventy-two hours, they formulated the U.S. position on territory and facilities. By the time they were finished, things like Pier 20, the Diablo Power Station, and the Coco Solo commissary building were as familiar to them as the house next door.

The morning after he got back to Washington, Kozak met with Ambassador Bunker and gave him the treaty text and agreement worked out in Panama. He also provided copies to the department's legal adviser and the Pentagon. At a meeting in Bunker's office later that morning, Kozak explained to the ambassador and General Dolvin the horrible confusion surrounding the treaty annexes. He urged Dolvin to send a lawyer and some cartographers to Panama to put the agreement into proper shape. The general argued that putting the agreement on paper was a job for State. Kozak responded with some heat that drafting what amounted to a bases agreement was a Pentagon specialty, to say nothing of drawing maps. Bunker finally interceded and Dolvin agreed to send some people. Steve

---

*The complexity of the task is clear from reading *Documents Associated with the Panama Canal Treaties*, Department of State Publication 8914, released September 1977. It includes the two Implementing Agreements and their seven Annexes.

Lucas, the savvy army lawyer, flew to Panama the next day. That freed Gerri Chester to return to Washington for the final treaty review.

Sol Linowitz had gone to his country retreat in upper New York State for a well-earned rest while the treaty writing was moving ahead. It proved to be less than the vacation he had hoped for. He found himself on the phone almost hourly taking calls from the White House and Ambassador Bunker, from Panama's always active envoy Gabriel Lewis, and from other quarters. He finally abandoned the idea of getting a little rest and moved back to the fray.

When Linowitz went to his office above Washington's Farragut Square, his first visitor was Mike Kozak, who delivered a copy of the treaty draft and the attached agreement. While they were discussing the documents, the phone rang. Linowitz took the call while Kozak continued going through the draft, marking sections he particularly wanted the veteran lawyer to check. He heard Linowitz say: "Please hold on a minute. Mike Kozak is here and he's working on the draft." Sol turned to Mike and asked, "When can you have this thing finished?" Mike explained there were quite a few unresolved issues on Lands and Waters, and numerous mechanical problems, including language confirmation (ensuring that the English and Spanish versions said the same thing). He also pointed out that the Panamanian cabinet would be reviewing the text and might raise last-minute problems. Assuming all those matters were overcome, Sol said, when could it be completed? If everything went well, Kozak guessed it might be done in ten days, but two weeks would be better.

Sol asked: "How about September 7?" That was two weeks off. "Well, that sounds pretty good," said Kozak. Sol took his hand off the mouthpiece. "I've got assurances we'll have it done on the seventh," he said. When he hung up, he turned to Kozak. "Well, we're committed now," he said. "But to whom?" Mike asked. "Who were you talking to?" Sol replied, "That was the president." Kozak gulped. "If I'd known that," he said, "I would have suggested two months."

Kozak dashed back to the State Department, told Bunker about the newly fixed deadline, then went to his office and got on the phone—to the Pentagon, to General Dolvin, to Panama. As he said later, "We really got cracking." As the Americans went to work, the target date was leaking. Ambassador Lewis heard it from one of his friends in the White House, and that evening the Panamanian government announced that General Torrijos would be signing the new Panama Canal Treaty on September 7 in Washington at OAS headquarters.

The next day, Gerri Chester flew home from Panama leaving Wyrough, Lucas, and the others to deal with the Panamanians on the annexes. On Friday, she joined forces with Kozak to complete the final dash to a treaty. That evening, the Panamanian team—Escobar, Royo, Ahumada, López-

Guevara, and de la Rosa—arrived at National Airport. For the next week, the two sides worked almost around the clock to put the finishing touches to the first major U.S. treaty in twenty-four years.

They started with the preamble and went through every sentence of each article. With the aid of professional interpreters, they assured that the English and Spanish drafts said the same things. There were constant efforts by both sides to make the language more precise and eliminate any ambiguity that could cause future trouble.

As they worked away at the treaty, unresolved issues percolated up from the teams working on Lands and Waters in Panama. After a few days, Bunker concluded: "This is crazy, trying to operate in two forums. We ought to get them up here." He discussed it with Escobar, who concurred. The word came to the embassy, and Wyrough and the U.S. military team caught the next plane for Washington. Edwin Fábrega and his technical assistants followed close behind.

One problem thrown into the negotiators' laps was a seemingly trivial yet highly emotional one. It concerned use of military post offices and commissaries by canal employees. It had been agreed for months that the separate postal system and commissaries run by the Canal Zone would be abandoned. But company officials were arguing that the post offices in downtown Balboa and Colón be retained as U.S. military post offices. If that was out of the question, they wanted to have at least separate windows and P.O. boxes retained for exclusive use by American employees. They also wanted company grocery stores near the housing areas at both ends of the canal to continue operating as army stores.

I did not realize what difficulties this created until I got an impassioned phone call one evening late in August from Gabriel Lewis. The ambassador was furious and the more he talked about it, the louder his voice rose and the stronger his language became. I was soon holding the receiver a foot from my ear to save my eardrums from permanent damage. I tried to calm him down. I could see that retaining a U.S. post office in the center of Balboa would be offensive to any Panamanian, but what was the harm of having a window set aside where one could buy U.S. stamps and mail a package home?

"It's just more of the same thing we've been trying to get rid of for fifty years," he roared. "Separate windows, separate facilities, special privileges."

Gabriel had always been tough on the main issues in the treaty—on sovereignty, perpetuity, and other sensitive matters. But I had never seen him so emotionally aroused as on this question of post offices and grocery stores. I could see his basic point and I promised to look into the problem and do what I could. But I urged him not to make a minor difficulty into a test of whether the treaty itself was good or bad. "But it is a test," he said.

"A test of whether all this talk about sovereignty, and independence, and fairness is real, or just talk."

I called Sol Linowitz and described my talk with Gabriel. I told him that it was certainly not worth endangering the new arrangement for the sake of minor conveniences. I could see no good reason why canal workers couldn't use a little more gas to buy their stamps, as most Americans did. Perhaps the only answer was some kind of interim arrangement on the commissary problem that would gradually wean the Zonians away from their sheltered past. He promised to try to work something out.

By September 1, the negotiators had completed work on the basic canal treaty and most of the implementing agreements. Some troublesome annexes still were not completed, but the broad understanding was finished. The Panamanians felt they had enough in hand to go home and get final approval from their government. The afternoon they flew to Panama, there was one more trying session in the State Department on the "colonial nature" of post office and commissary privileges. Ambassador Lewis was still arguing they should end the day the treaty went into effect. His colleagues recognized this was nonsense, but they were by then reluctant to try to moderate his position. "Gabriel is absolutely crazy on this subject," one of them said, "and we can't talk to him any better than you can."

With Linowitz doing a masterful job of accommodating the seemingly irreconcilable, a final solution was found. The Balboa and Cristóbal Post Offices would be Panamanian, but the U.S. forces would have space there "for bulk mail sorting and as postal distribution points." Procedures would be worked out by the U.S.-Panama Joint Committee, but there would be no separate "Americans only" window. The former Canal Zone commissaries in Balboa and Coco Solo would continue to function, but as U.S. Army commissaries and only for six months, though the time could be expanded to thirty months "unless the two Parties otherwise agree."

Meantime, invitations had gone out to the heads of all governments in the hemisphere (except Cuba) to witness the signing of the Panama treaties. By the beginning of September, most had accepted, from Canada's Prime Minister Pierre Trudeau on the north to Chile's military President Augusto Pinochet Ugarte to the far south. There were two notable holdouts—President José López Portillo of Mexico and Brazil's General Ernesto Geisel. Both pleaded urgent business at home that prevented their travel that week. Mexico sent its foreign minister, Santiago Roel, and Brazil's representative was Vice President Adalberto Pereira Dos Santos.

By the Labor Day weekend, official Washington's attention had shifted from policy to protocol. With fourteen presidents, three prime ministers, and high-level representatives of nine other countries about to descend on the capital, the official planners and arrangers were under incredible strain.

They were making lists, charts, and diagrams into the small hours of every night. Thousands of people, from security specialists to pastry cooks, were worrying about their particular role in the extravaganza. It would be the largest assemblage of foreign leaders in our nation's capital since the funeral of former President Eisenhower. More chiefs of state in the Western Hemisphere had not been in one place together since President Johnson went to Punta del Este in 1967.

With all that going on, one would have assumed the business of making a treaty had ended. Not so. On Saturday night, September 3, Ambassador Lewis called Kozak and Chester at about 10 o'clock. Could they come over? López-Guevara had called from Panama and had something urgent to discuss. When they arrived, Gabriel picked up his red phone and got Carlos on the line. The lawyer explained that General Torrijos had been reading the treaty and had come across a phrase he really did not like. It would have to be changed. The Americans groaned. Carlos explained it was the second sentence in Article IX, the one that said that Panamanian law would not be applied to events that occurred in the Canal Zone before the new treaty went into effect. Torrijos thought the wording was terrible—"the laws of the Republic of Panama shall not be applied . . ." How could it be changed? The Americans promised to look at it and see what might be done. Carlos explained it was not the principle—the Panamanians knew something of the kind had to be included. But the wording was unfortunate.

It was impossible at that hour to reach those who had to be consulted for a wording change in the treaty. One problem was that Herb Hansell, the legal adviser, had already sent the text to the printers. At that point, any change was a major change. Kozak and Chester attacked the problem with customary ingenuity. They reworded the article to say that Panamanian law *would* apply to previous events in the Zone but "only to the extent specifically provided in prior treaties and agreements." That meant, of course, that it did not apply at all since previous treaties gave Panama no real jurisdiction in the Zone. But it had a nice positive ring, and that was what the Panamanians wanted. All concerned agreed to the meaningless change early Sunday morning. It was the last revision in the text of the Panama Canal Treaty.

The next day, Monday, September 5, there was controlled pandemonium at Tocumen airport as the clock moved to 2:00 P.M. General Torrijos was about to leave for Washington and it seemed that half the population of the capital was either going with him or was there to say good-bye. He had kindly invited Mili and me to join him on the flight and we were in the middle of the milling, laughing crowd. Everyone was either drinking champagne, shaking hands, embracing family, or trying to make sure their luggage had gone aboard the Air Panama jet. It was a carnival without music. The only unsmiling face I noticed was that of the general's long-suffering, sensitive wife, Raquel. She appeared far from sure the demands of the days ahead were going to be fun. Raquel was a private person, happiest at home with family or close friends. Her husband's flamboyant public life held no appeal for her.

The lively mood continued through the flight to Washington. There were thirty-seven people in the official party, but Torrijos had invited an additional eighty Panamanians to make the trip and witness history in the making. There were, in addition to a large press contingent, leading representatives of business, labor, the government, Church, university students, and a considerable technical staff.

The entire group was keyed up. People wandered up and down the aisle, drinks in hand, joking with friends, discussing the treaties, and feeling proud to be part of the moment. Torrijos ambled through the plane, stopping here and there to visit with his guests, obviously delighted with events and fully aware he was riding into history.

The Panamanian jet made a smooth landing at Andrews Air Force Base and taxied to a stop near the roped-off reception area. The welcoming committee was headed by Secretary of State Vance and his wife, Gay. After the handshakes and introductions, Vance led the General along a red carpet to the microphones. A military band played the two national anthems, and Vance made a brief but warm welcoming speech. Torrijos responded, saying he was happy the United States had decided to "correct an error instead of prolonging an injustice for eternity." The ceremony completed, we climbed into the cars of the motorcade and made the quick trip into Washington with police motorcycles clearing the way.

We pulled to a stop on Jackson Place facing Lafayette Square across from the White House. The carefully restored brick townhouse assigned to the Torrijos family was the alternate guest house for foreign visitors (Blair House was undergoing repairs). The only person Torrijos had said he particularly wanted to see during his visit, except for President Carter, was Gen. George Brown, the JCS chairman. As we walked into the Jackson Place house, I saw the tall air force general standing by the fireplace in the living room. The two military men greeted each other warmly. Two years earlier, on Contadora Island, the generals had sized each other up, listened carefully to what the other had to say, and decided they liked what they heard.

The three of us went to a separate room, ordered drinks, and reminisced. Torrijos recalled that Brown had asked him to keep things quiet until the political process could work, and he had done so. Brown remembered he had told Torrijos that he was sure a good treaty would come out in time, and it had. "We both kept our word," the Panamanian leader said. The JCS chieftain reminded Torrijos that the battle was not over yet; there was going to be a long, hard struggle to get the treaties approved. "I don't have to tell you, General, that any outbreak of violence in your country during this fight is not going to help either of us," Brown said. Torrijos nodded. "I know," he said. "Don't worry."

There was considerable discussion of what the treaties meant in terms of increasing military cooperation between the two countries. Both men made clear their intention to see that military planning, joint exercises, training, and, if need be, defense of the Canal would be carried out in a spirit of full sharing and mutual trust. As I listened to the exchange, I hoped those responsible in both countries over coming years would have the same attitude reflected at that table in Jackson Place.

Brown rose to go, and the two officers shook hands again. Torrijos said: "I will see you at the signing ceremony and maybe we can talk some more." Brown told him he would not be there. Torrijos was surprised. "Why not?" he asked. "Because the bastards didn't invite my wife," Brown said curtly. Then he walked stiffly out of the room. Torrijos just stood there, staring after the departed general. Then he snapped his heels together and saluted the empty doorway. "That is a man," he said.

The next morning at 10 o'clock, the four men who had negotiated the treaties assembled in the Department of State to initial the final texts. It is the diplomatic way in which envoys tell the heads of their governments: these are finished and correct and good; they are ready for your signature. It was a simple ceremony, deliberately designed not to detract from the formal signing by Carter and Torrijos the following evening. As he held his pen to put his *EB* on the documents, the veteran diplomat Ellsworth Bunker said: "We have come to the end of a very long road." Panama's Rómulo Escobar said it was "a very happy day." Then they went to work putting their initials on the two treaties and the agreements to implement them. Escobar and Royo signed for Panama; Bunker for the United States. Sol Linowitz, the man whose drive and imagination had been so essential to the successful conclusion, sat quietly next to Bunker looking on. He did not sign because his commission as ambassador and negotiator had formally expired. It was an absurdity, of course, and everyone in the room knew it, but such are the strange ways of protocol.

While that ceremony was taking place, a small group had assembled at Jackson Place for the next event. Foreign Minister González-Revilla, Ambassador Lewis, and I were to accompany General Torrijos to the White House. It was no great surprise to me, but it flustered the Secret Service when the general added a few good friends to the entourage. We drove around two blocks, entered the southwest gate, and came to a stop on the driveway closest to the Oval Office. President Carter was standing under the portico talking with Vice President Mondale and National Security

Adviser Brzezinski. He greeted Torrijos with a broad grin and a hearty handshake. The president and the general led the way inside.

President Carter was obviously delighted with the visit of so many Latin American leaders. He thought it would be helpful in dramatizing for the American people the fact that the new treaties, while made with Panama, were an expression of his administration's interest in better relations with the hemisphere as a whole. He was grateful to Torrijos for the general's effective work in encouraging his Latin American neighbors to come. It will, he told Torrijos, be "a great help to me in getting the Senate to ratify the treaties."

Torrijos reminded Carter that while the president had only to worry about one hundred members of the Senate, he had to be concerned with his entire population. Under the Panamanian Constitution of 1972, any treaty concerning the Panama Canal had to be approved by all eligible voters in a plebiscite. Carter asked how that was going to work and Torrijos told him he planned to go to every nook and cranny of his country—"by plane and helicopter, by jeep and by horseback"—to talk with all his people. He said his message would be that though the treaties were not perfect, "they are much better than what we have now." He said he thought he could guarantee success, despite the fact that some Panamanians did not like the treaty and "some don't like me" and would cast negative votes on that basis.

Torrijos reported to Carter what he had told the U.S. negotiators in Panama: "We are selling the same product, but we're selling it to two different customers." Carter laughed and told his guest: "Then we'll have to use two different advertising campaigns."

I had sat in on a fair number of talks between presidents of the United States and foreign leaders and diplomats, but this was the most candid and open I had experienced. One explanation was the nature of the men involved. Another was the freshness of the experience for both leaders. Carter had then been in the White House less than eight months and the diplomatic stage was still unfamiliar. Torrijos had been in power for nine years, but almost all of his attention had been directed to internal affairs. For both, summitry was a relatively new ball game. Whatever the reasons, the talk flowed freely and there was unusual candor on both sides.

"To be honest," said Torrijos at one point, "I never thought we would get to a treaty. In the past, we were always talking around the problem, not getting down to the real issues." I knew the man well enough to realize that he spoke not to flatter—though it sounded that way—when he said: "Some people don't live up to their ideals. You do. This has been an act of valor on your part." Torrijos was not overstating things. At that moment, Jimmy Carter was displaying incredible political courage by putting the prestige of his newly won office on the line in a cause that was certainly less than popular, that was misunderstood by two-thirds of the American people, and that was a ready-made target for opportunists and demagogues.

The case was never put more simply or briefly than when he told Torrijos: "It is the right, the fair, the decent thing to do. And the American people are fair and decent."

And there was never a more apt description of his action than the one Torrijos gave: "It's like jumping out of an airplane without a parachute."

The meeting had been programmed for thirty minutes. It had by then gone on for almost an hour. Still the president did not wish to call an end to it; he was enjoying every minute. Carter asked Torrijos about conditions in the rest of Latin America and for suggestions about what he might do in his meetings with other Latin American leaders that would be useful in the hemisphere. Torrijos repeated something he had told General Brown the night before. Some of our neighbors, he said, are arming themselves at great expense instead of spending their money on improving the condition of their people. But they are doing it "in the name of the United States," saying that that is what you want. "They are confusing the arms race with their real problems," he said, "and only you can tell them otherwise." He argued that the best people to propose a change in that course would be "representatives of the Pentagon instead of politicians." They listen to the Pentagon, he said, more than to diplomats. He was saying something most diplomats who worked in Latin America stoutly refused to admit, and that recent presidents and secretaries of state had failed to recognize. It was true, nonetheless.

The congenial meeting finally came to an end, and the president gave Torrijos several copies of his book *Why Not the Best?* "They are not very good," he said, "but they sold much better after I was elected." He also gave Torrijos a picture of Panama and the southern Caribbean taken from outer space. It showed in dramatic fashion that Panama provided the path between Atlantic and Pacific. Keeping that path open was what the new treaties were all about. Carter and Torrijos walked together down the path to the general's waiting car. The two men had come, in slightly more than an hour, to feel they had found a partner they could trust.

The next thirty-six hours were chaos for all concerned, not least for the innocent citizens of the District of Columbia who were subjected to more sirens, more traffic jams, more interruptions of normal routine than even jaded residents on the Potomac were accustomed to. Every hour, it seemed, another limousine with police escorts was pulling into the southwest gate of the White House. And if one of the two dozen foreign leaders was not going to see Jimmy Carter, he was looking at the Capitol Building or the Lincoln Memorial. There were planned and spontaneous press conferences going on in every part of town, at embassies and in editorial offices.

Harassed reporters, attempting to cover all bases, were trying to get to President Pinochet for a Chile story, to Prime Minister Trudeau for his latest views on Quebec separatism, to Torrijos for an exclusive side of the Panama story. Everywhere one went within two blocks of the White House or along Embassy Row or at the State Department, one was likely to have to wait while a motorcade passed. No one will ever know how many sprained ankles resulted from tripping over television cables that wormed across every scene of action.

That second evening, Alejandro Orfila, the secretary general of the OAS, was host at a massive reception for all the visitors—and half of Washington—at his organization's headquarters, the stately old Pan American Union Building on Constitution Avenue. There was a magnificent buffet—if you were lucky enough to reach it—laden with pâté, smoked ham, Alaskan crab, sliced beef, huge platters of empanadas. Six or seven bars catered to the thirsty throng.

Torrijos, who hated crowded receptions, was surrounded by reporters and cameras wherever he went. Mrs. Carter, who was representing her husband, moved smoothly through the crowd as though it were a Democratic rally in Chicago or Denver, shaking hands graciously and chatting with the folks. For military chieftains like Paraguay's Gen. Afredo Stroessner, Argentina's Lt. Gen. Jorge Rafael Videla, and Bolivia's Gen. Hugo Banzer Suárez, leaders unaccustomed to having strangers freely approach them, it was a trial. Fortunately, most people present did not recognize most of the visiting heads of state. They stood in corners of the room surrounded by people from their embassies and a few diplomats, then left quietly after a decent interval.

In the middle of the night, two bombs exploded in downtown Washington, one in a large flower pot on a traffic island not far from the White House, the other close to the Soviet Embassy on Sixteenth Street. A group of anti-Castro Cubans claimed responsibility and there was no indication the explosions had any connection with Panama or the treaties. Nonetheless, the bombs gave security officials a sleepless night and made the visitors more than a little uneasy when they heard about them the next morning.

Despite their understandable nervousness, the visiting leaders went through their scheduled meetings without any cancellations. The Council of the Americas, an organization of U.S. business leaders active in Latin America, hosted a luncheon for the visiting delegations at the Kennedy Center. Mrs. Carter took Mrs. Torrijos and the other wives for a cruise down the Potomac and a visit to Mt. Vernon, George Washington's stately home.

That evening, the main event, the central reason for all the frenetic activity of the past days, was at hand. The leaders of the hemisphere gathered at 6:00 P.M. in Secretary General Orfila's office for a reception. While the presidents and prime ministers and other dignitaries sipped champagne and chatted amiably among themselves, the other invited guests were slowly filling up the main ballroom, transformed overnight into an auditorium.

At a few minutes before 7 o'clock, Orfila led President Carter and General Torrijos and the other government leaders into the hall from a side door and up onto the dais, which filled the front of the hall. There were thirty-nine chairs lined up behind the long, baize-covered table that ran the length of the hall. Large crystal chandeliers glistened from above but their glow was made trivial by the powerful glare of the television lights that flooded the scene. In the front row of spectators sat Lady Bird Johnson, the widow of the president who had first promised a new treaty, and Former President Gerald Ford, who had reaffirmed that pledge. Former Vice President Nelson Rockefeller, a good friend of Latin America, was there, and next to him Henry Kissinger who had approved the principles that underlay the new arrangement. There were members of the Senate, who would have to approve or disapprove the treaties, and members of the House who thought they, too, should have a voice in the matter. There was some quiet muttering among members of Congress about being "pressured" by the attendance of all the Latin American leaders—which was, of course, precisely what the White House sought with the display of hemispheric unanimity.

Secretary General Orfila occupied the center chair with Carter on his right and Torrijos on his left. The men who had negotiated the treaties were given places of honor behind their chiefs, Ambassadors Bunker and Linowitz flanking the U.S. president, Rómulo Escobar Bethancourt and Aristides Royo near Torrijos. The visiting chiefs of government and national representatives were ranged on either side the length of the table.

Orfila welcomed the participants and spectators to the Pan American Union, headquarters of the OAS. It was, he said, "your house." In flowery Spanish, he hailed the new treaties as "the turning of a new page in American history."

President Carter said the new pacts "will assure a peaceful and prosperous and secure future for an international waterway of great importance to us all." He said they also marked "the commitment of the United States to the belief that fairness, not force, should lie at the heart of our dealings with the nations of the world." The president stated that the 1903 treaty, soon to be replaced, "has become an obstacle to better relations with Latin America." He called the new arrangement "a symbol of mutual respect and cooperation."

In his response, General Torrijos was considerably more outspoken. He recalled that President Theodore Roosevelt had assured Panamanians in 1904 that "we have not the slightest intention of establishing an independent colony in the Canal Zone." Yet that was what had happened. "Deep within them," Torrijos continued, "what nourished the hopes of Panamanians and fortified their patience throughout these many years was the firm conviction that the people of the United States have no colonialist ambitions, for you were once a colony and fought heroically for your liberty."

Torrijos said the plain truth was that the new treaties did not have the unanimous support of his people. The twenty-three–year transition period meant "8,395 days during which time United States military bases will remain, turning my country into a possible strategic target for reprisal." And he admitted quite bluntly that the Neutrality Treaty placed Panama "under the Pentagon's defense umbrella." That provision, he warned, "if not administered judiciously by future generations, could become an instrument of permanent intervention."

In closing, he recognized the realities of American politics and addressed himself to the members of the Senate who would soon be judging the treaties. He reminded them of a statement attributed to Abraham Lincoln: "A statesman is one who thinks of future generations; a politician is one who thinks of the next election.*

"I return to my country," said Torrijos, "convinced the future of our relations rests in the hands of excellent statesmen."

What the press had been calling "the week of Panama" had reached its climax. Herb Hansell, the State Department's legal adviser, and Ambassador José Watson, Panama's chief of protocol, had been standing by with the leather-bound copies of the treaties. They stepped forward and placed opened copies in front of Carter and Torrijos for their signatures. Each wrote his name four times, on each of the two treaties in both English and Spanish. That done, the two men rose and shook hands and Torrijos impulsively hugged the U.S. president in the traditional Latin *abrazo*. There was prolonged applause as everyone in the room stood to hail the major change in U.S.-Panama relations.

Then the crowd slowly dispersed, the two central figures, their wives, and the other top-level visitors to the White House for an elaborate state dinner; the foreign ministers, ambassadors, members of cabinets, and others to the State Department where Secretary Vance and his wife were entertaining the second echelon of visitors.

In front of the White House and on the Ellipse, some people had gathered to voice their protests—more against the presence of right-wing dictators from the hemisphere than against the Panama treaties. When the Park Police arrested the young man who was organizing the demonstration in front of the Executive Mansion with shouts from a bullhorn, the

---

*The maxim should have been credited to James Freeman Clarke, not Lincoln.

chants in English and Spanish quickly died out and the marchers went home.

There were significantly stronger protests in Panama. Even before the treaties were signed, an estimated fifteen hundred university and high school students paraded in downtown Panama City. Carrying placards denouncing the "Dirty Treaty" and urging "No U.S. Bases," the young demonstrators tried to move on the Foreign Ministry. They were met by a strong force of National Guardsmen wielding rubber truncheons and carrying tear-gas canisters who waded into the middle of the crowd and quickly dispersed them.

In the Canal Zone, when the news arrived that the treaties had been signed, about five hundred Zonians expressed their sentiments with "a funeral procession." Carrying candles and a black box labeled "democracy," they marched to the memorial for George Goethals, the engineer who directed the construction of the canal. They placed their candles on the stone base of the memorial, listened to angry speeches, and sang "The Battle Hymn of the Republic" and "Home on the Range." Then they went home, frustrated and unhappy with the changes that were coming.

In most of Panama City and the other towns, there was a mood of celebration. Much of the population watched the signing ceremony on live television. As it ended, sirens moaned from fire station roofs and other public buildings. People driving cars honked their horns and shouted to each other: "It's done; it's done." Long-planned parties began and went on, and on, into the night.

If a new era had not yet been born, it had been conceived.

CHAPTER 17

The Battle for Two-Thirds

"A man must carry knowledge with him if he would bring home knowledge."

—Samuel Johnson (Boswell's *Life of Johnson*)

AFTER two grueling months in Washington, I had returned to Panama the last day of June 1977. My first task was to take care of a visiting senator who had arrived the same day: William L. Scott, Republican of Virginia. His short biography told me he was a lawyer, had spent most of his working life as a government attorney, practiced law privately for several years, then went into politics, winning election to the House of Representatives in 1966. He narrowly won a Senate seat in 1976. A poll of reporters who covered the Congress had rated him among the ten least effective members of the upper house; another survey put him at the end of the line in overall competence.

Because Scott was a member of the Armed Services Committee, the main burden for his care fell to the Southern Command. But at the embassy we wanted every visiting congressman to have a chance to learn as much as possible about Panama and the treaties. I believed that visitors from Washington should meet as many well-informed Panamanians and Americans as we could line up. The night after their arrival, Mili and I gave a dinner for the senator and his wife, Inez. The guests included Panama's minister of housing and four leading businessmen. It gave Scott a chance to ask about the local political scene and the economic situation. We ended up talking mostly about shopping opportunities in Hong Kong, Bangkok, and Indonesia.

Ever an optimist, I thought Scott might handle a one-on-one situation better and that contact with a knowledgeable Panamanian might help broaden the narrow base from which he looked at Panama. My choice for the challenge was Fernando Eleta, one of the most intelligent and worldly of men, a businessman and horse breeder, an engineer and student of history. He had enough areas of expertise to find common ground with almost anyone. I took Scott to Eleta's spacious home and we went directly to his comfortable study. Eleta began by telling the senator it might be useful to recall a little of the background of the controversy. He then recounted some of the events of Panama's birth as a nation and the way the original treaty with the United States was produced.

It was a quite accurate, lucid, and unemotional account of the events of 1903 and 1904. Fernando was laying the groundwork for his central thesis—which was close to the heart of all Panamanians—that our basic contract was unequal and unfair. But he never had a chance to get to that point. After listening to five minutes of history, Scott interrupted his host to say: "I just want you to know that I disagree with everything you are saying."

It was probably the most inane remark I ever heard from anyone in public life. The man was hearing historical facts, things anyone making a judgment on Panama should know. Reasonable men could disagree about the meaning of past events; to pretend they had not happened was utterly incredible. Fernando looked at me with a puzzled expression. I tried to explain that what he had said was historical reality, not political argument. But Scott was adamant. "We have to keep things the way they are," he said. I realized that trying to expose the man to reason and history and a civilized neighbor had been a waste of time. I made a feeble excuse for our departure, and we left. I took him back to his quarters to let him get on with his shopping.

Fortunately for the country, there were many good and thoughtful visitors. I think immediately of William F. Buckley, Jr., the columnist and editor of the *National Review*. Buckley had written several columns critical of the Panamanian government and of any new arrangement. But he believed in first-hand evidence and I gather it bothered him that he was writing about a scene he had not looked into with his own eyes. He came to Panama in late 1976 to remedy that deficiency. He was curious, skeptical, questioning, all the things a good investigator must be. And he brought to the task a command of Spanish and an understanding of Latin American history and attitudes rare among our visitors.

The group I assembled for Buckley was of the same caliber as those who met with the senator from Virginia but the difference in the evenings was vast. The guest-of-honor asked penetrating questions, understood the answers, and sifted the evidence for himself. He picked up a dozen matters he wished to look into more deeply. I arranged meetings with General Torrijos and President Lakas and the two conversations exposed facets of the Panamanian problem he had not previously considered. He went into the Canal Zone and talked with residents there; he conferred with numerous Panamanians. Buckley explored, listened, pondered, and in the end concluded that a change was overdue and just. Then, though it differed with what he had said earlier, he wrote his new perception. A man of not only intellect but also courage, Buckley defended the new arrangement as one that would promote the U.S. national interest, not weaken it. He realized, as jingoists have never understood, what Tennyson meant by saying that, in keeping Freedom's oak alive and strong, "that man's the true Conservative who lops the moulder'd branch away."

Panama City was never high on the list for official junkets. The real *aficionados* of travel to the isthmus were the members of the House Panama Canal Subcommittee, who visited semiannually to see how the canal was getting on, then went fishing, golfing, or shopping with the assiduous help of their hosts in the Zone. But for the average member of Congress, Panama was about as attractive as Sri Lanka or Bulgaria. Then came the treaties.

From February 1977 through January 1978, the U.S. Embassy devoted more man-hours to the care and feeding of the Congress than to any other task. They came in one's and two's, and as many as ten at a time. In less than a year, we hosted half the U.S. Senate, dozens of representatives, and a multitude of congressional staffers. We also had to attend to a steady stream of media people, countless nonlegislative officials, civilian and military, and representatives of interested organizations, from the American Legion to the U.S. Chamber of Commerce. Driving in from Tocumen airport in late 1977, Senator Robert Byrd asked me about the large number of visitors he had heard were coming through. I told the majority leader: "Senator, I sometimes think that we're not running an embassy. What we're operating is the biggest travel bureau in the Western Hemisphere."

I assumed, until proved wrong, that all visiting members of Congress came to see and learn as much as possible. I reckoned that those interested in pure "junketeering" were likely to go to capitals that offered far more lively attractions. So our guiding rule in planning schedules for the many visitors was to give them maximum exposure to all sides of the problem. We provided extensive embassy briefings covering the political situation, Panama's economic condition, the military significance of the canal, and a status report on the treaty negotiations at that moment. We always left plenty of time for questions on anything that particularly concerned the congressmen. Those were usually lively and useful sessions.

We arranged with our colleagues in the Canal Company and Southern Command for detailed discussions of canal operations and of the mission and readiness of U.S. forces in the area. The schedule normally included a helicopter tour so the visitors could see what the canal looked like and how it operated.

We considered it crucial that our visitors hear not just the U.S. view of the canal and our relations with Panama. To get the full flavor of the controversy, the lawmakers had to hear what Panamanians thought and felt.

Consequently, part of the program was a series of face-to-face meetings with officials of the Torrijos government, private businessmen, representatives of the professions and the Church, and students. For larger groups, and for senators in leadership positions, we arranged meetings with General Torrijos or President Lakas, sometimes with both.

To ensure that all segments were heard, we set up meetings with residents of the Canal Zone, usually the more active and vocal citizens among them. Finally, we got the visitors together with American businessmen who had lived and worked in the Republic for some time, many for decades.

Though there was scattered mumbling about the rigor of the schedules, most senators and representatives appreciated the breadth of views they had been exposed to. One described it as "the best cram course on a foreign policy issue that I've ever taken."

Among the several hundred visitors to the isthmus in those years, there was great variety. There were the bright and the dim, the serious and the frivolous, the open-minded and those with blinders. In any such large group, there was a minority who were opinionated, arrogant, or prejudiced, or all three. The majority were serious, inquisitive, searching for a balanced view of a complicated question, and trying to decide how they should vote.

One large group of congressmen and staffers arrived in the middle of February 1977 headed by John M. Slack, a West Virginia Democrat who chaired the Appropriations Subcommittee that oversaw the State Department budget. The ostensible purpose was to look at embassy operations, and three members of Slack's subcommittee were in the group. But five other representatives joined the caravan, two from the Panama Canal Subcommittee and one each from Appropriations, Interior, and Public Works. It was evident that the canal issue and the treaties were the main attraction so we provided a detailed briefing on them. Ambassadors Bunker and Linowitz were on Contadora for the first round of talks under the Carter administration and I invited them to Panama City to talk with the Slack group. We had a long exchange of views in the study at the residence.

As the Slack delegation prepared to leave Panama, they held a press conference in the diplomatic lounge at the airport. It went smoothly except for one member, Robert K. Dornan, the Republican representative from California's 27th District. The former talk-show host, who from the outset was opposed to the treaties, found the microphones and TV cameras irresistible. He used the occasion to attack the Panamanian government for its dictatorial ways and the lack of freedom. He also took the opportunity to deliver a gratuitous insult to President Lakas, whom he described as "powerless" and "a figurehead." While his fellow delegates squirmed, he went on in that vein.

It was one of the worst public exhibitions of arrogance and bad taste I ever saw by a member of Congress. I was tempted to interrupt the proceedings, apologize for the man's gaucherie, and end the conference. But that, I knew, would only draw heavier attention to the incident. So I walked out of the room.

What is wrong with a congressman's speaking his mind? Absolutely nothing—when he is in the halls of Congress, in committee, in his home district, or in his own country. But when he is on foreign soil, he is a guest in the country concerned. As an official, elected or appointed, he should know that his words can be interpreted, more often misinterpreted, as the voice of the United States.

The second thing wrong with Dornan's diatribe was that he did not know what he was talking about. He had been in Panama three days and was in no position to comment on the inner workings of a very complicated political situation. That there were wrongs that needed attention was unquestionable. But one does not correct errors or excesses with insults. His outburst made the job of those who were trying to work quietly for change all the more difficult. Finally, his affront to President Lakas was an outrage. He did not know that Lakas was, in many respects, the man who kept the wheels of government turning in Panama on a day-to-day basis. Certainly he was the dominant figure in economic policy. He was also the principal anchor and source of stability for the large and potent business community. Moreover, the Texas-educated engineer was perhaps the best friend the United States had in government circles in all of Latin America. This was the man Dornan tried to undercut with his ill-informed statement.

Mili and I stood at the foot of the ramp to say farewell to our guests. Impervious to the implications of his performance, Dornan came along to say good-bye. I told him in some detail what I thought of his statement. He said he did not think it was "so bad." "Congressman," I told him, "you have just left a huge pile of broken crockery on the floor. I am going to have to clean it up and I don't appreciate it one little bit."

The other congressmen pointedly remained at a distance. When the Californian climbed into the plane, they stepped forward to say good-bye and thank us for an interesting, useful visit. One leaned over and whispered, "I'm sure you told that SOB what the rest of us would like to have said. We can't be as frank with another congressman as you can. But what he did was an outrage. Thanks." It was a small but sour incident in what had been an otherwise constructive few days.

The senator who unquestionably knew the most about the Panama Canal was Mike Gravel. The Democrat from Alaska had visited Panama several times and had studied the operations and traffic pattern of the waterway in depth. A man sensitive to the aspirations of the less favored, he believed Panama deserved a better deal as a matter of justice. As a realist, he knew that a revised treaty was the best insurance for keeping the canal open. And as an Alaskan, he realized that keeping the canal operable was the best way to move his state's petroleum to the refineries of the U.S. Gulf and East coasts. In fact, the deeper he got into his canal study the more Gravel became convinced the best solution to the whole problem would be construction of a sea-level canal, one that could easily handle the huge oil tankers and the navy's aircraft carriers as well as all other ships.

Gravel was in town when the House Subcommittee on Latin American Affairs came to call. The delegation of five Democrats and three Republicans was led by its chairman, Rep. Gus Yatron of Pennsylvania. Mili and I gave a reception to introduce the visiting legislators to a number of Panamanians with different backgrounds and outlooks. The guests included three cabinet ministers, several politicians, a couple of newspaper editors, some businessmen, and the chief of the National Bank. One can learn a good deal about a congressman at such an affair. Does he talk or listen? What kinds of questions does he ask? Does he seek out those who might know something useful? Does he talk about problems at home or try to learn about problems locally? Is he friendly? Or pompous? Or happy to sit in a corner drinking gin-and-tonic?

There were clearly some pros in the group and some who would have been happier at home. Ben Gilman, the moderate Republican from a district just northwest of New York City, moved from one group to another, stopping always to ask a couple of good questions. Stephen Solarz, a Brandeis graduate from a Brooklyn district, was gathering information in every encounter, probing for new insights, sometimes playing devil's advocate to see what reactions he would get. Gravel was working the group with great skill, garnering political information here, stirring interest in a sea-level canal there.

The biggest disappointment was the head of the House subcommittee. Yatron, from a district northwest of Philadelphia, received his political training in the Pennsylvania House (4 years) and Senate (8 years). Then the principal figure in the House of Representatives on Latin American affairs, he had little knowledge of and less interest in what was happening in the hemisphere. His chief of staff, a former priest in the Orthodox church, could talk of little else than the situation in Cyprus. Yatron's preoccupation was what the voters in his 6th District might think. The suggestion that he give them some basis for thinking in a broader perspective had no apparent effect.

Talking with Yatron about Latin America was doubly disappointing because of contrast. His predecessor as head of the subcommittee was the lively, astute, knowledgeable Dante Fascell. The veteran congressman from Miami understood the issues in Latin America better than anyone else on Capitol Hill. Fascell had moved to the more prestigious International

Operations Subcommittee, but his loss to the Latin American area was devastating.

Another visit stands out in memory—perhaps because it so perfectly illustrated the narrow desire of members of Congress to be able to tell their colleagues "I was there" when discussing a foreign policy issue. The participants were three staunchly conservative Republicans who made a brief trip to the Canal Zone in August 1977. The senior senator was the elderly but still vigorous Strom Thurmond of South Carolina, the "Dixiecrat" candidate for president in 1948. One companion was North Carolina's Jesse Helms, a one-time radio and TV commentator who, by hard work, advocacy of right-wing causes, and an ability to amass vast financial support, had made himself a figure of power in his party. The third member of the trio was the bright but equally conservative junior senator from Utah, Orrin Hatch.

The three were on the isthmus for a day and a half, almost entirely in the Canal Zone, overflying the canal, getting military briefings, and talking with residents of the Zone. We offered to arrange meetings with Americans or Panamanians in the Republic from any categories the senators chose—protreaty or antitreaty, progovernment or antigovernment. But it was apparent from the outset that the minds of these senators were closed, that they wanted no detailed discussions with anyone who might differ with their rigidly held views. Their only request, more to satisfy protocol than for serious discussion of the treaties, was for a meeting with President Lakas—and that produced a near disaster.

As I described him earlier, Panama's president was a tough, Texas-educated engineer. He was an honest, undiplomatic, outgoing man, most of whose views of the United States were shaped by his experiences as a college student in Fort Worth and the Texas Panhandle. When Lakas spoke of U.S. policy in a complimentary way, the senators thought he was trying to soft-soap them. When he contrasted growing up in Panama's multiracial society with the segregation of our southern states, the senators later professed to be offended by the president's "racism" though his intent was just the reverse. Unfortunately, in the long discussion Lakas used a few words and phrases that were common in the American vocabulary for more than a hundred years but recently have diminished in use because of their racist connotations. The Panamanian had learned the words in his youth and assumed Americans, especially from the South, still used them (as indeed many do).

Without asking the president's permission, or even telling him, the senators recorded the session on what I had assumed was a small radio. Back in Washington, they turned the tape over to a newspaper columnist who used it to accuse Lakas of "offensive, racist and archaic American jingoistic language." It was amazing to read that "no American politician even privately uses the language the tape recordings show Lakas using." I wondered which politicians the writer associated with. I had certainly heard the same, and much worse, language used by U.S. senators, congressmen, and, indeed, presidents of the United States. It was a revelation to learn that the three senators were "stunned" by the language. They certainly gave no sign of it at the time. Thurmond had built his political career on a staunch defense of segregation and states' rights. Helms was one of the few members of the Senate who had no blacks on his personal staff. Surely in their travels they had heard those words before.

The affair was offensive in several ways. It was a display of egregious taste for U.S. senators to tape a conversation with a head of state without his knowledge or approval. There would have been howls of rage if the reverse had happened. To pass along such tape to the press was a compounding of low-road politics. And for the columnist to write drawing on lurid words and exaggerated reactions with no effort to discover what Lakas was really trying to say showed a marked lapse in journalistic standards.

A week after the Thurmond delegation's visit, the other senator from South Carolina arrived in Panama. The contrast was notable. Ernest "Fritz" Hollings, a graduate of the Citadel, a lawyer and one-time governor of his state, was a tough-minded, intelligent, no-nonsense politician. He was what is known as a senator's senator, so highly thought of by his colleagues that he nearly beat Robert Byrd in the contest for majority leader in 1976. He listened closely to briefings on the Panama situation, absorbed everything like a sponge, and asked penetrating questions. His primary concern, clearly, was the security of the United States. Would the new treaties promote or weaken American access to the interoceanic waterway now and in the future? Ten years before, Hollings had opposed a new arrangement with Panama. But he had done a lot of thinking and considerable studying since and was not sure he had been right.

He pressed hard for answers with the Panamanians he met, and he did the same with President Lakas. He grilled Lt. Gen. Phil McAuliffe and his Southern Command staff mercilessly for facts and estimates. When he left Panama, I had no idea how Hollings would come out on the treaty question. I only knew we had been dealing with a serious and thoughtful man, and when he cast his vote, it would be enlightened and honest. I told my colleagues in the embassy that if Hollings came down in favor of the treaties, they had a chance; if he opposed them, they were dead.

A few weeks later, I received a letter from the senator thanking us for the way his visit was handled. He included a newsletter he had just sent to his constituents. I was jolted by the first sentence: "Do you want to give the Panama Canal away? NO! I don't either." We're in trouble, I thought. Then I read on. "Neither does President Carter. If President Carter's treaty is not giving it away, what is it doing? *Keeping it to use!* Given the present circumstances, the two new treaties are the only reliable and fair way for the United States *to keep the Canal to use.*" There followed four fact-filled, tightly reasoned pages that covered every key treaty question. It was vastly better and more persuasive than the "fact sheets" then being produced in the White House and State Department. Hollings had done his homework, searched his conscience, and made a tough decision.

The program to educate the Congress on the Panama treaties was by no means confined to visits to the isthmus. A large part, indeed the major part, of the campaign was conducted in Washington. While a new administration was settling in, shifts and adjustments were taking place on Capitol Hill as a new Congress organized itself. One of many changes was the selection of Senator Paul Sarbanes of Maryland as chairman of the subcommittee on Western Hemisphere Affairs succeeding Gale McGee of Wyoming, who had failed in his bid for reelection. The brilliant (Harvard Law, Rhodes Scholar) and thorough Sarbanes was fortunate, as he moved into Latin American affairs, to have the counsel of one of the most experienced staffers on the Foreign Relations Committee. Robert Dockery was one of those valuable staff members who understood thoroughly both his area of responsibility and the arcane workings of the Congress.

At their first working session, Dockery reviewed all the main issues in U.S.-Latin America relations—trade problems, nuclear energy policy, Cuba, Chile, Panama, human rights, terrorism, and the rest. He knew that the White House had ordered a fresh look at the Panama issue, and he read, correctly, the selection of Sol Linowitz to be a treaty negotiator as a sign of serious intent. The Foreign Relations staffer recommended that Sarbanes' first act as chairman should be a closed subcommittee meeting on Panama. "You should invite Bunker and Linowitz to come up," he told the Maryland senator, "and find out where we're headed." Sarbanes, a believer in the Confucian dictum that "the cautious seldom err," took the suggestion under advisement, as he did most new proposals. But after considering it, the senator decided Dockery's advice was good and he acted on it.

The landmark meeting was held behind closed doors in early April. The Sarbanes subcommittee was the host but the entire membership of the Foreign Relations Committee was invited—and most attended. Bunker and Linowitz laid out in detail the kind of treaty they were seeking, and explained why they thought such a pact was in the national interest. They were then subjected to a barrage of questions by such old hands at congressional grilling as Javits of New York, Case of New Jersey, and Church of Idaho. That grueling, two-hour session, as much as any other single influence, helped persuade the negotiators that canal security was the most sensitive treaty issue in congressional circles. That, plus heavy pressure from the Pentagon, convinced Bunker and Linowitz that protection of the canal had to be handled as an issue separate from all other problems.

After that closed-door session, the campaign to win the understanding of senators took concrete shape. The guiding geniuses behind the effort were two exceptional Foreign Service officers, Curt Cutter and Larry Pezzullo of the State Department's Congressional Liaison Office. Both had political savvy and the kind of direct, candid approach to the Congress that is appreciated on the Hill. Neither had served in Panama, but both had spent many years in Latin American affairs and knew the territory well.

After the meeting with the Foreign Relations Committee, Cutter and Pezzullo decided it was essential to get Majority Leader Byrd involved. The West Virginia senator was initially skittish about the venture. He had been one of the signers of the Thurmond resolution, which opposed any surrender of U.S. rights in Panama, and he was far from persuaded a new treaty was desirable. But Byrd was willing to listen to the arguments. In fact, under urging from his chief aide, Hoyt Purvis, Byrd agreed to make his inner office, just off the Senate floor, available as the "classroom" for a series of meetings, or seminars, on the treaty question. The goal was to get as many senators as possible to attend those gatherings to discuss the Panama problem in depth.

The next problem for Cutter and Pezzullo was to enlist the "teachers" for the Senate seminars. The only logical candidates were the negotiators themselves. No one else at the top echelon of the Department had their grasp of treaty problems and the negotiating history. No one of lesser stature would have attracted the attention of busy senators. However, the two ambassadors were not especially eager to make the kind of commitment of time that the Cutter-Pezzullo program demanded. They were busy working out the treaties with the Panamanians and that required concentration and large chunks of time. Though the intellectual exercise had some attraction, the idea of going over the same ground again and again was not appealing. As one who had worked closely with Linowitz said: "Sol likes to do a thing once, and do it well, and then move on." Nonetheless, both ambassadors recognized the crucial importance of persuading senators of the reasons for, and justice of, a new Panama policy. They finally agreed to the meetings in Byrd's sanctum.

Over the next months, at least half a dozen times, Bunker and Linowitz went to Room 209 on the Senate side of the Capitol and met with eight or nine, sometimes as many as twelve, senators. They described the goals the United States was seeking and provided an up-to-the-minute description of the negotiations. Then they fielded questions from the inquisitive and sometimes critical senators. The mechanics and timing of the sessions were the work of Alan Cranston, the majority whip from California. Byrd himself still harbored nagging doubts about the treaties and he did not want to seem to be leading a campaign to drum up support. But he attended several sessions, usually sitting at the back of the room with a yellow pad on his lap, taking copious notes, occasionally asking a pointed question. By the time the treaties were signed, about seventy senators had taken part in one or more of the Bunker-Linowitz "seminars" under the stained-glass window of Byrd's inner office. Several participants later admitted that those frank sessions had influenced considerably their final votes.

The days following the elaborate treaty-signing ceremony in the Pan American Union were one of those quiet periods when one knew some fresh explosion was about to detonate. The morning of September 16, I was reading the local papers, enjoying my second cup of coffee, and listening with one ear to the CBS news broadcast on Armed Forces Radio. When I heard the word *Panama*, I shoved the papers aside and listened more closely. The voice on CBS was saying that the Senate Intelligence Committee had received "potentially explosive information" about wiretapping of the Panamanian Embassy in Washington and "blackmail" in the negotiations. The fanciful account claimed the United States had "bugged" the embassy, that the Panamanians had discovered it, and that they had then used their find to blackmail the U.S. side into making concessions at the negotiating table. It was an incredible tale, but clearly it was going to cause trouble.

I called Washington and found that Bunker had been asked to appear before the Senate Intelligence Committee that same day. In his cool, detached way, Bunker told the committee headed by Hawaii's Daniel Inouye that the story was a total fabrication, that nothing like the purported events had ever happened. Whoever had launched the red herring obviously hoped to sabotage the treaty effort. The notion that men like Ellsworth Bunker and Sol Linowitz could have been pressured by that kind of crude device was patently absurd. Anyone who knew them for ten minutes would have known it was impossible, and the Panamanians had known them both well for some time.

Nonetheless, the committee wanted to nail the story down and Inouye and his colleagues realized that one quick hearing would not suffice. Linowitz had been scheduled to make a major speech to the prestigious Economic Club of Detroit that Monday, but he canceled his appearance and flew to Washington over the weekend. On Monday, he and Bunker, together with CIA Director Adm. Stansfield Turner and National Security Agency chief Adm. Robert Inman, went behind closed doors to talk with the Senate's intelligence panel. Majority Leader Byrd sat in. After long discussion and stiff questioning, the meeting adjourned and Chairman Inouye told the press there was absolutely no evidence or any reason to believe that intelligence activities had had any effect whatsoever on the treaty negotiations. That killed the story, and the antitreaty forces looked for other ways to push their cause.

Ten days later, in Washington to testify before the Foreign Relations Committee, I had dinner with my friend Gabriel Lewis. As we sat in his lounge, I asked him about the "blackmail" flap. He walked behind the couch and dramatically pulled aside the draperies. There, still hanging from long wires, were two "bugs." I looked at them closely, and smiled. "Gabriel, my friend," I said, "that kind of device went out of style fifteen years ago. If I were going to bug you, I certainly wouldn't do it that way." He asked me who could have done it. "I don't know," I said. "Maybe the Cubans wanted to know what was happening in our negotiations." It set him thinking.

Near the end of the evening, he told me: "You know, maybe CBS did it. They sure had the story fast after we found the damn things." I laughed and told him I didn't think CBS was relying on bugging to get its stories. Who put the "bugs" in the ambassador's room remains a mystery to all but those who did it. It certainly was not the U.S. negotiators or anyone associated with them.

The Senate Foreign Relations Committee began hearings on the Panama Canal Treaties on September 26, 1977. It was one of the longest, most intensive congressional investigations of a foreign issue in recent history. It went on for three weeks and the senatorial panel heard seventy-nine witnesses. Eighteen spoke for the administration, fourteen were members of Congress, and the remaining thirty-seven were public witnesses representing every shade of opinion on the controversial treaties. In addition to the large number of people who appeared before the committee, countless others submitted written statements, which were printed in the final report.

One reason for the extensive hearings was to make sure no one could later claim that some important matter, indeed *any* matter, had been neglected. Every member of the Senate panel realized how sensitive the Panama treaties were to public opinion. However strongly a senator may have wished to back the treaties as the right thing to do, he also wanted to protect his political flanks. Exhaustive hearings were one way to do that.

The lead-off witnesses on the first day were Secretary of State Vance and the treaty negotiators, Bunker and Linowitz. Room 318 in the Russell Office Building was filled with spectators, including a large contingent of reporters. The front of the chamber, including the senatorial dais and the witnesses' table, was flooded in light for the television cameras. Committee members had turned out in force and the only notable absentee was Hubert Humphrey, who had returned to his beloved Minnesota to die. Chairman Sparkman called the session to order at 9:36 A.M.

To underline the importance of the hearings on the first major treaty in many years, each senator present delivered a short statement. They were, expectably, noncommittal, all wanting to hear testimony of witnesses pro and con before making a final decision. The one exception was the absent senator from Minnesota. Chairman Sparkman read a message from Humphrey in which the candidate for president in 1968 said he had "pledged to the President my full and active support for the treaties." They would, he told his colleagues, "be viewed abroad by friend and foe alike as a sign that we can make necessary accommodations to a changing world."

Vance, Bunker, and Linowitz each then made opening statements urging approval of the treaties.* That done, the questioning began. The senators were interested in everything about the two treaties—how they were negotiated, what various articles meant, whether U.S. authority was diminished, and, if so, whether it mattered. But it became apparent in the first half hour that the senators were preoccupied by a few central issues and, before the hearings ended, it appeared the fate of the treaties could depend on those questions. One concerned the rights of the United States to protect the canal; a related one was whether the Panamanians fully understood those rights. A second focus of Senate questioning was the right of U.S. warships to pass through the canal ahead of commercial traffic. There, too, senators wanted to know if Panama's interpretation of our rights was the same as ours. There were hundreds of other questions, but those two areas were the ones on which the Foreign Relations panel was concentrating.

What had attracted the senators' attention were some unfortunate and quite misleading statements made in Panama by that country's chief negotiator, Rómulo Escobar Bethancourt. A week after the agreement in principle, Escobar had held a news conference to explain the pacts. As a politician, he wanted to make them as palatable as possible to his compatriots. As often happens in any country, he thought he was speaking to a domestic audience and did not calculate the likely repercussions of his statements in the United States. He said, for example, "The neutrality pact does not provide that the United States will say when neutrality is violated." He also seemed to be denying that "expeditious passage" meant "priority passage" for U.S. warships.

When I heard what Rómulo had said, I knew it was going to cause trouble. I reported his remarks to Washington and suggested we consider immediately how to neutralize them. After talking it over with Ambassador Bunker, we decided we had to protest immediately to the Panamanians. I went to see Foreign Minister González-Revilla, and Bunker discussed it with Ambassador Lewis in Washington. We told both of them

---

*Their statements and the report of the entire hearings are contained in *Panama Canal Treaties: Hearings before the Committee on Foreign Relations, United States Senate, Ninety-fifth Congress* (Parts I, II, and III).

that Rómulo's interpretation of key parts of the treaty did not square with what was said in the treaties or with what the negotiators of both sides had clearly agreed upon. I told Nico that it was going to "raise bloody hell" if Rómulo continued to say those things and that it would put the treaties in jeopardy. Bunker told Lewis the same. In a few hours, we both had assurances that Rómulo would not be repeating his politically inspired interpretations. And indeed he did not thereafter try to make the treaties acceptable by distorting the essential meaning of key articles.

We thought the brief misunderstanding had been more than taken care of at the signing ceremony in Washington when General Torrijos had said publicly: "We have agreed upon a neutrality treaty that places us under the protective umbrella of the Pentagon." Ambassador Linowitz quoted those words in his statement to the Senate committee to underline the point. The general was saying it was the United States and its military power that would be the decisive guarantor of the canal's security and neutrality, and that the United States would decide when that neutrality was threatened.

But that was not enough for some senators. Nor was the assurance that Escobar would not repeat his disclaimers. Sen. Howard Baker, for example, asked if we could get a statement in writing from the Panamanian government saying that Escobar's explanation of the treaties was not that government's position. As an experienced politician, Baker had to know how difficult it was for heads of governments to repudiate close friends and top advisers. (The Bert Lance case was then in the headlines and President Carter was finding it impossible to turn his back on an old friend. Most previous presidents had had similar problems with some advisers.) Nonetheless, Baker pressed the point relentlessly.

"It is far, far too early to judge my position and the Senate's position on this treaty," he told the witnesses, "but I will say that, unless we can have a clear understanding that these statements are not the interpretation placed on these treaties by the Panamanians, the chances for advice and consent are greatly diminished."

Baker raised another controversial point. He told Vance and the ambassadors that he wanted to see the "negotiating transcript, the minutes of the negotiation" as well as "memoranda, cable traffic between negotiators and the State Department and the White House" and presidential review memoranda "and the like." In other words, the complete negotiating record. As he knew perfectly well, the senator from Tennessee was advancing demands that involved not merely the Panama Canal talks but the totality of the government's conduct of foreign relations and the constitutional question of separation of powers.

A special difficulty for the administration was that the request for background data came from Baker and from his colleague, Sen. Claiborne Pell of Rhode Island. Both were highly regarded by the State Department and the White House as serious and constructive legislators. Certainly most of us would have had no qualms about taking the full record to their offices and letting them read all or any part of it. It would, I am sure, have set to rest any concerns they may have had about the meaning of various articles and whether the Panamanians understood them and agreed. That, unfortunately, is not the way things work on Capitol Hill.

The Congress, as every newspaperman in Washington knows, is a sieve. If the administration had acceded to the Baker and Pell requests, what would have happened would have been quite different from what those two gentlemen intended. Copies of the negotiating record would have gone to them and to their fourteen colleagues on the committee. It would have been available to the senators' personal staffs and members of the committee staff as well. Within twenty-four hours, excerpts of the record would likely have appeared in columns and news stories. Some accounts would have been the product of careful analysis; others would have been sensational. In either case, the confidentiality of the negotiating process would have been destroyed. And for every disclosure that came out, accurate or distorted, Panama would have produced its own angry retaliation.

If we had released the text of the Panama negotiations to the Senate, and thereby to the world at large, we would undoubtedly have ended up renegotiating sections of the agreement. More important, the action would have made incredibly more difficult the task of every diplomat and official who tried to work out any problem with any foreign government for the next several years. If negotiators fear their every word may be in tomorrow's newspapers, they are going to be rigid, superpatriotic, and unbending in their demands. Nor are they likely to back away from any position once they take it. Under those circumstances, any chance for success is minimized if not eliminated. Men as experienced as Pell and Baker should have understood that.

Like most such controversies, this one ended in a compromise. The State Department gave the senators summaries of negotiating sessions and a few excerpts that covered essential points. One of the ironies of the whole affair was that no organization or agency in Washington is more protective of its internal records and its behind-closed-doors activities than the Congress of the United States. Committees of the Senate and the House guard the proceedings of their executive sessions as though they were the crown jewels. Yet those discussions are rarely as sensitive as negotiations with a foreign government.

The next day, the committee's witnesses were from the Pentagon—Secretary of Defense Brown, JCS Chairman General Brown, Vice Chief of Naval Operations Adm. Robert Long, and Lt. Gen. Denis P. McAuliffe, commander-in-chief of the Southern Command in Panama. The heart of the military's view of the new Panama treaties was briefly stated by General

Brown when he said: "U.S. military interests in the Panama Canal are in its use, not its ownership . . . Our capability to defend the Panama Canal will be enhanced through cooperation with the government of Panama. The new treaty provides a basis for such cooperation . . ." SOUTHCOM commander McAuliffe put it even more succinctly: "The most effective defense of the canal can be obtained in conjunction with a friendly Panama."

Questioning of the Defense panel concentrated, naturally, on the military aspects of the treaties. Did the pacts give the Defense Department what its leaders and the Joint Chiefs believed they needed to protect the canal? What were the most likely threats to the waterway? What problems would the military expect if the treaties were not approved? In case of an attack, who would be responsible for conducting defense measures?

The committee members, some of the most experienced politicians in the land, were fully aware that the testimony they were hearing was a decisive element in their work. Those inclined to favor the treaties knew they had no chance for success if the country's military leaders had any serious reservations. Every member of the committee was by then being bombarded with letters and postcards from antitreaty constituents. What better way to respond to those often emotional and occasionally irrational attacks than to be able to say: "The top military men in the country support these treaties."

Support them they did, and not begrudgingly, but with vigor and with facts. One of the more telling arguments was that the Department of Defense was not a latecomer to the treaty-making process. Secretary Brown and General Brown and the others had not merely read the final version of the canal pacts and found them acceptable; they had played an active role in developing the treaties and in approving all the essential features as negotiations progressed. Lt. Gen. Tom Dolvin, a deputy negotiator since autumn 1975, was the voice of the Pentagon in the inner circles of the negotiations. Indeed, the concept for assuring U.S. rights to protect the canal was a joint Defense-State product known as the "Brown and Brown formula."

Most critics of the treaties were totally unaware of the close collaboration between State and Defense that had produced the pacts. When they heard that the Joint Chiefs of Staff supported cooperation with Panama, their immediate response was that the military leaders had been "intimidated" or that they were "protecting their jobs." It was an insulting charge and one the top military men deeply resented. When Sen. Dick Clark of Iowa raised this matter, General Brown met it head on.

He began by citing the rules under which senior military officers operated. They gave their best advice to the secretary of defense and to the president, he said, but once a decision was made they supported it. If they opposed the action strongly, they retired and argued against it on the outside. At the same time, he said, they were obliged to answer any questions by a congressional committee "fully and factually." It had been in that context, in congressional hearings, that he and others had opposed administration decisions to halt production of the B-1 bomber and to pull troops out of Korea.

In regard to the Panama treaties, Brown said: "I have personally worked very diligently for four years to achieve these treaties . . . We have worked hard for this treaty because we feel it is right." Admiral Long and General McAuliffe echoed his sentiments. Secretary Brown then intervened to say to Senator Clark: "The kind of charge to which you are referring . . . is an insult to our senior military officials. I believe it is not helpful to the debate, any more than it would be helpful to the debate if the proponents of the treaty were to question the motives, the integrity, or the honesty of those who oppose it."

I testified on the treaties the next day, appearing together with Secretary of the Army Clifford Alexander and Harold Parfitt, governor of the Canal Zone and president of the Panama Canal Company. The committee had heard the secretary of state describe the foreign policy implications of the new treaties. They had received a detailed report on the treaties themselves from the men who negotiated them. And the senators had explored the security and military implications with the secretary of defense and top-ranking military officers. Alexander and Parfitt would be discussing the technical aspects of the new pacts and their operational implications for the canal.

"What I would like to do," I told the committee, "is to look at this matter from the vantage point of the isthmus of Panama. How did we get where we are? Where do we go from here? What course best serves our fundamental interests? How do Panamanians look at all this?" Until then, the discussion had focused on what the treaties meant for us, what they would do for the United States. It seemed to me the senators should also give some thought to what the new arrangement meant to Panama. Having worked on the isthmus for three and a half years, I was in a better position to provide that than the other witnesses.

"Opponents of the treaties would have you believe," I said at one point, "that Panama's key goal is to take over the canal. That, I submit, misses the whole point, the whole explanation of Panamanian attitudes. They want a canal that works well as much as we do. They have pride in it; they benefit from it. The issue, as seen through Panamanian eyes, is not the canal at all. Rather, it is the presence in a friendly country of a zone governed by the United States. It is an area over which Panama—the country in which it is located—has absolutely no control of any kind. If a Panamanian is caught speeding or is involved in an accident, he gets a ticket from a foreign policeman. If the offense is serious enough, he is tried in a foreign court, under a foreign code of laws.

"You and I can well imagine what the reaction would be of an American faced with such a situation. Suppose, for example, that history had dictated that the Mississippi River and a strip of territory on each side were controlled by a foreign power. Suppose that in going from Illinois to Missouri, or from Louisiana to Texas, you had to cross that strip. And imagine, if you will, that you broke the law in some fashion—by speeding or having a taillight out, or whatever—and you were arrested by a French gendarme or a Mexican policeman. It does not take great imagination to know what our reactions would be. Yet that is the situation that our Panamanian friends have found themselves in for the past seventy years. That is what they have for so long wished to see changed."

The hearing went on for more than three hours. Some of the brightest members of the Senate were on that panel and their questions were informed, pointed, and aimed at eliciting useful information. I was especially glad the session permitted some exploration of the Panama question from viewpoints that went beyond "What's good for us?" or "What does it offer that we don't already have?" We got into several wide-ranging discussions of Panamanian politics and General Torrijos and the U.S. role in Latin America. I particularly enjoyed a colloquy with Sen. Joseph Biden of Delaware, one of the smartest of the younger senators. For three days, witnesses and senators had been talking about the U.S. right to "intervene" in Panama if the canal were threatened. Biden's questions gave me a chance to expose the difference between "intervention" as used by the senators and military witnesses and "intervention" in the Latin American vocabulary.

"'Intervention' in Panama and in the minds of the Latin Americans has a very special meaning," I told Biden. "When Latin Americans think about intervention they think of foreign troops coming in, killing their people, removing their government or replacing their government, taking over and running the show, and that is the context of 'intervention' for the last 150 years in Latin America.

"They remember the Spanish, they remember the French in Mexico, they remember Haiti and Nicaragua, and all the rest of it. When they talk about 'intervention' that hits a very sensitive nerve, and it is bloody difficult for any Panamanian to say: 'Yes, we have given the United States the right to intervene.'

"Now when *we* are talking about 'intervention,'" I continued, "we are talking about a very different thing. We are talking about fulfilling a specific treaty obligation to protect the Panama Canal, not to destroy Panama or replace the government, but to protect that canal . . . All these countries that use the canal want to have it protected, want to have it open and safe, and would be quite happy if the United States did protect it."

Biden asked me why, then, were they "so damn upset now with our presence—not Panama, but our Latin American friends?" I told him:

"They are not upset by the U.S. operation of the canal. They are upset by the presence of a slice of territory in which the country on both sides has absolutely nothing to say about what goes on."

Biden responded: "You have—at least for me—in a matter of two minutes succinctly stated what I think is the essence of this dispute that is going on." Soon after, the hearing ended, and senators and witnesses, reporters and staff people went their separate ways. As I rode to the State Department that evening, I thought back over the hours of questioning. We had thrown at least a little light into some of the previous shadows, covered some ground that had not been touched earlier.

It is impossible to live in Washington and follow the workings of government without becoming occasionally cynical about congressional hearings. Often they seem like little more than carefully staged dramas aimed at giving politicians a chance to appear on the evening TV news. Frequently, one gets the impression that the senators or representatives have long since determined their stand on the issue at hand and are simply using the public hearings to buttress their positions, pro or con. Since publicity is the life blood of political careers, politicians and their staffs look eagerly for provocative questions, and the areas that are most sensitive and newsworthy.

Fortunately, there are exceptions to the general rule. When the action of the committee involves a matter of broad national policy or when it has attracted widespread public attention, hearings are likely to be much more thorough than in the normal run of congressional business. Much depends, too, on the quality of the committee itself. In the years since World War II, the Senate's Foreign Relations Committee had attracted more than its share of good minds and serious lawmakers. It was also blessed with a staff that was well above average during those years. The result was that hearings before that committee were likely to be considerably more thoughtful and revealing than most.

Still, one has to wonder what effect congressional hearings have in broadening public perceptions and knowledge. Few Americans, busy making a living, raising a family, paying their bills and taxes, keeping up with their favorite sports, and worried about where the economy is headed, have time to read proceedings of congressional hearings or watch them on television (when they appear). Even the largest, most prosperous newspapers provide only superficial coverage of such discussions; smaller papers give none. I daresay the extensive antitreaty mail campaign, based almost entirely on emotion rather than reason and designed to generate fear rather than understanding, reached far more Americans than did the detailed hearings before the Senate committee. It was infinitely easier to shout "We bought it, we built it, and we should keep it" than it was to ask "Why is there a problem?" and then try to find out.

The purpose of congressional hearings is not to educate the public at large at all, though some legislators continue to argue that dubious point. The main objective is to inform the legislators themselves, to give them the facts and background necessary to reach a sensible conclusion. They also provide a useful barometer for members of Congress that tells them how far out they are sticking their political necks in supporting or opposing an issue. Hearings on the Panama Canal Treaties served both those objectives well.

The Foreign Relations Committee hearings revealed some troublesome problems in treaty interpretation. Those difficulties developed not because of the treaties themselves and their essential meaning, but because of what some Panamanians had been saying about them. Statements by chief negotiator Escobar and legal adviser López-Guevara muddied the waters of the debate in the U.S. Senate more, I am sure, than either of those gentlemen ever imagined. What happened was that both men doffed their diplomatic hats and became politicians. In talks with students and fellow lawyers, and even before the National Assembly, their purpose was to "sell" the treaties. In doing so, they put the best possible light on every article from a Panamanian point of view. Neither had any notion, though they should have, that their words would be rigorously scrutinized in the United States and, specifically, in the Senate.

For example, in one of his dissertations on the treaties, Escobar had insisted they did not give the United States the right to "intervene" in Panama. Given the Panamanian interpretation of "intervention," he was right. But several senators took his phrase to mean that the treaty denied the United States the right to go in and protect the canal, which was absurd. In a sense, it was just the opposite of what Escobar had really said. His point, made before the Assembly and other audiences, was that the United States was a large and immensely strong nation, a "Super Power," and that fact gave the "Colossus of the North" the authority to "intervene" where it chose. The new treaties could not convey, he argued, what the United States already had. Nonetheless, Senators Baker, Stone, Pell, and others were concerned about what looked like a divergence in interpretation.

Another vexed problem flowing from the Escobar and López-Guevara pronouncements in Panama concerned the right of U.S. Navy ships to transit the canal "expeditiously." We read that to mean that the warships of the United States (and of Panama) would have priority going through the canal if they needed it. Secretary Vance made our interpretation even more explicit. In the opening session of committee hearings, the secretary said he read the provision to mean "that our ships, our warships, could go to the head of the line." The Panamanians seemed to dispute that approach. Noting that the Americans wanted the right to "go through first," Escobar had said, "We cannot go that far." But in the same speech, he had admitted that "expeditious passage" meant "passage as quickly as possible." One would have thought the quickest way to go through would have been to go to the head of the line. He never explained the difference but the senators professed to see one.

After the senatorial grilling of administration witnesses, and in the wake of requests for the negotiating record, the administration knew it had a problem on its hands. Logic and legal citations were not enough to quell senatorial demands for clarification. Early in October, Bunker and Linowitz went to the Panamanian Embassy for a talk with Ambassador Lewis. They explained the difficulty to Gabriel and asked if there was some way to get General Torrijos to straighten out the mess. Sol had drafted a statement he thought would meet the requirements and he handed it to Lewis, who agreed to forward it to the general. Torrijos was, at the moment, on his way to Israel on an official tour that would include stops in Belgrade, Madrid, Paris, Rome, Stockholm, Helsinki, Bonn, and London.

President Carter was beginning to feel the heat of senatorial pressure. Talk of amending the treaties was widespread. Some senators felt that was necessary to nail down any possible misunderstanding on key issues. Carter knew that amending the treaties would open a Pandora's box in both the United States and Panama. To block that dangerous course, he sent an urgent message to Torrijos on October 11 asking him to come to Washington to try to solve the problem. The general knew from his ambassador that Carter was not exaggerating the difficulty and he arrived in Washington the evening of October 13.

At 8 o'clock the next morning, the president and Torrijos met in the Oval Office. The beleaguered chief executive explained the troubles he was having with the Senate and the need for clarity on the defense clauses. Torrijos understood the difficulty and was sympathetic, but he said he thought the matter had been clarified when he had stated, at the signing ceremony, that the treaties placed his country "under the umbrella of the Pentagon." He told Carter that statement had created great trouble for him among his critics at home. Nonetheless, he appreciated Carter's problem and said he would go along with a joint statement if that would ease the struggle in the Senate. He explained, however, that he did not think he could do it before the national plebiscite on the treaties, which was scheduled for October 23. He told Carter he was already being criticized for making too many concessions to the United States and it would look like he was bending even further under Yankee pressures.

After forty minutes, the two leaders walked into the adjoining Cabinet Room where their top advisers were waiting. Carter explained the situation, as he and Torrijos had discussed it. He suggested perhaps there could be a secret agreement between them that would describe the meaning of the treaties unambiguously. In deference to Torrijos' internal problem, it could be made public after the plebiscite had been held. As the president spoke, Sol Linowitz shook his head in disagreement. Carter noticed the gesture and asked Linowitz what he was thinking.

Linowitz knew firsthand how great the pressure was in Senate circles to get an unambiguous delineation of U.S. security rights. Some senators were seeking a U.S. definition that would be added to the treaty in a reservation. That, in turn, would have required formal Panamanian acquiescence through negotiation and certainly would have delayed the Panamanian plebiscite. Members of the upper house who took that position had contradictory motives: one group thought it would enhance chances for ratification; another group thought it might so irritate the Panamanians that they would resist the proposal or break off negotiations entirely.

Knowing that, Linowitz argued that the course Carter had suggested would only encourage those who favored a reservation. He thought it would be a major setback if Torrijos left town without reaching some kind of mutual agreement with Carter, and without having that agreement known to the members of the Senate. The president repeated Torrijos' reasons for feeling reluctant. Linowitz then suggested that the two sides work out a statement that would clarify the disputed phrasing in the treaty beyond any question. The U.S. side would handle the statement in its own way, to best meet its needs; Torrijos could use it in his own time and fashion when he returned to Panama. Without that kind of joint effort, Sol told the president and the Panamanians, the campaign to win Senate ratification would become hopelessly snarled and conceivably made impossible.

Rómulo Escobar, the man whose words had created most of the problem in the first place, said he thought the only real difficulty was the timing of an announcement and the way it was handled. He said he thought it would be better if President Carter made the U.S. announcement in Washington and General Torrijos made his in Panama. Torrijos supported that approach and it was accepted.

President Carter then made a point that would prove crucial in succeeding months, though it received little attention in that session in the White House. He insisted that the joint understanding must receive publicity in Panama. "It is important for the people and for the Senate to know that the Panamanian people will vote on October 23 on treaties that we both understand the same way," he said. "It will be better to get 70 percent of the vote in Panama and get ratification [in the Senate] than to get 90 percent in Panama and *not* obtain ratification." Having been badly burned by the freewheeling statements of Escobar and others in Panama, the president also said it was important that, once an understanding had been worked out, no one on either side "say anything to contradict the meaning of that understanding."

Once it was agreed that a joint declaration was necessary, the president and Torrijos asked Linowitz and Escobar to work it out. While Carter escorted the Panamanian leader to his car, the two negotiators with an interpreter sat at the cabinet table and composed an understanding. At Sol's request, they used a statement Carter had made some days earlier as their basic text. The wording on defense rights and responsibilities was quickly agreed. Rómulo's draft of a paragraph on "nonintervention" created problems and required some careful rephrasing. The toughest nut was "expeditious passage." Linowitz tried several approaches and Escobar countered with others. Finally, the Panamanian asked, "What is it you really want to say?" Linowitz explained that what he was looking for were words that would, without being too stark, say that U.S. ships in an emergency could go to the head of the line. "Well," said Rómulo, "why don't we just say that?" Sol was amazed, but immediately wrote it out just that way and Rómulo accepted it. What emerged from the Cabinet Room deliberations were wonderfully nonlegalistic words that anyone could understand.

Rómulo called the embassy, read the agreement to Torrijos, and got his assent. Linowitz then took the understanding to President Carter for his approval. The president was sitting in the small, hideaway office next to the Oval Office with Hamilton Jordan and Jody Powell. Carter read it over, and was delighted. "It's stronger than the one we originally proposed," he said. He called Senator Byrd, told him about the agreement, and said he would like Ambassador Linowitz to go to the Hill to discuss it.

Linowitz sped to the Hill in a White House limousine and went directly to Byrd's office. There he showed the agreement to the majority leader and explained how it had been negotiated. Byrd was highly pleased and thought it would help greatly in the Senate debate. Linowitz went from there to a meeting with key members of the Senate Foreign Relations Committee and showed them the understanding. They, too, welcomed the result. The only problem mentioned, raised by Sens. Howard Baker and John Glenn, concerned use of the phrase "territorial integrity." They wondered how we could insert military forces to protect the canal without violating Panama's territorial integrity. Linowitz explained that what was involved was *intent*. Obviously, in sending forces to protect the waterway, we would have to *use* Panamanian territory. What we were doing here, he said, was assuring the Panamanians we would not be assigning troops to the isthmus to invade the country or annex any territory.

We had some quick consultations with the Panamanians about possible substitute phrases, but by then Torrijos and his advisers were as nervous as the senators about using words that might rise up to haunt them. We decided to leave the statement as it was drafted. Linowitz then appeared before a hastily summoned press conference in the White House to reveal the understanding reached between Carter and Torrijos. It was an item on all the TV network news programs that evening.

The Carter-Torrijos Understanding reached on October 14, 1977, was an essential element in clarifying some perceived obscurity in the original agreement. It was also absolutely necessary to win Senate approval of the treaty. Indeed, it eventually became an integral part of the treaty in the course of Senate deliberations, with the full concurrence of the Panamanians. The understanding said:

> Under the Treaty Concerning the Permanent Neutrality and Operation of the Panama Canal [the Neutrality Treaty], Panama and the United States have the responsibility to assure that the Panama Canal will remain open and secure to ships of all nations. The correct interpretation of this principle is that each of the two countries shall, in accordance with their respective constitutional processes, defend the Canal against any threat to the regime of neutrality, and consequently shall have the right to act against any aggression or threat directed against the Canal or against the peaceful transit of vessels through the Canal.
>
> This does not mean, nor shall it be interpreted as a right of intervention of the United States in the internal affairs of Panama. Any United States action will be directed at insuring that the Canal will remain open, secure and accessible, and it shall never be directed against the territorial integrity or political independence of Panama.
>
> The Neutrality Treaty provides that the vessels of war and auxiliary vessels of the United States and Panama will be entitled to transit the Canal expeditiously. This is intended, and it shall so be interpreted, to assure the transit of such vessels through the Canal as quickly as possible, without any impediment, with expedited treatment, and in case of need or emergency, to go to the head of the line of vessels in order to transit the Canal rapidly.

News stories about the understanding reached Panama quickly but editors and bureaucrats who determined policy for official press organs were unsure how to handle it. The independent *La Estrella* printed a full account, including the text of the agreement, but the others were nervous, waiting assurance that Torrijos was truly behind the move. Their doubts were removed three days later when Escobar held a press conference and explained the new understanding fully. Only then did the other newspapers describe the matter in detail. What really clinched the fact that the understanding with Carter was Panamanian policy was a press conference by General Torrijos two nights before the plebiscite. Carried live on television to all parts of the country, the general's appearance was seen by most Panamanians. The understanding was read in full, and Torrijos endorsed it heartily. When the Panamanian people went to the polls on Sunday, October 23, to pass judgment on the Panama Canal Treaties, they knew what it said and what it meant. In that vote, two-thirds of the Panamanian voters said "yes" to the new arrangement.

Five days after President Carter and General Torrijos reached their agreement, the Foreign Relations Committee heard from Ambassadors Bunker and Linowitz on the understanding. In an hour-and-a-half session, the negotiators carefully explained what each sentence in the understanding meant and why it was included. Several senators wondered why the agreement was not signed by either party. Senator Church pressed the point, and Ambassador Linowitz replied: "The reason it was not signed, Senator, was because it was felt that it added nothing to the treaty itself, that it was a statement issued by the leaders of both countries saying: 'This is what we understand the treaty means.' It was not felt there was any need for signing it as a separate document." That seemed to put the issue to rest, though it was raised occasionally during the Senate debate.

Sen. Robert Byrd's personal journey through the Panama maze—from opponent, to skeptic, to strong supporter—was a crucial part of the Panama story. Absent the majority leader's imprimatur, the Panama pacts would still be languishing in a senatorial pigeonhole. With his support, they went to the head of the Senate's action list.

In the early and mid-1970s, the impulse to get a new arrangement with Panama came under two Republican presidents. As a leading Democrat on the Hill, Byrd viewed the treaty-making drive as a Republican initiative, even though it had begun under Lyndon Johnson. The West Virginian also knew from his mail that the issue was not popular with many of his constituents. But when Democrat Jimmy Carter occupied the White House and made Panama his Number One priority in Latin America, Byrd felt he had to take a fresh look.

The start of that new look began with the senatorial "seminars" conducted by Bunker and Linowitz. The quiet, often stern appearing, majority leader frequently attended those sessions. Obviously, he knew his role would be central to any successful treaty effort and he wanted to be on solid ground before he took a stand. He gave a couple of my colleagues a compressed but accurate analysis of the outlook. "You're not going to get a treaty without me," he told them, "and you're not going to get a treaty without Senator Baker. If you have both of us, you *might* get a treaty."

But even when the basic principles of the new treaties had been agreed upon in early August, Byrd still had not made up his mind. Two weeks later, President Carter sought to nudge the majority leader into positive action and invited him and his wife, Erma, to the White House for dinner. Before and after the meal, the president and the most powerful man in the Senate talked about Panama. Carter explained his reasons for seeking a new relationship with Panama, the justice of that cause, and the meaning it would have for U.S. relations in the rest of the hemisphere. Byrd listened carefully, then explained how difficult it would be to win Senate approval for such a politically unpopular action. He still made no promises and, as he said the next day: "I told him the treaty has an uphill road to travel for ratification."

Once the treaties were signed (in September), room for maneuver on Byrd's part narrowed sharply. He was going to have to bite the bullet—either back the Democratic president's hand or declare himself in opposition and thereby kill the treaties. Carter and his principal advisers had decided it was politically imperative to get action on the Panama arrangement by the spring of 1978. Otherwise the issue was going to distort, and be distorted by, the congressional election in the fall.

Byrd was, by then, leaning toward the treaties but he still harbored serious reservations—especially regarding U.S. defense rights and Panama's General Torrijos. He wanted to reassure himself on both counts and decided he could only do so by going to Panama. Known as both a thorough and cautious legislator, Byrd decided to share both the work and the responsibility with six of his Democratic colleagues. They were Walter Huddleston (Kentucky), Spark Matsunaga (Hawaii), Howard Metzenbaum (Ohio), Donald Riegle (Michigan), Paul Sarbanes (Maryland), and James Sasser (Tennessee). Only Sarbanes was from Foreign Relations. The others represented a wide range of senatorial committee interests, from Agriculture to Veterans Affairs. Of the six, only Matsunaga had publicly declared his intention to support the treaties.

CODEL (Congressional Delegation) Byrd arrived in Panama on November 9. In addition to the senators, ten others were in the group—three from Byrd's staff, three from the State Department, two from Defense. Most interesting was the inclusion of two of the sharpest political operators on the Hill, Bill Hildenbrand, the secretary of the Republican minority in the Senate, and Howard Liebengood, a top assistant to Senator Baker. When I saw their names, I knew that Baker was doing some advance scouting, obviously with Byrd's cooperation.

On the drive into the city, Senator Byrd and I went over the plans for the visit and he approved the entire schedule. We talked a bit about the treaties and it was clear that the majority leader was still struggling with the problem. "Frankly, I still have some serious questions," he told me. "I hope this trip will resolve them." I apologized for the rigorous schedule that left practically no time for leisure. "Don't worry," Byrd said, "that's what we're here for, to work."

We went to the embassy for a briefing by the Country Team. I knew these visitors did not want or need a history of Panama or an analysis of the economy. We kept it short and then jumped right into questions and answers. Every member of the Byrd delegation was intelligent and thoughtful. They also arrived in Panama as one of the best briefed groups on record. On the flight from Washington, Ambler Moss, Sol Linowitz' deputy during the negotiations who had recently returned to State to help with congressional relations, spent two and a half hours giving the senators facts and background. He explained all the essential features of the treaties, discussed how they had been negotiated and how the two countries looked at the crucial questions. The results of that thorough cram session were evident in the sharp questions the senators asked.

That evening, I gave a dinner for the visitors and introduced them to a group of leading Panamanians—government officials, businessmen, lawyers, educators. I divided the guests into seven tables with senators, staff, Panamanians, and a handful of Americans from the community well mixed. The conversations at each table were lively, probing, informative. At the end, I offered a toast welcoming our visitors and urging that both sides work toward better understanding. Senator Byrd responded with an eloquent description of American politics and with some thoughts our Panamanian guests badly needed to comprehend. "What you have to understand," he told them, "is that any senator voting for these treaties will pay a high political price. He will gain absolutely nothing personally by doing so. Therefore, you have to be tolerant and patient in bringing people around to understanding these problems and to taking this difficult decision."

They could pretend otherwise; they could ask about politics and human rights; they could study the balance sheet of the Canal Company; and they could check out the readiness of the 193rd Brigade. But what every member of Congress who came to Panama wanted more than anything else was to meet Gen. Omar Torrijos Herrera. They had heard all the epithets in common use—"dictator," "strongman," "tyrant." They had read the gossip—about his capacity for hard liquor, his womanizing, his alleged friendships with Castro and Qaddafi. Many had seen news stories and commentaries about his drive to improve the lot of his countrymen, especially in the countryside.

He was a complicated mix of good and bad, of openness and mystery, sophistication and naïvete. But probably the most compelling attraction was power. Here was a man who had seized it by force, held it for (by then) nine years, used it with moderation, and, by all appearances, retained the support of his people throughout. For men whose life is politics, there is no greater magnet than power, for themselves and in others. It holds a special fascination, to say nothing of its ability to attract headlines.

On their second day in Panama, the seven senators went from morning to night in the company of Panama's leader. We flew first to the San Blas Territory on the northeast coast, the home of the Cuna Indians. The Cuna are a proud and independent people who, almost miraculously, have managed to retain their ancient ways and tribal structure into the modern era.

We landed on a dirt airstrip in San Blas while the senators, used to big jets and long paved runways, gulped and held tight to the arms of their seats. Then we climbed into small boats, badly overcrowded and swaying with the uneven loads, to cross the lagoon to the island that was our destination. The Cuna, never too fond of the Panamanians, had raised an American flag in front of the local school—as a gesture of welcome to the visitors and a mark of defiance to the legal authorities. An angry National Guardsman took it down, but Torrijos called attention to the incident. He told the senators they were in the midst of some very strong-willed people.

What followed was a scene that Gilbert and Sullivan would have loved. It was a town meeting, a congressional hearing, a piece of light opera, and grass-roots politics combined. I had seen Torrijos at that kind of affair in towns and villages across the isthmus, so I knew it was standard practice for Omar. But I knew some of the senators wondered if it was not elaborately staged for their benefit. After a few minutes, they knew it could not have been planned.

The central figure in the drama was a stern-faced, middle-aged Cuna woman who represented the matriarchal tradition of the tribe. She stood in the sun facing Torrijos, who sat under an awning surrounded by the senators and the other guests. She wore the traditional, high-necked, heavily brocaded dress of the tribe in black, gold, and red. There was a gold ring in her nose and around her neck hung a small fortune in finely worked gold necklaces.

Torrijos began the session jovially, commenting on the friendly reception and wondering if there were any problems. The Cuna princess responded in her native tongue, which was then translated into Spanish. She welcomed the distinguished visitors and said it was a proud day for her and her people. Then she took Torrijos at his word. "You asked about problems," she said. "I will tell you what they are." She then launched into an extensive catalog of complaints—too much interference from the central government, she said; too many orders and not enough help; an unreliable water supply (from the mainland); poor health care for the children, much less than for the Panamanians. It went on, with Torrijos trying to explain but regularly being cut off by the tough-minded, outspoken Cuna leader.

The visitors from Washington could not believe what they were hearing. Having grown up paying obeisance to the glories of the American town meeting, few had ever lived through one. Here, on a remote island in the Caribbean, in the company of a supposed iron-fisted dictator, they were seeing grass-roots democracy in action. It was totally different from anything they had heard or imagined. They would think of the scene later as they heard colleagues in the Senate who had never met Torrijos mouthing tired clichés about Panama's "tinhorn dictator."

From San Blas, the Byrd party and the general flew to the city of Los

Santos on the Azuero Peninsula, southwest of Panama City. The citizens of Los Santos, in the heart of good cattle and farming country, were celebrating the 156th anniversary of Panama's declaration of independence from Spain. It was another eye-opener for the visiting politicians. Here was the much maligned "dictator" walking up the dusty main street of a provincial capital with no car, no ring of bodyguards, no one pushing the crowds aside. He was surrounded by children who pulled on his trouser legs, touched his canteen, laughed when he picked one of them up to ask a question.

Byrd and the other senators walked along in Torrijos' wake, shaking outstretched hands, returning the greetings of the people. A ragtag band was playing traditional Panamanian music. The people were drinking beer, dancing, laughing. It was dusty, hot, lively, friendly—nothing like what the Americans had expected. By then, their ties were gone, stashed in the pockets of the jackets they were carrying over their arms. The senators knew a master politician when they saw one and they were adjusting to the mood.

But the senators never forgot why they were there. On the plane ride from San Blas, and again on the trip from Los Santos to Torrijos' seaside house at Farallon, they grilled the general unmercifully. What about political freedom and free elections, they asked. Why have you sent some of your people into exile? When are you going to step down as ruler? Why do you have relations with Cuba?

I was amazed at Torrijos' restraint and patience. I was also surprised by the occasional rudeness of otherwise thoughtful men. Some were confirming by the minute the picture much of the world has about the arrogant "ugly American." I knew the general's gut reaction would have been to open the plane door and drop a couple of them into the Pacific. But he held his stiff Indian face, answered quietly, tried to be reasonable. He knew how much was riding on the opinions of these men. But when I saw his molars grinding, I intervened, tried to soften the questions, and in a few cases gave an answer that allowed the general to sit back and regain his composure. What was surprising was the insensitivity of some of these otherwise sophisticated men. If they had tried the same tactics with a de Gaulle or a Brezhnev or a Castro, they would have been shown the door.

To be fair, Senator Byrd himself usually probed with care. Paul Sarbanes put even sharp questions in ways that were not offensive. And Spark Matsunaga could never, I think, be rude. But there is something about the congressional experience—perhaps sitting so much in chairs that are above floor level and looking down at witnesses—that produces a kind of superior, judicial attitude. Many legislators come to think they are prosecuting attorneys, judges, and juries as well. They could have asked the same questions, elicited the same information, without putting themselves on pinna-

cles of moral righteousness. But power and grace are rarely balanced evenly
in any man.

The questioning went on for three hours and it was intensive and detailed. As they walked from the seaside house at Farallon, one senator told
a CBS reporter: "It was one of the toughest interrogations that could be
made of any man." Senator Metzenbaum, one of the more vigorous questioners, commented: "I feel it is just to say that General Torrijos has impressed all of us favorably, particularly by his honesty and frankness." If
their final meeting with the general went as well as the one just concluded,
he said, "I would not have any difficulty in confirming that I would vote
for the ratification of the treaties."

The next day was crammed with activities. The senators flew over the
canal in helicopters, then received a briefing on the military situation from
General McAuliffe. They met with Governor Parfitt and Canal Company
officials for a discussion of canal operations and the impact of the treaties.
We had arranged for each senator to meet separately with small groups of
Canal Zone residents to hear their side of the story. Later in the day, the
visitors conferred with leading Panamanians to get their views.

That evening, President Lakas welcomed the senators and staff to the
presidencia and hosted an elaborate reception and dinner. Despite the formal setting, it turned out to be one of the more relaxed and convivial
events of the visit. Lakas was in high spirits and moved easily through the
crowd, booming out greetings in the accents of Texas. He made it a point
to visit with each of the senators and thanked them for taking the time and
trouble to come to his country and look into the treaty problem personally.
The top level of the government was there and that gave the senators a
chance to explore aspects of Panamanian society they otherwise might
have missed—economic problems, labor, housing, banking, and foreign
relations.

The dinner was sumptuous and lively talk flowed around the long table
in the State Dining Room. A small orchestra played softly from the balcony overhead. I had told the president that Senator Byrd's favorite hobby
was playing country music on the fiddle. During the meal, Lakas and Byrd
got along famously and, after the toasts had been exchanged, the president
pressed his visitor to honor the others with a tune. Byrd finally relented
and a violin was commandeered from the orchestra. The West Virginia
statesman played "Turkey in the Straw" and the prolonged applause led to
several encores. People were tapping their feet and drumming on the table.
The Panamanian *presidencia* had never seen anything quite like it. When
Byrd finally returned the violin to its owner, Lakas took off his necktie and
handed it to the majority leader as a gesture of thanks, and of friendship.
Byrd reciprocated.

As I sat listening to the West Virginian playing the fiddle in the home of the Panamanian president, I believed he had finally made up his mind. At that moment, he seemed to have concluded that the new treaties and U.S. friendship with Panama were political goals worth pursuing, though he knew it would be costly to him and all who went that way.

Stories about the Byrd delegation's visit to Panama, the senators' intensive questioning of Torrijos, and the general's patience and his forthcoming answers appeared in newspapers across the United States. One man who read them was a gruff, popular, politically conservative actor named John Wayne. From his home in Newport Beach, California, Wayne sent Torrijos a cable congratulating the general for his "frankness and open-mindedness with our Senate committee" and also for his "patience with some of our leadership who would use this sensitive situation for political expediency." Wayne said he thought Torrijos' actions would persuade many Americans "of the honesty and decency of your intentions and the dignity of the Panamanian people."

Duke Wayne became involved in the Panama issue almost by accident, though he was one of very few public figures embroiled in the matter who knew Panama intimately. He had visited the isthmus many times over a period of forty years and his first wife was Panamanian. When the Panama treaties were signed in Washington, Wayne sent messages to both President Carter and General Torrijos congratulating them and hoping the new arrangement would serve the best interests of both countries.

Torrijos' overeager advisers saw a chance to grab a headline and put out the story that the veteran Hollywood figure was backing the treaties (which he was not at that point). The erroneous story irritated the crusty old actor, generated some vicious hate mail (which irritated him even more), and stirred him to take a real interest in the treaties. I was with Torrijos the day after Wayne's message arrived and he showed it to me. I told him that few Americans' support would mean more to the success of the treaties than that of Duke Wayne, an authentic folk hero. The general said he wanted to send Wayne a message, told me what he wanted to say, and asked me to put it into English. I wrote it out on the back of a scratch pad. Torrijos told Wayne: "I see the new treaty as the opening of a very new period in history—a period in which Panamanians and Americans are working together to keep the canal open to all the world. It will be a time in which anyone who tries to destroy the canal will have to stand against us both." He begged Wayne to "help your fellow countrymen . . . know that we have a great future ahead of us as friends and partners."

That same day, at Torrijos' urging, a Panamanian businessman and friend of Wayne, Arturo McGowan, called the Duke in Newport Beach and asked how he could help on the treaty problem. Wayne asked McGowan to come to California to talk about the new agreement in detail. He wanted to know much more about it than he did. McGowan went immediately, taking along two men who had worked on the treaty and the Status of Forces Agreement.

For two days, they were closeted with the outspoken old screen veteran, going over every article in the treaties, answering his tough questions, finally convincing him the deal was fair and balanced and good for both sides. At the end of that intensive study, Wayne said he was ready to back the new pacts. McGowan returned to Panama and gave the news to Torrijos and the general gave it to the press. Soon, Wayne's Newport Beach telephone was ringing every ten minutes. U.S. reporters wanted confirmation or a denial. Wayne told them it was true, he was supporting the treaties "if what I understand about them is true." One West Coast reporter began his story: "Actor John Wayne won't be saddling up to join Ronald Reagan in his fight against ratification on the Panama Canal Treaty. Wayne has signed on with the pro-treaty outfit."

From then on, Wayne and Reagan were engaged in a running verbal gunfight on the issue. The Duke believed his friend Ronnie had been pushed into an extremist position by the pressures of the 1976 campaign and he begged him to reconsider his stand. "My reaction," Wayne wrote, "was that the Rockefeller group was doing the same thing to you they had done to Goldwater, trying to make you look like a warmonger by bringing up a subject which you had not had time to review." He offered to have McGowan call on Reagan to analyze the treaty and give Panama's viewpoint. Reagan declined the offer and that prompted Wayne to write a scathing letter. He recalled the many ways he had helped Reagan's career—from the days of bitter fights with left-wingers in the Screen Actors Guild, which Reagan headed, to the actor's political campaigns. Against that background of active assistance, to say nothing of long friendship, he thought the former California governor at least owed him a hearing on the Panama issue.

In the same letter, Wayne told Reagan: "The Panamanians have always been a friendly country to us. I am sure it is quite embarrassing to General Torrijos to be called a 'tinhorn' dictator, and I didn't feel that was your style. I hope they weren't your words. That is more the style of a liberal punk who doesn't have to answer for his words." Wayne was clearly furious. He attacked Reagan's notion of making the canal the responsibility of the Inter-American community rather than turning it over eventually to Panama. That course, Wayne claimed, "opens up a wider area for leftist governments to become involved . . . It is exactly what the Commie line is suggesting for the Canal."

Wayne was by then getting a flood of mail, some from acquaintances of long standing, others from people who had admired him from afar, asking about his stand on the Panama question. He sat down and composed in the next days a three-page statement that gave his views. It was not fancy, as the man was not. It was not graceful, as he was not. But it was honest and direct and impressive, as he most certainly was. No one but the Duke himself could have written it.* He sent it off in answer to every letter that complained of his position. He also sent it, with a covering letter, to every member of the Senate. No doubt it gave some of the fainthearted an injection of new courage.

Reagan, stung by Wayne's attack, finally agreed to see McGowan. But three weeks after Wayne's rather harsh letter, Reagan spoke to a group of Orange County, California, doctors and repeated his by then familiar attack on the treaties, with his own peculiar version of history and of those documents. When the possibility was raised of the canal's being closed if a new approach were not adopted, he passed it off as "an empty threat." "The canal represents three-quarters of Panama's gross national product," he said (which was not even close to the truth). "They wouldn't dare close the canal." He did not know Torrijos or the Panamanians, of course. Nor had he read speeches in the British Parliament of two hundred years before in which it was confidently asserted that "those raggedy colonists" in Massachusetts and Virginia would never revolt because it would destroy them economically.

The next event in the Wayne versus Reagan controversy began with a letter Reagan signed in late October for the Republican National Committee which concentrated on the Panama issue and ended with an appeal for money. The Reagan letter was an incredible document, filled with misstatements, distortions, inaccuracies. It drove Duke Wayne up the wall. He took it apart, statement by statement, paragraph by paragraph. Then he fired off a letter to Reagan pointing out the errors of his former friend's ways. To put no fine point on it, he told Reagan that "most of the alarming things that you are saying are untruths." He attached to his letter a five-page, single-spaced rebuttal of Reagan's major points. As the outspoken Wayne put it: "Now I have taken your letter, and I'll show you point by God damn point in the Treaty where you are misinforming people. This is not my point of view against your point of view. These are facts."

There was a note of real regret in Wayne's letter to a man he once had backed fully. "You have lost a great and unique 'appointment with history,'" he told Reagan. "If you had given time and thought on this issue, your attitude would have gained you the image of leadership that I wished for you, rather than, in the long run, a realization by the public that you are merely making statements for political expediency."

In the attachment to his letter, Wayne picked nine of Reagan's principal contentions and argued that each was either "false" or "complete untruth"

---

*John Wayne's statement is in Appendix B.

or "completely misleading." One example will suffice. Reagan had alleged of the Neutrality Treaty: "Once ratified, there's no guarantee our Naval Fleet will have the right of priority passage in time of war." In fact, that right did not then exist under the 1903 treaty but, as Wayne pointed out, was spelled out clearly in Article VI of the new pact. Moreover, President Carter and General Torrijos had agreed that U.S. Navy ships would not only have priority but could even go to "the head of the line" in case of need. That understanding was reached and widely publicized two weeks before Reagan signed his fund-raising letter.

From early November through December and on until the end of January, the U.S. Embassy in Panama played host to an unrelenting flow of official and unofficial visitors. Of all those many sojourns to the isthmus, none was more important than that of Sen. Howard Baker, the Republican leader in the Senate. Though the Democrats controlled the upper house, a treaty required the votes of two-thirds of that body and it was obvious that without significant Republican backing (which meant Baker's backing) the Panama treaties had no chance.

When the Panama issue had moved to the front of the political stove in the summer of 1977, Baker at first hoped he could postpone making a decision on it. A few days after the treaties were signed on September 7, he told an ABC broadcaster: "I have decided not to decide on that issue for the moment because it is too important to make a snap judgment." He would not make a decision, he said, "until I know what I am talking about." The Panama treaties clearly put Baker in an uncomfortable position. As minority leader, he had to consider and try to blend the disparate views of fellow Republicans in the Senate. That was close to impossible. How could one find any common ground on an issue as emotional as that between a Hatfield and a Helms, or a Goldwater and a Javits?

On top of trying to juggle divergent political inclinations among his colleagues, Baker had personal political aims to consider. He clearly was going to be a candidate for the presidential nomination in 1980. As a wise observer of politics, he knew that coming down hard on an unpopular issue could severely hamper his bid for the nation's highest office. But Baker was also one of that rare breed of national politicians who believed the only legitimate end of politics was to serve the national interest—as one is given the wisdom to see that interest. And so he agonized over what to do.

What finally convinced Baker he could no longer duck the Panama issue was the growing pressure from political competitors and from the ultra-conservative wing of his own party. For example, Sen. Robert Dole of Kansas, President Ford's running mate in 1976, clearly had his eye on his party's nomination. He was making speeches attacking the treaties and also, with little subtlety, criticizing the minority leader's failure to take a stand. Even more direct was the assault from the Republican extreme right, typified by North Carolina's Jesse Helms, a master of political over-simplification. Talking to the Florida Conservative Union in mid-September, Helms said the Tennessee Republican was "squirming like a worm on a hot brick" over the Panama issue. Noting that Baker had "his own political ambitions," Helms said the minority leader was going to have to handle "such pseudo Republicans" as New York's Javits and New Jersey's Case.

It was typical Helms venom. He knew that few in his audience would remember that men like Javits and Case were serving the Republican cause in state legislatures and in the Congress when Helms was a little-known radio news broadcaster and a member of the Democratic Party.

The repeated barbs from Dole, Helms, and others finally got under Baker's skin. He decided he had to look into the Panama situation, learn as much as he could, and develop a position based on his own study. By the end of the year, Baker concluded any serious look had to include a visit to the scene and talks with as many of those directly involved as possible. General Torrijos had previously invited him to come to Panama but Baker had declined. Now he got the invitation revived, and accepted.

To give himself the benefit of thoroughly researched positions for and against the treaties, Baker hired two consultants to brief him on every aspect of the treaties. To argue for the treaties, he selected William D. Rogers, a partner in the law firm of Arnold and Porter and a former under secretary of state. The antitreaty brief was the responsibility of Roger Fontaine, a conservative academic from Georgetown University's Center for Strategic Studies. Before and during Baker's trip to Latin America, Rogers and Fontaine provided the minority leader with arguments on every significant portion of the Panama Canal and neutrality treaties.

Senator Baker and his party arrived at Panama's Tocumen airport a few minutes after 1:00 P.M. on January 3, 1978. Traveling with him were two Republican colleagues from the Senate, John Chafee of Rhode Island and Jake Garn of Utah. Chafee, a Yale-educated ex-Marine, former governor and secretary of the navy, strongly favored the new treaties. Garn, a Utah-born Mormon and staunch conservative who had been Salt Lake City's mayor, opposed the new pacts just as vigorously. Another member of the group was Frank Moore, President Carter's chief liaison man with the Congress.

The Baker visit differed little from those that preceded and followed, though it was somewhat longer, four full days. The added time gave Baker, Chafee, and Garn more opportunity than most visitors had to talk with Panamanians and Americans who favored or opposed the treaties. The highpoint, as usual, was their extended conversations with General Torrijos. After touring the countryside, including a visit to crowded Colón with its heavily black population and high unemployment, the general took the American visitors to his seaside villa at Farallon. There he provided his

guests with a buffet and cool drinks, then took the senators and a few officials off for a private confab in the cool, tile-floored living room.

It was a good talk, unmarred by the kind of probing on internal Panamanian business that dominated the Byrd delegation's sessions. On the
other hand, it exposed Torrijos much more to the realities of Senate politics and the main problems that would attend ratification. After initial
sparring, Baker bluntly told Torrijos that the treaties as written, without
any change, would not win Senate approval. Torrijos was surprised and
pushed for an explanation. He had already submitted the treaties to his
people for popular approval and had won the support of two-thirds of the
voters. If the treaties were changed significantly, he told Baker, he would
have to resubmit the documents to another poll, and that would be a
nightmare.

He seemed relieved when Baker explained that what he had in mind was
the need to incorporate into the treaties, or the ratification documents, the
clarifications Torrijos and President Carter had agreed to in October.
"There can be no doubt about our right to use force to protect the canal,"
Baker explained. "And in time of emergency, our navy ships have to be able
to get through the canal as fast as possible." The general told the senators
he thought there was no serious problem. What Baker had been describing
was precisely what he and President Carter had agreed to in the White
House. Baker said he realized that but he and some of his colleagues were
not satisfied with an unsigned statement on such important issues. Somehow they had to be incorporated into the treaties so there was no misunderstanding. If not, he said, the Senate would not give its advice and consent. There followed some intense consultation between Torrijos and a few
advisers. The general then told Baker and his Senate companions that he
thought there would be no serious problem, that there would surely be
some way to work his agreement with Carter into the treaties.

That was the heart of the Baker-Torrijos talk, though several other
points were discussed in the three-hour session. In part, Baker wanted to
pin down those controversial issues so there could be no effective attack on
their meaning in the coming Senate debate. In part, too, he wanted some
kind of personal impact on the treaties. Before he was willing to defend the
new arrangement he needed to protect himself politically and he believed
that closing what many critics had called "loopholes" in the original document was a good way to do it.

Torrijos led the way to the patio and then some yards farther to a stile
over a stone seawall where dozens of reporters and photographers were
waiting. The general clearly was pleased with his talk with Baker and felt
he had won the minority leader's backing. He expressed his gratitude for
that development in his impromptu remarks. That nearly caused an explosion at the end of a smooth and useful day. When an interpreter told Baker

what Torrijos had said, the senator was infuriated. He felt, quite rightly, that any statement about his position on the Panama treaties should come from him. Second, he had not told the general he would support the highly charged arrangement, only that he would *not* support it without the kind of change he advocated. Torrijos had jumped to a hasty conclusion and almost lost an invaluable ally.

Baker moved to face the press and said flatly he had not made a commitment to back the treaties. That, in turn, embarrassed Torrijos, and he stalked off, stony-faced, to his house. Baker then softened what had come across as a rather harsh rejection. He explained that if there were appropriate "modifications" in the treaties, that might satisfy him and win the necessary backing of two-thirds of the Senate. The tense moment passed, and Torrijos and Baker shook hands cordially when the visitors left for Panama City a few minutes later.

As soon as the airplane and helicopters carrying the senators and their staff men had taken off for the capital, Torrijos went into a huddle with his advisers on the porch of his house. One immediate product was an editorial in one of the government-directed newspapers the next day. Its heading was: "I am not dogmatic, gentlemen of the Senate." The editorial stressed Torrijos' flexibility and admitted that some senators had "reasonable objections" to the treaties. Baker clearly had made his point.

The next two days gave the Baker group a chance to meet a wide variety of Americans and Panamanians, in and out of government, pro and con the treaties, in the Republic and in the Canal Zone. The final meeting with Torrijos was scheduled for Saturday morning just before the senators' departure. Another snafu developed that threatened briefly to alienate Baker and end his visit on a sour note. The senators' meeting with the general had been planned for the La Siesta motel, less than five minutes from the airport terminal. At the last minute, we got word that the general's helicopter had a mechanical problem and he could not fly. Instead, he asked Baker and his party to go to Farallon for the meeting. That did not set well with the minority leader and some of his staff. They suspected the general was playing games, keeping them dangling, and showing who was boss. I was sure that was not the case but I had a difficult time convincing the Tennessee senator and his people. I explained that Torrijos' acceptance of Baker's demand for modification of the treaties had been both tough and embarrassing for the general. He knew he would be criticized vigorously by many of his own people and he wanted to ease into the new position slowly and carefully. If he went to La Siesta, he would immediately be surrounded by reporters, Panamanian and foreign, and they would push him hard on his "about face." Baker, who had had more than his share of problems with political and press pressures, appreciated Torrijos' position better than most people and decided to go to Farallon.

Despite the ruffled feathers on the American side, the final meeting with Torrijos went well. He was in a good mood, friendly, and as jovial as he ever got. He and Baker reaffirmed their understanding on the treaty, though neither had any firm ideas on how to do it. Torrijos explained he wanted it done in a way that would not necessitate holding another national plebiscite, which, he said, would cost "$500,000 that we do not have." Before leaving for other Latin American capitals, Baker told waiting reporters that he was inclined to support the treaties if the changes he proposed could be worked out. It was his way of putting the Baker stamp on the final product and it gave him the talking points he needed to fend off his increasingly strident critics.

The news of Baker's conditional support for the treaties spread rapidly through Washington. It raised a problem for his Democrat counterpart, Senator Byrd, who still had made no public declaration of backing for the Democratic president's principal foreign policy initiative. After consulting his staff and some key colleagues in the Senate, Byrd decided he had to move. He called Baker, who by then was in Brazil, and told him of his decision. The two Senate leaders decided to work together to get the required "advice and consent." Byrd announced his decision at his regular weekly news conference on January 13. He told the reporters he was "cautiously optimistic" the treaties would get the necessary two-thirds vote though he admitted there would be "a difficult battle."

Echoing the words of the chairman of the Joint Chiefs of Staff and other witnesses before the Foreign Relations Committee, Byrd said that "the treaties are the best means of assuring continued access to the canal and use of the canal—and that is our primary concern."

With Byrd and Baker finally enlisted to lead the coming "hot battle" (as Byrd called it), the White House and protreaty forces in general were greatly heartened. It took considerable political courage for the two Senate leaders to take the course they did. They knew from their mail, from the polls, and from the press that the Panama treaties were not popular. Both were shrewd politicians who realized they were sticking their necks out and risking their political futures.

It was vastly more dangerous for Baker than for Byrd, of course. The Senate's Democratic leader could always fall back on the defense that he was merely backing the play of his party's man in the White House. There was no such refuge for Baker. The strongest opposition to the treaties came from within his own party. As a man with presidential aspirations, he saw several of his potential rivals—notably Ronald Reagan and Senator Dole—trying assiduously to curry popular support with oversimplified and often misleading assaults on the Panama treaties.

Baker could have stood aside, remained in the shadows of the treaty controversy, and let the Senate debate take its normal course. At the end, he could have voted aye or nay like his ninety-nine colleagues. That would have been the easy course, but it held no appeal for Baker. The Tennesseean was mild in manner, unfailingly polite, congenial, soft spoken, a man to whom others looked for common sense and fairness. But behind that rather bland exterior was a politician of rare intellectual and moral courage. Deep inside, Baker knew that the 1903 treaty with Panama had been an exercise in power politics and undisguised domination of the weak by the strong. The struggle to right that imbalance and to develop new rules for a modern relationship was not one he could merely watch from the sidelines.

With the protreaty banners figuratively raised over the offices of the majority and minority leaders of the Senate, the stage was set for the longest, most detailed, and certainly most rancorous foreign policy debate in the Congress in more than fifty years. The United States of America was about to prove whether it could temper vast power with simple justice, whether wisdom could prevail over prejudice, and whether it could look forward as a nation or would insist on looking back nostalgically to an outdated past.

CHAPTER 18

The Great Debate: Act One

"There is no political mileage in voting for these treaties, and there is no doubt in my mind but that every Senator who votes for these treaties will, to some extent, suffer a loss of support among his people."

—Sen. Robert C. Byrd (Dem.-W.Va.) to the Senate, March 16, 1978

It was late 1977. Senator Byrd and his colleagues had been to Panama and gone. The visit of Minority Leader Baker was just ahead. Panama's Omar Torrijos was resting at his seaside home at Farallon, trying to make sense of the flood of recent events—the signing ceremony in Washington, his visits with European political leaders, his second trip to the U.S. capital when he agreed with President Carter on U.S. defense rights. Then there were the visitors—some friendly, some rude, but all of them prying and demanding. Finally, there was the situation in his own country—budget stringency, growing unemployment, little new investment, increasing discontent.

As he lay in his hammock on the open, wind-washed veranda, the Panamanian general tried to put it all in some order. These crazy Americans, he thought, don't really understand our problems or us. He was by then enjoying his second scotch-and-soda, and was well launched on one of his more philosophical flights. It was the kind of thoughtful mood that occasionally swept over that unusual, erratic, sensitive, ill-educated, brilliant man who was a conundrum to most who knew him.

As he talked, one of his cronies suggested the Americans should hear what he was saying. No sooner said than done. The general picked up his phone and called Ambassador Lewis in Washington. The general said he had some ideas he wanted to convey to Carter and the U.S. leadership. "Of course, General," Lewis said, and quickly turned on the tape recorder that he kept handy. It saved taking laborious notes that were never complete, and that he sometimes had trouble deciphering.

"I want to convey to the highest leaders of that country what our real situation is," Torrijos began, "the country's real situation apart from Omar Torrijos' real situation. I believe there is nothing left to do that I have not done. Nevertheless, I am ready to do what they feel has to be done in order to help them with the ratification."

There followed about forty minutes of monologue that was profoundly, authentically Torrijos. It lacked any semblance of organization. He skipped from one subject to another with no transitions. He threw in references that only someone who knew Panama's history would grasp. The range of his discourse was from high statesmanship to nearly maudlin self-pity. It was, nonetheless, the voice of a unique leader speaking from his heart. It told much about the man's thoughts and mood as the battle for ratification shaped up.

The following excerpts from Torrijos' "Meditations"* help reveal what was going through the mind of Panama's chieftain as his, and his country's, relations with the United States moved toward the political crucible:

"I am fully convinced that ratification is not a magic wand nor the panacea that will place us in front of a cash pipeline, that will solve all our problems. More than money, I want us to recover a climate of confidence, the climate of investment we used to have but which has gone as the canal became an area of dissension in the hemisphere . . .

"I know this is not a warlike people, not a people that likes to shed blood. But remember this: people can be transformed in twenty-four hours, in minutes, in an instant. When they see no hope, they can change from peaceful people into the most violent . . .

"I am beginning to believe that I have hurt my people, hurt the country, by insisting on calm, no more hatred, that I am going to solve things . . . Under another regime, if several dozen incidents had occurred, the case would already have had a solution.

"It is no secret to the United States, because its intelligence services have reported on it, that parallel to the negotiations, we have been training the youth and special troops . . . in order to seek a solution through loud action should every peaceful solution fail. All of Central America would break out in flames . . .

"That was the tactic. But when I undertook my commitment with the Americans, when I made friends with General Brown, whom I esteem highly, upon perceiving Carter's moral quality, when I realized . . . that I was facing not just another ruler, but a new attitude, I confess to you that against them . . . I could not fight . . .

"I would lose the war, my tranquility, and my life. But that great power [the United States] would lose all prestige, something the Soviet Union would automatically capitalize on for its own benefit . . .

---

*The full text is in the collection of papers used in preparing this volume, which will be deposited in the Lyndon Baines Johnson Library at the University of Texas at Austin.

"The Soviets have been making signals of friendship, but I am no fool. I know the price the socialist world charges for aid. They would stay here and no one, no one, could get them out of here ever . . ."

Of the senators he had met recently, Torrijos commented: "They impressed me well, even though I had to show great patience, an almost Franciscan patience. Otherwise one could not stand being interrogated about his private life, the internal life of his country, being reprimanded, being told there is no democracy here, that I am this, that I am the other . . ."

About Panama's economic condition: "Internally, the uncertainty caused by the delay in ratification of the treaty . . . has resulted in serious impairment of the country's economy. I have problems with my establishment. Right now, the rate of growth is zero. This year, 15,000 students will be graduating from high school and will have no hope of finding jobs. What will become of them? . . ."

Finally, a poignant personal cry: "I have never felt myself so much in hiding . . . I'm living like an ascetic, like a misanthrope, like a hermit. I go into the mountains to meditate alone . . . Sometimes I wonder if I'm trying to escape reality . . . I know when a leader runs away from reality, he is treading dangerous ground."

He concluded: "I want you to tell me what else I can do. Don't tell me that you're going to give me money. I don't want money. I want a healthy investment climate. As Mao Tze-tung said: 'Don't give a hungry man a fish; teach him how to fish.'"

There was a pause. Then the general said: "That's it, Gabriel. Do what you think is best." Then he rang off. The ambassador stopped the recorder and flipped on the rewind switch. As the small machine whirred, he leaned back in his chair. He knew he had just heard a piece of Panamanian history. As a friend of Torrijos, he had heard a cry for help. But as a practical matter, he had no idea what to do with what he had heard.

Lewis realized that if he spread the document widely he would be criticized for "propagandizing" the legislature. He knew, too, that many people would not really grasp what Torrijos was trying to convey. Treaty opponents would label it a threat—though that clearly was not Torrijos' intent. He decided the matter needed sensitive handling. Lewis gave the tape to Lucho Noli, a veteran Associated Press correspondent who had recently retired and was then doing some public relations work for the embassy. That night, Noli translated the Torrijos ruminations into English.

The next day, Ambassador Lewis went to the White House and gave Hamilton Jordan, the president's top aide, a copy of Torrijos' uninhibited outpouring. It was, he said, "an important and highly sensitive document" intended only for President Carter and those closest to him. "It will tell you exactly how the general feels," he said. Jordan promised that the president would get it immediately.

The "Meditations of General Torrijos" caused an immediate stir in the White House. President Carter, Jordan, and the few others they consulted believed it revealed a Panamanian leader who was discouraged, emotional, skeptical of U.S. intentions. Knowing how easy it would be for the Panamanian political cauldron to boil over, they worried that a Torrijos in that mood might let it, or cause it, to happen. That would have been disastrous for treaty prospects in the Senate. The president decided to send Jordan to Panama to visit with Torrijos and calm him down.

The president's youthful Georgian assistant arrived at Tocumen on December 8, 1977, and we immediately went off to meet the general at the latter's unofficial headquarters on Fiftieth Street. Jordan used the next hours to convince Torrijos that nothing had higher priority in the Carter administration than getting early approval for the settlement with Panama. He explained the difficulties being encountered in the Congress and the tough battle that lay ahead in persuading two-thirds of the Senate to back the president's policy. He praised Torrijos for his handling of the Byrd delegation and urged him to be as forthcoming with the others that would follow. President Carter had total confidence in Torrijos' ability to cope with visitors, however trying it might be, he said. He begged the general to have the same confidence in Carter's management of the Washington end of the complicated game. What was needed above all, Jordan argued, was a few months of tranquility and patience so the political scenario could move to the conclusion both Carter and Torrijos wanted.

The Jordan visit had a positive effect on Torrijos. First, he was pleased that President Carter had sent his top assistant to see him. Second, he genuinely liked the young Georgian and his open and informal approach to problems. He found himself believing it when Jordan told him the Panama question was at the top of Carter's agenda. I saw Jordan's trip as a decided plus, especially as I knew Torrijos was at the ragged edge of frustration. Because of Jordan's proximity to the president and his temperament, I felt no one from Washington could reassure Torrijos more convincingly.

Jordan did make one mistake, as he later admitted, by being enticed to visit the Canal Zone with Torrijos as tour director. The Panamanian general was not a popular figure to the Zonians, and it riled those who saw him looking over the locks. They were further irritated when they realized that the man at his side was the principal aide to the president of the United States. Except for that minor gaffe, Jordan's visit went well and he returned to Washington two days later.

The day after Jordan came, a quiet, unassuming senator from Arizona named Dennis DeConcini arrived in Panama with his wife, mother, and younger brother. Fully occupied with the president's top assistant, I had less time than I wished to spend with the new arrival from Phoenix. There was no way that anyone could know that the mild-mannered young man would, three months later, do more to endanger the work of thirteen years of painstaking diplomacy than anyone else.

January 15, 1978, was Super Bowl Sunday. The Dallas Cowboys were playing the Denver Broncos for the NFL championship in the New Orleans Superdome. A lifelong football fan, I had some unprintable thoughts about the Senate Foreign Relations Committee whose members were to arrive in Panama just before kickoff. A welcome reprieve came in a message saying the senators would not arrive until midnight.

In truth, I welcomed the visit of the prestigious committee. Its collective judgment on the Panama treaties could decide whether they prospered or died. Moreover, the incoming senators included some whom I admired most in the upper house. Chairman John Sparkman of Alabama and the leading Republican, Clifford Case of New Jersey, were past their prime, but both were decent, thoughtful men who had served the nation well. Frank Church of Idaho, Jack Javits of New York, and Paul Sarbanes of Maryland had abilities that would have enhanced any parliament in the world. Rhode Island's Claiborne Pell, a former Foreign Service officer, was unique in his understanding of diplomacy, and Charles Percy of Illinois was both an idealist and a hard-headed businessman. The one I missed most was Minnesota's Hubert Humphrey, who had died two days before. His departure from the arena was an irreparable loss to the Senate, to the country, and to the often disparaged craft of politics.

The committee's visit was unremarkable despite its importance. By that time, I am sure all members of the delegation had decided to support the treaties. They wanted the reassurance that only first-hand inspection and personal contact would provide. It supplied ammunition they could use when they had to speak on the Senate floor or with their colleagues in the cloakroom.

On the final day of the visit, we flew to Contadora for a meeting with General Torrijos. Panama's "strongman" received the committee members in the Presidential Suite of the new hotel. He was in slacks and a sport shirt, and the senators had shed their coats in the tropical heat. For an hour and a half, they probed for Torrijos' views on dozens of treaty matters and he answered at length. The central question—and the senators served it up in a multitude of ways—concerned U.S. rights to protect the canal. Torrijos kept reminding the legislators of his statement that the treaties put Panama "under the Pentagon's defense umbrella," and of his later agreement with President Carter in October. Torrijos told the senators his country had given more on those matters than it really wanted to, and the giving had caused him considerable pain. The American solons seemed to be pressing for additional concessions, trying to get one more pound of flesh that would make their task slightly easier in Washington.

I was surprised to hear some of them brace Torrijos on the sea-level canal option, for example. That gave the United States a veto over any other country's building a waterway on the isthmus. In return, we agreed not to build a canal elsewhere in Central America. It was something the U.S. negotiators had pushed for and the Panamanians had reluctantly accepted. We made the "concession" not to talk with others about a new canal only because the engineers and technicians who had looked at the problem had given firm assurances that Panama was the *only* logical place to build a sea-level canal.

Nonetheless, some senators felt that agreeing to not even talk about building a canal elsewhere was somehow a diminution of U.S. power and freedom of action. They told Torrijos that "the United States must be able to talk to anyone about anything." They were taken aback when he told them: "Fine. You talk to anyone you like and we'll do the same. Frankly, my people don't like this article at all. If we take it out, I'll be a national hero." The only reason Torrijos did not agree on the spot to eliminate the article was that deletion of part of the treaty already approved by his people in a plebiscite could have forced another costly nationwide vote. That was something he wanted to avoid for both budgetary and political reasons.

Sitting on the sidelines and listening to the exchange between the general and the senators, I was impressed again with the difficulties of political dialogue between such disparate characters. The Americans, most of them lawyers, were looking at the fine print, searching for "correct interpretations," and anticipating domestic political fights. Torrijos, the untutored politician and populist, looked at the "spirit" of the new arrangement. The men from Washington wanted to nail down every unanswered question; Torrijos believed many imponderables could never be nailed down. It was impossible for those sophisticated veterans of the legislative process to see the issues through the eyes of a single-minded, emotional, Latin American leader who was looking at the "big picture" of a new order in U.S.-Panama dealings. Nor could Torrijos, who had never seen a truly independent and democratic legislature at work, have hoped to comprehend what occupied the visiting lawmakers. Both sides were staring at the same problems, but using different lenses and seeing quite different images.

At least the exchange was conducted with cordiality on both sides. Torrijos reassured the senators on several matters that concerned them deeply. They, in turn, impressed him as serious men who truly sought a fair arrangement between the two countries. Most important, all the senators left the encounter with a view of Torrijos quite different from the one they held before, a view based mainly on cartoons and gossip and political propaganda.

We went directly from the meeting to the dining room of the hotel for lunch. A large contingent from the Panamanian government was on hand, and they gathered around the senators in clusters, talking mainly about the prospects for ratification of the treaties. In one corner, a couple of senators and some staff members ringed General Torrijos. They were discussing Panama's economic problems and the effect approval of the treaties would have on those difficulties. Into the midst of the loud talk and laughter strode a tall American whose walk was almost as distinctive as his rugged face and gravelly voice. It was John Wayne, who was in town visiting Panamanian friends.

The room was transformed. The laughing stopped and voices died out. All eyes shifted to the big American who was pumping Torrijos' hand and laughing. I was reminded of White House days when President Johnson walked into a crowded room and the same thing happened. Senators, used to being the center of attention on their own turf, edged toward the new arrival to shake his hand, exchange a few words, and get a picture taken. They knew, far better than the Panamanians, that here was a man who spelled patriotism with a capital *P* to millions of his fellow citizens, and courage for all who knew of his gritty fight against cancer. A picture with John Wayne was pure gold in the political bank.

After lunch, Torrijos thanked his guests for coming to Panama and expressed his confidence in the statesmanship he was sure they would demonstrate toward the treaties. He repeated what he had said in Washington four months earlier: "A politician thinks of the next election. A statesman thinks of the next generation." Chairman Sparkman responded with his committee's gratitude for Torrijos' hospitality and candor, and gave his assurance that the Senate "will do what it thinks is right." The general then urged John Wayne to say a few words.

The actor stood and his big, 6′4″ frame towered over the head table. "I didn't come here to make a speech," he said. "I'm sure the people in this room hear enough speeches every day of their lives." But he said he was there, and he was talking, because he believed the new treaties were "the right thing to do." He described his long association with Panama and his conviction that the American and Panamanian people should be friends and partners.

Wayne told his listeners that the canal issue had produced the first hate mail he ever received, and it hurt him. But he was trying to answer every letter and explain why he thought the treaties were good for the United States. He said one of his biggest disappointments was his failure to convince his old friend Ronald Reagan that a new deal for Panama was just and long overdue. He recalled the two actors' long association and the endless hours he had devoted to "moving Ronnie away from the left-wing toward the center."

"But," he added with a grin, "I never counted on so much momentum." The room exploded in laughter and Wayne sat down. He knew a good curtain line when he gave it.

After a brief press conference, the senators flew to Tocumen and thence to Washington. A week later, they began their markup sessions* on the Panama Canal Treaties. The ratification process had begun in earnest.

As the impending battle in the Senate took shape, the State Department and White House realized it would be a donnybrook. Clearly the Panama treaties could not be "business as usual" and all the bases—public opinion, domestic politics, the Senate debate, diplomacy, international attitudes— would have to be covered. Though all were important, the Senate would be the crucial arena; that was where the game would be won or lost.

Two men recognized it better than most. One was Doug Bennett, the State Department's shrewd assistant secretary for congressional relations. The other was Bennett's deputy, Ambler Moss, who had worked hard as Sol Linowitz' assistant and then returned to State to help with the ratification struggle. Bennett and Moss worked out an ingenious scheme to strengthen protreaty forces in the Senate debate. They knew there was no shortage of intelligent, articulate, thoughtful senators who wanted the treaties to succeed. What they would need most was ammunition to counter the inevitable antitreaty onslaught that would come from equally dedicated and convinced critics.

Bennett and Moss concluded that a small, highly qualified treaty resource team should operate on Capitol Hill during the Senate debate. The team would have to be able to provide treaty details, legal arguments, interpretations, historical background, technical data, anything an inquisitive senator might ask for. With White House blessing, Bennett outlined his idea to Senator Byrd and won his cooperation. Vice President Mondale agreed to let the treaty support team operate out of a small office in his large suite on the Senate side of the Capitol. Byrd's staff also located an unused office near the Senate floor where most of the real work would be done.

Meantime, Moss was enlisting the team that he would head. His first selection was Mike Kozak, the State Department lawyer who had lived through the treaty negotiations since 1971. He brought to the task a familiarity with every phrase in the two treaty documents, most of which he had helped write, as well as a first-class mind and the courage to make decisions. The second selection was Larry Jackley, a tough-minded infantry

---

* In congressional parlance, "markup" is the process in which the responsible committee prepares a piece of legislation for submission to the full House or Senate for final action.

colonel who had commanded troops in the Canal Zone, understood the
military elements in the treaties as well as any man alive, and provided superb liaison with the Pentagon. Moss' third choice was Betsy Frawley, a
bright and talented woman who had learned the political ropes working in
Ted Kennedy's campaign in Massachusetts and later on a congressional
staff. She had recently joined State's congressional office.

Moss, Kozak, Jackley, and Frawley came to be known as the "Gang of
Four." From mid-January until the end of the treaty fight, they put in excruciating hours at their command post and in the halls and offices of the
Senate. If the debate on the Panama treaties displayed an uncommonly
high quality of technical detail, legal precision, and solid historical background, it was due in no small measure to the "Gang of Four" and the
wisdom of senators in using them. Though their names were never mentioned in the *Congressional Record*, their ideas and even their words filled
many of its pages.

We had agreed by mid-January that the Carter-Torrijos agreement of
October should be included in some fashion in the Neutrality Treaty. I
had discussed it with Torrijos in December and had told the State Department that a Senate "understanding" using Carter's and Torrijos' own
words would create no problem at the Panama end. The general went somewhat further with Senator Baker and the Foreign Relations Committee,
hinting that an "amendment" covering the agreement would cause no
trouble. What was not agreed was the precise way such a revision should
be carried out.

This issue became the first order of business when the Foreign Relations Committee met on January 26 for markup of the two Panama Canal
Treaties. The centerpiece of that first session was the appearance of Majority Leader Byrd, who reaffirmed his support for the treaties. But he underlined that his backing depended on inclusion, in some fashion, of the
Carter-Torrijos agreement. Later in the meeting, Minority Leader Baker
took the same stand.

The next day, the committee assembled in Room 4221 of the Dirksen
Office Building to go over the treaty in detail and draft its recommendations to the full Senate. Topic number one was how to incorporate the
Carter-Torrijos Understanding into the Neutrality Treaty. Frank Church,
the Idaho Democrat who had been picked by Chairman Sparkman to lead
the floor fight for the treaties, believed he had a solution. First, he felt it
was important that any amendment adhere as closely as possible to the language Carter and Torrijos had used. Any deviation in language would
open the door to a charge that what the Senate was approving was not
exactly what the Panamanian people had accepted in their plebiscite on
October 23.

Church proposed taking the first two paragraphs of the Carter-Torrijos agreement and adding them verbatim to Article IV of the Neutrality Treaty. That article contained the American and Panamanian pledge to maintain a "regime of neutrality" for the Panama Canal. Carter and Torrijos had said that meant both countries had "the right to act against any aggression or threat directed against the Canal or against the peaceful transit of vessels through the Canal."

Church's second proposed amendment would have added the final paragraph of Carter-Torrijos to Article VI, which gave U.S. and Panamanian warships the right to "transit the Canal expeditiously." The president and the general had agreed that was intended "to assure the transit of such vessels through the Canal as quickly as possible . . . and in case of need or emergency, to go to the head of the line of vessels in order to transit the Canal rapidly."

At that delicate point, liaison between the Department of State and the embassy in Panama broke down. Without consulting us, or giving me a chance to explore the matter with Panamanian authorities, the State Department told Church and the committee that it preferred another solution. State thought it would be better to put the Carter-Torrijos Understanding into a separate treaty article (Article IX) at the end of the Neutrality pact. That way, the argument went, the Panamanian people would more clearly recognize that the "change" was something they had considered in advance of their vote on the treaty. It was a case of the State Department trying to read another nation's mind—without consulting that nation or the Americans who knew it.

I was not immediately aware that things on Capitol Hill were slipping off the track. Our reports on the committee's markup sessions were sketchy at best. Moreover, we had our hands full with a delegation of ten senators who had just arrived on the isthmus. The group was led by Alan Cranston, California's senior senator and the Democrats' majority whip. Except for its leader, who had been in the Senate for ten years, CODEL Cranston was composed of relative newcomers. The senior Republican was Vermont's Robert Stafford, who had been elected in 1972. Five of the ten had been in the upper house one year or less.

The other members of the Cranston group were John Danforth (Rep.-Mo.), John Durkin (Dem.-N.H.), Wendell Ford (Dem.-Ken.), H. John Heinz III (Rep.-Penn.), Kaneaster Hodges (Dem.-Ark.), Patrick Leahy (Dem.-Ver.), John Melcher (Dem.-Mon.), and Daniel Patrick Moynihan (Dem.-N.Y.).

The Cranston group arrived in Panama the afternoon of January 27. In Washington, the Foreign Relations Committee was discussing the Neutrality Treaty and deciding to add the Carter-Torrijos Understanding as a new numbered article. That evening I invited the visiting senators to dinner to give them a chance to meet a cross section of Americans and Panamanians. In the middle of dinner, an embassy officer came in with a message telling me of the committee's decision to add an article. After dinner, I took Cranston aside and showed him the cable. I told him I thought the decision was unwise and would cause problems with the Panamanians. At least it was something I thought he would want to ask General Torrijos about the next day. He agreed it should be explored.

Saturday morning, we took off early from the tiny Paitilla Airport and flew to Panama's interior. It was a typical day with Omar Torrijos. The senators and their entourage traipsed down dusty village streets in the general's wake. They passed through crowds of smiling, curious Panamanians who watched the unusual parade of visitors, wondering what they were doing there. Some senators got the notion that the people and the bands and the banners had all been arranged for their benefit, which was not true. Torrijos would have been there whether the senators had been in town or not.

The populist Panamanian leader wanted to get the men from Washington away from the tall buildings and the comfortable hotels of downtown Panama City and expose them to the real Panama. He wanted them to see that the stores were not filled with luxury goods, that no one wore suits and few even had leather shoes, that most of the hands were calloused and the faces burned from long hours in the cane and rice fields. When Torrijos talked about "helping my people," these were the ones he spoke of. He hoped senators with half an eye would see. Most did; some did not.

We ended the tour at Torrijos' house in Farallon and he sat down with the senators to answer their questions. Cranston immediately raised the Foreign Relations Committee's action the day before in recommending an additional article to the treaty. Torrijos told the senators he had no problem with the substance of the committee's proposal, that is, including his agreement with President Carter in the treaty. But making it a new and separate article gave him serious concern.

One senator asked if adding a new article would force Panama to have a new plebiscite on the treaty. Rómulo Escobar, the lawyer and treaty negotiator, said he thought such a major alteration would indeed require a new vote. Torrijos told the senators he felt the Carter-Torrijos language should be included in an "understanding" or put into a separate annex—anything but a new, numbered article.

Torrijos then said that if it was unavoidable that a new plebiscite be held on the question, he would hold one. But he warned the senators that it would be "expensive and dangerous." It was the first and only time I ever heard Torrijos say he might be willing to hold a second referendum on the treaties, though I knew the prospect gave him nightmares. He was pleading with the ten senators to find some other solution.

On the way back to Panama City, Senator Cranston and I discussed what should be done about the controversial new article. I suggested the best approach would be to let me lay the groundwork; then for him to meet with the Panamanian negotiators and reach an accommodation. He agreed. After his talk with Torrijos, Cranston knew something had to be done.

That evening, the senators went off to meet groups of Panamanians who opposed Torrijos, then to dinner with U.S. businessmen who lived and worked in the Republic. I began trying to find the right kind of needle and thread to sew up the rent that had developed. First, I called Acting Secretary of State Christopher and reported on the talk with Torrijos. I explained that Cranston had agreed we should try to find some formula that would meet our needs and, at the same time, not create problems for the Panamanians. Since the committee had already voted to recommend a new article for the treaty, Christopher doubted we could get them to reverse course. I reminded him that Cranston was the second-ranking Senate democrat. I was sure that, if we found something he could accept, Church and the others would see the wisdom of it.

I called a few friends to get their views on the Carter-Torrijos Understanding and the way it might be included in the treaty without doing political damage. Finally, I called Gabriel Lewis, who had come for the Cranston visit, and invited him over for a drink. We thrashed out the problem at length and concluded the best thing would be to talk with the Panamanian negotiators and try to find an answer. He volunteered to arrange the meeting in his house the next day.

I stayed up late rereading the treaty language, staring at the formula the Senate committee had adopted, and recalling what Torrijos had told the senators earlier in the day. By midmorning Sunday, the approach that made the greatest sense to me was to take the most direct route. Why not simply add that portion of the Carter-Torrijos agreement that related to Article IV to that article? The same with Article VI. The additions would simply say that "President Carter and General Torrijos agreed on October 14, 1977, that the above paragraph should be interpreted as follows: x x x."

That afternoon, I went to Lewis' house. He and Panamanian negotiators Escobar and Royo were waiting. Royo explained that they preferred putting the Carter-Torrijos agreement into an annex to the treaty. "If we add another article," Royo told me, "it almost forces us to have another plebiscite. The critics will say that a treaty with nine articles is not the same as one with eight, which is what we voted on."

I told the Panamanians I saw their point, but it seemed to me that adding a new annex, with a letter instead of a number, was almost as bad as adding a new article. "I have an idea that might make it simpler than either of those two ways," I said. Then I outlined the suggestions of adding explanatory amendments to the two articles, amendments that would simply embody the language the general and our president had used before the October plebiscite. "The Panamanian people knew that language before they voted," I argued, "and if we simply add it as an 'explanation' or 'clarification' we are not changing anything essential. But if we add a new article or a new annex, the critics are bound to jump on it as 'a substantive change.'"

Escobar and Royo looked at me for a minute, then at each other. "Let us think about this," Royo said, and he and Escobar walked into the next room. Gabriel gave me a coke and said, "I think you found the answer." We clinked glasses and I said, "I hope so."

In about ten minutes, Escobar and Royo came back to the living room. They had been on the phone and I assumed it had been with Torrijos. "We think," Royo told me cheerfully, "that your approach is the best one. It cuts out the need for a new article or a new annex, but it puts in what has to be added. We won't have to have a new plebiscite for two small 'explanations' that everyone knew about."

"Now," I said, "I'm going to ask Senator Cranston to come over here. I suggest you lay out this approach and tell him this is the way you want to do it. I'm sure he'll go along."

Cranston and his colleagues were then meeting with residents of the Canal Zone and would soon be returning to the Holiday Inn to change for dinner. I sent a message to the majority whip asking him to stop at Ambassador Lewis' house on his way to his hotel. Meantime, I went to the embassy and sent an "immediate" cable to Christopher explaining what had happened and outlining the formula. Then I dashed back to Gabriel's house. In a few minutes, Cranston appeared with Senator Stafford, the senior Republican in the delegation.

Royo and Escobar told the senators they had been considering the problem of getting the Carter-Torrijos agreement into the treaty without forcing a new plebiscite. They thought an entirely new article, as the Foreign Relations Committee had suggested, would greatly complicate matters for them. Even their own idea of a treaty annex had major drawbacks, they admitted. They had concluded that the best way was simply to insert the Carter-Torrijos wording into the treaty itself as "explanations" or "clarifications" of Articles IV and VI. Cranston and Stafford asked a few questions, then agreed to the Panamanian approach. They said they would recommend it to the Senate as the best way to deal with the matter.

True to his word, Cranston relayed the proposal to Senator Byrd, who passed it along to Senator Church. From the plane the next morning, Republican Stafford called Senator Baker to urge the new approach. Baker, in turn, passed the word to Senator Case, the senior Republican on Foreign Relations. By midmorning, the committee voted to reconsider its decision on a new article and decided instead to recommend amendments to Articles IV and VI.

The Foreign Relations Committee, by a vote of 14 to 1, recommended that the Senate give its advice and consent to the Panama Canal Treaties. Instead of adding the two changes it thought should be made, as committees normally do, it merely recommended them to the full Senate. That left the door open for the changes to be offered from the floor. That deviation from normal procedure met a specific request from Majority Leader Byrd and Minority Leader Baker.

Both had gone on record as saying they would only support the treaties if "significant changes" were made in the security provisions. They wanted to propose those changes themselves to underline that their pledges were being carried out. Hence, one week later, the revisions recommended by the committee were submitted to the Senate as "Leadership Amendments" sponsored by Byrd and Baker. Seventy-six of their colleagues promptly joined as co-sponsors, powerful evidence of the political appeal of the two security clarifications.

Frustrated by the obvious protreaty trend they saw in the Foreign Relations Committee, Senate foes of the treaties looked for an outlet for their views. They found it in the Armed Services Committee. Headed by the venerable John Stennis of Mississippi, the committee was loaded with anti-treaty senators—John Tower, Strom Thurmond, Barry Goldwater, William Scott, Jesse Helms, Jake Garn, and Harry Byrd. Obviously, the Armed Services Committee had a legitimate interest in what happened to the Panama Canal and in arrangements for its security. But, as the record demonstrated, its study of the Panama question went far afield from military affairs and concentrated more on political, economic, and psychological factors than on the safety of the waterway. To his credit, Stennis tried to preserve a fair balance among the committee's many witnesses. But most of the testimony and the vast majority of questions were antitreaty in nature. By then, public and press attention had focused on the upcoming debate in the Senate and on White House maneuvers in support of the new pacts. The antitreaty effort in Armed Services never won the attention its sponsors had hoped for.

I often received summaries of congressional hearings and read them with interest. One such summary caught my attention and I asked for a full transcript. It was the testimony of former Deputy Secretary of Defense William Clements, who appeared before the Armed Services Committee on January 31. Having taken part in the Clements-Brown meeting with General Torrijos in 1975, I was interested to learn what the former Defense official had to say. When I read the report, I was amazed.

To establish his credentials, he noted that in 1975 the Panama issue had come before the National Security Council "of which I was a member for four years." In fact, he had never been a member of the NSC. Deputy secretaries occasionally attend NSC meetings with, or as substitutes for, their secretaries, but they are not members.

More to the point was his testimony on the treaties and his alleged role in their making. Clements told the committee about his visit to Panama and described it as "a fruitful trip in the spirit that we impressed upon Mr. Torrijos that a singlemost thing in any treaty negotiation had to be the security of the canal and as it affected our national security and our strategy on a worldwide basis." The truth was that the "singlemost thing" that Clements and Brown impressed upon Torrijos was that he could not expect a new treaty until the political situation in the United States had been sorted out, and that would not be before the fall of 1976.* The main discussion concerned the need to keep things moderated in Panama. Certainly there was no talk of "worldwide strategy."

The most surprising element in the Clements testimony was his reference to a security clause for the Panama treaty which he credited to the Defense Department under his leadership. He described it in a way that could only have led senators to conclude it had stemmed directly from the Clements and Brown talk with Torrijos. In fact, that conversation occurred in September 1975 and the draft he referred to was not even written until nine months later. The formula cited by Clements said: "In the event of any threat to the neutrality or security of the Canal, the Parties shall consult concerning joint and individual efforts to secure respect for the Canal's neutrality and security through diplomacy, conciliation, mediation, arbitration, the International Court of Justice, or other peaceful means. If such efforts would be inadequate or have proved to be inadequate, each Party shall take such other diplomatic, economic or military measures as it deems necessary in accordance with its constitutional processes."

Clements told the committee he found that "a very clear clause," describing it as "adequate and acceptable at that time." Military men, diplomats, and lawyers with whom I discussed it, then and later, found major flaws in the Clements formula. The Pentagon itself insisted it be scrapped.[†] First, it required the United States to "consult" with Panama before it did anything. Then it obliged us to try a range of vague maneuvers—diplomacy, conciliation, mediation, and so on—before we took any serious action. Only after such efforts "proved to be inadequate" would the United States have been free to take military measures to protect the canal. The Clements "Christmas tree" clause on security was significantly less "clear"

---

* See pp. 292–294.
† See pp. 368–369.

and "adequate" than the actual treaty language, which he criticized as "improper, in my opinion, and totally unacceptable." The language adopted by the Senate was: ". . . each of the two countries shall, in accordance with their respective constitutional processes, defend the Canal against any threat to the regime of neutrality, and consequently shall have the right to act against any aggression or threat directed against the Canal or against peaceful transit of vessels through the Canal."

Clements claimed his formula was "acceptable at that time." Chairman Stennis asked him: "Acceptable to both sides?" The former deputy secretary of defense replied: "Yes, sir. Now that clause remained in the treaty as proposed until some time after January 20, 1977."

In truth, the Clements security clause was *never* accepted by the Panamanians. Indeed, it was never even presented to them. Nor was it adopted by the U.S. negotiators themselves. Ambassador Bunker and his advisers studied the Clements proposal carefully and, on July 14, 1976, the U.S. negotiator wrote Clements that "based upon my experience to date, I believe that Panama would have considerable difficulty with your proposal as formulated." He also informed the deputy secretary that he had no intention of tabling *any* formal proposals with the Panamanians until after the November elections. It was a polite way of telling Clements that his suggestion was a nonstarter.

Suspecting he had uncovered a rich vein to mine, antitreaty Sen. Jesse Helms pursued the security arrangement with Clements. "Now, General Torrijos was in agreement with this at that time," Helms said. "Is that correct?" Clements replied: "Yes, sir; he was." Yet Torrijos had never seen the Clements proposal, let alone approved it. In the debate on the Senate floor, Helms repeatedly referred to the alleged "Torrijos agreement," which, in fact, never existed. And he vigorously extolled the virtues of the Clements security formula, which was demonstrably inferior to that contained in the treaty. Treaty advocates tried to meet head on and rebut every antitreaty argument raised on the floor. These were two they missed.

The morning of February 8, 1978, senators rode to their offices along slippery streets with snow piled high on both sides. Two nights before, the capital had suffered the biggest blizzard of the year. But though they saw the snow, and worried about skidding, the minds of most senators were doubtlessly absorbed with what lay ahead of them on the floor of the upper house. That day, the one hundred members of the Senate would begin debate on whether to give their advice and consent to the Panama treaties. For Senators Byrd and Baker, it would challenge their skill as leaders to guide the controversial measures through the Senate maze to final approval. For the floor managers, Idaho's Church and Maryland's Sarbanes, it would be a supreme test of mental agility and persuasiveness, to say nothing of physical stamina. Similarly, for leaders of the antitreaty forces,

Alabama's James Allen and Nevada's Paul Laxalt, it would measure their ability to persuade one-third of their colleagues to reject the pacts.

One thing colored the proceedings that first day, and every day thereafter. For the first time in Senate history, the debate was carried live on radio. The Senate had given permission for the Public Broadcasting Corporation to provide gavel-to-gavel coverage of the debate. Once that arrangement was made, Panama's lively radio entrepreneurs lined up simultaneous broadcasting of the debate in Spanish. A case can be made that it was a blow for freedom of speech. A case can also be made that it had a deleterious effect on both the debate in the Senate and political relations with Panama.

The Senate was forced to consider the Panama Treaties under a procedure known as Committee of the Whole. That meant the Senate would hear and debate each article of the treaties in order, voting up or down any amendments or reservations thereto. It was a cumbersome procedure that had regularly been set aside by unanimous consent for fifty-five years. In the case of the Panama Treaties, the opponents refused to accede to any effort at streamlining or simplifying the debate. The result was to give each senator the opportunity, and responsibility, for voting yea or nay on each article in both treaties—and on any proposed changes. It was unwieldy but thorough, and it pinpointed what each senator did on every treaty item. It left little room to hide, which some senators deeply regretted.

What happened next was sound parliamentary procedure, and a media disaster. Alabama Sen. James Allen, a staunch treaty opponent and recognized master of procedural intricacies, took the floor to make sure the rules were clearly understood. There followed a long series of complicated questions on which the presiding officer, Vice President Mondale, was called to rule. Any hope Senate leaders and the producers of the PBS broadcasts may have entertained that the Panama debate would start off on a high level of interest died quickly. A typical Allen inquiry: "In considering each treaty by articles, as the rules provide, with committee amendments, if any, to be considered first, would it not be necessary to consider amendments from the floor of the Senate as to an article and to have a vote on such article before amendments of any sort to the next succeeding article could be offered or considered in the Senate?" After twenty minutes of that, one could see eager listeners all over America either falling asleep or turning on the TV sets to get "General Hospital." The leadership would have preferred to deal with that kind of technical detail before the Senate went on the air for the first time in its history. But Allen relished the moment and continued for nearly an hour.

Finally, the central business of the day was made central. The vice-president recognized the senior senator from Alabama, John Sparkman, chairman of the Foreign Relations Committee. The distinguished, gray-haired politician, then 78 years old, rose to present to the Senate the Panama treaties. In a soft voice, he told his Senate colleagues: "Mr. President, the Committee on Foreign Relations has reported favorably the Panama Canal Treaty and the Treaty Concerning the Permanent Neutrality and Operation of the Panama Canal with recommendations to each. The Committee reached its decisions after long and careful consideration of the issues and the viewpoints of all concerned. I have no hesitation in recommending strongly that the Senate give its advice and consent to these treaties as reported by the Committee."

Sparkman then described the main political, security, and economic issues involved, and his reasons for feeling that the treaties provided appropriate answers. He concluded by inserting in the *Congressional Record* the texts of the treaties and of the numerous related documents that made up the full treaty package.

Sparkman was followed by Clifford Case of New Jersey, ranking Republican on the committee, one of the most decent and honorable men in the Senate. In his twenty-three years in the upper house, Case had established a reputation as a compassionate and liberal lawmaker. It was no surprise that he came out in favor of the treaties. His concluding statement was: "Evaluating the treaties has some similarities to buying a house. Few are perfect and have all the features one would like. It took thirteen years to hammer out the treaties. We did not get everything we wanted, nor did the Panamanians. But a new structure was created with a stronger footing."

The first formal words of opposition came from Michigan's Sen. Robert Griffin, who described himself as "the only and lonely member of the Committee on Foreign Relations who voted against approval of the treaties." Griffin readily admitted that our relationship with Panama needed "major revision," but he argued that the pacts worked out by Bunker and Linowitz were unsatisfactory. The senator's principal concern was with the security of the canal, the danger of some future takeover by the Cubans or Soviets, and the possible exodus of skilled American workers that might occur if the treaties were approved. He suggested the Senate recommend the reopening of negotiations with the Panamanians to achieve the revisions he sought.

The leader of the Senate fight against the Panama treaties was Nevada's genial, soft-spoken Paul Laxalt. He had been in the Senate only three years and had won his seat by a paper-thin margin of 624 votes, but he had made friends and garnered considerable respect. A long-time friend of Ronald Reagan, Laxalt had managed the Californian's presidential campaign in 1976. He had recognized then the emotional appeal the canal issue had for millions of Americans. It did not surprise his Senate colleagues, or the press gallery, that in his first statement of the debate, the Nevada politician relied heavily on emotional arguments.

He emphasized the strategic importance of the canal and the need to keep it tightly under U.S. control. To him, the new treaties represented "a grievous risk of loss within twenty-two years, and an almost certain loss after that time, of a vital strategic and economic asset." He never faced the question whether the loss he feared might occur even sooner without the treaties than with them. Laxalt also devoted considerable time to castigating the Torrijos regime in Panama. He said, for example, that "General Torrijos' connections to Havana and, by extension, Moscow are well documented." A competent intelligence officer could have told Laxalt that the "documentation" he implied did not exist. The U.S. government had "connections" with Moscow that were many times more elaborate than those of Panama. As for Cuba, Torrijos had gone to Havana and talked with Castro—as had dozens of U.S. senators. The Panamanian strongman admired some things Castro had done, especially in education and health care. But Torrijos had also said that Cuba's system would never work in Panama. I was present when Torrijos told Laxalt that Castro was a "friend who gives me good advice" and Laxalt quoted that description in his Senate statement. He did not say that the main suggestion Castro had made was to "be patient and don't push the Americans too hard."

Laxalt's final point was that by agreeing to the Panama treaties the United States would somehow be displaying weakness and "backing down" under pressure. He said he thought "our friends would view Senate ratification of the proposed treaties with contempt and pity." He was never asked just who those "friends" were. The leaders of every government in Latin America had endorsed the new treaties. The governments of all principal canal users, the United Kingdom, Japan, West Germany, and the others, had made known their approval. They saw the course the United States was following as wise and farsighted.

Laxalt spent considerable time trying to "prove" the Canal Zone was sovereign U.S. territory. South Carolina's shrewd Fritz Hollings punctured the argument in a brief exchange. He asked whether it was not true that a child born to a Panamanian couple in Laxalt's Nevada would be a U.S. citizen. Laxalt admitted Hollings was right. The South Carolinian then noted that a child born to the same couple in the "sovereign" Canal Zone would not be an American citizen. Laxalt confessed that was true. "Well, the Senator has answered the question," Hollings said.

The next morning, discussion of the treaties resumed at 11 o'clock. Senator Scott of Virginia announced that he had conducted a poll among his state's voters and that 87 percent of those who responded were opposed to the treaties. "The American people are opposed to these treaties," Scott claimed. "I urge my colleagues that they get in close touch with those they represent before casting their vote on the matters before us."

That infuriated Majority Leader Byrd, who was about to declare his support for the treaties. Senators traditionally treat their colleagues with elaborate courtesy on the floor and in committee, but one can tell from the words when there is a chill in the senatorial air. Byrd's remarks were draped with icicles. "As one who has represented the people of the State of West Virginia for a period now going on thirty-two years," he asserted, ". . . may I say to the able Senator from Virginia, I think I know what my responsibilities are to the people of West Virginia and to the people of the United States."

Byrd went on to quote approvingly the words eighteenth-century Irish statesman and writer Edmund Burke addressed to his constituents: "Your representative owes you not only his industry but also his judgment, and he betrays rather than serving you if he sacrifices it to your opinion."

Byrd continued for the edification of Scott and those of like mind: "I am not going to betray my responsibility to my constituents. I owe them not only my industry but I also owe them my judgment. That is why they sent me here. If I am to reach a judgment based only on the number of names on a petition or upon the weight of the mail, what we need is a computer and a set of scales, not a Senator . . ."

In any case, Byrd continued, he doubted the picture Scott had given of public opinion was accurate. He cited a Gallup Poll published just the week before. It showed that 45 percent of the people favored the treaties and 40 percent opposed them. Among the "better informed"—defined as those who could answer three rather rudimentary questions about the canal and the treaties—57 percent approved and only 39 percent opposed the treaties while 4 percent had no opinion.

As the majority leader moved into his statement in support of the treaties, one tactic of treaty opponents became apparent. After the first few minutes, Nevada's Laxalt asked Byrd to yield the floor for a question. Then he asked another. Hatch of Utah joined in the interruptions. Byrd was able to pronounce little more than a sentence or two before one of the treaty critics stood up to ask a question or make a statement. Helms joined the exercise, then Allen. They succeeded in breaking the flow of the majority leader's statement—as they obviously wished to do—and in testing his patience sorely. They also provided the gallery and the radio audience with constant reminders that the treaty foes were active.

This tactic, soon replicated by treaty supporters, helped to often turn the Panama treaties debate—which had the potential for providing one of the truly great discussions of Senate history—into a petty shouting match, a parody of serious parliamentary inquiry. It could have displayed the Senate to the American people and the world as a genuinely great deliberative body. Instead, it showed those who listened that the Senate could be a cockpit of small-minded men seeking the limelight, grasping for "points" like high school debaters. Truth and even good taste frequently suffered in the process.

Anyone who knew a little Panamanian history had to be amazed to hear Senator Laxalt proclaim that the 1903 treaty "was welcomed by all Panamanians." What Panamanians welcomed was their own independence, and the U.S. pledge to protect it. What they hated was the grant of sovereign rights over a strip of their territory in perpetuity. The man who signed the treaty, Frenchman Bunau-Varilla, was a despised figure in Panamanian history from the day he put his name to the treaty.

When Senator Byrd mentioned that the man who signed the 1903 pact was not a Panamanian, he and most of his colleagues were astonished to hear Senator Helms' comment: ". . . since the senator is so concerned about a non-Panamanian signing the 1903 treaty, I would remind him that Henry Kissinger was not born in this country. And Mr. Kissinger signed the Kissinger-Tack agreement." Byrd, like most who heard the remark, was nonplussed. "I beg the Senator's pardon?" he said. Helms answered tartly: "Henry Kissinger negotiated for this country, and he was not born here." Byrd replied: "Henry Kissinger is a citizen of this country." Senator Hatch intervened to change the subject.

The debate rarely descended to that low level, nor did it reach the heights many expected. There were moments when eloquence held sway, when the power of words and logic dominated the proceedings for a brief time. But they were rare. All the principal arguments for and against the two treaties were raised in the first three days—about a dozen on each side. So were the diversionary arguments, the "red herrings": Should the treaty be in English only? Why did the Senate have no chance to confirm appointment of negotiator Sol Linowitz? Why not consider the Canal Treaty before the Neutrality Treaty? Did the United States have "sovereignty" in the Canal Zone or "the rights of sovereignty"? Was Torrijos involved in drug trafficking? From then until a few days before the Senate voted, the debate ploughed the same ground again and again. It became an exercise in boredom, for the senators and for those who listened.

Decentralization of power in the Congress, which had begun ten years before, was one part of the problem. Another part was a relatively weak president who took office without close links to the Congress, and never succeeded in forming them. A third element that made the fight for treaty approval an uphill one was a White House staff that was energetic but unseasoned, intelligent but inexperienced, and, almost to a person, unfamiliar with the workings of the Washington political mill. Jimmy Carter was the first president since Calvin Coolidge who had never worked in

Washington until sworn in as chief executive. The key members of his staff suffered the same disability.

That staff, which had helped transport an obscure Georgia politician from near anonymity to the presidency, was at least attuned to the requirements of public relations. They lined up visits to the White House by opinion leaders from thirty-five states. The invitees were selected in most part by the senators concerned, and they were composed mainly of newspaper editors, television and radio station managers, key politicians from the states involved, and large contributors who had backed the senators in past campaigns. By all accounts, those elaborate briefing sessions were highly successful.

At a typical gathering, treaty negotiator Sol Linowitz described the treaties and explained what they did for the United States. The chairman of the Joint Chiefs of Staff explained the military implications and advantages. Secretary of State Vance went over the diplomatic profit that would accrue from the new arrangement. National Security Adviser Brzezinski described the impact we expected on our overall posture in Latin America and the world. Then the president himself explained why a new arrangement with Panama was the honorable and wise thing to do. The reaction among those who attended was almost universally positive.

Those White House gatherings supplied a bit of starch for the backbones of some senators, especially the timid and fearful. They did little to meet the real political and public relations challenge: to convince a majority of the American people—who had been bombarded with superpatriotic slogans—that the treaties were good for the United States under any political, military, or economic criterion. A Citizens Committee for the Panama Treaties, headed by the venerable W. Averell Harriman, failed to meet the challenge. It never mobilized the energy, resources, or imagination required to counter the well-financed and highly active opposition. A speakers program developed by the State Department had more, but limited, success. The overall effort failed to counteract one of the most elaborately planned and financed propaganda campaigns of modern times. The antitreaty forces were bombarding the American people with pamphlets and forecasts of doom. Neither the White House nor the Citizens Committee seemed to realize that the battle, a large part of it, was being waged in the mailboxes of the United States.

Beginning in late January, and continuing through the entire Senate debate, we maintained close contact daily, often hourly, with the State Department. By that time, the administration had designated Deputy Secretary of State Warren Christopher to mastermind the political offensive on the Hill. Christopher was a fine lawyer, an intelligent and thoughtful man. But he went to Washington with little more than an astute outsider's awareness of the intricacies of the congressional snake pit. That he succeeded as well as he did was a tribute to his qualities of mind and his dedication. But President Carter would probably have been well advised to make leaders in the Senate itself his principal lieutenants for the battle, rather than an official of the executive branch, however capable.

As one senator after another raised questions about the treaties with the State Department or concocted possible treaty changes, Christopher and his principal aide in the treaty struggle, Herbert Hansell, the department's legal adviser, relayed them to us for comment. We gave them our best estimate of likely Panamanian reactions. If a reservation or understanding was proposed, we told Washington whether Panama would be inclined to accept it or reject it, or whether some careful rewording might make it palatable. When the actual debate started, I urged the State Department to let me take the Panamanians more fully into our confidence. When that was approved, I set up a system of consultation with the Panamanians involving the foreign minister and Torrijos' main legal advisers on treaty matters.

It permitted us to get back to individual senators and to the leadership not merely with "we think this is what the reaction will be," but rather "the Panamanians tell us this is what they think." In many cases, it helped discourage actions that would have created serious problems. It also enabled us to get Panamanian approval for understandings that swayed some votes in the Senate. The first day of our secret consultations in Panama, I explained to Christopher: "You should know, at the outset, that the basic GOP [government of Panama] position is that the Panama Canal Treaties have been negotiated and signed, and that *any* changes or modifications are less than welcome. They exclude from this appraisal the statement of understanding reached by President Carter and General Torrijos on October 14, 1977. I have explained ad nauseum the imperatives of the legislative process in our system, and the need—if we are to achieve positive advice and consent from the Senate—to accommodate at least some of the concerns advanced by various senators, and especially by the leadership, who are working hard to win ratification. I have managed to overcome the basic inclination of this government to be negative as regards any modifications, but it has been an uphill climb."

One of the first issues we raised with the Panamanians concerned the priority passage of U.S. naval ships through the canal "in case of need or emergency." Some senators were concerned about who would decide there was "need" or that "an emergency" existed. They wanted an understanding that "determinations of need or emergency shall be made by the nation operating the vessel." I explained the problem to the Panamanians. I was then able to tell the State Department: ". . . the Panamanians believe that this was clear in the text and in the negotiating record. However, if it is necessary for tactical legislative purposes, they have no problem with the 'understanding' as phrased . . ." One problem up; one problem down.

Another example demonstrated how the system worked. The Neutrality Treaty provided that after Panama took control of the canal, at the beginning of the year 2000, the only military forces and defense sites on the isthmus would be Panamanian. For them, the withdrawal of foreign troops and bases was a prime goal. But some U.S. senators were worried. Suppose, they said, conditions in the world and in the Caribbean are such in the mid-1990s that both Panama and the United States believed a continued U.S. military presence around the canal would be useful for both countries? Does not the new treaty prevent that? Shouldn't we leave the door open to that possibility? To meet that need, Georgia's Sen. Sam Nunn and others backed an understanding that "the United States shall, no later than January 1, 1996, enter into discussions with the Republic of Panama with a view to making, in accordance with constitutional processes, arrangements to facilitate appropriate U.S. actions to maintain the canal's neutrality, including providing to the Republic of Panama such military assistance as the two parties may consider necessary or appropriate." It was neatly contrived. It said nothing about U.S. troops or bases, but it left the door open to their presence after A.D. 2000 if both countries decided they were needed.

I explained all this to my Panamanian colleagues. Then I reported their reaction to Washington: "As the Panamanians pointed out to me, this opens the door by implication to the possibility of trying to arrange for the existence of U.S. bases in Panama after the treaty period. This, they said emphatically, would be a 'political nuclear explosion' in Panama. . . . My Panamanian counterparts admit privately that some such negotiations may indeed be necessary, even desirable, at some point in the future. But they cannot give their approval at this point to something that will obviously create serious political problems for them here." I added my private estimate: "This proposal, if adopted by us, would be roundly denounced by the present government of Panama. But they would not let final treaty approval founder on this rock. They would likely say that this government had not accepted this proposal; if some future Panamanian government wished to enter into negotiations on this matter, it would be the affair of that future government."

That is pretty much the way it turned out. In fact, with much explaining and patient negotiating, we convinced the Panamanians to accept language even more explicit, including the words "agreements or arrangements for the stationing of any United States military forces or the maintenance of defense sites." But Torrijos and his spokesmen consistently took the position that they would never reach such an agreement; if future Panamanian leaders wished to do so, it was their business. The arrangement satisfied Panamanian pride, and Senate requirements.

During those weeks, the State Department passed along to the embassy those matters Christopher and his colleagues felt were most urgent or likely to receive serious attention in the Senate. They did not burden us with the many statements and proposed amendments (more than thirty in the first two days of debate) that they considered trivial or unlikely to get much attention. Their judgment was excellent and it made our job considerably easier. There was, however, one glaring mistake and it threatened to destroy the Neutrality Treaty.

Tucked away in the "additional remarks" section of the *Congressional Record* on February 9 was a little-noted statement and a proposed amendment offered by Arizona's Junior Sen. Dennis DeConcini. He referred to the threat to canal security from third countries, then added: "I have been equally bothered by the possibility that internal Panamanian activities might also be a threat to the waterway, should we give it up. Labor unrest and strikes; the actions of an unfriendly government; political riots or upheavals—each of these alone or in combination might cause a closure of the Canal." He then filed for future consideration an amendment. It stated: "If the Canal is closed, or its operations are interfered with, the United States of America shall have the right to take such steps as it deems necessary to reopen the Canal or restore the operations of the Canal, as the case may be."

The department did not send the DeConcini statement to Panama. We saw the proposed amendment two weeks later, after it had been revised and when it threatened to blow everything out of the water. If we had seen it, we would certainly have raised warning flags, because the implication of what DeConcini was saying was totally destructive of the kind of partnership that was our goal.

No summary can re-create the full flavor and tone of the protracted Senate debate on the Panama treaties. There were moments of eloquence and drama; vastly more moments of turgid prose and dull repetition. One thing future historians who dig through the thousands of pages will discern will be the unremitting trickle of poison fed into the stream of the debate. Those noxious injections were a combination of arrogance, chauvinism, self-righteousness, and contempt. The targets were Panama, its people, its government, and its leader, General Torrijos—above all, Torrijos. The verbal assault on an erstwhile partner did more than anything else to diminish the quality of the debate and, more important, the final result.

It was a deliberate choice. The senators involved were too artful not to know what they were doing. There were, of course, an unthinking few who knew no other way, had no other tools. But the tacticians among treaty foes were shrewd, experienced men. They knew that the Panamanians, certainly Torrijos, were sensitive, proud, and emotional. If a steady barrage of insults could force the Panamanians into some exaggerated response, an insulting speech, even violence, then the goal of destroying the treaties would be neatly done for them. That they were systematically curdling the milk of any future relationship with Panama seems not to have occurred to them, or at least they did not care.

Nevada's Laxalt described Torrijos as "an unstable dictator who is a close confidant of Fidel Castro." Utah's Jake Garn talked of "some future dictator who replaces General Torrijos." Laxalt then cast doubt on the intelligence and ability of everyone on the isthmus when he said, "Panama does not now have, and cannot have within the short period of time required, the skilled personnel to fill adequately the jobs of those who will leave their present jobs, whether voluntarily or under duress." It was said that the Panamanian government was "shot through with mismanagement" and that it had an "abysmal human rights record." Jesse Helms spoke of "the brutality of the *guardia* and Panamanian justice." Utah's Hatch described Panama as one of the "antiethical powers" and claimed it would shut down the Canal "to embarrass the United States."

The steady stream of vilification had no noticeable effect on the debate or on the opinions of other senators. They had looked into those matters on visits to the isthmus and by other means and had, for the most part, resolved them to their own satisfaction. But the counterpoint of criticism may well have influenced the attitude of Americans who tuned in. It most certainly had a baleful effect on Panamanians who listened to the debate, at first with interest, then with amazement, and finally with disgust. They could not understand what they and their little country, where ties with the United States were broader and deeper than any place else in Latin America, had done to deserve such undisguised contempt and venom. The quality of the Senate debate, with its poisonous minor theme, did more to create a mood of bitterness and anti-American feelings than anything that had happened in more than ten years. And it certainly made more difficult the job of those Americans and Panamanians who had, for a long time, been quietly extolling the virtues and advantages of a freely elected legislature. "If this is what we'd get," one Panamanian told me, "maybe we're better off with what we have." And another, a good friend of the United States and not an admirer of Torrijos, said: "Don't these supposedly brilliant men realize what they're doing? They're insulting me and every other Panamanian and they are creating sympathy and support for Torrijos whom they profess to dislike."

I had heard from friends that on two occasions General Torrijos had picked up the radios on which he had been listening to the Senate debate and smashed them on the floor in utter frustration. I went to see him. I knew if Panama's leader let his emotions govern his actions, years of patient work were going to disappear. Though usually the coolest member of his entourage, the general had a threshold of tolerance that once crossed could produce an explosion.

It was midafternoon, and though Omar rarely drank before 5 o'clock, he had a hefty scotch in his hand. I told him I had come over to see what he thought of the Senate debate and asked if he had listened to the statements of Senators Byrd and Baker. He had. "Those are real men," he said. "They came down; they talked to us; and they learned a lot. They talked like statesmen, not politicians." He was not to be diverted for long. "But they're not the only ones I've listened to," he said. "Who are some of these other bastards? I've never met most of them. Where do they get their ideas? Why didn't they have the guts to talk to me directly? I know some of them came down to the Zone, but they never came into Panama. How did they learn so much about us without talking to us?"

He was in a vile mood but I thought it best to let him get things off his chest. I merely reminded him of the many senators who had come to Panama and *had* talked with him and many other Panamanians. "And they are fighting hard for the treaties," I said.

"Yes, I know and I appreciate what they're doing," he said. "Church and Sarbanes and Gravel—people like that—they know what they're talking about. They understand. But what about these other loudmouths? Who is this Allen who keeps talking about 'dictator Torrijos'? Has he ever been here? Who is Helms? I never saw him. I remember Laxalt, though. He was polite and nice and asked good questions. Now he's back in Washington and talking like a tiger. Why didn't he talk to me that way?"

The general was pacing up and down, letting off steam. I wanted to put things into better perspective. "Look, Omar," I said, "we're talking about politicians who are in a touchy business in a big capital. I admit some of them may be 'looking more to the next election than to the next generation.' But you know that all the people in high positions in your government aren't geniuses either. Suppose you had this kind of debate in Panama right now. Do you know how many stupid statements would be made? I've heard some of your people talk about my country in an insulting prejudiced way. And they don't know Connecticut from California. You're a commander; you have to look at the big picture."

"You're right, Bill," he said. "But this is Panama. This is a little country. You people are supposed to be the leaders of the free world. So you're supposed to be smarter and fairer and more experienced. The big brother has to take care of the little brother, not kick him in the teeth."

I then told Torrijos what had been on my mind for a week or more. "Look, Omar, you are getting mad about this damn debate," I said. "Maybe that's what these fellows really want. They don't like the treaties so they want to beat them any way they can. I'm not sure, but I don't think they can do it in the Senate, and maybe they don't think so either. But if they can get you furious, if they can get your people hopping mad, then maybe something will happen down here that will make their job easier. And just maybe that's what they're hoping for."

It was as though I had shot a rifle in the quiet room. Torrijos stopped and spun around to look at me. He put down his glass. He lit a cigar and stared at the other side of the room. "Mother of God," he said. "Of course that's what they want. They want me to be stupid. And I almost . . ." He stopped. Then for the first time that day, he smiled, raised his glass in a salute, and drained it. Soon after, I left.

Of all the innuendo scattered through the speeches of treaty opponents, the item that riled Torrijos most was the suggestion that he or members of his family might be involved in the illicit drug traffic. That rumor had been circulated for several years by Torrijos' enemies. It had been passed along to several members of Congress and some journalists and thereby found its way into a few columns and into the *Congressional Record*. U.S. narcotics agents, always eager to pursue any solid leads to international trafficking, had looked into the allegations against Torrijos and found the evidence so flimsy that further investigation was considered a waste of time.

The most damning "proof" concerned not Omar Torrijos at all but his brother Moises, then Panama's ambassador to Spain. Two Panamanians had been nabbed at New York's Kennedy Airport in 1971 with 155 pounds of heroin concealed in their luggage. One of them, the son of the Panamanian ambassador in Taiwan, apparently told the arresting agents that Moises Torrijos had helped expedite his diplomatic passport and had been aware of the smuggling scheme. On that basis, a grand jury delivered a sealed indictment against Moises in 1972.*

For those who knew him, Moises Torrijos was an unlikely candidate for the role of international drug trafficker. As those who know that degrading business point out, successful drug running requires meticulous planning, detailed intelligence, usually split-second timing, total secrecy, and ruthless execution when necessary. Moises had none of those qualifications. Like his brothers, he loved to drink and to play. But he had nothing of his brother Omar's discipline. As one Panamanian told me: "Anyone who went into the drug business with Moises would be courting disaster. And those people aren't fools."

Kansas Sen. Robert Dole chose to champion this sorry subject and to press it as part of the attack on the Panama treaties. During the 1976 cam-

---

*The young man on whose testimony the indictment was rendered later recanted and claimed he had been "forced" by the narcotics agents who questioned him to implicate Moises Torrijos. He did so in hopes of easing his own punishment. See the *New York Times*, February 24, 1978. Whether he lied then or earlier, or on both occasions, is not clear.

paign, some reporters had given Dole the sobriquet "the hatchet man." He was a master at picturing himself as the most sweetly reasonable of men, while all within earshot of his deft strokes knew his target was somebody's jugular. No one else in the Senate could so adroitly drag a red herring into a debate, all the while denying that was what he was doing.

Dole called dramatically for a rare closed-door session of the Senate to discuss the drug charges. The leaders of the floor fight knew Dole's move was a "fishing expedition" to divert attention from the central business. But they also knew that the American people took the drug threat seriously and that the Kansan's vague allegations should be pinned down quickly. They may have surprised him by immediately concurring in a secret session. Senator Byrd proposed it be held on February 21 at 10 o'clock and the Senate agreed unanimously to that arrangement.

We had worked hard to develop close relations with the Panamanians in drug enforcement, and the effort was paying off handsomely. But with the drug question on the front burner in Washington, I wanted details. I called in the drug enforcement agents on my staff and we went over the reports for the last several years. In 1976, Panama had imprisoned thirty-two major drug traffickers. The next year, the number increased 25 percent, to forty-one. In only the first seven weeks of 1978, twenty-four drug merchants had been arrested. During that time, Panama had seized and destroyed more than two hundred pounds of refined cocaine, a quantity the agents told me had a street value of more than $22 million. The Panamanians had also arrested and turned over to our custody more than a dozen Americans connected with drug conspiracy cases in the United States. I passed this information on to Washington with the comment that it was "hardly the record of a country that is 'soft on drugs.'" The State Department relayed our report to interested senators.

Promptly at the appointed hour of ten on February 21, the Senate gallery was cleared and the huge oaken doors at the entrance to the upper house swung shut. Only senators and a few carefully screened members of the Senate staff were allowed to enter. Indiana's Sen. Birch Bayh of the Intelligence Committee introduced his group's twenty-page report on the drug situation in Panama and the various allegations to which Senator Dole had referred. There followed fourteen hours of discussion, questions, clarifications. When the massive doors finally swung open at the end of the second day, weary senators wandered off to their offices or home for dinner.

It was quickly apparent that, as *Time* magazine reported, "the great drug drama turned out to be something of a bust." The many senators who were lawyers realized that the so-called evidence was largely rumor and hearsay, nothing that would stand up in any court. "There was no smoking gun found in Torrijos' hand," said California's Cranston, "and besides, he's not going to be around in the year 2000." Even staunch treaty foes found the secret session a waste of time. "I don't think it changed any minds," said Alabama's Allen. Dole's carefully plotted strategy had failed.

In addition to trying to talk the treaties to death, regularly insulting the Panamanians, hoping for some adverse incident, and raising unsubstantiated allegations, the opponents of the treaties used another technique. They offered amendments that had a superficial appeal to Americans but that the proponents knew would either be rejected by the Panamanians or force holding a new plebiscite, thereby possibly getting the Panamanians to turn down the treaties. In the Senate and among treaty specialists and reporters, those proposed revisions got the name "killer amendments," for their real purpose was not to improve the treaties but to destroy them.

The first of the "killers" was introduced by Senator Allen. It provided that U.S. military forces would continue to be based in Panama after the year 1999 "if the President of the United States deems it necessary for the defense of the Canal . . ." Warren Christopher sent us a copy of the amendment together with a possible substitute that the administration hoped to get some other senator to sponsor as an "understanding." The latter said the Neutrality Treaty did not preclude the two governments from agreeing that continued U.S. military assistance to Panama might be desirable after 1999.

Several things bothered me about the proposed substitute for Allen's "killer." Until then, Senators Byrd and Baker and the other managers of the treaty battle had staunchly resisted *any* significant change in the Panama pacts. The only exceptions were the leadership-sponsored amendments to Articles IV and VI. Wise in the ways of the Senate, those men knew that once the "no changes" dike was breached they would be swamped with proposals for additional revisions.

I was convinced the senators were absolutely right. I could foresee having to accept one or two carefully worded understandings at the last minute if they would influence several crucial votes. But Allen's challenge was made in the third week of February and we knew the final vote was several weeks away. I believed the administration was caving in prematurely.

That was on my mind when I wrote our appraisal for Christopher. The heart of my estimate was in the final paragraph:

> We really should not try to play this kind of game with this little country. I am certain we have numerous friends in the Senate who would be prepared to take on the proposed "killer" amendment, and kill it as it deserves. But let us face this kind of challenge head on, not try to find some "middle ground" which means a watering down of the real intent of the treaties as written. The Panamanians have been pushed to the wall, as you know. They are sick and tired of being urged to meet our standards. I really think the question we now face is whether Senatorial arrogance or a real spirit of even-handed treatment

and genuine partnership is to prevail. I therefore urge that we not knuckle under to Allen but stand up and fight him.

I added a personal footnote: "I'm sure a good Irishman like Pat Moynihan would be willing to take him on. And if he needs ammunition, I will be happy to supply it."

The footnote never reached Moynihan, but I was told our message did stiffen resistance in the State Department and the White House to this and later "killer amendments." When the compromise understanding emerged much later in the Senate debate, the requirement for the United States to initiate defense talks late in the century had been dropped. The Allen amendment was soundly defeated. A week later, another Allen proposal—that U.S. troops in Panama in 1999 could stay there if the United States were at war—was defeated 57 to 38. A week after that, another "killer"—that enemy ships not be allowed through the canal in wartime—was rejected 52 to 40. All of Allen's "killer amendments" had several things in common: they sounded wonderful to any patriotic American; they irritated the Panamanians, as intended; they solved no problems that could not have been dealt with perfectly well under the treaties as written. The Senate rightly consigned them to the dustbin.

Debate on the Neutrality Treaty dragged on through February and March. Thousands of words were printed in the *Congressional Record*. There were innumerable prepared statements, and considerably more legalistic interventions. Yet the debate never reached the peaks of eloquence that many expected.

It was ironic that, of all the statements made, the one most likely to be included in anthologies of great Senate speeches did not even deal with the Panama issue as such. Its central theme was the low level to which American politics had sunk in the recent past, and it threw a spotlight on some of the grubby corners of that field of action. It was courageous exposure of the tactics used by a handful of vicious and narrow-minded political manipulators whose main weapons were exaggeration, distortion, prejudice, and fear.

The man who made that speech was Sen. Thomas J. McIntyre of New Hampshire. He had labored in the Senate with quiet distinction for sixteen years. McIntyre was known to his colleagues as a thoughtful, rather conservative legislator and a hard-working member of the Senate's Armed Services and Banking committees. He had served his country with gallantry in World War II as an officer in the U.S. Third Army.

McIntyre began his remarkable speech by stating simply:* "Mr. President, despite the threats of political reprisal from the radical right, I intend

---

*For the full text, see *Congressional Record*, March 1, 1978, pp. S2592–2595.

to vote to ratify the proposed Panama Canal Treaties." He then went on to explain how "six months of hard study" had led him to that decision. But McIntyre's central theme was not the Panama Treaties; it was the way the issue was being fought in the American hinterland. His target was the Radical Right, just as he and all senators who favored the treaties were their targets.

The New Hampshire senator began by repeating the caution signal that Eric Sevareid, the veteran CBS correspondent, had raised in his farewell broadcast a few months earlier. Sevareid's concern was the paradoxical rise of "dangerously passionate certainties" in a time when there were no easy answers.

Senator McIntyre told his colleagues:

> I see abundant evidence that these "dangerously passionate certainties" are being cynically fomented, manipulated, and targeted in ways that threaten amity, unity, and the purposeful course of government in order to advance a radical ideology that is alien to mainstream political thought.
>
> Already we have seen the vigor of the two-party system sapped by this phenomenon. More and more Americans appear unwilling to abide by the essential ethic of the party system—that willingness to tolerate differing views within the party, and to accept the party platform, however unpalatable some of its provisions, in order to advance a general political philosophy.
>
> As a result, the traditional role of the parties is slowly being usurped by a thousand and one passionately committed special interest, splinter faction and single issue constituencies.

What concerned McIntyre even more was the arrogance of the ultra-rightists "born of the conviction that they and they alone have a corner on patriotism, morality, and God's own truths, that their values and standards and viewpoints are so unassailable they justify any means, however coarse and brutish, of imposing them on others."

To know any man, it helps to know his enemies. McIntyre's most vitriolic critic was William Loeb, the passionately conservative publisher of New Hampshire's biggest newspaper, the *Manchester Union Leader*. Loeb had been seeking McIntyre's political scalp for more than a dozen years, and he saw in the Panama controversy a chance to capture it. It was Loeb who, when the oil embargo of 1973 began, called the leaders of the Arab world "heathen swine."

The other principal McIntyre attacker was New Hampshire's ludicrous Gov. Meldrim Thomson. Born in Pittsburgh, raised in Georgia, and a publisher of textbooks, Thomson had become a darling of publisher Loeb. With no experience in elective office, he became governor in 1972. Thomson was as close to a political primitive as U.S. gubernatorial politics had seen in the last half of the twentieth century. A self-styled expert in foreign policy, though he had never lived or worked abroad, Thomson had accused the Carter administration of following a "pro-Communist course," had attacked the State Department as "un-American," and had hailed South Africa's Prime Minister Vorster as "one of the great world statesmen of today." These, and others of like mind and quality, were the people who had determined that a Thomas McIntyre should not be in the U.S. Senate.

McIntyre delivered his own political epitaph:

> If you want to see people of dignity, integrity and self-respect refuse to seek public office for fear of what might be conjured or dredged up to attack them or their families, stand aside and be silent.
>
> If you want to see confidential files rifled, informants solicited, universities harassed, "enemy hit lists" drawn up, stand aside and be silent . . .
>
> If you want to see the fevered exploitation of a handful of highly emotional issues distract the Nation from problems of great consequence, stand aside and be silent . . .
>
> If you want this Nation held up to world-wide scorn and ridicule because of the outrageous statements and bizarre beliefs of its leaders, stand aside and let the Howard Phillips,* the Meldrim Thomsons and the William Loebs speak for all of us.

The Senate was not totally silent, at that moment. Majority Leader Byrd immediately rose to say that McIntyre's speech was "among the two or three speeches I have heard in thirty-two years in public office that have had a genuine impact on my thinking, on me personally, and I believe on all who have had the privilege to listen to it." And New York's Senator Moynihan, an admirer of powerful truth, said: "The speech we have just heard could have been made in the Roman Senate in the days of its honor, and it has enhanced this Chamber as no other speech I have heard this year."

But whether any significant number of senators truly recognized the political death knell that McIntyre was sounding for himself and for some of them was doubtful. They would have done well to heed his words more closely. Later that year, some of them, and two years later, even more, would know how right their perceptive neighbor from New Hampshire was. If they had joined forces then to fight the influences McIntyre described so well, the outcome might have been different.

By the beginning of March, everyone concerned with the Panama treaties—and that included the entire Senate and most of the population of Panama—was bored to death with the tiresome debate. Virtually everything that could be said about every feature of the Neutrality Treaty, pro and con, had been said, not once but many times. As the *Washington Star*

---

* National director of the Conservative Caucus.

commented on March 2: "Eleven tedious days into the debate, a new argument is an oddity. A new 'fact'—a statement stipulated to by both sides—is even rarer." Vermont's perceptive Senator Leahy likened the proceedings to a soap opera. You could miss a couple of hours or a couple of days, he said, and find that nothing essential had passed you by.

It was not just that senators and listeners alike were growing bored, but tempers were becoming frayed on both sides. Traditional senatorial courtesy was beginning to sound more and more strained and stilted. Senators were combing the lexicon for polite equivalents to "my distinguished colleague is lying in his teeth." In Panama, everyone with a radio seemed either disgruntled or dismayed. The debate to which they had looked forward with so much interest had rapidly turned into a sour mixture of insults and nit picking.

Treaty proponents and the Senate leadership recognized the delaying tactics perfectly well. Majority Leader Byrd informed his colleagues that "unless more rapid progress is made" he was going to start scheduling evening sessions and meetings on Saturdays, and might shorten the Easter recess. That got the Senate's attention. Members of Congress detest night sessions, treasure their weekends, and consider the recesses as precious times for mending political fences at home or for trips abroad. Byrd's skillful wielding of his scheduling powers enabled him, with Senator Baker's cooperation, to win unanimous consent from the Senate on March 6 that the upper house would vote on ratification of the Neutrality Treaty by 4:00 P.M. on March 16.

By the end of the first week in March, the mood in the White House and the State Department toward the Panama debate had undergone a marked change. The move had been gradual, nothing one could attribute to any single event, meeting, speech, or poll. Nonetheless, the optimism of the first weeks of the Senate sessions had turned into evident concern. When Senator Proxmire gaveled the Senate to order on February 8 and the great debate began, the White House congressional liaison office counted fifty votes as certain for the Neutrality Treaty. Within ten days, the number had risen to sixty, and all concerned were elated. But then the vote-count needle stopped like the hands of an unwound clock. Meantime, the estimate of those firmly opposed had risen from twenty-five to thirty. The administration needed sixty-seven votes and the battle centered on the decisions of the remaining ten "uncommitted" senators.

The president and his advisers concluded they could not count on things like party loyalty, awareness of the situation in Panama, regard for the president's leadership role in foreign affairs, or old-fashioned statesmanship to swing the waverers into line. Most of the holdouts were either desperately nervous about their personal political futures or hard-eyed opportunists who wanted to enhance their status in their home states and in the Senate. It was going to take a combination of realistic politics and some minor concessions to the nervous and the ambitious. That meant, among other things, a much more direct role for the president.

For those with a sensitive nose for the scents of politics, the first indication that something new was in the wind had nothing to do with Panama. That first week in March, the White House reversed itself on a plan to buy copper for the national stockpile of strategic metals. Until then opposed, the administration decided to back the purchase of $250 million worth of copper. That was good news in Arizona and Montana. Dennis DeConcini was from the former; Paul Hatfield from the latter. A week later, the White House quietly changed its stand on a $2.3 billion emergency farm bill that was of special interest to Senator Talmadge, chairman of the Senate Agriculture Committee. The White House denied any connection between those shifts and the drive for votes on the Panama treaty. But one administration official was quoted by the *New York Times* as saying: "I hope the Panamanians will get as much out of these treaties as some Senators."

President Carter had led the many White House briefings for visiting state delegations and he had gone on nationwide television to extoll the Panama treaties. But beginning in early March, he played a much more direct role in the treaty fight. He called many senators to either persuade them to support the new pacts or to encourage those already committed not to waver. He invited at least a dozen senators to the Oval Office for personal talks. On Friday, March 10, for example, he met separately with Republicans Brooke and Schweiker and Democrat Hatfield. Two nights before, Nebraska's Senator Zorinski and his wife were added at the last minute to the guest list for a White House dinner for Yugoslavia's Marshall Tito.

What effect all that personal attention had on the final treaty vote is questionable. Despite overused clichés about "wheeling and dealing" and "arm twisting," personal contacts between a president and a member of Congress on matters of policy are an expression of the political art. If the president is to succeed, he needs great finesse, a thorough understanding of the character of the man with whom he is dealing, an awareness of the congressman's problems and needs, of his strengths and his weaknesses. Those skills do not come easily, and Jimmy Carter had little chance to develop them. Nor did any of his top staffers. My evidence indicated that Carter's one-on-one contacts with the Senate were less than triumphant.

The first sign of a break in the administration's theretofore rigid stance against treaty changes occurred at a lunch on March 9 in Senator Byrd's office. Vice President Mondale attended along with Democratic Whip Cranston and floor leader Frank Church. Warren Christopher was there to advise on treaty provisions and policy. The guests were five Democratic holdouts: Long of Louisiana, Nunn and Talmadge of Georgia, Kentucky's

Ford, and DeConcini from Arizona. The talk revolved around two problems. One was the demand for arrangements to keep U.S. military forces in Panama after the year 2000. The other did not concern the Neutrality Treaty at all but rather the provision in the second treaty that prohibited the United States from negotiating with other countries on a possible sea-level canal.

Christopher called me earlier that day to get an update of my views on a provision for post-2000 canal defense. I told him any amendment by the Senate that provided for the continued presence of U.S. troops after the treaty expired would be rejected by Panama. Obviously it would have forced a new plebiscite by the Panamanian people. "And I have no doubt," I told the deputy secretary, "that a new plebiscite that turned on this provision would be resoundingly defeated by the Panamanian public."

Knowing his and the administration's difficulties with some senators on this vexed question, I told Christopher: "I wouldn't rule out the possibility of finding acceptance from the Panamanians of some general understanding that left the door open for the two countries to work out mutually advantageous and commonly agreed methods for assuring that the neutrality of the canal would be jointly guaranteed in the twenty-first century." Torrijos would not like it, to be sure, but I believed I could convince him of its advantages if crucial votes swung on the outcome. I explained to Christopher I was stressing "mutually advantageous" and "commonly agreed" and "jointly guaranteed." The element of mutuality was essential.

On the sea-level canal option, I told Christopher I thought the senators were being "damn fools" to abandon our exclusive rights in a future Panama Canal so that we could talk with the Nicaraguans or Colombians, where the experts said any canal would be incredibly more expensive. The change those senators were talking about would, of course, release the Panamanians to talk with anyone they wished to about a future canal. We were trading something for nothing, in my judgment. But I told Christopher that if pride and false patriotism forced such a revision, Torrijos and the Panamanians would welcome it. They thought the original provision was unduly restrictive on *them*.

The Thursday lunch gave the senators a chance to explain why they thought a U.S. military presence after the year 2000 was needed, and the leadership and Christopher an opportunity to underline why it endangered the treaty. At that point, a few senators were still insisting on a treaty amendment. The same group met the next day, and at that session Vice President Mondale argued persuasively against an amendment. The senators pulled back and seemed willing to accept a "reservation" or "condition." But they left no doubt there had to be some provision for dealing with posttreaty defense and U.S. involvement. It became equally clear that the administration—which had successfully fought off all treaty changes—had shifted ground and was ready to accept something along that line. The question became not whether it would be done but what words would be used.

During the first two weeks of March, the White House staffers made two serious mistakes. First, they were persuaded that Sam Nunn and veteran senators like Long and Talmadge were their real problem. They discounted the importance of Arizona's DeConcini, who had been in the upper house less than two years. The White House liaison staff concluded that, if old hands in the Senate could be persuaded, neophytes like DeConcini would surely go along. The second error was in assigning primary responsibility for dealing with DeConcini to State's Warren Christopher. It had nothing to do with ability, intelligence, or background—which Christopher had in abundance. In the end, even President Carter proved incapable of dealing with DeConcini. The results would have been significantly different, I believe, if the task of corralling the young maverick from Arizona had been given to some veteran of Senate roundups, a Byrd or a Hollings, a Jackson or a Muskie. That course was never chosen; the White House thought it knew better.

Admittedly, DeConcini was under heavy pressure in his home state. Even Arizona's prestigious and usually courageous Barry Goldwater had retreated in the face of heavy pressure from the well-organized, well-heeled, and vociferous antitreaty forces. When I talked with Goldwater the year before in his office, he freely conceded a new, more evenhanded arrangement with Panama was long overdue. After listening to a briefing by Bunker and Linowitz on details of the new treaties later in 1977, the Arizona Republican told them he had not totally reversed position but that they had moved his view "about 160 degrees." But when reports circulated that Goldwater was considering supporting the treaties, conservative political action groups unleashed their artillery. The GOP standard bearer in 1964 was deluged with letters, postcards, and phone calls. The clamor, especially from old friends and financial supporters, was too much to withstand. Finally, in September, Goldwater announced his opposition to the new treaties. He claimed to be unhappy about some of the security provisions, though he was never too specific about what he would like to see changed.

Goldwater's emergence as a treaty opponent put additional heat on his young, Democratic colleague. DeConcini began telling questioners at meetings in Arizona that he could not support the treaties without "substantial amendments." DeConcini was listed on the White House nose-count chart in February as "uncommitted but leaning negative." At that point, one of the big guns in the protreaty camp in the Senate should have been asked to have a quiet private talk with the junior senator from Arizona. Instead, during the week of March 6, the White House assigned the task to the State Department.

When Christopher saw DeConcini the next day, he found the senator in a demanding mood. He insisted the treaty be altered in two respects. First, he wanted an amendment giving the United States the right to keep at least three military bases in Panama for five years after the treaty expired. Whether for five years or for five minutes, DeConcini's proposal violated both the spirit and the letter of the treaty and would have been immediately rejected by the Panamanian government. The Arizonian either knew that or the countless briefings he had heard, in Panama and in Washington, had gone in one ear and out the other. More likely, he was playing a card he knew he would lose but in return for which he hoped to gain much.

The second change DeConcini insisted on was "a specific guarantee that the obstruction of the canal arising out of internal Panamanian activities can be swiftly and adequately dealt with." To meet that need, DeConcini was pushing the amendment he had introduced with little fanfare into the Senate hopper on February 9. Christopher did not attack DeConcini's two proposals frontally, as they probably should have been addressed. After all, the senator was endangering thirteen years of careful negotiation and a foreign policy initiative that his party's president had given top priority. In judging possible threats to the canal in the future, and the ability of the United States to meet those threats, the forty-year-old senator was setting his judgment above that of the experienced diplomats who had worked out the treaty, of the Joint Chiefs of Staff, of a majority of his fellow senators, and of the president as well. He should probably have been told quite bluntly that if he persisted in his arrogant approach, the treaties were going to fail and the consequences, which would have been dire for the United States, for Panama, and for world commerce, would be laid directly on his doorstep.

That was not done. Perhaps it could not have been done. DeConcini by then had become a regular fixture on the evening network television shows and his voice was heard often on radio news broadcasts. He seemed to love that kind of exposure. For the media, looking for something to add a little spice to an otherwise dull story, a maverick senator who appeared to be bucking his colleagues and the White House was ready-made for exploitation.

The hope in the White House and at the State Department was that DeConcini would be satisfied with a reservation on post-2000 security for the canal. He had been a leading advocate of that provision and administration strategists reckoned that, with that won, he might drop his second demand. That was the farthest thing from DeConcini's mind. He was getting wide media attention and relishing it. He told reporters the price for his vote on the treaty was incorporation of his two changes. "I won't go without both of them," he said.

The political maneuvering then going on between the administration and a few senators was making the Panamanians nervous and suspicious. Ambassador Lewis was sure he was not getting the full story of the behind-the-scenes actions. Though he was on the phone constantly with Christopher and Hamilton Jordan, he said he was getting more information from the *Washington Post* and the *Washington Star* than from the administration. Unfortunately, the news accounts often contained inaccuracies or exaggerations that compounded his uneasiness.

Lewis' concerns colored the views of Torrijos and those around him and they, too, became suspicious and fearful. I had my hands full trying to reassure them and to counsel patience. I kept telling the general and his advisers that "President Carter is your friend," and "Senators like Byrd and Baker and Church want a good treaty as much as you do," and "No one is going to cut Panama's throat after we have come this far." But the credibility of my reassurances was undercut by the news from Washington where it seemed a few senators did indeed want to "cut Panama's throat." At the end of most of those trying days, usually late at night, Ambassador Lewis and I consulted by phone. We shared such information as we had, and usually signed off by telling each other that the next day had to be better than the one just ending.

Occasionally, of course, we argued. I remember he was outraged by a story in the *Washington Star* that said Senate leaders had accepted a proposal that "the treaties would not go into effect unless Panama agreed to discuss further the possibility of American troops remaining in what is now the Canal Zone."

"That," Gabriel said in some heat, "is just another form of perpetuity. And I tell you that a perpetuity treaty written in 1903 is better for Panama than one written in 1978!"

I told him the story was wrong. All that was being considered was a provision that left Panama and the United States free to work out future canal security at some distant date, say 1998, and then only if both countries agreed. Finally I told him: "Gabriel, I agree with you that it's stupid. Twenty years from now, if the canal is in danger, your children and mine will make some kind of arrangement, just as we did. But if leaving that door open now gives us a couple of votes on the big issue, why not do it?" He swore a gentle oath. "Yes, you're right," he said. "I just don't think some of these damn senators think about it the way you and I do." I told him he was most assuredly right.

The second weekend in March, Christopher kept trying to whittle down DeConcini's elaborate demands but with little success. A few words were deleted and a few added that helped take the rougher edges off the

Arizona senator's chauvinistic proposal, but nothing was done to change its basic thrust. The senator seemed to enjoy the elaborate attention he was getting, and he played a diddling game. One afternoon, he would tell Christopher a suggested change seemed all right; the next morning he would call to say he had changed his mind.

Meantime, I had explained to Washington that we had a serious and growing problem in Panama. The Senate debate was bad enough. But Torrijos and his advisers had become increasingly concerned about the elaborate game being played around proposed amendments, reservations, and conditions. Ambassador Lewis obviously was not getting the details he needed for a comprehensive report. We needed badly to convey to the Panamanians the full flavor of the mood in the Senate and the problems treaty supporters faced.

That weekend, Christopher and Carter's aides decided it would be wise to send Ambler Moss to Panama to brief the Panamanians. Ambler had been leading the effective information group supplying background material to senators on questions that arose in the debate. When the idea was raised with me, I welcomed it. If anyone was aware of Senate maneuvering, it was Moss. I also believed that sending a special representative to explain Senate developments would underline our concern and our sense of partnership. Christopher cleared the Moss visit with Senator Byrd early Monday morning, and Ambler was on a plane a few hours later.

At the same meeting with Byrd and other senators, the final touches were put on the condition relating to a possible U.S. military presence after the year 1999. Because Georgia's Senator Nunn was up for reelection later in the year, it was agreed he should be the principal sponsor. As revised at that meeting, the reservation provided "that nothing in this treaty shall preclude Panama and the United States from making, in accordance with their respective constitutional processes, any agreement or arrangement to facilitate performance at any time after December 31, 1999, of their responsibilities to maintain the regime of neutrality established in the treaty, including agreements or arrangements for the stationing of any U.S. military forces or maintenance of defense sites after that date in the Republic of Panama that Panama and the United States may deem necessary or appropriate."

After the meeting, Christopher called Ambassador Lewis. He told him Ambler Moss was on his way to Panama. He also explained the final shape of the Nunn reservation. Like all Panamanians, Lewis was troubled by any mention of a foreign military presence after the treaty expired. But Christopher explained that "anything less than this and we'll have the treaty defeated here." Lewis wondered if, with that reservation, the treaty would be ratified. Christopher told him that with it the chances were "better than even"; without it, he said the treaty would lose. Later, the ambassador spoke with Hamilton Jordan. He got the same assessment: the Nunn reservation was "the difference between ratification and no ratification."

Ambler Moss arrived in Panama that night and he and I stayed up late discussing developments in the Senate. It was invaluable to get his first-hand account of the debate, the personalities, the issues, and the political forces at work. His sharp eye and trained legal mind uncovered nuances in the Senate drama that never came through in sterile official reporting. That talk with Ambler gave me the full flavor of the DeConcini reservation and what its author really intended. The Arizona senator was talking not about threats to the canal from Soviet submarines or Cuban paratroops, but such things as a slowdown in transits brought on by a labor dispute. It was ludicrous, and dangerous, but that was what the political tyro from Arizona had in mind.

The next morning, Moss and I met with Torrijos' principal advisers on treaty affairs—Foreign Minister González-Revilla, Escobar, Royo, López-Guevara, and Rory González. We met in Rory's spacious house, just off the sixth fairway of the former Panama Golf Club. Ambler gave a detailed description of the Senate debate, the fractious mood, the problem of egos, the political ambitions that had to be catered to. He told the Panamanians bluntly that at that moment the administration did not have enough votes to prevail. To get crucial votes from several undecided senators, some accommodation of their demands would be essential. He praised Panama's patience during the many provocative Senate sessions. Their silence had helped treaty defenders greatly, and had frustrated treaty critics who hoped for an explosion on the isthmus. Unfortunately, he said, the same restraint would be necessary during the debate of the second treaty.

The Panamanians listened carefully but with considerable reserve. It was well and good to talk about their patience, they said, but the steady flow of poison that came from some senators was creating serious political problems for Torrijos. The press and many citizens were criticizing the government for not responding to the numerous snide remarks and allegations made on the Senate floor. They could not guarantee the general's patience would last forever.

Despite the frosty background, the Panamanians were more cooperative than I had expected when we got down to specific cases. They recognized that the Nunn reservation on post-1999 military arrangements imposed no real obligation on Panama. Nor did it change the treaty itself. Still, they said, it "altered the psychological expectations of the Panamanian people" with its reference to a "military presence," which they thought had been ended once and for all. Royo said they would like to give us wording that they thought would meet our problem while doing minimum damage to Panamanian sensibilities. I told the treaty advisers we would receive their suggestion gladly, but could make no promises that it would alter the final outcome. Christopher had told me "we do not have any real room for maneuver on this," and I was determined not to give the Panamanians any false hopes. Still, the Panamanian view deserved a hearing.

The second issue, the sea-level canal option and the insistence of some senators that the United States be free to discuss it with other countries, gave the Panamanians no problems. They had agreed to it originally as a concession to us and had never really liked it. Their only concern was that outright deletion would be a "substantive change" that might require a new plebiscite. The Panamanian lawyers agreed to try to find a formula that would meet our requirements and theirs.

Where we ran into a stone wall was on the DeConcini reservation. Based on press reports and information from their embassy, they had concluded DeConcini was not merely restating or underlining the treaty provisions on protection of the canal's neutrality. As one of the Panamanians put it, the Arizona senator was "permitting U.S. intervention in Panama on the slightest pretext—a strike, a landslide, anything." The advisers' comments were vitriolic.

In our report to Washington, made within the hour, we said that the DeConcini reservation was "flatly unacceptable" and "if adopted would cause rejection of the treaty." Ambler and I felt Washington should have an unvarnished description of the Panamanian government's view. It was as clear a warning flag as language would allow.

That afternoon, we went back to Rory González' house for a follow-up session. The Panamanian group had expanded. Ricardo Bilonick, Ambassador Lewis' deputy in the Washington embassy, had arrived. Colonel Contreras was there to represent the National Guard. Two or three others who had been involved in the treaty negotiations were also present. As I informed Washington, "the atmosphere was a bit more relaxed than it had been in the A.M." and the Panamanians seemed "somewhat more forthcoming."

"It was clear, nonetheless," I cabled, "that there are limits in treaty adjustments and interpretations beyond which they feel they cannot go."

Regarding the sea-level canal problem, the Panamanians seemed eager to go along with us in eliminating the restrictions we had imposed on ourselves. But they believed that all the formulations proposed to that point represented "a major change" and were thus unacceptable. They agreed to give it additional thought and to find some middle ground both sides could accept.

On the DeConcini proposal, I informed Washington that "the Panamanians repeated their strong feeling that this would be totally unacceptable to their Government." They insisted that "no government could grant such a right to another nation and maintain its national pride."

Most of our talk concerned the Nunn reservation, keeping the door open to U.S. military participation in canal defense on the scene after the treaty expired, if the two countries agreed. It was still giving the Panamanians heartburn. They had no trouble with the general idea, but for internal political reasons, they wanted to get rid of the phrase "military presence." Less than an hour after we broke up, Royo called me to pass along the formula he and his colleagues had worked out. They felt it met our needs, but made the formula politically more palatable to them. The Panamanians proposed "that nothing shall preclude the United States and Panama, in accordance with their respective constitutional processes, from entering into future negotiations for the purpose of reaching any agreement to facilitate performance, at any time after December 31, 1999, of their responsibilities to maintain the regime of neutrality established in the treaty, including agreements on military cooperation as the United States and Panama may deem necessary or appropriate."

I passed Panama's wording on to Washington, but I had no great expectation it would be accepted. By then, the Nunn formula seemed to be locked in concrete. I urged Royo not to be too optimistic.

Our long sessions with the Panamanians revealed their desire for honest consultation to the very end of the treaty trail. We had had that during the lengthy negotiations. But once the treaties were signed, the rules of the game seemed to change and the close contacts we had—to the benefit of both sides—were allowed to dwindle. Some Americans in the White House, the Senate, and the State Department took the view that ratification was *our* business, not that of the Panamanians. A major foreign policy issue was magically converted into an internal affair.

The Panamanians never understood that. They believed that when the Senate decided to interpret a treaty article or inject an understanding on matters not covered in detail, it was as much Panama's business as had been the original agreement. They simply wanted to talk things over, to get our ideas and explain theirs, and to make sure that treaties they had already approved were not altered in any central way. It was not an unreasonable wish.

In the early stages of the Senate debate, there was, in fact, a good deal of consultation, as we have seen. And it worked exceedingly well. But as the Senate worked its way toward the voting deadline, the process disintegrated. The ability of the U.S. Embassy to explain to Panamanian officials precisely what a particular senator was demanding, and why, diminished. Panama's ambassador in Washington was gradually cut off from the close consultation he had enjoyed for a year.

During those critical days, a flood of official cables was coming into the embassy, but many contained the texts of understandings or reservations that would be killed or "tabled." We began to find newspaper reports more revealing than official messages. After Moss and I met with the Panamanians, for example, we read a story from that morning's *Washington Post*. It dealt with the administration's "substantial concession" to Senator De-Concini. And it quoted the Arizona Democrat as saying he was not satisfied with what the White House was offering. He predicted that "the Administration would do what it had to to please him," said the *Post*.

When I read it, I called the State Department and requested that the two cables we had sent earlier in the day be passed to top officials in the White House. I wanted to be sure that at least Hamilton Jordan, Zbig Brzezinski, and congressional liaison chief Frank Moore were aware of Panama's determination to reject a treaty that contained DeConcini's proposal. The request was either lost in the bureaucratic mill, or the authorities at State did not wish to alarm the White House.

Wednesday, March 15, 1978, will live in the memory of a handful of Americans and Panamanians as the day the patiently sought, painstakingly pursued "new deal" in U.S.-Panama relations approached total collapse. The previous evening, State's deputy secretary had told DeConcini that the Arizonian's reservation was acceptable to the administration. But the suspicious DeConcini wanted that assurance from the highest authority in the land. Accordingly, at his request, DeConcini was given an appointment with the president that Wednesday morning.

Carter was by then fearful that his first major move in foreign policy was on the brink of failure. His aides had convinced him DeConcini's vote was critical for success, especially as the Arizona senator was said to have the votes of "two others" in his pocket. (One was Montana's Paul Hatfield, who had been in the Senate less than two months. The second dependent vote was a mystery; I later heard at least four names mentioned.)

At the meeting in the Oval Office, DeConcini proposed the condition he and his staff had been working on for weeks. The words he demanded were: ". . . notwithstanding the provisions of Article V or any other provision of the treaty, if the Canal is closed, or its operations are interfered with, the United States of America and the Republic of Panama shall each independently have the right to take such steps as it deems necessary, including the use of military force in Panama, to reopen the Canal or restore the operations of the Canal, as the case may be."

DeConcini told the president his reservation was needed to clarify the "ambiguity" he saw in the Neutrality Treaty, even with the leadership amendment. He also warned that, without the proposed change, he would not vote for the treaty. The president asked Christopher if DeConcini's revision would create any problems with Panama. The deputy secretary admitted it would, but he thought it was something that could be "handled." It was probably the most misleading advice the normally cautious diplomat ever gave Carter.

I later asked Christopher about this in light of the two extremely strong warnings I had sent the previous day. He thought there had been "some misunderstanding about the ambassador's advice on this." His recollection was that "although there was certainly an indication that the Panamanians would have difficulty . . . there was an implication that, at the end of the day, it could be digested." There was no such implication in my messages. Christopher was confusing what we had reported many days before on the original DeConcini reservation regarding a possible U.S. military presence after 1999 (what later became the Nunn reservation). I had said that probably could be worked out, as it was. On the DeConcini proposal discussed with the president, I had said it was "unacceptable" and would probably lead to rejection of the treaty.

In any case, having received Christopher's assurances, the president told the Arizona senator he would accept his addition to the treaty. DeConcini left the White House a happy man and word of Carter's endorsement of his proposal was promptly in the hands of the reporters.

Though the president and his aides seemed not to have realized the depth of the problem they had created in Panama, they at least suspected that some "massaging" of Panamanian egos might be useful. As soon as DeConcini had left the Oval Office, the president wrote a letter to General Torrijos and sent it by cable to me for delivery.

It was a long message recalling the progress made since the two leaders met in Washington the previous October, and noting that the Senate was "now approaching the end of its debate on the Neutrality Treaty." Carter warned Torrijos that "the Senate will almost certainly attach a number of reservations, conditions or understandings reflecting certain of its concerns." The president assured the Panamanian leader: "We have made every effort and have been successful to date in ensuring that these will be consistent with the general purposes of our two countries as parties to the treaty." He urged Torrijos to "examine them in this light." Carter did not mention the Nunn reservation (which was giving the Panamanians some pain) or the more onerous DeConcini proviso (which would create consternation), or why he had felt obliged to accept them.

Soon after the president's meeting with DeConcini, Hamilton Jordan called Ambassador Lewis and asked him to come to the White House. Lewis explained that Panama's ambassador to the United Nations, Jorge Illueca, was with him and he wanted to bring him along. The two diplomats then drove to the White House and went to Jordan's office in the West Wing.

The president's assistant told the Panamanian ambassadors that President Carter had reached an agreement that morning with Senator DeConcini. He also handed Lewis the original of the president's letter to Torrijos. The Panamanians complained that the U.S. side was accepting reservations and conditions without any consultation with Panama and that, they claimed, "violated our understanding" on working things out together. Lewis said Jordan and his colleagues were going out of their way "to save President Carter's dignity." But he and Illueca had to be concerned with General Torrijos' "dignity."

Hoping to calm the Panamanians, Jordan called Warren Christopher, who was then on Capitol Hill in the vice-president's office. He asked the deputy secretary to meet with the Panamanians and to give them the text of the DeConcini condition that had just been accepted. The Panamanians drove to the Capitol and went to Mondale's office. There Christopher gave them copies of the Nunn and DeConcini reservations and went over the wording of each. Panama was by then inclined to accept the Nunn proposal on future security arrangements, but Lewis and Illueca told the two Americans that the DeConcini approach was an insult. Christopher argued that he considered the condition was "not too bad." Lewis said he would report to General Torrijos, who would have to decide. But he said he thought the Americans were shifting responsibility to Panama instead of themselves rejecting changes that were clearly offensive.

Witnesses said Lewis and Illueca were obviously infuriated when they walked out of the vice-president's office. It was probably at that point that Christopher realized fully what a Pandora's box he had opened by bowing to DeConcini's threats.

When they got back to the embassy, Ambassador Lewis tried to locate Torrijos. The general was on an inspection tour in Colón and away from any phones. Lewis contacted Aristides Royo and Rory González, who were standing by on Torrijos' orders at Rory's house. Knowing some of his colleagues thought he was sometimes too emotional, Lewis asked Illueca to describe what they had just been through. The U.N. ambassador said the situation was "serious" and he gave Royo and González a full account of the morning's events. He read them the letter from President Carter, which Royo took down in his special shorthand, and then described the DeConcini condition, which he said "violated our understanding."

Rory then managed to contact Torrijos in Colón. He told the general about the call from the two ambassadors, and Torrijos was soon talking with his diplomats in Washington. Once again, Illueca went over the details of his and Lewis' visits to the White House and to Mondale's office. The Panamanian leader said: "I think we should tell Carter to be honest and tell us [what's happening]. If he can't go ahead with our agreement, don't go. We want *the* treaty, not just any treaty."

As he thought about the whole affair, DeConcini in particular, Torrijos grew more heated. "If he can't make it, he should tell me," Torrijos said of Carter. "That would be honest. I will not let them camouflage 'perpetuity.'

We want the treaty we approved in October. Even if they dress it up as a clown, it will still be perpetuity." Finally, he said he was going to denounce the DeConcini reservation to the world press.

Lewis by then was back on the phone. The general told the ambassador: "Call Rómulo [Escobar] and tell him to start preparing a statement to that effect." Torrijos said he would sign it as soon as he got to Panama City. He told Lewis he would make his statement at six o'clock. The ambassador asked if he should inform the White House of what was coming. Torrijos said he should.

Lewis called the treaty advisers in Panama City and relayed Torrijos' instructions. He and Illueca then wrote out a message summarizing Torrijos' views. Gabriel called Hamilton Jordan, told him he had a message from Torrijos, and asked for an appointment with the president. Jordan called back almost immediately to say they should come to the White House right away.

Meantime, in Panama City, Torrijos' instructions had created pandemonium among the assembled treaty advisers. Escobar and Royo could see all their hard work on the treaties going down the drain of history. They, López-Guevara, and Rory González were certain Torrijos' denunciation of DeConcini would be regarded as a condemnation of the Senate itself. In the vote due the next day, the Senate would certainly refuse to approve the Neutrality Treaty. That, in turn, would lead to riots and bloodshed in Panama that would make the 1964 outburst look mild by comparison. Surely, they thought, there must be some way to undercut the reservation without destroying a lifelong goal in the process. "But we still have to prepare a statement for Omar," someone said. "Leave that to me," Escobar said as he sat down at a typewriter.

When Ambassadors Lewis and Illueca arrived at the White House, they were met by Jordan and escorted directly to the Oval Office. Lewis told the president he had a message from General Torrijos and he proceeded to read it.

"In the name of the Government of Panama," he began, "the Embassy of Panama transmitted to the Head of the Government of Panama the letter President Carter addressed to him, as well as the information received from your Administration this morning through Vice President Mondale, Presidential Adviser Hamilton Jordan and Deputy Secretary of State Warren Christopher regarding the Nunn and DeConcini reservations.

"He [Torrijos] asked me, as his Ambassador, to deliver the following message to you: 'The Head of Government of Panama considers that this type of reservation that will be introduced in the Senate is not acceptable because it disguises perpetuity. General Torrijos prefers to know frankly whether the Government of the United States is or is not in a position to obtain ratification from the Senate without affecting the text of the original treaties.'

"General Torrijos will make a public statement today at 6 P.M. putting the world on notice that any draft of a reservation, amendment, condition, or whatever unilateral understanding is prepared by the Senate will not be acceptable to Panama."

Lewis explained that he meant any change that altered the treaties in a fundamental way.

The president was taken aback. He had been advised only that morning that any problems brought on in Panama by DeConcini would be "manageable." Apparently they were anything but that. It was after 4 o'clock and Torrijos would be on television and radio denouncing the treaty condition in less than two hours. Carter immediately summoned Secretary Vance, National Security Adviser Brzezinski, Warren Christopher, and several members of his own staff.

When his advisers had assembled, the president outlined the difficulties just raised by the ambassador and instructed them to "find a solution to the problem." There was a brief discussion of a possible Senate resolution which would make clear that nothing in the treaty, including DeConcini's addition, gave the United States the right to interfere in Panama's internal affairs. Christopher went to Capitol Hill to find out whether such a resolution had a chance.

Another, less orderly, meeting was underway in Panama. Torrijos had flown across the isthmus by helicopter and landed behind Rory González' house. The general stormed in in a foul mood. He was damning the Senate, and every tenth word was "DeConcini" led or followed by an unprintable expletive. Carter seemed to be bailing out, he exclaimed, and "he wants to use my parachute—except I don't have one left." Torrijos said he wanted the original treaties, the ones he and Carter had agreed to, not some patched-up documents that insulted his country. He looked at Rómulo and asked him if he was getting it all down. "Yes, my General," said the lawyer sitting at the typewriter. Rory handed Torrijos a drink and the others started talking to him quietly. Royo showed a special brand of courage that day. "You may think that I'm a traitor," he began, "but I don't think this is the best way to handle this problem." Torrijos was surprised, but he listened. Royo said he felt sure there was some way to cope with the DeConcini problem that did not destroy everything. Others chimed in with similar thoughts. A consensus grew: we need to look harder at this; possibly something can be done in the Senate; maybe Carter can help; perhaps there are things we can do as well.

Torrijos was slowly persuaded he should wait a bit. If there was some way to neutralize DeConcini without shattering the entire new arrangement, he decided it was probably worth a try. At that point, the phone rang.

In the Oval Office, President Carter had decided that he could not just sit and wait. He ordered a phone call to Panama City. In a few minutes, the operator was on the line saying she was ringing General Torrijos' number. When the general came on the phone, the president said: "General, this is Jimmy Carter."

He explained that he had just talked to Ambassador Lewis and he now understood the unhappiness in Panama with the DeConcini proposal. The heart of his message was: we are going to try to do something about it; give us a chance to work things out; the treaties are too important to us both to lose them at this late stage. Torrijos was cordial and receptive, but he had to explain why the DeConcini condition was offensive to all Panamanians. He repeated what he had told Lewis: "We want the treaty you and I worked out last October; we don't want just any treaty." Carter said he understood perfectly and he promised to do something about it before the second treaty was approved, sooner if possible. Torrijos thanked the president for that assurance and promised to do nothing to make the job more difficult.

When Carter hung up, he said in Spanish, "Ese general es muy buen hombre" [That general is a very good man]. Ambassador Lewis replied: "Yes, he is a very good man. But he can't accept DeConcini because that would be political suicide. You wouldn't want a good man to commit suicide, would you?" Carter grinned and said he certainly would not.

At the other end, Torrijos replaced the phone and turned to Rómulo. "Have you written anything?" he asked. The sharp lawyer said he had not. "I can't get this damned machine to work," he said in frustration. He had deliberately fouled up the new typewriter and the ribbon looked by then like a long string of black spaghetti. Torrijos laughed. "Don't bother," he said. "We're not going to say anything tonight. Carter says he's going to do something. Let's give him a chance. He's a good man."

By that slim margin, thanks to the quick action of President Carter and the restraint of Omar Torrijos—plus the magic of Alexander Graham Bell's invention—no blood flowed on the streets of Panama and the Canal Zone that night.

The embassy had picked up bits of information and a host of rumors, but our first solid information came in a phone call at 6:30 P.M. from Ambassador Lewis. He ran down the events of what he called "the toughest day in my life." In about fifteen minutes, we had the flavor and the facts we needed. Gabriel said he was then waiting for the "wording we need" from Panama.

He then told me there was a plan afoot for Hamilton Jordan and Warren Christopher to fly to Panama the next day to "explain everything" to

General Torrijos. I told him bluntly that was "a loser." At that moment, the problem was in Washington, not Panama.

Half an hour later, Lewis received a call from Panama. Royo and the other lawyers had worked out language they thought would effectively pull the teeth of the DeConcini proposal. They hoped it, or something like it, could be converted into an amendment by the leadership in the Senate. It read: "As stated in the Treaty of Neutrality, the United States does not have the right to intervene in the internal affairs of the Republic of Panama. The conditions, reservations and understandings which have been amended to* this resolution of ratification are not intended or interpreted by the United States to mean that it has the right to intervene except to reaffirm the right of both Panama and the United States to maintain the neutrality of the Canal."

Ambassador Lewis had the proposal typed up and sent it to Hamilton Jordan's office. When he received it, Jordan called the ambassador to promise "we will do the best we can" but he would not know whether it was possible until noon the next day. The White House was nervous about the political implications. Jordan explained they did not want to hit Majority Leader Byrd with any "surprises." Jordan's second point was that accepting the Panamanian approach might give the appearance that President Carter was "acting under Panamanian pressure." Nonetheless, Jordan said it would be done "if there is any way of doing it without blowing it all out of the water." Lewis responded: "If not, Omar will have to turn it down."

While Lewis and Jordan were talking, Christopher was on the Hill making one last effort to moderate DeConcini's condition, but it was like applying a Band-Aid to a severed artery. The real battle had been lost that morning when the president accepted DeConcini's demand. Christopher asked the senator for two minor changes which he hoped might soften Panama's disappointment. He wanted to insert the phrase "in accordance with constitutional processes" to reassure Panamanians that any use of force would be considered at the highest level of government. He also asked DeConcini to take out the words "in Panama" which seemed to underline that Panama might be the enemy. The Arizona senator told Christopher he would "think about it overnight" and let him know in the morning.

That night, Gabriel called to share ideas, but more than anything else to release the frustration that had been building in him. He recounted the day's events in detail—his visit to the White House and the talks with the president and his advisers; his bitterness about U.S. willingness to accept a

---

*They meant "added as amendments to."

condition that threatened the treaty, without even consulting Panama; his impression that the U.S. leadership was "like a bunch of generals who are in a losing battle"; his fear that his own government might, in the end, reluctantly accept DeConcini without a real fight. He told me that, if that happened, he was going to resign as ambassador and fight the treaty as a private citizen. I got him to promise not to "do anything rash or abrupt" until he and I had a chance to discuss it further.

The day of reckoning finally arrived for the Treaty Concerning the Permanent Neutrality and Operation of the Panama Canal, to give it its formal title. On March 16, 1978, treaty advocates were fearful some last-minute shift would destroy all they had battled for through weeks of dreary debate, and months before that. The opponents were equally edgy, afraid they had lost but hoping some miracle would provide victory at the final bell. The best bet was that the vote would be 67 to 33, but even experts were admitting that could shift two or three votes either way.

Christopher was at the White House that morning, and Senator De-Concini reached him at 8:30 A.M. The Arizonian said he had spent a largely sleepless night studying the treaty and considering Christopher's request for minor changes. He regretted he could not agree with them. Christopher reported that to the president, and Carter thereupon called De-Concini to say the administration would stand by its agreement with him—provided he would vote for the treaty. DeConcini said he would if the Senate adopted his condition.

The Senate met at 9 o'clock. By previous agreement, Indiana's Richard Lugar made a fifteen-minute speech on the fiscal woes of New York City and argued against excessive federal involvement. That done, the Senate turned its attention once again to the Neutrality Treaty. One after another, senators took the floor to extol or castigate the treaties. They were sometimes lively, more often dull, but careful listening showed no new argument being raised, pro or con.

There was only one development of real interest. Between 9:30 A.M. and 1:00 P.M., four senators who had kept silent on their intentions finally revealed them. Oklahoma Republican Henry Bellmon and two Democrats, Dale Bumpers of Arkansas and Montana's Paul Hatfield, told the Senate they planned to vote for the treaty. Democrat Wendell Ford of Kentucky declared himself opposed. When Hatfield made his statement a few minutes before 1 o'clock, the protreaty "head counters" entered his name on their tally sheets as Vote No. 67, the necessary margin of victory. Then they crossed their fingers.

In the middle of the debate, I received a letter General Torrijos had written to President Carter the night before. We translated it quickly and sent it to the State Department for transfer to the White House. Torrijos thanked Carter for his letter and for the good talk they had had earlier that evening. The general said he was grateful for Carter's assurance that reservations in the Senate "will not detract from the content of what was agreed upon" in the original treaty and in their October understanding. Responding to Carter's plea for patience, the general said that "the Government of Panama will proceed to study carefully these reservations and will take its position once the Senate had voted on both treaties.

"I do wish, nevertheless, to point out," Torrijos continued, "that such a study will be based on the following concepts: for Panama, any reservation would be unacceptable which blemished our national dignity, which altered or changed the objectives of the treaty, or which was directed at hindering the effective exercise of Panamanian sovereignty over all of its territory, the transfer of the Canal, and military withdrawal on December 31, 1999."

He put the president on notice that the Panamanians would never accept "words, misplaced commas or ambiguous sentences" that might be interpreted as "occupation in perpetuity disguised as neutrality, or intervention in their internal affairs." It was a polite but undisguised warning that the DeConcini approach was unacceptable to Panama. Torrijos was also saying his country would give the administration and the Senate time to correct their own error and make good the president's word.

Christopher was at the White House that morning meeting with a nervous Hamilton Jordan. Both were dismayed by the sharply negative reaction from the Panamanians over their concession to the Arizona senator. They went over the wording received the night before from Panama. Christopher then drafted a possible understanding to defang DeConcini's handiwork. It read: "None of the amendments to the Resolution of Ratification is intended to or shall be interpreted to contravene the principle of non-intervention in the internal affairs of Panama affirmed in the Memorandum of Understanding of October 14, 1977, nor shall the United States and Panama be prevented from negotiating any agreements or arrangements in the future which are in the mutual interests of the two countries."

Christopher drove to the Hill and showed the newly minted reservation to Senator Byrd. The majority leader insisted the matter be considered with great care. Though he hinted that such a modification might be offered near the end of the debate that day, he did not endorse it wholeheartedly. He wanted additional consultation. In the next hour, the new language was shown to a number of treaty supporters—Church, Nunn, and Baker among others. They told Christopher they saw value in the proposal, but he found them "nervous" about putting it into the Senate hopper at that late hour. Their fear was that it would be read as a direct repudiation of DeConcini and, if pushed, might lead to loss of his vote and Hatfield's on the treaty itself. In the end, they concluded it was not worth the risk. If anything was to be done about neutralizing DeConcini's initiative, it was going to have to be accomplished in connection with the second treaty.

A central problem was that none of the senators, even key players like Byrd, Baker, and Church, knew the depth of Panamanian bitterness about the DeConcini proposal and what it implied. None had been shown my cables on Panama's rejection of the DeConcini proposal. Nor were they told of Torrijos' strong reaction. When they heard the day before that President Carter had accepted DeConcini's condition, they all assumed it had Panamanian blessing. In fact, one senator who was central to the treaty battle recalled being told by Christopher that Panama had agreed to DeConcini's demand. When they learned later about Panamanian unhappiness and, in fact, that Panama had told us DeConcini was "unacceptable," ensuing bitterness with the White House was profound among protreaty senators. But on March 16, most senatorial impatience was directed at what they thought was Panamanian pique that would probably pass.

In that atmosphere, it was impossible to generate any serious move to undercut the DeConcini ploy. Vice President Mondale and others made some discrete soundings but the results were negative. Maryland's Sarbanes said he and his colleagues concluded that what the Panamanians wanted at that moment "really would just blow everything up." Hamilton Jordan called Ambassador Lewis to give him the bad news. They could try for a new reservation, "the one you suggested," said Jordan, "but if we lose, we'll probably lose the whole treaty."

"If you think we might lose the whole treaty," Lewis responded, "I don't want to take the responsibility. I want to consult the general."

Lewis then got Foreign Minister González-Revilla on the phone. He told him what Jordan had said—that putting new language in as Panama wanted would probably mean losing the treaty itself. The minister consulted Torrijos, then came back on the Washington line. "Omar says don't put it in," he reported. The general's feeling was that if they could not get the votes it was better not to try at that time.

Lewis called Jordan to pass along Torrijos' reaction—that it was best to drop the subject for the time being and to deal with it later. Lewis also informed Carter's aide that Torrijos had decided a trip to Panama at that point by Jordan and Christopher was not a good idea. He felt it would "raise expectations" among his people that would not be realized. The real reason was that the visit would have been interpreted by Panamanians as additional Yankee pressure on the general. That was the last thing Torrijos needed at that delicate moment. A disappointed Jordan informed the president and asked the military aide's office to call off preparations for the special flight that evening.

That afternoon, Mili, Ambler Moss, I, and a few embassy officers gathered at the residence to hear the final hours of the Senate debate. We were relaxed because we assumed, despite the confusion of preceding days, that the necessary votes were in hand. The by-then familiar voices spilled out of the radio we had installed for the occasion—Robert Byrd's polite mountain accents, the smooth oratory of Idaho's Church, the mellow drone of Alabama's Allen. Most of the dialects of America were encapsulated in those hours, from Vermont to California, from snare drums to syrup.

The critical moment finally arrived. The presiding officer was Sen. James Abourezk of South Dakota. He banged his gavel, asked senators and staff members to stop talking, and then recognized the senator from Arizona, Mr. DeConcini. I wondered if he would handle his proposal to the Senate with grace, or if he would use it to beat the Panamanians over the head. The answer came quickly.

DeConcini said there had been considerable discussion of possible future threats to the canal from third parties, especially communist countries. But he said he was "equally bothered by the possibility that internal Panamanian activities might also be a threat to the waterway." He used most of the same words he had inserted in the *Record* one month earlier, listing domestic developments that might close the canal. He recalled a "sick-out" by canal employees in February 1975 which "disrupted the efficient operation of the canal."

The senator from Arizona went on, rubbing salt in the political wound: "The amendment contains a very specific reference to the use of military force in Panama. I believe these words are absolutely crucial because they establish the American right—which I am not convinced is adequately provided for either in the body of the treaty or the leadership amendment—to take military action if the case so warrants. It further makes it clear that the United States can take military action on Panamanian soil without the consent of the Panamanian Government."

The senator, who had been in Washington for fourteen months, was interpreting the treaty in a manner diametrically opposed to that of the experienced men who had negotiated it. He was saying that the Senate leadership and the Committee on Foreign Relations were unanimously wrong in what they had told their colleagues. And he was telling the generals and admirals on the Joint Chiefs of Staff that they did not understand their military rights under the treaty they had helped shape.

Treaty supporters were strangely mute, many of them laboring under the delusion that Panama had accepted the DeConcini condition, and that it was the price for two needed votes. Treaty opponents were not slow in recognizing what DeConcini really meant. Senator Allen got DeConcini to admit that his reservation added up to "a major change in the treaty itself." Allen then glided smoothly to his own proposition—that DeConcini's proposal "shall have the same effect as an amendment to the treaty." By then, treaty backers realized they were being boxed in. They rallied their forces and defeated Allen's amendment by a vote of 62 to 36.

But no one seemed willing to address the DeConcini reservation on its merits; rather they appeared to accept it as an embarrassing necessity. The Carter administration and the Senate seemed to be missing the central meaning of DeConcini's proposition. Obviously it would be offensive to the Panamanians, whom we were trying to make our partners and allies. Equally important, DeConcini was embarrassing the United States, talking like an assistant secretary of war in 1903, and representing the worst of past attitudes rather than the best of future policy.

Moss and I were tempted to call friends in the Senate to point out things that seemed to be escaping their attention. DeConcini had mentioned the "sick-out" in 1975, which had slowed canal traffic to a crawl and forced a backlog of hundreds of ships. He did not mention that the protesters were American workers. Was DeConcini saying military force should have been used to break up that "interference" in the canal's operation? What would the AFL-CIO, the parent organization of the U.S. unions involved, have said about that? What would the Congress have said?

Even more to the point, DeConcini's condition gave the right to use military force to end any closure of the canal or interference with its operations to both the United States and Panama. Did that mean that if a U.S. labor union, the pilots, for example, slowed down traffic through the canal to back a claim against management, the Panamanian National Guard should use force to break up that action? Under DeConcini's proposal, that would have been a Panamanian right. Members of the U.S. Senate appeared not to have thought of that possibility.

When I reached for the phone, my wife put her hand on my arm and told me to wait. "You're here and you don't know everything that's been happening in Washington," she said. "Maybe this is the only way to get the first treaty, and DeConcini can be dealt with later. You could stir things up and maybe lose the treaty." I knew she was right, so I put down the phone and went back to listening to the radio.

At last, two members of the Senate said some of the things that others were thinking. One was Howard Metzenbaum of Ohio. He described the reservation, then said: "That reads to me as if we were saying that if the canal is not operating properly, if there is some mechanical breakdown, for example, we can and should send in the troops in order to make it operate.

"I think that is wrong," the Ohio senator said. "I think it violates all the concepts that we have been talking about for days on end. . . . I think it violates the respect we owe the people and the government of Panama, now and after the year 2000."

The other senator who spoke out was Edward Kennedy of Massachusetts. "I am opposed to his amendment," he told the Senate. "It stirs up what is already an emotional issue in Panama, without adding to rights of the United States already recognized by the treaty." Kennedy warned the Senate that the DeConcini amendment could be construed to give the United States the right of military intervention "on almost any pretext." Said the Massachusetts senator: "A strike, a slowdown, even inefficient operation of the canal could—but must not—be used as a pretext to use force, in order to 'restore the operations of the canal.'"

Those lone voices of dissent having been heard, the Senate voted to approve DeConcini's amendment by a vote of 75 to 23. It was without a doubt the most mismanaged segment of the entire Panama treaty debate. First, it should have been recognized much earlier that what DeConcini was talking about in February threatened the entire spirit of the new treaties. That danger having been recognized, the task of reasoning with the senator should have been handled by experts in the ways of the Senate. If the problem had been properly described, Byrd, Church, Cranston, Sarbanes, and a few others surely could have devised a solution. Instead, inexperienced staff work caused the rebellion of one junior senator to be raised to the level of presidential politics. When the problem finally reached the Oval Office, either the president himself was misled about the violent reaction he could expect from Panama, or his handling misled all but a handful of senators. Neither possibility flatters either the president or those around him.

As the Senate clock moved toward 3:00 P.M. that afternoon, the visitors' gallery was rapidly filling with the curious, the concerned, and the connected. At least two dozen Senate wives were there to share a moment in history with their husbands. Ambassadors Ellsworth Bunker and Sol Linowitz, the treaty architects, were in front-row seats. The press gallery had been jammed for some time. On the floor, Alaska's Mike Gravel was dissecting with scalpel and ax a speech Ronald Reagan had made on national television five weeks earlier. But there was so much confusion on the floor, and in the galleries, that few could follow Gravel's carefully documented statement. In any case, the time for oratory had passed; there were no votes then to be influenced one way or the other.

Vice President Mondale was in the chair. When Gravel finished, he rapped for order. "The hour of 3 o'clock having arrived," he said, "the time between now and 4:00 P.M. shall be equally divided between and controlled by the senator from Idaho [Church] and the senator from Nevada [Laxalt]." The last lap had begun. Church immediately yielded fifteen of his thirty minutes to the Senate's Republican leader, Howard Baker of Tennessee. The minority leader described the difficulty all senators faced in reaching a decision on the Panama treaties and commended his fellow senators for the way they had conducted the debate. Then Baker asked the central question: why should the Senate give its advice and consent to the Neutrality Treaty?

"I believe that our opportunity to continue to have the quiet use and enjoyment of the Panama Canal for many years to come," he said, "is greatly enhanced and improved by the adoption of these treaties—by this step forward in the relations between our two countries . . ."

Baker concluded by disagreeing sharply with those who had argued that most Americans opposed the Panama treaties. "The American people want to do what is best for our country," he said, "and in this case, Mr. President, I believe, and I believe a majority of Americans believe, that what is best for our country is not to cling to the status quo but to move forward with an improvement in our use and enjoyment of that great and historic canal."

Control of the floor then passed to Nevada's Laxalt, who had led the treaty opponents through the long debate. Laxalt knew that the die had been cast by then and no amount of oratory was going to alter the outcome. He decided to share the historic spotlight with ten of his colleagues who had backed him in opposition through the dreary weeks. He gave two or three minutes each to Senators Griffin, Wallop, Stevens, Melcher, Stennis, Dole, Harry Byrd, Bartlett, Thurmond, and Allen. Each summarized why he was against the Neutrality Treaty. The arguments were those advanced over and over again in the previous weeks. Griffin argued that the two countries interpreted the treaty differently and that the United States should force Panama to hold another plebiscite. Dole complained that, at the outset, the administration had opposed any change whatsoever in the treaty, then shifted ground and accepted reservations and amendments in order to garner votes. Thurmond called the Panama treaties "the big giveaway of the century."

Floor manager Laxalt reserved the final minutes for himself. It was a rare opportunity to move into the spotlight and to show himself as a statesman, looking not at the day but at the future. He muffed it badly, starting with a long and whining complaint against the Senate for not accepting the many proposed treaty changes his fellow opponents had offered. Laxalt followed with a dissertation on the nation's security that suggested U.S. power would disintegrate if we gave up the Canal Zone. He dragged in the red herring of a future Soviet naval base or Cuban troop emplacements—as though the United States would not resist such advances whether the treaty was approved or not. And he concluded with a political warning to his fellow senators. Noting he was not up for reelection that year, Laxalt said: ". . . if I were, I would not want to go back to Nevada and have to explain a vote for this treaty to my constituents."

Students of Senate practice, and senators most of all, know that oratory is not what makes the legislative machinery turn. But there are those rare occasions when the Senate should present itself to the people and to the world as something more than a collection of manipulators, technicians, or specialists in minutiae. As time ran out, it was left to Senate Majority Leader Byrd to raise the level of discourse; his was the burden of presenting the upper house of the Congress as most Americans, romantically and unrealistically, like to think of it.

He began by quoting the words Shakespeare assigned to Brutus before the battle of Phillipi:

> There is a tide in the affairs of men,
> Which, taken at the flood, leads on to fortune;
> Omitted, all the voyage of their life
> Is bound in shallows and in miseries.
> On such a full sea are we now afloat.
> And we must take the current when it serves,
> Or lose our ventures.

"Today, in the Senate," said Byrd, "we have reached such a tide and we must take the current which now serves, or lose our ventures."

Even witnesses to many Senate debates were moved when they heard the quiet senator from the hills of West Virginia say: ". . . nothing can be politically right if it is morally wrong. In my judgment, it is not only economically right, not only commercially right, not only right from the standpoint of the security interests of our country, not only politically right, but it is morally right that we vote to ratify these treaties, and thus live up to the principles that we have so long espoused among nations."

Byrd warned those who would vote for the treaty that "your badges of courage may be the dents in your armor." But he offered some words of comfort: "He who undertakes to conduct the affairs of a great government as a dedicated, faithful public servant, if sustained by the approval of his own conscience, can rely with confidence upon the candor and the intelligence of a free people, and can bear with patience the censure of disappointed men.

"We have searched for truth," said Byrd, "and both sides lay claim to the answer to the ultimate question, the ultimate question being: what is in the best interests of the United States of America?"

When Byrd had finished, Michigan's Griffin made one final effort to scuttle the treaty. He proposed an amendment that would have sent the Neutrality Treaty back to the president with the Senate's advice that it be renegotiated. Senator Church's comment was brief and sharp. "Mr. President," he said, "if the Senate were to adopt this proposal, we would not go back to the bargaining table. In all probability, we would go back to the trenches." Thereupon the Senate voted 67 to 33 to table Griffin's proposal.

At last, the moment of truth had come. Senator Byrd called for "the yeas and nays on the resolution of ratification." Senators were talking to their neighbors, and the vice-president called them to order. People in the gallery were chatting and Mondale instructed them to be silent. The clerk commenced calling the role. Every member of the Senate was in his seat and called out his "aye" or "nay" for all to hear. On that first roll call, all but three senators voted. Two had passed deliberately; one inadvertently. Wisconsin's Gaylord Nelson was talking with a colleague and claimed he had not heard his name called. The two deliberate passes were by West Virginia's Byrd and Randolph. The majority leader believed his should be the decisive sixty-seventh vote so that none of his colleagues would bear the onus of providing the margin of victory. Randolph, who had pledged his vote if it were "absolutely necessary," held out for that reason. Byrd and others wished to spare him, if possible, because the veteran senator faced a tough reelection fight that fall.

The vote at the end of the roll call was 66 for ratification, 31 against. Byrd then provided the crucial sixty-seventh vote. Nelson's "yea" made it 68. Randolph could then breathe a sigh of relief and deliver the thirty-second vote against. "On this vote," said the vice-president, "the yeas are 68 and the nays are 32. Two-thirds of the senators present and voting having voted in the affirmative, the resolution of ratification is agreed to."

There were some whoops in the gallery. Wire service reporters and others close to their deadlines dashed out to file stories. Senators stood and shook hands with each other, sharing congratulations or commiserations as appropriate.

When the most controversial treaty in sixty years was finally approved by the Senate, one would have thought all who had a hand in that success would have been toasting the event until the early hours of the next day. It had, after all, been fourteen years in the making. But that day, any real sense of triumph was missing. In the Senate, the feeling was more one of relief than of self-congratulation among those who had won. In Panama, where what had just happened had been a dream for seventy-five years, there was resentment that narrow-minded men had deprived the moment of its expected joy. Torrijos himself was disappointed that a staunch partner had seemed to cave in to expediency. He made no public statement, and the next morning, he flew to his village retreat deep in the mountains of Coclé.

In Washington, opponents of the new arrangement were persuaded the close vote promised better things on the next round. Nevada's Laxalt rushed to the press gallery to tell reporters he was "very optimistic" about his faction's chances on the second treaty. The protreaty forces, he claimed, had already "fired their best shot." He predicted that when his Senate colleagues went home for the Easter recess they would find their constituents "raising hell." The man who had led Ronald Reagan's campaign in 1976 obviously had his eyes on the Senate races in 1978 and, more important, on the national campaign two years later. With that focus, what happened in Panama mattered little.

The only place where the victory generated unalloyed joy was in the White House. The president and his aides were acutely aware of Carter's sinking popularity among the American people. His approval rating in the polls was lower after one year in office than that of any predecessor in the past twenty-five years. In the days before the Panama treaty vote, more than one White House staffer was quoted as saying: "We need a big one, a big victory." Hence, the almost desperate efforts by the president and his congressional staff during the closing days of the debate to harvest the required votes. Hence, too, the elation that swept through the Oval Office and the West Wing as soon as the 68–32 result was recorded. Bottles of white wine and beer were discretely opened (the Carters frowned on anything stronger), paper cups were raised, and the victory was toasted. It was the first good reason for rejoicing in the Carter White House for many months.

While his assistants were celebrating, President Carter walked to the White House press room to make a statement. "The people of our nation," he began, "owe a debt of thanks to the members of the United States Senate for their courageous action taken today in voting for the Panama Canal Neutrality Treaty." He said he was "confident that the Senate will show the same courage and foresight when it considers the second treaty. This is a promising step toward a new era in our relationships with Panama and with all of Latin America."

To ease some of the pain on the isthmus, Carter said: "While the right of the United States and Panama to act against any threat to the regime of neutrality is assured by this treaty, it does not mean that there is a right of intervention, nor do we want a right of intervention, by the United States in the internal affairs of Panama."

As he walked from the room, one reporter called out: "How does it feel to win one?" The president stopped and smiled. "It feels good—I think," he said.

While those in the White House were congratulating each other and the president for garnering the needed votes, experts in the Senate were more sparing in their praise. In fact, some senators believed that Carter's frantic public wooing of such junior senators as DeConcini and Zorinsky, and the impression that deals were being made right and left, had nearly snatched defeat from the jaws of victory. Minority Leader Baker told the press that administration efforts had not influenced a single Republican vote, except perhaps for Massachusetts Senator Brooke "and we nearly lost him."* Meantime, Senator Byrd reportedly told his personal staff that without inept and too obvious White House lobbying, plus the hints of political deals, he could have assembled seventy votes for the treaty.

In Panama, there was none of the exuberance that attended the signing of the Panama treaties the previous September. Torrijos stayed in the house on Fiftieth Street with his friends and advisers and sent treaty negotiator Rómulo Escobar to meet the press and speak for the government. Rómulo called the new treaty "a triumph for the Panamanian people and for General Torrijos." As for the changes inserted by the Senate, Rómulo told the Panamanians: "The fundamental objectives that Panama pursued have not been changed by these reservations that the senators introduced." Escobar was putting the best possible face on what he, Torrijos, and most Panamanians saw that evening as little more than half a loaf.

Hamilton Jordan called Ambassador Lewis just after the vote to invite him to the White House for a cup of cheer. Lewis, still bitter about the DeConcini surrender, really did not want to go. He called Torrijos. The general understood his ambassador's feelings, but he urged Lewis to "go ahead and visit with them" and to pass along Panama's feelings. Torrijos said the White House and the American press should know "there is no euphoria here." The attitude was that of a people "who have recovered their dignity, even if it was like taking a laxative." Torrijos concluded by expressing again his disappointment that Carter had found it necessary to "go with DeConcini." He said he had always felt the president "would use conviction, not wheeling and dealing, to gain his ends."

About that time, a small group of students assembled on the campus of the university. The school was in recess and only about thirty hard-core members of the leftist faction had rallied for the protest. They burned a copy of the treaty and shouted, "Yankees go home," but hardly anyone was listening. Still, it was a straw in the wind.

We passed Escobar's remarks along to Washington as soon as we heard them. I then sent my own interpretation and a warning to the State Department. "We are greatly encouraged," I wrote, "by this early (and considered) reaction by Torrijos. The Panamanian Government is making a noble effort to swallow the DeConcini reservation, which is merely the bitterest of a number of not-very-appetizing reservations and understandings. We must not assume that just because they appear to have been swallowed, that the Panamanians will be able to keep them down. Once the substance

---

*Brooke had left a meeting with President Carter infuriated by what he interpreted as an effort to make a deal for his vote. He was brought back into the protreaty camp only through the skillful handling of the competent Republican staff in the Senate.

of the reservations is fully understood here, the opposition will surely go to work to undermine both Torrijos and the treaties."

The most bitter opposition to the DeConcini reservation came, not from anyone in the political opposition, but from Torrijos' ambassador to Washington. Gabriel's anger was not significantly reduced by his visit to the White House that evening. And later, when Hamilton Jordan, Frank Moore, and other White House staffers dropped in at the Panamanian Embassy for a party, none of them was able to deaden Lewis' pain. By the next morning, he was in a barely controlled fury.

In that mood, the ambassador flew to Miami. He talked to friends, there and in Panama, then went to the airport to continue his journey. A few reporters were waiting for him and he made a statement praising the new treaty but blasting the DeConcini addition as blatant interference in his country's internal affairs. Then he flew to Panama.

Mili and I were helping celebrate "United States Day" at the annual fair in David. When we got back to Panama City on Saturday, I found a message from Gabriel asking me to come over. I found him in an even worse mood than when we had talked two days earlier. When he used the word "DeConcini" it came out as an expletive. "There has to be some way, Gabriel, that this can be handled," I told him, "without blowing everything up." He refused to be mollified. "It's an insult to me and to every Panamanian," he said. "This kind of thing was bad enough in 1903. But in 1978, there's no excuse. This isn't the way friends treat each other."

I reminded him the treaty said the United States did not have the right to intervene in Panama's affairs. He knew that. I recalled that President Carter had said the same thing *after* the treaty had been approved. He knew that, too. He told me he was not worried about a president like Carter ("he's a moral man"). But he wondered, and worried, about what would happen in the future with a president who thought like DeConcini or Laxalt or Helms. "Talk it over with Omar," I said. "I think he'll want to wait before he does anything drastic." Gabriel had said he would be seeing the general the next day.

The next morning, Gabriel, Ricardo Bilonick, and Jimmy Arias flew to the interior in a small chartered plane. They landed at the crude airstrip at Coclecito, the village that was Torrijos' refuge from the pressures and problems of government. In Omar's house, which resembled a rundown hunting lodge, the ambassador described the events of the recent past as he saw them. He recounted the final stages of the Senate debate and characterized the main participants in some detail. Gabriel also provided an assessment of the administration team responsible for shaping and carrying out strategy in the fight for the Panama treaties.

Ambassador Lewis and his colleagues talked with Torrijos at length about the DeConcini reservation. It was not the wording of the proposal that aroused them so much—though the reference to the use of military force in Panama rankled. It was DeConcini's "clarifying" speech in which he referred to such things as "labor unrest and strikes" and to "political riots or upheavals" as possible excuses for using military power. The Panamanians at Coclecito that day, all acutely aware of the history of their country and of the numerous instances in which the United States had intervened to "protect law and order" or to "insure honest elections," were reading DeConcini as authorizing more of the same.

As the discussion continued, General Torrijos became progressively more irritated. He was offended by what DeConcini had said and what the Senate had done. Most of all, he was disappointed that "my friend Carter" had accepted DeConcini with no consultation with him. The ambassador and his colleagues left Coclecito with the impression Torrijos had agreed to make a statement roundly denouncing the DeConcini reservation. He had instructed Gabriel to get together with his other advisers immediately "and work things out."

The only communications worth the name that Torrijos maintained in his village retreat was the radio link to National Guard headquarters. He sent word over the network to contact his key advisers and have them meet Ambassador Lewis at his home that night. Late that afternoon, a National Guard jeep drove up to a villa in Cerro Azul where Rory González, Foreign Minister González-Revilla, and Finance Minister Pérez Balladares were playing dominoes. The Guard officer told Rory and Nico they were wanted in Panama City at Gabriel Lewis' house by 7 o'clock. The same message went to Education Minister Royo, Labor Minister Ahumada, and others in their scattered weekend retreats. Not knowing what was in the wind, they all flew or drove back to Panama City.

Ambassador Lewis told the assembled group he had talked to the general and that his instructions were to "stop the presses." Torrijos wanted to put out a strong statement denouncing the DeConcini reservation and threatening to kill the Neutrality Treaty. Lewis said Omar wanted the group to prepare a declaration and get it into the next morning's newspapers.

The advisers were flabbergasted. They thought Torrijos and Lewis were being too emotional. One recalled that the government had put out a statement only two days before promising to say nothing about the treaties until both documents had been acted on by the U.S. Senate. The kind of statement Lewis was talking about would cause chaos in Panama and in Washington, they argued. It was a long and heated session. Finally, Rory González told the ambassador that he and the others were not in agreement with him or with the general. They would not cooperate. "It was," Rory recalled later, "the only time that we ever unanimously said no to the general." The meeting broke up in some confusion and bitterness.

That night, someone in the group contacted Torrijos, told him what had happened, and urged him to assemble his key advisers to consider next steps. A meeting was arranged at Farallon on Monday morning to work out Panama's strategy for the coming battle on DeConcini and the second treaty.

That same night, Gabriel called to tell me what was happening. He explained that Torrijos had wanted to put out a statement denouncing DeConcini and saying Panama could not accept a treaty with his reservation. But he said that the key advisers opposed the move and they were going to assemble the next day to work out a plan. Then he asked me a seemingly unrelated question. What did I think of Bill Rogers? Bill, a partner in the law firm of Arnold and Porter, had been assistant secretary of state and later under secretary of state for economic affairs under Kissinger, and had served briefly as the protreaty advocate in Senator Baker's entourage when the minority leader was determining his stand on the Panama issue.

"You know that Bill Rogers is a friend of mine," I told the ambassador. "He's one of the brightest, most able people I know. He understands Panama and Latin America. And he knows the Washington scene better than most. Why do you ask?"

Gabriel said: "Oh, nothing. I just had an idea and I wanted to sound you out. Maybe Bill could help us in this mess."

I told him I did not know what he was thinking about, but if anyone in Washington could be helpful, I could not think of a better candidate than Bill Rogers. "That's what I thought," he told me. I hung up the phone puzzled. Only later did I understand what he had in mind. It proved to be a move that was decisive to the fate of the second treaty and to U.S.-Panama cooperation in Washington.

Meantime, in the United States, treaty opponents were laying out their own strategy for the second round. The day after the Senate vote, the Conservative Political Action Conference met in the nation's capital and the Panama issue was high on the agenda. Governor Reagan was the main speaker and he promised that "the fight has just begun." Senate strategist Paul Laxalt told the cheering ultraconservatives he thought the second treaty would be rejected. "We will start again on Monday with amendments," he promised. The keynote of the meeting, and the theme that emerged as the most potent weapon the antitreaty forces could wield, was expressed by Utah's Jake Garn. Senators who differed with the conservative view, said Garn, should be threatened with "political extinction."

The barricades were going up and the opposing forces on the Panama Treaty were taking their places behind them. It promised to be a bloody, no-holds-barred struggle.

CHAPTER 19

The Great Debate: Act Two

"Perhaps the people of Panama are overreacting . . . But perhaps their reaction is not so inexplicable in view of Latin America's historical concern over U.S. intervention in their internal affairs . . . And perhaps it is not so unwarranted in light of repeated statements during this debate . . ."

—Sen. Frank Church to the Senate, April 10, 1978

THE White House celebration of the Neutrality Treaty victory was a short-lived hurrah. Even as they toasted their success, President Carter and his top aides knew they were in trouble. Frank Moore and his congressional liaison staffers were already getting blunt questions from puzzled, irritated senators. Reports from Panama reflected that country's disappointment, and Washington journalists were beginning to ask about the "DeConcini fiasco." If the Carter team had any lingering doubts, they were washed away by what they heard that evening from Americans and Panamanians as well.

The critical chorus began at a party at Vice President Mondale's house. In the middle of a small circle of Americans, an unhappy Hamilton Jordan confessed: "You know, the president told me today he should have seen the problem with that DeConcini thing and not accepted it. He said he'd been foolish not to see it." Jordan berated himself for not anticipating the trouble that would flow from the "interventionist" reservation. "I should have seen it, too," he said.

Mike Kozak, who had been working on Capitol Hill for two months, tried to make the president's aide feel a little better. "We should have told you more about that problem," he said. Then he asked: "Didn't you see Ambassador Jorden's cables?" The Georgian said he had not. "He sent in two cables saying 'absolutely no,'" Kozak explained. "He checked it out with the Panamanians. They said they would have to reject the treaty over it."

"My God," the surprised Jordan said, "we never saw those."

Later that night, at a long and liquid reception at the Panamanian ambassador's residence, criticism of the addition to the treaty continued. Anyone within earshot of Ambassador Lewis was left in no doubt how he and other Panamanians felt about DeConcini's handiwork. His wife, Nita, even asked some guests if they knew where the senator lived; she was thinking of organizing a picket line.

The talk that evening made Jordan and his colleagues realize what a mare's nest had been created. Everything they heard over the next forty-eight hours reinforced that awareness. Our reports from the embassy told them and the State Department how fetid the atmosphere was in Panama. I spoke with Ambassadors Bunker and Linowitz and was amazed to learn they had not even been consulted on the president's decision. The day after the vote, Ambler Moss flew back to Washington, the memory of Panamanian reactions to DeConcini fresh in his mind. On the plane, he talked with a fellow passenger, lawyer Carlos López-Guevara. Carlos told him how close Torrijos had come to denouncing the treaty the night before the vote. He also described several heated sessions among treaty advisers in which tempers had flared more than once over the "colonialist" reservation and Carter's acceptance of it.

On Monday, March 20, Torrijos and his inner circle met at Farallon to consider next steps. One thing they decided they needed desperately was advice from someone who knew the Washington scene well and understood the inner workings of the U.S. government. When Ambassador Lewis proposed Bill Rogers, the general and several others snapped up the suggestion. Lewis called Rogers at his office at Arnold and Porter and asked if it would be appropriate for his government to enlist the counsel of an American legal firm in the coming treaty struggle. Rogers assured him it would be. Would Arnold and Porter take it on, he asked? Rogers said he would have to consult his partners, but he felt certain the firm would be happy to act in an advisory capacity. He explained that he was then packing for a trip to Japan. Lewis begged him to delay his journey and to come to Panama immediately. It was a matter of the greatest urgency, he insisted. Rogers said he would consider it and promised to give his decision within the hour. Rogers then contacted sources in the administration and on the Hill and they urged him to accept Panama's offer. When Lewis called back, Rogers said he was delaying his Japan trip and would go to Panama the next day.

I had told Washington that Torrijos had assured us nothing drastic would happen until Panama could sort things out and see how the Senate handled the second treaty. But those around the president were desperately worried that a volatile Torrijos might say or do something to upset an already wobbly applecart. To forestall any rash move by the irritated general, Carter decided to write another letter and to talk with him personally.

The president's letter came in a cable the evening of March 20 and I delivered it immediately. Carter cited Torrijos' earlier statement that his government "will not take any action until the Senate has acted on both treaties." The president lauded that as "a wise and prudent course." He promised to urge the Senate to resist any amendments to the second treaty as well as "any reservations or conditions which are inconsistent with the basic purposes and spirit of the treaty." Carter concluded with another plea for restraint, saying, "It will be important for us to follow your wise counsel to be calm and to withhold judgment until the treaties can be considered in their entirety." He really meant "you" not "us." When I delivered the letter, I told Torrijos the president would be calling him at 9:30 the next morning. He said he would be waiting.

The only justification for a call from the president at that point would have been to tell Torrijos the administration had found a way to mitigate the DeConcini reservation. Obviously that was not the purpose. "Defanging" DeConcini was not yet an element in the White House scenario. Only later would it become part of the political mythology that the administration accepted DeConcini's addition to the treaty only to secure his and a few other votes, and that his mischief would be neutralized in the second treaty. In fact, neither Carter nor anyone in his inner circle had the vaguest notion at that time how they could possibly undo the damage they had allowed DeConcini to inflict.

The next morning, I was at my desk reading cables when the phone rang. The White House operator told me the president was coming on the line. Carter said he was about to talk with Torrijos and wondered if there was anything he should know. I told him things were quiet at the Panama end, but Torrijos and his advisers were still upset about the DeConcini matter. "Anything you can tell him that shows we understand their unhappiness and that we will make it clear that intervention is not our intention would be helpful," I told the president. He said he understood and would do his best to ease their concern.

When he had Torrijos on the line, President Carter repeated most of what was in his letter the previous evening. The debate on the second treaty had begun, he said, and we should all be patient and see how that developed. Torrijos told Carter he was deeply concerned about the DeConcini reservation, and even more about the words the senator had used in explaining his "horrible" addition to the treaty. Carter called the general's attention to the statement Senator Church had made on March 16— that the DeConcini proposal only elaborated on but did not change the essence of the treaty's intention. The president urged Torrijos not to jump to any conclusions, or take any action, until the Senate completed work on the second treaty. The general repeated his pledge to consider the two treaties as "a package." But he told Carter it was important they find some way to neutralize DeConcini's reservation and his intimidating statements. The president agreed to try, but gave no indication how that might be done.

That night, Bill Rogers arrived in Panama to advise the Panamanian government. Soon after arrival at Tocumen airport, he and Paul Besozzi, an assistant from his law firm, were conferring with Ambassador Lewis, his aide Ricardo Bilonick, and Jaime Arias. Rogers suggested the flaws in the DeConcini reservation might be corrected by a statement in the instruments of treaty ratification reaffirming the principle of nonintervention in U.S. policy. Arias contended that would be inadequate. The DeConcini view had been accepted by the Senate, and only action by the upper house could erase the impression that support had left with everyone. As they talked it over, a three-point approach took shape: a Senate resolution disowning DeConcini's harsh language; U.S. reaffirmation of nonintervention in its policy toward Panama and Latin America; reendorsement by the Organization of American States of the principle of noninterference.

The following day that approach was discussed with Panama's treaty advisory panel and received general approval. Rogers put the proposal into a memorandum for General Torrijos and the document was translated into Spanish.

At 9 o'clock the next morning his advisers gave Torrijos the memo. A bit later, Rogers was summoned for a talk with the general. The full group then reconvened and the three-part strategy was adopted as official Panamanian policy. Education Minister Royo took the next plane to Caracas to brief Venezuelan President Carlos Andres Pérez. Torrijos was especially eager that his Venezuelan ally be fully informed because Pérez was to meet President Carter the following week.

Another Latin American leader, Costa Rica's Daniel Oduber, was in Panama during those days and Lewis and Rogers described the three-step formula to him. He endorsed it enthusiastically. From the earliest days of treaty negotiations until the U.S. Senate completed action on the new pacts, Torrijos went to great lengths to keep his nearest neighbors—Colombia, Costa Rica, and Venezuela—fully informed of every development. It was a notable example of informal and highly effective cooperation among friendly regimes. It also kept three of Latin America's rare democratic governments firmly enlisted in Panama's treaty cause.

Those who hoped the quality of Senate debate on the second Panama treaty would rise above the level of petty wrangling were sorely disappointed. There were, to be sure, moments of eloquence and drama, even of humor. But they were few. For the most part, the debate followed the course of the previous months, one dull, lengthy, repetitious speech after another. The antitreaty forces were like boxers who kept flailing away with roundhouse blows, hoping one would finally land. Despite repeated protestations that all they wanted was "to improve these flawed agreements," their clear intention was to destroy them. They kept hoping they would uncover some argument that would set off alarms around the country and generate a storm of public reaction their colleagues could not ignore. It never happened. They hoped, too, that outrageous statements and insults might generate some ill-considered response in Panama that would do their work for them. That, too, never happened though the brink was approached more than once.

The deliberately provocative approach of treaty opponents was apparent in almost every proposed amendment or revision. The initial week of discussion provided a good sampling. Kansas Sen. Robert Dole offered the first amendment on the floor. He noted that under the Neutrality Treaty only Panama would have military forces on the isthmus after the year 2000. But what about the next twenty-two years? Dole wanted an amendment that would force Panama not to invite any foreign troops into its country during those two decades. It was an attempted invasion of sovereignty that any nation would resist. But Dole was undeterred by appeals to reason or citations of what was normal in the relations of sovereign states.

"I defy anybody who opposes this amendment," he argued, "to tell us what they are going to do if Cuban troops are invited into Panama."

Indiana's Birch Bayh responded by citing U.S. actions in the Cuban missile crisis in 1962, in the Dominican Republic in 1965, and in Guatemala in the 1950s. "We have not been bashful," said Bayh. "And frankly we have not looked for a whole lot of treaties and international precedents to rely on. And I suggest . . . that once this treaty is ratified, or is not ratified, we are going to take whatever steps are necessary, adjacent to that canal, in order to protect it."

The Senate rejected the Dole amendment. Something puzzled me greatly about the argument. The United States had, for decades, been providing training in the Canal Zone for military forces from almost every country in Latin America, schooling in everything from vehicle maintenance to strategic planning. If Dole's amendment had passed, that program would have had to be abruptly terminated—though we had fought successfully to retain it under the treaty. No senator even mentioned the subject. Dole himself seemed unaware that the legislative machete he was wielding had two edges.

Three-fourths of the suggested treaty revisions came from rabid opponents, whose clear purpose was to destroy, not improve. In one revealing colloquy, Senator Byrd pressed Alabama's Allen to tell the Senate whether he would vote for the treaties if all of his proposed revisions were adopted. Allen tried to evade the question, but finally admitted he had decided many years earlier to oppose any significant change in the Panama Canal arrangement. That same mind-set was shared by perhaps twenty other senators. Nothing short of the arrangement imposed by Teddy Roosevelt early in the century would have truly satisfied them. Under those circumstances, meaningful dialogue was next to impossible.

A separate book would be needed for detailed analysis of the many efforts made to alter the Panama Canal Treaty. In all, 105 amendments were filed with the Senate clerk and 29 of them were raised on the floor and debated there. About 40 reservations were similarly introduced of which 11 finally were considered and voted on. And there were more than 30 understandings of which 7 were discussed. Almost all the changes were defeated or tabled. The protreaty forces under Byrd and Baker had the votes needed to reject the frivolous and the destructive.

The Senate did adopt some additions that reaffirmed or clarified treaty provisions. In a few cases, they addressed concerns the leadership recognized were shared by a considerable number of senators. In others, the suggestions did no significant harm to the pact and helped assure the originators would vote for the final product. In all cases, we were able to discuss the changes in advance with the Panamanians, explain the reasons for their introduction, and provide reassurances that the basic thrust of the treaty itself was not being violated. In some cases, we provided arguments that persuaded senators to alter their proposals to accommodate legitimate Panamanian concerns.

The jousting over treaty changes took an inordinate amount of the Senate's time. But there were really only two central questions facing the upper house during the second phase of the Great Debate: Would the Panama Canal Treaty garner the necessary two-thirds vote needed for ratification? And could Senate leaders find some way to neutralize the DeConcini reservation without alienating crucial votes? Most everything else was secondary and would end in history's wastebasket.

We kept assuring the Panamanians that something would be done to ameliorate DeConcini's one-sided statement of rights. We did so more on the basis of faith that something *had* to be done rather than knowledge of any concrete steps being taken. In fact, in the days immediately following approval of the first treaty, there was resistance in Washington to any serious discussion of corrective steps. Christopher and Hansell, the action officers in the final stages of the first debate, took the view that any move to undercut DeConcini risked losing votes on the second treaty. That view tended to close minds and make the search for a remedy nearly impossible.

The Panamanians decided finally to take their case to Washington. Ambassador Lewis and Aristides Royo flew to the capital the last weekend in March. On Monday, March 27, they went to the White House for a meeting with Hamilton Jordan. They gave him the memorandum worked out the previous week outlining their three-part suggestion for handling DeConcini. The president's aide promised to study their suggestions carefully and discuss it with his colleagues. But he told them that getting the Senate to reverse itself posed formidable problems. The Panamanians got much the same reaction later that day when they talked with Frank Moore, the congressional liaison chief.

The next day, the two Panamanians went to the State Department for a long and friendly session with Ellsworth Bunker. Bunker listened sympathetically and promised to do what he could to promote some corrective action in the Senate. He also raised some of the nagging trivia that were still creating problems on the Hill—Panama's outstanding debts to the Panama Canal Company for various services, guarantees of future payments on Panamanian bonds, and the settlement of outstanding disputes with two private U.S. companies. By then it was clear the Senate wanted to eliminate the treaty restriction on U.S. discussions of a possible future isthmian canal with countries other than Panama. Bunker raised this with Lewis and Royo and confirmed what I had reported earlier—that Panama would be delighted to release the United States from that limitation if Panama, too, were freed from its obligation to give the United States first priority.

Bunker asked Ambler Moss and Mike Kozak to follow up with the Panamanians on the several subjects he had discussed. But when they raised such matters as water rates, or the sea-level canal option, or the backing for Panamanian bonds—as they did at considerable length—the conversation inevitably veered back to the central problem: neutralizing DeConcini. The two Americans did their best to reassure Royo and Lewis that "something will be done." But they were in a ticklish position because they knew perfectly well that nothing *was* being done. The White House staff and State Department officialdom were still hunkered down in the political storm cellar hoping the whole affair would go away and that Panama would, in the end, find it could accept the onerous reservation.

Nor did there seem to be any hope for igniting early senatorial interest in the problem. Congress was in the midst of its Easter recess and almost all senators were back home mending political fences. Moreover, Bill Rogers had temporarily withdrawn as an adviser to the Panamanian government. Before he went further, he felt he had to have assurance from the Justice Department that there was no "conflict of interest" in a former State Department official acting as counsel to a foreign government. He went off for a holiday in the Bahamas to await Justice's decision. That left still another channel for mediation temporarily closed.

At that moment, Moss and his "Gang of Four" seemed to be almost the only people in Washington who understood the problem we faced in all its aspects. Late one afternoon, Ambler called to describe the stone walls they were encountering. Hardly anyone would admit the treaties were in serious danger. Those who did had no idea what to do about it. The White

House and the top level at the State Department wanted desperately not to make any waves. Nor were they prepared to admit that a grave mistake had been made in handling the senator from Arizona. In the Senate, not a few members were still laboring under the delusion that Panama had accepted the DeConcini condition and was now backing away from it.

Moss asked if I would talk to Senator Sarbanes and give him my view of the situation. He said that on his two trips to Panama the Maryland senator had formed a good opinion of my candor and understanding of the local scene. I told him I would be delighted to talk to Sarbanes. There was no one in the Senate I respected more. Moreover, I thought he, as a leader of the floor fight, should know everything that was going on.

That evening, Sarbanes called from Baltimore. He wanted to know the real story on Panama's reaction to the Senate condition. I told Sarbanes bluntly there was no reason for anyone to have imagined that DeConcini's doctrine would be acceptable on the isthmus. The fact was that I had sent two cables stating just the reverse—that DeConcini's reservation could cause Panama to reject the treaty. I had been amazed to learn the president had been persuaded to accept the Arizonian's condition.

If tone of voice can indicate complexion, the usually restrained senator from Maryland was livid. He felt he and his fellow senators had been misled, and that the White House had mismanaged the whole affair. I asked if there wasn't some way in the second treaty to undo the damage. He confessed he did not know how, but obviously he and others were going to have to focus on it. He asked if Panama might change its mind. I told him that, on the contrary, the view in Panama then was even harder than it had been, but the Panamanians were waiting for us to correct our own misstep. Sarbanes said he would be talking to his confreres to see what could be done.

During those days, we were going through much the same kind of experience our colleagues in Washington had with Lewis and Royo. But in Panama City, it was a daily occurrence, or almost so. On March 29, for example, I had a long meeting with Foreign Minister González-Revilla and several members of Panama's treaty team. We went over in detail the main items of pending business, things that were causing trouble in the Senate. We agreed on a way to settle Panama's outstanding debts to the Canal Company. I impressed on them the need to resolve outstanding claims by the two U.S. companies. And they agreed that payments on Panamanian bonds—part of the portfolio of the Kentucky state teachers retirement fund and of some U.S. insurance companies—would continue to be backed by canal annuities.

As we talked through the afternoon, the compass of our conversation swung irrevocably back toward the all-powerful magnet of their concern: the DeConcini condition. I talked of the utility to both sides of maintaining the close consultation we had developed; they reminded me consultation had broken down in the final days of debate on the first treaty, and DeConcini's "disaster" had been the result. I reminded them of the hectic atmosphere that prevailed in Washington during those wild final hours; they pointed out that the political problems they faced were just as troublesome for them as those we had in Washington.

I reported the progress made on the agenda of technical problems requiring action on Panama's part. Then I reminded the State Department once again that the DeConcini "bone" was still stuck in Panama's throat and that "something will have to be done to make clear it did not give the U.S. a right to intervene in Panamanian internal affairs." The foreign minister had warned that "the addition of any similar proposal in the Canal Treaty would certainly be rejected by Panama."

I added a footnote to underline that what the minister and his colleagues had told me were not casual views but reflected "Torrijos' own feeling that he has been pushed to the wall and cannot, in dignity, be pushed much further." It was crucial that officials at State and in the White House understood that when Senator Allen said of Torrijos, "He is going to accept these reservations and be overjoyed at doing so," he was totally, and dangerously, wrong.

Torrijos was disappointed by the failure of the Carter White House to give him any assurances it would neutralize DeConcini's "interventionism." He was also frustrated by the apparent failure of even protreaty senators to understand how offensive the DeConcini affair was. Working with a handful of his closest advisers, the general developed a plan he thought would put some subtle pressure on the administration in Washington.

It was a typical Torrijos reaction. When things were going badly with Washington, the general searched for an international spotlight. He was persuaded little Panama could not stand alone against the "Colossus of the North." Its only hope was to enlist support from sympathetic governments around the world and thereby appeal to the American conscience. No leader of any small country has used this ploy to greater effect in the last thirty years than did Omar Torrijos.

The Panamanian general wrote a letter in late March to the president or prime minister of almost every country in the world. The Torrijos letter noted the U.S. Senate's approval of the Neutrality Treaty on March 16. He quoted the two leadership amendments which were based on his understanding with President Carter. The principles inherent in those amendments, wrote Torrijos, flowed from "generally accepted norms of international law which are effectively consecrated in multilateral international agreements." He cited the U.N. Charter, the OAS Charter, and the Rio Pact. Next came the text of the DeConcini amendment. To determine what that treaty change meant, the general wrote, one only had to read what the senator himself said about it. There followed citations from De-Concini's speech to the U.S. Senate. Since the addressee governments would be asked to back the treaty, wrote the Panamanian general, "we have considered it our duty to inform you of this situation about which we have already publicly expressed our deep concern."

That was it. No requests for action or public statements. Torrijos left it to the recipients to decide where justice lay and what, if anything, they should do about it. He knew, of course, that in time reactions would get back to authorities in Washington through the diplomatic grapevine. He calculated they would be favorable to his cause.

On March 28, Panama's ambassador to the United Nations, Jorge Illueca, sent a letter to Secretary General Kurt Waldheim. He enclosed a diplomatic note and four attachments: the Senate's resolution of ratification of the Neutrality Treaty; Senator DeConcini's statement to the Senate; Senator Kennedy's comments on DeConcini's amendment; and a communiqué from Panama's Foreign Ministry issued the previous day on the treaty question.

Ambassador Illueca's note to Waldheim paraphrased Torrijos' letter with some slight elaboration. He cited the DeConcini amendment and what the author had said about it. He noted, with approval, Senator Kennedy's comments. And he concluded by saying it was only proper for all members of the international community to study the problem since they would be asked to endorse the treaties.

Illueca asked for distribution of his letter and its attachments to all members of the General Assembly. Those familiar with the paper mill that is the U.N.'s document center realize what that meant. Thousands of copies poured out of the duplicating machines—several for each country's U.N. Mission, one for every reporter and news agency, copies for foreign ministries around the world, others for libraries and research centers. They were stacked on tables and crammed into envelopes. Yet nothing happened.

It was one of those inexplicable lapses in news coverage that occasionally occurs. Those who saw the Panamanian document did not recognize it as news. Those who would have spotted it immediately as part of the continuing treaty struggle apparently never read it. For a full week, the Torrijos letter and Illueca's note remained the exclusive property of diplomatic circles. Those who later accused the Panamanians of using the U.N. channel as a pressure play against the administration and the Senate missed a key fact. If that had been the main purpose, the story would have been in the Washington press the next day. Lewis and Bilonick had demonstrated unusual skill in attracting media attention anytime they felt it important. In this case, they did nothing.

Word of Panama's initiative began to seep through the system at midweek. The first intimation I had came from Herb Hansell, State's legal adviser, the afternoon of April 4. He told me generally what had happened and said, "It looks like Panama is engaged in building a case internationally." I told him it was news to me but that if Panama had launched a "campaign" they were certainly being "strangely quiet about it at this end of the line." Hansell asked if I could get a copy of Torrijos' letter to world leaders. I told him I would try, but that the Panamanian Embassy or our U.N. Mission in New York would be quicker sources.

On Wednesday, April 5, Ambassador Lewis called me from Washington. He had just talked with Colonel Noriega, Torrijos' G-2, who had told him about planned antitreaty demonstrations in Panama City. What bothered Gabriel was the news that ultraleftist students opposed to the treaties were being supported financially by anti-Torrijos factions in the business and professional community. He was also concerned that the demonstrations might take on an anti-American tone and that any real trouble would stir up strong reactions in the Senate, to the detriment of treaty prospects. The element that brought the leftists and conservatives together was DeConcini's demeaning amendment, Gabriel argued. The best way to take the heat out of the antitreaty bandwagon was to "handle the DeConcini problem."

I told him I knew about the antitreaty manifestation planned for the seventh and was sure Torrijos and Noriega would not let it get out of hand. In any case, I told my diplomatic colleague, there was no possible way to "handle DeConcini" in the next two days. He agreed. What he wanted was just some kind of reassuring statement—by Senator Byrd, the White House, anyone in a key position—to indicate that "something is being done about it." He said he planned to raise the matter that afternoon with Frank Moore. I encouraged him to describe the situation to Frank, but warned against using the danger of public demonstrations in Panama to try to force positive actions. That approach, I cautioned, would certainly be counterproductive.

The White House congressional staff occupied a comfortable suite of offices on the second floor of the West Wing. When they walked into his office a few minutes after 4 o'clock, Moore greeted Lewis and Bilonick with the latest word from the Senate. The leadership had won agreement from pro- and antitreaty forces to end debate on the second treaty on April 14. They would vote on the Resolution of Ratification no later than 6:00 P.M. on April 18. The Panamanians welcomed the news.

The ambassador then told Moore he was worried. Since his return to Washington a week earlier, it was his clear impression that people in Washington, especially on Capitol Hill, failed to understand "Panamanian reality." "They think that everything is calm," he said, "and that Torrijos and his government are not encountering serious problems because of what the senators are doing here." The truth was quite different, he said. Lewis then described the coalition of antitreaty students and antigovernment businessmen who had joined forces in "a common front against the DeConcini amendment."

Lewis said the main purpose of his visit was to find out if the U.S. side was preparing a draft resolution that could neutralize the effect of DeConcini's amendment. If so, when could he receive a copy to send to Panama? After all, it was his country that was most directly affected. Moore indicated there would be no great problem. He said State's Christopher would have a draft ready the next day. It would reaffirm U.S. adherence to the principle of nonintervention, a feature of the U.N. Charter. As soon as it was ready, Moore wanted first to get Senator Byrd's reaction. He said the majority leader had agreed in principle to such a resolution, but the senator wanted to see the text before making any final commitment. When Lewis asked when such a resolution might be presented to the Senate, Moore said it would have to be the following week.

The Panamanians left the White House in an optimistic mood. Moore had given them their first assurance that something finally was afoot to balance DeConcini. From the embassy, the ambassador reported to the foreign minister on his encouraging talk with Moore. Within a week, the Panamanians were disillusioned to learn that the resolution the administration was considering was a "sense of the Senate" opinion separate from the treaty and having no real legal effect.

April 6 was a day almost everyone connected with the Panama treaties could have very well done without. Before it was over, nerves were frazzled, old friends were calling each other names, and the Panama Canal Treaty teetered on the rim of destruction. The White House went into a 24-hour seizure of nervous prostration. Normally restrained senators were reacting to rumors like squirrels in a hound's backyard. The Panamanians, who had created the problem, did not know what to make of the unexpected hubbub. How, they asked, did so little become so much?

A few reporters had finally heard about Panama's U.N. presentation the week before and were asking for details. The Panamanian Embassy responded by providing copies of Illueca's note to Waldheim and its attachments. The word reached Capitol Hill and suddenly Illueca's rather innocuous diplomatic initiative was converted into a Panamanian "rejection" of the Neutrality Treaty.

The senatorial storm had not yet burst when Ambassador Lewis went to Capitol Hill that morning to meet with Senators Cranston and Church in the majority whip's office. Warren Christopher was with the senators. Lewis was accompanied by Ambassadors Illueca and Nander Pitty, Panama's envoy to the OAS. Lewis made an impassioned plea for some action by the Senate to moderate DeConcini's doctrine of intervention.

"What we are after," he told the senators, "is the elimination of the existing colonial-type relationship, and the renewal of a friendly relationship. That was the object of the new treaties. And that was why President Carter was so happy about inviting the presidents of Latin America to be witnesses [to the treaty signing].

"But in Latin America," he went on, "the word 'intervention' is outrageous. The people of Latin America don't care if Panama gets five cents or a dollar from tolls. But they want to be sure that Panama doesn't commit itself to an interventionist treaty. I mean that is outmoded. I would rather stick to the 1903 treaty than to come all the way to 1978 with the same type of thing."

Christopher asked the Panamanian ambassador if he did not agree that "the treaty specifies that the United States could intervene in Panama." Lewis said it specified "that the United States should take action to maintain the neutrality of the canal." Illueca noted that DeConcini had talked about "action in Panama," not about "protecting the canal's neutrality." The Panamanians argued there was a distinct difference.

Lewis finally told the Americans: "Look, you are human beings, and you're bound to make mistakes now and then. And you made a mistake. Somebody misinformed you. And you people voted for something that is against what you have already approved—the Charter of the United Nations, the Charter of the Organization of American States, and a lot of other treaties and conventions that you have signed."

When he heard that, Church said: "Gabriel, I agree with you 100 percent." Cranston said he agreed, too. The senator from Idaho suggested that if DeConcini violated the U.N. and OAS charters, it should be possible to "draft something that would cover that . . . as part of the resolution on ratification of the second treaty." Christopher did not agree. He was doubtless sensitive because he had pushed the DeConcini condition in the first treaty, and had helped convince senators like Church and Cranston to go along. He was also afraid of losing votes on the second treaty if the condition were weakened. He told the group he was unwilling to "make any change in the meaning of the first treaty, including any of its amendments or reservations."

"Well," said Lewis, "I'm happy to know where you stand." He reminded Christopher that "President Carter has all along expected that we treat each other as equals. That's what he has been spreading in Africa [where Carter was then on a visit]. And that's what we are after, a friendly relationship of equals."

The session ended on that sour note. Lewis said he left the Capitol feeling that "Christopher was more interventionist than DeConcini." Christopher left thinking the Panamanian ambassador was too emotional and that his direct dealings with U.S. senators created new problems.

From his embassy, Ambassador Lewis called Hamilton Jordan and gave a vivid account of his visit to the Hill. Lewis reported that Cranston and Church had agreed with him that something should be done to modify the DeConcini condition. But he said he was "shocked" by Christopher's reaction. He quoted the State Department official as saying he would not write "anything that would try to change the meaning of the first treaty." "In that case," Lewis said, "we're in danger of ending up with two treaties that your partner can't accept." He begged Jordan to get the administration behind the kind of solution Senator Church had mentioned—a reservation to the second treaty reaffirming that "the United States under no circumstances would violate the Charter of the United Nations, the Charter of the OAS, et cetera, in regard to territorial integrity and the political independence of countries."

Jordan assured him that "we're going to try to do that." But he said there was a problem. If the move was seen as a purely "liberal" initiative, "then we're going to lose DeConcini and some of the conservatives." It had to be done with great care, he insisted. If it were viewed only as a tactic "to undercut the DeConcini thing," it might cost eight or ten votes on the second treaty. Jordan argued that the effort had to be handled "very quietly" and be done "through the conservatives as well as the liberals." He said he would discuss the matter the next morning at a foreign policy breakfast with the president, Secretary Vance, and NSC chief Brzezinski and would get back to the ambassador after that.

Later that afternoon, Frank Moore called the embassy to say that Senator DeConcini was putting out a press release concerning Panama's message to the United Nations. He was saying he would not vote for the second treaty unless it was clear Panama had accepted his condition. Bilonick argued that the U.N. message said only what DeConcini himself had said, and what Senator Kennedy had commented. "Why does that change his mind?" Bilonick wondered. Moore said he did not know, but he felt "everybody needs to lie low for awhile on this thing."

By late afternoon, what was being called "the U.N. thing" was being spread around Capitol Hill. DeConcini and others were claiming that Panama was rejecting his amendment. Antitreaty senators were delighted with what looked like a propaganda windfall. The rumors and exaggerations even influenced the usually careful Sen. Howard Baker, who was in Houston for a political speech. When a CBS reporter asked him about Panama's U.N. initiative, the minority leader responded: "Our friends in Panama ought to know that just the twitch of an eyelid, just the slightest provocation or expression that these treaties, or this treaty in this form, is not acceptable to Panama, and this whole thing could go down the tube." It was, I believe, the only time in the entire trying debate that Baker lost his usual cool and acted on the basis of incomplete information. Nonetheless, it could be argued—and was by Baker supporters—that the Panamanians needed a splash of cold water at that point. Their emotions were rising to a dangerous point. It was one thing to press insistently for rectification of DeConcini's error; it was quite another to depict the entire Senate as responsible for a massive mistake.

At the White House, Jordan and Moore heard the CBS report on Baker's statements in Houston. The presidential aides immediately called Ambassador Lewis. When he heard what Baker had said, Lewis guessed that "he probably heard about the U.N. thing." Moore confirmed that it was "all over the Hill." Jordan noted that senators and some newsmen were widely interpreting the U.N. document as a rejection of the treaty. It was playing into the hands of the opposition. He wondered what could be done to correct the Senate's impression. Lewis volunteered that his embassy or Panama City could say, "We are not rejecting any treaty." Jordan said the Panamanians would have to do it soon. Moore told the ambassador, "We are just hanging on by our fingernails." Lewis reminded the Americans that DeConcini was a serious problem for his country, but he said he would give serious thought to what his country could do to ease the problem on the Hill. Moore reminded him: "We only have to lose one vote."

The ambassador quickly got on his direct line to Panama and reached the foreign minister. He reported his conversation with Jordan and Moore, and also told González-Revilla about the adverse reaction on Capitol Hill to the U.N. document. Lewis suggested a public statement that would make clear Panama had not rejected the first treaty and was waiting for the Senate to act on the second. The minister promised to explore that option.

The next morning fit Milton's description of "confusion worse confounded." It did not help that, when senators looked at their newspapers over their first cup of coffee, they found stories of the Panamanian move at the United Nations, with the tone of "rejection" dominant. The *Washington Post*'s treatment was typical: "Panama Raises Challenge to Treaty" with a subhead "Statement Hits U.S. 'Right' to Intervene." Actually, the Illueca note neither "challenged" nor "hit" anything. It gave the wording of the treaty; quoted what DeConcini had said; repeated Senator Kennedy's comments; and left conclusions up to the recipients.

The White House was inundated by phone calls from the Hill asking what was happening. Had the Panamanians turned down the first treaty? The pressure produced frenzy in some circles. Bob Pastor of the NSC called the ambassador and told him: "We're about to lose everything unless you people issue a denial over there." Lewis tried to reassure him by saying Panama planned to reaffirm the statement it had made on March 17 after the first treaty.

Lewis got on the phone and began discussing the wording of his government's statement with the foreign minister. In ten minutes, Pastor called back. He begged the ambassador to issue a simple "no" in answer to the question "Has Panama rejected the treaty because of DeConcini?" Lewis said he was not going to answer any questions or issue any denials; he was going to release his government's statement. He thought that would make it clear.

The NSC aide said he thought the Panamanians did not realize what was happening on the Hill. "Our friends are about to desert us," he said. The treaty managers were threatening to call off the debate if Panama had rejected the first treaty. He asked if the ambassador wanted both treaties to "go down the drain." Obviously not, Lewis replied. Pastor said they were not going to get something to compensate for DeConcini "by deserting your friends, by pulling the ground from under them." Lewis denied he was "deserting any friends." All Panama had done, he insisted, was to publish a document at the United Nations and it said "only what DeConcini and Kennedy had said." Lewis told Pastor he had to get to work on his government's statement. Pastor warned that "if you don't get it out soon, you may as well forget it."

González-Revilla called with the text of the ministry statement. He read it to the ambassador. The first paragraph was a reminder that the position of the Panamanian government remained as General Torrijos had described it to President Carter three weeks earlier—Panama would not approve or reject anything until the U.S. Senate had finished its debate and voted on the second treaty. The second paragraph said: "The present statement is made because our Government believes that the Panamanian people voted on two treaties and not just one. It is also made to deny news [reports] to the effect that our Government has already taken an official position regarding the approval or rejection of the Neutrality Treaty. Said information, built on speculation, has been spread abroad by foreign news services with the purpose of confusing and distorting the firm conviction of the Panamanian Government on this important issue."

With that in hand, Ambassador Lewis called Hamilton Jordan at the White House. He said Panama wanted to help in any way possible on the Hill, but he urged Jordan to "get people busy on some kind of approach that would be 'an umbrella' over the DeConcini thing." Jordan said that would be tough. He and Moore had believed they had an answer two days before, but things had changed. Lewis asked what he thought the chances were for a corrective resolution. Jordan said he reckoned "right now they are 10 percent." Senator Byrd had told Moore that to put any resolution in at that point would lose votes for the second treaty. Lewis then read him the statement just received from Panama, which he planned to release immediately, and Jordan said he thought it was fine. A member of the embassy staff then read the statement slowly to Jordan's secretary so she could take it down in full.

When the Senate convened at 11 o'clock that morning, the controversy surfaced immediately. Minority Whip Ted Stevens of Alaska took the floor to call attention to Panama's message to the United Nations and to General Torrijos' letter to heads of government. He urged Senator Byrd to produce the documents for the information of all senators. Admitting he had not seen the documents in question, Stevens nonetheless said of Torrijos: "It appears to me that he is trying to create an international climate in which he can disregard the conditions placed upon the ratification of these treaties by the U.S. Senate through either the leadership amendment or reservations such as the DeConcini reservation."

The State Department had already sent copies of the Panamanian documents to the Hill and in minutes they were in Senator Byrd's hands. The majority leader took the floor and inserted into the *Congressional Record* the entire package—Illueca's note to the U.N. secretary general, the four attachments he had included, and the text of General Torrijos' letter to various heads of governments.* Byrd also added the Panamanian government's communiqué of that morning, which the White House had sent to the Hill. The documents were immediately circulated to all senators. Byrd's fast action helped defuse what had been an angry situation one hour earlier. When they read what the Panamanians had actually written, most senators realized they had been misled by rumors and exaggerations. It was one more tempest in the senatorial teapot, but it had tested many nerves and caused some premature graying in the protreaty ranks and at the White House.

I was following the evolving drama on the Hill but my main concern at that moment was the antitreaty demonstration that we knew was being mounted in the city. When such demonstrations occurred, we never knew whether they would be aimed at our embassy, at the Canal Zone, or at the Panamanian government. To be on the safe side, I released all personnel except the Marines, the military staff, and a few key officers. As it turned out, our precautions were unnecessary. The three hundred or four hundred young demonstrators, representing the Socialist Revolution League and the Camilo Torres Circle, moved to the Santa Ana Plaza in the center of town under the watchful eyes of the National Guard. They raised an effigy of President Carter by rope to a limb of a plaza tree and then burned it. The speeches called for rejection of the treaties. The harangues over, the

---

* A footnote for historians: the treaty text that Illueca used misquoted the DeConcini amendment, and the error was repeated in Byrd's insertion in the *Congressional Record*. Illueca's attachment said that "the United States of America shall have the right to take such steps" etc. The actual treaty condition said that "the United States of America and the Republic of Panama shall each independently have the right to take such steps" etc. It was a strange omission, and strange, too, that no one noticed it.

students marched from the plaza carrying banners: "Panamanians organize and fight the treaties" and "Torrijos, we demand another plebiscite." Evidently, the extreme left in Panama saw things much the same as the extreme conservatives in Washington. Both wanted the treaties killed. The burning of Carter's effigy was designed to stir nationalist emotions in the United States, just as senatorial insults of Panama had as their goal an irrational response on the isthmus.

That same day, Bill Rogers returned from the sun-swept Bahamas and quickly learned how chaotic the treaty business had become. The morning newspapers told the story of Panama's U.N. initiative, and a few phone calls revealed that there was consternation on the Hill among treaty supporters. He got the Panamanian side of the story from Ambassador Lewis. In the middle of the day, Rogers had a call from Herb Hansell, who was then at the Justice Department pursuing the matter of Rogers' representation of the Panamanian government and whether it would involve a conflict of interest. Hansell suggested they meet at the State Department with Christopher at 5:30 P.M.

At that session, the State officials told Rogers that Justice thought there would be a conflict if the lawyer dealt directly with U.S. officials on Panama's behalf, but not if he merely advised the Panamanians. That approach was not what either the Panamanians or Rogers had in mind. Nor would it have suited U.S. interests at that point. It was clear that Christopher and the White House wanted Rogers in the act. The deputy secretary freely acknowledged that his own relations with the Panamanians had deteriorated and that a new channel was badly needed in Washington. He urged Rogers to lend his "good offices" for that purpose, representing neither party but acting as a go-between to expedite and smooth communications. Rogers agreed to think it over but said two things should be understood: he would not take it on if the only purpose was to urge the Panamanians to stay quiet and not make waves; it was apparent something had to be done on the second treaty to "make DeConcini compatible with the principle of nonintervention."

Rogers went from the State Department to the Panamanian Embassy to talk with Gabriel, who was getting ready to go to Panama. He described the State Department's "good offices" proposal. The ambassador said that Torrijos and the Panamanian government would be happy if Rogers undertook that role. He was especially pleased that Rogers agreed that something substantive needed to be done about the DeConcini condition. Rogers told Lewis he thought the Panamanians should avoid doing or saying anything for the moment until the dust had settled on Capitol Hill. By then, Senator Byrd had circulated Panama's U.N. papers and that had taken considerable steam out of the issue, but there was still a residue of rancor among some legislators. Lewis promised nothing would be heard from Panama for the next few days, but he said he and Torrijos and others would be watching to see what the Senate did.

Lewis left for the airport with his U.N. and OAS colleagues Illueca and Pitty. They were joined by Carl Rowan, the widely circulated newspaper columnist, who was bound for the isthmus to get a firsthand look at the situation and to talk with Torrijos.

That relations between the Carter White House and the Panamanian Embassy had disintegrated was evident when the *Washington Star* hit the newsstands on Saturday. A front-page story was headlined: "Panama's Lobbying Could Backfire." It began with a dramatic lead: "Public posturing and ham-handed lobbying efforts by Panamanian officials are threatening to unravel the slim majority in the Senate on record in support of the new Panama Canal Treaties." What followed was a long and scathing attack on General Torrijos and Ambassador Lewis and their tactics in recent weeks. Strictly speaking, it was not a news story at all but an editorial. If a significant number of senators were as irritated as the story alleged, it was strange none was quoted. As a group, senators are not notably reluctant to speak out on matters they feel deeply. The only senatorial quotation was Howard Baker's statement in Houston two days earlier.

Indeed, the story named *no* sources, only "some administration officials," "an official," or "one source." The screen of anonymity was quite dense. A curious reporter might have wondered why he was being fed those allegations of near disaster. Those who knew what was happening realized there were, indeed, a handful of U.S. officials who were distressed by Panama's U.N. move and Ambassador Lewis' contacts with the Senate. They were unhappy mainly because Panamanian actions had accomplished what they themselves had failed to do, or did not want to attempt—that is, to convince senators that something had to be done about the DeConcini reservation.

There was one glaring omission in the story, which a good editor should have seen and questioned. The report was a thousand-word criticism of the Panamanian government and its ambassador. Yet no one from that government, including the ambassador, was asked for a comment or reaction.

That same morning, Bill Rogers met with Christopher and said he would undertake the "good offices" role. Rogers also told the deputy secretary once again that something had to be done in the second treaty to modify the DeConcini condition. He said the Panamanians would not sit still too long unless they felt a good faith effort was being made in that direction. Christopher explained he was toying with the idea of suggesting something DeConcini could add to a reservation he planned to offer on the second treaty. That sounded like putting a wolf in charge of the sheep.

Rogers was not then too familiar with the intricacies of the Senate fight or with the anathema the name DeConcini was to Panama. He thought it was a good road to pursue; he would soon learn it was a dead end.

Rogers made one other demand. That was that he be "the exclusive channel of communication between the entire U.S. government and the Panamanian government." It was not, he assured Christopher, a matter of personal ego but a move to assure there was totally accurate communication between the two governments. In a matter so sensitive, he argued, "misunderstanding is the greatest enemy." Christopher agreed and assured Rogers he would see to it the department and the White House cooperated.

The new go-between's demand was understandable if somewhat unrealistic. Christopher wisely never even raised it with me, knowing it would never have worked at the Panama end. Nor would I have accepted it, as I am sure he also knew. He and Herb Hansell were in touch with me several times a day to discuss possible Senate amendments and likely Panamanian reactions. The consulting machinery we had set up in Panama was an effective means to explain Senate moves and to get authoritative Panamanian opinions thereon. In addition, as Christopher and others well knew, I was spending much time and energy convincing a volatile Omar Torrijos and his advisers not to do things that could have destroyed the treaties before the Senate completed its work.

In Washington, it made sense to limit the number of contacts, but even there it raised problems of efficiency, to say nothing of bent egos. Rogers used young lawyers in his firm to handle daily routine. They, in turn, had to deal with people in the government who knew vastly more than they did about the Panama treaties. Some of those sources of information— men like Ambler Moss and Mike Kozak—also knew Ambassador Lewis and other Panamanians much better than did Rogers. At the outset, the go-between would have been wise to seek out such people and enlist their help as part of his team rather than treating them as remote information assets. He should have realized, too, that trying to confine Gabriel Lewis to a single channel of information and contacts was like attempting to harness a Caribbean hurricane. At least the Rogers approach did deter Gabriel from unwelcome needling of nervous officials in the White House. It also provided a much smoother operational channel between the State Department and the embassy in Washington. Both were useful. But Rogers' major accomplishment transcended such bureaucratic hassles.

Though Panama's move at the U.N. produced an outpouring of bitterness from the Carter administration, it proved salutary to the treaty cause, though hardly anyone recognized it at the moment. For it caused several key senators to realize something had to be done about the DeConcini condition. The realization also began to crystalize that, if anything were to be done, the Senate itself would have to do it. The White House and State

Department found it impossible to admit they had made a gross mis-calculation. An increasing number in the Senate, both members and staff, recognized the problem, but perceived no solutions. It was the frustration a doctor feels in diagnosing a disease but having no medicine to cure it.

One man who felt that frustration deeper than most was Mike Kozak. That weekend, he went home agonizing over a problem no one seemed ready to meet frontally. As much at home with a toolbox as with a legal text, Mike sublimated his concerns by repairing the plumbing in his aging house in Arlington. But repairing leaky faucets and replacing a faulty joint could not erase the nagging concern. Finally, he put down his wrench and, with plumbing on his mind, told himself: "Damn it, I can't just let it go down the drain. I have to do something, even if it's fruitless." He washed up, told his understanding Eileen he was going to the office, and drove off to the State Department.

In his small and littered cubicle on the fifth floor, Kozak took off his coat, thought for a few minutes, then started to write. Knowing well the Senate's problem, he wrote as though a member of that body were speaking. As the words poured out, the unknown senator was saying: "We are not taking anything back; we aren't repudiating DeConcini. It's just that the Panamanians don't understand what we intended. So we have to come up with a statement to clarify what we really meant."

On Monday morning, Kozak went to the office early and had his product put into neat and error-free type. He showed it to his colleague Ambler Moss for comment. Ambler liked it, but he noted that it deviated from the current party line at State—which was to sit tight and hope the Panamanians would come to accept DeConcini. "I don't care," Kozak said. "This is more important than my own situation." Unlike some timorous souls in the capital, his concern was with the treaties' fate, not his own. Kozak and Moss gave a copy of the statement to Doug Bennett, chief of State's congressional affairs office. Then they went to the Hill.

While the floor debate rambled on, Kozak showed his statement to Hoyt Purvis, Senator Byrd's top aide. Purvis read it, then admitted he had done something along the same lines himself. But for political reasons, Byrd felt he should not be too far in front of the movement to modify DeConcini. The majority leader's assistant suggested Mike try it out with Senator Church. Kozak went to the Idaho senator's office and tossed his paper on the desk in front of Ira Nordlick, a principal Church staffer. While Nordlick read, Kozak paced. When he finished reading, the senator's man realized it could provide a crucial turning point.

"Well, I just don't know what his attitude is going to be," Nordlick said. "But we'll show it to him, and then we'll just have to wait and see." It was all Kozak could ask. Nordlick carried the speech to Church, and Kozak went back to S-205, the operations center of the "Gang of Four."

Church read the draft and recognized it was what he and others had been searching for, an elegant and closely reasoned argument for undoing the damage that misinformation had produced a month before. Church went to the Senate floor and, with leadership cooperation, won recognition from the chair.

"Mr. President," he began, "I wish to take some time this afternoon to address a subject which, I believe, is weighing heavily on the minds of most of us who are well aware of the deep concern which has emerged during the last few days in Panama concerning the action we took on the Neutrality Treaty on March 16." Church then recalled the various efforts the Senate had made to "clarify" and "strengthen" the first treaty through amendments, reservations, and understandings.

"It is highly regrettable, however," Church went on, "that in the course of strengthening the Neutrality Treaty—by removing the ambiguities that we found in it—we appear to have introduced a new ambiguity which is causing grave concerns among the people of Panama."

The senator from Idaho then explained the contradictory views in Washington and in Panama of "intervention." He argued that "the U.S. policy of intervention is long gone" and he cited U.S. adherence to the U.N. Charter and other international agreements that prohibited interference in the internal affairs of other countries. He quoted DeConcini himself as saying, "It is not our expectation that this change gives to the United States the right to interfere in the sovereign affairs of Panama." Church thought objections raised in Panama were not to "what the Senate in fact intended" but rather to an "interpretation the Senate did not have in mind—and in fact disclaimed."

Church suggested the Panamanians might be "overreacting" or interpreting the reservation "out of context." In any case, he said, "they are reading an intention into our language that was not actually there." But that reaction, he argued, was "not so inexplicable" in view of the long history of U.S. and other foreign interference in Latin America's affairs. What then was to be done? The answer was in four sentences:

> Let us find an appropriate way to reassure the people of Panama that our intention was not to nullify the specific pledge of nonintervention in the internal affairs of Panama, which 85 Senators voted to incorporate into the treaty.
>
> Let us find a way to reaffirm the specific commitment to respect Panama's territorial integrity and political independence which we similarly voted to incorporate in the treaty.
>
> Let us find a way to tell all the nations of this hemisphere that we have not in one afternoon nullified the last 40 years in the history of the United States–Latin American relations.
>
> Let us make clear to the world that we are not seeking for ourselves the kind of rights the Soviets claimed in Czechoslovakia in 1968.

Church called on the Senate to "find an appropriate way to communicate its true intention to the people of Panama and to thus promptly resolve the misunderstanding that has arisen."* When he sat down, New York's Pat Moynihan took the floor to congratulate him for "what in history may prove to be the critical address in this long, crucial debate." That sounded like hyperbole to some. In fact, it was closer to the truth than even New York's junior senator may have realized. The fate of the Panama Canal Treaty would be determined by the skill of Senate leaders in attenuating the DeConcini condition without alienating two votes.

The extremes of the coming parliamentary struggle were expressed in the next few minutes by two senators. One was Alaska's Mike Gravel, one of twenty-three senators who had voted against the DeConcini reservation. Gravel told his fellow senators: "As I read the DeConcini amendment, I feel bad that we did not put up a greater fight at that time. I think we were all concerned with just winning. But I think the issue now is a little greater than that. I think I would rather have seen the treaty go down to defeat than have something that now I think casts a serious, serious shadow on the Neutrality Treaty." He urged the Senate to eliminate the ambiguity caused by the Senate itself.

Alabama's Senator Allen was equally vehement in opposing any change. He told his colleagues: "The door is closed, Mr. President, on legislative history for the DeConcini amendment because that amendment has been agreed to, it has become a part of the resolution of ratification of the Neutrality Treaty, and it has been approved by the U.S. Senate. And all dialogue here on the floor cannot change the meaning of the DeConcini amendment . . . It is just like trying to restore Humpty Dumpty. It cannot be done."

In the following week, jousting between those two points of view would determine the fate of the Panama treaties.

The Church speech and the statements by senators like Moynihan and Gravel finally forced the White House and the State Department out of their storm-cellar mentality and to the realization that something had to be done. By then it was evident that changing DeConcini meant risking the loss of some votes; but not changing might mean even more lost votes.

Facing that painful dilemma, Warren Christopher called the next day and asked me to set down what would satisfy Panama on the DeConcini issue. It was not difficult. I had talked with Torrijos about the problem, and with most of his advisers. Many outside the government had given us their opinions. A handful of able political officers had been feeding their

---

*The text of Church's speech is in the *Congressional Record*, April 10, 1978, pp. 9426–9428.

gleanings into the mill for several weeks. That afternoon, I sat at the typewriter and put our conclusions into seven paragraphs.

"The ideal would be to get DeConcini expunged from the books," I wrote. But I assumed that was technically and politically impossible. The next best approach would be "a Senate reservation, coequal with DeConcini, making it clear that the DeConcini reservation does not authorize what its author says it does." The wording of such a countermove would be all-important, I argued. "Subtle logical argument is lost in a situation such as this one," I explained. "The issue in Panama is one of mass politics, not scholarly deliberation by lawyers or statesmen. Whatever the Senate may do must be comprehensive and effective in terms of this political reality."

Some officials in Washington had wondered if we could not get over the DeConcini hurdle by having the president make some kind of antiinterventionist statement. I told the department that would not wash. Panamanians were not concerned about what Jimmy Carter would do; they considered him an honorable, decent man. Their worry was what might happen in the future if an aggressive and insensitive administration in Washington tried to use DeConcini's doctrine to inject itself into Panama's internal business. The report concluded: "We seriously doubt that statements by President Carter—or anyone else—that are not legally binding will create conditions here in which the treaties have a chance for life."

That day, Washington was buzzing about reports in the press describing the meeting in the White House six days earlier between Ambassador Lewis and Frank Moore. The "transcript" had Lewis and Moore discussing possible Senate action to counteract DeConcini. The report had fallen into the hands of treaty opponents and was being used as "proof" that a move was afoot to "water down DeConcini." But no one could make too much of the document, in part because of doubts about its authenticity. The White House issued a statement by Moore labeling the document inaccurate and incomplete.

Moore claimed, for example, that he told the Panamanians "in no way would an amendment undercutting the legality of the DeConcini amendment be adopted by the United States Senate." That was a shrewdly crafted sentence since the effort to modify DeConcini was never aimed at undercutting the "legality" of the reservation but rather its "intent." In any case, neither the ambassador nor Bilonick remembered Moore saying that. They did recall his telling them a resolution to "clarify" DeConcini's handiwork was being drafted by Warren Christopher, and that they might get a copy of it the next day.

The press handled the mysterious memo with restraint because reporters were not sure of its authorship. It could have been a clever invention of treaty opponents. In fact, it was quite genuine. Bilonick had written it in Spanish immediately after the White House session. It did not pretend to be a full transcript but covered what the Panamanians saw as the main points of the meeting. When heat arose over its disclosure, the embassy claimed the memo had been stolen from Bilonick's briefcase. If true, the Panamanians could have claimed it was a phony memo. A thief would not have stepped forward to dispute them. I suspected the report had been leaked deliberately by someone in the embassy, probably Bilonick, to "prove" that something was being done about DeConcini. When they realized how badly they had embarrassed Moore, and perhaps their own cause, the story of the "stolen memo" was concocted. In the end, the leak did no real harm, but it did rasp White House sensitivities anew and gave treaty foes something else to play with.

On Monday, April 10, the day the "stolen memo" was circulating among reporters and senators, Ambassador Lewis returned to Washington with columnist Carl Rowan. Two days of tramping through the Panamanian countryside, talking to both Americans and Panamanians, and long sessions with General Torrijos had convinced the veteran journalist that the Panama treaties were good for both sides. From then on, he was an outspoken advocate of the new arrangement. Lewis returned to his embassy and plunged into the familiar maelstrom.

He met almost immediately with the newly designated go-between, Bill Rogers. Lewis described the Panamanian scene—the widespread opposition to DeConcini, Torrijos' increasingly impatient attitude, and his own certain conviction that the treaties would be rejected by his countrymen unless "interventionism" was repudiated.

The silver-haired American lawyer gave Lewis an account of events in Washington. The need to correct DeConcini had finally, reluctantly, been recognized. He had met that morning with Christopher and Hansell, and they had drafted a possible addition to the resolution of ratification. It said that any actions taken to protect the canal would be undertaken "to the maximum extent feasible in consultation and cooperation with the other party." More important, such actions would *not* be "for the purpose of intervention in the internal affairs of the Republic of Panama, or intrusion upon its territorial integrity or political independence." It was not perfect, Rogers admitted, but it was a major step toward overcoming what both sides finally recognized as the biggest obstacle to accommodation.

Lewis told the American that Torrijos thought a meeting between specialists would be helpful in solving their common problem. He wanted Rogers to sit down with Aristides Royo, the treaty negotiator, to develop an answer to the DeConcini difficulty. The ambassador and the go-between recognized such a gathering would have to be secret.

No sooner had the U.S. intermediary left than the Panamanian ambassador went out the rear door to his car. He had arranged another "secret" meeting on his own. Trying to get Gabriel to put all his eggs in one basket was like trying to knead mercury. When he returned to Washington that afternoon, Lewis had called Sen. Mike Gravel. Much as he trusted Rogers, the ambassador believed Gravel could provide a more intimate appraisal of the Senate's mood at that moment. The ambassador and Bilonick drove down Calvert Street, turned right on Connecticut Avenue, and went to the heart of Washington. At Harvey's restaurant, a famous capital eatery, they were shown to their reserved table. As arranged, Gravel was there dining with the mayor of Anchorage and other Alaskan friends. He got up and joined the Panamanians.

Lewis told Gravel about his trip to Panama and the sour mood he had found. The Panamanians wanted the treaties badly, he said, but they could not stomach the arrogance that DeConcini represented. At the same time, Lewis was concerned that, if Panama appeared too rigid on something the Senate had approved, his country was going to be blamed for killing the treaties. "And you know damn well, it isn't our fault," he told Gravel.

The senator from Alaska knew what the Panamanian ambassador was feeling. Gravel blamed the White House and the Senate itself for not recognizing immediately that DeConcini's proviso represented a departure from more than forty years of U.S. foreign policy. He told Lewis he thought Panama should stick by its guns. If it came to a showdown, he assured the ambassador, he and like-minded colleagues would kill the treaty in the Senate rather than shift responsibility to Panama. "If there's any blame," he said, "it should fall on us, not on you."

One senator who was ignoring Panamanian opinion or feelings was Dennis DeConcini. Having nearly destroyed the first treaty, he declared his intention to add two reservations to the second treaty. As it turned out, both were rather innocuous. But the fact that the name DeConcini would be attached to them inclined the Panamanian government to reject them even without knowing what they provided. One DeConcini addition specified that provisions for joint military planning and a combined board for canal defense did not water down U.S. rights to protect the canal unilaterally. That was precisely what the treaty said and what administration spokesmen had been explaining for five months. His other contribution was to specify that payments to Panama under the treaty could not be made from the U.S. Treasury "without statutory authorization." Since the treaty provided those payments would come from canal operating revenues, not from the U.S. Treasury, it was meaningless.

Some Carter tacticians saw in DeConcini's proposal on defense an opportunity to kill two birds with one stone. They rewrote his reservation, saying what he wanted to say about unilateral military rights—which gave the administration no real problems. Then they added language specifying that canal protection would never be used to intervene in Panama's internal affairs. It seemed a clever ploy, but it was doomed, as the authors should have known. The language was shown to DeConcini later that day, and, predictably, he found it unacceptable. At that moment, Senate leaders and treaty managers realized that if DeConcini's handiwork were to be undone they were going to have to do it. The process of developing a leadership reservation to undercut DeConcini began.

The next morning, Rogers, Lewis, and Bilonick were on their way to Dulles International Airport. The Panamanians had chartered a Learjet for their secret mission and chose Dulles instead of the more heavily trafficked Washington National Airport. The plane was hired in the name of Ricardo Paredes, Bilonick's maternal family name. The three men boarded the jet at the private plane area and flew off to Florida. Instead of landing at Miami International Airport, they put down at the nearby Opa-Locka field, a former military airbase converted to civilian use. There they met Panamanian lawyer Jimmy Arias, who was in Miami on legal business. The four drove to a house owned by Bilonick in a Miami suburb.

About the same time, Panamanian treaty negotiator Aristides Royo flew into Miami. He was met by a Panamanian consular officer, passed through the diplomatic exit, and was driven to the Bilonick house. For the next three hours the ambassador and the four lawyers talked about what could be done about the DeConcini reservation.

Rogers explained that senators fighting for the treaties appeared convinced that something was going to have to be done to take the rough edges off the earlier treaty condition. They finally realized the depth of Panamanian objections. Just that morning, he told them, he had received the draft of a possible corrective move. It said that nothing in either Panama treaty "shall be interpreted as a right to intervene in the internal affairs of the Republic of Panama or to violate its territorial integrity or political independence." In the secret negotiations that began that day, this version came to be known as "Appendix A."

Royo, Arias, and the two diplomats were delighted when Rogers put that phrasing on the table. The words themselves were good; more important, they were proof that Panama's umbrage had finally penetrated to the Americans. What bothered the Panamanians mainly was the use of the words "shall be interpreted." As Jimmy Arias put it: "We need something stronger than that. We're less concerned with the way your rights are 'interpreted' than we are with the way they are 'used.'" After long discussion, he and Royo suggested a firmer guarantee: that U.S. actions "shall never be directed against the political independence or the territorial integrity of the Republic of Panama."

The session broke up and Lewis, Rogers, and Bilonick flew back to Washington from Opa-Locka. Royo returned to Panama to report to Torrijos and the treaty team. Arias remained in Miami to finish his legal business.

The next morning, Lewis and Rogers met in the latter's office on Nineteenth Street. As they considered their next move, the jangling of the phone interrupted them. It was the State Department calling. Could Rogers meet with Christopher and Hansell at 11:45 A.M.? He could. In the deputy secretary's office on the seventh floor, Christopher outlined the state of play on the Hill and gave Rogers a written version of the text they had discussed the previous morning. Rogers, in turn, relayed Panama's worries about the simple "shall be interpreted" language. Back at his office, Rogers did a six-paragraph memo for Ambassador Lewis summarizing his talk with Christopher and including the official text of Appendix A:

> Nothing contained in this treaty or the Treaty Concerning the Permanent Neutrality and Operation of the Panama Canal, and the resolutions of advice and consent related thereto, shall be interpreted as a right to intervene in the internal affairs of the Republic of Panama or to violate its territorial integrity or political independence.

Rogers assured the Panamanians there was goodwill on the U.S. side and that "all are concerned to do everything possible to work the problem out." He reported that Senate leaders felt a solution would be easier once debate ended on treaty changes two days later. The report went to Panama on the embassy's telephoto machine.

That afternoon, things looked tolerably bright for a change. Three hours later, the wind had shifted 180 degrees. The source of trouble, as it had been for weeks, was Dennis DeConcini. Christopher and others had explained to the Arizonian how sensitive the moment was, both in dealing with Panama and in the Senate itself. DeConcini professed to understand and had promised to remain quiet. But the appeal of media exposure proved too much for his resolve. That evening, he spoke at length with National Public Radio, with CBS, and with several newspapermen. He described his two amendments, which he pictured as "toughening" and "clarifying" the treaty. Asked about Panama's negative reaction to his earlier reservation, the senator told reporters, "It's not my problem what Panama thinks."

When Christopher called to ask why he had broken his pledge to remain quiet, DeConcini's only excuse was that he was under "great pressure" to speak out. The fact that an appointment with the president earlier that day had been abruptly canceled might have influenced his response to the journalistic "pressure." The administration's explanation was that the two sides were still too far apart to make such a meeting useful. In fact, the White House belatedly had realized that the first Carter-DeConcini meeting had been a disaster. Moreover, it had finally sunk in that top-level courting of the junior senator was giving him press attention and bargaining power which he was using to make life miserable for the administration.

Protreaty forces in Washington were upset with DeConcini, especially after his broken promise to remain silent for a decent interval. In Panama, the reaction was explosive. As a consequence of his various statements, including his intention to introduce new changes to the second treaty, DeConcini had pushed the Panamanians close to the breaking point. The last straw was his appearance on CBS news that evening. The ambassador reported that event to his colleagues in Panama City, where they were sitting around talking with General Torrijos. The reaction was swift and unmistakable. Lewis called Bill Rogers at home.

"Look, Bill," he told the American, "these people in Panama blew their stack with the DeConcini thing. And they say they want you to tell them [the administration] informally tonight." The good news was that Panama was happy about the statement on nonintervention that Rogers had sent that afternoon. But as for DeConcini and his reservations, "they don't want to hear anything else from DeConcini." If the Carter people accepted the Arizonian's additions, and if nothing was done about a resolution of nonintervention, "then that's the end of it." Panama planned to write a detailed diplomatic note expressing its unhappiness with what was going on in Washington, including a listing of the many demands Panama was being asked to accept in silence. Lewis quoted the foreign minister as saying that, from Panama's viewpoint, "it would be better if DeConcini voted against the treaty and the president found another vote somewhere."

Rogers called the State Department to convey this latest development. Christopher was at a dinner for the president of Rumania, so he talked with Hansell instead. He described the talk with Lewis, and Hansell said he would convey the news to Christopher as soon as he was available. When Christopher received the disturbing report, he asked Rogers to come to his office early the next morning.

The phone rang in our quarters at 9:15 that night. It was earlier than usual, but I felt sure it was Gabriel. Before I picked up the phone, I made sure I had a good writing pad and several pencils handy—and the makings of a stiff nightcap. Then I took the black instrument off its cradle and said, "Hello." The familiar voice came into the earpiece.

"Look, Bill, this situation is out of hand now," he said. There followed a description of the Arizona senator on television and the announcement about his two new treaty amendments. In Gabriel's version, DeConcini was laughing as he spoke into the CBS microphone and he indicated that "he didn't give a damn if the Panamanians like it or not." It was clear, the ambassador said, that the legislator was enjoying "being the star of the show" and he was appealing to emotions by saying, "Panama can't dictate to the U.S. Senate."

"He's trying to make our distrust of him into a fight with the Senate," Gabriel said, "and that is a lie, as you know. We want these treaties and we want to work with the Senate. He's fighting both of us."

He was called to the other phone and, while he was gone, Bilonick read me the text of the two DeConcini reservations. They were, with minor word changes, the same as those described earlier.* The problem was not the words; it was the authorship. Gabriel came back on and said he had been talking with a White House official who, he said, was in "a very depressed mood." The reason: "Everything he hoped could be done today had failed." The official had described the situation in graphic terms. DeConcini had the Carter administration in a vise, and was squeezing hard. No one seemed to know what to do about it.

Gabriel asked what I thought of the DeConcini additions. I told him frankly I could not see that they changed anything essential. He felt it was "immaterial," that it was "a matter of principle."

"We're sick and tired of DeConcini," he said. "You reach a point, when you fill a glass with so much water, that it won't take another drop. This is the last drop—today."

He then said that Panama was going to deliver a note the next day outlining its full position. He said the note would probably be delivered to me. I told him I thought a diplomatic note was a bad idea. The problem was in the Senate, not in government-to-government relations. The kind of protest he was talking about would only help treaty opponents. "It's a bad situation, I know, Gabriel," I told him. "But we've got to stay cool and figure out how to handle it." The first requirement was for the Senate to make clear the United States had no interest in intervening in Panama's internal affairs, and it seemed that path was being pursued actively. Once that was accomplished, everything else would seem unimportant.

Gabriel's rational side accepted that, but his emotional sphere was in control. He recalled I had worked for President Johnson and he wished that "someone with Johnson's guts were running this show." He was sure LBJ would have known how to handle DeConcini. I told him he was right "except that Lyndon Johnson would have had seventy-two votes going in." Gabriel remembered that, after the note on the first treaty, Hamilton Jordan and others had boasted they had at least three votes they could have called up if necessary. "Maybe it's time to call up those votes," I suggested. We broke off then because his other phone was ringing.

---

* See p. 585.

I immediately called a few people in the Panamanian government, said I had heard there might be a diplomatic protest in the works, and advised that such a move would hurt them and us. I explained my reasons, and they agreed. By the next day, it was apparent that treaty proponents were doing their best to put an antiintervention resolution together, and the idea of a protest note was quietly dropped.

The *Washington Post* set the Panama kettle boiling merrily the morning of April 13 with a slashing editorial attack on Senator DeConcini. Referring to future historians, the *Post* speculated: "How was it, they may ask, that the treaties, with their immense diplomatic and political freight, came to hinge on the ill-informed whims of a 40-year-old freshman senator of no previous renown, of no known international awareness, or little experience of any kind beyond minor administrative posts in Arizona?" The newspaper found him "a lightweight whom serious senators should regard as an institutional embarrassment." The editorial also took President Carter to task for his inept handling of the Arizona politician. It said he had "blundered sorely in failing to anticipate the explosive Panamanian reaction" to his acceptance of DeConcini's amendment. He could not, "in honor," offer Panama a package "that he and everyone else knows is absolutely offensive to virtually every segment of Panamanian society." It was up to the president to impress on DeConcini that, "if he persists in his ways, the wreckage will be on his hands and on the hands of those other senators so cynically playing his game."

Everyone concerned with the Panama issue had read or heard about the *Post* editorial before the working day had gone an hour. Critics of DeConcini thought it said what had badly needed saying for a month. Friends of the senator thought it was grossly unfair. Treaty advocates hoped it would make the Arizona politician realize what a destructive game he had been playing. Treaty foes hoped it would so incense him that he might shift his vote. Because of senatorial courtesy, no member of that body could possibly have endorsed the editorial in public. Indeed, soon after the session began that day, half a dozen of DeConcini's colleagues, pro- and antitreaty alike, took the floor to defend their colleague's character and integrity against the "unwarranted attack" by the press. When I asked one senator about the editorial a year later, he told me, "The language may have been a little extreme, but in general it said what about half the members of the Senate had been thinking privately."

Bill Rogers went to the State Department that morning for the meeting with Christopher. He laid out the Panamanian position as he had received it the night before. It was a tight, three-point brief: first, Panama could not accept the two new DeConcini additions; second, a clear declaration by the Senate on nonintervention was "essential"; third, the Panamanians hoped that President Carter would "stand and fight." Torrijos and Company "would rather lose the treaties on this clear issue of principle than have them adopted in their present form."

The deputy secretary told Rogers that he and the White House understood Panama's reaction, that nothing with the Arizona senator's name on it would be welcome. As for the nonintervention reservation, Christopher had talked with Senator Church about it the night before and the Idaho politician was fighting hard for it. The liberal group in the Senate were all in favor, and Church thought he could win over most of the "undecideds." But Christopher warned that the result would be close, and would probably not be decided until the following Monday or Tuesday.

The go-between went to the embassy and told Ambassador Lewis about his talk with Christopher and his account was sent to Panama in a few minutes. The Foreign Ministry translated it and sent the report to Torrijos. The general read it in a mood considerably more tranquil than the one he had passed through the night before.

In the White House, the reverse was true. Perhaps it was the stinging editorial he had read in the *Post* that morning. Maybe the critical comments made by some senators were getting under his skin. In any case, President Carter was described that morning as being "fed up." He called Hamilton Jordan to the Oval Office and told him he thought he should go on national television that evening. He wanted to urge the Senate to adopt some kind of resolution reaffirming the longstanding U.S. policy of not intervening in the internal affairs of other countries.

Back at his office, Jordan called a meeting of officials involved in the treaty fight and told them of the president's inclination. The reactions were mixed. As always happens when a president floats an idea, some automatically judged it "great." A few were less convinced. They wondered if senators might not resent being publicly nudged by the White House. Also, it would certainly have appeared to some on the Hill that Carter was trying to put the onus on the Senate for his own gross error in adopting DeConcini's treaty change in the first place.

Later, Vice President Mondale and some Carter operatives raised the president's idea with key senators. The reaction was universally negative— from Byrd, Church, and others. In fact, the Senate leaders told the Carter people rather bluntly that they thought it was time for the administration to stand aside from the problem and let them handle it. The feeling was strong that the White House had mismanaged DeConcini badly on the first treaty and might well do the same again. Based on that, Frank Moore advised the president to drop the idea of a televised statement. When he heard the senators' reaction, the president quickly agreed.

The debate in the Senate was grinding to an end. That day would be the last for discussing individual articles in the treaty and any amendments thereto. The debate was ending as it had begun a month earlier, and as it had continued through long, dreary, windy days—with desperate but futile efforts by treaty foes to kill it. The main weapon selected for the attempted "pacticide" on that final day was an amendment offered by Senator Dole of Kansas. Instead of the two and a half years' transition period for replacement of U.S. legal jurisdiction with Panamanian, Dole proposed a twelve-year transition. He argued that without such an extended period most Americans working on the canal were going to leave. He cited an informal poll indicating 70 percent of canal workers had expressed that intention. It may have been one of the most misleading pieces of "evidence" introduced in the Senate debate. In any event, it was obvious Dole's proposal, if adopted, would have guaranteed Panama's rejection of the treaty. And that, of course, was what he wanted.

New York's Pat Moynihan rose to respond. The eloquent senator from the Empire State said he was responding "to the thoughtful and reasoned statement of the Senator from Kansas." He then went on to suggest with great subtlety that it was neither. Rather it was "a needless insult to Panama," he argued. A man with considerable experience overseas, Moynihan said Americans in the Canal Zone "are going to have to accept the normal circumstances that living in another country involves, which means being subject to its laws."

The Dole amendment was soundly defeated by a voice vote. The Senate continued on its dreary course toward sundown, and the end of a debate that by then had bored and tired even those who had sought to drag it out.

The real business of the Senate that day was going on behind the scenes. It was senatorial surgery designed to draw the fangs of the DeConcini amendment without its author, or others, feeling excessive pain. The Senate leadership was recasting "Appendix A" to reflect both senatorial and Panamanian views. Working at times in the majority leader's office, at times in the vice-president's office, Senators Byrd, Church, and Sarbanes, with kibitzing from other senators and the vice-president, composed a new resolution.

At 3:30 P.M., Warren Christopher called Bill Rogers at the Panamanian Embassy. He dictated the text of the new resolution, which came to be called "Appendix B." It read:

> The right of the United States to take action to assure that the Canal shall remain open, secure and accessible, pursuant to the provisions of this treaty and of the Neutrality Treaty, and the resolutions of advice and consent related thereto, shall not be interpreted as a right of intervention of the United States in the internal affairs of the Republic of Panama, and shall never be directed against the political independence or territorial integrity of the Republic of Panama.

Rogers typed the resolution from his notes and Lewis sent it to Panama. While the document was being readied for transmission, Rogers spoke with Foreign Minister González-Revilla. He told the young Panamanian that "the gap is being closed." He said it could be closed further if Appendix B could be accepted. He described the pressure that had developed on the Hill and said he needed Panama's approval "in three hours."

The ambassador and Rogers were sitting in the comfortable sitting room of the residence sipping a sundown scotch and reviewing the day's events when the phone interrupted their musings at almost exactly 5 o'clock. It was Aristides Royo calling from Panama. He said his government was prepared to accept Appendix B but they were still fretting over the phrase "shall not be interpreted." Royo said they would prefer other words— "does not grant" or "shall not permit" or something of that kind.

The American lawyer knew what the Panamanians were getting at and promised to look for a solution. After trying countless words and phrases, he finally went back to the agreement between Carter and Torrijos. The two leaders had affirmed that the right to protect the canal "does not mean, nor shall it be interpreted as, a right of intervention of the United States in the internal affairs of Panama."

Rogers called Royo and proposed the Carter-Torrijos phrasing. With the addition of "does not mean," Royo accepted for Panama. Rogers then called Christopher and told him the new leadership resolution was acceptable to Panama provided the words "does not mean" were inserted. Christopher promised to try to get the Senate leaders to buy that. If they did, he wondered if Panama would then be willing to accept the two DeConcini reservations. Rogers said his guess was that "this will produce a package that will be acceptable."

The long annual holiday for Panama's schools was coming to an end and classes were to resume the next week. There were widespread rumors that, when the students reassembled, there would be demonstrations, possibly riots, with the U.S. Embassy as a prime target. The potential for violence was on Ambassador Lewis' mind that evening when he called Hamilton Jordan at the White House. They talked briefly about the Senate resolution and Jordan's judgment was that "we'll either have a good treaty or no treaty at all." Lewis then pointed out that Panamanian schools would be reopening on Monday and there was a likelihood of large protests against the treaties. He wondered if it would be possible "to get some kind of signal down to Panama from Washington that things are moving along in a favorable way." Senator Byrd normally held a news conference on Saturdays and Lewis wondered if the majority leader would be willing to "say something useful" to calm emotions on the isthmus. Jordan promised to inquire.

While Lewis and Jordan were talking about it, Senator Byrd was doing it. He told an enterprising reporter from the *New York Times* that the Democratic leadership planned a reservation to the second treaty "restating the U.S. policy of nonintervention in Panama." He said it would be done to counter the angry reaction to the DeConcini reservation. Byrd even provided essential details, giving the reporter an accurate paraphrase of the language he and others had worked out earlier that day.

"Just to get 67 votes for a treaty, and then to have it rejected and have the United States roundly criticized by all the Latin American countries, and the world, would harm the United States and the Senate," he told the *Times*.

Amazingly, central players in the treaty drama, including Ambassador Lewis, missed the *Times* account. Much later in the day, he was still pressing Bill Rogers and others to get the majority leader to say the kind of thing Byrd had already said. The ambassador, normally an avid reader of all the major papers, may have been sidetracked by an item in the *Washington Post* that morning. It reported that two senators who had voted for the first treaty were in rebellion against the Carter administration. One was the feisty James Abourezk from South Dakota. The other was California's S. I. Hayakawa. Both were said to be considering a negative vote on the Panama treaty.

Lewis also read with some surprise the defense of Senator DeConcini that appeared in the *Post* that morning in letters from two senators. One, from Utah's antitreaty Orrin Hatch, was an attack on the "vicious, irresponsible and demeaning" editorial of the previous day. He defended his colleague as "one of the most ethical, decent, fine men in the Senate." Hatch thought the *Post* owed an apology to both DeConcini and the Senate.

The other letter, from Michigan's Don Riegle, a strong treaty supporter, was more revealing. He defended his fellow senator as an "intelligent and decent man," and criticized the *Post* for attacking the wrong target. It should have vented its anger at the White House, not at one senator, wrote Riegle. For the first time in any public forum, he laid out what he and many senators saw as the real problem. He wrote:

> When President Carter agreed to support the DeConcini reservation without alerting treaty supporters in the Senate about the intense negative reaction the White House had received privately from Panama, the White House seems to have attempted a daring and unwise double finesse. It first finessed the Senate's treaty supporters by failing to disclose the intensity of the Panamanian reaction to the DeConcini reservation, and allowed the vote to go forward on schedule in order to grab a quick and narrow victory on the first treaty. The second finesse was then to say to Panama that the DeConcini reservation was an accomplished fact and would have to be lived with.

There is obvious sleight-of-hand in all this that has now put the entire treaty package in genuine jeopardy.

In two carefully drafted paragraphs, the astute senator from Michigan had exposed the key element in the debate on the second Panama treaty. Dozens of reporters who had been covering the story for months had either written around that central fact, or ignored it completely.

The Senate had agreed to go into recess Thursday night until noon on Monday. That gave the protreaty leaders additional time to work on their new resolution. Byrd, Church, and Sarbanes had to avoid alienating DeConcini and those who had backed his stand. But they also had to placate more than half a dozen senators who thought the Arizonian's condition was a catastrophe. The latter were threatening to vote against the second treaty unless the interventionist language was modified. The treaty managers walked a tightrope, and there was no safety net beneath them, only the dark chasm of treaty defeat and the gloomy events they knew would follow.

They met at noon on Friday in the majority leader's office with DeConcini and five Democratic senators who had voted with him—Hatfield of Montana, Hodges from Arkansas, Louisiana's Long, and Nunn and Talmadge from Georgia. Each was given a copy of Appendix B, which had been developed the day before, and the discussion commenced. Some senators, DeConcini in particular, took exception to the "shall not mean or be interpreted as a right of intervention" phrasing. The Arizona senator thought that left the door open for some future Panamanian government to argue that *any* move by the United States to keep the canal open was "intervention." Similarly, he argued against saying that U.S. actions would not be directed against Panama's "territorial integrity." Panamanians might contend that any introduction of U.S. forces violated their "territorial integrity," he claimed.

DeConcini's approach illustrated the difficulty of conducting foreign policy by committee. His suspicious and legalistic approach might have been appropriate if the matter at hand had been a business contract or an arms agreement with an adversary like the Soviet Union. But if one is trying to build a relationship based on cooperation and trust—as we were in Panama—you help destroy your own chances of success with proclaimed suspicions about the other party's motives.

The elders in the majority leader's office recognized the mistake their young colleague was making, but senatorial courtesy prevented any lectures on so elementary a point. Besides, they were all feeling sorry for him because of the pasting he had taken from the *Washington Post* the day before. And so all hands went to work to find words to meet the objections raised yet preserve as much of the previous draft as possible. Byrd and the others recognized, of course, that they needed DeConcini's vote on the second treaty and the best way to get it was to keep him "on the team."

What emerged was "Appendix C." Byrd gave it to Christopher after the meeting, and the deputy secretary in turn called Bill Rogers and asked him to go to the White House. There, in Hamilton Jordan's office, the go-between was handed a copy of the senators' product. It stated:

> Pursuant to its adherence to the principle of nonintervention, any action taken by the United States of America in the exercise of its rights to assure that the Panama Canal shall remain open, neutral and secure, pursuant to the provisions of this Treaty and the Neutrality Treaty and the resolutions of ratification thereto, shall be only for the purpose of assuring that the Canal shall remain open, secure and accessible to the ships of all nations, and shall not have as its purpose interference in the internal affairs of the Republic of Panama, or infringement of its independence or its sovereignty.

Most people reading "B" and "C" would have seen no significant distinction. That night, talking with Panama City, Bill Rogers argued that "as a matter of law" there was little difference between the two versions. But the central point—and Rogers recognized it fully—was that what was being hammered out was not law, not a contract, but a political document. If there had been no difference, the senators would not have rejected "B" and written "C."

What were the differences? Clearly "B" was more restrictive. U.S. actions in protecting the canal would never be "directed against the political independence or the territorial integrity of the Republic of Panama." Version "C" spoke not of U.S. action and its effects but of its "purpose." Such action would be "only for the purpose" of keeping the canal open and would not "have as its purpose interference in [Panama's] internal affairs." The Panamanians would have as many problems with the "purpose" concept as they had with the "shall not be interpreted" approach. If American forces ever went into Panama, Washington might define the "purpose" as one thing, while Panamanians saw the "purpose" quite differently.

There was one other notable difference. "B" mentioned Panama's "territorial integrity." The senators dropped the phrase completely and spoke of Panama's "independence" and "sovereignty." DeConcini had said the Panamanians might some day interpret any U.S. move in protecting the canal as a violation of their "territorial integrity." The Panamanians were concerned that some future U.S. administration might move in to "protect" the canal and use that as a pretext for a revived Canal Zone in violation of their "territorial integrity." The search for a Senate resolution was deepening concerns on both sides instead of alleviating them.

As Rogers was walking out of the White House with Appendix C in his pocket, Hamilton Jordan called Ambassador Lewis to give him the news. He read the text of the senators' draft and told the ambassador, "I think it solves our problem." Lewis asked: "If that thing is accepted, do they have the votes?" Jordan said they did. Then he added: "One more thing; this is probably the best we can get out of the Senate." The ambassador asked how many votes the administration thought it had. Jordan told him "sixty-seven, maybe sixty-eight."

Jordan quoted the last phrase of Appendix C and said he thought it gave Panama "plenty of ammunition to work with." Lewis said he would study the proposal carefully. Jordan again said: "But, my friend, if you come back and say 'we have to have another phrase or another clause' the whole thing is going to blow up again." Lewis told him Bill Rogers was at the door and he wanted to consult with the lawyer.

Rogers quickly summarized his meeting at the White House. Then he sat at a typewriter and wrote a report of the events for the Panamanian treaty group. As usual, it began "Dr. Reyes reports:"—Reyes was the code name Rogers had adopted for his behind-the-scenes role. He told the Panamanians that Senator Byrd believed he had the votes necessary for approval of a new nonintervention resolution. Rogers attached the latest leadership draft, Appendix C. Byrd hoped to have Panama's response that evening. The majority leader planned to have a press conference the next morning, but only if the nonintervention matter was settled by then.

"Dr. Reyes" told the Panamanians that Senator Church, who had done much of the negotiating with wavering senators, would "find it difficult to make changes in Appendix C" but he did not want that taken as "an ultimatum." Rogers also passed along White House plans provided the treaty was approved the following Tuesday. In that case, the president intended to make a statement in Spanish on television for all of Latin America. He had also promised a letter to General Torrijos emphasizing the U.S. pledge never to intervene in Panama's internal affairs. Carter expected to announce plans to travel to Panama "in the near future" to exchange the treaty ratification documents with Torrijos.

Lewis put the report on the telecopier for transmission to his Foreign Ministry. Rogers called Christopher to tell him the new draft was on its way to Panama and that he was pressing the Torrijos team for an early answer. The lawyer then asked the deputy secretary a crucial question: "How negotiable is this really?" He was wondering how to handle things if the Panamanians came back with minor changes, or even a rewritten draft.

Christopher admitted that when people said something was not negotiable they often meant only "back up and think it over." In this case, he told Rogers, "this is virtually nonnegotiable." He explained the wording had been shown to six or seven wavering senators, and if it were changed, "they would have to go back through that process." Church had told Christopher he felt they had "stretched it to the end." The deputy secretary did not rule out one or two minor changes, but he thought anything more would endanger the delicate balance in Senate maneuvers.

From 5 until 7 o'clock that evening, lawyers Royo, Escobar, and López-Guevara, the foreign minister, and a few other advisers pored over the document they had received from Washington. A consensus slowly formed around the notion of a modest revision. The group was unanimous in wanting a reference to Panama's "territorial integrity" in the resolution.

While the Panamanians were working, and arguing, Rogers and Lewis were talking in the ambassador's sitting room. Perhaps from that talk, more likely from the sixth sense of a good lawyer and diplomat, Rogers felt the outcome might be more auspicious if the Panamanians had more time. On the other hand, he did not want to suggest any delay if that would complicate what Byrd and the other senators were trying to do. He called Christopher with those musings.

The deputy secretary said he had no ready answer. He doubted that, if he gave the majority leader Panama's response that night, Byrd would immediately go to his colleagues with it. The West Virginia senator would probably want to get "some indication of general acceptability," Christopher thought, "before he goes to the 'liberals' who have been causing most of the trouble."

It was the first admission that the Senate leadership's real problem was then less with the DeConcinis and Hatfields than with the most avidly pro-treaty members of the upper house. They were insisting that unless the Panama Treaty made clear it was not the intention of the United States to interfere in Panama's internal affairs, they could not in good conscience vote for it. The group included Senators Culver, Gravel, Haskell, Kennedy, McGovern, Moynihan, and, perhaps, even Frank Church, who was leading the fight for the treaties. If DeConcini was Byrd's Scylla, this group made up his Charybdis.

After voicing these considerations, Christopher concluded that, "if two or three hours would improve the chances of a favorable reaction, we ought to take them. That's my bottom line." Rogers said that was where he had hoped his fellow lawyer would come out.

He immediately called Royo. They talked about the formula in general terms. Then Rogers told him that he and his colleagues should not feel they were under any kind of "artificial deadline."

"In other words," he said, "if you need more time for deliberate and careful analysis, take the time."

But at that juncture, the Panamanians were under as much pressure as the Americans to get things moving. An impatient Omar Torrijos, pacing the enclosed porch at the Fiftieth Street house, was pushing his advisers to "get this thing settled." Royo told the American lawyer that "we feel that in maybe half an hour you'll get your answer." They would send their response by "the little toy we have," a reference to the telecopier.

Thirty minutes later, the minister called to say they were ready to transmit. In a few minutes, the ambassador and the U.S. go-between were looking at Panama's counterproposal. The first nine lines, ending with the words "ships of all nations," were exactly as drafted by Church and the other senators. Royo and his colleagues had redrafted the remainder to read: "This does not mean nor shall it be interpreted as the right of interference in the internal affairs of the Republic of Panama, or infringement of its political independence, its territorial integrity, or its sovereignty." The Panamanians had deliberately put their draft into almost the precise words of the Carter-Torrijos Understanding. The new wording was labeled "Appendix D" in the expanding file on the Senate resolution.

Rogers was relieved because the changes were less drastic than he feared they might be. Still, knowing how sensitive were the negotiations going on under Byrd's aegis, he realized any revision could create difficulties. He called Christopher at the State Department and read the paragraph received from Panama. The deputy secretary said he would pass it along to the senators for their consideration, but he felt the rewording created "formidable problems."

Rogers raised another point. The Panamanians had suggested a direct meeting between Ambassador Lewis and Senator Church might be useful. They named Church because he seemed to be doing most of the drafting on the proposed resolution. They also knew the Idaho senator was dedicated to a fair treaty. Rogers pointed out that such a session would give the U.S. side an opportunity to explain the difficulties it was encountering with temperamental senators. Christopher saw the advantages of such a meeting, and he agreed to try to set it up the next day.*

Saturday, April 15 was to have been "D Day" (*D* for *DeConcini*, for Appendix *D*, and for *Decision*). Ambassador Lewis woke up early, showered, put on a well-tailored suit, even wore a favorite tie. By 7:30 he had devoured his breakfast, swallowed his vitamins and other assorted pills,

---

*In his memoirs, President Carter admitted "it had been impossible to deal with DeConcini directly." As a result, he wrote, he decided that Ambassador Lewis and Warren Christopher should work on the problem with Senate leaders, "letting them deal with DeConcini." (See Carter's *Keeping Faith* [New York: Bantam Books, 1982].) That is not the recollection of other major participants in those events. The decision that they, not the White House, should cope with DeConcini was made by the senators themselves, especially Senators Byrd, Church, and Sarbanes. The proposal for direct contact between the key senators and Ambassador Lewis was made by the Panamanian envoy, conveyed by Rogers and Christopher, and accepted by the Senate leaders. President Carter made neither decision but acquiesced in both.

skimmed through two newspapers. But he was especially edgy that day because of the meeting he thought would be held on Capitol Hill.

At half past eight on what he remembered as "a screamingly beautiful Saturday morning," Bill Rogers had a call from Christopher. He wanted to check the wording of the last phrase in Appendix D, and Rogers read it to him. He also wanted to know if the Senate version, Appendix C, was really unacceptable to Panama. Rogers assured him it was. The State official thought the difference between the two was minor, "just a matter of words." Rogers explained that was not the way the Panamanians saw it. They attached considerable importance to "territorial integrity" and they thought the formula on the "purpose" of U.S. action was a considerable retreat from the wording Byrd and the others had originally proposed. Christopher raised the possibility of President Carter's calling General Torrijos, but Rogers argued strongly against the idea. It would not be helpful, he thought, for the president to try to convert Torrijos to the new resolution and be refused, as he probably would be. Christopher accepted that judgment.

The go-between called Ambassador Lewis to relay his talk with Christopher. He asked about a possible Carter-Torrijos talk. Lewis was emphatic: "It would be the greatest mistake at this point." Rogers said that was what he had told Christopher. He mentioned that the deputy secretary was trying to set up a meeting for them with Vice President Mondale. Lewis was delighted because "he knows how the Senate works." Rogers left for the embassy immediately.

A few minutes after 9, Christopher called the embassy to say that a meeting that day was impossible. Sen. Dick Clark was in trouble in his reelection bid, and Byrd, Church, and others had flown to Iowa to help him with appearances around the state. They would not be back in Washington until 9:00 P.M. or later. But Church had agreed to a meeting Sunday morning in his office. Christopher said he was arranging a talk with Vice President Mondale after the session with Church.

Though he had set up the meeting with Church, Christopher was uneasy about it. He knew Panama's ambassador could be, on occasion, abrasive and strong willed. He also knew how much was riding on the success of the treaties in terms of the president's foreign policy as well as Carter's image as a successful manager. Through daily contacts with the White House staff, he had absorbed much of their nervousness about the slightest misstep. He suggested that he and Rogers get together to review the bidding on the entire exercise. Rogers proposed lunch at the Jockey Club in the gracious old Fairfax Hotel on Massachusetts Avenue.

Only a handful of people knew about the planned Lewis-Church meeting and all of them realized it could determine whether there was going to be a treaty. President Carter had gone to Camp David for a weekend of intensive meetings with his cabinet and principal advisers on overall administration policy. He knew early Saturday that the planned meeting had been put off for twenty-four hours. General Torrijos was standing by at his house on Calle Cincuenta with a handful of aides and cronies. When his ambassador called to say the session with the senators had been put off until Sunday, the general jumped into his helicopter and flew to Contadora Island for the day.

Rogers' luncheon with Christopher reflected the administration's mood. The senior diplomat was fearful the solution to the DeConcini problem, which he had thought was in hand twenty-four hours earlier, was about to come unstuck. He spent much of the time extolling the advantages of Appendix C and insisting the differences between it and "D" were relatively minor. Rogers explained that the Panamanians did not see it that way. They believed, for example, that elimination of "territorial integrity" was a deliberate weakening of the resolution. They saw it as a test of whether the United States was willing to abandon past interventionist inclinations. Christopher urged Rogers to explain to the Panamanians that the difference between respect for "sovereignty" and for "territorial integrity" was small or nonexistent. The go-between promised to do his best but was not sanguine such an attempt would have any effect.

He was quite right. When he returned to the ambassador's residence, he told Lewis about the lunch and started to discuss the administration's view of Appendix C. It was evident neither the ambassador nor his colleagues in Panama wanted to hear a legal analysis of the concept of sovereignty at that moment. Lewis and Rogers agreed to wait and see what happened at the meeting with Senator Church the next morning.

Soon after, there was another indication that the administration was suffering a case of nerves. Hamilton Jordan called Lewis and said he had just talked with the president at Camp David. There was something he wanted the ambassador to "factor into your thinking." Carter had been talking to a number of senators, and, Jordan said, "he hopes this thing will be wrapped up soon, or it's going to unravel." He admitted that the president had "sounded nervous." Jordan added his own estimate: "The longer this thing is up in the air, the shorter the time we have to push it through."

Lewis reminded him that he had gotten "all dressed up" that morning, thinking he was going to work. Then he found that Byrd and the others had flown off to Iowa. The White House aide admitted that was "our fault, not yours." Lewis assured him he knew how important the time element was and he could tell the president the Panamanians would do everything possible to accelerate things.

One of the most critical moments in the long pursuit of new Panama treaties was at hand. By then, some of the worry that had infected the U.S. side for two days had spread to Panama. Foreign Minister González-

Revilla called the ambassador early Sunday morning to discuss the forth-coming session.

Torrijos and those around him knew that Lewis was probably the most effective ambassador their country had ever sent to Washington. But they also knew their friend had a quick temper and was easily offended. The minister's first admonition to the envoy was that he should exercise "great calm." Panama wanted no risk of a breakdown in the delicate negotiations on anything but the central issue. González-Revilla said there was one basic question the ambassador should ask: "Is it the intention of the United States to intervene in the internal affairs of Panama?" If the answer was no, as Panama assumed, the remaining problem was to "figure out some way of putting that into writing."

The ambassador said the senators might tell him: "We will take your language, but what if it means we don't have 67 votes?" Lewis said he thought Panama's answer should be: "Take our language and we'll take our chances." González-Revilla agreed, but urged the ambassador not to give any "spur-of-the-moment answers." Lewis said there was not enough time left to play with the matter. In that case, the minister said, "go ahead as we have discussed."

By 10 o'clock, Bill Rogers had joined Lewis at the residence. Soon after, Christopher called to say the meeting would be at 11 in Senator Church's office, room 208 in the Senate. The meeting with the vice-president would be an hour and a half later.

Finally, it was time to go. Lewis, Rogers, and Bilonick walked down the steps in front of the residence and climbed into the ambassador's official car. If some curious reporter was lying in wait and asked where they were going, the ambassador was primed to say: "Doesn't everyone go to Church on Sunday?" But the street was empty. They drove across town and stopped in front of the Senate side of the Capitol. A police guard at the entrance directed them to S-208.

Waiting in the ornate, high-ceilinged old office were Majority Leader Byrd, Senators Church and Sarbanes, and Deputy Secretary Christopher. The ambassador explained he was under instructions from his government to insist on the inclusion of words to protect his country's "political inde-pendence" and "territorial integrity" in the second treaty. For that reason, he found it necessary to reject the resolution (Appendix C) which the sena-tors had proposed, a copy of which Church had just handed them. For Panama, he said, it was better to defeat a treaty that might cause future problems between the two countries than to accept one in which such problems were inherent.

Church explained that the draft resolution was a compromise developed at considerable pain with half a dozen uncommitted senators whose votes were necessary. Then Byrd delivered a brief lecture on his favorite theme:

that no senator had anything to gain by supporting the treaties, indeed had much to lose. Lewis responded that the problem of Panama was that of "two million Panamanian senators," the entire population. "For them, what is at stake is not their own political future but the destiny of their country," he said. "For them, bad treaties could be the ruin of their country." Those rhetorical admonitions delivered, the two sides got down to business.

Byrd had a copy of Appendix C in one hand, and a pen in the other. He put the paper on the coffee table in front of the ambassador. The majority leader ran his hand down the text two-thirds of the way and said: "We're in agreement down to here, I gather." The ambassador said that was right. "And you want to change the rest?" Lewis said that, too, was correct. Byrd then knelt on the floor beside the low table and began questioning Lewis and lining out some words and writing in others. Church joined in; so did Sarbanes. Christopher and Rogers remained in the background watching the amazing scene. It was the only time in history a majority leader of the Senate and a foreign ambassador had negotiated wording that would become part of an international treaty. But it was done for a very simple reason, which everyone in S-208 understood: there was no other way to save the treaties.

For the senators and the Panamanians huddled around the coffee table in Church's office, the goal was a product as close as possible to their own original that would satisfy the other party. Deep down, both wanted something that would win Senate support and get the treaty passed. One thing that inspired patience and encouraged accommodation among the senators was their unanimous belief that White House failure to get Panamanian consent earlier had jeopardized the entire project. They were determined not to repeat that egregious mistake. What permitted Ambassador Lewis to accept changes was his profound awareness that the men he was dealing with—Byrd, Church, and Sarbanes—were champions of a truly new relationship between their country and his.

So they worked away at the paper before them, haggling, explaining, and compromising. Appendix C was one sentence; the Panamanian version was two. Senator Byrd saw no reason to make it too complicated and the ambassador agreed. The Senate draft had said "shall not have as its purpose." The Panamanians countered with "does not mean nor shall it be interpreted as." Byrd's editorial pen produced: "shall not have as its purpose or be interpreted as." Both "C" and "D" had opposed "interference" in Panama's affairs. Under prodding from Lewis, Byrd changed it to "intervention," a stronger, more despised concept in Panama. Byrd put "interference" in later as a substitute for "infringement." The real battle came as they addressed the final phrase in the draft.

As noted earlier, some senators had argued that "territorial integrity" might be used by a future Panamanian government to claim the United States had no right to send military forces onto any part of its territory without permission. Byrd and his colleagues argued at length that "sovereignty" subsumed "territorial integrity" and that they had sound political reasons to avoid the latter. The lawyers present concurred that "sovereignty" was the more encompassing term. Byrd finally agreed to a gesture in Panama's direction by using the phrase "sovereign integrity." Ambassador Lewis, convinced that "sovereignty" was more important than "territory," agreed. I never saw the phrase used elsewhere, or found a lawyer who differentiated between "sovereignty" and "sovereign integrity." But no matter. It sounded good, satisfied all hands, and opened the way to agreement, which is the purpose of words in politics.

One other modest change was made. Both "C" and "D" had referred to actions to keep the canal "open, secure and accessible." Panama asked that "neutral" be added to the list, and it was done. Senator Church then sat at a typewriter and tapped out the agreement. It was passed around and one further alteration was proposed and accepted. Someone suggested the reference to keeping the canal open to "the ships of all nations" was superfluous. It was deleted. Sarbanes then manned the typewriter and wrote the final version, with copies for both sides. It was "Appendix E," the last in the secret series, and it read:

> Pursuant to its adherence to the principle of nonintervention, any action taken by the United States of America in the exercise of its rights to assure that the Panama Canal shall remain open, neutral, secure, and accessible, pursuant to the provisions of the Panama Canal Treaty, the Treaty Concerning the Permanent Neutrality and Operation of the Panama Canal, and the resolutions of ratification thereto, shall be only for the purpose of assuring that the Canal shall remain open, neutral, secure, and accessible, and shall not have as its purpose or be interpreted as a right of intervention in the internal affairs of the Republic of Panama or interference with its political independence or sovereign integrity.

Byrd rose from his awkward kneeling position before the low table and found that his back and shoulder were knotted. A thoughtful Senator Church applied a hasty massage that soon had the majority leader standing upright. Byrd said he wanted the Panamanians to realize that the new proposal was going to encounter some rough going in the Senate. At the same time, he said, he was not accustomed to losing. Like the captain of a ship, he would manage the affair in such a way that "the vessel will not be sunk." He and the other senators assured the Panamanians there would be no further changes on their side. Lewis thanked the majority leader and his colleagues and said he would send the new proposal to Panama immediately. He would inform them as soon as he had an answer, which he hoped would be positive.

Bilonick went from the meeting to National Airport to catch a plane to Panama. The ambassador, Rogers, and Christopher rode in the latter's limousine down Capitol Hill and out Massachusetts Avenue. They turned into the grounds of the old U.S. Naval Observatory. On a hill, certainly one of the loveliest spots in all of Washington, stood Admiral's House. By act of Congress in the mid-1970s, the beautiful mansion had been designated the official residence of U.S. vice-presidents. The visitors were welcomed by Vice President Mondale.

The mood was cheerful, relaxed, upbeat. The vice-president told the ambassador he had talked with President Carter and the president had underlined the fact that "he doesn't intend to preside over a reinstitution of a colonial foreign policy; he wants to put an end to it." Mondale said Panama had nothing to fear from the United States. "The age of interventionism is over," he said. The ambassador said that was why he and his government had been so disappointed in the DeConcini reservation. He then handed Mondale a copy of the draft resolution just worked out with Byrd, Church, and Sarbanes. Mondale read it and said he thought it was "fair and equitable."

The ambassador told the vice-president: "We have to have a treaty package that my country can accept with pride." Mondale said that was the only kind of treaty that would work, and he thought it was what the Senate would produce. Lewis then told Mondale he thought it was important that General Torrijos have a letter from President Carter emphasizing the principle of nonintervention. He hoped he could receive such a message as soon as the Senate voted on Tuesday. Mondale promised to raise the matter with the president over the weekend. He explained he was leaving immediately for Camp David for the two-day review of administration policy.

When Lewis and Rogers arrived at the ambassador's house, the two men began to compose a report for Torrijos and his government. Lewis insisted on a full account of the meeting in Church's office and of their session with Mondale. He said it was important for the general to have "the flavor as well as the facts." He wanted to make sure those in Panama City appreciated why it was impossible to get every word they wanted into the final resolution. The ambassador attached the text of the proposed leadership amendment so laboriously concocted on the Hill that morning. The completed document was transmitted from the embassy at 5:30 P.M.

While his report was being encoded, Lewis called the foreign minister to give him the high points and to say that the full account would soon be in his hands. He said official Washington hoped to have Panama's response before they went to bed that night so Byrd and his colleagues "can go to work early tomorrow." A few minutes later, Lewis called General Torrijos and gave him a similar account of the day's happenings. Omar said it had been an important day and then, with tongue in cheek, he told the ambassador: "You should relax—just like the GI's relaxed the night before the Normandy invasion."

While he waited nervously for word from his government, the restless ambassador used the phone. One call was to President López Michelsen of Colombia, a longtime business associate. It almost caused a new disruption. The ambassador told his old friend about the late developments, including the rephrased Senate resolution. López told Lewis the U.S. ambassador in Bogotá had come to see him that day to try to win his support for a resolution that obviously was not the one the Panamanian envoy was talking about. The mild-mannered Colombian was upset that the Americans had come to him with wording that was outdated. The Panamanian ambassador was furious that the U.S. side seemed to be maneuvering behind his back to win support for a formula his country had already rejected.

The envoy's angry musing was interrupted by a message from Panama. It was cryptic in both senses of the word: it was brief and it was in code. The first line was the crucial one. Taken from a well-known Panamanian song, a *tamborito*, it said: "La mula tumbo a Genaro"—The mule has thrown Genaro (a well-known jockey). It was code the ambassador and Minister Royo had worked out days before and meant: "Panama accepts the wording you submitted." The other two lines were not so disguised. One said: "There will be no leaks here"; and the other: "We expect there will be no surprises at the last minute."

As soon as he read the message, the ambassador called Hamilton Jordan at Camp David. "I just got word from Panama," he told the presidential aide. "What did they say?" Jordan asked expectantly. "They accept the wording," Lewis told him. "That's very good," said Jordan. There was one other thing, Lewis said: "They don't want any surprises at the last minute." Jordan told the ambassador he understood, but he was worried about Byrd's being able to "get what he said he'd get." Lewis said that was the Senate's problem. "We're not going to settle for anything less than that," he told Jordan, "so don't come with anything else because that's my gentlemen's agreement with Byrd."

Lewis then picked up his red phone, the direct line to Panama, and got Omar Torrijos on the line. He said the general's message had been received and had been delivered to the president at Camp David. Torrijos said he had read carefully Lewis' report of his morning session, including Senator Byrd's reference to himself as "a captain who would bring his ship in without sinking it." Torrijos told his ambassador: "Tell Senator Byrd that if he brings the ship in, I will make sure that the pier is in the right place and waiting to receive it." He then coined a phrase that would be used often over the next forty-eight hours. "Tell the senator and the White House," he told Lewis, "that we think this is a dignified solution to a difficult problem."

The ambassador then called Bill Rogers to tell him Panama had accepted the formula worked out that morning, and he passed along the comments Torrijos had made, including his reference to "a dignified solution to a difficult problem." Rogers, in turn, called Warren Christopher at Camp David to convey Panama's acceptance and the Torrijos statements. It was then 9 o'clock in the evening. The deputy secretary called Senator Church to pass along the good news. Senator Byrd was not available, and Christopher decided to inform the majority leader first thing the next morning.

Meantime, Ambassador Lewis was calling still another old friend, President Oduber of Costa Rica. The two had known each other for twenty years. Gabriel recounted the day's events—the meeting on the Hill, the new "antiinterventionist" resolution, and Panama's acceptance of the senators' proposal. He then told the Costa Rican leader of his talk that evening with López Michelsen and of the U.S. ambassador's effort to sell an outdated draft resolution. By then, Lewis' irritation had been salved considerably by Panama's acceptance of the new wording, but Oduber added another abrasion. He told the Panamanian that the U.S. envoy in San José had come to him that day on the same mission as his colleague in Bogotá. He said he realized from his close contacts with Lewis and Torrijos that what the American was touting was not the latest language. He was displeased with the apparent U.S. effort to enlist his support for an outdated formula.

Lewis was not merely displeased, he was furious. He saw himself and his country as victims of a "two-faced game." Determined to register a protest, he called Camp David but was told Hamilton Jordan was in a meeting. Then he called Bill Rogers to vent his spleen. The ambassador told the lawyer of his talks with the Latin American presidents and of their unhappiness with the U.S. initiatives. He suggested that Rogers call Christopher and tell him that "if he keeps that up, I'm going to resign tomorrow." Rogers was surprised by the report. It was apparent to him that whoever had sent the messages was, as he told the ambassador, "way behind times." He advised Lewis to cancel his call to Camp David and let him straighten things out.

When Gabriel called me a bit later, he was still fuming. He told me the whole story of his talks with Presidents López and Oduber. I explained what I thought probably had happened. No doubt the messages went to the other capitals some days before, I said, when Appendix C was the only thing on the table. Our people probably considered it helpful for the other presidents to know what was happening. If they reacted positively to the wording, it would aid Torrijos. I was putting the best face I could on what looked like a gaffe. But Gabriel was not buying it. "They weren't trying to inform them," he said; "they were trying to convince them, and get them to convince Torrijos."

I could understand my Panamanian friend's pique, but I felt he was overplaying it. We were too near the end of a historic journey to let a relatively minor diplomatic miscalculation become a roadblock rather than a mere pothole. Because I regarded him as a brother, I wanted to pull him back to reality.

When he told me that "the only one I want out of this" was the deputy secretary of state, I blew the whistle. "Look, Gabriel," I said, "you can't get my friends in the State Department 'out of the way' any more than I can get [and I named several people in his government who had been thorns in my side] out of the way here." He stopped short. "Yes, you're right, Bill," he said finally. "We're just going to have to live with it," I added. "Yes, I know. But damn it, it's frustrating," he said. "Don't talk to me about 'frustrating,'" I said. "You ought to try it at this end of the line." He laughed, then, because he knew exactly what—and whom—I was talking about. The problem was back in focus.

At midnight, a message went from the State Department to our ambassadors in Bogotá, Caracas, and San José thanking them for their help but saying, "We would like to minimize additional efforts which might only upset delicate agreement." It was a wonderfully diplomatic way of saying: "Don't do anything more."

Monday, April 17, 1978, was what racehorse fans call the "clubhouse turn" for the Panama treaties. It was the beginning of the final stretch to the wire, the grueling, pounding run that separates champions from platers. When it was over, connoisseurs of political horseflesh would know which were the thoroughbreds and which were the also-rans who lacked the heart or the wind for the final test.

Early that morning, Christopher called Senator Byrd from Camp David to tell him the Panamanian government had accepted the resolution. He informed the majority leader that the Panamanians had dubbed it "a dignified solution to a difficult problem." Byrd asked Christopher to come into town right away to talk with him and other senators. The deputy secretary boarded a helicopter and was in Byrd's office shortly after 10:00 A.M.

With Christopher's report confirmed in person, Byrd invited two senators in for a talk, Kaneaster Hodges of Arkansas and Patrick Leahy of Vermont. Both were reasonable, thoughtful men—and both were friends of DeConcini. Byrd showed them the wording he had developed Sunday with Ambassador Lewis and both found it an excellent reaffirmation of the U.S. policy of nonintervention as well as confirmation of the U.S. right to protect the Panama Canal. With Byrd's encouragement, the two went off to discuss the new resolution with their Arizona colleague.

While the subtle Senate chess game was proceeding, move by move, things were neither so orderly nor restrained at the U.S. Embassy in Panama. At midmorning, about one hundred leftist students from the university marched down Avenida Balboa and assembled in front of the solid old building. Antitreaty, anti-American, and anti-Torrijos chants filled the air. Banners carried slogans against U.S. bases and for a new plebiscite. Two students with battery-powered bullhorns were leading the cheers and the targeting was equally divided between the United States and the Torrijos regime. When you have been through a few such demonstrations, you are sensitive to the change in mood most mobs undergo. A stage is reached when shouted imprecations lose their force and cease to satisfy. At that point, an angry crowd is likely to either move on to its next target or turn to means other than vocal cords.

From my third-floor vantage point, I knew that point had finally been reached. Then I saw students in the center of the group pull back and form an open circle. A white-shirted student stood at the far side of the open space in a half crouch. He took three quick steps toward the embassy and let fly with a missile of some kind. Then I heard the crash of breaking glass. Then came another, and another, and another. Fortunately, the heavy steel mesh we had installed on all outside windows kept anything from coming into the building.

I told one of my embassy officers that breaking bottles against a building could not provide too much satisfaction. A Marine Guard who had been on the first floor came in with the answer to our puzzlement. The bottles were not empty; they were filled with paint—red, white, and blue paint.

We had called the National Guard and the troopers had turned out in force. They let the bottle throwing continue for some time. But when some of the mob entered the embassy grounds and tried to climb the flagpole, the soldiers reacted quickly. They pushed them into the street, then threw a few canisters of tear gas at the edge of the throng. In minutes, the students were beating a retreat down the avenue. They ended up at the Foreign Ministry for another shouting exercise—but without paint.

I walked outside to survey the damage. Nothing had been broken, but the front of the splendid old building looked like a second grader's finger painting. It was another $5,000 repair bill for the long-suffering Panamanian taxpayers. But they didn't know it, and the students didn't care.

It was noon by then. In Washington, the Senate was assembling for its penultimate day of debate on the Panama Canal treaty. But even before Senator Proxmire, acting president pro tempore, had gaveled his colleagues to order, the real work of the day was well begun. A group of reporters cornered the majority leader outside his office, and Senator Byrd told them he planned to introduce a reservation to "clarify" U.S. rights to protect the canal. He disclosed that the wording had been approved by the

Torrijos government. It was the first confirmation that the Senate leadership intended to modify the DeConcini reservation in a manner acceptable to Panama. It took no time at all for that word to filter through the cloakrooms and Senate offices.

Pro- and antitreaty forces quickly came to the obvious conclusion: there would be a treaty acceptable to Panama or there would be no treaty. The easy option, which had appealed to a few short-sighted senators—pass the treaty and have Panama turn it down—had gone up in smoke. The revolt of half a dozen liberal senators made that impossible. A source in the Senate leadership put it starkly to the *Washington Star* that morning: "After all that work," he said, "we saw that the blood could be on our hands after all . . . In the eyes of the world, it would be the Senate that had tried, first, to shove something demeaning down the Panamanians' throats, and then rejected the treaties when they wouldn't swallow it."

It was what was happening behind the scenes in the Senate that day that really mattered. What senators on the floor were putting each other through, and what was going out on public radio, was froth, as those sophisticated politicians knew full well. Some were proposing reservations that would enable them to tell their constituents, "Yes, I voted for the treaties, but I made them better." The antitreaty forces were still introducing changes in the vague hope one might slip through and create chaos. A few suggested additions were well meant, offered by senators who intended to vote for the second treaty and designed to make it marginally easier for their colleagues to vote aye.

One of the latter was introduced by Louisiana's Russell Long and it concerned the sea-level canal option. Long and other senators objected to the notion that the United States could be bound not to talk with any other country about anything it chose. It was a reaction of pure chauvinism, with no strong logical base. Geography, engineering, and politics all argued that Panama was the only viable site for any future isthmian waterway. But pride and nationalism outweighed reason, and Long's amendment made it easier for his colleagues to approve the treaty. The revision was approved 65 to 27.

Another "vote easing" amendment was offered by South Carolina's Hollings, one of the ablest of Senate "insiders." His proposal dealt with Paragraph 4(c) of Article XIII, which provided a contingent payment of $10 million a year to Panama if it were available from operating surpluses. There was a "carryover" principle in the paragraph: if revenues were inadequate to make the payment in one year, a surplus in the next or succeeding years would be used to make it up.

Hollings' amendment was designed to ensure that any such accumulation of contingent payments did not become, at treaty's end, an obligation of the U.S. Treasury. In negotiating the treaty, Ambassadors Bunker and

Linowitz had made that point on many occasions and the Panamanians understood it perfectly well. The ambassadors had restated the position frequently in congressional testimony and Panama's negotiator on economic matters in the treaty had supported the Bunker-Linowitz interpretation in a speech in San Francisco a few months earlier. So there was no doubt that both sides interpreted it the same way.

But Hollings wanted to nail down the understanding with 16-penny spikes. He wanted to eliminate any lingering doubts in the mind of some colleagues that the United States might owe Panama as much as $200 million at the end of 1999. That is what his amendment did. The popularity of his move was evidenced by the vote, 90 to 2.

With such efforts to improve the treaty marginally, and with contrasting attempts to undercut it, the Senate passed its official day. What was happening away from the floor was vastly more significant. First, there was the effort by the leadership to sell its new resolution to DeConcini and to the coalition of anti-DeConcini senators. Equally intriguing was the campaign to bring back to the protreaty fold two senators who had suddenly decided to gain attention for favorite causes by threatening to vote against the treaty and a third who was wavering badly.

The waverer was Nevada's Howard Cannon, who was concerned about public opinion in his conservative state. The two mavericks were liberal James Abourezk of South Dakota and conservative S. I. Hayakawa of California. All three had voted for the Neutrality Treaty because they considered it a just and farsighted agreement. But then they saw other senators bargaining with President Carter on a variety of unrelated issues. Abourezk and Hayakawa decided they were missing a chance offered by Fate to press their cases on matters dear to them.

For the dedicated South Dakotan it was energy. A staunch advocate of consumers' interests, Abourezk strongly opposed the plan to deregulate natural gas prices. He had led the filibuster in the Senate against deregulation and was bitterly disappointed when Carter shifted position in the middle of that thirteen-day effort and came out in favor of it. Then the administration committed a glaring error. Energy Secretary Schlesinger set up ostensibly "secret" White House meetings of Senate and House committeemen to work out a unified energy bill that would reconcile differences between the two houses. Abourezk, a member of the Senate Energy Committee, was not invited to those conclaves. He heard about the meetings, of course, as soon as they began.

Bitter about the administration's flip-flop on gas, incensed at being excluded from the policy deliberations, Abourezk decided to strike back. He called Dan Tate, a congressional lobbyist in the White House, denounced the effort to develop an energy policy in secret, and announced he was going to vote against the Panama Canal Treaty. The reverberations were felt immediately in the Executive Mansion. That night at about 6 o'clock, President Carter called Abourezk. The senator recalled the conversation in detail.

"Jim, I hear you're upset with me," said Carter.

"Well, Mr. President, I am," the senator answered. He explained that he had awakened at 3:00 A.M. that morning. "Then," he said, "I couldn't get back to sleep because I was so upset about those meetings you and Schlesinger have been holding at the White House. So I wrote out a statement announcing that I'm going to vote against the Panama Canal treaty."

"Well, Jim," Carter responded, "if you ever have any problems like that again, just call me and we'll talk."

It was not clear whether he meant waking up at 3:00 A.M. or being mad about energy. Abourezk started laughing about the double meaning. "No, I'm serious," Carter said. "Please call me, any time of the day or night."

Abourezk admitted later that he knew in his own mind he was going to vote for the Panama treaty no matter what happened. But, at that moment, he had the White House buffaloed, and he enjoyed every minute of it. An intense lobbying effort began the next morning to bring the South Dakotan back to the treaty fold.

An early caller at the senator's office was energy Secretary Schlesinger. It was an ill-advised move on the part of the White House planners. Known to many in Congress and the press as one of the brightest but more self-important figures on the Washington scene, Schlesinger apparently treated the visit as an onerous chore. He told the senator he was there "because the president told me to be here."

"That's all he told you?" Abourezk asked.

"That's essentially it," the secretary replied. He added that "we're not going to have any more meetings in the White House." Neither Schlesinger nor Carter seemed to understand Abourezk's objection was not to meetings but to the effort to develop an energy policy for the United States in secret—and without his participation.

The senator went from that unsatisfactory session to another meeting. On the way, he told several reporters he planned to vote against the treaty. Schlesinger had deepened not eased the administration's problem.

California's Hayakawa was going through the same kind of revolt. Always unpredictable, he was an outspoken supporter of a "strong" and anti-communist foreign policy. His most quoted statement from the 1976 senatorial campaign concerned the Panama Canal: "We stole it fair and square." Something in the brilliant, erratic legislator—perhaps a better sense of history than most, or a strong sympathy for the underdog in human events—led him to vote for the first Panama treaty. Then, like Abourezk, he saw a chance to make his voice heard on other matters that concerned him. Like the South Dakotan, he let it be known his vote for the second treaty was not assured. Hayakawa was particularly irate about the administration's decision to halt production of the B-1 bomber and its failure to vigorously oppose communist inroads in Africa.

Alarm bells sounded in the offices of White House congressional workers. Hayakawa was invited to a meeting with the president on Monday. Carter explained the importance of the Panama treaties to U.S. policy and its relations with Latin America. He assured the Californian that his opinions on other foreign policy matters would be heeded as never before. Meantime, several top administration officials were calling Abourezk to woo his vote and give assurances that his views on energy would get a hearing. Pleased by the unaccustomed attention, but still skeptical of the promises, the two continued to hold out. On the eve of the final vote, Hayakawa told a few reporters: "No one will know my vote until I cast it. I won't know either until I vote. I await my decision with eager anticipation." Abourezk also played his enigmatic role to the end.

Actually, neither vote was seriously in doubt but both senators concealed that fact with consummate skill. On Sunday, in an appearance on "Face the Nation," Minority Leader Howard Baker had said only one Republican vote, Hayakawa's, was in any doubt among those who had voted for the first treaty. "And I'm not at all sure that we will lose him," Baker added. The next morning, he sent one of his best political operatives, Bill Hildenbrand, to see the California senator. And Baker himself talked with Hayakawa. Later that day, when an executive-branch official complained there might not be enough protreaty votes, Hildenbrand smiled enigmatically and said: "Well, don't be so sure of that." Knowing how supremely careful the Senate staffer was about such things, the official from downtown relaxed. Hildenbrand obviously knew something administration lobbyists scurrying around the Hill were not aware of.

Hildenbrand had political antennae as finely tuned as any on Capitol Hill. One thing he may have known was that there had been a showdown that afternoon that changed some calculations. From early morning, the Democrats' first team—Byrd, Cranston, Church, and Sarbanes—had been promoting the new leadership amendment. Because the Panamanians had accepted the formula, liberal senators like Gravel, Kennedy, Haskell, and others had signed on. The final barrier was DeConcini himself. Byrd and others met him that afternoon. He was still trying to get wording closer to his own, especially the damaging reference to "the use of military force in the Republic of Panama." Byrd looked at his young colleague with eyes as cold and barren as a West Virginia mineshaft. "It has to be like this, Dennis," he said grimly. "I will not accept any changes." The Arizonian had been in the Senate for only fifteen months, but he knew what the wrath of the majority leader could do to an aspiring young senator's career if turned against him full blast. He looked at the other grim faces and cold eyes and concluded the resolution was just fine.

Once Byrd had his Democratic troops in line, he gave a copy to Minority Leader Baker. The Tennesseean read it, said it gave him no problems, and told reporters its acceptance by the Senate was certain. The long struggle to repudiate interventionism was nearly ended.

Byrd's performance that day had been masterful. Most senators in his position would have been congratulating themselves on a smooth and effective job. But the majority leader, a supremely cautious man, was still uneasy about the final outcome. He called the president that evening, taking him away from a country music festival then going full-blast on the White House South Lawn. Byrd told Carter of his talk with DeConcini and assured him the leadership resolution was guaranteed of passage. But the majority leader said he was concerned about two Democratic colleagues, namely Abourezk and Cannon. The president did not return to his guests and the country music until he had called the two wavering senators once again. Abourezk was invited to the White House the next morning for another chat. Cannon asked for support for a treaty reservation on financial arrangements and the president promised to look into it.

On the Senate floor, the long day was grinding to an unspectacular end. After countless votes, approving or rejecting mainly meaningless proposals, the Senate recessed at 10:02 P.M. Weary senators rode home through darkened streets—some pleased, some disappointed, all knowing they would write history the next day.

That night was a short one for everyone concerned with the Panama treaties. Despite a late night of country music, President Carter arose early the next morning and was in his office before 7 o'clock. General Torrijos took his customary early morning hike, showered and dressed, and went off to the *presidencia* to join top government officials. Panama's Ambassador Lewis had consumed his breakfast—and the morning papers—and was on his beloved telephone by 8 o'clock. Even I, who regularly worked late at night, was in my office while the overnight cables were still being sorted. And the U.S. Senate, accustomed to assembling decorously at noon, heard the presiding officer's gavel at 7:30 that morning.

In the White House, the atmosphere was tense. The president's prestige and political influence were riding on the outcome of that day's events. All around him knew that, and were walking on eggs. Ambassador Lewis got a strong whiff of the prevailing mood when he called Hamilton Jordan early that morning. Gabriel was pressing to get a draft of the letter the president had promised to send to General Torrijos. Jordan was unusually abrupt with his diplomat friend. He could not see any draft "until the president has seen it and signed off," he told the Panamanian. "Besides," he added, "we don't have the votes right now." He explained Abourezk was "talking funny and so is Hayakawa." The White House had no political leverage on either one, he complained.

On the Hill, the Senate's day began with a remarkable statement by the author of the principal mischief, Arizona's DeConcini. In time generously ceded by the majority leader, the senator professed to be alternately "amazed," then "puzzled," finally "shocked" by the controversy his reservation had stirred up. It was, he contended, with elaborate citation, no different from what the Senate Foreign Relations Committee had described as U.S. rights under the treaty. With every sentence in his extensive self-justification, DeConcini was proving what many around him had privately been contending—that he was an unimaginative man with a good legal mind and an inoperative psychological antenna. He appeared not to have read what the press had been reporting and what many of his colleagues in the Senate had been saying for weeks. If the Arizona senator had simply said that he never intended that the U.S. Army should be used as an instrument for strike breaking in Panama, he would have won plaudits from his fellow senators. Later in the day, he would not only vote for but also co-sponsor the leadership amendment that said in effect that the DeConcini approach was not the policy of the United States.

While Hamilton Jordan was complaining about the "funny" attitude of Senator Abourezk, the South Dakota senator was in the Oval Office talking with President Carter. "What can I do for you, Jim?" the president asked. "Can we invite the president of Lebanon over?"

The senator, of Lebanese ancestry and an advocate of a more balanced U.S. policy in Middle East affairs, was taken aback. He admitted later that "it was hard to deal with something like that because his values were totally different from mine."

"Well, that's no big deal," he told the president. "I mean it would be nice to have him over and all that. But that's not the issue. The issue is the Natural Gas Bill right now."

Carter said he had told Schlesinger "to work something out on that."

"Well, he didn't," said Abourezk. "And I don't think he is going to."

The president would not, could not, then change his position on gas deregulation. He did promise the senator there would be no more "secret" meetings in the White House on the matter, and that Abourezk's views would get full consideration. The senator said he told the president that was not enough and that he was "holding out" on the Panama treaty. Carter argued that failure of the Panama treaties would have a devastating effect on the ability of the United States to carry out an effective foreign policy. Abourezk responded that the effect on American consumers of gas deregulation was more important to him. It was a standoff, but the pressure on Abourezk continued.

So did the wooing of Nevada's Cannon. The White House staff had informed the treaty forces on the Hill about Cannon's interest in a reservation requiring the new Panama Canal commission to pay the U.S. Treasury interest on government funds invested in the canal. At a desk in Vice President Mondale's office, lawyers Moss and Kozak developed wording to satisfy Cannon. They carefully left the door open for the Congress to eliminate the interest payments if it chose to do so. Mondale then asked Senator Sarbanes to confer with his Nevada colleague but not to offer support for the new reservation unless the veteran legislator from Nevada promised to vote for the treaty.

Some hours later, the Maryland senator returned to Mondale's office to report on his talk with Cannon. He showed the vice-president the final wording he and Cannon had agreed on. He explained that he had not secured a firm pledge from Cannon to back the treaty but added: "If we don't give this one to him, I don't think we have much hope of getting his vote." Mondale understood and let Cannon have his reservation, adopted that afternoon.

Meantime, President Carter was also pursuing the Cannon vote. A devout Mormon, Cannon had heard a rumor that his church elders opposed the Panama treaty. The president called Salt Lake City and learned that the Church of Jesus Christ of Latter-day Saints had taken no formal stand on the treaties. He also spoke to at least one Nevada newspaper editor in Cannon's behalf. With all the attention he was getting from fellow senators and the president—always balm to a politician's ego—Cannon inched ever closer to an affirmative vote on the second treaty.

Throughout the morning, the Senate was routinely debating, then tabling or defeating, reservations and understandings offered as last-gasp attempts by treaty opponents to kill the Panama treaty. The principal authors of those final desperate efforts were Senators Curtis, Dole, Helms, and Thurmond. At noon, the Senate took up the most meaningful treaty change. Senator Byrd was recognized and called up Amendment #36, the so-called leadership reservation to the Panama Treaty.* In addition to Byrd, it was sponsored by Minority Leader Baker and by Senators Church, DeConcini, Gravel, Javits, Leahy, Sarbanes, and Sparkman.

Inclusion of DeConcini as a co-sponsor was a stroke of genius on Byrd's part. In the ensuing debate, Allen, Laxalt, Helms, and others tried to "prove" that the leadership resolution meant "watering down" the DeConcini reservation. With the Arizona senator inscribed as a sponsor of the new measure, that was impossible. DeConcini himself insisted the Byrd-Baker addition did not alter the fundamental intent of his original proposal.

---

*For text, see p. 604.

Much of the debate that followed was superficial. Two of the wisest senators put their fingers on the core of the dispute. One was New York's Javits, who had voted against the original DeConcini reservation. He told his fellow senators that the DeConcini proviso was wrong, and that he had voted in opposition because it could become a "hunting license" for some future president and Congress to use the slightest pretext to meddle in Panama's internal politics. He believed the leadership resolution made clear such interference was not the intent of the Congress or the purpose of the United States.

The other astute senator was South Carolina's Hollings. He approached the matter from a quite different viewpoint. He favored the leadership move because it was a restatement of time-honored U.S. policy and, as a realistic politician, he knew it was necessary to win approval of the treaties, which he favored. But he had concurred in the DeConcini reservation for reasons precisely opposite those his New York colleague had given. Hollings' fear was that some future president and Congress would comb through the treaty language and the associated debate to find reasons to do nothing, even if the canal was truly threatened, on grounds that the cause of danger was "a domestic incident." He then spoke probably the truest words uttered during the entire debate on the future attitude of the United States toward the Panama Canal: "We cannot jockey here for the exact wording each senator would want. We all have to agree that no language will force us *in* or force us *out*. It depends on the measured judgment at the particular time—the intent, the steel, the determination, and the will of a national Congress."

To the superficial eye, Panama City looked perfectly normal that afternoon. Buses and taxis were running, people were shopping, stores and offices functioned as usual. But the entire top layer of the government and the business, political, and professional leadership of the country were in a state of suspended animation. All ears were glued to radios that dispensed the final hours of the Senate debate. There was tacit recognition among Panamanians that the outcome was going to determine their own individual futures in the short run, and also the long-run prospects for their country. A turning point in history was close at hand and most Panamanians seemed to recognize that awesome fact far better than did most of those in Washington who would soon be making the fateful decision.

Omar Torrijos was at the *presidencia*, joking with his governmental advisers, listening occasionally to the broadcast debate, and alternately pleased and depressed by what he heard. He did not understand the parliamentary intricacies of what was happening, but he grasped a central fact—the fight to kill the treaties still had not ended. He did not understand why that should be. It baffled him that his friend Jimmy Carter, occupying the most powerful office in the free world, should have so little influence in his own legislature. The elaborate doctrine of "checks and balances" had not been part of his political education. In frustration, he left and returned to his house on Fiftieth Street to spend the rest of the day. Only his treaty negotiators, Royo and Escobar, accompanied him.

By prearrangement, President Lakas had gone to Colón, his old stamping ground, while Torrijos remained in Panama City. If the treaties were approved, the two men would direct the celebrations in those two principal cities. And if things went bad? I suspected, with no evidence beyond instinct, that Omar wanted his old friend on the other side of the isthmus. If the treaties were rejected, the general planned some actions that he knew Lakas would oppose energetically, and the president was the only person in Panama who could intimidate Omar Torrijos.

While the Senate mill was slowly grinding away, separating the grain of policy from the chaff of obstruction, almost every senator's office was a noisy, chaotic scene. Radios blared with the maunderings from the floor. Phones rang incessantly. The antitreaty camp of conservative Republicans had organized one of the largest write-in, call-in campaigns in U.S. political history. At the last minute, the Democratic National Committee had awakened to the challenge and, in the final two days, prominent Democratic politicians and fund raisers in twelve key states made almost five thousand phone calls to buttress the courage of the protreaty forces.

One senator who was a particular target of that campaign was South Dakota's Abourezk, who had become the new DeConcini in terms of media and lobbying attention. To escape the clamor and the incessant questions and pressure, the South Dakotan left his office and found refuge in the Senate cloakroom. In minutes, he was joined by his good friend, Sen. John Culver of Iowa. Culver was a strong treaty supporter, and Abourezk was certain the democratic leadership had assigned his chum and neighbor to "babysit me"—that is, to lobby him unmercifully. A few days earlier, Culver and Ted Kennedy had pulled Abourezk from an Energy Committee hearing to belabor him with arguments for the Panama treaties.

In the cloakroom, which he had hoped would be a safe retreat, Abourezk was once again bombarded by Culver's determined arguments. Suddenly, he was called to the cloakroom phone and he went into the booth to take the call with some relief. Even then, he found no surcease. The call was from President Carter, making one last impassioned plea for the South Dakotan's support. It was embarrassing for Abourezk. He knew he was going to vote for the treaty, but he wanted to keep the heat on the White House because of the gas deregulation problem. "You don't have to plead with me," he told Carter. "After all, you're the president of the United States."

Culver, meanwhile, had decided his colleague was using the phone call to evade him. So he gathered up some paper towels, stuffed them into the cracks around the phone booth door, and lit them with a match. As smoke filled the confined area, Abourezk let out a pained shout of protest. An alarmed president asked: "What's the matter?" Abourezk yelled into the phone: "It's just that damn John Culver trying to smoke me out." That ended the phone call, and a puzzled president never realized what had happened.

Coughing and laughing, Abourezk walked out of the phone booth and told Culver he had had enough. They walked together to the Senate floor. Abourezk got hold of Majority Leader Byrd to tell him he was going to vote for the treaty but that he wanted fifteen minutes to explain his position. Byrd promised to try to arrange it.

After all the delays, interruptions, and inconsequentia, the Senate finally addressed its second-most important task of the day—a vote on the leadership amendment. Allen moved to table that amendment and his proposal was defeated 79 to 21. The time had come to bite the bullet. The clerk read the role and the wording so painfully arrived at was approved by a vote of 73 to 27. The Senate's decision that U.S. intervention in Panama's internal affairs would play no part in our future relations was thus firmly imbedded in the new treaty structure.

The last gasp of treaty obstruction came, as it had on the first treaty, from Michigan's Griffin. He proposed again that the Senate advise the president that the Panama treaties be renegotiated. His proposal was tabled by a vote of 64 to 36.

The Senate had decided the previous day, by unanimous consent, that the vote on the Panama treaty would occur at 6:00 P.M. and that it would be preceded by one hour of debate evenly divided between proponents and opponents. That neat schedule was totally disrupted by long speeches, unforeseen amendments, and unanticipated roll-call votes. Majority Leader Byrd tried desperately to reinstate the planned format by asking unanimous approval for holding a full hour of final debate to be followed immediately by the vote. It was not to be. Time had nearly expired and an impatient Senate was not willing to delay things any more. Louisiana's Long voiced the opinion of most senators at that moment:

> We have debated these treaties for almost two months now. Mr. President, it would be an insult to the intelligence of Senators to think anyone is going to change his mind at this late date.
> We have people here who want to know the final vote count. Radios are tuned in all around the country. The galleries are packed. Everyone wants to know what will happen. Anyone who makes a speech now will be doing a very unpopular thing.

The Senate roared with laughter, and Byrd knew his effort to change the rules was a lost cause. He did manage to get Abourezk about one minute of his own remaining time—enough only for the South Dakotan to lambast the administration's energy policy in three paragraphs, and to say he planned to vote for the Panama treaty. Then the time ran out. Everything that appears after that point in the *Congressional Record* was not voiced on the floor of the Senate but submitted in writing and inserted as though it had been spoken.

The hour was 6:00 P.M. Vice President Mondale was presiding and ordered the clerk to call the role. It began with Abourezk and ended with Zorinsky. The final count was precisely what it had been two months earlier on the Neutrality Treaty—68 votes for and 32 against. The vice-president intoned: "Two-thirds of the senators present and voting having voted in the affirmative, the resolution of ratification, as amended, is agreed to." To lock it in and prevent any later reconsideration, Senator Church moved to reconsider the vote, and Byrd moved to lay Church's motion on the table. Those parliamentary niceties attended to, Senate approval of the Panama treaties was fixed in the history of the Republic.

There was applause from the galleries and the vice-president made no attempt to gavel it down. Senators rose from their desks and congratulated each other. Byrd and Baker shook hands and were surrounded by their followers. Church and Sarbanes were hailed for a masterful job of floor management. It had been one of the most demanding assignments in recent Senate history and everyone on the floor that evening recognized it.

When the roll call started, President Carter had walked out of the Oval Office to his secretary's office, where a radio was reporting each senator's response. He stood with Hamilton Jordan, press secretary Jody Powell, and NSC chief Brzezinski. As soon as the crucial sixty-seventh vote was recorded, the president called Senator Byrd and told him: "You're a great man. It was a beautiful vote." The president and all around him were elated. It was the first major foreign policy victory of the Carter administration, and those in the White House that evening hoped it would be the precursor of many more.

In Panama, the excitement and satisfaction were even more profound. For Omar Torrijos it was the end of a long trail and he knew that from that moment on he would have a major place in his country's history. During the final hour he had paced the floor of the large glass-enclosed sitting room where he and his cronies gathered almost every night. He was making comments, some in praise, some unprintable, as he heard the by-then familiar names and voices in the final debate. Warmed by his own emotions, and by the scotch he was imbibing in liberal quantities, the general reacted strongly to those who had called him "dictator" or who had cast doubts on Panamanian intelligence or ability. He was equally quick to praise those who had talked of Panama as a friend and ally. As soon as the vote was final, he was on the phone to Ambassador Lewis in Washington.

"Tell President Carter and Senator Byrd that we accept the treaties as the Senate passed them," he told Gabriel. "And tell them we're going to make them work."

Lewis called Hamilton Jordan to tell him that he had a message for the president from Torrijos and that he was on his way to deliver it. In twenty minutes, he was in the Oval Office with President Carter, along with treaty negotiators Bunker and Linowitz, passing along Torrijos' message. He and the others walked in the president's wake to the White House press office. To the waiting reporters and the sound cameras, Carter said: "This is a day of which Americans can always feel proud; for now we have reminded the world and ourselves of the things that we stand for as a nation.

"These treaties," the president said, "can mark the beginning of a new era in our relations not only with Panama but with all the rest of the world. They symbolize our determination to deal with the developing world, the small nations of the world, on the basis of mutual respect and partnership." He said the Panamanian ambassador had just informed him that General Torrijos accepted the treaties with the changes made by the Senate. The Panamanian leader had invited him to visit Panama and Carter said he would "like very much to accept."

The vote in the Senate set off a huge round of celebrations in many parts of the capital city even before the president made his statement. Everyone involved in the Panama treaties battle wanted to relax, unwind, celebrate a notable victory. In the Senate, the vote marked the end of a long, dreary struggle of three months, nearly seven if one counted the beginning of public hearings by the Foreign Relations Committee. In the White House and State Department, the Senate's decision ended a fifteen-month climb to the first foreign policy pinnacle of the Carter administration. And for a small handful of people it was the culmination not of months but years of patient toil in the diplomatic vineyard. To those at the Panamanian Embassy, of course, what happened the evening of April 18 represented a dream not of months, or even years, but lifetimes.

The mood, the revelry, the laughter were like those in a college town when the home team has just won the final game of the year. On the Hill, the first stop of the inner circle who had worked hardest during the debate was at the office of Minority Leader Howard Baker. An elaborate buffet was laid out on tables for the hungry visitors. It indicated that the Tennessee politician and his staff had no doubt what the outcome of the vote would be. From there, many senators and staffers went to the Foreign Relations Committee room where a more impromptu bash was underway. Word went around that a small party was going on at the White House so that became the next port of call. While sampling the wine and cheese in the West Wing, Ambler Moss looked around the room, thought something was amiss, then realized what it was. Neither Howard Baker nor any other Republican who had supported the treaties had been invited. A small thing, but a revealing incident that helped explain why the Carter White House never really mastered the art of dealing with Congress.

From the small, rather sedate assembly at the Executive Mansion, many of those present went off to the crowded, noisy, cheerful party at the Panamanian Embassy. The large rooms of the residence were jammed with people—Panamanians and Americans, the vice-president, many senators, Ambassadors Bunker and Linowitz, officials from the State Department, staffers from the Hill, Hamilton Jordan and others from the White House, and dozens of reporters who had been covering the story for months. Three bars worked overtime to slake the thirst of the laughing guests. In the middle of it all, Ambassador Lewis shouted into the telephone sharing the moment with friends and family in Panama.

As of 6:17 P.M., official Washington had stopped listening to the radio or paying any attention to the news. The time for celebration was at hand. It was just as well; many would not have enjoyed the latest report from Panama.

I had invited all the top embassy officials to our house to listen to the final scene in the Senate. We had been confident of the outcome, and twenty seconds into the roll call, with Abourezk, Cannon, and DeConcini recorded as ayes, all doubt was erased. Toasts and mutual congratulations were shared. I told that redoubtable and energetic group that, without their skill and hard work, the care and feeding of nearly half the Senate, the close and detailed liaison with the Panamanians, the multitude of suggestions to Washington, the outcome would not have been the same. They could enjoy the quiet satisfaction of knowing that, without them, history would have been written differently.

Meanwhile, Omar Torrijos had gone to the Holiday Inn on Paitilla Point to meet the press. It was the same room where agreement in principle on the treaties had been reached the previous August. The event was carried on every radio and television station in the country. A colleague grabbed my arm and said, "Omar is making a statement," so we gathered around to listen.

He began by saying: "I feel proud that I have fulfilled my mission." He described the treaties as "the greatest, the most awaited, and the most discussed triumph" in Panama's history. He sat behind a microphone-laden table flanked by his two treaty negotiators, Royo and Escobar. He was wearing a suit and tie instead of his usual uniform. One could see that he was tired and tense. His cheeks were sunken and his fingers drummed on the table in front of him.

Suddenly, the accumulated bitterness of three painful months poured forth. "Never in our Republic's life has a Panamanian been more insulted than me," he told his listeners. "Never has a country been subjected to so much disrespect as Panama. No people has ever seen crude power so closely as we saw it through the conservatives who are a dishonor to a nation of such dignity as the United States."

What surprised us, and shocked many of his fellow countrymen, was Torrijos' declaration that "today, the canal was placed within two votes of being destroyed." If the Senate had turned down the Panama treaty that evening, he said, "tomorrow we would have started our struggle for liberation, and possibly tomorrow the canal would not be operating any more.

"The armed forces had decided," said their commander, "that if the treaty had been rejected, or amended in an unacceptable way, then we would not negotiate anymore."

There was more of the same in a long, rambling diatribe. The tone of threat was mixed with high praise for the agreements and what they meant to Panama. He called the treaties "a new pact of mutual respect that places a fixed date on the end of the colonialism we have known throughout our independent life." He also announced that all Panamanians then in exile could return home the following day. And he promised to restore political parties to their rightful place as participants in the nation's business. Then came more bellicosity. If the United States ever invaded Panama, using protection of the canal as an excuse, said the general, "they would find the canal destroyed by the time they got here."

Finally, blessedly, it was over. Torrijos' public display of *machismo* and execrable taste had converted one of the most joyous moments in decades into an occasion for rancor. I knew he was lashing out at a handful of senators who had attacked him and his country with repeated displays of arrogance and disdain that brought no honor to them or the Senate. But the general did not distinguish himself or his country by using the same methods. The occasion was a test of his maturity and statesmanship, one of the few that even his closest friends would later admit he failed miserably. The irony was that his real targets were not listening to him; many of his best friends were.

I had been invited to join the Panamanian inner circle to celebrate the birth of the new treaties. I drove to the house on Fiftieth Street in a black mood. What bothered me was not what Omar had threatened. I had long known that Panama had the power to put the Panama Canal out of business any time it chose and we were expecting major trouble if the second treaty had failed. It was that the man who had proved himself a political genius on so many occasions, a man I admired for much that he had done for his country, had on this occasion proved to have such incredibly bad judgment. His chest thumping had played into the hands of his most violent critics, in Panama and in Washington. It certainly had damaged the thing he knew Panama needed most at that time—an atmosphere of stability, confidence, and reliability in order to attract much-needed foreign investment.

Omar's second home was a maelstrom that night. People were jammed in like sardines. You had to shout to be heard because everybody else was shouting. Bodies were stacked three-deep at the big bar. I walked around greeting old friends and sharing congratulations on the big event. Torrijos finally spotted me and came over to exchange an *abrazo*. "We finally got it, Bill," he said. His face was flushed, his eyes a little out of focus. But he was clearly on a cloud of elation. "Yes, Omar," I said. "A great moment in your history and ours." His eyes focused quickly. He knew from my face and tone that I had heard him on the radio. And he knew what to expect if we talked very long. "Don't worry," he said and winked. "Nothing's going to happen . . . now." Then he turned and joined friends at the other side of the room. He wanted to relax, not think. He wanted the adulation of those who would tell him what a great man he was, not someone who would tell him he had goofed. A few minutes later I went home.

I drove through streets filled with people dancing to music from scattered bands and blaring radios. Sirens at the city's firehouses were wailing, and firecrackers exploded on every street corner. Now and then I passed trucks parked along the streets busily dispensing beer and rum to the happy crowds. People were shouting "Long Live the Treaties" and "Long Live Omar." It was Carnival multiplied several times. The fun and the dancing would go on all night.

Two days later, Torrijos asked me to come to see him. We met, as we so often did, in the big bedroom of his "second home." He was still recovering from the revelry of recent days, but he was in good spirits. He said he had heard that I was about to go to Washington and he wanted me to deliver several messages. The most important was a cordial invitation for the president to visit Panama soon (Torrijos suggested May 12 as a good day). He asked me to assure Carter that the political situation in Panama would be "under control" and that the people and government would welcome the U.S. president enthusiastically. He planned to invite the presidents of Costa Rica, Colombia, and Venezuela as well. Did Carter see any problems with that? He went on with a list of ten or twelve questions—about the president's visit, the future of the Canal Zone, and other matters. It was a filibuster.

When he finally ran down, I asked him, "Where do we go from here?" I said I had in mind the unhelpful statements he had made two nights before. "You know they helped your enemies and hurt your friends, don't you?" I asked. He nodded several times. Then he said we could be sure there would be "no more of those."

"Please tell President Carter the canal has never been better protected than it will be from now on," he said. He told me he wanted especially to reassure Senators Byrd and Baker of that and to thank them for what they had done to make the treaties possible. He asked me to help him with letters to the two, and I took notes as he described what he wanted to say. Later I typed drafts in English on his office typewriter. The next day, I received the finished and signed versions, and Omar asked me to deliver them in person to the two senators. The letters to the senators were as close to an apology and an explanation as Omar Torrijos ever offered for anything he ever said. A key paragraph in the letter to Senator Byrd read:

> If anything that I have said over the past few days has caused you pain, please understand that a man who leads a people who have been subjected to a steady flow of criticism, of denigration by men who lack your wisdom, finds it hard to simply sit back and accept insults. But please know, too, my dear Senator Byrd, that I believe we have entered on an entirely new era, one in which our two countries are partners, are friends, are going to work together to make the future better for both our peoples. And you should know, also, that the Canal has never been safer, more secure than it is at this moment— and as it will be far into the future.

Was Omar Torrijos serious when he claimed that the Panama Canal had been "within two votes of being destroyed"? One year later, I asked the general that blunt question. He assured me he meant every word he had used that night in April 1978. He told me small special units of the National Guard had been trained to incapacitate the waterway if Panama's hopes had been destroyed. He said that those units were "in the field" the night he spoke. Using a special code, he called them back before there could be "any mistakes." Two Panamanians who were extremely close to the general assured me such recall orders did go out the night of April 18.

Another, equally close to the general, told me that regardless what plans may have been made, he was sure Torrijos would have pulled back from the brink at the last minute. "If he had done that [closed the canal]," he said, "it was we Panamanians who were going to go hungry. Omar knew that and I don't think he would have put that kind of pain on his own people."

My estimate was this: Panama had the capacity to inflict grievous damage on the canal and its orderly operation. Special units of the Guard were trained to carry out that kind of action. If Torrijos had given the order—or not withdrawn the order—it would have been done. At 10 o'clock in the morning, after meeting with several advisers, Torrijos would have been reluctant. At 6 o'clock at night, after three months of insults and personal attacks, acting on impulse and out of bitterness, he could have done it, and probably would have.

The Senate's approval of the Panama treaties avoided that possible disaster. Otherwise, the Panama Canal might very well have been closed. And we might have had fifty thousand or more young Americans on the isthmus, trying to restore the waterway, killing Panamanians, and being killed in turn. That was the potential catastrophe that 68 senators prevented on April 18, 1978.

CHAPTER 20

"The President Is Coming"

"We, the people of the United States, and you, the people of Panama, still have history to make together."

—President Jimmy Carter, at the exchange of instruments of ratification, Panama City, June 16, 1978

MANY years ago, I had lunch with an old friend, a man who had spent his entire working life in the diplomatic service of our country. I had recently moved from writing about foreign affairs to the role of active participant, and I wanted to learn all I could about the arcane diplomatic world he knew so well. We had been talking about some of the problems that confront envoys abroad, and I asked him: "What's the worst thing that can happen to an embassy?"

"Chip" Bohlen thought a moment, then said: "I suppose the very worst thing is to have the embassy attacked and occupied by a mob bent on destruction. Even an attack that doesn't succeed is a nightmare.

"The second worst thing," he went on, "is to have some major development in your country—a sudden shift in government, a coup, some 180-degree turn—that you didn't expect, and didn't tell Washington to look out for.

"The other major disaster," he said with puckish humor, "is a visit from the president of the United States."

I laughed at his joke, and my wise friend just smiled. The memory of that talk came back with a crash in the middle of 1978. I realized the wily diplomatic veteran had not been joking at all.

When I arrived in Washington on April 24, six days after the Senate approved the Panama treaty, I found mixed feelings. The euphoria that attended the Senate's vote had not yet worn off. But the bad taste left by General Torrijos' boast about putting the Panama Canal out of commission lingered on. The general thought his friendly message to President Carter would undo the damage; I knew he was wrong. His letters to Senators Byrd and Baker were, in this case, vastly more important. The unthinking wound he had inflicted was considerably deeper on Capitol Hill than on Pennsylvania Avenue. For that reason, my first priority was to deliver the Byrd and Baker letters as quickly as possible.

The reactions of the majority and minority leaders were similar. Both realized that what the Panamanian general had written would ease their difficulties considerably. Byrd read long excerpts from the Torrijos letter into the *Congressional Record* a few days later. When word of Torrijos' conciliatory, if not apologetic, gesture spread around town, the atmosphere cleared considerably. By the time I left for Panama at the end of the week, I knew President Carter would accept Torrijos' invitation for a visit, not on May 12 as Omar had proposed, but in the middle of June.

On Tuesday, May 2, I called the embassy's Country Team into session and told them: "The president is coming. The purpose, of course, is the exchange of instruments of ratification of the treaties. He'll be here about the middle of June, probably the sixteenth. God knows how many people will be coming with him, but there will be quite a few, you can count on that. We're all going to have our hands full." I selected Virgil Moore, our veteran administrative officer, to be control officer for the presidential visit. He would have to pull, or try to pull, all the many loose ends into some kind of coherent whole. Fortunately, Virgil had worked on several Kissinger trips to the Middle East so he had some feel for the complications we would face. For the rest of the staff, it would be their baptism of fire with a presidential visit, but they were all competent people and I was not concerned about how they would perform.

I realized later that my assumptions about the Carter tour were too optimistic. I had seen many state visits, and had been a party to President Johnson's travels through half a dozen Asian capitals in 1966. Against that background, a two-day trip to the isthmus looked like a piece of cake. I did not realize what a decade had wrought in terms of presidential travel. In 1966, a half dozen able operators from the White House had gone out in advance and made all the arrangements with a minimum of confusion. As I remembered it, our biggest difficulty concerned leasing a large houseboat for the accompanying press contingent in the harbor at Wellington, New Zealand. What had happened to the press corps and to the White House in twelve short years was a revelation.

The first intimation of change came in a cable from Washington that told us a group of people would be arriving to help prepare for the Carter visit. What jolted me was the news that this would not be the usual "advance group" but the "preadvance group." It was a new refinement in arranging presidential trips. The second surprise was that it would not be two or three planners, but a contingent of twenty-nine people. "My God," I told Virgil, "with twenty-nine people, we could plan the Normandy invasion."

The group was headed by Phil Wise of the White House staff and Evan

Dobelle, State's chief of protocol. The others were from the Secret Service, the press office, the White House Communications Agency, plus transportation specialists, secretaries, and "assistants." The day after the group arrived, we had a meeting in the Holiday Inn with the Panamanians concerned with arranging the president's visit—Colonel Noriega of the National Guard, who was responsible for security; Ambassador Watson, Panama's protocol chief; Ambassador Lewis, who had just returned from Washington; other top officials. The session was a minor disaster. Wise, Dobelle, and the others were accustomed to situations wherein all that was needed was the magic phrase "the White House wants" and it was accomplished. To them, Panama City was no different from Pittsburgh or Peoria.

Early on, the Panamanians proposed having President Carter stay, and the formal ceremony occur, on the island of Contadora, where most of the treaty making had been done. It was a rather romantic notion, but not totally illogical if one were dealing with an official party of fifty or even one hundred persons. We knew that it would be twice that large, and that the visiting press corps would be more than two hundred. The logistics problems on Contadora would have been impossible. But rather than gently dissuading the Panamanians with quiet arguments based on numbers of people, transportation complications, and communications difficulties, the visiting Americans squashed the proposals as "impossible" and "incredible."

"It just wouldn't work, so forget it," said one of the visitors. The talk then moved to more technical questions—transport from the airport, security arrangements, the president's schedule from arrival to departure. When the number of "we want" and "we'll need" and "we'll have to have" demands became overwhelming, I reminded the visitors they were in Panama as guests and that what Panama needed and wanted was just as important as what they thought was required. That changed the tone for the moment, but I knew it was temporary.

After the first general meeting, the real professionals in the preadvance group—a few Secret Service men and communications experts—got together with Panamanian counterparts and began working out the central problems of the coming visit. After a few days, the preadvance group flew back to Washington. I estimated the cost of that exercise to the American taxpayers in the neighborhood of $50,000. They had done nothing that my embassy staff, with three specialists from Washington, could not have done faster, better, and cheaper—and certainly with less wear and tear on both sides.

Meantime, planning for the real purpose of the visit was moving ahead. Ambassador David Popper, General Dolvin, Mike Kozak, and others came to Panama to work out with Carlos López-Guevara and Panamanian lawyers the texts of the various documents that would be exchanged. There were five "instruments" in all. Two affirmed U.S. ratification of the Neutrality and Panama Canal treaties; two others did the same for Panama. The fifth was a joint document—the Protocol of Exchange of Instruments and Ratification. Compiling the documents was more a challenge to lawyerlike precision and editorial care than to negotiating skill or imagination. Nine-tenths of the four ratification documents were an orderly listing of the various amendments, reservations, conditions, and understandings added by the U.S. Senate as the price of its approval.

The only new feature in the documents was an expression of Panamanian pride and self-protection. Having listened to the Senate debate as one U.S. proviso after another was tacked on to the treaties, the Panamanians considered it only fair for them to add a couple of their own. In its ratification instruments and in the joint protocol, Panama stated its own "understandings" of the treaties. One was that there were "positive rules of public international law" to which both the United States and Panama were parties. They mentioned specifically articles of the U.N. and OAS charters. Those articles ruled out the use or threat of force between member states and interference in another country's internal affairs.

Panama's second understanding was more general. It was that actions by either country under the two treaties would be taken "in a manner consistent with the principles of mutual respect and cooperation on which the new relationship established by those treaties is based." It was an elegant way of saying: "The treaties are a partnership, and partners don't act without consulting each other." It did not rule out unilateral action, which the United States had insisted upon from the outset. It did suggest such action would stretch the rules of the game and should be considered only in extremis.

Popper and his colleagues returned to Washington and submitted the documents, leaving more than enough time for State Department and White House approval. There followed a bureaucratic snafu that defied logical explanation. The stack of carefully drafted papers went into "in" boxes in the legal adviser's office, State's Executive Secretariat, Ambassador Bunker's office, and the Panama Desk. The latter two quickly read and approved them. The Secretariat, responsible for getting major papers approved and sent to other parts of the government, just sat on the ratification papers. When pressured, the usually efficient seventh-floor staff finally admitted the Panama documents had been misplaced. At last they unearthed them and sent the package to the White House. There, too, they disappeared for a time in the maw of the National Security Council apparatus.

While the bureaucratic mill ground, then stopped, then ground again slowly, time was passing. The president had a date in Panama on June 16. But the papers he had to sign there were not yet approved. At that point, another internal argument erupted. Should congressional leaders approve the documents before the president saw them; or should Carter give his OK before they went to the Hill? Kozak, whose chronometry was better than most, solved the dilemma swiftly. He stuffed the ratification documents into his briefcase, went to the Hill and showed them to key people in the leadership and on the Foreign Relations Committee, winning unanimous backing. He went back to the department to report that the ratification instruments had been squared away on the Hill.

As they passed through the bureaucracy, the treaty documents underwent only minor changes, one short phrase suggested for another, a different word for one used in the first draft. But even those insignificant revisions would have to be explained to and approved by the Panamanian authorities. Meanwhile, the clock kept ticking.

As the available time shrank from weeks to days, it became clear the final drafting of the official documents would have to be done in Panama. Everyone in Washington who had to approve them had read the papers. The Panamanians had not. I received a cable from State asking if Political Counsellor Elkin Taylor could be freed from other work to shape the final instruments with the Panamanians. I agreed and we set aside working space and reserved two typewriters. Kozak's secretary, Joan Vanderlyke, who was thoroughly familiar with the treaties, would join Elkin in the final push to produce the formal instruments. Their main job would be to make sure the English and Spanish versions said the same things.

A few hours before Joan was to leave for Panama, State's legal adviser, Herb Hansell, had an acute attack of nervous second thoughts. The Panama treaties were the first international agreements he had dealt with as State's principal legal officer, and he wanted to take no chances of anything going wrong. He called a meeting in his office to announce: "We'll have to do all the instruments here," he said. "We'll just give them to the Panamanians when we arrive." His listeners could not believe what they were hearing. Kozak pointed out that the signing would take place about twenty minutes after the U.S. party's arrival in Panama. That made little impression on Hansell. He wanted the papers produced under his direct supervision. No one understood why. Two days later, after countless arguments and reassurances from Bunker's office and others, Hansell finally realized something had to be done and he relented. Joan took off for the isthmus less than seventy-two hours before the final signing occurred.

Ten days before the big event, the White House advance party arrived. It was headed by Dan Lee, a member of Appointment Secretary Tim Kraft's staff and a specialist in "advancing." He was accompanied by members of the White House organization, especially the press office, as well as communicators and Secret Service agents. Each day, a few more people arrived from Washington and my staff was kept busy booking additional hotel rooms, renting cars, and catering to the other logistical needs of the growing throng. Before it was over, almost ninety people were involved in advancing the president's visit.

People were one thing; matériel was another. One afternoon, a huge C-5A transport plane, called a Galaxy, roared down the runway at Howard Air Force Base and pulled to a stop at one of the cargo hangars. It carried two presidential helicopters, 45,000 pounds of communications gear, and sixty men. With crisp military efficiency, the huge stock of equipment was unloaded from the plane onto six big trucks. The vehicles and their precious burden of the most modern communications equipment drove across the Thatcher Ferry Bridge into downtown Panama City and pulled in at the freight entrance of El Panamá Hotel, where the president would stay. Installation of a White House phone system began that night. Meantime, at Howard Air Base, thirty-two of the best helicopter crewmen in the world went to work to make *Marine One* and *Marine Two*, the presidential choppers, ready to fly.

In Panama City, Dan Lee and his team, guided by the embassy's Virgil Moore and a few aides, were going over every square foot of space the president and his party would cover. They inspected the arrival scene at Tocumen airport. They checked the route, time, and distance from the airport to the New Panama Coliseum, where the signing ceremony would occur. They looked over Cinco de Mayo Plaza, where the big popular gathering would be held. They went into the Canal Zone and surveyed the scene at the Miraflores Lock, where President Carter was slated to see the waterway in operation. Distances from point A to point B to point C at speed X were clocked with stopwatches and dutifully recorded in the planning book.

As I watched all these meticulous calculations being made, I had to wonder if anyone had ever stepped back from the charted statistics and asked: "Does it make any real difference if the motorcade arrives at 3:47 P.M. or 4:15 P.M.?" I remembered Lyndon Johnson stopping the procession of cars through downtown Manila to get out and shake hands with people and talk to them. It fouled up the schedule, to be sure, but it added value to the trip downtown, for him and for the onlookers. What could possibly account for this American dedication to the split-second timing of such events? Had we, perhaps, developed an entire generation hopelessly influenced by the countdown clock at Cape Canaveral? Or the relentlessly expiring timepieces of several thousand football stadiums? Reading a presidential travel schedule in the second half of the twentieth century was like reading the record of a biological experiment in a well-run laboratory.

There was a time, still remembered by perhaps one-fifth of the reporters in Washington, when the press covered the president of the United States as it covered most other people and major events. When he traveled, a handful of reporters on the White House beat went along—at considerable expense to their companies. Most reporting was done by correspondents and news bureaus at the scene. In the last twenty-five years, that has changed markedly. The press, which boasts endlessly and emphatically about its freedom and its independence, has become a subsidized adjunct of government. Most reporters, especially the younger ones, take the resulting perquisites and spoon feeding as a kind of God-given right that attends their assignment to the White House, the Pentagon, the State Department, and the other institutions of government. It was not always so, but few remember it otherwise.

The fault is not with the press alone. No vice can flourish without supply and demand. Politicians have learned that their survival depends in considerable measure on the volume and quality of their public exposure. It was natural, almost inevitable, that presidents and those around them should conclude that the more they catered to the media, the better the final results. If fifty reporters covered their doings, it was good; if five hundred wrote or commented about them, to say nothing of filming their every move, so much the better. Hence the move to bigger and better press rooms, smooth travel arrangements, the best possible communications. A sizable part of the tab for those bigger, better, smoother, more felicitous arrangements was paid by the U.S. taxpayers.

The extent to which the press had become an appendage of government was nowhere more evident than in a trip abroad by an American president. First off, the U.S. government became a charter service in arranging for one or more jet transports to carry the press where the president was going, and at the right time. Most of the time and effort in lining up such a charter were provided by government employees. Then the U.S. government, usually the U.S. Embassy concerned, became a travel agency, booking hotel rooms and arranging transportation. Obviously, the press corps needed a press room to work in. That meant renting rooms for that purpose, setting up desks and typewriters, installing telephones. Providing paper and carbons and wastebaskets was all part of the service. People had to be standing by to answer questions—"How many people in Panama?" and "Who was that guy standing next to the president at the airport?" and "Where do I find a good local restaurant?"

On a presidential trip, there are two castes in the news community. One is the White House press corps; the other is "all the others," whether non-American or American. Buses, trucks, platforms, even stepladders reserved for the former are "off limits" to the latter. People are assigned to keep "aliens" from encroaching on White House press facilities. Let some poor Panamanian or Mexican or Venezuelan photographer climb up on a "White House" photo truck and he is quickly reminded he is poaching on reserved territory. Steely-eyed American reporters who pride themselves on getting at "the real truth" never seem to notice or to think anything is amiss.

Whenever a president appears outdoors, there is always a "rainy day scenario." In Panama, if rain interfered with the arrival ceremony, plans had been made to welcome the president inside the Tocumen terminal building. The night before arrival, it occurred to someone on the White House staff that photographers would need stepladders inside to take pictures over the heads of the crowd. They called our public affairs officer to insist twenty-four stepladders be kept in readiness at the airport. That meant buying the ladders and hiring a "stepladder officer" to pass them out in case of rain. When we handed the bill to the White House press office, the response was: "We're not going to take the ladders with us, so we're not going to pay for them."

We had hired a dozen Panamanians to handle the suitcases, camera bags, and other paraphernalia of the incoming media representatives, 225 strong. A budget-conscious White House staffer thought it was excessive. "You really have to watch expenses," he told one of my officers. "This is the taxpayers' money, you know." We fired four baggage handlers and saved $50. Ten hours later, the same youngster from the White House insisted we build a soundproof booth for interpreters to handle the planned meeting of heads of government in the Panama Hotel. That cost $700 and the booth was never used.

The incidents and the confusion—to say nothing of mounting costs—seemed endless. There was, for example, the saga of the flatbed truck. The motorcade planners had decided that when President Carter's limousine was about one hundred yards from the reviewing stand in Cinco de Mayo Plaza, the bubble top would be lifted. The U.S. president and General Torrijos could then stand up in the opening to wave to the throng. That priceless moment had to be recorded for posterity, to say nothing of the 6:00 P.M. television news. The only way it could properly be done was to have the photographers on a vehicle moving parallel to the motorcade route during those crucial one hundred yards. That meant renting a flatbed truck. But it could not be just any old truck, or any random driver.

Bright and early one morning, a week in advance of the big event, Public Affairs Officer (PAO) Steve Dachi went to a truck park where the needed vehicle could be hired. He patiently rode around two blocks in six different trucks until he found one that did not backfire and whose engine sounded reasonably tuned. He also tested drivers until he discovered one who could drive at a steady eight miles an hour in second gear without jerking or stalling. But those were only Steps One and Two.

Because the driver would be close to the president and General Torrijos—for all of thirty seconds—he had to have a special security clearance. Nor was his truck usable as it was. So the press photographers would not be shooting through or around each other, we had to build a three-level platform on the flatbed. Then a five-step stairway was attached to the back so the press could climb aboard without strain. Finally, heavy rope had to encircle the platform so no one would fall off. Installation took two days, so we had to rent the truck for those days, plus the day of the parade, plus one more day to restore the venerable flatbed to its original condition. When a White House Transportation Office staffer saw the bill for four days for a truck that was to be used for less than a minute, he screamed in protest.

The day the president arrived, an embassy officer had to go to the driver's home (he had no telephone) to make sure he was awake, dressed, and ready to drive his big truck to its appointed spot well in advance of its moment in the sun. Because the vehicle and driver would be so near the presidential cavalcade, a Secret Service agent had to occupy the front seat and give instructions. We had to assign an interpreter so the non-English-speaking driver could understand the orders from the non-Spanish-speaking agent. We also arranged for a small security force to make sure no "unauthorized personnel" (i.e., none of the thousands of Panamanians crowded into the square for a look at Carter and Torrijos) climbed aboard the "White House Press Only" truck.

When the critical moment arrived, everything worked like a well-oiled machine. A bus unloaded fifty or so shouting, shoving photographers and they boarded the flatbed. At a signal, the trusty driver inched his huge vehicle ahead at the prescribed speed. Carter and Torrijos waved to the crowd, and the scene was recorded on dozens of films—movie and still, black and white and color. You may have seen it on television news that night. It lasted exactly five seconds.

There are reasons a presidential visit takes on aspects of a three-ring circus. Those reasons, though moderately valid, have been twisted almost beyond recognition. The process confirms Parkinson's Third Law: Expansion means complexity and complexity decays. I first heard the phrase "the White House is where the president is" more than thirty years ago. It is still being used by bureaucrats to explain fantastic expenditures for communications on every presidential trip. Of course the proposition is true. Our political system permits no delegation of executive authority whether the president be out of Washington, or out of the country. But what does it mean in the real world?

Some scholar may one day investigate how many phone calls the last six or seven presidents received while traveling abroad that had to be answered in twenty seconds, or twenty minutes, or even two hours. I suspect the answer would be "none" but it could be "two or three." Since White House switchboards have been set up everywhere from the Elysée in Paris to a tent in the desert of Iran, from the Imperial Palace in Bangkok to a hill

in the Panama Canal Zone, one wonders how much of it was really necessary. Was it cost-effective?

The truth is that 90 percent or more of the calls that go through such
switchboards do not involve the president at all. They provide a wonderfully fast way for White House assistants to keep in touch with their offices
at home. I found that putting a call through "Washington Switch" halved
the normal time required to contact the capital. One of the first calls on the
splendid network set up in Panama was made by a junior assistant in the
press office to wish her boyfriend in Washington a happy birthday. It was a
magnificent luxury for all who could use it. That it served any essential
national purpose is questionable. The president's real needs for communications could be met at one-tenth the present cost. He and his top aides
could still have the best communications in the world; the rest of the gravy
train could be disconnected.

The second feature of presidential travel that adds to the circus atmosphere is the security element. Any American would agree that the safety
of our president is a primary concern. We have been through tragedy and
near tragedy too often not to have this factor weigh heavily with us all. The
question is whether we protect our political leader in the most effective
way without, at the same time, diminishing what he and our nation are
trying to accomplish. Having watched presidential protection in many
capitals, I am not certain our methods don't do as much harm as good. In
Panama, for example, President Carter was making a positive impression
on the populace of that small country; behind his back, the U.S. Secret
Service was rubbing raw the nerves of half the Panamanian government, to
say nothing of the presidents of Mexico, Venezuela, and Costa Rica. How
do the two balance in terms of the best interests of the American people?

One problem with the Secret Service is that its personnel are trained
and conditioned to work in Washington and the continental United
States. When the president comes to town, they are kingpins. They tell
local police forces what is needed, and it is done. Their president is the
president of the people with whom they are dealing, and everyone wants
to protect him. In the process, they become domineering, arrogant, and
demanding. They come to expect unquestioning cooperation and obse-
quious responses to every stated need. They forget they may be in Tokyo
not Toledo, or Panama City, Panama, not Panama City, Florida. Americans usually accept being insulted by "the White House"; many foreigners
do not.

No country's chief executive and other top officials travel abroad more
than those of the United States. To protect them effectively, the U.S. Secret Service clearly needs an external security branch. Its personnel should
understand much more than the use of weapons, crowd control, and modern communications. Its agents should have some comprehension of inter-

national politics, psychology, and one or two foreign languages. A dram of humility would help; a dollop of humor would add much.

Ask diplomats, foreign correspondents, businessmen who have lived and worked abroad for many years which countries do the most effective, least publicly apparent job of executive protection. You will hear about the British and Canadians, the French and Israelis, the Japanese and Australians, even the Soviets. The U.S. Secret Service is well down most such lists. One glaring historical fact seems to have been lost: the president of the United States is safer in almost any foreign capital—whether Paris or Panama City—than he is in Washington, D.C., and his safety there depends far more on the effectiveness of local security forces than it does on the Secret Service.

The third ring in the circus of presidential travel is the press, more correctly the media. Technological change has transformed coverage of presidents and of most news to a process of sight and sound and immediate impact rather than careful analysis and a detached accounting of events. In the process, the media have become not merely chroniclers of events but increasingly obtrusive participants in those events. Presidents and other politicians have been gradually converted to the proposition that unless their words and deeds are recorded on film and soundtrack, they have not really happened. It was an inevitable conversion when increasing numbers of Americans began to get most of their information about their nation, their world, even their hometowns from some twenty-three minutes of televised news at the end of a long, hard day.

In earlier times, only a handful of reporters accompanied a touring president. The senior wire service correspondents and a small group representing the major newspapers and magazines made up the traveling press corps. Large organizations like the Associated Press, United Press, International News Service, *New York Times*, *Chicago Daily News*, *Baltimore Sun*, and the radio news companies, CBS and NBC, had bureaus in the major world capitals. The main burden of coverage fell on reporters stationed where the president was visiting. In those days, most news organizations considered it much too expensive to send a reporter overseas to cover anything less than a war.

Then came television. Beginning in the late 1950s and proceeding in quantum jumps since, coverage of U.S. presidents has become big business, big in terms of money and of people. When air time is worth $100,000 per minute, sending reporters and cameramen halfway round the world becomes an incidental expense. But whether all this is wise or foolish, and whether it provides a balanced picture of what is happening in the world, is not the subject of this account. My concern was with the impact the new American press had on Panama and on the story of the treaties.

No capital in the world can absorb without notable strain an influx of more than two hundred foreign reporters, photographers, and media technicians. The smaller the country, the more the strain. It becomes particularly unbearable when the visiting newspeople do not simply come into town to cover a story, but insist on being treated as members of the visitor's official party. Nestled comfortably under the protective wing of a solicitous government, they are free from concern about any essential need—housing, transportation, communications, access to the scenes of action. They no longer have to fight for their "rights" and "requirements"; their guardian angels in the White House press office do that for them. The really "free" reporters, who came in to cover the Panama treaties story from such varied capitals as Caracas and Bogotá, London, Paris, and Rome, Tokyo and Mexico City, watched the shepherding of their American brethren with wry amusement, no little envy, and some obvious resentment.

To meet the housing requirement, we reserved the entire Holiday Inn, Panama City's second-largest hotel, for the White House press. We set up on the first floor an elaborate press room with all the necessary equipment—desks, phones, teletypes, supplies. There was space for White House Press Secretary Jody Powell to brief the reporters. Duplicating machines churned out schedules, texts, and statements by the thousands. Top-level information specialists from other embassies in the hemisphere had come in and were standing by to answer questions, provide background, supply linguistic assistance.

Moving the huge White House press corps, 225 strong, from place to place was a challenge. We hired six air-conditioned buses (half the available supply in Panama) plus about seventy cars—to say nothing of the famous flatbed truck and the countless motorcycles needed to rush film to the airport to catch the next flight to Miami. Transmission of words and pictures by satellite was monopolized by the U.S. media for twenty-four hours.

Our greatest difficulties were not with the working press itself—though its vast size and logistics requirements posed formidable demands on a small country and a small embassy. The reporters and photographers were there to do a job and, with only a few exceptions, went about it in a thoroughly professional way. Our biggest headaches came from a group of largely inexperienced people in the White House press office. They were mainly youngsters who had earned their spurs working on the Carter campaign. For those pains, they were rewarded with jobs in the White House for which many were clearly unqualified in terms of experience and proven skills. What they lacked in ability they made up for with arrogance.

They never recovered from the tunnel vision that afflicts those in partisan political campaigns. The only criterion was: does it help make our man look good? Anything else was trivial or a diversion. The measure of "looking good" had to do almost exclusively with what appeared on America's television tubes the next day, or in tomorrow's editions of the *Washington Post* and the *New York Times*. It had not yet sunk in for many of the White House advance workers that Mr. Carter had already been elected, that he was then president of the United States, and that things that harmed U.S. interests in general could also harm "our man."

How does one insult a host country and individuals from a dozen others? One way would be to tell local authorities that the backdrop they erected for the signing ceremony was "impossible" and would "look terrible on television." Another would be to tell them that a block of seats reserved for members of their National Assembly had to be used for television cameras. Still another would be to inform reporters from the host country and a dozen others that they were not welcome in the White House press center. Or you could assign security guards to every bus, truck, press box, and camera stand to make sure no interlopers tried to share the privileged facilities of the White House press corps.

If those things failed to alienate everyone concerned, you could tell those hosting the coming meeting that all the lights in their 11,000-seat coliseum had to be changed so that film would register the "healthy pink skin tones" of those on the stage. Or you could inform a government that planned to assign the five deluxe suites (one on each floor) in its best hotel to the five visiting heads of government that the president of the United States had to have one entire floor and all the rooms above and below his "for security reasons." To make absolutely sure that you made a maximum of enemies, you could tell the host government's chief of protocol that you, not he, would decide who would be on the stage behind the principals at the signing ceremony.

These were not hypothetical actions; they all happened. They were some of the worst, but only a sampling, of the examples of insolence and flawed judgment that typified methods used in preparing the president's visit. It was not, to be sure, a phenomenon exclusive to the Carter presidency. The same, or similar, things happened under his predecessors and are happening today. One can only hope that some future president or his principal aides will take a penetrating look at the methods used to arrange presidential travel. They could save the taxpayers a bundle, and improve the reputation of the United States significantly. In the process, they would make "our man" look very good, indeed.

Despite all the tribulations and broken crockery, plans for the exchange ceremony moved forward. The routes had all been plotted, the vehicles reserved, the supplies laid in. The National Guard band had marched across the asphalt runway and played the "Star-Spangled Banner" and Panama's national hymn so often they were hearing the notes in their sleep. The Panamanian phone company had installed at least two hundred extra lines into the El Panamá and Holiday Inn hotels to satisfy official and press requirements. Carpenters hammered away late into the night to complete the three-story-high reviewing stand in front of the International Hotel on Cinco de Mayo. Electricians were changing the lights in the roof of the coliseum, and interior decorators were putting up a new backdrop in front of the original blue and white vertical stripes. It was Wednesday evening, and it appeared everything would be ready in time for the president's arrival Friday afternoon.

I took our basset hound, Anayansi, out for a walk before dinner, and as we wandered through the grounds I heard some shots in the distance. They came from the direction of the university only about half a mile away and they sounded like handguns or small-bore rifles. Back inside, I called the duty officer to ask if he had any reports of trouble. He had not. I told him to alert the embassy's Military Group commander and to check on what was happening. We had expected some difficulties because earlier that day antitreaty students occupied the El Carmen cathedral half a block from the hotel where President Carter would be staying.

In about an hour, I received a report. A radical student organization had organized a rally of antitreaty students at the architecture and law schools. Progovernment students intervened and tried to break up the gathering. There were fistfights, and rocks and bottles were thrown by both sides. A few progovernment students sneaked away from the melee and returned with guns. Witnesses claimed that at first the gun-wielding demonstrators fired into the ground and the air as a warning. At that, the antitreaty forces went off to get weapons from their own hidden caches. Most students ran for cover when the shooting became serious. When they learned of the confrontation on the university grounds, many of the antitreaty demonstrators who had occupied the nearby cathedral left that sanctuary to join their fellows. The police quickly sealed off the church grounds so they could not return.

Shots were still being exchanged when I received my report on the tragedy. Outbursts continued sporadically for almost four hours. The police, as reluctant as authorities throughout Latin America are to invade university territory, finally decided the deadly affair had continued too long. Two students had been killed and more than a dozen wounded. *Guardia* troops swept over the university grounds, arresting students they found with guns, and herding others out the gates. They picked up some of the better-known activist leaders for questioning. The authorities then padlocked the gates to the university and put the grounds off limits for any kind of gatherings or demonstrations. They also closed the National Institute, the well-known high school that had become a center of political radicalism.

Questioning of students involved in the fight and reports from informants in the student body convinced Panamanian authorities that the occupation of the El Carmen church and the outburst at the university had been actively promoted by anti-Torrijos elements. Among the most prosperous and resentful of those elements were those Panamanians who had been forced into exile by Torrijos and allowed to repatriate only after the U.S. Senate approved the Panama treaties. Ex-President Arias was the best known of the exiles and he had returned to Panama only four days before. In a well-planned, but partly spontaneous demonstration, an estimated 100,000 Panamanians had turned out to welcome the aging political maverick. The main purpose of the anti-Torrijos forces was clearly to discourage the visit of President Carter, create doubt about the validity of the treaties, and give Torrijos and his government a black eye on the world stage and in Panama.

Our own investigation confirmed most of the government's charges. Returned exiles had aroused and paid students to create a hostile atmosphere on the eve of the U.S. president's visit. But the government itself had done much to promote the protreaty and pro-Torrijos manifestations at the university. There was responsibility, and blood, on both sides. One central fact, almost always ignored in reports of riots, certainly in this one: the students who occupied the El Carmen cathedral and took part in the fight at the university represented three one-hundredths of 1 percent of the population of Panama.

The next morning, I received several frantic calls from Washington. What was going on? Should the president's trip be canceled? I explained what had happened and what it meant. We had talked with men we trusted in the Panamanian government and they assured us the previous night's violence was a one-time outburst that would not be repeated. I passed that assurance to my colleagues in Washington along with my own estimate that the president would have an unmarred visit. To cancel his trip at that point, I argued, would be an unvarnished disaster—for him, for Panama, and for U.S. policy. The president and his advisers decided to go forward as planned.

The day before six foreign heads of government arrive in town, any town, is likely to be a hairy one for all concerned. Panama City on June 15 was no exception. Half the Panamanian government had spent a nearly sleepless night going over last-minute details and worrying about what they might have forgotten. It was the same for those in the U.S. Embassy and the White House advance party. Vehicles and communications were checked one final time. Schedules were reviewed for possible gaps and delays.

The luckiest people were those who had specific things to do during the long wait. Technicians replacing all the light bulbs in the coliseum had their hands and minds occupied. Drivers made sure their gas tanks were filled and that engines had plenty of coolant. Communicators fiddled endlessly with line checks and antenna adjustments. The National Guard combed every inch of every floor in every building on Cinco de Mayo Plaza. The last holdouts in the El Carmen cathedral bowed to the persuasion of Archbishop Marcos McGrath and ended their thirty-hour sit-in. They walked slowly out of the church behind him, assured of his personal protection.

In the Canal Zone, the atmosphere was as gloomy as it was festive in Panama. Residents there were watching what they regarded as a splendid way of life coming to an end. For some, people who had spent a lifetime in the Zone, not a few of whose fathers and even grandfathers had worked on the canal, it was an emotional wrench. Others had simply fallen in love with a system that gave them subsidized housing; plentiful and cheap recreation; food pegged at New Orleans prices; no local income, property, or sales taxes; and inexpensive medical and dental care. It was an economy that made a $20,000 salary the equivalent of $30,000 to $40,000 in an average U.S. city. Actually, most economic advantages of working on the canal would not end when the treaties took effect; they would in a few years, of course, for those employed by the Zone government—policemen, firemen, other service personnel.

Despite the widely felt disappointment, many Zonians realized their privileged way of life could not last forever. They knew it was time for a new arrangement, and a few even welcomed it. Many others, though admittedly unhappy about the change, were willing to give the new order a fair trial, hoping it would work smoothly, suspecting it probably would not in many ways. At least they were prepared to wait and see.

The die-hard opponents of any change were vocal, bitter, and apparent. Unused to the ways of democracy in their authoritarian world—there were no elected local or area officials in the entire Zone—many Zonians were not accustomed to majority rule or to losing gracefully in politics. They came to hate President Carter for backing the treaties, to revile the Senate for approving them, and to dislike any fellow American who had anything to do with the change in their status. When it was announced that the president would visit the Zone and make a speech, irate Zonians declared their intention to stay away. They were like resentful children deprived of a favorite toy. What mattered was what happened to them, not what was good for their country.

Friday, June 16, 1978, finally arrived. It was hot, like most days on the isthmus, and humid, like all days. Clean-up crews were washing off or painting over the last of antitreaty, anti-Carter slogans on downtown walls. General Torrijos and the top officials in his government were at Tocumen airport, where, every hour, they welcomed another visiting chief executive, first from Costa Rica, then Jamaica, Colombia, Venezuela, and, finally, Mexico.

President Carter flew that morning from Washington to Atlanta, where he stopped off to address the annual convention of the Southern Baptist Church. The president told his fellow Baptists that "a person who knows he is strong can afford not to have to prove it." That was true of nations as well, he said, and he used the new agreement with Panama as an example of the kind of strength he thought the United States should exhibit. After his speech, the president returned to the airport from the Omni Coliseum and boarded *Air Force One* again for the flight to Panama.

At 2:00 P.M., the chartered jet carrying the main body of the White House press corps arrived at Tocumen. The reporters and photographers were escorted to the large roped-off area reserved for them. Fifteen minutes later, a DC-9 landed with twenty-five of the official U.S. party, four congressmen and their wives, a dozen high-level officials from the executive branch, and several top staffers from Senate committees. Then came a big C-137 bearing forty-one more of the White House party—eleven senators and their wives, treaty negotiators Bunker and Linowitz and their wives, and other high-ranking officials, including U.N. Ambassador Andrew Young and Deputy Secretary of Defense Charles Duncan.

Air Force One was scheduled to land at 3:00 P.M. and precisely at that hour the wheels of the big presidential jet touched down on the runway at Tocumen. It slowed, then turned onto the taxiway and eased to a stop directly in front of the terminal building, where we all were waiting. When the boarding ramp was rolled into place, Panama's chief of protocol, Ambassador Watson, and I walked up the steps and into the plane to welcome President Carter and his wife to Panama. When the president and his lady appeared at the plane's open door, they were greeted with a roar of welcoming shouts and applause. Hundreds of young schoolchildren assembled for the occasion were waving American and Panamanian flags. The crowds in front of the terminal and on the second-floor balcony were shouting: "¡Viva Jeemy Carter!" and "¡Viva los Estados Unidos!" "Long Live the United States" was something my predecessors and I had not heard too often on the isthmus in recent decades.

Standing at the bottom of the ramp, at the edge of a long strip of red carpet, waiting to greet President and Mrs. Carter were Omar Torrijos and his wife, Raquel, President Lakas and Fanny, Colonel Garcia (head of the National Guard), Foreign Minister González-Revilla and Maria Elena, and my wife, Mili. After the *abrazos* and handshakes, Torrijos and Lakas led the Carters along the flower-strewn carpet to the reviewing stand. Everyone stood at attention while the National Guard band played the much-rehearsed national anthems of the two countries.

Carter quickly won over the crowd by addressing them in Spanish. They ignored the Georgia accent and cheered when he said: "For sixty-five

years, Panama and the United States have been friends. Now we will also
be partners and we will give an example to the world of the way in which
nations can solve their differences peacefully and for the benefit of both."
He said the long, and often painful, trek to the treaties had been a case of
"peaceful and successful negotiations that has few parallels in history."

The end of the speechmaking brought one of the greatest tests for embassy, Panamanian, and White House planners. More than 175 U.S. visitors, at least 100 Panamanian officials, and 225 White House press representatives had to be moved the ten miles from Tocumen airport to the
coliseum in twenty minutes. Getting that many people into the right cars
and buses was a logistics nightmare. That it happened with hardly a hitch
was a tribute to meticulous planning and a product of vast good luck.

The roofed coliseum looked like the scene of a national political convention. Huge strips of blue and white material hung from the ceiling to the
floor behind the main platform. But directly behind the long table for the
key participants and the main observers was a solid curtain of blue, a concession to the photographers, who hate contrasting backgrounds. The gallery seats were filled by about four thousand Panamanians, mainly government servants, representatives of civic groups from the countryside, and
friends of high officials.

Dwarfing the central stage where the main business would be conducted was a huge, tiered platform set aside for the White House press. A
much smaller platform was reserved for the Panamanian and "other" press.
The large delegation of visiting U.S. vip's had a reserved section on the
other side of the central aisle, directly in front of the main stage. Because of
the bloated demands on space for press purposes, there was limited seating
for Panama's National Assembly and many of its members ended up in the
gallery. Even the diplomatic corps, usually honored guests at such affairs,
had fewer seats than necessary and some ambassadors had to stand. It was,
as one of my colleagues said, "a triumph of American ethnocentrism."

When President Carter and General Torrijos arrived at the coliseum,
they were directed to what is inelegantly called, in White House schedules,
"holding rooms." That is where high officials wait for the right time for
their entrances. It gives them a place to relax, comb their hair, check their
speeches, or whatever else before entering the main arena. Meantime, the
other players had a chance to get into the building and find their assigned
places on or before the stage.

When most people had been seated, I led the nine-man U.S. official delegation to our seats just behind the long table reserved for the heads of
government. In the group were U.N. Ambassador Andrew Young; Security Adviser Zbig Brzezinski; Sen. John Sparkman, the chairman of the
Foreign Relations Committee, who was bowing out of public life; Con-

gressman Ralph Metcalfe, chairman of the Panama Canal subcommittee, who died four months later; Deputy Defense Secretary Charles Duncan. Then came two Americans whose names and faces meant something in Panama and without whom there would have been no treaties—Ambassadors Ellsworth Bunker and Sol Linowitz. The last official was Senator Jack Javits, the ranking Republican in the delegation.

The list was drawn up by protocol, not by common sense. Two men who obviously should have headed up the U.S. representation were not even in Panama—Majority Leader Robert Byrd and Minority Leader Howard Baker. A wise president would have insisted they be at his side on that historic occasion. And at least three men sitting in the VIP section had worked harder for the treaties than most of those on the stage—Senators Frank Church and Paul Sarbanes and Deputy Secretary of State Warren Christopher.

Those on the Panamanian side of the stage had all played major roles in the treaty-making process—negotiators Rómulo Escobar Bethancourt and Aristides Royo and advisers and occasional negotiators Carlos López-Guevara, Nicolás Ardito Barletta, Edwin Fábrega Velarde, Adolfo Ahumada, and Rory González. The other Panamanian delegate was the just retired ambassador to Washington, my friend Gabriel Lewis. All had been at the center of the treaty business for a long time. I saw the unmistakable hand of Omar Torrijos in their selection; his criterion was common sense.

The preliminaries were over and it was time for the main event. A voice on the public address system announced the president of Costa Rica, Rodrigo Carazo Odio. The recently elected president of one of the few democratic nations in the hemisphere walked down the red carpet to the stage and took his place at the long table. He was followed by the presidents of Colombia, Mexico, and Venezuela and the prime minister of Jamaica. With the visitors in place, the president of Panama, Demetrio B. Lakas, was introduced. The big, grey-haired man lumbered down the aisle and took his place on the stage.

Then came the announcement that set off vocal Roman candles: "General Omar Torrijos Herrera and President of the United States Jimmy Carter." The coliseum exploded with cheers and applause. The two men walked in, waved to the crowd, and walked on stage to their chairs.

The formal proceedings were brief and to the point. Ambassador Watson gave Torrijos a series of leather-bound documents and pointed out where he should sign. Three feet away, Herb Hansell was presenting similar documents to President Carter. Both leaders had to sign the English and Spanish versions of the "Protocol of Exchange of Instruments of Ratification Regarding the Treaty Concerning the Permanent Neutrality and Operation of the Panama Canal and the Panama Canal Treaty." A process of fourteen years was finally terminated in less than five minutes.

The two men stood and shook hands, and the applause was deafening throughout the large auditorium. For us Americans it was a kind of self-congratulation on finally having done something that was just and long overdue. For the Panamanians, it was the hailing of a new day that they and their parents and grandparents had dreamed of, yet hardly dared think would ever come.

Torrijos shook hands with all the members of the U.S. delegation. Carter did the same with the Panamanians. Then the two leaders walked off the stage together and followed the red carpet to the rear of the coliseum. The applause and cheering continued, and the American and Panamanian principals responded with waves and smiles. They finally reached the sanctuary of the "holding rooms."

The other presidents filed out through the nearest exit, and the rest of us then made our way slowly outside to the waiting cars and buses. There we waited, and waited. No one knew what was causing the delay. When Carter and Torrijos finally emerged and walked to the big presidential limousine, the holdup was explained. The Panamanian strongman had changed from the white business suit he had worn for the signing ceremony into the gleaming white dress uniform and gold braid of Panama's only general. It was the outfit he invariably wore in public appearances before his people. Besides, his suit had been badly rumpled after six arrival ceremonies in the sweltering heat at Tocumen airport.

With the central characters aboard, the long motorcade began to move slowly through nearby streets headed for downtown Panama City. By the time we reached Vía España, Panama's principal east-west thoroughfare, the sidewalks on both sides were filled with people. They were waving flags and hands, and shouting "Viva Jeemy; Viva Omar" at the top of their lungs. Every now and then, we passed small musical groups playing traditional songs while the people danced. They stopped to wave and cheer as the vast procession passed by; then they resumed the festivities.

Well down Vía España and halfway to our destination, the long motorcade glided to a stop. After a while, when nothing moved, I got out of my car to see what was happening. The street ahead was clear but a group of people were gathered around the lead car talking and gesticulating. I saw President Carter alight and walk over to the sidewalk to say hello and shake a few hands. Then I spotted Colonel Noriega, Panama's chief of security, in the center of the group around the lead car.

A frantic call had come in from the U.S. Secret Service detail at Cinco de Mayo. They were recommending that the president not go to the plaza because of the huge crowd. "There is no security here," one of them was saying. Noriega urged them not to worry. "There is no problem," he said. "We have control of the situation." After a long discussion, the head of the Secret Service detail and the president decided to go ahead as planned. The motorcade resumed its slow passage toward the heart of the city.

The ride along Panama's streets had been triumphant for Carter and Torrijos. At least fifty thousand people had lined the route from the coliseum. But nothing quite prepared any of us for what met our eyes once we reached the plaza. Every square foot of the vast open area was occupied by cheering, singing Panamanians. Some were farmers bussed into the city by the government from as far away as Chiriquí province. Many were government workers who had been encouraged to attend. But the majority were residents of nearby areas—El Chorrillo, Curundu, Santa Ana, and Exposición—and quite a few had come from outlying parts of the city.

The effort to keep the street open alongside the International Hotel had finally collapsed in the late afternoon under Panamanian impatience and the press of human bodies. When the president's car reached the hotel entrance, the motorcade could go no further. Carter and Torrijos had been waving to the crowd through the open roof of the Lincoln. When the caravan halted, they climbed down from their perch and walked into the hotel. The rest of us did the same, pushing our way through laughing, cheerful Panamanians. Inside the hotel, we went up to the fourth floor, the level of the reviewing stand.

Carpenters and painters had been busy for a week erecting and finishing the huge structure. It covered two-thirds of the front of the hotel and it rose forty feet above street level. At its center, facing the street, was a large reproduction of the national seal of the Republic. Above the stand, covering another four floors of the International Hotel, was a monstrous mural in garish colors. It depicted a ship about to enter one of the locks of the canal. At the very top was the slogan "This is the triumph of the people," something Torrijos had said when the treaties finally were approved.

At street level, one saw dozens of grinning faces and sweaty bodies. From forty feet up, you saw a sea of heads from one side of the plaza to the other and as far as the eye could reach. Even the side streets were jammed with people for block after block. Then there were the banners and placards, hundreds of them, mostly white with black or red lettering. Unlike years past, they were mainly hopeful, cheerful, rarely critical of the United States. They said such things as "The Treaties Represent the Hopes of the People" and "Today Is Our Day of Dignity." One announced: "The Carter-Torrijos Treaties Mark the End of the Colonial Enclave." Many repeated favorite Torrijosisms, such as "It Is More Noble to Correct Injustice Than to Perpetuate It."

One small placard introduced a note of sadness for those who saw it and understood. Carried by a student, it said simply: "Rodríguez Presente" (Rodríguez is here). Rodríguez was one of the students killed in the gunfight at the university two nights before.

There were considerably more than 200,000 people in the plaza and the surrounding streets. Many had been there all day, and most for at least five hours. One would have expected them to be limp and wilted after all that time in what at ground level was at least 100 degrees Fahrenheit. Not so. A few of the frail did collapse in the oppressive heat and were quickly treated by the emergency medical teams standing by. Some others fell victim to the massive amounts of beer and rum that were being consumed. But the vast majority were laughing, dancing, cheering, waving flags and banners. For them, and for most Panamanians, it was a day that would never be forgotten. It was not unlike what many citizens of Philadelphia must have felt as witnesses to history on a July day 202 years earlier. Looking out at that vast crowd, I was certain young Panamanians fifty years hence would be reading about that day and that crowd in their history books.

Torrijos handled the throng with a mastery developed over the previous decade, often in that same setting though under vastly different circumstances. He joked with them and praised them. When he said he wanted to offer a kiss and applause for Mrs. Carter, the lid would have blown off the plaza—if there had been a roof.

I had never seen Torrijos so satisfied, so manic. And why not? On that day, a man of modest background from the province of Veraguas moved into a niche in his country's history that dozens of politicians and leaders before him had dreamed of. He had succeeded where all of them had failed. He had restored to Panamanian sovereignty a strip of territory across the middle of the country that for seventy-five years had been in alien hands. Moreover, he had done it by peaceful means, not with the use of the force that was his official vocation. It was an accomplishment that would live as long as Panama and its people survive.

While Torrijos was carrying on his lively dialogue with the crowd, I noticed a Secret Service agent shoving and standing in front of President Lakas. I walked over and tapped him on the shoulder. I told him quietly who I was and that the man he was jostling was the president of Panama. If he continued, I was going to file a formal complaint with his boss. The young man apologized and backed off. The irony was that the 6' 1", 260-pound Panamanian executive provided far better protection for the president on that flank than did the slim young agent.

Torrijos began introducing each of his foreign guests to the crowd, and the neighboring presidents hailed the new treaties and congratulated Panama and the United States for finding a just solution to a longstanding problem. When he introduced President Carter, the roar of approval from the vast crowd was long and loud. Carter smiled and waved in response to the ovation. Then he pleased the crowd even more by once again speaking in Spanish.

"This day," he began, "marks the beginning of a new partnership between Panama and the United States. The new treaties embody our mutual commitment to work together to assure that the Panama Canal shall always remain open, secure, and accessible to the vessels of all nations."

Carter praised the role that the other nations represented there had played in finding a fair agreement. He said the treaties had breathed new life into old principles—"principles of peace, nonintervention, mutual respect, and cooperation." He urged that those principles become the basis for a new level of understanding in the Western Hemisphere.

It was a perfectly fine speech, full of honorable sentiments and good intentions. It reflected the Carter administration's hope that the agreement with Panama could be transformed into the first step in a broader, comprehensive policy for the entire hemisphere. But it was not the kind of address that patriotic and emotional Panamanians who had been standing in the sun for long hours really relished. They received the president's words with polite applause, nothing more. The only enthusiasm came with his final words: "¡Viva Panama!" That stirred a warm response.

Torrijos restored the mood with a few more light comments, and with words of praise for his countrymen—for their fortitude, their restraint, and their inherent wisdom. The crowd loved it. And with that, the rally—the largest gathering in Panama's history—came to an end. We filed down the stairs to the waiting motorcade. By then, the police had cleared the side street, and we drove back to the Hotel El Panamá.

The next item on the agenda was a meeting of the heads of government. It proved the worst fiasco of the Carter visit for reasons both central and trivial. The basic flaw was that the impulse for such a gathering came exclusively from Washington. For reasons that are obscure, there had emerged among some U.S. diplomats and, even more so, among politicians in the postwar world a conviction that no international meeting was significant unless it produced a "joint communiqué" or an "agreed statement." Even better was a "declaration" or even a "charter." No one in the White House seemed to realize that in the previous three decades that process had produced some of the most forgettable documents in history. The assemblage of seven Western Hemisphere leaders in Panama was simply too delectable a prospect for Washington planners to ignore.

When the idea of a multilateral meeting during the Carter visit was raised with me in mid-May, I opposed it. It seemed to me it would be taking a well-decorated Christmas tree and adding an unneeded string of lights and an extra pound of tinsel. Finalizing the Panama treaties, I argued, was an accomplishment sufficient unto itself.

What made sense to me, as I told Washington, would be a series of quiet bilateral talks between President Carter and the other leaders. They could have explored one or two problems of common interest, and gotten to know each other better. We could then have expanded on that base as we addressed larger issues at a later date.

Part of my recommendation was based on my opinion of what was best for President Carter and the United States in the prevailing atmosphere. The other part was my judgment as a reporter that the real news was the treaty story; that rich cake did not need the added frosting of a multilateral meeting.

The confusion began as soon as all hands were back at the El Panamá Hotel. The "schedule," that forced menu for international gatherings, had President Carter arriving at the hotel at 6:00 P.M., then proceeding to the "holding room," and finally leaving for the Panama Room at 6:14 for the meeting, which was to begin at 6:15. The president actually arrived long after the meeting was to begin, and he went to his room to wash up and rest. So did the other presidents and the Jamaican prime minister.

Bob Pastor of the National Security Council and White House aides who had pushed for the meeting of presidents had left the planning up to the White House advance group. Dan Lee, head of the White House advance, was accustomed to political trips, not international meetings. He thought the Panamanians would take care of the session. The Panamanians saw it as a U.S. initiative and did nothing. No one was in charge.

Some embassy officers were standing in the lounge next to the Panama Room waiting for something to happen. President López Michelsen of Colombia walked in looking somewhat baffled. He asked PAO Steve Dachi where the meeting was. "It's supposed to be there, Mr. President," Steve said, pointing to the door to the next room. "But when does it start?" asked the puzzled Colombian executive. "We don't know," said Steve. López walked down the hall, got on the elevator, and returned to his room.

A few minutes later, an aide to Venezuela's President Pérez wandered into the room. "What about the damned meeting?" he asked. Someone told him it was going to be in the next room, but no one knew when. He, too, ambled off to report to his boss.

A White House staffer rushed into the room obviously upset. He grabbed Dachi and said, "Please, Steve, get these presidents together so our man can come down." Steve went to the hotel manager and asked him to have the switchboard connect him with the several presidential suites. The poor man did not know which presidents were in which rooms, and the switchboard was so snarled with calls in and out that even the chief operator could not remember who was where. Steve finally sent runners to every floor to tell all the presidents they were wanted in the Panama Room.

After traveling with the motorcade to the hotel, Mili and I had gone home to change for the evening events. We got back to the El Panamá at 7 o'clock when the meeting of presidents had been scheduled to end. We found it just beginning. I went into the conference room to see how it was progressing. It was as dreary as I had expected, and feared, it would be. It had turned into a kind of rump session of the Organization of American States, with each participant declaiming on his country's particular problems and grievances. Torrijos was presiding, a role he neither liked nor did well. He was clearly bored, and so were most of his guests. But they all seemed like beginning skiers on a snowy slope—once started, they had no choice but to try to get to the bottom as best they could.

Part of their discussion concerned the planned joint declaration. It had first seen the light of day in mid-May in a draft in Washington that covered most of the generalizations then prevalent in the Carter administration regarding U.S. relations with Latin America. It proposed that the seven nations concerned pledge to take certain rather vague actions aimed at three goals: "to further world peace," "to promote greater respect for human rights," and "to increase the well-being of the poor."

By the time the assembled presidents in Panama had finished, they had produced a three-page monstrosity called the "Declaration of Panama." It covered everything from limitations on conventional armaments to promoting commodity agreements in the hemisphere. It was one of those elaborately phrased and flowery documents that fills the graveyards of diplomacy. It meant little at the time, and less since.

I listened for a time to the words of bored leaders trying to be polite. I looked at the $700 sound booth at the end of the room, which was not being used. I gazed at the faces of seven obviously bored politicians. Then I quietly slipped out the rear entrance.

Soon, the doors of the Panama Room opened and people began streaming out to the exits. Mili and I rushed to our car to catch up with the presidential caravan. We drove through the narrow streets of the old part of town and pulled to a stop in front of the *presidencia*. We walked past the honor guard at the entrance and went quickly up the stairs to the Yellow Hall, where Panamanian and American guests were milling about, sipping champagne and talking.

Soon after, the central figures appeared at the head of the hall—President Carter and Rosalynn, President Lakas and Fanny, and General Torrijos and Raquel. They had been in the Lakases' private quarters for the traditional exchange of gifts between leaders. Lakas toasted his guests and the new treaties with great warmth, and President Carter responded in kind. Then, surrounded by the usual clutch of U.S. and Panamanian security guards, the six principals walked downstairs to the waiting line of cars. The rest of us followed along and found our places in the long caravan.

As we walked down the steps of the *presidencia*, I found myself thinking of the elaborate communications center that the White House technicians had installed days before in a room just off the Yellow Hall. It had required considerable time, effort, and expense. It was, of course, never used. I remembered something that wise Senator Everett Dirksen once said: "A million here, and a million there, and the first thing you know you're talking about real money."

The motorcade roared off in a burst of sirens and carbon monoxide, headed for the old Panama Golf Club. There we would have dinner, entertainment, and some much-needed relaxation at the end of a hectic day. The choice of the Golf Club was a typical Torrijos gesture. For fifty years, the club had been, second only to the Union Club, the symbol of oligarchic domination of Panamanian society. On restful afternoons and long, sunny weekends, Panamanian businessmen, politicians, lawyers, and other members of the elite, together with American businessmen and foreign diplomats, gathered there to play golf, make deals, and rail against the military government. It was conveniently close to the center of town and was surrounded by the homes of some of Panama's wealthiest families. Omar Torrijos was acutely aware of the Golf Club and what it represented. He lived only a block away on Ninety-fifth Street.

Three years before, the government had bought the golf course and the clubhouse, intending to turn the area into a park and a recreational facility for Panama's poor. It was one of Torrijos' most quixotic gestures. The government never found the funds to turn the area into the recreational park he had envisaged. Meantime, what could have been a great attraction for golfing tourists—in a country desperately trying to promote tourism— was allowed to disintegrate. It was discouraging to pass by and see a handful of youngsters playing softball on the tenth fairway when they could have been accommodated far better on a dozen lots within half a mile. And for golfers, it was wrenching to watch motorscooters ripping up the once well-manicured greens of the old course. Meantime, most areas were vacant, gone to seed.

For the romantic Torrijos, a nongolfer, the once prestigious Golf Club remained a symbol of something he despised. And he would use it as a symbol that night, even if only a handful of the American guests understood what he was doing. He was telling his people that the enclave of the privileged was now public property to be used for national purposes, not for the select few. Everyone who thought about it knew, of course, that the dinner could have been handled with vastly less confusion, and probably less cost, at any one of Panama's better hotels. But that was not the Torrijos way.

There were about three hundred guests that night. The main table was an elongated U with the base serving as the head of table for President Carter, General Torrijos, President Lakas, and the other Latin American heads of state. Along the extended uprights of the U, American and Panamanian VIP's sat on both sides of the table. The floor space surrounded by the huge table on the Golf Club veranda was used later by the musicians and dancers who provided the entertainment. Tables for the majority of the guests were scattered throughout the club—on the balcony, in the old bar, and elsewhere.

It began in an orderly way, with everyone in his or her assigned seat. That lasted through the first round of drinks. Those seated away from the center table decided they had not come to visit with old friends or to talk with people they saw every week. They wanted to see Jimmy Carter and Rosalynn and Omar, and so they left their tables and gathered around the big table on the veranda. If one left his chair to walk across the room to say hello to friends, he was likely to find someone sitting in it when he got back. Waiters trying to serve the food were forced to walk through massed bodies around the table. By the time dishes reached guests, the food had cooled considerably.

The first course was a seafood dish, scallops and shrimp. When a waiter put his plate before Senator Abourezk, an American lady leaned over the lawmaker's shoulder and said, "My, that looks good." The gallant senator handed her the plate and said, "Here, take a bite." In about twenty seconds, she handed him back the empty plate. "It was delicious," she said. He made no more handouts. "I'd never seen anything like that dinner," he commented later. Nor had anyone else.

How President Carter or General Torrijos or some of the other celebrities managed to get anything to eat was a mystery. Perhaps they did not. People were approaching them every minute to say hello or to introduce a friend. Something of the same was going on in other parts of the party. Panamanians were starting up conversations with senators whom they had seen only on television. Americans were asking Panamanians about the inner workings of the Torrijos government and what the new treaties meant.

It was a revelation to Americans accustomed to the stiffness of state dinners at the White House. It was a dramatic reminder to denizens of the Northern Hemisphere that the formality that dominated international intercourse was not the accepted way for all of mankind, and might not even be the best way. The truth is that, for all the confusion, the violations of protocol, and even the cold food, that dinner in Panama was more congenial, more solid fun, than any dinner I remembered at the White House or in embassies around the world.

At the end of the meal, President Carter and General Torrijos exchanged toasts and everyone joined in. Then came the music, and the dancing, and relaxed talk on the outskirts of the festivities. All too soon, it was over. At 11 o'clock, in the words of the schedule, "The President and Mrs. Carter proceed to motorcade for boarding." Most of the Americans followed along to their cars and buses for the trip back to their hotels. A few of the adventurous stayed on and, with most of the Panamanians, kept the party going into the small hours. There was an obvious desire not to let that momentous day in the life of Panama end too quickly.

The next morning, President Carter and General Torrijos had breakfast together. Then they went off to the second meeting of hemisphere leaders—a restricted affair because Mexico's President López Portillo and Jamaica's Manley had already gone home. With that diplomatic nicety taken care of, President and Mrs. Carter went to the nearby Paitilla Airport and boarded *Marine One*, the presidential helicopter, for an aerial tour of the Panama Canal. Others followed along in *Marine Two* and I found myself acting as a tour guide for Washington colleagues who had never seen the Panama Canal. In forty-five minutes—after going from the Pacific Ocean to the Atlantic and back again—we landed at Fort Clayton.

The visit to the Canal Zone was by all odds the most difficult segment of his visit for President Carter. He realized the new treaties were unpopular with many Americans who worked on the canal. They had been flooding Congress with antitreaty mail, and some had threatened to leave as soon as the new arrangement went into effect. Reporters' interviews with Zone residents in the days before Carter's visit had told the president he was not their favorite politician and that many planned to boycott his appearance in their "homeland." Nonetheless, the president was determined to meet with Americans in the Zone, despite warnings that he might be subjected to insults and rudeness.

The choice of Fort Clayton as the site of the president's appearance helped greatly to ease the worst of the threatened problems. Because it was a military housing area, a sizable turnout was guaranteed. Most military personnel not working on the visit itself had been given the morning off, and they and their families could be expected to turn out to see their commander-in-chief. For the military, Panama was a tour of duty, not a way of life, and they looked at the treaties differently from those who worked on the canal or in the Zone government.

In the end, more than three thousand Americans turned out to greet President and Mrs. Carter. Despite the boycott threat, many were canal workers. I saw a few placards critical of the president and the treaties, but fewer than some had expected. One that seemed more popular than others was a picture of General Torrijos with the slogan: "Re-elect Carter: the best President Panama ever had." There were a few boos and catcalls when the president and his wife walked across the grass from the helicopter to the podium, but they were drowned out by the cheers and applause.

The president's statement was well crafted—conciliatory but not apologetic. He showed that he understood the strain that a changed way of life would impose on those living in the Canal Zone. He said that everything that could have been done to protect their rights had been done in the treaty negotiations. He noted particularly the guarantees of civil rights that had been written into the treaties and said he had emphasized their importance the day before in his talks with Panamanian authorities. He also pointed out that the terms and conditions of employment on the canal would be, under the treaties, "no less favorable than they are now." The right of collective bargaining was preserved, and for the next twenty-two years that bargaining would be with the U.S. agency that would continue to run the canal. Finally, those who wished to leave could take advantage of the early retirement option that would be provided.

"The Senate of the United States has acted," the president said, "and the treaties are now a fact. I am not here to justify them, or to suggest that if you understood the treaties better that you would like them. I know that you understand them because for you they are not just a distant and impersonal foreign policy abstraction, but something that alters your lives in a direct and immediate way."

Later, in what seemed the heart of the Carter message, the president said: "According to the treaties, the Canal will increasingly be a place of Panamanian employment. Some of you might leave very soon; others will remain for many, many years. I am relying on all of you to help make this transition as smooth as possible. That is your duty, your responsibility, and the people of both nations expect nothing less. You have never disappointed your country in the past. I am sure you will not do so in the future."

One Carter phrase could appropriately have been carved in granite at the entrances to the canal: "The future of this waterway will depend upon the cooperation and the understanding of both Panamanians and Americans."

He concluded his message to the Zonians by saying: "I am proud of what you have done in the past and what you are doing today, and I have complete confidence that you will continue to represent our nation in the finest spirit of dedication, of competence, and of goodwill in the years to come."

There was a loud burst of applause and people were waving to the president from the field and the nearby stands. A few ill-tempered jeers were lost in the noise of approval. The president and his wife waved back to the crowd, then left the platform and headed for the waiting motorcade. They stopped to shake hands with people jammed up against the ropes that lined their pathway. The interval gave the rest of the official party time to find and board their assigned vehicles.

The motorcade made the journey from Fort Clayton to the Miraflores Locks in five minutes. It had started to rain and most of the party took shelter in nearby offices and work sheds. President and Mrs. Carter walked across the top of the closed lock and went up into the locks control house. Canal Zone Gov. Hal Parfitt explained the operation of the locks and the engineering marvel they represented. A U.S. ship, *American Apollo*, was in the first lock and was raised to the second level as the president looked on.

The tour of the locks over, the motorcade drove to a nearby hill overlooking the Miraflores Locks. There, the president would lunch with a dozen residents of the Canal Zone, people who worked for either the Canal Company or the Canal Zone government. There had been complaints from the antitreaty forces that those picked to have lunch with the president were "safe" and would not "make waves" in their session with Carter. In fact, those selected had either opposed the treaties or felt they could have been improved. But they were intelligent, thoughtful people who realized they were dealing with a fait accompli. They could, and did, point out some of their concerns about the way the treaties would be implemented in the future, and that the president needed to hear. The kind of diatribe that some of the rabid treaty critics would have liked to engage in would have served no earthly purpose.

Lunch on the hilltop overlooking the canal lasted forty-five minutes. Then, led by the presidential limousine, we rode to Fort Clayton, where the big, comfortable helicopters were waiting. In fifteen minutes, we were at Tocumen airport. General Torrijos, President Lakas, and their wives were waiting for the Carters. We all stood at attention while the National Guard band once again played the national anthems.

It was time for handshakes, *abrazos*, exchanges of good wishes and thanks. President and Mrs. Carter climbed the boarding ramp, turned to wave to their hosts, to the flag-waving children, and to the Panamanians who lined the second-story balcony of the airport building. Then they disappeared inside and the door to *Air Force One* swung shut.

My bag had been loaded aboard because I was going to Washington to consult with colleagues at State on next steps in the treaty process. I kissed Mili good-bye, our sixth airport farewell in a year, and climbed up the stairway to the big plane's rear door. I stood for a moment, waving to my wife and the embassy staff, and watching briefly the last act of the Carter visit to Panama. Then I went to my seat.

When we reached cruising altitude, people released their seat belts and walked up and down the aisle, chatting with friends, reviewing the trip, laughing about all the strange things that had happened to them. Up front, the president and his closest aides were going over the visit and concluding it had gone better than even they expected. It was the first major achievement of the administration, and they were savoring it to the full. The questions were: How do we build on it? Where do we go from here?

I sat quietly in my seat, a bit numb. I had not had more than a few hours of sleep any night for more than a week and I felt drained. A kindly steward came along and asked what I would like. I ordered a vodka on the rocks, and in minutes it was there, with a slice of lemon on the side. I sipped it, looked out the window, sipped some more, and thought. Then I got a couple of sheets of paper out of my briefcase and began to write. It rambled a bit, but it said what was in my mind and heart:

Air Force One
June 17, 1978

Reflections of a tired Ambassador—

The visit is over and the President is on his way back to Washington. The man has courage. He handled the crowd at Clayton with guts—said all the right things. But his courage goes a lot deeper than that. He grabbed the Panama problem by the horns when a lesser man would have jumped behind the barricades. He could have slid away—as Ford did when the going got tough, and as Nixon did (because he never really gave a damn, and Henry didn't understand what was at stake in anything that was less than global).

He almost blew it all with DeConcini. The best example I know of a President relying on the judgment of amateurs who didn't know the score. But he recovered—thanks mainly to a man named Byrd who saved the bacon. I did my best to warn him but the warning was buried. Presidents really would be well advised to pay more attention to those designated as their "personal representatives" abroad. Nine times out of ten they could give better advice than neophytes on their staff. I have the feeling that FDR was the last President who used Ambassadors as they should be used.

It has been a long road. It goes back to 1972—my "secret mission" and the long talks with Torrijos. That's really where it started. Omar is another man of courage. He could have demagogued the issue over and over again—and he did sometimes. But he could have stirred up his people a lot more. And he could have created an unholy mess. Of course, it would have meant disaster for him and for his country, as well as for us. I'm sure he knew that and so he always skirted the brink, never went over. I hope I helped. He says I did—and I have to believe him.

So damn many characters have walked on and off the stage. Tony Tack—a patriot, but so concerned with what history would say that it kept him from making history. Ellsworth Bunker—the good, gray rock of Vermont who really got the show on the road. Morey Bell—a genius with a self-destruct button of ego. Rómulo Escobar—one of the few men I have known whose intellect and sense of history were strong enough to overcome deep-seated prejudice. Aristides Royo—lively, brilliant, ambitious, torn between left and right, a big ship with a small anchor. He and Rómulo made it happen—but mainly because they knew Omar wanted it. Nicky Barletta—the best mind in Panama, and maybe the best hope for the future. Nico González-Revilla— could have done so much but got into the big league too soon. Sol Linowitz—breathed fire and energy, single-minded, got it done over immense odds. Gabriel—my friend and partner, a real patriot; Panama is lucky to have him.

And the Senate—Byrd and Baker, without whom it would never have been. Church and Sarbanes, masters of the floor, protectors of the right—day after day after day. Allen's droning and needless insults. And those who wanted to kill the whole thing because they never understood the modern world or Panama—Hatch, Helms, Thurmond, Laxalt, Dole. And Goldwater, who really knew better.

Finally, it is done. The treaties are in the books and on Apr. 1 they take effect. A remarkable chance for our big country to become a real partner to a small country in an enterprise that benefits all. There is surely going to be trouble ahead in the rest of Central America. Revolution is stirring. Somoza is hanging on, but probably not for long, despite his backing in Congress. If we play the Panama card wisely, it could change the whole sorry mess. Otherwise, we open the door for Cuba, and Moscow.

Will we pick the right people to do the job? Will Panama do the same? Will the House of Representatives make it easy or hard? Or impossible? I don't trust people like Bauman and Murphy, or Hansen or Dornan. No doubt their axes are being sharpened. They are wreckers, without vision or common sense. They will try to destroy, without any understanding of what it means for the future. God save us from crafty, unseeing men.

I hope the White House will stay on top of the fight in the House. They can't afford to rest on their oars. But I have a feeling that they will. They are savoring the victory now—but it will get away from them if they relax.

Anyway, that's for the future. I won't be in it. It is time for a new team. I wish them well.

The man up front can rightly feel a good deal of satisfaction. So can everyone else who played a role in it. We don't often have a chance to write a good page in history. Let's hope it survives and prospers—as it should. God knows that small men, petty men, evil men will try to besmirch what has been done. I hope the next generation will fight them—as we did.

WJJ

I stuffed the pages into my pocket, finished my drink, and pushed the "recline" button on the arm of the seat. In seconds, I was asleep. The steward shook me awake as we were descending for our landing at Andrews Air Force Base outside Washington. The long flight was over. It was only five hours, but it seemed more like four-plus years. It seemed so because it was.

Epilogue

Wʜᴇɴ legislation to implement the Panama Canal Treaty went to the U.S. House of Representatives in early 1979, that increasingly unmanageable body became a shambles. All the concerns that had nagged at me on the flight to Washington with President Carter six months earlier were realized, and then some. The actions in the House were something between a misfortune and a disaster. Almost the only good thing to be said for the denouement is that there *was* one and that legislation was approved at the eleventh hour that at least allowed the United States to continue operating the Panama Canal.

In its handling of the implementing legislation, the Carter White House repeated several mistakes it had made on the treaties themselves. The president's political advisers grossly underestimated the opposition on the Hill, to say nothing of the depth of feeling that characterized that opposition. Instead of demanding expert advice and help from congressional leaders, the administration fell back on its own expertise—which was not notably acute on legislative affairs. Finally, one of the great political ironies of recent decades, the president and his men had to rely on an unreconstructed critic of the Panama Canal Treaty to shepherd through the House the legislation to put that pact into effect. It was a move calculated to save as much as possible from what was beginning to look like a sinking ship. But it was like expecting Captain Bligh to boost morale on H.M.S. *Bounty*.

One thing the Carter administration produced was a first-class draft law. That was no surprise. The State and Defense lawyers who wrote it knew every sentence of every article in the Panama treaties. Their proposed legislation was designed to carry out the letter and the spirit of the new arrangement. In a way, it may have been *too* meticulously crafted.

Everyone connected with the Panama situation, and many of their sisters and cousins and aunts as well, it seemed, wanted the right to read and approve every draft of each paragraph. Back and forth the papers went, from State to Defense to White House, then back to the point of origin.

The number of chops that had to be affixed to each draft was one reason for the languor of the process, despite the fact that the bulk of the proposed law had been completed while the Senate was still debating the canal treaty. More important was the certainty in administration circles (House leaders had given an unequivocal warning) that nothing was going to be done on treaty implementation until the politicians in the House had passed through their biennial test at the polls in November 1978. What that self-imposed delay did, of course, was to open the way for treaty opponents to get in first with their versions of implementing legislation.

Get in they did. New York's John Murphy, chairman of the Merchant Marine and Fisheries Committee, introduced H.R. 111, a full-dress treaty implementation bill that differed sharply from the administration's outlook on many important problems. Idaho's George Hansen, labeled by a leading political handbook as "one of the authentic zanies in the Congress,"* put several bills into the House hopper—all aimed at supporting Hansen's view that not a cent of money or an inch of territory could be turned over to Panama without explicit approval from the House. Ron Paul, an eccentric libertarian from Houston who wanted to cut most or all U.S. ties with the rest of the world, introduced a bill that imitated Hansen's. There were others.

Those several drafts of antitreaty, antiadministration legislation were printed and circulated to all representatives. Their authors buttonholed colleagues in the corridors and cloakrooms and gradually won support. It was claimed, for example, that one of Representative Hansen's efforts had attracted some 180 co-sponsors. By the time President Carter's entry reached the House, it was already trailing the opposition badly, especially the Murphy bill.

It was January 23, 1979, before the administration was ready to move ahead with its Panama scenario. On that date, President Carter sent the newly drafted implementing legislation to the Speaker of the House and the president of the Senate. In an accompanying letter, the president asked for "urgent consideration and timely passage" of the bill. "To assure a smooth transition and continued efficient Canal operation once the new Treaties come into force," the president wrote, "the legislative framework—in which the agencies responsible for operating and defending the Canal will be operating—must be established well in advance so that they may make the necessary plans and preparations." He warned that any untoward delay would make conversion to the new system of operation and defense "less efficient and more costly."

---

*M. Barone and G. Ujifusa, *The Almanac of American Politics, 1982.*

The administration proposal was numbered H.R. 1716 in the House and was parceled out in four sections to appropriate House committees: International Relations (later renamed Foreign Affairs), Merchant Marine and Fisheries, Post Office and Civil Service, and Judiciary. The House leadership asked the four panels to report back no later than April 10.

In the Senate, the administration's bill was assigned to the Armed Services Committee. In part, that was because the implementing legislation was largely technical and focused on the future operations of the waterway. It was assumed those operations would continue to be the responsibility of the U.S. Army, certainly of the Defense Department. In addition, Senate leaders felt considerable sympathy for the Foreign Relations Committee, which had borne the weight of the long fight for treaty ratification the previous year. Majority Leader Byrd and his leadership team believed Foreign Relations had served the Senate above and beyond normal duty. The new Foreign Relations chairman, Frank Church of Idaho, faced a tough reelection battle the next year, and the last thing he needed at that moment was additional publicity as the point man in another Panama skirmish in the Congress.

It was quickly apparent that assignment of the Panama legislation to Armed Services was more of a prune than a plum to its members. One after another, those in the Democratic majority pleaded other business and invoked their seniority to avoid handling the bill. The job eventually went to the panel's newest member, Sen. Carl Levin of Michigan. He had just defeated incumbent Robert Griffin, who had been a staunch treaty foe.

The Panamanians, at least the government and a fair number of the politically alert, were watching those strange machinations in Washington from the early autumn of 1978 onward. They were puzzled and vaguely apprehensive. Like most people in the hemisphere, including the vast majority of U.S. citizens and the media as well, they assumed the Panama treaties issue was settled. In their minds, all that remained was a collection of household chores that had to be spelled out in order to convert general principles into specific actions. Yet long experience had persuaded many Panamanians that American officials, especially members of Congress, were an erratic, unfathomable breed capable of strange and unpredictable behavior. So while they told themselves that the big job was completed and the worst was over, many Panamanians were braced for more unpleasant surprises from the capital city on the Potomac.

Meanwhile, the Torrijos government was putting its own house in order. Under the Constitution of 1972, the term of President Demetrio B. Lakas was expiring in 1978 and he could not succeed himself. I have explained that Lakas was not the figurehead executive that some observers blithely assumed. His role was not fully comprehended by many, probably most, of those who commented on Panamanian politics. Despite that, the central authority, the final decision-making power, belonged to Omar Torrijos. Often he chose not to wield it. But it was there when he needed or wanted it.

From 1977 on, Torrijos was under heavy pressure from friends, followers, and hangers-on to become president, making him national leader in name as well as fact. He vacillated for a long time, sometimes attracted to the notion of joining the world's recognized chiefs of state. More often, he was turned off by the prospect. He knew himself well enough to realize he would be miserable presiding over cabinet meetings. And the demands of protocol—receiving the credentials of newly arrived ambassadors, for example—would have driven him to distraction.

Above all else, Torrijos was a realist and he knew that his National Guard was the most powerful coherent force in the country. As its commander, he could act on his whims and pursue his dreams. Once he turned over the reins to others, who could predict what might happen? Torrijos had told several U.S. senators who visited Panama in 1977–78 that he intended to withdraw gradually from the center of the political stage and to move his country increasingly toward civilian rule. His decision not to run for president was in line with that promise. And though American and Panamanian cynics reacted with skepticism to his pledge when they heard of it, the fact was that his intervention in political decisions after 1978 was significantly less common than it had been in the previous decade.

My feeling was that Torrijos had decided to slowly disengage from the political wars but that he wanted to make sure he was in a position to move in effectively should that prove necessary. I also had the feeling when I left Panama in August 1978—and again two months later when I met him while on a special mission to Central America for the secretary of state—that Omar Torrijos had grown weary of political battles. Things that once excited him had become a bore. His senses and his mind were dulled by the repetition of stimuli. He had traveled the world and met its leading statesmen. He had hosted the president of the United States. He had concluded treaties that ended the unbearable inferiority of 1903—and thereby had marched into the history of his country and the hemisphere. He was then dabbling with affairs in Central America, but even that failed to spur his interest as much as lesser things had only a few years earlier. It was no surprise to learn that he was spending an increasing amount of time in the remote village of Coclecito, where he was free from the vexations and pressures of the capital.

Having decided not to become president himself, Torrijos chose one of his inner circle to replace Jimmy Lakas in the post. No one openly campaigned for the assignment but there were at least half a dozen men around Torrijos who hoped that fortune, and the general, would smile upon them.

The hopes of the other eager aspirants were shattered when Omar announced that he thought Aristides Royo, who had helped negotiate the Panama treaties, would make a good president. His choice as vice-president was Ricardo de la Espriella, chief executive of the Banco Nacional and a strong supporter of President Lakas in the twin causes of economic development and fiscal responsibility. Many Panamanians and not a few foreign observers thought the roles of Royo and de la Espriella should have been reversed, that the banker-economist would have made the better president; the balancing role as vice-president should have gone to the leftist lawyer Royo. But that was not the way Omar Torrijos saw things, which was what counted.

Once Torrijos' decision was announced, the election of Royo and de la Espriella by the Assembly of Community Representatives (what passed as a national legislature) was automatic. The two took office on October 11, 1978.

One thing Torrijos did not have to worry about, unlike President Carter, was getting laws and regulations to carry out Panama's obligations under the Panama Canal Treaty. The many lawyers who had helped negotiate the treaties, and others working under their direction, quickly drafted the rules that codified Panama's participation in the modernized arrangement with the United States. With a minimum of consideration and no wrangling, the new laws were approved by the Legislative Council headed by Torrijos.

Needless to say, the procedure in Washington was a far cry from that in Panama City. Most bills that pass through the committee machinery in Congress undergo some alteration. In this case, with four House panels involved instead of the usual one, the administration's draft law for treaty implementation was revised, rewritten, and altered in ways that were unprecedented. The intent of some key portions of the bills was not merely changed but reversed. The principal source of mischief was the committee on Merchant Marine and Fisheries. Because that committee (and its Panama Canal subcommittee) had been dealing with waterway affairs for decades, the other panels and members tended to defer to it on the treaty problem. Also, the aggressiveness of its domineering chairman, New York's John Murphy, cowed many of his colleagues, including other committee chiefs.

What President Carter and his political advisers came slowly to realize (when it was too late) was that Murphy and those working with him had no desire or intention to produce the kind of law the White House wanted. From the day the administration's bill went to the Hill in January, through the final months of winter and into the spring, the Merchant Marine and Fisheries Committee hacked away at the legislation with amendments, additions, and deletions. It became obvious that the Carter legisla-

Epilogue

tion lacked sufficient support to survive in anything close to its original form and that the bill proposed by Congressman Murphy (H.R. iii) had considerably more backing. When it was clear they had no other realistic choice, the Carter forces dropped their own bill and agreed to use the Murphy draft as the basis for future discussions. The final incongruity was White House acceptance of the legislator from Staten Island, a man who opposed the Panama treaties vehemently and distrusted the Panamanians, as floor manager for the implementing legislation. With that, Mr. Carter and his advisers put their sheep in the wolf's tender care.

As the fight proceeded, the differences between what the Carter administration wanted and what an aggressive, well-organized antitreaty faction in the House would allow stood out sharply. A dozen or more issues became the battlegrounds on which the contending forces waged their campaigns. In reviewing those issues, it is important to remember that the differences were not between two well-meaning contenders who desired the same end but differed only in how to achieve it. Many House members wanted if at all possible to scuttle the Panama Canal Treaty, not implement it. Others wanted to punish the president and his supporters for not giving the House a decisive voice in treaty ratification, a role that the courts and a majority of legal scholars argued the House did not have under the constitution. One other goal of the antitreaty group was to ensure that the House would have a dominant voice in Panama Canal matters for the remainder of the century.

This latter insistence, to be dealt a hand regardless of the game, has been increasingly evident in congressional politics. In a world of growing complexity, our elected representatives are insisting on their right to dabble in matters often beyond their competence. Traditional, even constitutionally prescribed, distinctions between the executive and legislative branches of government are more and more ignored or flouted. Then, when members of Congress face these responsibilities that are beyond their ability or too much of a drain on their time, their answer is to add people to their personal or committee staffs to do the job. The result: an increasing amount of the public business is being done by anonymous and unelected but well-paid staffers who are unknown to the voters who pay them but essential to the congressmen who hire them.

One of the longest, most bitter skirmishes between administration and antitreaty forces in the House concerned the kind of organization that would run the Panama Canal. The treaty said only that the United States would carry out its canal responsibilities "by means of a United States Government agency called the Panama Canal Commission, which shall be constituted by and in conformity with the laws of the United States of America."

The Carter administration wanted a straightforward approach to management requirements. Since 1951, the Panama Canal had been operated efficiently by a government corporation known as the Panama Canal Company. The Carter forces believed the new commission should take the same form. It would be self-sustaining and receive no appropriations from Congress. It would set tolls for transiting ships based on its estimates of its obligations. The commission could borrow up to $40 million to meet any unexpected needs, but any such borrowing had to be repaid with interest to the U.S. Treasury. A business-type accounting system would be used as required by the Government Corporation Control Act.

That approach clashed with the mood of the House and the plans of Chairman Murphy. What they wanted was House involvement in, if possible control over, every significant step in the operation of the Panama Canal for the next twenty years. Murphy took care of it nicely in his proposed bill by making the canal commission an appropriated fund agency of the U.S. government. In its simplest terms, that meant all tolls collected from ships passing through the canal would be paid into the U.S. Treasury. All money expended by the commission—to pay its personnel, to buy supplies (from paper clips to anchors), to widen a channel, or to widen a stairway in a warehouse—had to be studied, approved, and funds appropriated for by congressional committees and by both houses of Congress.

Nearly thirty years earlier, the Congress had recognized that procedure as cumbersome and unnecessary and had adopted the more efficient corporate form of management. But the House of Representatives in 1979 was in a mood to turn back the clock, and it did. An operation of demonstrated efficiency was thereby converted into one that easily could become cumbersome, wasteful, and needlessly complicated.

Another argument, fully as vitriolic, developed over the question of transferring property to Panama. The treaty provided that certain lands and facilities would go to Panama the day the new pact went into effect. Others would be handed over on a phased basis during the treaty period. The United States also agreed that if certain lands or buildings became superfluous to its needs later on they would revert to Panama. Everything not transferred to Panama earlier would be handed over at the treaty's end in 1999.

That relatively simple, self-executing transfer of properties displeased many House members mightily. A few knew, and the others had it drummed into their ears ceaselessly for two years, that Article IV, section 3, of the Constitution gave Congress the power to dispose of territory and property belonging to the United States. It was that constitutional provision that House members argued ad nauseam had been violated by the Panama treaty. They refused to accept two hundred years of history and the long-standing legal view that there was another equally valid way for the government to dispose of property and that was via a treaty approved by the Senate. Only a few months earlier, in answer to a suit brought by several members of Congress, the federal court of appeals in the District of Columbia had ruled that transfers of federal property by the treaty route were completely proper and legal. The Supreme Court had refused to review the lower court's decision, thereby validating it. Even that failed to deter some extremist members of the House who were determined to destroy the Panama treaty at whatever cost.

Typical of that rocklike resistance to either law or common sense was the position of Illinois' ultraconservative representative, Philip Crane. Only one hour before the House voted on the implementing legislation, Crane proposed an amendment to postpone the transfer of *all* property to Panama until the canal treaty expired in 1999. It was one of the more cynical and irresponsible contributions to a debate that suffered no shortage of those qualities. Crane's admitted goal was to try to force the president and the Senate to work out a completely new arrangement with Panama.

Representative Murphy pointed out that Crane's proposal would be a clear violation of the Panama treaty. Then one of the House's brighter members, Georgia's Elliott Levitas, dissected Crane's amendment—and several similar offerings—using history, law, and reason as his instruments. It was one of the forensic high points in a generally banal debate. The House defeated the Crane proposal resoundingly, 248 to 177.

The form of the canal commission and the transfers of property were only two of the many targets picked by those in the House who hoped to wreck the Panama treaty. Early on, for example, the House tried to insist there be no change in the size or disposition of U.S. military forces in Panama. That was designed to prevent their being moved to new areas or vacating defense sites that were promised to Panama in the treaty. President Carter finally sent a message to the House insisting that U.S. national interest required the moves.

The treaty provided for an annual payment of $10 million to Panama for canal income and up to $10 million additional from canal profits that might remain after all normal expenses had been paid. A group of representatives set out to make that second payment impossible. They did it by piling on one expense after another that had to be paid by canal tolls before the so-called contingency payment could be made to Panama. The administration had planned to drop the requirement that the canal operation provide the U.S. Treasury with an annual payment of interest on the original cost of building the canal. Most economists and students of canal operations argued that the U.S. government and the American people had been paid many times over for the roughly $350 million it cost to build the canal. The savings to U.S. armed forces during World War II alone were many times that amount.

That carried no weight with a majority of members of the House of

Representatives. They calculated that $20 million a year in interest would give the Treasury about $400 million over the life of the treaty. That was significantly more than the total cost of canal construction from 1903 to 1914. For some members, it was a useful argument when it came to explaining their treaty votes back home. For a handful of vindictive congressmen, it was just one more way to make it slightly harder for the new treaty to work as it was intended.

The House took other steps as well either to tighten its control over the canal or to deliver gratuitous insults to the Panamanians who would be our partners on the waterway for the next twenty years. When the Panama treaties were being negotiated, Ambassadors Bunker and Linowitz had made clear to the Panamanians that no economic benefits beyond those related to operation of the canal could be part of the treaty agreement. At the same time, the Carter administration and the negotiators wished to make the point that there were benefits attached to being a friend and a partner of the United States. When the Panama treaties were signed, Secretary of State Vance sent the Panamanian government a letter outlining the things Washington hoped to do for its small ally—investment guarantees for housing, loan guarantees for productive projects in the private sector, loans and insurance from the Export-Import Bank to stimulate U.S. trade with Panama, and repayment guarantees for a military sales program to modernize Panama's National Guard, which would be sharing the burden of canal defense with U.S. forces. Every item was a loan or a guarantee or insurance; there were no gifts or cash.

As soon as the treaty implementation legislation went to the House, members of that body began to slash at every proposal that came their way involving Panama. Whether it was military assistance (which the U.S. armed forces strongly favored) or steps to improve education and health care in Panama's rural areas, the House cut or eliminated the proposal. The lower house seemed intent on proving the opposite of the Carter doctrine—that it did *not* pay to be a U.S. ally.

Another tactic adopted by some congressmen was to insist that all U.S. expenses under the new treaty should be paid by tiny Panama. For example, we were turning over some military areas, including barracks and training grounds, to the National Guard. That meant providing new quarters for the U.S. forces being relocated. Antitreaty legislators demanded that Panama pay the bill. We had promised U.S. canal workers that they would be given an early retirement program as an incentive to continue working until they were eligible. Many congressmen said, "Yes, but let the Panamanians pay for it."

The battle over military costs was abandoned only when the representatives finally realized that under the treaty the facilities were to be transferred to Panama "without charge." But the additional costs for early retirement were added to the expenses of canal operations. Thus, it was one more item that had to be paid from canal revenues *before* the Panamanians could collect on the contingency payment, the second $10 million in the treaty. The goal of the antitreaty elements was to make sure Panama never collected on that promised money.

Many other things were done by the House, or at least attempted, to undercut or destroy the atmosphere of partnership that the president and his negotiators had tried to create with Panama. Under the treaty, the new canal administrator was to get his policy guidance from a board of directors, five Americans and four Panamanians. The House tried to insist that all members of the board be approved by the U.S. Senate. They were frustrated to learn that Panama had the right to pick its own directors.

The House then set out to make the supervisory board as much of a U.S. rubber stamp as possible. It named the secretary of defense as the president's agent for dealing with the canal commission. It demanded that U.S. members of the board could vote only "as directed by the Secretary of Defense or his designee." The regulations of the new board, including the schedule of meetings, had to be approved by the defense secretary. A quorum for the conduct of business was defined as a majority of board members "of which a majority of those present are nationals of the United States." The control of the defense secretary over the Panama Canal Commission and its board of directors was markedly tighter than it had been in pretreaty years. The notion of a canal being run by men of good will from both countries operating as a team was rudely trampled under by a majority in the House of Representatives who understood little and cared less about such things as partnership, mutual advantage, and cooperation in foreign affairs.

The preceding pages provide only a sampling of ways in which a legislative body can twist and undermine a president's foreign policy. Almost the only thing that kept the lower house of the Congress from wreaking total havoc on the Panama treaties was the unwelcome realization that they were a fact and that they would enter into force on October 1, 1979, with or without implementing legislation. Without the new law, the United States would have had two grim choices come October. One would have been to leave Panama; the other, to violate our solemn word, and international law, and use military force to hold the waterway. Needless to say, the latter would certainly have led to the Panama Canal being closed to us and to all world shipping, a major catastrophe. Those were the appalling alternatives that 435 members of the House of Representatives faced, and some of their number toyed with so cavalierly, in the summer of 1979.

While the treaty drama was being played out in the committees and halls of Congress, another play was going on within the plan. The scene was Central America, especially Nicaragua. What was happening there had more to do with developments in the House than many members of that body even guessed, and more than a usually penetrating press began to understand.

By the autumn of 1978, the Carter administration had decided that the days of the Somoza dictatorship were numbered. Enemies were closing in on the once all-powerful ruler, and even many of his friends and followers were transferring their money and themselves to Miami, Mexico, Western Europe, or other Latin American capitals. The curtain was slowly descending on one of the longest running political shows in the Western Hemisphere. The question by then was not whether Somoza would leave but when, and under what circumstances.

Even Somoza, whose family had ruled Nicaragua for more than forty years, realized the glory days were over. He insisted, nonetheless, on keeping his grip on the presidency until his term expired in 1981. His demand convinced many that the 52-year-old tyrant was losing not only power but his hold on reality as well.

Washington's main concern was that the Nicaraguan leader would hold on to power until all of the moderate, middle-of-the-road, noncommunist political forces in the country were either destroyed, forced into exile, or pushed into the arms of the Marxist-led faction of the Sandinista rebels. The U.S. government wanted Somoza to agree to accept mediation by other governments in the hemisphere, mediation that would end the killing in the countryside and arrange for a peaceful transfer of power to noncommunist political elements in Managua while they still existed.

I had retired by then and was settling down in Austin, Texas, to write and relax when I was called back to active duty. The president and Secretary Vance wanted me to do three things: convince some Latin American governments to join us in mediating the Nicaraguan civil war; persuade Somoza to accept our peace-making effort; prevail upon those governments that were helping the anti-Somoza forces with material and moral support to reduce their actions and give the mediation effort a chance to succeed.

In ten days of shuttle diplomacy, we accomplished all three. Five governments (Colombia, Costa Rica, El Salvador, Honduras, Guatemala) agreed to take part in mediation if asked, and if Somoza agreed. Somoza himself balked at first but finally agreed to the peace-making exercise. And those who had been sending help to the Nicaraguan rebel forces (Costa Rica, Panama, Venezuela) agreed to pull back for a time and give the diplomatic approach a chance to work.

I flew home pleased with an outcome that Washington had thought was unlikely if not impossible. But I still had considerable misgivings about chances for an orderly, early outcome. I knew that once the diplomatic process began Somoza could find many ways to delay and obstruct it. I also regarded it as ominous that twice in our several talks he had referred to the many friends he had in government circles in Washington. Also, Venezuelan President Carlos Andrés Pérez had told me that in their last meeting Somoza had boasted to him that he had "more friends in Congress than Jimmy Carter has." Was the Nicaraguan ruler depending on pals in the U.S. Congress to help keep him in power? It seemed more than likely.

One of those pals was particularly well placed to lend a hand. He was Congressman Murphy, the floor manager of the Panama legislation. Both West Point graduates, he and Somoza had been close friends for years. Another Somoza admirer was Texas Congressman Charles Wilson. A graduate of Annapolis, Wilson visited Nicaragua often and had a close relationship with its ruler. There were numerous other members of the Somoza fan club on Capitol Hill.

The effort to make Panama implementing legislation a hostage in exchange for a revision in the administration's policy toward Nicaragua was apparent. Early in June, the Panama Canal subcommittee held hearings on reports that Panama was smuggling guns to communist rebels in Nicaragua. The day before it voted on Panama treaty implementation, the full House held a secret session—its first in 150 years—to study the same allegations. In both cases, the evidence was too flimsy to win much support for the antitreaty faction's demand that the implementing legislation be set aside.

There was no doubt that Panama (along with Costa Rica, Venezuela, and others) was providing support to Somoza's opponents. It was also evident that there were communists among the anti-Somoza coalition and that they dominated some groups within it. But it was equally clear to all but the blindly prejudiced that the great majority of those who wished an end to Nicaraguan tyranny and oppression were not communists—and many were strongly anticommunist. Superior organization and tighter discipline enabled the communists to survive the trials of civil strife longer and with more organizational coherence than most of their rivals. Many of the others—liberal politicians, intellectuals, students, professionals, businessmen—were gradually forced into silent conformity, into exile, or into the welcoming embrace of the Sandinistas.

There was a glaring incongruity in this campaign. Right-wing extremists in the House were criticizing Panama almost daily. And at the other end of the capitol, Senators Helms and Thurmond were thumping the anticommunist drums. Yet oil-rich Venezuela was giving Somoza's enemies vastly more material aid than was Panama and it was never mentioned in the Congress. Nor was there any reference to democratic Costa Rica, which provided sanctuary for rebels fleeing Nicaragua. Members of Congress were using a double standard to judge our neighbors.

President Carter was soon aware of the way the Panama debate was being used by friends of the strongman in Managua. In his memoirs, he wrote of legislators who "were supporters of President Anastasio Somoza in Nicaragua and saw a chance to trade Panama treaty votes for support for his faltering regime."* He did not write that they may have succeeded in some measure. Once it became apparent that the mediation plan was going to break up on the rocks of Somoza's obstinacy, the U.S. administration pulled back from its anti-Somoza posture and waited for history to take its course. It did not wish to risk its Panama policy.

The desperate effort to help Somoza by using the Panama issue continued to the very end. On June 21, the day the House voted on the implementing legislation, Rep. Charles Pashayan of California introduced an amendment for that purpose. It required no payments be made to Panama, under the treaty or outside it, if the president *or* Congress determined that "Panama is interfering in the internal affairs of any other state." It clearly demonstrated that Pashayan did not understand foreign policy or elementary psychology. Still, his incredible proposal was not laughed out of court as it would have been in earlier Congresses.

Congressman Murphy knew there had to be legislation to carry out the Panama Canal Treaty. When an amendment was a clear violation of that pact, he was usually ready to point that out and oppose it. In this case, helping out his beleaguered friend in Managua took precedence over making U.S. policy work. Though the Pashayan amendment was a flagrant violation of the treaty's letter, Murphy backed it and helped win House approval. The provision was later deleted at Senate insistence.[†]

What congressional friends of Somoza did—by urging him to hold out, by suggesting that Washington's position might be reversed, by constantly reaffirming their support for him—was to gradually weaken the noncommunist opposition in Nicaragua. They helped importantly to push the anti-Somoza uprising into the hands of the very leftists and communists they spent so much time attacking.

At the very end, even Somoza found their advice incredible. In early July, Idaho's Hansen and Georgia's Larry McDonald flew to Managua to urge Somoza to stand fast, telling him he had plenty of backers in Washington. A few days later, a skeptical Somoza had flown in panic to Miami (where he had prudently deposited some of his vast wealth). He left be-

---

*Jimmy Carter, *Keeping Faith*, p. 181.
† Readers will doubtless see distinct irony in the efforts of the U.S. House of Representatives to condemn Panama for lending some limited assistance to rebels in Nicaragua. Four years later, it was the United States that was supplying such assistance on a vastly larger scale. Some congressmen who were most scathing in their verbal assaults on Panama for "violating international law" became the most ardent supporters of intervention by the United States.

hind the sort of political chaos the United States had been trying to forestall for more than a year. It was the deluge that generally follows the collapse of absolutism.

By May 1979, the president and his staff and the Democratic leadership on the Hill knew unmistakably what they should have realized six months earlier—the Panama legislation was in deep trouble in the House. On May 17, the House voted to consider the implementing legislation by the slim margin of two votes, 200 to 198. That badly shook Speaker Thomas P. O'Neill and Majority Leader Jim Wright. They and other leaders decided to have no more votes on the Panama question until the administration took steps to shore up its position in Congress and with the public.

Most of the machinery used to rally support for the Panama treaties the year before was revitalized. Hamilton Jordan, the president's aide, whose greatest talent was mobilizing popular opinion, went to work to gain better understanding of the pending legislation. Officials from State and Defense used speaking engagements around the country to win backers for the cause. The program of White House briefings, which had been quite successful the previous year, was revived, with representatives rather than senators as the targets.

Whether in meetings at the White House or during question periods at lectures across the country, the president and other administration spokesmen ran into one question far more than any other. It was money—how much will the treaties cost? how much are we paying Panama to take our canal? and others in that vein.

Actually, the financial aspect of the Panama treaties was handled with great care in the negotiating process. From the outset, everyone on the U.S. side emphasized to their Panamanian counterparts that the one thing we could not agree to was any payments to Panama from the U.S. Treasury. As I once told my friend Gabriel Lewis, "We are going to turn the canal over to you in twenty years; but we can't pay you for the privilege." The treaties were drafted with that consideration very much in mind. The Panamanians did not like our approach and thought it was most unfair. But they understood it perfectly well.

The public affairs aspect of the financial question was bobbled badly after the treaties were drafted. In their zeal to underline the fact that U.S. taxpayers were not paying anything to Panama, one administration official after another overstated the case. Secretary of State Vance, for example, told a Senate committee that "the treaties require no new appropriations, nor do they add to the burden of the American taxpayer." Deputy Secretary Christopher and Ambassadors Bunker and Linowitz said the same in committee hearings and other public appearances. They presumed, correctly in my judgment, that their listeners were interested mainly in what the United

States might be paying Panama under the new arrangement. But they did misstate the facts. Obviously there would be some costs in the many adjustments required by the new treaties—in moving U.S. military forces from one part of the old Canal Zone to other parts of Panama, for example.

It was totally fallacious, however, for antitreaty spokesmen in the House and Senate to contend—as they did repeatedly—that the administration's original error was never corrected. In early February 1978, Secretaries Vance and Brown of State and Defense and Secretary of the Army Alexander sent a letter to all senators estimating that the cost of implementing the treaties would be approximately $350 million. That did not include the loss of interest to the Treasury, which would have raised the cost to roughly $750 million. Additionally, the Senate Armed Services Committee had estimated implementation costs at $1.23 billion. The Senate Budget Committee supplied a third estimate to the upper house—$712 to $720 million—before the end of February. All the estimates were available to all senators from six to nine weeks *before* they voted on the Panama Canal Treaty.

This was well known to members of the House, certainly to those who took an active part in the debate. But the antitreaty, anti-Panama, anti-administration activists—congressmen like Robert Bauman (Md.), Robert Dornan (Cal.), George Hansen (Id.), William Dannemeyer (Cal.), Ken Kramer (Col.), Steven Symms (Id.), and William Carney (N.Y.), all Republicans—gave the misleading impression they had never heard of those estimates of treaty costs. It was almost impossible to read more than four or five pages of the *Congressional Record* without encountering a statement from one or the other of them saying, in effect, "We were told this treaty wasn't going to cost the taxpayers a dime, and we were lied to." They knew better, but it was too tempting for political sloganeers to pass up. Fortunately, there was a small band of representatives who knew the facts and, to the discomfort of the extremists, insisted on putting them into the record. Outstanding among them was David Bowen, a Harvard and Oxford graduate who represented Mississippi's 2nd District. Though not an admirer of the Panama treaties, he insisted they had to be made to work—in the interests of the United States and of world commerce. He mastered treaty details probably better than any other representative and he fought tirelessly in subcommittee and committee and on the House floor to get implementing legislation that would carry out the basic intent of the Panama agreement. Others in the small but effective group who led the fight for a good bill were Representatives Les AuCoin (Ore.), David Bonior (Mich.), and Elliott Levitas (Ga.), all Democrats. They did considerably more to defend the basic principles of the treaty, and the bill that would make it live, than did the ostensible shepherd of the legislation, Congressman Murphy. Two others who performed yeomanly service were Clem Zablocki (Wis.) and Ed Derwinski (Ill.), chairman and a senior Republican, respectively, of the Foreign Affairs Committee. They intervened regularly to object when an amendment would egregiously violate the treaty's words or spirit.

By mid-June 1979, the Carter administration was on the horns of a painful dilemma. The president and those around him had been working hard to sway votes in the House and to alter perceptions in the public at large. The effort had been modestly successful, but it fell short of what White House strategists had hoped for. The other "horn" was the painful fact that time was running out for the implementing legislation. The treaty was going into effect on October 1, and many things had to be done before then, things that could only be accomplished with legislative sanction. Officials in both State and Defense departments were predicting dire consequences if management personnel were not selected and in place, if promised guarantees to the labor force were not in effect, and if the transfer of such functions as health care and education from the old Canal Zone government to the Department of Defense was not completed.

The decision was made to go forward, ready or not. Speaker O'Neill and his aides believed there was sufficient support to push the legislation through, but no one was taking any bets. Floor manager Murphy promised to do his best to get the bill passed without further damaging alterations or additions. But the fractious, often mean spirited, debate that had prevailed until then in committee and on the floor itself provided no solace to anyone who hoped for an early and constructive outcome.

What many in the House, executive departments, and White House hoped would be the final act began at midday on June 20. Almost immediately, Maryland's Bauman proposed and won approval for the secret session mentioned earlier. The purpose was to discuss allegations of Panamanian gunrunning in Nicaragua. The closed-door meeting, the first of its kind since 1830, lasted an hour and a half. The data aired was neither so new nor so surprising to cause a majority of representatives to turn against the implementing bill or even to delay its consideration. At that meeting, the House leadership for the first time entered the lists actively and pleaded with the members to act responsibly on implementation.

One representative notably unmoved by appeals for prompt action to carry out U.S. responsibilities under the treaty was Idaho's George Hansen. Always a loose cannon on the legislative deck, Hansen had a proclivity for involving himself in international problems that he did not understand, much to the embarrassment of the House and the executive branch. For example, when U.S. diplomats were held hostage in Iran, the irrepressible man from Pocatello flew off to Teheran to do his own negotiating. Among other things, he promised supporters of the Ayatollah Khomeini he would organize congressional hearings to look into alleged U.S. misdeeds under the Shah. The Iranians knew, of course, that their unexpected visitor was speaking with absolutely no authority from his own government. Naturally he got nowhere, only further muddying waters that were already badly roiled.

Hansen was emotionally opposed to the Panama treaties even as they were being negotiated. When the pacts were before the Senate for consideration, Hansen demonstrated his disapproval in a typically flamboyant way. He hired a huge flatbed truck, which was parked occasionally at the Capitol, at other times across the street from the State Department. Atop the truck's bed was a pile of bricks painted gold, or pieces of wood painted to look like bricks painted gold. A garish sign said the "gold" represented the $4 billion the Panama treaties were going to cost the U.S. taxpayer. He later upped his estimate of the cost to $26 billion.

The Idahoan's "bill" for treaty costs was a mishmash of fact and fancy, mostly the latter. He was, for example, charging as a cost to the United States the value of all property in the Canal Zone that would be returned to Panama. Hansen set the figure at $20 billion though the basis for that estimate was never explained. Hansen did not understand, as Teddy Roosevelt and almost every succeeding president did, that, while we had purchased title to some land in the Canal Zone, Panama remained the sovereign power. The property was being restored to its rightful owners who had let us use it for seventy-five years—and would continue to let us use much of it for the next twenty.

Hansen had written his own legislation to implement the Panama treaty. It provided that all costs of the new arrangement—real and imagined, including the fanciful cost of Canal Zone property—had to be borne by Panama. Hansen's approach was a flagrant violation of the treaty. Any thinking member of the House had to realize it would be rejected by Panama. Moreover it would have led to the closing of the Panama Canal. It was no surprise that Hansen would propose such an atrocity. What was shocking was that 180 fellow representatives agreed to act as co-sponsors. Even so, reason finally prevailed and adroit maneuvering by Representative Murphy led to adoption of his own bill and the shelving of Hansen's disastrous draft.

Final debate on H.R. 111 lasted almost five hours on June 21. Again, there were many attempts to alter the bill in ways that ran across the grain of the treaty. But floor manager Murphy had his troops under a tight rein and every effort to undo his handiwork was defeated, though several times by only narrow margins. At the close, Maryland's Bauman made one final effort to defy Murphy's strategy. He proposed sending the bill back to committee with instructions to include the Hansen amendment in its later report. The desperate gesture was rejected by the House 216 nays to 210 yeas. The Murphy bill was then approved 224 to 202, but the battle to implement the Panama Canal Treaty was far from over.

Once the House completed action, the Senate went to work. The Armed Services Committee held hearings the following week and on July 17 sent its approved bill to the full Senate. The legislation, based heavily on the draft President Carter had sent up in January, was considerably closer to what the administration wanted than the version adopted in the House. The Senate bill made the canal commission a government corporation. The Armed Services Committee also refused such House-favored elements as requiring transfers of property to win congressional approval and putting a military officer in charge of the canal in case of war. The Senate found these and other House amendments inconsistent with the Panama Canal Treaty.

Nine days after the committee gave its approval, implementing legislation passed the Senate by a vote of 64 to 30. In every important respect, it was the bill approved by Armed Services. The two implementing bills then went to a conference committee of the two houses so differences could be worked out. Anyone who thought that would be either quick or easy could not have been listening to discussions in the House over the previous several months.

In proposing or supporting extreme amendments to the Murphy bill, conservatives in the House were doing two things. One was to weaken the Panama Canal Treaty and make life as difficult for the Panamanians under that treaty as possible. The other was to produce an implementing measure so slanted that House conferees could "compromise" on certain points with the Senate while still coming up with a final product as close to their antitreaty views as possible. Opposition leader Bauman spoke quite openly of the tactic during the debate, for example, when he said, "My feeling is that [sic] let us go to the other body in conference with the toughest possible bill." The House further strengthened its conferees by approving 308 to 98 instructions to stand fast on such things as congressional approval for property transfers, making the Panama Canal Commission an appropriated funds agency, and severe limitations on payments to Panama.

Conferees from the Senate and House labored through August and well into September, trying to accommodate their differences. When their report was ready, it went to the two houses and the Senate approved it 60 to 35 on September 20. In the House that day, the story was quite different. As had happened often before, the discussion was less concerned with implementing legislation than with attacks on the Panama treaty and alarmist diatribes against communist plots to close the Caribbean to our shipping. It provided a splendid ego trip for Bauman, Hansen, and like-minded rightists in the House but it shed little light on the real business of the day, the conference committee report on H.R. 111.

The radical right was helped greatly by the announcement from the White House a few days earlier that a brigade of Soviet troops had been located in Cuba. President Carter and his advisers overreacted to that intelligence without carefully calculating what it meant and what they could do about it. "The status quo is unacceptable," said the president, without having a strategy to change the situation. In the end, he had to accept Moscow's explanation that its forces were in Cuba with no aggressive intent but only on a training mission. But on September 20, the news was fresh and the ultrarightists in the House were sounding the alarm.

"With Soviet combat troops in the Caribbean, do we dare give away the Panama Canal?" asked Congressman Hansen. Bauman waved the red flag a bit stronger with talk of "3,000 combat-ready Soviet troops only minutes away from the Canal Zone." Another Bauman ally, Floyd Spence of South Carolina, appealed further to the House's manliness, saying: "Torrijos has recently said that if we are not out by October 1, they will push us out. Well, I am here to tell you I want to see him push us out." (The Panamanian leader had said no such thing. He had said that he and his compatriots planned to enter the Canal Zone on October 1—as all Panamanians had dreamed of doing for seventy-five years.)

There was more in that same vein—that the Caribbean was becoming a Soviet lake and that we needed the toughest possible bill to keep little Panama in line. In the end, the House voted 203 to 192 to reject the conference report, thereby forcing the Senate into still another effort at compromise.

What was happening in the House of Representatives during those months, indeed during most of the late 1970s? It has perplexed many people, even members of that body. A peevish, quarrelsome atmosphere, once rare, had become the norm. The quality of debate, rarely as high as in the Senate, had deteriorated. There was less respect for truth and a depressing acceptance of exaggeration and distortion. There was even a readiness to wink at outright discourtesy which, in earlier times, would have been ruled unacceptable by a Sam Rayburn or a John McCormack. What had produced that strange brew?

Many specialists have commented on factors that influenced House actions and atmosphere—the effects of Watergate, for example, and the congressional role in Vietnam. Others have stressed House sensitivity over the apparent bypassing of its responsibility for disposing of federal property. Finally, no doubt the Panama treaties were unpopular with many Americans. A flood of mail pouring into congressional offices had made that point and had impacted on many legislators. But there was an additional element. Not mentioned in the Congress-and-foreign-policy literature I have seen, it was crucial in understanding what the House did on the Panama legislation and the manner of its doing. The unnoticed ingredient, without which the outcome would have been quite different, was the character, style, operating methods, and influence of one member of the House. He was Robert Bauman of Maryland.

Bauman went to the House of Representatives as a result of a special election in his Chesapeake Bay district in 1973. He was 36 years old and national chairman of the ultraconservative Young Americans for Freedom. As a fledgling lawyer, he had served as a Republican staffer in the House for four years and thus knew the Hill well even before his election. He quickly gained a reputation for extreme conservatism and for his mastery of parliamentary procedure. Bright, arrogant, snide, aloof, and dour, he stirred no great liking among his colleagues. He did win a degree of respect, albeit tinged with uneasiness and fear.

Reading the record of House deliberations on the Panama legislation, I had the nagging feeling that I had heard or read debates remarkably close to these in style though different in content. Then I remembered. It was the early 1950s and I was reading a speech by a senator from Wisconsin named Joe McCarthy. Though quite different physically—McCarthy was tall, big boned, heavy handed, crude in manner while Bauman was short, chubby, fast of tongue, slow of foot—it was amazing how similar the two were as political operatives. Bauman never achieved the influence or power McCarthy had, but by 1979 he was well on his way to that kind of notoriety.

McCarthy's principal crusade was against communists, real or imagined, in government. Bauman's *bête noire* was big government, our own and all others. He was especially antagonistic toward communist, socialist, or liberal governments, or those he presumed to be in those categories. One of the towering incongruities of the Panama episode was that the Canal Zone government, which Bauman coddled and defended like a mother hen, was the most perfect example of socialism in the Western Hemisphere. He never understood that.

One of Joe McCarthy's favorite targets was the State Department. Bauman followed his ideological mentor in that, as in so much else. When another congressman described some part of the Panama treaty as sensible or helpful to the United States, Bauman was likely to make some slighting reference to the other member "and your friends in the State Department." When a senior member of the Foreign Affairs Committee defended certain treaty provisions, Bauman snidely suggested he be given "the Cy Vance award," implying he was a dupe of the secretary of state.

In sports, a "cheap shot" is a blow delivered when an opponent is not looking or when he cannot retaliate. Bauman, like McCarthy before him, was a master of the political cheap shot. He delivered them freely, not just at the State Department but at any individual or group on his rather extensive hate list. Surprisingly, he even used his bullying tactics against fellow members of the House in violation of the politeness norms that usually prevail in that body. Though he had been in the House for only six years, the victims of his scornful humor included senior House members, some committee chairmen.

It is amazing to read the House debates during that period and to encounter the deferential attitude accorded Bauman, even by some who were the butt of his jokes and the targets of his criticism. Several things help explain it. First, members of the House were only about fourteen months away from their next election when the Panama bill debate reached its climax. The political wave of new right sentiment was growing and did not reach its climax for another year. Bauman, a leading light in the American Conservative Union and in the entire conservative movement, had an important voice in selecting vulnerable Democratic targets and advising on the allocation of funds by various political action groups. In looking at Bauman, members of the House saw a man who could make their political life more difficult or considerably easier. Some sought his support; others shied from his enmity. Without him and his energetic leadership of the opposition, members of the House told me, the Panama implementation bill would have passed in June not September and the transition on the canal would have been vastly smoother and more efficient.

The members of the new conference committee went back to work and in four days settled on what would be their final report. In truth, it changed very little. It adopted the House demand that three members of the board of directors of the new Panama Canal Commission be private citizens with experience in shipping, port operations, and labor matters, respectively. The Senate conferees refused to require the president to turn management of the canal over to a military officer in case of war. They agreed the president *could* take that step if he wished to. The report also took a stand against retroactive taxation by Panama of U.S. businesses or individuals though the Panama treaty already prohibited such taxation.

On September 25, a bored Senate approved the conference report by a 63-to-32 vote. The next day, Congressman Murphy introduced the same proposal in the House. He was acutely aware that five days later the Panama treaties would be in operation. A majority of his colleagues appeared to share his concern. But many members of the House, led by Bauman and Hansen, were ready to express their opposition to the new pacts by voting against implementing them.

Murphy defined the critical moment in stark terms: "A time bomb is ticking away and the hour is short. We have a duty and an obligation to perform—we must honor the sacred word of our country. The treaty is the law of the land and, whether we like it or not, it goes into effect on October 1.

"On October 1," he continued, "there will be no payroll, no schools, no hospitals and, in short, no legal means of continuing the operation of the canal unless this vital legislation has been passed."

Aware of how narrow the margin was between victory and defeat, and responding to a plea for help from the president, the Democratic leadership in the House finally stirred itself. Majority Leader Jim Wright of Texas went to the microphone to urge his fellow legislators to have the courage to vote for what they knew was right, not what public opinion seemed to favor. He said he had talked with twenty or thirty representatives that week and they had told him: "Yes, Jim, I understand that. I want the bill to pass. I know it is in the best interest of the United States. But my constituents misunderstand it, and I can't vote for it."

Wright said such men were selling America short and selling their constituents short. He had more confidence in representative democracy. "I believe we will demonstrate that its members still possess the force of character not to cringe in fear when they know that hostile opinion is mistaken and based on misinformation," he said, "but rather to use their honest judgment and to follow their best informed opinion and to do what is right."

He was followed at the microphone by "Tip" O'Neill. The silver-haired Speaker from Massachusetts used his potent voice to stir colleagues who were still wavering. After recalling some of the history of U.S. acquisition of rights in Panama—and of economic power in the Caribbean area in general—the Speaker urged support for the implementing bill. "We will have kept our commitments," he said, "and I think we are going to witness a friendlier Western Hemisphere." He concluded: "I think an aye vote is the right vote."

The final count was 232 votes in support of the committee report and 188 against it. It was astounding that 188 members of the House of Representatives could have voted, in effect, to turn over the Panama Canal to Panama on October 1 or to use military force to prevent that outcome. That was what they said with their votes, though many later denied it was their intention. Privately, they maintained they were just voting against the Panama treaties as an emotional gesture. They claimed that if the decision had been close they would have voted otherwise. Even Congressman Bauman told one U.S. official that he favored having the bill pass "because I didn't want to have any blood on my hands."

The next day, September 27, 1979, President Carter signed the implementing legislation into law. He accompanied it with a carefully crafted statement giving his view that nothing in the bill would compel him or any later president to take any action that was inconsistent with "the terms and the intent of the treaties." With the president's signature affixed, the United

States was at long last ready to turn the blueprint of those treaties into reality.

October 1, 1979, marked the end of an era in U.S. history that was defined at each end by the dream of a president. Teddy Roosevelt's vision was of a canal connecting the Atlantic and the Pacific. Jimmy Carter's was of a foreign policy in which justice superseded selfishness. When the Panama Canal opened in 1914, the Rooseveltian dream became reality. It is always hard to judge whether ideals have been achieved. But at least President Carter believed he had taken a huge step toward his goal when he signed the Panama Canal Act of 1979.

The first day of October was an end and a beginning for Panama as well. For seventy-six years, the Panamanians had lived with a foreign government occupying and ruling a huge slice of their territory in the very heart of their country. Most political speeches and much of the poetry during that time had expressed one facet or another of the national dream—that the day would come when every inch of Panama's soil would once again be Panamanian, that they would truly be masters in their own house, and that the flag of the Republic would fly proudly over every home and farm and factory from Costa Rica to Colombia.

Vice President Mondale led a large delegation of Americans to the isthmus for the massive celebration. Included were members of Congress, other government officials, and private citizens who had close connections with either Panama or the treaties. Presidents of the original Contadora group—Colombia, Costa Rica, Mexico, and Venezuela—attended with their national delegations. There were outdoor meetings and indoor gatherings, receptions and dinners and postdinner parties. It reminded most of us of the festival atmosphere that marked the visit of President Carter to Panama the year before.

Of all the events during the historic celebration, one lives longest in my memory and I am sure meant the most to the Panamanians who took part. It was the sunrise march up Ancon Hill. President Royo led the way with members of his cabinet, colonels from the National Guard, other government officials, and visitors from abroad. Following along behind were several thousand ordinary citizens on a march they would tell their grandchildren about. At the top of the hill, the highest point in Panama City, a huge flag was unfurled. Specially made for the occasion, it was at least fifty feet long and thirty feet wide. When it was raised on the massive flagstaff, the largest banner in the country could be seen from every building (almost every streetcorner) in the capital city. As of that moment, as Royo said for all to hear, "a state within a state no longer exists."

The one person strangely absent from the walk to the top of Ancon was the man everyone expected to see leading the parade: Omar Torrijos. For years, he had talked about "walking into the Zone" once Panama was whole again. Just a few weeks earlier, he had declared his intention to lead his people into the Zone whether the implementing legislation was approved by the U.S. Congress or not. I asked him later why he had not done the expected thing. He said he had decided that it was a wonderful chance to put the civilian government in the limelight. He had told many people he intended to withdraw gradually from the center of the political stage, and October 1 offered a perfect opportunity to show he meant what he had said. "Besides," he said with a laugh, "I knew the Zonians were upset enough that day. I didn't want to make it even harder for them."

Fate, in the form of voter disapproval, dealt unkindly with some senators who favored the new Panama treaties. In 1978, seven who had voted for the new pacts went down to defeat at the polls. In 1980, the citizens' disapproval was even stronger. Eleven senators who backed the treaties lost their bids for reelection, along with the president, who had made a new deal for Panama a centerpiece of his foreign policy.

Another kind of fate dealt even more severely with some leading enemies of the treaties in the House of Representatives. I mention it as a footnote, not because it sheds new light on the Panama saga. But it is part of the story that a reporter or historian cannot ignore. Certainly students in the future will recount the facts and probably speculate at length on their meaning.

Robert Bauman of Maryland, leader of the Republican opposition to the Panama implementing legislation in the House, had a promising future in politics. In 1979, many political columnists were persuaded he would be a candidate the next year for Senator Mathias' seat in the upper house. If not in 1980, then surely in 1982 against Paul Sarbanes. In early October 1980, Bauman was arrested and charged with soliciting sex from a teenage boy in Georgetown. He fought back, blaming his indiscretion on his heavy drinking. It was not enough and he lost to Democrat Roy Dyson in November. Almost three years later, Bauman, since divorced, admitted that he was and had been gay all along.

Congressman John Murphy was caught in the FBI's Abscam scandal. He was indicted before the 1980 election, lost the election, and was then convicted. He now is serving time in a federal prison.

Representative George Hansen had admitted in 1975 that he was guilty of filing late and false campaign expense reports. He was sentenced to two years in jail but the sentence was later suspended and he paid a fine of $2,000. The federal judge said Hansen was not "evil," merely "stupid." In 1983, Hansen was indicted by a federal grand jury on several counts of submitting untruthful statements of financial disclosure. If convicted, he could be sentenced to five years' imprisonment on each of the counts.

Another bitter critic of the Panama implementing bill was Florida's Richard Kelly. Like Murphy, he was caught in the Abscam net. He appeared on national television happily cramming $50,000 in bribe money into his pocket. He too is serving time in a federal prison.

Less prominent than his brother Philip, Daniel Crane of Illinois was no less active in attacking the Panama treaties and in opposing the bill to implement treaty provisions. In 1983, he was censured by the Ethics Committee for carrying on a sexual affair with an underage female page on the House staff. The committee censured another congressman at the opposite end of the political spectrum from Crane. Gerry Studds of Massachusetts was cited for an affair some years previous with a male page. Unlike the others, Studds had supported the passage of workable implementing legislation.

Charles Wilson of Texas, a close friend of Murphy and an ardent admirer of Nicaragua's Somoza, was one of the three House members subjected to lengthy investigation for alleged cocaine use on Capitol Hill. The Justice Department announced in mid-1983 that it had insufficient evidence to prosecute the three men. The House Ethics Committee investigation of the same charges was continuing, however.

The most tragic fate befell archconservative Larry McDonald of Georgia, head of the John Birch Society. He was a passenger on the ill-fated Korean Air Lines Flight 007 that was shot out of the sky by a Soviet fighter plane over the Sea of Japan on September 1, 1983.

From October 1 on, the Panama Canal was under new management. The old Panama Canal Company was no more; the Panama Canal Commission was the new operator. The United States, Panama, and the entire world of shipping were luckier than they knew, certainly more fortunate than they could reasonably expect. In the normal course of events, the president might have named a highly political, technically incompetent person as administrator of the canal. On the Panamanian side, Torrijos could have done the same, picking perhaps one of his personal cronies as deputy administrator. That did not happen, mainly because the leaders on both sides wanted the new arrangement to work. Both were wise enough to know that bungled operation of the waterway would damage their reputations in history.

President Carter's choice was Lt. Gen. Denis P. McAuliffe, one of the ablest and brightest men in the top levels of the U.S. Army. Phil had been commander in chief of the Southern Command in Panama since 1975 and knew the scene, the problems, and most of the main players. A graduate of West Point with a master's degree in electrical engineering, he had no problem understanding the technical details of canal operation. Service in both Europe and Asia had given him an excellent understanding of political realities and requirements. Finally, as a high-ranking soldier of un-blemished reputation, McAuliffe commanded respect from such members of Congress as Bauman, Hansen, and Murphy who would have made life miserable for a civilian, especially a political appointee.

Torrijos' nominee for the number-two spot in the canal management was as much a stroke of genius as Carter's choice had been. Fernando Manfredo was a businessman with strong links to the private sector. He had served Panama with distinction as minister of commerce for half a dozen years. The reader will recall that he was one of Panama's chief nego-tiators during the futile treaty talks of 1971–72 and an adviser to the nego-tiating team after 1974. That experience gave him not only a detailed un-derstanding of canal operations but also a deep awareness of political sensitivities among Americans, especially those who lived in the Canal Zone and worked on the canal.

McAuliffe and Manfredo worked together like brothers and partners. It was almost as though they had trained together for years to undertake the many tasks they faced in their new assignments. Their strengths comple-mented each other's neatly. McAuliffe's experience as a commander of var-ied units, his engineering background, his sensitivity to the workings of U.S. politics—these and more fitted him admirably for his task (in the words of the treaty): "to manage, operate, maintain, improve, protect and defend the Canal."

Manfredo brought to the assignment experience in running an enter-prise, a deep knowledge of both government and business, sensitivity to labor's rights, thorough knowledge of the Panamanian government's rules and practices, and a warm, outgoing personality. He was one of the hard-est working members of the Panamanian government during the years I dealt with it. Manfredo's understanding of the United States plus his excel-lent English helped greatly in establishing good working relations with the American hierarchy in the canal organization.

The technical skills and personalities of McAuliffe and Manfredo made the transition to the new system of management smooth and surprisingly effective. It could have been a disaster, of course, and many people in both countries were freely predicting it would be. During the debate in the Sen-ate many antitreaty spokesmen gloomily forecast that the proposed part-nership with Panama would create chaos. Senator Dole, for example, pre-dicted that 70 percent of the canal work force would walk out if the new treaty was approved. In fact, during the first year of operation under the new pact, only 275 workers quit and another 216 opted for the early retire-ment that the treaty provided. That was about 4 percent of the canal com-pany and Zone government work force in October 1979, and 16 percent of the U.S. workers. It was not very different from the normal turnover in the labor force during the previous ten years.

During that first year of operation under new management, the canal not only continued to be operated smoothly but it also moved record tonnage—171 million long tons of cargo—between the oceans. Nearly fourteen thousand ships transited the waterway and their average size was the largest in the sixty-seven years of canal operations. Another record was also set: $303 million in tolls were paid by canal users. In the last month of the transition period, March 1982, an average of forty-two ships passed through the canal every day and that was the highest monthly average in ten years.

In addition to keeping the canal operating as a vital link in world commerce, McAuliffe and Manfredo and their management team launched an ambitious program of training to improve the skills of the work force. A key reason for that program was the Panama Canal Treaty's mandate that "the Republic of Panama shall participate increasingly in the management and protection and defense of the Canal." The commission has been spending more than $5 million a year on its training program for employees. Besides training, the new managers have promoted qualified Panamanians to positions of higher responsibility than ever before. As of this writing, Panamanians head the commission's electrical division, dredging division, canal improvements division, and the office of public affairs. Panamanians now fill more than 70 percent of the skilled jobs on the canal and the number is growing steadily. Of every six jobs that become available, five are filled by Panamanians. It appears that the doom sayers and cynics who once predicted that "the Panamanians will never be able to run the canal" are in for a rude awakening.

If things were moving relatively smoothly on the canal, the same could not be said of Panama itself. President Royo was a bright lawyer and had been an able negotiator during the treaty talks. He was less than a stunning success as his country's chief of government. Omar Torrijos had made the same mistake with him that he had with a few other choices for important jobs; that is, he gave heavy responsibilities before the man was ready. In the case of Royo, it was unreasonable to expect that a 38-year-old lawyer with neither political nor business experience could suddenly become an effective national executive. The reality was quickly evident to the business community in Panama and, not long after, to the leadership of the National Guard. For some time, Torrijos refused to acknowledge that reality because it represented his own misjudgment.

Royo's failure to provide strong and imaginative leadership was only one of Panama's problems, one more burden for Torrijos to bear. Another concern that was putting premature touches of gray in the general's dark hair was the failure of Panama's economy to revive. Torrijos had assumed for years that, once new pacts were drawn up with the United States, his small country's economic woes would be over. With the main source of tension removed, he pictured a flood of foreign investors trampling over each other to invest in new factories and in expanding old businesses. It was an unrealistic dream, of course.

Someone once said, "Nothing is more nervous than a million dollars." There was good reason for the uneasiness of investors in 1980 and 1981. The United States and most other industrial countries were sliding into recession. Unemployment was growing. Interest rates were high and many banks were in trouble, including some of the largest banks in the world whose massive loans to Mexico, Brazil, Venezuela, Poland, and other debtors were not being repaid. In that climate, hopes of attracting huge investments were a pipe dream.

Omar Torrijos had another nagging worry on the international front. In 1978–79, he had worked closely with his Venezuelan and Costa Rican neighbors to supply arms and moral support to the anti-Somoza rebels in Nicaragua. One reason for that backing was Torrijos' conviction that Somoza was an antidemocratic tyrant who had used power to enrich himself, not to help his people. Another thing that impressed the Panamanian leader was the personality of Commander Zero, Eden Pastora, a top commander in the Sandinista movement. In their many long talks, Torrijos came to believe that Pastora and he were brothers, that they looked at the world through similar eyes, and that they wanted the same thing—a better life for their people, honest government, and freedom.

By 1981, Torrijos had not changed his mind about Pastora, who, by all accounts, had remained honest and idealistic. As one promise after another made by the Sandinista leaders in Managua was broken, Pastora's disillusion with his fellow revolutionaries grew, finally developing into an open break. Watching developments in Nicaragua with first surprise and then anger, Torrijos experienced disappointment as great as Pastora's. The general told me and several of his friends that he thought his blind support for the Sandinistas had been his most serious foreign policy mistake. He did not regret the end of the Somoza dictatorship. But he believed that he and others should have been more insistent that the newly installed Nicaraguan junta live up to its solemn promises to hold free elections, spend money for education and health rather than on a huge military machine, and guarantee basic human rights. In his blacker moods, Torrijos wondered if his involvement in Nicaragua had not produced more harm than good.

All those pressures, and others we shall probably never know about, pushed Omar Torrijos into periods of deep gloom in 1981. At the height of the Senate debate, the general had complained often of "living like a hermit" and "getting away so people won't ask me so many questions." But he was a social butterfly in 1978 compared to his routine three years later. He was spending an increasing amount of time in the countryside with only a few close friends, sometimes only members of his personal staff. He spent countless weekends at Coclecito, the tiny village in the hills of remote Coclé province. Sometimes he went to Contadora island where he could relax with friends like Gabriel and Nita Lewis. Occasionally, he would fly off to the most distant parts of his small country—to Bocas del Toro or Almirante, to Puerto Armuelles on the Pacific coast, or to villages on the Azuero peninsula or his old hometown of Santiago. Sometimes even the general staff of the National Guard did not know where he had gone.

Friends reported him to be gloomier than they had ever seen him, at times so deep in thought he was hard to arouse. Always a heavy drinker, Torrijos was imbibing more than ever. His frequent trips and the bottle helped him fend off whatever devils were pursuing him during that unhappy time.

Around the end of June or early July, a change came over the troubled general. He became more open and unusually kind, not a trait usually attributed to him. He spoke to friends with great affection about his wife, Raquel, regretful of the anguish he had caused her over many years. He gave the sergeant who kept his clothes clean, his shoes polished, and his bar well stocked money to buy a small farm, something the man had dreamed of for years. At least a dozen people who talked with Omar during those weeks said it was as though he were saying good-bye.

On Friday, July 31, 1981, the general had a toothache. He went to a favorite dentist in Penonomé, the provincial capital of Coclé. Relieved of the discomfort, he decided to fly to Coclecito for the weekend. When he got to the airport, it was raining and he insisted that his daughter, who had been going to travel with him, remain behind in Penonomé. The plane took off with seven persons aboard—the pilot and co-pilot, a crewman, two bodyguards, the dentist, and the general.

By the time the plane reached Coclecito, the rain was falling in sheets, a typical tropical downpour. They went down to try for a landing but, though it was a little after noon, the visibility was nearly zero. A more experienced pilot would probably have told the general it was hopeless to try to land in that weather and insisted they go to an airport that was open. Instead, the young airman went down for another try, but again it was futile. He pulled up to clear the mountains that surrounded the valley, but not fast enough, not high enough.

A tall tree sheared off one wing and the plane nosed into the side of the mountain only fifteen feet from the top. The fuel tank exploded turning the smashed aircraft into a funeral pyre. All aboard died instantly.

That afternoon, National Guard headquarters tried to reach the general to make some routine reports. They learned he had not landed at Coclecito as expected. They then called other airports where he might have put down. No luck. Late in the afternoon, a farmer walked into a rural outpost of the Guard. He had tramped all the way from his remote farm to report that he had heard a plane overhead about 12:30 P.M. and then an explosion. He could not tell exactly where it was, just somewhere in the hills.

The Guard sent out search parties along the country roads and into the hills. But it was dark by then and they found nothing. A helicopter search the next morning located the wreckage but reported there was no sign of survivors. No landing was possible at the immediate site but a military rescue team went overland, climbing the hill to the scene. They removed the charred bodies. At 1 P.M. that afternoon, a shocked nation learned by radio and television that Omar Torrijos Herrera was dead. Within minutes, the sad tidings had traveled around the world.

It will take time, perhaps another generation, for the real story of Omar Torrijos to be written. Most of what has been recorded to date has been like a shadow—very flat and out of proportion. What has been put down about the man has come from those who loved him too much, or hated him too deeply. Time will remedy that and a more balanced, fair appraisal will come forth.

It is too much to expect that those who followed him, who served him, who gave a large piece of their lives to his cause would readily admit that he made major mistakes and abused his powers. Similarly, it is almost impossible for those who suffered at his hands to acknowledge that he probably did more for Panama than any chief executive in the nation's history. Like most dynamic men of politics, Torrijos was either saint or devil to those who encountered him at close range.

The decision by Torrijos and his fellow officers in the National Guard to interfere in the political process in 1968 was based in large part on their need to survive. If they had not acted, Omar would have gone off to El Salvador as military attaché and then been separated from the Guard. He could easily have ended up teaching school or running a cantina in Santiago. The same fate awaited those who acted with him. But they did act, and the pattern of Panamanian politics was changed forever.

Torrijos and Lakas and the others who manned the key posts in government beginning at the end of 1968 shaped a regime that was unique in Panamanian history. They insisted their administration do what previous governments had only talked about. They put more money into education, especially into rural education and vocational training, than had any previous government. They did more in a few years to raise the level of health care in both cities and rural areas than had ever been done. They built roads and made central marketing possible for many Panamanian farmers for the first time. They wrote a liberal banking law and laid the groundwork for establishment of the biggest banking center in Latin America. Future historians will delineate the accomplishments and the failures in detail, I have no doubt.

Omar Torrijos' second and probably greatest achievement was the two new treaties with the United States governing the future of the Panama Canal and providing the guidelines for future relations between the two countries. Treaties had been worked out in 1967, to be sure, but the Panamanian government at that time had neither the strength nor the will to fight for their approval. Only Torrijos' determination and full backing made the treaties of 1977 possible.

Omar's final legacy was his dream of Panama's future. Of all institutions, only the National Guard commanded his total loyalty and dedication. But his affection for the country and its people was even deeper, especially for the poor, for the farmers, for the lower third of humanity that always seems to be working harder than anyone else and getting less for it. Much as he loved the National Guard, he was convinced in his final years that it should get out of politics and return to its proper role in society.

What was that proper role? He touched on it in several of our talks and he spoke at even greater length to close Panamanian friends. Torrijos believed the appropriate place for the military was in the barracks if (it should be emphasized *if*) the civilian rulers were doing their job correctly. He rather denigrated military rule, whether of the left or of the right, whether in Cuba or in Nicaragua, in Peru or in Paraguay. Even his own use of military power to carry out governmental action provided no source of pride. He rather thought it was too bad that it was necessary.

Torrijos wanted the National Guard to be the instrument for protecting the homeland, especially for defending the canal. But he was utterly convinced that it should be, as well, a mechanism for helping the Panamanian people, particularly those in remote areas, through civic action—building bridges, repairing roads, putting up schools and health centers. Its third function, as he saw it, was watching the political process from a distance and making sure that the civilian politicos did what the law required and the people expected. He always left the door open for involvement of the military forces if the kind of contract he assumed existed between the people and the government was violated.

It is problematical whether that part of the Torrijos dream will survive and prosper. No one understood his hopes better than his colleagues in the National Guard, yet barely seven months after his death, the members of the joint staff joined together to force the removal of Col. Florencio Flores, a good and decent man who was the legitimate successor as Guard commander. Flores' retirement date was not far off and his fellow officers could have waited for his graceful departure. But personal ambition proved stronger than institutional loyalty, something Torrijos would have deplored.

That was in March 1982. Less than five months later, one day before the anniversary of Torrijos' death, the general staff asked for and received President Royo's resignation. The reason given for Royo's abrupt departure was poor health, a debilitating throat infection. More to the point was his failure to develop good working relations with the Guard, plus his involvement in a huge scandal in the social security system, a disgraceful affair in which millions of dollars were misdirected into private hands from public funds. Royo went off to the United States for medical treatment, then on to Spain where he served as Panama's ambassador. He was succeeded by the vice-president, Ricardo de la Espriella, who had served long and ably as the chief executive of Panama's National Bank.

The man who followed Flores as commandant of the National Guard was Gen. Rubén Darío Paredes. He was the only officer who had served both at the top level of the Guard and as a minister of the government (in agriculture). His experience in the cabinet post gave him a taste for politics as well as useful exposure to the workings of government. Encouraged by friends and several old-line politicians, Paredes retired from his military post in early August 1983 to run for president. In less than a month, convinced he could not win and fed up with growing intrigue, he repented of his decision and withdrew from the race. His chief rival, Arnulfo Arias, back in Panama from exile, still lusting for political power, and determined to oppose any military candidate, also indicated he might withdraw. That left the political scene in a state of confusion as the final lines of this chronicle are written.

The Panama odyssey is near its end. We have traveled the high road of policy and politics to the Ithaca of our journey, the treaties and the formation of a new partnership. During the trip, we have traversed not a few low roads as well, segments where mistakes were evident and human failings and foibles all too apparent.

We have had the pleasure of seeing a few political leaders at their best: Jimmy Carter making the righting of an old wrong the keystone of his foreign policy; Omar Torrijos balancing left and right in a masterful juggling act that Machiavelli would have admired. And, too, we have seen their worst: Carter using an inexperienced staff instead of seasoned congressional professionals in his biggest political battle; Omar sullying the moment of his greatest triumph with shallow bravado and empty threats.

At every stage from 1964 until the treaties went into effect in 1979, there were people in both countries who performed with skill, acted without selfishness, and completed one essential job after another. Their reward is in the fond memory of those who know what they did. It is also in the dents in their armor inflicted by unworthy foes and outrageous fortune.

During this long journey, long in time and in events, we have seen some of the less attractive public characters of our time—the arrogant and the petty, the venal and the sycophantic, those for whom personal advantage weighed more than national good. That is not to say that the Panama Canal Treaties could not have been, or were not, opposed by honorable men on sound political, historical, economic, or sociological grounds. They could have been, and they were.

Nonetheless, it is a sad fact that so little of the opposition was thoughtful, intelligent, perceptive, sensitive, or openminded. To listen to Jesse Helms, Strom Thurmond, or Bob Bauman, the choice facing the U.S. Congress was between the wondrous splendors of perpetual U.S. domination in Panama or the satanic alternative of friendship and cooperation with a small country. Any change was seen by them and those who followed them as a step into the fiery furnace.

Enough now of reliving the past and toting up the pluses and minuses. The reader can make his or her own good judgment. And history, and this historian, will be content with that. But before closing, I must ask the central question that faces us all at the end of any reliving of history. What have we learned? If mistakes were made, how do we avoid them the next time around?

The first and most obvious lesson I discern is that we can never know enough about any serious problem our country faces. It was appalling to me throughout the Panama treaty debate that emotions were so high and the level of information so low. Of the hundreds of letters I received during those years, only a few came from people who understood what the proposed treaties were all about. The same was true of the many communications to members of Congress. Most of the writers would have had great difficulty locating the Panama Canal on a map let alone describing even one of the central issues in the treaty debate.

We cannot continue to enjoy the blessings of liberty unless we come to understand a great deal more than we usually do about the top issues that face us. We have to read more, think more, know more, and to that end we have to begin putting pressure on our newspapers, radio stations, and television outlets to give us more of the information we need. During the Panama treaties debate, what people needed was not ill-informed editorials, with which we were inundated in all but a few cities. What was in short supply was basic information—about history, about Panama, and about the treaties.

Is that likely to change? I see few indications that point in that direction. The advent of all-news television and the programming on public television are hopeful signs. But most of us want to be entertained, not educated. A society that pays its teachers less than its garbage collectors cannot be too serious about being informed, or perhaps even about surviving.

It became clear during the Panama debates that the American people needed desperately to know more about what was happening in Congress. We pay little or no attention to daily developments in our principal legislative bodies. We elect our representatives and senators and then, for the most part, we forget about them for two or six years—unless they do something dramatic or get into serious trouble. Why do our local newspapers not give us at least a weekly summary of what our congressmen and senators are doing and how they are voting? Why can't local television stations tell us what is happening in Congress in at least half the detail they offer about a big fire or a barroom murder? The simple answer is that they think we are more interested in fires and murders—and no one has told them any different.

The final lesson is perhaps the most important. That is that the Congress is going to have to do something about the Congress. Clearly it is getting out of hand. Not only is it becoming difficult to get coherent action from the Congress but it is also sometimes toilsome to get any action at all. There are problems in both chambers, but the real crisis is in the House of Representatives. There procedures have become chaotic and discipline has been cast aside.

It may be that the old system of seniority and party discipline was abused at times by hard-headed and prideful congressional veterans. But at least there was a modicum of order, and serious business was handled in a serious manner. Today, no one seems to be in charge. The experience of the Speaker and the accumulated knowledge of veteran committee chairmen can be enlisted only in extremis. The House is composed of 435 individual fiefdoms. Every member seems to be chairman of his or her own small subcommittee, and the degree of refinement and specialization has become absurd. The members strike one as being a collection of loose cannons rolling unlashed across the deck seeking something to crash into at the earliest opportunity.

Nor are the members of Congress content to confine their lack of discipline and proclivity for loose talk to their home pastures. Throughout the year, especially during recesses, one can encounter a wandering representative in almost every obscure capital in the world—more often, of course, in Paris, London, or Rome. Under cover of "congressional investigations," they force themselves on the officials of host governments demanding this or that action, explanation, justification. They frequently end by thoroughly confusing the folks with whom they deal and setting back the foreign policy of the United States by several degrees, often more. When you have 435 secretaries of state you are assured of having a chaotic foreign policy.

Members of the Congress need to remind themselves, or be reminded by their constituents and the press, that the constitution assigns responsibility for determining and carrying out foreign policy to the president. It gives the Senate a role in approving treaties and giving its consent to the appointments of ambassadors and other top-level officials. And both houses have the power of control over the purse strings. But that is a far cry from what now prevails.

Politicians are drawn by the magnet of television as by no other attraction. It is a successful day, indeed, when the congressman's face is seen on the evening news, and doubly successful when his words are carried as well. So it is that the legislators follow the news like children trailing the Pied Piper. Is today's crisis in Lebanon? Expect to see a dozen of the people's representatives on the spot watching the incoming shells and providing the Marines, who are there to do a job, with a royal pain. Or is the problem in Central America? Immediately we see eager congressmen grilling some hapless president in Honduras or El Salvador. And if no high-level official is available, then a military commander or a mayor will have to do.

It provides marvelous salve for the politicians' egos. And it supplies the raw material for dozens of speeches on the floor of the House or to private groups for a fee. It also gets the vote seeker's face and name before the public, which is the real name of the game. But that it contributes anything to the taxpayer in the form of better legislation or wiser policy judgment is highly questionable. I have watched the process of congressional travel for forty years, and I can count on one hand the cases where there was a clear and obvious advantage to the legislative process and to the pursuit of policy. Moreover, at least in my possibly jaundiced eyes, things are getting worse, not better, with the arrival on our political scene of wild-eyed extremists and single-issue politicians for whom any cause but their own is unimportant.

I am reminded of the comment made by Arthur Larson, a wise observer who was director of the U.S. Information Agency under President Eisenhower. Looking at the multivoiced confusion that we call politics, Larson said: "It must be very comfortable to be an extremist. You don't have to think—just shout."

The American people are fortunate that the Panama Canal Treaties were negotiated and approved before the current babble took over in the halls of Congress. Today those pacts, which were carefully crafted to serve a major national purpose, would not be approved. And we would now have on our hands a desperate situation alongside which our current difficulties in Central America and the Middle East would seem like a Sunday picnic. I believe most Americans have no idea how close we came to disaster. Those who have traveled on the Panama odyssey to this final anchorage will know what we gained—and what we prevented. And that was the reason for this long journey.

A smiling General Omar Torrijos waves to admirers on arrival at a provincial town. The Panamanian leader spent more time in the countryside with his people than had any previous head of government in the isthmus—probably more than any other figure in Latin American politics. (Photo by Rogelio Achurra)

Rioting erupted along the Canal Zone–Panama border on January 9, 1964. The next morning, President Lyndon Johnson met in the Roosevelt Room with his principal foreign policy advisers to plan the U.S. response. Standing facing the president is National Security Adviser McGeorge Bundy. Flanking the president, *left to right*: Under Secretary of State George Ball, Secretary of State Dean Rusk, the president, Secretary of Defense Robert McNamara, and Secretary of the Army Cyrus Vance. Within hours, Vance and other officials were flying to Panama. (White House photo by Okamoto)

President Johnson met in the Oval Office with his Panama negotiator, Ambassador Robert Anderson, on June 23, 1966. The former treasury secretary reported on progress made in working out a package of three treaties—one on canal operations, another on defense arrangements, and a third on the possible construction of a new waterway. At this point, the president and Anderson were both hoping for an early conclusion to the treaty talks, but it was not to be. (White House photo by Okamoto)

Ambassador Ellsworth Bunker arrived in Panama on September 7, 1975, to launch an important round in the revived Panama treaty talks. He was met at Tocumen airport by the Panamanian negotiating team, then flew to Contadora Island. In the airport's lounge, *left to right*: Deputy Foreign Minister Carlos Ozores, Foreign Minister Tony Tack, Ambassador Bunker, deputy U.S. negotiator S. Morey Bell, Panama's Ambassador to Washington Nicolás González-Revilla, and U.S. Ambassador William J. Jorden. (USIS photo)

The new U.S. negotiating team—Ambassadors Ellsworth Bunker and Sol Linowitz—arrived in Panama on February 14, 1977, to undertake the first round of canal treaty talks under the Carter Administration. On the tarmac at Tocumen airport, *left to right*: Deputy Foreign Minister Carlos Ozores, U.S. Ambassador William J. Jorden, Ambassador Bunker, Ambassador Linowitz, Foreign Minister Nicolás González-Revilla, and deputy U.S. negotiators Lt. Gen. Welborn "Tom" Dolvin and S. Morey Bell. (USIS photo)

President Jimmy Carter met with the Panamanian treaty negotiators in the Cabinet Room on July 29, 1977. It was at this meeting that the president told the visiting envoys that the treaties then in their final stages were "generous, fair, and appropriate" and went as far as he could go. *On the left*: Ambassador Gabriel Lewis Galindo, Panamanian negotiators Rómulo Escobar Bethancourt and Aristides Royo, and State Department interpreter Tony Hervas. *On the right*: President Carter and, to his right, Secretary of State Cyrus Vance, Vice President Walter Mondale, and Security Adviser Zbigniew Brzezinski. To the president's left: Ambassador Bunker, Ambassador Linowitz, and NSC staff member Robert Pastor. (White House photo)

U.S. and Panamanian negotiators announced they had reached agreement in principle on the new Panama Canal Treaties on August 10, 1977. In a press conference at the Holiday Inn in Panama City, they disclosed the long-sought understanding to the Panamanian and world press. On the couch facing a battery of microphones and cameras, *left to right*: Rómulo Escobar Bethancourt, Ellsworth Bunker, Sol Linowitz, and Aristides Royo. (USIS photo)

The new Panama Canal Treaties were signed at the Pan American Union Building in Washington on September 7, 1977. Host for the occasion was Alejandro Orfila, secretary general of the Organization of American States (center). President Jimmy Carter and General Omar Torrijos, assisted by protocol officers, are signing the two treaties. Behind them are the treaty negotiators: Sol Linowitz and Ellsworth Bunker for the United States, Rómulo Escobar Bethancourt and Aristides Royo for Panama. (Photo by Rogelio Achurra)

President Jimmy Carter and General Omar Torrijos face a cheering crowd in the
New Panama Coliseum on June 16, 1978. They had just signed documents—the
instruments of ratification—that officially put the Panama Canal Treaties into
effect. For the U.S. president it marked the success of his first major foreign
policy initiative and possibly the most important of his administration. For Torrijos and the Panamanians it was the realization of a lifelong dream. (Photo by
Rogelio Achurra)

More than 100,000 Panamanians hail President Carter and General Torrijos in
Cinco de Mayo Plaza on June 16, 1978, the day the Panama Canal Treaties were
formally ratified. It was the largest crowd ever assembled in one place in Panamanian history. President Carter scored a hit with the crowd by addressing them in
Spanish. Between the president and Torrijos (in uniform) is the general's wife,
Raquel. To the general's right is Mexican President José López Portillo. (Photo
by Rogelio Achurra)

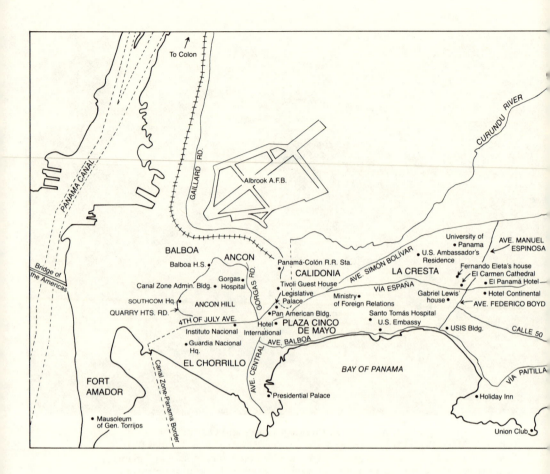

To Colon

PANAMA CANAL

CURUNDU RIVER

GAILLARD RD.

Albrook A.F.B.

Bridge of the Americas

BALBOA

ANCON

University of Panama

AVE. MANUEL ESPINOSA

U.S. Ambassador's Residence

Balboa H.S.

Panamá-Colón R.R. Sta.

AVE. SIMÓN BOLIVAR

CALIDONIA

LA CRESTA

Fernando Eleta's house

El Carmen Cathedral

El Panamá Hotel

Gorgas Hospital

Canal Zone Admin. Bldg.

Tivoli Guest House

VÍA ESPAÑA

Hotel Continental

Legislative Palace

Ministry of Foreign Relations

Gabriel Lewis' house

AVE. FEDERICO BOYD

SOUTHCOM Hq.

ANCON HILL

GORGAS RD.

Pan American Bldg.

Santo Tomás Hospital

QUARRY HTS. RD.

Hotel International

PLAZA CINCO DE MAYO

U.S. Embassy

USIS Bldg.

CALLE 50

4TH OF JULY AVE.

Instituto Nacional

AVE. CENTRAL

AVE. BALBOA

VÍA PAITILLA

Guardia Nacional Hq.

EL CHORRILLO

BAY OF PANAMA

FORT AMADOR

Canal Zone-Panama Border

Presidential Palace

Holiday Inn

Mausoleum of Gen. Torrijos

Union Club

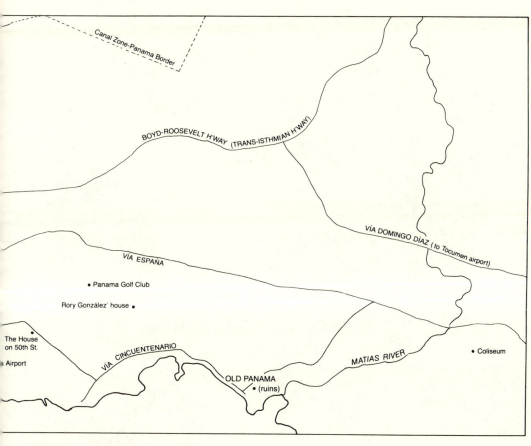

Canal Zone-Panama Border

BOYD-ROOSEVELT H'WAY (TRANS-ISTHMIAN H'WAY)

VÍA DOMINGO DÍAZ (to Tocumen airport)

VÍA ESPAÑA

• Panama Golf Club

Rory González' house •

The House
on 50th St. •

Airport

VÍA CINCUENTENARIO

MATÍAS RIVER

• Coliseum

OLD PANAMA
• (ruins)

PANAMA CITY

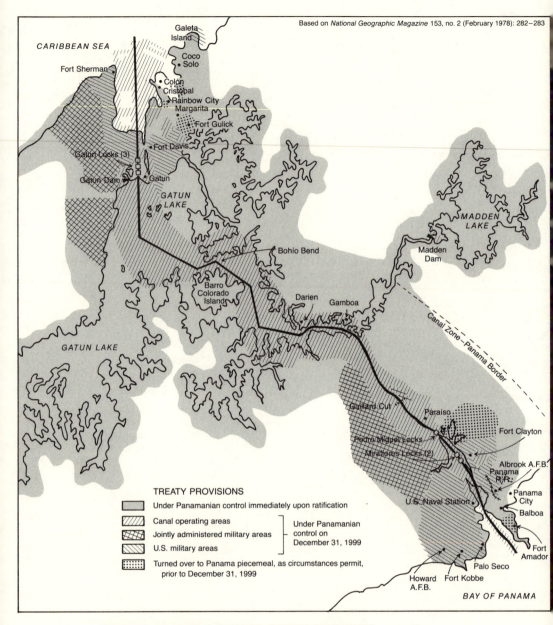

Based on *National Geographic Magazine* 153, no. 2 (February 1978): 282–283

CARIBBEAN SEA

Galeta
Island

Coco
Solo

Fort Sherman

Colón
Cristóbal
Rainbow City
Margarita

Fort Gulick

Fort Davis

Gatun Locks (3)

Gatun Dam

Gatun

GATUN
LAKE

MADDEN
LAKE

Bohío Bend

Madden
Dam

Barro
Colorado
Island

Darien

Gamboa

GATUN LAKE

Canal Zone–Panama Border

Gaillard Cut

Paraíso

Fort Clayton

Pedro Miguel Locks
Miraflores Locks (2)

Albrook A.F.B.
Panama
R.R.

Panama
City

U.S. Naval Station

Balboa

TREATY PROVISIONS

Under Panamanian control immediately upon ratification

Canal operating areas

Jointly administered military areas

Under Panamanian
control on
December 31, 1999

U.S. military areas

Turned over to Panama piecemeal, as circumstances permit,
prior to December 31, 1999

Fort
Amador

Palo Seco

Howard
A.F.B.

Fort Kobbe

BAY OF PANAMA

EFFECT OF THE PANAMA CANAL TREATIES
ON THE GOVERNANCE OF THE CANAL ZONE

Appendix A

ON MAY 21, 1973, Panama's Foreign Minister Juan Antonio Tack wrote a letter to U.S. Secretary of State William P. Rogers. He delivered the letter to Secretary Rogers in Buenos Aires on May 24. The two diplomats were in Argentina to attend the inauguration of newly elected President Héctor Campora. In his letter, Minister Tack stated the principles he thought should serve as a basis for a new canal treaty between his country and the United States. They were:

1. The 1903 treaty must be abrogated. The two countries are willing to conclude an entirely new interoceanic canal treaty.

2. The concept of perpetuity is rejected. The new treaty concerning the lock canal shall have a fixed termination date.

3. The exercise of any type of jurisdiction by the United States in Panamanian territory shall quickly cease at the end of the transition period agreed upon.

4. The so-called Canal Zone shall be returned to full Panamanian jurisdiction. The Republic of Panama, as territorial sovereign, is willing to grant the Government of the United States, for the duration of the new treaty on the interoceanic canal, the right to use the lands and waters proved to be essential for the operation and maintenance of the canal, the transit of ships, and the protection of vital installations.

5. The Republic of Panama shall have a just and equitable share in the benefits in proportion to the total benefits that the United States and world trade derive from Panama's geographic location.

6. The activity of the United States Government shall be limited to the administration of transit through the interoceanic waterway. The activities of the United States Government shall be those which have a direct relation to the operation, maintenance, and protection of the Canal, as shall be specified in the treaty.

7. The United States of America shall exercise, in the facilities for protection, such activities as may be expressly stipulated in the treaty, for the duration of the treaty.

8. The Republic of Panama is willing to include in that same treaty provisions authorizing the Government of the United States to construct a sea-level canal along what has been designated Route 14, on the following conditions:

(a) The United States will notify Panama of its decision to construct a sea-level canal along Route 14 within a reasonable period to be negotiated following the entry into force of the new treaty, and if it should fail to do so, its right in that respect would lapse;

(b) Panama would retain full jurisdiction in the area that would be occupied by the sea-level canal; and

(c) with respect to the sea-level canal, the life of the treaty shall have a limited duration with a specified duration date.

(The origin of the above principles and the story of Tack's letter to Rogers is described on pp. 203–206.)

The principles negotiated by Minister Tack and U.S. Ambassador Ellsworth Bunker on Contadora (November 1973–January 1974) and announced publicly by the Panamanian foreign minister and Secretary of State Henry Kissinger on February 7, 1974, were the following:

1. The treaty of 1903 and its amendments will be abrogated by the conclusion of an entirely new interoceanic canal treaty.

2. The concept of perpetuity will be eliminated. The new treaty concerning the lock canal shall have a fixed terminal date.

3. Termination of United States jurisdiction over Panamanian territory shall take place promptly in accordance with terms specified in the treaty.

4. The Panamanian territory in which the canal is situated shall be returned to the jurisdiction of the Republic of Panama. The Republic of Panama, in its capacity as territorial sovereign, shall grant to the United States of America, for the duration of the new interoceanic canal treaty and in accordance with what that treaty states, the right to use the lands, waters, and airspace which may be necessary for the operation, maintenance, protection, and defense of the canal and the transit of ships.

5. The Republic of Panama shall have a just and equitable share of the benefits derived from the operation of the canal in its territory. It is recognized that the geographic position of its territory constitutes the principal resource of the Republic of Panama.

6. The Republic of Panama shall participate in the administration of the canal, in accordance with a procedure to be agreed upon in the treaty. The treaty shall also provide that Panama will assume total responsibility for the operation of the canal upon the termination of the treaty. The Republic of Panama shall grant to the United States of America the rights necessary to regulate the transit of ships through the canal, to operate, maintain, protect, and defend the canal, and to undertake any other specific activity related to those ends, as may be agreed upon in the treaty.

7. The Republic of Panama shall participate with the United States of America in the protection and defense of the canal in accordance with what is agreed upon in the new treaty.

8. The United States of America and the Republic of Panama, recognizing the important services rendered by the interoceanic Panama Canal to interna-

tional maritime traffic, and bearing in mind the possibility that the present canal could become inadequate for said traffic, shall agree bilaterally on provisions for new projects which will enlarge canal capacity. Such provisions will be incorporated in the new treaty in accord with the concepts established in principle 2.

Appendix B

THE following statement was prepared by actor John Wayne and was sent to many people who wrote to him asking about or criticizing his stand on the Panama Canal Treaties. He also sent a copy of the statement to each member of the U.S. Senate. Wayne wrote the statement on or about October 10, 1977.

STATEMENT REGARDING PANAMA CANAL TREATY

My interest in Panama goes back to the 40's. I have friends on both sides of their political spectrum. As a matter of fact, my first introduction to the Panamanian situation was in the 30's when Harmodio Arias was president. He was probably the best liked figure in all of South America and one of the very few presidents who has ever completed a term up to and since that time. His wife and his son Tito, then about 12 years old, visited me in California. Another son, Tony, was Godfather to one of my daughters. I am only going into these personal things to show you that I have had reasons to give attention to our relationships down there.

I have followed the Panamanian situation since the time the State Department insured us losing good relationships with Panama by changing their policy and charging extremely high prices for tuition for the children of several Panamanian families to go to Canal Zone schools. These families were continually involved in the leadership and administration in Panama. I think it would have been quite obvious with their children attending our schools that they would have our point of view. I wrote a letter to our Administration at that time to apprise them of this situation. Nothing was done.

You say that it is a blow to you to learn from the press that I favor the surrender of the Panama Canal. I certainly did not. I was appalled when General Eisenhower did just that and gave the sovereignty of the Canal away by allowing the Panamanian flag to fly there; but at that time, neither Congress, nor the press, nor the conservatives uttered any kind of cry. I did, but it was a voice in the wilderness.

In checking to find the reason for President Eisenhower's actions, I found out that although we had the rights to the ownership and jurisdiction of the Canal that Panama had not surrendered sovereignty of same. I also found out that the United States in the Arias-Roosevelt Treaty of 1936, ratified by our Congress in 1939, recognized the sovereignty of Panama in the Canal Zone as it was originally stated in the 1903 agreement.

Under negotiations during the Kennedy Administration, it was further agreed that any place within the civil area that the American flag flew, there must be a Panamanian flag raised.

Our people in the Zone tried to avoid this by removing flag poles. This started irrational actions by both sides. During those student riots which took place in 1964, our then president, Lyndon B. Johnson, told the world that there would be a gradual return of the Canal to Panamanian possession. There were still no outcries from the people who are now complaining, but the above acts plus common decency to the dignity of Panama demanded a re-evaluation of our Treaty.

Now, let's take the Treaty for what it is. We do not give up one active military installation for the next quarter of a century. We do transfer to Panama in the civil Canal area such governmental activities as police and fire protection, civil administration, post offices, courts, customs, garbage collection, and maintenance of certain areas which are not necessary to manage the Canal. The Canal will continue to be run by an American agency. The Board of Directors of that entity will be comprised of nine members—five members of the Board, American, and four Panamanians who will be selected by the United States from a list proposed by Panama. This Board of Directors will not have any authority on our military bases which we will have there for a quarter of a century to insure this Treaty.

The Treaty insures all American citizens working in the Canal their continuing jobs to retirement and the continued uses of their rented homes at the present rate which averages around $150 per month including all their utilities, garbage collection, sewerage, upkeep of the grounds and maintenance including gardening lawns and painting of buildings. This is guaranteed to each until retirement or completion of their contracts.

When the Canal Company transfers these responsibilities to Panama, they will also transfer $10,000,000 a year of the toll charges to take care of them. I doubt if this will cover the costs. So does our government. Therefore, this United States Canal Company Agency which will still be running the Canal for the next 20 years will be instructed to raise the toll charges 30 cents per ton or about $1/100$ of a cent and a half per pound to be given to Panama to cover such contingencies as inflation and to insure the above responsibilities plus rental for the 120,000 acres which these United States will continue to hold for its military installations and also the use of a 4,000 square kilometer water shed as a water reservoir to take care of our civil and military needs in the area. This added toll charge could amount to $40,000,000 in the years to come; but not one cent of it will come out of our pockets.

None of this will cost the American taxpayer one cent. We will not be required to pay $1 to Panama when this Treaty is put into effect.

I explained to the press when I was interrogated that I am only one of 200,000,000 private citizens of the United States and that I am not presuming to establish our foreign policy. I suggested that perhaps the facts as I have presented them to you might be put in a more enlightening manner to our citizens.

Regarding Communism, quite obviously, there are some Communists in General Torrijos' administration as there have been and probably still are in ours. Back in the days of McCarthy, it was proven that a great number of people in our government were Communists. For his high-handed manner with the use of the Committee, he was censored [*sic*]; but the truth of his findings was never questioned.

There will always be accusations and counter-accusations in this area. General Torrijos has never followed the Marxist line. Even in his speech when he visited Cuba, he stated that Castro had insured schooling and developed a system of feeding his people but at a high social cost. Because of this he stated that what was aspirin for Cuba was not necessarily the right medicine for Panama which is putting it about as plainly as possible when you are visiting in a foreign country that you are not agreeing with their methods.

Such rumors and accusations mushroom to a degree that it is hard for anyone to defend themselves. General Torrijos' government has not followed the Marxist line. He does have his Escobar Bethancourt as we have our Andrew Young, neither of whom were elected by either populus. A quarter of a century from now—when and if this agreement is carried out to the letter of the law—and we decide that it is proper to remove military installations, Escobar Bethancourt will be an old and forgotten character; and Young will probably be relegated to some posh job in our civil service from which he cannot be fired or taken care of by some liberal foundation as was Hiss.

I hope that the pragmatic view that I have of this situation is understandable. I have carefully studied the Treaty, and I support it based on my belief that America looks always to the future and that our people have demonstrated qualities of justice and reason for 200 years. That attitude has made our country a great Nation. The new Treaty modernizes an outmoded relation with a friendly and hospitable country. It also solves an international question with our other Latin American neighbors, and finally the Treaty protects and legitimates fundamental interests and desires of our Country.

—John Wayne

Appendix C

Following is the text of the treaty dealing with the neutrality of the Panama Canal. It was signed in Washington on September 7, 1977, by President Jimmy Carter and Panamanian General Omar Torrijos Herrera. President Carter submitted the treaty to the U.S. Senate on September 16, 1977, for its advice and consent. The only alterations in the treaty text were the two "clarifications" of Articles IV and VI based on the Carter-Torrijos understanding of October 14, 1977. The maneuvering that led to those changes is described on pp. 504–509. The Senate approved the treaty on March 16, 1978.

TREATY CONCERNING THE PERMANENT NEUTRALITY AND OPERATION OF THE PANAMA CANAL

The United States of America and the Republic of Panama have agreed upon the following:

ARTICLE I

The Republic of Panama declares that the Canal, as an international transit waterway, shall be permanently neutral in accordance with the regime established in this Treaty. The same regime of neutrality shall apply to any other international waterway that may be built either partially or wholly in the territory of the Republic of Panama.

ARTICLE II

The Republic of Panama declares the neutrality of the Canal in order that both in time of peace and in time of war it shall remain secure and open to peaceful transit by the vessels of all nations on terms of entire equality, so that there will be no discrimination against any nation, or its citizens or subjects, concerning the conditions or charges of transit, or for any other reason, and so that the Canal, and therefore the Isthmus of Panama, shall not be the target of reprisals in any armed conflict between other nations of the world. The foregoing shall be subject to the following requirements:

(a) Payment of tolls and other charges for transit and ancillary services, provided they have been fixed in conformity with the provisions of Article III(c);

(b) Compliance with applicable rules and regulations, provided such rules and regulations are applied in conformity with the provisions of Article III;

(c) The requirement that transiting vessels commit no acts of hostility while in the Canal; and

(d) Such other conditions and restrictions as are established by this Treaty.

ARTICLE III

1. For purposes of the security, efficiency and proper maintenance of the Canal the following rules shall apply:

(a) The Canal shall be operated efficiently in accordance with conditions of transit through the Canal, and rules and regulations that shall be just, equitable and reasonable, and limited to those necessary for safe navigation and efficient, sanitary operation of the Canal;

(b) Ancillary services necessary for transit through the Canal shall be provided;

(c) Tolls and other charges for transit and ancillary services shall be just, reasonable, equitable and consistent with the principles of international law;

(d) As a pre-condition of transit, vessels may be required to establish clearly the financial responsibility and guarantees for payment of reasonable and adequate indemnification, consistent with international practice and standards, for damages resulting from acts or omissions of such vessels when passing through the Canal. In the case of vessels owned or operated by a State or for which it has acknowledged responsibility, a certification by that State that it shall observe its obligations under international law to pay for damages resulting from the act or omission of such vessels when passing through the Canal shall be deemed sufficient to establish such financial responsibility;

(e) Vessels of war and auxiliary vessels of all nations shall at all times be entitled to transit the Canal, irrespective of their internal operation, means of propulsion, origin, destination or armament, without being subjected, as a condition of transit, to inspection, search or surveillance. However, such vessels may be required to certify that they have complied with all applicable health, sanitation and quarantine regulations. In addition, such vessels shall be entitled to refuse to disclose their internal operation, origin, armament, cargo or destination. However, auxiliary vessels may be required to present written assurances, certified by an official at a high level of the government of the State requesting the exemption, that they are owned or operated by that government and in this case are being used only on government non-commercial service.

2. For the purposes of this Treaty, the terms "Canal," "vessel of war," "auxiliary vessel," "internal operation," "armament" and "inspection" shall have the meanings assigned them in Annex A to this Treaty.

ARTICLE IV

The United States of America and the Republic of Panama agree to maintain the regime of neutrality established in this Treaty, which shall be maintained in order that the Canal shall remain permanently neutral, notwithstanding the termination of any other treaties entered into by the two Contracting Parties.

ARTICLE V

After the termination of the Panama Canal Treaty, only the Republic of Panama shall operate the Canal and maintain military forces, defense sites and military installations within its national territory.

ARTICLE VI

1. In recognition of the important contributions of the United States of America and of the Republic of Panama to the construction, operation, maintenance, and protection and defense of the Canal, vessels of war and auxiliary vessels of those nations shall, notwithstanding any other provisions of this Treaty, be entitled to transit the Canal irrespective of their internal operation, means of propulsion, origin, destination, armament or cargo carried. Such vessels of war and auxiliary vessels will be entitled to transit the Canal expeditiously.

2. The United States of America, so long as it has responsibility for the operation of the Canal, may continue to provide the Republic of Colombia toll-free transit through the Canal for its troops, vessels and materials of war. Thereafter, the Republic of Panama may provide the Republic of Colombia and the Republic of Costa Rica with the right of toll-free transit.

ARTICLE VII

1. The United States of America and the Republic of Panama shall jointly sponsor a resolution in the Organization of American States opening to accession by all nations of the world the Protocol to this Treaty whereby all the signatories will adhere to the objectives of this Treaty, agreeing to respect the regime of neutrality set forth herein.

2. The Organization of American States shall act as the depositary for this Treaty and related instruments.

ARTICLE VIII

This Treaty shall be subject to ratification in accordance with the constitutional procedures of the two Parties. The instruments of ratification of this Treaty shall be exchanged at Panama at the same time as the instruments of ratification of the Panama Canal Treaty, signed this date, are exchanged. This Treaty shall enter into force, simultaneously with the Panama Canal Treaty, six calendar months from the date of the exchange of the instruments of ratification.

DONE at Washington, this 7th day of September, 1977, in the English and Spanish languages, both texts being equally authentic.

PROTOCOL TO THE TREATY CONCERNING THE PERMANENT NEUTRALITY AND OPERATION OF THE PANAMA CANAL

Whereas the maintenance of the neutrality of the Panama Canal is important not only to the commerce and security of the United States of America and the Republic of Panama, but to the peace and security of the Western Hemisphere and to the interests of world commerce as well;

Whereas the regime of neutrality which the United States of America and the Republic of Panama have agreed to maintain will ensure permanent access to the Canal by vessels of all nations on the basis of entire equality; and

Whereas the said regime of effective neutrality shall constitute the best protection for the Canal and shall ensure the absence of any hostile act against it;

The Contracting Parties to this Protocol have agreed upon the following:

ARTICLE I

The Contracting Parties hereby acknowledge the regime of permanent neutrality for the Canal established in the Treaty Concerning the Permanent Neutrality and Operation of the Panama Canal and associate themselves with its objectives.

ARTICLE II

The Contracting Parties agree to observe and respect the regime of permanent neutrality of the Canal in time of war as in time of peace, and to ensure that vessels of their registry strictly observe the applicable rules.

ARTICLE III

This Protocol shall be open to accession by all States of the world, and shall enter into force for each State at the time of deposit of its instrument of accession with the Secretary General of the Organization of American States.

Appendix D

Following is the text of the Panama Canal Treaty signed in Washington on September 7, 1977, by President Jimmy Carter and Panamanian General Omar Torrijos Herrera. President Carter submitted it, together with its companion pact on canal neutrality (in Appendix C), to the Senate on September 16, 1977, for that body's advice and consent. The Senate approved the treaty on April 18, 1978.

PANAMA CANAL TREATY

The United States of America and the Republic of Panama,

Acting in the spirit of the Joint Declaration of April 3, 1964, by the Representatives of the Governments of the United States of America and the Republic of Panama, and of the Joint Statement of Principles of February 7, 1974, initialed by the Secretary of State of the United States of America and the Foreign Minister of the Republic of Panama, and

Acknowledging the Republic of Panama's sovereignty over its territory,

Have decided to terminate the prior Treaties pertaining to the Panama Canal and to conclude a new Treaty to serve as the basis for a new relationship between them and, accordingly, have agreed upon the following:

ARTICLE I

ABROGATION OF PRIOR TREATIES AND
ESTABLISHMENT OF A NEW RELATIONSHIP

1. Upon its entry into force, this Treaty terminates and supersedes:

(a) The Isthmian Canal Convention between the United States of America and the Republic of Panama, signed at Washington, November 18, 1903;

(b) The Treaty of Friendship and Cooperation signed at Washington, March 2, 1936, and the Treaty of Mutual Understanding and Cooperation and the related Memorandum of Understandings Reached, signed at Panama, January 25, 1955, between the United States of America and the Republic of Panama;

(c) All other treaties, conventions, agreements and exchanges of notes between the United States of America and the Republic of Panama concerning the Panama Canal which were in force prior to the entry into force of this Treaty; and

(d) Provisions concerning the Panama Canal which appear in other treaties, conventions, agreements and exchanges of notes between the United States of America and the Republic of Panama which were in force prior to the entry into force of this Treaty.

2. In accordance with the terms of this Treaty and related agreements, the Republic of Panama, as territorial sovereign, grants to the United States of America, for the duration of this Treaty, the rights necessary to regulate the transit of ships through the Panama Canal, and to manage, operate, maintain, improve, protect and defend the Canal. The Republic of Panama guarantees to the United States of America the peaceful use of the land and water areas which it has been granted the rights to use for such purposes pursuant to this Treaty and related agreements.

3. The Republic of Panama shall participate increasingly in the management and protection and defense of the Canal, as provided in this Treaty.

4. In view of the special relationship established by this Treaty, the United States of America and the Republic of Panama shall cooperate to assure the uninterrupted and efficient operation of the Panama Canal.

ARTICLE II

RATIFICATION, ENTRY INTO FORCE, AND TERMINATION

1. This Treaty shall be subject to ratification in accordance with the constitutional procedures of the two Parties. The instruments of ratification of this Treaty shall be exchanged at Panama at the same time as the instruments of ratification of the Treaty Concerning the Permanent Neutrality and Operation of the Panama Canal, signed this date, are exchanged. This treaty shall enter into force, simultaneously with the Treaty Concerning the Permanent Neutrality and Operation of the Panama Canal, six calendar months from the date of the exchange of the instruments of ratification.

2. This Treaty shall terminate at noon, Panama time, December 31, 1999.

ARTICLE III

CANAL OPERATION AND MANAGEMENT

1. The Republic of Panama, as territorial sovereign, grants to the United States of America the rights to manage, operate, and maintain the Panama Canal, its complementary works, installations and equipment and to provide for the orderly transit of vessels through the Panama Canal. The United States of America accepts the grant of such rights and undertakes to exercise them in accordance with this Treaty and related agreements.

2. In carrying out the foregoing responsibilities, the United States of America may:

(a) Use for the aforementioned purposes, without cost except as provided in this Treaty, the various installations and areas (including the Panama Canal) and waters, described in the Agreement in Implementation of this Article, signed this date, as well as such other areas and installations as are made available to the United States of America under this Treaty and related agreements, and take the measures necessary to ensure sanitation of such areas;

(b) Make such improvements and alterations to the aforesaid installations and areas as it deems appropriate, consistent with the terms of this Treaty;

(c) Make and enforce all rules pertaining to the passage of vessels through the Canal and other rules with respect to navigation and maritime matters, in accordance with this Treaty and related agreements. The Republic of Panama will lend its cooperation, when necessary, in the enforcement of such rules;

(d) Establish, modify, collect and retain tolls for the use of the Panama Canal, and other charges, and establish and modify methods of their assessment;

(e) Regulate relations with employees of the United States Government;

(f) Provide supporting services to facilitate the performance of its responsibilities under this Article;

(g) Issue and enforce regulations for the effective exercise of the rights and responsibilities of the United States of America under this Treaty and related agreements. The Republic of Panama will lend its cooperation, when necessary, in the enforcement of such rules; and

(h) Exercise any other right granted under this Treaty, or otherwise agreed upon between the two Parties.

3. Pursuant to the foregoing grant of rights, the United States of America shall, in accordance with the terms of this Treaty and the provisions of United States law, carry out its responsibilities by means of a United States Government agency called the Panama Canal Commission, which shall be constituted by and in conformity with the laws of the United States of America.

(a) The Panama Canal Commission shall be supervised by a Board composed of nine members, five of whom shall be nationals of the United States of America, and four of whom shall be Panamanian nationals proposed by the Republic of Panama for appointment to such positions by the United States of America in a timely manner.

(b) Should the Republic of Panama request the United States of America to remove a Panamanian national from membership on the Board, the United States of America shall agree to such request. In that event, the Republic of Panama shall propose another Panamanian national for appointment by the United States of America to such position in a timely manner. In case of removal of a Panamanian member of the Board at the initiative of the United States of America, both Parties will consult in advance in order to reach agreement concerning such removal, and the Republic of Panama shall propose another Panamanian national for appointment by the United States of America in his stead.

(c) The United States of America shall employ a national of the United States of America as Administrator of the Panama Canal Commission, and a Panamanian national as Deputy Administrator, through December 31, 1989. Beginning January 1, 1990, a Panamanian national shall be employed as the Administrator and a national of the United States of America shall occupy the position of Deputy Administrator. Such Panamanian nationals shall be proposed to the United States of America by the Republic of Panama for appointment to such positions by the United States of America.

(d) Should the United States of America remove the Panamanian national from his position as Deputy Administrator, or Administrator, the Republic of Panama shall propose another Panamanian national for appointment to such position by the United States of America.

4. An illustrative description of the activities the Panama Canal Commission

will perform in carrying out the responsibilities and rights of the United States of America under this Article is set forth at the Annex. Also set forth in the Annex are procedures for the discontinuance or transfer of those activities performed prior to the entry into force of this Treaty by the Panama Canal Company or the Canal Zone Government which are not to be carried out by the Panama Canal Commission.

5. The Panama Canal Commission shall reimburse the Republic of Panama for the costs incurred by the Republic of Panama in providing the following public services in the Canal operating areas and in housing areas set forth in the Agreement in Implementation of Article III of this Treaty and occupied by both United States and Panamanian citizen employees of the Panama Canal Commission: police, fire protection, street maintenance, street lighting, street cleaning, traffic management and garbage collection. The Panama Canal Commission shall pay the Republic of Panama the sum of ten million United States dollars ($10,000,000) per annum for the foregoing services. It is agreed that every three years from the date that this Treaty enters into force, the costs involved in furnishing said services shall be reexamined to determine whether adjustment of the annual payment should be made because of inflation and other relevant factors affecting the cost of such services.

6. The Republic of Panama shall be responsible for providing, in all areas comprising the former Canal Zone, services of a general jurisdictional nature such as customs and immigration, postal services, courts and licensing, in accordance with this Treaty and related agreements.

7. The United States of America and the Republic of Panama shall establish a Panama Canal Consultative Committee, composed of an equal number of high-level representatives of the United States of America and the Republic of Panama, and which may appoint such subcommittees as it may deem appropriate. This Committee shall advise the United States of America and the Republic of Panama on matters of policy affecting the Canal's operation. In view of both Parties' special interest in the continuity and efficiency of the Canal operation in the future, the Committee shall advise on matters such as general tolls policy, employment and training policies to increase the participation of Panamanian nationals in the operation of the Canal, and international policies on matters concerning the Canal. The Committee's recommendations shall be transmitted to the two Governments, which shall give such recommendations full consideration in the formulation of such policy decisions.

8. In addition to the participation of Panamanian nationals at high management levels of the Panama Canal Commission, as provided for in paragraph 3 of this Article, there shall be growing participation of Panamanian nationals at all other levels and areas of employment in the aforesaid commission, with the objective of preparing, in an orderly and efficient fashion, for the assumption by the Republic of Panama of full responsibility for the management, operation and maintenance of the Canal upon the termination of this Treaty.

9. The use of the areas, waters and installations with respect to which the United States of America is granted rights pursuant to this Article, and the rights and legal status of United States Government agencies and employees operating

in the Republic of Panama pursuant to this Article, shall be governed by the Agreement in Implementation of this Article, signed this date.

10. Upon entry into force of this Treaty, the United States Government agencies known as the Panama Canal Company and the Canal Zone Government shall cease to operate within the territory of the Republic of Panama that formerly constituted the Canal Zone.

ARTICLE IV

PROTECTION AND DEFENSE

1. The United States of America and the Republic of Panama commit themselves to protect and defend the Panama Canal. Each Party shall act, in accordance with its constitutional processes, to meet the danger resulting from an armed attack or other actions which threaten the security of the Panama Canal or of ships transiting it.

2. For the duration of this Treaty, the United States of America shall have primary responsibility to protect and defend the Canal. The rights of the United States of America to station, train, and move military forces within the Republic of Panama are described in the Agreement in Implementation of this Article, signed this date. The use of areas and installations and the legal status of the armed forces of the United States of America in the Republic of Panama shall be governed by the aforesaid Agreement.

3. In order to facilitate the participation and cooperation of the armed forces of both Parties in the protection and defense of the Canal, the United States of America and the Republic of Panama shall establish a Combined Board comprised of an equal number of senior military representatives of each Party. These representatives shall be charged by their respective governments with consulting and cooperating on all matters pertaining to the protection and defense of the Canal, and with planning for actions to be taken in concert for that purpose. Such combined protection and defense arrangements shall not inhibit the identity or lines of authority of the armed forces of the United States of America or the Republic of Panama. The Combined Board shall provide for coordination and cooperation concerning such matters as:

(a) The preparation of contingency plans for the protection and defense of the Canal based upon the cooperative efforts of the armed forces of both Parties;

(b) The planning and conduct of combined military exercises; and

(c) The conduct of United States and Panamanian military operations with respect to the protection and defense of the Canal.

4. The Combined Board shall, at five-year intervals throughout the duration of this Treaty, review the resources being made available by the two Parties for the protection and defense of the Canal. Also, the Combined Board shall make appropriate recommendations to the two Governments respecting projected requirements, the efficient utilization of available resources of the two Parties, and other matters of mutual interest with respect to the protection and defense of the Canal.

5. To the extent possible consistent with its primary responsibility for the protection and defense of the Panama Canal, the United States of America will en-

deavor to maintain its armed forces in the Republic of Panama in normal times at a level not in excess of that of the armed forces of the United States of America in the territory of the former Canal Zone immediately prior to the entry into force of this Treaty.

ARTICLE V

PRINCIPLE OF NON-INTERVENTION

Employees of the Panama Canal Commission, their dependents and designated contractors of the Panama Canal Commission, who are nationals of the United States of America, shall respect the laws of the Republic of Panama and shall abstain from any activity incompatible with the spirit of this Treaty. Accordingly, they shall abstain from any political activity in the Republic of Panama as well as from any intervention in the internal affairs of the Republic of Panama. The United States of America shall take all measures within its authority to ensure that the provisions of this Article are fulfilled.

ARTICLE VI

PROTECTION OF THE ENVIRONMENT

1. The United States of America and the Republic of Panama commit themselves to implement this Treaty in a manner consistent with the protection of the natural environment of the Republic of Panama. To this end, they shall consult and cooperate with each other in all appropriate ways to ensure that they shall give due regard to the protection and conservation of the environment.

2. A Joint Commission on the Environment shall be established with equal representation from the United States of America and the Republic of Panama, which shall periodically review the implementation of this Treaty and shall recommend as appropriate to the two Governments ways to avoid or, should this not be possible, to mitigate the adverse environmental impacts which might result from their respective actions pursuant to the Treaty.

3. The United States of America and the Republic of Panama shall furnish the Joint Commission on the Environment complete information on any action taken in accordance with this Treaty which, in the judgment of both, might have a significant effect on the environment. Such information shall be made available to the Commission as far in advance of the contemplated action as possible to facilitate the study by the Commission of any potential environmental problems and to allow for consideration of the recommendation of the Commission before the contemplated action is carried out.

ARTICLE VII

FLAGS

1. The entire territory of the Republic of Panama, including the areas the use of which the Republic of Panama makes available to the United States of America pursuant to this Treaty and related agreements, shall be under the flag of the Republic of Panama, and consequently such flag always shall occupy the position of honor.

2. The flag of the United States of America may be displayed, together with the flag of the Republic of Panama, at the headquarters of the Panama Canal

Commission, at the site of the Combined Board, and as provided in the Agreement in Implementation of Article IV of this Treaty.

3. The flag of the United States of America also may be displayed at other places and on some occasions, as agreed by both Parties.

ARTICLE VIII

PRIVILEGES AND IMMUNITIES

1. The installations owned or used by the agencies or instrumentalities of the United States of America operating in the Republic of Panama pursuant to this Treaty and related agreements, and their official archives and documents, shall be inviolable. The two Parties shall agree on procedures to be followed in the conduct of any criminal investigation at such locations by the Republic of Panama.

2. Agencies and instrumentalities of the Government of the United States of America operating in the Republic of Panama pursuant to this Treaty and related agreements shall be immune from the jurisdiction of the Republic of Panama.

3. In addition to such other privileges and immunities as are afforded to employees of the United States Government and their dependents pursuant to this Treaty, the United States of America may designate up to twenty officials of the Panama Canal Commission who, along with their dependents, shall enjoy the privileges and immunities accorded to diplomatic agents and their dependents under international law and practice. The United States of America shall furnish to the Republic of Panama a list of the names of said officials and their dependents, identifying the positions they occupy in the Government of the United States of America, and shall keep such list current at all times.

ARTICLE IX

APPLICABLE LAWS AND LAW ENFORCEMENT

1. In accordance with the provisions of this Treaty and related agreements, the law of the Republic of Panama shall apply in the areas made available for the use of the United States of America pursuant to this Treaty. The law of the Republic of Panama shall be applied to matters or events which occurred in the former Canal Zone prior to the entry into force of this Treaty only to the extent specifically provided in prior treaties and agreements.

2. Natural or juridical persons who, on the date of entry into force of this Treaty, are engaged in business or non-profit activities at locations in the former Canal Zone may continue such business or activities at those locations under the same terms and conditions prevailing prior to the entry into force of this Treaty for a thirty-month transition period from its entry into force. The Republic of Panama shall maintain the same operating conditions as those applicable to the aforementioned enterprises prior to the entry into force of this Treaty in order that they may receive licenses to do business in the Republic of Panama subject to their compliance with the requirements of its law. Thereafter, such persons shall receive the same treatment under the law of the Republic of Panama as similar enterprises already established in the rest of the territory of the Republic of Panama without discrimination.

3. The rights of ownership, as recognized by the United States of America, enjoyed by natural or juridical private persons in buildings and other improve-

ments to real property located in the former Canal Zone shall be recognized by the Republic of Panama in conformity with its laws.

4. With respect to buildings and other improvements to real property located in the Canal operating areas, housing areas or other areas subject to the licensing procedure established in Article IV of the Agreement in Implementation of Article III of this Treaty, the owners shall be authorized to continue using the land upon which their property is located in accordance with the procedures established in that Article.

5. With respect to buildings and other improvements to real property located in areas of the former Canal Zone to which the aforesaid licensing procedure is not applicable, or may cease to be applicable during the lifetime or upon termination of this Treaty, the owners may continue to use the land upon which their property is located, subject to the payment of a reasonable charge to the Republic of Panama. Should the Republic of Panama decide to sell such land, the owners of the buildings or other improvements located thereon shall be offered a first option to purchase such land at a reasonable cost. In the case of non-profit enterprises, such as churches and fraternal organizations, the cost of purchase will be nominal in accordance with the prevailing practice in the rest of the territory of the Republic of Panama.

6. If any of the aforementioned persons are required by the Republic of Panama to discontinue their activities or vacate their property for public purposes, they shall be compensated at fair market value by the Republic of Panama.

7. The provisions of paragraphs 2–6 above shall apply to natural or juridical persons who have been engaged in business or non-profit activities at locations in the former Canal Zone for at least six months prior to the date of signature of this Treaty.

8. The Republic of Panama shall not issue, adopt or enforce any law, decree, regulation, or international agreement or take any other action which purports to regulate or would otherwise interfere with the exercise on the part of the United States of America of any right granted under this Treaty or related agreements.

9. Vessels transiting the Canal, and cargo, passengers and crews carried on such vessels shall be exempt from any taxes, fees, or other charges by the Republic of Panama. However, in the event such vessels call at a Panamanian port, they may be assessed charges incident thereto, such as charges for services provided to the vessel. The Republic of Panama may also require the passengers and crew disembarking from such vessels to pay such taxes, fees and charges as are established under Panamanian law for persons entering its territory. Such taxes, fees and charges shall be assessed on a nondiscriminatory basis.

10. The United States of America and the Republic of Panama will cooperate in taking such steps as may from time to time be necessary to guarantee the security of the Panama Canal Commission, its property, its employees and their dependents, and their property, the Forces of the United States of America and the members thereof, the civilian component of the United States Forces, the dependents of members of the Forces and the civilian component, and their property, and the contractors of the Panama Canal Commission and of the United States Forces, their dependents, and their property. The Republic of Pan-

ama will seek from its Legislative Branch such legislation as may be needed to carry out the foregoing purposes and to punish any offenders.

11. The Parties shall conclude an agreement whereby nationals of either State, who are sentenced by the courts of the other State, and who are not domiciled therein, may elect to serve their sentences in their State of nationality.

ARTICLE X

EMPLOYMENT WITH THE PANAMA CANAL COMMISSION

1. In exercising its rights and fulfilling its responsibilities as the employer, the United States of America shall establish employment and labor regulations which shall contain the terms, conditions and prerequisites for all categories of employees of the Panama Canal Commission. These regulations shall be provided to the Republic of Panama prior to their entry into force.

2. (a) The regulations shall establish a system of preference when hiring employees, for Panamanian applicants possessing the skills and qualifications required for employment by the Panama Canal Commission. The United States of America shall endeavor to ensure that the number of Panamanian nationals employed by the Panama Canal Commission in relation to the total number of its employees will conform to the proportion established for foreign enterprises under the law of the Republic of Panama.

(b) The terms and conditions of employment to be established will in general be no less favorable to persons already employed by the Panama Canal Company or Canal Zone Government prior to the entry into force of this Treaty, than those in effect immediately prior to that date.

3. (a) The United States of America shall establish an employment policy for the Panama Canal Commission that shall generally limit the recruitment of personnel outside the Republic of Panama to persons possessing requisite skills and qualifications which are not available in the Republic of Panama.

(b) The United States of America will establish training programs for Panamanian employees and apprentices in order to increase the number of Panamanian nationals qualified to assume positions with the Panama Canal Commission, as positions become available.

(c) Within five years from the entry into force of this Treaty, the number of United States nationals employed by the Panama Canal Commission who were previously employed by the Panama Canal Company shall be at least twenty percent less than the total number of United States nationals working for the Panama Canal Company immediately prior to the entry into force of this Treaty.

(d) The United States of America shall periodically inform the Republic of Panama, through the Coordinating Committee, established pursuant to the Agreement in Implementation of Article III of this Treaty, of available positions within the Panama Canal Commission. The Republic of Panama shall similarly provide the United States of America any information it may have as to the availability of Panamanian nationals claiming to have skills and qualifications that might be required by the Panama Canal Commission, in order that the United States of America may take this information into account.

4. The United States of America will establish qualification standards for skills,

training and experience required by the Panama Canal Commission. In establishing such standards, to the extent they include a requirement for a professional license, the United States of America, without prejudice to its right to require additional professional skills and qualifications, shall recognize the professional licenses issued by the Republic of Panama.

5. The United States of America shall establish a policy for the periodic rotation, at a maximum of every five years, of United States citizen employees and other non-Panamanian employees, hired after the entry into force of this Treaty. It is recognized that certain exceptions to the said policy of rotation may be made for sound administrative reasons, such as in the case of employees holding positions requiring certain non-transferable or non-recruitable skills.

6. With regard to wages and fringe benefits, there shall be no discrimination on the basis of nationality, sex, or race. Payments by the Panama Canal Commission of additional remuneration, or the provision of other benefits, such as home leave benefits, to United States nationals employed prior to entry into force of this Treaty, or to persons of any nationality, including Panamanian nationals who are thereafter recruited outside of the Republic of Panama and who change their place of residence, shall not be considered to be discrimination for the purpose of this paragraph.

7. Persons employed by the Panama Canal Company or Canal Zone Government prior to the entry into force of this Treaty, who are displaced from their employment as a result of the discontinuance by the United States of America of certain activities pursuant to this Treaty, will be placed by the United States of America, to the maximum extent feasible, in other appropriate jobs with the Government of the United States in accordance with United States Civil Service regulations. For such persons who are not United States nationals, placement efforts will be confined to United States Government activities located within the Republic of Panama. Likewise, persons previously employed in activities for which the Republic of Panama assumes responsibility as a result of this Treaty will be continued in their employment to the maximum extent feasible by the Republic of Panama. The Republic of Panama shall, to the maximum extent feasible, ensure that the terms and conditions of employment applicable to personnel employed in the activities for which it assumes responsibility are no less favorable than those in effect immediately prior to the entry into force of this Treaty. Non-United States nationals employed by the Panama Canal Company or Canal Zone Government prior to the entry into force of this Treaty who are involuntarily separated from their positions because of the discontinuance of an activity by reason of this Treaty, who are not entitled to an immediate annuity under the United States Civil Service Retirement System, and for whom continued employment in the Republic of Panama by the Government of the United States of America is not practicable, will be provided special job placement assistance by the Republic of Panama for employment in positions for which they may be qualified by experience and training.

8. The Parties agree to establish a system whereby the Panama Canal Commission may, if deemed mutually convenient or desirable by the two Parties, assign

certain employees of the Panama Canal Commission, for a limited period of time, to assist in the operation of activities transferred to the responsibility of the Republic of Panama as a result of this Treaty or related agreements. The salaries and other costs of employment of any such persons assigned to provide such assistance shall be reimbursed to the United States of America by the Republic of Panama.

9. (a) The right of employees to negotiate collective contracts with the Panama Canal Commission is recognized. Labor relations with employees of the Panama Canal Commission shall be conducted in accordance with forms of collective bargaining established by the United States of America after consultation with employee unions.

(b) Employee unions shall have the right to affiliate with international labor organizations.

10. The United States of America will provide an appropriate early optional retirement program for all persons employed by the Panama Canal Company or Canal Zone Government immediately prior to the entry into force of this Treaty. In this regard, taking into account the unique circumstances created by the provisions of this Treaty, including its duration, and their effect upon such employees, the United States of America shall, with respect to them:

(a) determine that conditions exist which invoke applicable United States law permitting early retirement annuities and apply such law for a substantial period of the duration of the Treaty;

(b) seek special legislation to provide more liberal entitlement to, and calculation of, retirement annuities than is currently provided for by law.

ARTICLE XI

PROVISIONS FOR THE TRANSITION PERIOD

1. The Republic of Panama shall reassume plenary jurisdiction over the former Canal Zone upon entry into force of this Treaty and in accordance with its terms. In order to provide for an orderly transition to the full application of the jurisdictional arrangements established by this Treaty and related agreements, the provisions of this Article shall become applicable upon the date this Treaty enters into force, and shall remain in effect for thirty calendar months. The authority granted in this Article to the United States of America for this transition period shall supplement, and is not intended to limit, the full application and effect of the rights and authority granted to the United States of America elsewhere in this Treaty and in related agreements.

2. During this transition period, the criminal and civil laws of the United States of America shall apply concurrently with those of the Republic of Panama in certain of the areas and installations made available for the use of the United States of America pursuant to this Treaty, in accordance with the following provisions:

(a) The Republic of Panama permits the authorities of the United States of America to have the primary right to exercise criminal jurisdiction over United States citizen employees of the Panama Canal Commission and their dependents, and members of the United States Forces and civilian component and their dependents, in the following cases:

(i) for any offense committed during the transition period within such areas and installations, and

(ii) for any offense committed prior to that period in the former Canal Zone.

The Republic of Panama shall have the primary right to exercise jurisdiction over all other offenses committed by such persons, except as otherwise provided in this Treaty and related agreements or as may be otherwise agreed.

(b) Either Party may waive its primary right to exercise jurisdiction in a specific case or category of cases.

3. The United States of America shall retain the right to exercise jurisdiction in criminal cases relating to offenses committed prior to the entry into force of this Treaty in violation of the laws applicable in the former Canal Zone.

4. For the transition period, the United States of America shall retain police authority and maintain a police force in the aforementioned areas and installations. In such areas, the police authorities of the United States of America may take into custody any person not subject to their primary jurisdiction if such person is believed to have committed or to be committing an offense against applicable laws or regulations, and shall promptly transfer custody to the police authorities of the Republic of Panama. The United States of America and the Republic of Panama shall establish joint police patrols in agreed areas. Any arrests conducted by a joint patrol shall be the responsibility of the patrol member or members representing the Party having primary jurisdiction over the person or persons arrested.

5. The courts of the United States of America and related personnel, functioning in the former Canal Zone immediately prior to the entry into force of this Treaty, may continue to function during the transition period for the judicial enforcement of the jurisdiction to be exercised by the United States of America in accordance with this Article.

6. In civil cases, the civilian courts of the United States of America in the Republic of Panama shall have no jurisdiction over new cases of a private civil nature, but shall retain full jurisdiction during the transition period to dispose of any civil cases, including admiralty cases, already instituted and pending before the courts prior to the entry into force of this Treaty.

7. The laws, regulations, and administrative authority of the United States of America applicable in the former Canal Zone immediately prior to the entry into force of this Treaty shall, to the extent not inconsistent with this Treaty and related agreements, continue in force for the purpose of the exercise by the United States of America of law enforcement and judicial jurisdiction only during the transition period. The United States of America may amend, repeal or otherwise change such laws, regulations and administrative authority. The two Parties shall consult concerning procedural and substantive matters relative to the implementation of this Article, including the disposition of cases pending at the end of the transition period and, in this respect, may enter into appropriate agreements by an exchange of notes or other instrument.

8. During this transition period, the United States of America may continue to

incarcerate individuals in the areas and installations made available for the use of the United States of America by the Republic of Panama pursuant to this Treaty and related agreements, or to transfer them to penal facilities in the United States of America to serve their sentences.

ARTICLE XII

A SEA-LEVEL CANAL OR A THIRD LANE OF LOCKS

1. The United States of America and the Republic of Panama recognize that a sea-level canal may be important for international navigation in the future. Consequently, during the duration of this Treaty, both Parties commit themselves to study jointly the feasibility of a sea-level canal in the Republic of Panama, and in the event they determine that such a waterway is necessary, they shall negotiate terms, agreeable to both Parties, for its construction.

2. The United States of America and the Republic of Panama agree on the following:

(a) No new interoceanic canal shall be constructed in the territory of the Republic of Panama during the duration of this Treaty, except in accordance with the provisions of this Treaty, or as the two Parties may otherwise agree; and

(b) During the duration of this Treaty, the United States of America shall not negotiate with third States for the right to construct an interoceanic canal on any other route in the Western Hemisphere, except as the two Parties may otherwise agree.

3. The Republic of Panama grants to the United States of America the right to add a third lane of locks to the existing Panama Canal. This right may be exercised at any time during the duration of this Treaty, provided that the United States of America has delivered to the Republic of Panama copies of the plans for such construction.

4. In the event the United States of America exercises the right granted in paragraph 3 above, it may use for that purpose, in addition to the areas otherwise made available to the United States of America pursuant to this Treaty, such other areas as the two Parties may agree upon. The terms and conditions applicable to Canal operating areas made available by the Republic of Panama for the use of the United States of America pursuant to Article III of this Treaty shall apply in a similar manner to such additional areas.

5. In the construction of the aforesaid works, the United States of America shall not use nuclear excavation techniques without the previous consent of the Republic of Panama.

ARTICLE XIII

PROPERTY TRANSFER AND ECONOMIC PARTICIPATION BY THE REPUBLIC OF PANAMA

1. Upon termination of this Treaty, the Republic of Panama shall assume total responsibility for the management, operation, and maintenance of the Panama Canal, which shall be turned over in operating condition and free of liens and debts, except as the two Parties may otherwise agree.

2. The United States of America transfers, without charge, to the Republic of

Panama all right, title and interest the United States of America may have with respect to all real property, including non-removable improvements thereon, as set forth below:

(a) Upon the entry into force of this Treaty, the Panama Railroad and such property that was located in the former Canal Zone but that is not within the land and water areas the use of which is made available to the United States of America pursuant to this Treaty. However, it is agreed that the transfer on such date shall not include buildings and other facilities, except housing, the use of which is retained by the United States of America pursuant to this Treaty and related agreements, outside such areas;

(b) Such property located in an area or a portion thereof at such time as the use by the United States of America of such area or portion thereof ceases pursuant to agreement between the two Parties.

(c) Housing units made available for occupancy by members of the Armed Forces of the Republic of Panama in accordance with paragraph 5(b) of Annex B to the Agreement in Implementation of Article IV of this Treaty at such time as such units are made available to the Republic of Panama.

(d) Upon termination of this Treaty, all real property and non-removable improvements that were used by the United States of America for the purposes of this Treaty and related agreements and equipment related to the management, operation and maintenance of the Canal remaining in the Republic of Panama.

3. The Republic of Panama agrees to hold the United States of America harmless with respect to any claims which may be made by third parties relating to rights, title and interest in such property.

4. The Republic of Panama shall receive, in addition, from the Panama Canal Commission a just and equitable return on the national resources which it has dedicated to the efficient management, operation, maintenance, protection and defense of the Panama Canal, in accordance with the following:

(a) An annual amount to be paid out of Canal operating revenues computed at a rate of thirty hundredths of a United States dollar ($0.30) per Panama Canal net ton, or its equivalency, for each vessel transiting the Canal after the entry into force of this Treaty, for which tolls are charged. The rate of thirty hundredths of a United States dollar ($0.30) per Panama Canal net ton, or its equivalency, will be adjusted to reflect changes in the United States wholesale price index for total manufactured goods during biennial periods. The first adjustment shall take place five years after entry into force of this Treaty, taking into account the changes that occurred in such price index during the preceding two years. Thereafter, successive adjustments shall take place at the end of each biennial period. If the United States of America should decide that another indexing method is preferable, such method shall be proposed to the Republic of Panama and applied if mutually agreed.

(b) A fixed annuity of ten million United States dollars ($10,000,000) to be paid out of Canal operating revenues. This amount shall constitute a fixed expense of the Panama Canal Commission.

(c) An annual amount of up to ten million United States dollars ($10,000,000) per year, to be paid out of Canal operating revenues to the extent that such revenues exceed expenditures of the Panama Canal Commission including amounts paid pursuant to this Treaty. In the event Canal operating revenues in any year do not produce a surplus sufficient to cover this payment, the unpaid balance shall be paid from operating surpluses in future years in a manner to be mutually agreed.

ARTICLE XIV

SETTLEMENT OF DISPUTES

In the event that any question should arise between the Parties concerning the interpretation of this Treaty or related agreements, they shall make every effort to resolve the matter through consultation in the appropriate committees established pursuant to this Treaty and related agreements, or, if appropriate, through diplomatic channels. In the event the Parties are unable to resolve a particular matter through such means, they may, in appropriate cases, agree to submit the matter to conciliation, mediation, arbitration, or such other procedure for the peaceful settlement of the dispute as they may mutually deem appropriate.

DONE at Washington, this 7th day of September, 1977, in duplicate, in the English and Spanish languages, both texts being equally authentic.

A Note on Sources

Unlike most histories, this record of the Panama problem and of U.S.-Panamanian relations over recent decades is based heavily on the memory and records of virtually all the main participants in both countries. The list of the many people who generously provided detailed recollections of their participation in these events is contained in the interviews section of Sources. In addition to their oral descriptions, many supplied me with pertinent documents related to the events described herein.

As the senior staff member concerned with Latin American affairs on the National Security Council from 1972 to 1974, then as U.S. ambassador to Panama for four and a half years, I naturally read all significant reports, cables, and memorandums relating to Panama during that time. In preparing this account, I read parts of that voluminous record to refresh my memory and to confirm, deny, or supplement my main impressions. My notes and selected documents were read and approved for use by the security review staff of the NSC. Needless to say, my personal files (letters, notes, daily calendars, and the like) served wonderfully to jog memory and to confirm dates and events.

Officials of the government of Panama and countless former officials and private individuals gave generously of their time in recounting those parts of the history in which they played active roles. Equally important, many gave me invaluable documentation—everything from scribbled notes and memos of phone conversations to the full negotiating record of the 1971–72 round of treaty talks. In some cases, it was possible to get negotiating documents more readily from Panamanian officials than from our own government. Their extensive cooperation helped make possible the detailed account that is contained in these pages. It also enabled me to write the Panama treaties story from the viewpoint of Panama as well as that of the United States.

The extensive treatment of the Senate debate on the Panama treaties in Chapters 18 and 19 was based on a careful reading of the *Congressional Record* from the day the treaties were introduced in September 1977 until the final vote on April 18, 1978. More important, because most of what really mattered in those months was going on behind the scenes, were the recollections of the key players—senators, congressional staffers, administration officials working on the Hill, White House aides, and a handful of Panamanians.

Obviously, no attempt to reconstruct anything in modern history can ignore what was being reported of the event in the news media. Often those reports divulge matters that do not appear in the official record. It is also important for the historian and for the reader to know what part of the story was receiving attention—and therefore what the general level of public awareness was at the time. The U.S. and Panamanian periodicals whose accounts of major events from 1964 to 1978 I read in preparing this narrative are listed in Sources. As is apparent in this account, I was as interested in what was *not* reported as in what made Page One.

A word on quotations. There is no imagined dialogue in these pages. What was said in Senate debates comes from the *Congressional Record*. The words used in negotiating sessions come from the transcripts of those meetings. Letters, documents, and memorandums are the sources of many of the quoted sections. Telephone and other conversations in which I was a participant are based on my notes of those talks. Quotations from other phone conversations are from the notes of one or both participants that I considered reliable. In other cases (meetings, private talks, and the like), I have put statements in quotation marks when one participant gave them as his or her best recollection and when at least one other witness agreed that those words, or others with the same meaning, were indeed used. In those few cases, I felt that quoted dialogue captured the true flavor of the moment better than indirect discourse.

As the reader will have noted, I have used a minimum of footnotes in this book. I did so deliberately. I wrote this volume in the hope that as many of my fellow citizens as possible would get a better appreciation of what surely was one of the most misunderstood chapters in our recent history. I did not wish to burden those readers with citations in every paragraph of where a quotation came from or where he or she could read more deeply into a given subject. Nor have I wished to buttress any conclusions with references to those who agreed with a given point of view. That approach has, it seems to me, discouraged far too many people from reading works they might otherwise have enjoyed.

The second reason for the paucity of footnotes is economic. The kind of annotation a purist might desire would have added at least fifty pages to this volume, which is already long enough. That would have added considerably to the final cost, which is already high enough. Hence, I decided to pursue the frugal course.

Still, I feel an obligation to that relatively small but quite important number of readers who may wish to know more and to delve deeper into matters concerning U.S. relations with Panama in the twentieth century. To serve that special interest, I plan to put on file in the Lyndon Baines Johnson Library in Austin, Texas, the full text of this book as well as the longer, more detailed penultimate draft of some 1,600 pages. Attached thereto will be most of the documents and background materials I have used in preparing this book—as many as the limits of confidentiality imposed by their donors will allow. I hope that will contribute to the needs of scholarship and to the pursuit of further knowledge of these lively and crucial events.

Sources

Books Providing Useful Background

Carter, Jimmy. *Keeping Faith*. New York: Bantam Books, 1982 (pp. 152–185).

Cornford, F. M. *Micro-cosmographia Academica*. Cambridge: Bowes & Bowes, 1908.

Crabb, Cecil V., Jr., and Pat M. Holt. *Invitation to Struggle: Congress, the President and Foreign Policy*. Washington: Congressional Quarterly Press, 1980 (chap. 3, pp. 65–88).

DuVal, Miles P., Jr. *Cadiz to Cathay*. New York: Greenwood Press, 1968 [first published 1940].

———. *And the Mountains Will Move*. Westport: Greenwood Press, 1968 [first published 1947].

Eisenhower, Milton. *The Wine Is Bitter*. New York: Doubleday & Co., 1963.

Escobar Bethancourt, Rómulo. *Torrijos: ¡Colonia americana, No!* Bogota: Carlos Valencia Editores, 1981.

Frank, Thomas, and Edward Weisband. *Foreign Policy by Congress*. New York: Oxford University Press, 1979 (pp. 275–286).

Geyelin, Philip. *Lyndon B. Johnson and the World*. New York: Praeger, 1966.

Gunther, John. *Inside Latin America*. New York: Harpers, 1940.

Illueca, Jorge E. *Las actuales negociaciones sobre el canal de Panamá*. Vol. 3 in *Relaciones entre Panamá y los Estados Unidos*. Panama City: Biblioteca Nuevo Panamá, 1973.

Johnson, Lyndon B. *The Vantage Point*. New York: Holt, Rinehart & Winston, 1971 (pp. 180–184).

LaFeber, Walter. *The Panama Canal: The Crisis in Historical Perspective*. New York: Oxford University Press, 1978.

McCullough, David. *The Path between the Seas*. New York: Simon & Schuster, 1977.

Torrijos, Omar. *La quinta frontera*. Costa Riva: DUCA, 1978.

Weil, Thomas E., et al. *Area Handbook for Panama*. Washington: U.S. Government Printing Office, 1972.

Sources of More Specialized Information

Annual Reports of the Panama Canal Company and Canal Zone Government, 1974 through 1978.

Annual Reports of the Panama Canal Commission, 1980 through 1982.

Annual Reports to the Congress on the Panama Canal Treaties of 1977, 1981 through 1983.

Background Documents Relating to the Panama Canal, prepared by the Congressional Research Service of the Library of Congress. Washington: U.S. Government Printing Office, 1977.

Barone, M., and G. Ujifusa. *The Almanac of American Politics, 1982*. Washington: Barone & Co., 1981.

Barone, M., G. Ujifusa, and D. Matthews. *The Almanac of American Politics, 1980*. New York: E. P. Dutton, 1979.

Castillero R., Ernesto J. (ed.). *El canal: ¿Justícia panamena o internacional?* Panama City: Universidad de Santa María La Antigua, 1977. Contains a collection of statements on the Panama problem by religious groups in Panama and the United States.

A Chronology of Events Relating to Panama Canal. Washington: U.S. Government Printing Office, 1977.

Communiqués and press releases, Ministry of Foreign Relations, Panama, 1977–1978.

Documents Associated with the Panama Canal Treaties (Department of State, Selected Documents 6B). Washington: U.S. Government Printing Office, 1977.

Lyndon Baines Johnson Library, Austin, Texas. Material in the archives under the headings Panama, Panama Canal, Panama Riots, Central America, Foreign Policy, Organization of American States, and related subjects contain invaluable material on the riots of January 1964 and President Johnson's handling of the crisis that followed.

Panama Canal Treaties: Hearings before the Committee on Foreign Relations, U.S. Senate (Parts I, II, III). Washington: U.S. Government Printing Office, 1977.

Panama Canal Treaties: Hearings before the Committee on Foreign Relations, U.S. Senate (Part V.—Markup). Washington: U.S. Government Printing Office, 1978.

Report on the Events in Panama, January 9–12, 1964. Geneva: International Commission of Jurists, 1964.

Senate Debate of the Panama Canal Treaties. Washington: U.S. Government Printing Office, February 1979. A compendium of major statements, documents, record votes, and relevant events.

Texts of Treaties Relating to the Panama Canal (Department of State, Selected Documents 6A). Washington: U.S. Government Printing Office, 1977.

U.N. General Assembly Document A/33/73 of 30 March 1978. Note to the U.N. secretary-general from Panama's permanent representative, Ambassador Jorge E. Illueca, with four appendixes.

Newspapers and Magazines Useful for Descriptions and Background on Specific Events in the 1960s and 1970s

Panamanian
Crítica.
La Estrella de Panamá.
Matutino.
Star & Herald.

American
Miami Herald.
Newsweek
New York Times.
Time
U.S. News & World Report
Washington Post.
Washington Star.

Interviews

Panamanians
Alemán, Roberto R. Treaty negotiator, 1965–1967.
Ardito Barletta, Nicolás. Minister of Economic Planning.
Bilonick, Ricardo. Legal adviser, Panamanian Embassy.
Boyd, Aquilino. Ambassador to United Nations; Minister of Foreign Relations.
Eleta, Fernando. Minister of Foreign Relations.
Escobar Bethancourt, Rómulo. Treaty negotiator, 1977.
Fábrega, Edwin. Director of IRHE; treaty negotiator, 1975–1977.
González, Rodrigo. Businessman; personal friend and adviser of General Torrijos.
González Revilla, Nicolás. Ambassador to United States; Minister of Foreign Relations.
Illueca, Jorge E. Ambassador to United Nations.
Lakas, Demetrio B. President of Panama, 1972–1978.
Lewis Galindo, Gabriel. Ambassador to United States.
López-Guevara, Carlos. Lawyer; treaty negotiator; Ambassador to United States.
McGowan, Arturo. Businessman; adviser to Torrijos.
Manfredo, Fernando. Treaty negotiator, 1971–1972; Minister of Commerce; first Deputy Administrator of the Panama Canal Commission.
Noriega, Manuel A. Colonel in National Guard; Torrijos' chief of intelligence; promoted to General and National Guard Commander, 1983.
Royo, Aristides. Treaty negotiator, 1977; President of Panama, 1978–1982.
St. Malo, Guillermo de. Businessman; adviser to Torrijos.
Tack, Juan Antonio. Minister of Foreign Relations; treaty negotiator.
Torrijos Herrera, Omar. General and National Guard Commander; political leader of Panama, 1968–1981.

Americans
Abourezk, Senator James.
Anderson, Robert B.
Baker, Senator Howard.

Barkley, Richard.
Beckel, Robert.
Bell, S. Morey.
Bennett, Douglas.
Blacken, John.
Bunker, Ambassador Ellsworth.
Byrd, Senator Robert C.
Carter, President Jimmy.
Chester, Gerri.
Christopher, Warren.
Church, Senator Frank.
Culver, Senator John.
Cutter, Curtis.
Dachi, Stephan.
Dockery, Robert.
Dolvin, Lt. Gen. Welborn.
Fleming, Maj. Gen. Robert.
Gravel, Senator Mike.
Helms, Senator Jesse.
Hurwitch, Ambassador Robert.
Irwin, Ambassador John N., II.
Johnson, Maj. Gen. Chester.
Jordan, Hamilton.
Kozak, Michael.
Linowitz, Ambassador Sol.
McAuliffe, Lt. Gen. Denis P.
McPherson, Harry.
Mann, Ambassador Thomas.
Meyer, Charles.
Mondale, Vice President Walter.
Moore, Virgil.
Moss, Ambassador Ambler.
Mundt, Ambassador John.
Parfitt, Maj. Gen. Harold.
Parker, Maj. Gen. David.
Pastor, Robert.
Rogers, William D.
Sarbanes, Senator Paul.
Sheffey, Col. John.
Wyrough, Richard.

Index